The Design of Approximation Algorithms

Discrete optimization problems are everywhere, from traditional operations research planning problems, such as scheduling, facility location, and network design; to computer science problems in databases; to advertising issues in viral marketing. Yet most such problems are NP-hard. Thus unless P = NP, there are no efficient algorithms to find optimal solutions to such problems. This book shows how to design approximation algorithms: efficient algorithms that find provably near-optimal solutions.

The book is organized around central algorithmic techniques for designing approximation algorithms, including greedy and local search algorithms, dynamic programming, linear and semidefinite programming, and randomization. Each chapter in the first part of the book is devoted to a single algorithmic technique, which is then applied to several different problems. The second part revisits the techniques but offers more sophisticated treatments of them. The book also covers methods for proving that optimization problems are hard to approximate.

Designed as a textbook for graduate-level algorithms courses, the book will also serve as a reference for researchers interested in the heuristic solution of discrete optimization problems.

David P. Williamson is a Professor at Cornell University with a joint appointment in the School of Operations Research and Information Engineering and in the Department of Information Science. Prior to joining Cornell, he was a Research Staff Member at the IBM T.J. Watson Research Center and a Senior Manager at the IBM Almaden Research Center. He has won several awards for his work on approximation algorithms, including the 2000 Fulkerson Prize, sponsored by the American Mathematical Society and the Mathematical Programming Society. He has served on several editorial boards, including *ACM Transactions on Algorithms, Mathematics of Operations Research*, the SIAM *Journal on Computing*, and the SIAM *Journal on Discrete Mathematics*.

David B. Shmoys is a Professor at Cornell University with appointments in both the School of Operations Research and Information Engineering and the Department of Computer Science. He is currently Associate Director of the Institute for Computational Sustainability at Cornell. He is a Fellow of the ACM, was an NSF Presidential Young Investigator, and has served on numerous editorial boards, including *Mathematics of Operations Research* (for which he is currently an associate editor), *Operations Research*, *ORSA Journal on Computing, Mathematical Programming*, and both the SIAM *Journal on Computing* and *Journal on Discrete Mathematics*; he also served as editor-in-chief for the latter.

The Design of Approximation Algorithms

David P. Williamson

Cornell University

David B. Shmoys

Cornell University

CAMBRIDGE
UNIVERSITY PRESS

CAMBRIDGE
UNIVERSITY PRESS

32 Avenue of the Americas, New York NY 10013-2473, USA

Cambridge University Press is part of the University of Cambridge.

It furthers the University's mission by disseminating knowledge in the pursuit of
education, learning and research at the highest international levels of excellence.

www.cambridge.org
Information on this title: www.cambridge.org/9780521195270

© David P. Williamson and David B. Shmoys 2011

First published 2011

A catalogue record for this publication is available from the British Library

Library of Congress Cataloguing in Publication data

Williamson, David P.
The design of approximation algorithms / David P. Williamson, David B. Shmoys.
    p.   cm.
Includes bibliographical references and index.
ISBN 978-0-521-19527-0 (hardback)
1. Approximation theory.   2. Mathematical optimization.
I. Shmoys, David Bernard.   II. Title.
QA221.W55   2011
518´.5–dc22   2011001945

ISBN 978-0-521-19527-0 Hardback

Contents

II Further Uses of the Techniques

Preface

This book is designed to be a textbook for graduate-level courses in approximation algorithms. After some experience teaching minicourses in the area in the mid-1990s, we sat down and wrote out an outline of the book. Then one of us (DPW), who was at the time an IBM Research Staff Member, taught several iterations of the course following the outline we had devised, in Columbia University's Department of Industrial Engineering and Operations Research in Spring 1998, in Cornell University's School of Operations Research and Industrial Engineering in Fall 1998, and at the Massachusetts Institute of Technology's Laboratory for Computer Science in Spring 2000. The lecture notes from these courses were made available, and we got enough positive feedback on them from students and from professors teaching such courses elsewhere that we felt we were on the right track. Since then, there have been many exciting developments in the area, and we have added many of them to the book; we taught additional iterations of the course at Cornell in Fall 2006 and Fall 2009 in order to field test some of the writing of the newer results.

The courses were developed for students who have already had a class, undergraduate or graduate, in algorithms, and who were comfortable with the idea of mathematical proofs about the correctness of algorithms. The book assumes this level of preparation. The book also assumes some basic knowledge of probability theory (for instance, how to compute the expected value of a discrete random variable). Finally, we assume that the reader knows something about NP-completeness, at least enough to know that there might be good reason for wanting fast, approximate solutions to NP-hard discrete optimization problems. At one or two points in the book, we do an NP-completeness reduction to show that it can be hard to find approximate solutions to such problems; we include a short appendix on the problem class NP and the notion of NP-completeness for those unfamiliar with the concepts. However, the reader unfamiliar with such reductions can also safely skip over such proofs.

In addition to serving as a graduate textbook, this book is a way for students to get the background to read current research in the area of approximation algorithms. In particular, we wanted a book that we could hand our own Ph.D. students just starting in the field and say, "Here, read this."

We further hope that the book will serve as a reference to the area of approximation algorithms for researchers who are generally interested in the heuristic solution of discrete optimization problems; such problems appear in areas as diverse as traditional operations research planning problems (such as facility location and network design) to computer science problems in database and programming language design to advertising issues in viral marketing. We hope that the book helps researchers understand the techniques available in the area of approximation algorithms for approaching such problems.

We have taken several particular perspectives in writing the book. The first is that we wanted to organize the material around certain principles of designing approximation algorithms, around algorithmic ideas that have been used in different ways and applied to different optimization problems. The title *The Design of Approximation Algorithms* was carefully chosen. The book is structured around these design techniques. The introduction applies several of them to a single problem, the set cover problem. The book then splits into two parts. In the first part, each chapter is devoted to a single algorithmic idea (e.g., "greedy and local search algorithms," "rounding data and dynamic programming"), and the idea is then applied to several different problems. The second part revisits all of the same algorithmic ideas, but gives more sophisticated treatments of them; the results covered here are usually much more recent. The layout allows us to look at several central optimization problems repeatedly throughout the book, returning to them as a new algorithmic idea leads to a better result than the previous one. In particular, we revisit such problems as the uncapacitated facility location problem, the prize-collecting Steiner tree problem, the bin-packing problem, and the maximum cut problem several times throughout the course of the book.

The second perspective is that we treat linear and integer programming as a central aspect in the design of approximation algorithms. This perspective is from our background in the operations research and mathematical programming communities. It is a little unusual in the computer science community, and students coming from a computer science background may not be familiar with the basic terminology of linear programming. We introduce the terms we need in the first chapter, and we include a brief introduction to the area in an appendix.

The third perspective we took in writing the book is that we have limited ourselves to results that are simple enough for classroom presentation while remaining central to the topic at hand. Most of the results in the book are ones that we have taught ourselves in class at one point or another. We bent this rule somewhat in order to cover the recent, exciting work by Arora, Rao, and Vazirani [22] applying semidefinite programming to the uniform sparsest cut problem. The proof of this result is the most lengthy and complicated of the book.

We are grateful to a number of people who have given us feedback about the book at various stages in its writing. We are particularly grateful to James Davis, Lisa Fleischer, Isaac Fung, Rajiv Gandhi, Igor Gorodezky, Nick Harvey, Anna Karlin, Vijay Kothari, Katherine Lai, Gwen Spencer, and Anke van Zuylen for very detailed comments on a number of sections of the book. Additionally, the following people spotted typos, gave us feedback, helped us understand particular papers, and made useful suggestions: Bruno Abrahao, Hyung-Chan An, Matthew Andrews, Eliot Anshelevich, Sanjeev Arora, Ashwinkumar B.V., Moses Charikar, Chandra Chekuri, Joseph Cheriyan, Chao

Ding, Dmitriy Drusvyatskiy, Michel Goemans, Sudipto Guha, Anupam Gupta, Sanjeev Khanna, Lap Chi Lau, Renato Paes Leme, Jan Karel Lenstra, Jiawei Qian, Roman Rischke, Gennady Samorodnitsky, Daniel Schmand, Yogeshwer Sharma, Viktor Simjanoski, Mohit Singh, Éva Tardos, Mike Todd, Di Wang, and Ann Williamson. We also thank a number of anonymous reviewers who made useful comments. Eliot Anshelevich, Joseph Cheriyan, Lisa Fleischer, Michel Goemans, Nicole Immorlica, and Anna Karlin used various drafts of the book in their courses on approximation algorithms and gave us useful feedback about the experience of using the book. We received quite a number of useful comments from the students in Anna's class: Benjamin Birnbaum, Punyashloka Biswal, Elisa Celis, Jessica Chang, Mathias Hallman, Alyssa Joy Harding, Trinh Huynh, Alex Jaffe, Karthik Mohan, Katherine Moore, Cam Thach Nguyen, Richard Pang, Adrian Sampson, William Austin Webb, and Kevin Zatloukal. Frans Schalekamp generated the image on the cover; it is an illustration of the tree metric algorithm of Fakcharoenphol, Rao, and Talwar [106] discussed in Section 8.5. Our editor at Cambridge, Lauren Cowles, impressed us with her patience in waiting for this book to be completed and gave us a good deal of useful advice.

We would like to thank the institutions that supported us during the writing of this book, including our home institution, Cornell University, and the IBM T.J. Watson and Almaden Research Centers (DPW), as well as TU Berlin (DPW) and the Sloan School of Management at MIT and the Microsoft New England Research Center (DBS), where we were on sabbatical leave when the final editing of the book occurred. We are grateful to the National Science Foundation for supporting our research in approximation algorithms.

We are also grateful to our wives and children – to Ann, Abigail, Daniel, and Ruth, and to Éva, Rebecca, and Amy – for their patience and support during the writing of this volume.

Additional materials related to the book (such as contact information and errata) can be found at the website www.designofapproxalgs.com.

Finally, we hope the book conveys some of our enthusiasm and enjoyment of the area of approximation algorithms. We hope that you, dear reader, will enjoy it too.

David P. Williamson
David B. Shmoys
January 2011

PART ONE
An Introduction to the Techniques

CHAPTER 1

An Introduction to Approximation Algorithms

1.1 The Whats and Whys of Approximation Algorithms

Decisions, decisions. The difficulty of sifting through large amounts of data in order to make an informed choice is ubiquitous in today's society. One of the promises of the information technology era is that many decisions can now be made rapidly by computers, from deciding inventory levels, to routing vehicles, to organizing data for efficient retrieval. The study of how to make decisions of these sorts in order to achieve some best possible goal, or objective, has created the field of *discrete optimization*.

Unfortunately, most interesting discrete optimization problems are NP-hard. Thus, unless P = NP, there are no efficient algorithms to find optimal solutions to such problems, where we follow the convention that an efficient algorithm is one that runs in time bounded by a polynomial in its input size. This book concerns itself with the answer to the question "What should we do in this case?"

An old engineering slogan says, "Fast. Cheap. Reliable. Choose two." Similarly, if P $\neq$ NP, we can't simultaneously have algorithms that (1) find optimal solutions (2) in polynomial time (3) for any instance. At least one of these requirements must be relaxed in any approach to dealing with an NP-hard optimization problem.

One approach relaxes the "for any instance" requirement, and finds polynomial-time algorithms for special cases of the problem at hand. This is useful if the instances one desires to solve fall into one of these special cases, but this is not frequently the case.

A more common approach is to relax the requirement of polynomial-time solvability. The goal is then to find optimal solutions to problems by clever exploration of the full set of possible solutions to a problem. This is often a successful approach if one is willing to take minutes, or even hours, to find the best possible solution; perhaps even more importantly, one is never certain that for the next input encountered, the algorithm will terminate in *any* reasonable amount of time. This is the approach taken by those in the field of operations research and mathematical programming who solve integer programming formulations of discrete optimization problems, or those in the area of artificial intelligence who consider techniques such as A^* search or constraint programming.

3

By far the most common approach, however, is to relax the requirement of finding an optimal solution, and instead settle for a solution that is "good enough," especially if it can be found in seconds or less. There has been an enormous study of various types of heuristics and metaheuristics such as simulated annealing, genetic algorithms, and tabu search, to name but a few. These techniques often yield good results in practice.

The approach of this book falls into this third class. We relax the requirement of finding an optimal solution, but our goal is to relax this as little as we possibly can. Throughout this book, we will consider *approximation algorithms* for discrete optimization problems. We try to find a solution that closely approximates the optimal solution in terms of its *value*. We assume that there is some *objective function* mapping each possible solution of an optimization problem to some nonnegative value, and an *optimal solution* to the optimization problem is one that either minimizes or maximizes the value of this objective function. Then we define an approximation algorithm as follows.

Definition 1.1. *An α-approximation algorithm for an optimization problem is a polynomial-time algorithm that for all instances of the problem produces a solution whose value is within a factor of α of the value of an optimal solution.*

For an α-approximation algorithm, we will call α the *performance guarantee* of the algorithm. In the literature, it is also often called the *approximation ratio* or *approximation factor* of the algorithm. In this book we will follow the convention that $\alpha > 1$ for minimization problems, while $\alpha < 1$ for maximization problems. Thus, a $\frac{1}{2}$-approximation algorithm for a maximization problem is a polynomial-time algorithm that always returns a solution whose value is at least half the optimal value.

Why study approximation algorithms? We list several reasons.

- *Because we need algorithms to get solutions to discrete optimization problems.* As we mentioned above, with our current information technology there are an increasing number of optimization problems that need to be solved, and most of these are NP-hard. In some cases, an approximation algorithm is a useful heuristic for finding near-optimal solutions when the optimal solution is not required.
- *Because algorithm design often focuses first on idealized models rather than the "real-world" application.* In practice, many discrete optimization problems are quite messy, and have many complicating side constraints that make it hard to find an approximation algorithm with a good performance guarantee. But often approximation algorithms for simpler versions of the problem give us some idea of how to devise a heuristic that will perform well in practice for the actual problem. Furthermore, the push to prove a theorem often results in a deeper mathematical understanding of the problem's structure, which then leads to a new algorithmic approach.
- *Because it provides a mathematically rigorous basis on which to study heuristics.* Typically, heuristics and metaheuristics are studied empirically; they might work well, but we might not understand why. The field of approximation algorithms brings mathematical rigor to the study of heuristics, allowing us to prove how well the heuristic performs on all instances, or giving us some idea of the types of instances on which the heuristic will not perform well. Furthermore, the

mathematical analyses of many of the approximation algorithms in this book have the property that not only is there an *a priori* guarantee for any input, but there is also an *a fortiori* guarantee that is provided on an input-by-input basis, which allows us to conclude that specific solutions are in fact much more nearly optimal than promised by the performance guarantee.

- *Because it gives a metric for stating how hard various discrete optimization problems are.* Over the course of the twentieth century, the study of the power of computation has steadily evolved. In the early part of the century, researchers were concerned with what kinds of problems could be solved at all by computers in finite time, with the halting problem as the canonical example of a problem that could not be solved. The latter part of the century concerned itself with the efficiency of solution, distinguishing between problems that could be solved in polynomial time, and those that are NP-hard and (perhaps) cannot be solved efficiently. The field of approximation algorithms gives us a means of distinguishing between various optimization problems in terms of how well they can be approximated.

- *Because it's fun.* The area has developed some very deep and beautiful mathematical results over the years, and it is inherently interesting to study these.

It is sometimes objected that requiring an algorithm to have a near-optimal solution for *all* instances of the problem – having an analysis for what happens to the algorithm in the worst possible instance – leads to results that are too loose to be practically interesting. After all, in practice, we would greatly prefer solutions within a few percent of optimal rather than, say, twice optimal. From a mathematical perspective, it is not clear that there are good alternatives to this worst-case analysis. It turns out to be quite difficult to define a "typical" instance of any given problem, and often instances drawn randomly from given probability distributions have very special properties not present in real-world data. Since our aim is mathematical rigor in the analysis of our algorithms, we must content ourselves with this notion of worst-case analysis. We note that the worst-case bounds are often due to pathological cases that do not arise in practice, so that approximation algorithms often give rise to heuristics that return solutions much closer to optimal than indicated by their performance guarantees.

Given that approximation algorithms are worth studying, the next natural question is whether there exist good approximation algorithms for problems of interest. In the case of some problems, we are able to obtain extremely good approximation algorithms; in fact, these problems have *polynomial-time approximation schemes.*

Definition 1.2. *A* polynomial-time approximation scheme (PTAS) *is a family of algorithms* $\{A_\epsilon\}$, *where there is an algorithm for each* $\epsilon > 0$, *such that* A_ϵ *is a* $(1 + \epsilon)$-*approximation algorithm (for minimization problems) or a* $(1 - \epsilon)$-*approximation algorithm (for maximization problems).*

Many problems have polynomial-time approximation schemes. In later chapters we will encounter the knapsack problem and the Euclidean traveling salesman problem, each of which has a PTAS.

However, there exists a class of problems that is not so easy. This class is called MAX SNP; although we will not define it, it contains many interesting optimization problems, such as the maximum satisfiability problem and the maximum cut problem, which we will discuss later in the book. The following has been shown.

Theorem 1.3. *For any MAX SNP-hard problem, there does not exist a polynomial-time approximation scheme, unless* P = NP.

Finally, some problems are very hard. In the *maximum clique problem*, we are given as input an undirected graph $G = (V, E)$. The goal is to find a maximum-size *clique*; that is, we wish to find $S \subseteq V$ that maximizes $|S|$ so that for each pair $i, j \in S$, it must be the case that $(i, j) \in E$. The following theorem demonstrates that almost any nontrivial approximation guarantee is most likely unattainable.

Theorem 1.4. *Let n denote the number of vertices in an input graph, and consider any constant $\epsilon > 0$. Then there does not exist an $O(n^{\epsilon-1})$-approximation algorithm for the maximum clique problem, unless* P = NP.

To see how strong this theorem is, observe that it is completely trivial to get an n^{-1}-approximation algorithm for the problem: just output a single vertex. This gives a clique of size 1, whereas the size of the largest clique can be at most n, the number of vertices in the input. The theorem states that finding something only slightly better than this completely trivial approximation algorithm implies that P = NP!

1.2 An Introduction to the Techniques and to Linear Programming: The Set Cover Problem

One of the theses of this book is that there are several fundamental techniques used in the design and analysis of approximation algorithms. The goal of this book is to help the reader understand and master these techniques by applying each technique to many different problems of interest. We will visit some problems several times; when we introduce a new technique, we may see how it applies to a problem we have seen before, and show how we can obtain a better result via this technique. The rest of this chapter will be an illustration of several of the central techniques of the book applied to a single problem, the *set cover problem*, which we define below. We will see how each of these techniques can be used to obtain an approximation algorithm, and how some techniques lead to improved approximation algorithms for the set cover problem.

In the set cover problem, we are given a ground set of elements $E = \{e_1, \ldots, e_n\}$, some subsets of those elements $S_1, S_2, \ldots, S_m$ where each $S_j \subseteq E$, and a nonnegative weight $w_j \geq 0$ for each subset S_j. The goal is to find a minimum-weight collection of subsets that covers all of E; that is, we wish to find an $I \subseteq \{1, \ldots, m\}$ that minimizes $\sum_{j \in I} w_j$ subject to $\bigcup_{j \in I} S_j = E$. If $w_j = 1$ for each subset j, the problem is called the *unweighted* set cover problem.

The set cover problem is an abstraction of several types of problems; we give two examples here. The set cover problem was used in the development of an antivirus product, which detects computer viruses. In this case it was desired to find salient features that occur in viruses designed for the boot sector of a computer, such that the features do not occur in typical computer applications. These features were then incorporated into another heuristic for detecting these boot sector viruses, a neural network. The elements of the set cover problem were the known boot sector viruses (about 150 at the time). Each set corresponded to some three-byte sequence occurring in these viruses but not in typical computer programs; there were about 21,000 such sequences. Each set contained all the boot sector viruses that had the corresponding three-byte sequence somewhere in it. The goal was to find a small number of such sequences (much smaller than 150) that would be useful for the neural network. By using an approximation algorithm to solve the problem, a small set of sequences was found, and the neural network was able to detect many previously unanalyzed boot sector viruses. The set cover problem also generalizes the *vertex cover problem*. In the vertex cover problem, we are given an undirected graph $G = (V, E)$ and a nonnegative weight $w_i \geq 0$ for each vertex $i \in V$. The goal is to find a minimum-weight subset of vertices $C \subseteq V$ such that for each edge $(i, j) \in E$, either $i \in C$ or $j \in C$. As in the set cover problem, if $w_i = 1$ for each vertex i, the problem is an *unweighted* vertex cover problem. To see that the vertex cover problem is a special case of the set cover problem, for any instance of the vertex cover problem, create an instance of the set cover problem in which the ground set is the set of edges, and a subset S_i of weight w_i is created for each vertex $i \in V$ containing the edges incident to i. It is not difficult to see that for any vertex cover C, there is a set cover $I - C$ of the same weight, and vice versa.

A second thesis of this book is that *linear programming* plays a central role in the design and analysis of approximation algorithms. Many of the techniques introduced will use the theory of integer and linear programming in one way or another. Here we will give a very brief introduction to the area in the context of the set cover problem; we give a slightly less brief introduction in Appendix A, and the notes at the end of this chapter provide suggestions of other, more in-depth, introductions to the topic.

Each linear program or integer program is formulated in terms of some number of *decision variables* that represent some sort of decision that needs to be made. The variables are constrained by a number of linear inequalities and equalities called *constraints*. Any assignment of real numbers to the variables such that all of the constraints are satisfied is called a *feasible solution*. In the case of the set cover problem, we need to decide which subsets S_j to use in the solution. We create a decision variable x_j to represent this choice. In this case we would like x_j to be 1 if the set S_j is included in the solution, and 0 otherwise. Thus, we introduce constraints $x_j \leq 1$ for all subsets S_j, and $x_j \geq 0$ for all subsets S_j. This is not sufficient to guarantee that $x_j \in \{0, 1\}$, so we will formulate the problem as an *integer program* to exclude *fractional solutions* (that is, nonintegral solutions); in this case, we are also allowed to constrain the decision variables to be integers. Requiring x_j to be integer along with the constraints $x_j \geq 0$ and $x_j \leq 1$ is sufficient to guarantee that $x_j \in \{0, 1\}$.

We also want to make sure that any feasible solution corresponds to a set cover, so we introduce additional constraints. In order to ensure that every element e_i is covered, it must be the case that at least one of the subsets S_j containing e_i is selected. This will be the case if

$$\sum_{j: e_i \in S_j} x_j \geq 1,$$

for each e_i, $i = 1, \ldots, n$.

In addition to the constraints, linear and integer programs are defined by a linear function of the decision variables called the *objective function*. The linear or integer program seeks to find a feasible solution that either maximizes or minimizes this objective function. Such a solution is called an *optimal solution*. The value of the objective function for a particular feasible solution is called the *value* of that solution. The value of the objective function for an optimal solution is called the *value* of the linear (or integer) program. We say we *solve* the linear program if we find an optimal solution. In the case of the set cover problem, we want to find a set cover of minimum weight. Given the decision variables x_j and constraints described above, the weight of a set cover given the x_j variables is $\sum_{j=1}^{m} w_j x_j$. Thus, the objective function of the integer program is $\sum_{j=1}^{m} w_j x_j$, and we wish to minimize this function.

Integer and linear programs are usually written in a compact form stating first the objective function and then the constraints. Given the discussion above, the problem of finding a minimum-weight set cover is equivalent to the following integer program:

$$\text{minimize} \quad \sum_{j=1}^{m} w_j x_j$$

$$\text{subject to} \quad \sum_{j:e_i \in S_j} x_j \geq 1, \qquad i = 1, \ldots, n, \qquad (1.1)$$

$$x_j \in \{0, 1\}, \qquad j = 1, \ldots, m.$$

Let Z_{IP}^* denote the optimum value of this integer program for a given instance of the set cover problem. Since the integer program exactly models the problem, we have that $Z_{IP}^* = \text{OPT}$, where OPT is the value of an optimum solution to the set cover problem.

In general, integer programs cannot be solved in polynomial time. This is clear because the set cover problem is NP-hard, so solving the integer program above for any set cover input in polynomial time would imply that P = NP. However, linear programs are polynomial-time solvable. In linear programs we are not allowed to require that decision variables are integers. Nevertheless, linear programs are still extremely useful: even in cases such as the set cover problem, we are still able to derive useful information from linear programs. For instance, if we replace the constraints $x_j \in \{0, 1\}$ with the constraints $x_j \geq 0$, we obtain the following linear program, which can be solved in polynomial time:

$$\text{minimize} \quad \sum_{j=1}^{m} w_j x_j$$

$$\text{subject to} \quad \sum_{j:e_i \in S_j} x_j \geq 1, \qquad i = 1, \ldots, n, \qquad (1.2)$$

$$x_j \geq 0, \qquad j = 1, \ldots, m.$$

We could also add the constraints $x_j \leq 1$, for each $j = 1, \ldots, m$, but they would be redundant: in any optimal solution to the problem, we can reduce any $x_j > 1$ to $x_j = 1$ without affecting the feasibility of the solution and without increasing its cost.

The linear program (1.2) is a *relaxation* of the original integer program. By this we mean two things: first, every feasible solution for the original integer program (1.1) is feasible for this linear program; and second, the value of any feasible solution for the integer program has the same value in the linear program. To see that the linear program is a relaxation, note that any solution for the integer program such that $x_j \in \{0, 1\}$ for each $j = 1, \ldots, m$ and $\sum_{j:e_i \in S_j} x_j \geq 1$ for each $i = 1, \ldots, m$ will certainly satisfy all the constraints of the linear program. Furthermore, the objective functions of both the integer and linear programs are the same, so that any feasible solution for the integer program has the same value for the linear program. Let Z^*_{LP} denote the optimum value of this linear program. Any optimal solution to the integer program is feasible for the linear program and has value Z^*_{IP}. Thus, any optimal solution to the linear program will have value $Z^*_{LP} \leq Z^*_{IP} = \text{OPT}$, since this minimization linear program finds a feasible solution of lowest possible value. Using a polynomial-time solvable relaxation of a problem in order to obtain a lower bound (in the case of minimization problems) or an upper bound (in the case of maximization problems) on the optimum value of the problem is a concept that will appear frequently in this book.

In the following sections, we will give some examples of how the linear programming relaxation can be used to derive approximation algorithms for the set cover problem. In the next section, we will show that a fractional solution to the linear program can be rounded to a solution to the integer program of objective function value that is within a certain factor f of the value of the linear program Z^*_{LP}. Thus, the integer solution will cost no more than $f \cdot \text{OPT}$. In the following section, we will show how one can similarly round the solution to something called the dual of the linear programming relaxation. In Section 1.5, we will see that in fact one does not need to solve the dual of the linear programming relaxation, but in fact can quickly construct a dual feasible solution with the properties needed to allow a good rounding. In Section 1.6, a type of algorithm called a greedy algorithm will be given; in this case, linear programming need not be used at all, but one can use the dual to improve the analysis of the algorithm. Finally, in Section 1.7, we will see how randomized rounding of the solution to the linear programming relaxation can lead to an approximation algorithm for the set cover problem.

Because we will frequently be referring to linear programs and linear programming, we will often abbreviate these terms by the acronym LP. Similarly, IP stands for either integer program or integer programming.

1.3 A Deterministic Rounding Algorithm

Suppose that we solve the linear programming relaxation of the set cover problem. Let x^* denote an optimal solution to the LP. How then can we recover a solution to the set cover problem? Here is a very easy way to obtain a solution: given the LP solution x^*, we include subset S_j in our solution if and only if $x^*_j \geq 1/f$, where f is the maximum number of sets in which any element appears. More formally, let $f_i = |\{j : e_i \in S_j\}|$ be the number of sets in which element e_i appears, $i = 1, \ldots, n$; then $f = \max_{i=1,\ldots,n} f_i$. Let I denote the indices j of the subsets in this solution. In effect, we round the fractional solution x^* to an integer solution $\hat{x}$ by setting $\hat{x}_j = 1$ if $x^*_j \geq 1/f$, and $\hat{x}_j = 0$ otherwise. We shall see that it is straightforward to prove that $\hat{x}$ is a feasible solution to the integer program, and I indeed indexes a set cover.

Lemma 1.5. *The collection of subsets S_j, $j \in I$, is a set cover.*

Proof. Consider the solution specified by the lemma, and call an element e_i *covered* if this solution contains some subset containing e_i. We show that each element e_i is covered. Because the optimal solution x^* is a feasible solution to the linear program, we know that $\sum_{j:e_i \in S_j} x_j^* \geq 1$ for element e_i. By the definition of f_i and of f, there are $f_i \leq f$ terms in the sum, so at least one term must be at least $1/f$. Thus, for some j such that $e_i \in S_j$, $x_j^* \geq 1/f$. Therefore, $j \in I$, and element e_i is covered. $\square$

We can also show that this rounding procedure yields an approximation algorithm.

Theorem 1.6. *The rounding algorithm is an f-approximation algorithm for the set cover problem.*

Proof. It is clear that the algorithm runs in polynomial time. By our construction, $1 \leq f \cdot x_j^*$ for each $j \in I$. From this, and the fact that each term $f w_j x_j^*$ is nonnegative for $j = 1, \ldots, m$, we see that

$$\sum_{j \in I} w_j \leq \sum_{j=1}^{m} w_j \cdot (f \cdot x_j^*)$$

$$= f \sum_{j=1}^{m} w_j x_j^*$$

$$= f \cdot Z_{LP}^*$$

$$\leq f \cdot \text{OPT},$$

where the final inequality follows from the argument above that $Z_{LP}^* \leq \text{OPT}$. $\square$

In the special case of the vertex cover problem, $f_i = 2$ for each vertex $i \in V$, since each edge is incident to exactly two vertices. Thus, the rounding algorithm gives a 2-approximation algorithm for the vertex cover problem.

This particular algorithm allows us to have an *a fortiori* guarantee for each input. While we know that for any input, the solution produced has cost at most a factor of f more than the cost of an optimal solution, we can for any input compare the value of the solution we find with the value of the linear programming relaxation. If the algorithm finds a set cover I, let $\alpha = \sum_{j \in I} w_j / Z_{LP}^*$. From the proof above, we know that $\alpha \leq f$. However, for any given input, it could be the case that α is significantly smaller than f; in this case we know that $\sum_{j \in I} w_j = \alpha Z_{LP}^* \leq \alpha \, \text{OPT}$, and the solution is within a factor of α of optimal. The algorithm can easily compute α, given that it computes I and solves the LP relaxation.

1.4 Rounding a Dual Solution

Often it will be useful to consider the dual of the linear programming relaxation of a given problem. Again, we will give a very brief introduction to the concept of the dual of a linear program in the context of the set cover problem, and more in-depth introductions to the topic will be cited in the notes at the end of this chapter.

To begin, we suppose that each element e_i is charged some nonnegative price $y_i \geq 0$ for its coverage by a set cover. Intuitively, it might be the case that some elements can be covered with low-weight subsets, while other elements might require high-weight subsets to cover them; we would like to be able to capture this distinction by charging low prices to the former and high prices to the latter. In order for the prices to be reasonable, it cannot be the case that the sum of the prices of elements in a subset S_j is more than the weight of the set, since we are able to cover all of those elements by paying weight w_j. Thus, for each subset S_j we have the following limit on the prices:

$$\sum_{i:e_i \in S_j} y_i \leq w_j.$$

We can find the highest total price that the elements can be charged by the following linear program:

$$
\begin{aligned}
\text{maximize} \quad & \sum_{i=1}^{n} y_i \\
\text{subject to} \quad & \sum_{i:e_i \in S_j} y_i \leq w_j, \qquad j = 1, \ldots, m, \\
& y_i \geq 0, \qquad i = 1, \ldots, n.
\end{aligned}
\qquad (1.3)
$$

This linear program is the *dual* linear program of the set cover linear programming relaxation (1.2). We can in general derive a dual linear program for any given linear program, but we will not go into the details of how to do so; see Appendix A or the references in the notes at the end of the chapter. If we derive a dual for a given linear program, the given program is sometimes called the *primal* linear program. For instance, the original linear programming relaxation (1.2) of the set cover problem is the primal linear program of the dual (1.3). Notice that this dual has a variable y_i for each constraint of the primal linear program (that is, for the constraint $\sum_{j:e_i \in S_j} x_j \geq 1$), and has a constraint for each variable x_j of the primal. This is true of dual linear programs in general.

Dual linear programs have a number of very interesting and useful properties. For example, let x be any feasible solution to the set cover linear programming relaxation, and let y be any feasible set of prices (that is, any feasible solution to the dual linear program). Then consider the value of the dual solution y:

$$\sum_{i=1}^{n} y_i \leq \sum_{i=1}^{n} y_i \sum_{j:e_i \in S_j} x_j,$$

since for any e_i, $\sum_{j:e_i \in S_j} x_j \geq 1$ by the feasibility of x. Then rewriting the right-hand side of this inequality, we have

$$\sum_{i=1}^{n} y_i \sum_{j:e_i \in S_j} x_j = \sum_{j=1}^{m} x_j \sum_{i:e_i \in S_j} y_i.$$

Finally, noticing that since y is a feasible solution to the dual linear program, we know that $\sum_{i:e_i \in S_j} y_i \leq w_j$ for any j, so that

$$\sum_{j=1}^{m} x_j \sum_{i:e_i \in S_j} y_i \leq \sum_{j=1}^{m} x_j w_j.$$

So we have shown that

$$\sum_{i=1}^{n} y_i \leq \sum_{j=1}^{m} w_j x_j;$$

that is, any feasible solution to the dual linear program has a value no greater than any feasible solution to the primal linear program. In particular, any feasible solution to the dual linear program has a value no greater than the optimal solution to the primal linear program, so for any feasible y, $\sum_{i=1}^{n} y_i \leq Z_{LP}^*$. This is called the *weak duality* property of linear programs. Since we previously argued that $Z_{LP}^* \leq \text{OPT}$, we have that for any feasible y, $\sum_{i=1}^{n} y_i \leq \text{OPT}$. This is a very useful property that will help us in designing approximation algorithms.

Additionally, there is a quite amazing *strong duality* property of linear programs. Strong duality states that as long as there exist feasible solutions to both the primal and dual linear programs, their optimal values are equal. Thus, if x^* is an optimal solution to the set cover linear programming relaxation, and y^* is an optimal solution to the dual linear program, then

$$\sum_{j=1}^{m} w_j x_j^* = \sum_{i=1}^{n} y_i^*.$$

Information from a dual linear program solution can sometimes be used to derive good approximation algorithms. Let y^* be an optimal solution to the dual LP (1.3), and consider the solution in which we choose all subsets for which the corresponding dual inequality is *tight*; that is, the inequality is met with equality for subset S_j, and $\sum_{i:e_i \in S_j} y_i^* = w_j$. Let I' denote the indices of the subsets in this solution. We will prove that this algorithm also is an f-approximation algorithm for the set cover problem.

Lemma 1.7. *The collection of subsets S_j, $j \in I'$, is a set cover.*

Proof. Suppose that there exists some uncovered element e_k. Then for each subset S_j containing e_k, it must be the case that

$$\sum_{i:e_i \in S_j} y_i^* < w_j. \tag{1.4}$$

Let ϵ be the smallest difference between the right-hand side and left-hand side of all constraints involving e_k; that is, $\epsilon = \min_{j:e_k \in S_j}(w_j - \sum_{i:e_i \in S_j} y_i^*)$. By inequality (1.4), we know that $\epsilon > 0$. Consider now a new dual solution y' in which $y_k' = y_k^* + \epsilon$ and every other component of y' is the same as in y^*. Then y' is a dual feasible solution since for each j such that $e_k \in S_j$,

$$\sum_{i:e_i \in S_j} y_i' = \sum_{i:e_i \in S_j} y_i^* + \epsilon \le w_j,$$

by the definition of ϵ. For each j such that $e_k \notin S_j$,

$$\sum_{i:e_i \in S_j} y_i' = \sum_{i:e_i \in S_j} y_i^* \le w_j,$$

as before. Furthermore, $\sum_{i=1}^n y_i' > \sum_{i=1}^n y_i^*$, which contradicts the optimality of y^*. Thus, it must be the case that all elements are covered and I' is a set cover. $\quad\square$

Theorem 1.8. *The dual rounding algorithm described above is an f-approximation algorithm for the set cover problem.*

Proof. The central idea is the following "charging" argument: when we choose a set S_j to be in the cover, we "pay" for it by charging y_i^* to each of its elements e_i; each element is charged at most once for each set that contains it (and hence at most f times), and so the total cost is at most $f \sum_{i=1}^m y_i^*$, or f times the dual objective function.

More formally, since $j \in I'$ only if $w_j - \sum_{i:e_i \in S_j} y_i^*$, we have that the cost of the set cover I' is

$$\sum_{j \in I'} w_j = \sum_{j \in I'} \sum_{i:e_i \in S_j} y_i^*$$

$$= \sum_{i=1}^n |\{j \in I' : e_i \in S_j\}| \cdot y_i^*$$

$$\le \sum_{i=1}^n f_i y_i^*$$

$$\le f \sum_{i=1}^n y_i^*$$

$$\le f \cdot \text{OPT}.$$

The second equality follows from the fact that when we interchange the order of summation, the coefficient of y_i^* is, of course, equal to the number of times that this term occurs overall. The final inequality follows from the weak duality property discussed previously. $\quad\square$

In fact, it is possible to show that this algorithm can do no better than the algorithm of the previous section; to be precise, we can show that if I indexes the solution returned by the primal rounding algorithm of the previous section, then $I \subseteq I'$. This follows from a property of optimal linear programming solutions called *complementary slackness*. We showed earlier the following string of inequalities for any feasible solution x to the set cover linear programming relaxation, and any feasible solution y to the dual linear program:

$$\sum_{i=1}^n y_i \le \sum_{i=1}^n y_i \sum_{j:e_i \in S_j} x_j = \sum_{j=1}^m x_j \sum_{i:e_i \in S_j} y_i \le \sum_{j=1}^m x_j w_j.$$

Furthermore, we claimed that strong duality implies that for optimal solutions x^* and y^*, $\sum_{i=1}^{n} y_i^* = \sum_{j=1}^{m} w_j x_j^*$. Thus, for any optimal solutions x^* and y^* the two inequalities in the chain of inequalities above must in fact be equalities. The only way this can happen is that whenever $y_i^* > 0$ then $\sum_{j:e_i \in S_j} x_j^* = 1$, and whenever $x_j^* > 0$, then $\sum_{i:e_i \in S_j} y_i^* = w_j$. That is, whenever a linear programming variable (primal or dual) is nonzero, the corresponding constraint in the dual or primal is tight. These conditions are known as the *complementary slackness conditions*. Thus, if x^* and y^* are optimal solutions, the complementary slackness conditions must hold. The converse is also true: if x^* and y^* are feasible primal and dual solutions, respectively, then if the complementary slackness conditions hold, the values of the two objective functions are equal and therefore the solutions must be optimal.

In the case of the set cover program, if $x_j^* > 0$ for any primal optimal solution x^*, then the corresponding dual inequality for S_j must be tight for any dual optimal solution y^*. Recall that in the algorithm of the previous section, we put $j \in I$ when $x_j^* \geq 1/f$. Thus, $j \in I$ implies that $j \in I'$, so that $I' \supseteq I$.

1.5 Constructing a Dual Solution: The Primal-Dual Method

One of the disadvantages of the algorithms of the previous two sections is that they require solving a linear program. While linear programs are efficiently solvable, and algorithms for them are quick in practice, special purpose algorithms are often much faster. Although in this book we will not usually be concerned with the precise running times of the algorithms, we will try to indicate their relative practicality.

The basic idea of the algorithm in this section is that the dual rounding algorithm of the previous section uses relatively few properties of an *optimal* dual solution. Instead of actually solving the dual LP, we can construct a feasible dual solution with the same properties. In this case, constructing the dual solution is much faster than solving the dual LP, and hence leads to a much faster algorithm.

The algorithm of the previous section used the following properties. First, we used the fact that $\sum_{i=1}^{n} y_i \leq \text{OPT}$, which is true for any feasible dual solution y. Second, we include $j \in I'$ precisely when $\sum_{i:e_i \in S_j} y_i = w_j$, and I' is a set cover. These two facts together gave the proof that the cost of I' is no more than f times optimal.

Importantly, it is the *proof* of Lemma 1.7 (that we have constructed a feasible cover) that shows how to obtain an algorithm that constructs a dual solution. Consider any feasible dual solution y, and let T be the set of the indices of all tight dual constraints; that is, $T = \{j : \sum_{i:e_i \in S_j} y_i = w_j\}$. If T is a set cover, then we are done. If T is not a set cover, then some item e_i is uncovered, and as shown in the proof of Lemma 1.7 it is possible to improve the dual objective function by increasing y_i by some $\epsilon > 0$. More specifically, we can increase y_i by $\min_{j:e_i \in S_j}(w_j - \sum_{k:e_k \in S_j} y_k)$, so that the constraint becomes tight for the subset S_j that attains the minimum. Additionally, the modified dual solution remains feasible. Thus, we can add j to T, and element e_i is now covered by the sets in T. We repeat this process until T is a set cover. Since an additional element e_i is covered each time, the process is repeated at most n times. To complete the description of the algorithm, we need to give only an initial dual feasible solution.

$$y \leftarrow 0$$
$$I \leftarrow \emptyset$$
while there exists $e_i \notin \bigcup_{j \in I} S_j$ **do**
    Increase the dual variable y_i until there is some ℓ with $e_i \in S_\ell$ such that
$$\sum_{j:e_j \in S_\ell} y_j = w_\ell$$
    $I \leftarrow I \cup \{\ell\}$

Algorithm 1.1. Primal-dual algorithm for the set cover problem.

We can use the solution $y_i = 0$ for each $i = 1, \ldots, n$; this is feasible since each w_j, $j = 1, \ldots, m$, is nonnegative. A formal description is given in Algorithm 1.1.

This yields the following theorem.

Theorem 1.9. *Algorithm 1.1 is an f-approximation algorithm for the set cover problem.*

This type of algorithm is called a *primal-dual* algorithm by analogy with the primal-dual method used in other combinatorial algorithms. Linear programming problems, network flow problems, and shortest path problems (among others) all have primal-dual optimization algorithms; we will see an example of a primal-dual algorithm for the shortest s-t path problem in Section 7.3. Primal-dual algorithms start with a dual feasible solution, and use dual information to infer a primal, possibly infeasible, solution. If the primal solution is indeed infeasible, the dual solution is modified to increase the value of the dual objective function. The primal-dual method has been very useful in designing approximation algorithms, and we will discuss it extensively in Chapter 7.

We observe again that this particular algorithm allows us to have an *a fortiori* guarantee for each input, since we can compare the value of the solution obtained with the value of the dual solution generated by the algorithm. This ratio is guaranteed to be at most f by the proof above, but it might be significantly better.

1.6 A Greedy Algorithm

At this point, the reader might be forgiven for feeling a slight sense of futility: we have examined several techniques for designing approximation algorithms for the set cover problem, and they have all led to the same result, an approximation algorithm with performance guarantee f. But, as in life, perseverance and some amount of cleverness often pay dividends in designing approximation algorithms. We show in this section that a type of algorithm called a greedy algorithm gives an approximation algorithm with a performance guarantee that is often significantly better than f. *Greedy* algorithms work by making a sequence of decisions; each decision is made to optimize that particular decision, even though this sequence of locally optimal (or "greedy") decisions might not lead to a globally optimal solution. The advantage of greedy algorithms is that they are typically very easy to implement, and hence greedy algorithms are a commonly used heuristic, even when they have no performance guarantee.

$$
\begin{aligned}
&I \leftarrow \emptyset \\
&\hat{S}_j \leftarrow S_j \quad \forall j \\
&\textbf{while } I \text{ is not a set cover } \textbf{do} \\
&\quad \ell \leftarrow \arg\min_{j:\hat{S}_j \neq \emptyset} \frac{w_j}{|\hat{S}_j|} \\
&\quad I \leftarrow I \cup \{\ell\} \\
&\quad \hat{S}_j \leftarrow \hat{S}_j - S_\ell \quad \forall j
\end{aligned}
$$

Algorithm 1.2. A greedy algorithm for the set cover problem.

We now present a very natural greedy algorithm for the set cover problem. Sets are chosen in a sequence of rounds. In each round, we choose the set that gives us the most bang for the buck; that is, the set that minimizes the ratio of its weight to the number of currently uncovered elements it contains. In the event of a tie, we pick an arbitrary set that achieves the minimum ratio. We continue choosing sets until all elements are covered. Obviously, this will yield a polynomial-time algorithm, since there can be no more than m rounds, and in each we compute $O(m)$ ratios, each in constant time. A formal description is given in Algorithm 1.2.

Before we state the theorem, we need some notation and a useful mathematical fact. Let H_k denote the kth *harmonic number*: that is, $H_k = 1 + \frac{1}{2} + \frac{1}{3} + \cdots + \frac{1}{k}$. Note that $H_k \approx \ln k$. The following fact is one that we will use many times in the course of this book. It can be proven with simple algebraic manipulations.

Fact 1.10. *Given positive numbers $a_1, \ldots, a_k$ and $b_1, \ldots, b_k$, then*

$$
\min_{i=1,\ldots,k} \frac{a_i}{b_i} \leq \frac{\sum_{i=1}^{k} a_i}{\sum_{i=1}^{k} b_i} \leq \max_{i=1,\ldots,k} \frac{a_i}{b_i}.
$$

Theorem 1.11. *Algorithm 1.2 is an H_n-approximation algorithm for the set cover problem.*

Proof. The basic intuition for the analysis of the algorithm is as follows. Let OPT denote the value of an optimal solution to the set cover problem. We know that an optimal solution covers all n elements with a solution of weight OPT; therefore, there must be some subset that covers its elements with an average weight of at most OPT $/n$. Similarly, after k elements have been covered, the optimal solution can cover the remaining $n - k$ elements with a solution of weight OPT, which implies that there is some subset that covers its remaining uncovered elements with an average weight of at most OPT $/(n - k)$. So in general the greedy algorithm pays about OPT $/(n - k + 1)$ to cover the kth uncovered element, giving a performance guarantee of $\sum_{k=1}^{n} \frac{1}{n-k+1} = H_n$.

We now formalize this intuition. Let n_k denote the number of elements that remain uncovered at the start of the kth iteration. If the algorithm takes ℓ iterations, then $n_1 = n$, and we set $n_{\ell+1} = 0$. Pick an arbitrary iteration k. Let I_k denote the indices of the sets chosen in iterations 1 through $k - 1$, and for each $j = 1, \ldots, m$, let $\hat{S}_j$ denote the set of uncovered elements in S_j at the start of this iteration; that is, $\hat{S}_j = S_j - \bigcup_{p \in I_k} S_p$. Then we claim that for the set j chosen in the kth iteration,

$$
w_j \leq \frac{n_k - n_{k+1}}{n_k} \text{OPT}. \tag{1.5}
$$

Given the claimed inequality (1.5), we can prove the theorem. Let I contain the indices of the sets in our final solution. Then

$$\sum_{j \in I} w_j \le \sum_{k=1}^{\ell} \frac{n_k - n_{k+1}}{n_k} \text{ OPT}$$

$$\le \text{OPT} \cdot \sum_{k=1}^{\ell} \left(\frac{1}{n_k} + \frac{1}{n_k - 1} + \cdots + \frac{1}{n_{k+1} + 1} \right) \qquad (1.6)$$

$$= \text{OPT} \cdot \sum_{i=1}^{n} \frac{1}{i}$$

$$= H_n \cdot \text{OPT},$$

where the inequality (1.6) follows from the fact that $\frac{1}{n_k} \le \frac{1}{n_k - i}$ for $0 \le i < n_k$.

To prove the claimed inequality (1.5), we shall first argue that in the kth iteration,

$$\min_{j : \hat{S}_j \neq \emptyset} \frac{w_j}{|\hat{S}_j|} \le \frac{\text{OPT}}{n_k}. \qquad (1.7)$$

If we let O contain the indices of the sets in an optimal solution, then inequality (1.7) follows from Fact 1.10, by observing that

$$\min_{j : \hat{S}_j \neq \emptyset} \frac{w_j}{|\hat{S}_j|} \le \frac{\sum_{j \in O} w_j}{\sum_{j \in O} |\hat{S}_j|} = \frac{\text{OPT}}{\sum_{j \in O} |\hat{S}_j|} \le \frac{\text{OPT}}{n_k},$$

where the last inequality follows from the fact that since O is a set cover, the set $\bigcup_{j \in O} \hat{S}_j$ must include all remaining n_k uncovered elements. Let j index a subset that minimizes this ratio, so that $\frac{w_j}{|\hat{S}_j|} \le \frac{\text{OPT}}{n_k}$. If we add the subset S_j to our solution, then there will be $|\hat{S}_j|$ fewer uncovered elements, so that $n_{k+1} = n_k - |\hat{S}_j|$. Thus,

$$w_j \le \frac{|\hat{S}_j| \text{ OPT}}{n_k} = \frac{n_k - n_{k+1}}{n_k} \text{OPT}. \qquad \square$$

We can improve the performance guarantee of the algorithm slightly by using the dual of the linear programming relaxation in the analysis. Let g be the maximum size of any subset S_j; that is, $g = \max_j |S_j|$. Recall that Z_{LP}^* is the optimum value of the linear programming relaxation for the set cover problem. The following theorem immediately implies that the greedy algorithm is an H_g-approximation algorithm, since $Z_{LP}^* \le \text{OPT}$.

Theorem 1.12. *Algorithm 1.2 returns a solution indexed by I such that $\sum_{j \in I} w_j \le H_g \cdot Z_{LP}^*$.*

Proof. To prove the theorem, we will construct an *infeasible* dual solution y such that $\sum_{j \in I} w_j = \sum_{i=1}^{n} y_i$. We will then show that $y' = \frac{1}{H_g} y$ is a feasible dual solution. By the weak duality theorem, $\sum_{i=1}^{n} y_i' \le Z_{LP}^*$, so that $\sum_{j \in I} w_j = \sum_{i=1}^{n} y_i = H_g \sum_{i=1}^{n} y_i' \le H_g \cdot \text{OPT}$. We will see at the end of the proof the reason we choose to divide the infeasible dual solution y by H_g.

The name *dual fitting* has been given to this technique of constructing an infeasible dual solution whose value is equal to the value of the primal solution constructed, and such that scaling the dual solution by a single value makes it feasible. We will return to this technique in Section 9.4.

To construct the infeasible dual solution y, suppose we choose to add subset S_j to our solution in iteration k. Then for each $e_i \in \hat{S}_j$, we set $y_i = w_j / |\hat{S}_j|$. Since each $e_i \in \hat{S}_j$ is uncovered in iteration k, and is then covered for the remaining iterations of the algorithm (because we added subset S_j to the solution), the dual variable y_i is set to a value exactly once; in particular, it is set in the iteration in which element e_i is covered. Furthermore, $w_j = \sum_{i : e_i \in \hat{S}_j} y_i$; that is, the weight of the subset S_j chosen in the kth iteration is equal to the sum of the duals y_i of the uncovered elements that are covered in the kth iteration. This immediately implies that $\sum_{j \in I} w_j = \sum_{i=1}^{n} y_i$.

It remains to prove that the dual solution $y' = \frac{1}{H_g} y$ is feasible. We must show that for each subset S_j, $\sum_{i : e_i \in S_j} y_i' \leq w_j$. Pick an arbitrary subset S_j. Let a_k be the number of elements in this subset that are still uncovered at the beginning of the kth iteration, so that $a_1 = |S_j|$, and $a_{\ell+1} = 0$. Let A_k be the uncovered elements of S_j covered in the kth iteration, so that $|A_k| = a_k - a_{k+1}$. If subset S_p is chosen in the kth iteration, then for each element $e_i \in A_k$ covered in the kth iteration,

$$y_i' = \frac{w_p}{H_g |\hat{S}_p|} \leq \frac{w_j}{H_g a_k},$$

where $\hat{S}_p$ is the set of uncovered elements of S_p at the beginning of the kth iteration. The inequality follows because if S_p is chosen in the kth iteration, it must minimize the ratio of its weight to the number of uncovered elements it contains. Thus,

$$
\begin{aligned}
\sum_{i : e_i \in S_j} y_i' &= \sum_{k=1}^{\ell} \sum_{i : e_i \in A_k} y_i' \\
&\leq \sum_{k=1}^{\ell} (a_k - a_{k+1}) \frac{w_j}{H_g a_k} \\
&\leq \frac{w_j}{H_g} \sum_{k=1}^{\ell} \frac{a_k - a_{k+1}}{a_k} \\
&\leq \frac{w_j}{H_g} \sum_{k=1}^{\ell} \left(\frac{1}{a_k} + \frac{1}{a_k - 1} + \cdots + \frac{1}{a_{k+1} + 1} \right) \\
&\leq \frac{w_j}{H_g} \sum_{i=1}^{|S_j|} \frac{1}{i} \\
&= \frac{w_j}{H_g} H_{|S_j|} \\
&\leq w_j,
\end{aligned}
$$

where the final inequality follows because $|S_j| \leq g$. Here we see the reason for scaling the dual solution by H_g, since we know that $H_{|S_j|} \leq H_g$ for all sets j. $\square$

It turns out that no approximation algorithm for the set cover problem with performance guarantee better than H_n is possible, under an assumption slightly stronger than $P = NP$.

Theorem 1.13. *If there exists a c* ln *n-approximation algorithm for the unweighted set cover problem for some constant c < 1, then there is an* $O(n^{O(\log \log n)})$-*time deterministic algorithm for each* NP-*complete problem.*

Theorem 1.14. *There exists some constant c > 0 such that if there exists a c* ln *n-approximation algorithm for the unweighted set cover problem, then* P = NP.

We will discuss results of this sort at more length in Chapter 16; in Theorem 16.32 we show how a slightly weaker version of these results can be derived. Results of this type are sometimes called *hardness* theorems, as they show that it is NP-hard to provide near-optimal solutions for a certain problem with certain performance guarantees.

The *f*-approximation algorithms for the set cover problem imply a 2-approximation algorithm for the special case of the vertex cover problem. No algorithm with a better constant performance guarantee is known at this point in time. Additionally, two hardness theorems, Theorems 1.15 and 1.16 below, have been shown.

Theorem 1.15. *If there exists an* α-*approximation algorithm for the vertex cover problem with* $\alpha < 10\sqrt{5} - 21 \approx 1.36$, *then* P = NP.

The following theorem mentions a conjecture called the *unique games conjecture* that we will discuss more in Section 13.3 and Section 16.5. The conjecture is roughly that a particular problem (called unique games) is NP-hard.

Theorem 1.16. *Assuming the unique games conjecture holds, if there exists an* α-*approximation algorithm for the vertex cover problem with constant* $\alpha < 2$, *then* P = NP.

Thus, assuming P $\neq$ NP and the NP-completeness of the unique games problem, we have found essentially the best possible approximation algorithm for the vertex cover problem.

1.7 A Randomized Rounding Algorithm

In this section, we consider one final technique for devising an approximation algorithm for the set cover problem. Although the algorithm is slower and has no better guarantee than the greedy algorithm of the previous section, we include it here because it introduces the notion of using randomization in approximation algorithms, an idea we will cover in depth in Chapter 5.

As with the algorithm in Section 1.3, the algorithm will solve a linear programming relaxation for the set cover problem, and then round the fractional solution to an integral solution. Rather than doing so deterministically, however, the algorithm will do so randomly using a technique called *randomized rounding*. Let x^* be an optimal solution to the LP relaxation. We would like to round fractional values of x^* to either 0 or 1 in such a way that we obtain a solution $\hat{x}$ to the integer programming formulation of the set cover problem without increasing the cost too much. The central idea of randomized rounding is that we interpret the fractional value x_j^* as the probability that $\hat{x}_j$ should be set to 1. Thus, each subset S_j is included in our solution with probability

x_j^*, where these m events (that S_j is included in our solution) are independent random events. We assume some basic knowledge of probability theory throughout this text; for those who need some additional background, see the notes at the end of the chapter for suggested references.

Let X_j be a random variable that is 1 if subset S_j is included in the solution, and 0 otherwise. Then the expected value of the solution is

$$E\left[\sum_{j=1}^{m} w_j X_j\right] = \sum_{j=1}^{m} w_j \Pr[X_j = 1] = \sum_{j=1}^{m} w_j x_j^* = Z_{LP}^*,$$

or just the value of the linear programming relaxation, which is no more than OPT! As we will see, however, it is quite likely that the solution is not a set cover. Nevertheless, this illustrates why randomized rounding can provide such good approximation algorithms in some cases, and we will see further examples of this in Chapter 5.

Let us now calculate the probability that a given element e_i is not covered by this procedure. This is the probability that none of the subsets containing e_i are included in the solution, or

$$\prod_{j:e_i \in S_j} (1 - x_j^*).$$

We can bound this probability by using the fact that $1 - x \le e^{-x}$ for any x, where e is the base of the natural logarithm. Then

$$\Pr[e_i \text{ not covered}] = \prod_{j:e_i \in S_j} (1 - x_j^*)$$

$$\le \prod_{j:e_i \in S_j} e^{-x_j^*}$$

$$= e^{-\sum_{j:e_i \in S_j} x_j^*}$$

$$\le e^{-1},$$

where the final inequality follows from the LP constraint that $\sum_{j:e_i \in S_j} x_j^* \ge 1$. Although e^{-1} is an upper bound on the probability that a given element is not covered, it is possible to approach this bound arbitrarily closely, so in the worst case it is quite likely that this randomized rounding procedure does not produce a set cover.

How small would this probability have to be in order for it to be very likely that a set cover is produced? And perhaps even more fundamentally, what is the "right" notion of "very likely"? The latter question has a number of possible answers; one natural way to think of the situation is to impose a guarantee in keeping with our focus on polynomial-time algorithms. Suppose that, for any constant c, we could devise a polynomial-time algorithm whose chance of failure is at most an inverse polynomial n^{-c}; then we say that we have an algorithm that works *with high probability*. To be more precise, we would have a family of algorithms, since it might be necessary to give progressively slower algorithms, or ones with worse performance guarantees, to achieve analogously more fail-safe results. If we could devise a randomized procedure such that $\Pr[e_i \text{ not covered}] \le \frac{1}{n^c}$ for some constant $c \ge 2$, then

$$\Pr[\text{there exists an uncovered element}] \le \sum_{i=1}^{n} \Pr[e_i \text{ not covered}] \le \frac{1}{n^{c-1}},$$

and we would have a set cover with high probability. In fact, we can achieve such a bound in the following way: for each subset S_j, we imagine a coin that comes up heads with probability x_j^*, and we flip the coin $c \ln n$ times. If it comes up heads in any of the $c \ln n$ trials, we include S_j in our solution, otherwise not. Thus, the probability that S_j is not included is $(1 - x_j^*)^{c \ln n}$. Furthermore,

$$\Pr[e_i \text{ not covered}] = \prod_{j:e_i \in S_j} (1 - x_j^*)^{c \ln n}$$

$$\le \prod_{j:e_i \in S_j} e^{-x_j^*(c \ln n)}$$

$$= e^{-(c \ln n) \sum_{j:e_i \in S_j} x_j^*}$$

$$\le \frac{1}{n^c},$$

as desired.

We now need to prove only that the algorithm has a good expected value given that it produces a set cover.

Theorem 1.17. *The algorithm is a randomized $O(\ln n)$-approximation algorithm that produces a set cover with high probability.*

Proof. Let $p_j(x_j^*)$ be the probability that a given subset S_j is included in the solution as a function of x_j^*. By construction of the algorithm, we know that $p_j(x_j^*) = 1 - (1 - x_j^*)^{c \ln n}$. Observe that if $x_j^* \in [0, 1]$ and $c \ln n \ge 1$, then we can bound the derivative p_j' at x_j^* by

$$p_j'(x_j^*) = (c \ln n)(1 - x_j^*)^{(c \ln n)-1} \le (c \ln n).$$

Then since $p_j(0) = 0$, and the slope of the function p_j is bounded above by $c \ln n$ on the interval $[0, 1]$, $p_j(x_j^*) \le (c \ln n)x_j^*$ on the interval $[0,1]$. If X_j is a random variable that is 1 if the subset S_j is included in the solution, and 0 otherwise, then the expected value of the random procedure is

$$E\left[\sum_{j=1}^{m} w_j X_j\right] = \sum_{j=1}^{m} w_j \Pr[X_j = 1]$$

$$\le \sum_{j=1}^{m} w_j(c \ln n)x_j^*$$

$$= (c \ln n) \sum_{j=1}^{m} w_j x_j^* = (c \ln n)Z_{LP}^*.$$

However, we would like to bound the expected value of the solution given that a set cover is produced. Let F be the event that the solution obtained by the procedure is a feasible set cover, and let $\bar{F}$ be the complement of this event. We know from the previous discussion that $\Pr[F] \geq 1 - \frac{1}{n^{c-1}}$, and we also know that

$$E\left[\sum_{j=1}^{m} w_j X_j\right] = E\left[\sum_{j=1}^{m} w_j X_j \middle| F\right] \Pr[F] + E\left[\sum_{j=1}^{m} w_j X_j \middle| \bar{F}\right] \Pr[\bar{F}].$$

Since $w_j \geq 0$ for all j,

$$E\left[\sum_{j=1}^{m} w_j X_j \middle| \bar{F}\right] \geq 0.$$

Thus,

$$E\left[\sum_{j=1}^{m} w_j X_j \middle| F\right] = \frac{1}{\Pr[F]}\left(E\left[\sum_{j=1}^{m} w_j X_j\right] - E\left[\sum_{j=1}^{m} w_j X_j \middle| \bar{F}\right] \Pr[\bar{F}]\right)$$

$$\leq \frac{1}{\Pr[F]} \cdot E\left[\sum_{j=1}^{m} w_j X_j\right]$$

$$\leq \frac{(c \ln n) Z_{LP}^*}{1 - \frac{1}{n^{c-1}}}$$

$$\leq 2c(\ln n) Z_{LP}^*$$

for $n \geq 2$ and $c \geq 2$. $\qquad\qquad\square$

While in this case there is a simpler and faster approximation algorithm that achieves a better performance guarantee, we will see in Chapter 5 that sometimes randomized algorithms are simpler to describe and analyze than deterministic algorithms. In fact, most of the randomized algorithms we present in this book can be *derandomized*: that is, a deterministic variant of them can be created that achieves the expected performance guarantee of the randomized algorithm. However, these deterministic algorithms are sometimes more complicated to describe. In addition, there are some cases in which the deterministic variant is easy to state, but the only way in which we know how to analyze the algorithm is by analyzing a corresponding randomized algorithm.

This brings us to the end of our introduction to approximation algorithms. In subsequent chapters, we will look at the techniques introduced here – as well as a few others – in greater depth, and see their application to many other problems.

Exercises

1.1 In the set cover problem, the goal is to find a collection of subsets indexed by I that minimizes $\sum_{j \in I} w_j$ such that

$$\left| \bigcup_{j \in I} S_j \right| = |E|.$$

Consider the *partial cover problem*, in which one finds a collection of subsets indexed by I that minimizes $\sum_{j \in I} w_j$ such that

$$\left| \bigcup_{j \in I} S_j \right| \geq p|E|,$$

where $0 < p < 1$ is some constant.

    (a) Give a polynomial-time algorithm to find a solution to the partial cover problem in which the value is no more than $c(p) \cdot \text{OPT}$, where $c(p)$ is a constant that depends on p, and OPT is the value of the optimal solution to the set cover problem.

    (b) Give an $f(p)$-approximation algorithm for the partial cover problem, such that f is non-decreasing in p and $f(1) \leq H_{|E|}$.

1.2 In the *directed Steiner tree problem*, we are given as input a directed graph $G = (V, A)$, nonnegative costs $c_{ij} \geq 0$ for arcs $(i, j) \in A$, a root vertex $r \in V$, and a set of terminals $T \subseteq V$. The goal is to find a minimum-cost tree such that for each $i \in T$ there exists a directed path from r to i.

Prove that for some constant c there can be no $c \log |T|$-approximation algorithm for the directed Steiner tree problem, unless P = NP.

1.3 In the *metric asymmetric traveling salesman problem*, we are given as input a complete directed graph $G = (V, A)$ with costs $c_{ij} \geq 0$ for all arcs $(i, j) \in A$, such that the arc costs obey the *triangle inequality*: for all $i, j, k \in V$, we have that $c_{ij} + c_{jk} \geq c_{ik}$. The goal is to find a *tour* of minimum cost, that is, a directed cycle that contains each vertex exactly once, such that the sum of the cost of the arcs in the cycle is minimized.

One approach to finding an approximation algorithm for this problem is to first find a minimum-cost strongly connected *Eulerian* subgraph of the input graph. A directed graph is strongly connected if for any pair of vertices $i, j \in V$ there is a path from i to j and a path from j to i. A directed graph is Eulerian if the indegree of each vertex equals its outdegree. Given a strongly connected Eulerian subgraph of the input to the problem, it is possible to use a technique called "shortcutting" (discussed in Section 2.4) to turn this into a tour of no greater cost by using the triangle inequality.

One way to find a strongly connected Eulerian subgraph is as follows: We first find a *minimum mean-cost cycle* in the graph. A minimum mean-cost cycle is a directed cycle that minimizes the ratio of the cost of the arcs in the cycle to the number of arcs in the cycle. Such a cycle can be found in polynomial time. We then choose one vertex of the cycle arbitrarily, remove all other vertices of the cycle from the graph, and repeat. We do this until only one vertex of the graph is left. Consider the subgraph consisting of all the arcs from all the cycles found.

    (a) Prove that the subgraph found by the algorithm is a strongly connected Eulerian subgraph of the input graph.

    (b) Prove that the cost of this subgraph is at most $2H_n \cdot \text{OPT}$, where $n = |V|$ and OPT is the cost of the optimal tour. Conclude that this algorithm is a $2H_n$-approximation algorithm for the metric asymmetric traveling salesman problem.

1.4 In the *uncapacitated facility location problem*, we have a set of clients D and a set of facilities F. For each client $j \in D$ and facility $i \in F$, there is a cost c_{ij} of assigning client

j to facility i. Furthermore, there is a cost f_i associated with each facility $i \in F$. The goal of the problem is to choose a subset of facilities $F' \subseteq F$ so as to minimize the total cost of the facilities in F' and the cost of assigning each client $j \in D$ to the nearest facility in F'. In other words, we wish to find F' so as to minimize $\sum_{i \in F'} f_i + \sum_{j \in D} \min_{i \in F'} c_{ij}$.

(a) Show that there exists some c such that there is no $(c \ln |D|)$-approximation algorithm for the uncapacitated facility location problem unless $P = NP$.

(b) Give an $O(\ln |D|)$-approximation algorithm for the uncapacitated facility location problem.

1.5 Consider the vertex cover problem.

(a) Prove that any extreme point of the linear program

$$\text{minimize} \sum_{i \in V} w_i x_i$$

$$\text{subject to} \quad x_i + x_j \geq 1, \qquad \forall (i, j) \in E,$$

$$x_i \geq 0, \qquad i \in V,$$

has the property that $x_i \in \{0, \frac{1}{2}, 1\}$ for all $i \in V$. (Recall that an *extreme point* x is a feasible solution that cannot be expressed as $\lambda x^1 + (1 - \lambda) x^2$ for $0 < \lambda < 1$ and feasible solutions x^1 and x^2 distinct from x.)

(b) Give a $\frac{3}{2}$-approximation algorithm for the vertex cover problem when the input graph is planar. You may use the facts that polynomial-time LP solvers return extreme points, and that there is a polynomial-time algorithm to 4-color any planar graph (i.e., the algorithm assigns each vertex one of four colors such that for any edge $(i, j) \in E$, vertices i and j have been assigned different colors).

1.6 In the *node-weighted Steiner tree problem*, we are given as input an undirected graph $G = (V, E)$, node weights $w_i \geq 0$ for all $i \in V$, edge costs $c_e \geq 0$ for all $e \in E$, and a set of terminals $T \subseteq V$. The cost of a tree is the sum of the weights of the nodes plus the sum of the costs of the edges in the tree. The goal of the problem is to find a minimum-weight tree that spans all the terminals in T.

(a) Show that there exists some c such that there is no $(c \ln |T|)$-approximation algorithm for the node-weighted Steiner tree problem unless $P = NP$.

(b) Give a greedy $O(\ln |T|)$-approximation algorithm for the node-weighted Steiner tree problem.

Chapter Notes

The term "approximation algorithm" was coined by David S. Johnson [179] in an influential and prescient 1974 paper. However, earlier papers had proved the performance guarantees of heuristics, including a 1967 paper of Erdős [99] on the maximum cut problem (to be discussed in Section 6.2), a 1966 paper of Graham [142] on a scheduling problem (to be discussed in Section 2.3), and a 1964 paper of Vizing [284] on the edge coloring problem (to be discussed in Section 2.7). Johnson's paper gave an $O(\log n)$-approximation algorithm for the unweighted set cover problem, as well as approximation algorithms for the maximum satisfiability problem (to be discussed in Section 5.1), vertex coloring (Sections 5.12, 6.5, and 13.2), and the maximum clique problem. At the end of the paper, Johnson [179] speculates about the approximability of these various problems:

> The results described in this paper indicate a possible classification of optimization problems as to the behavior of their approximation algorithms. Such a classification must remain tentative, at least until the existence of polynomial-time algorithms for finding optimal solutions has been proved or disproved. In the meantime, many questions can be asked. Are there indeed $O(\log n)$ coloring algorithms? Are there any clique finding algorithms better than $O(n^\epsilon)$ for all $\epsilon > 0$? Where do other optimization problems fit into the scheme of things? What is it that makes algorithms for different problems behave in the same way? Is there some stronger kind of reducibility than the simple polynomial reducibility that will explain these results, or are they due to some structural similarity between the problems as we define them? And what other types of behavior and ways of analyzing and measuring it are possible? (p. 278)

There has been substantial work done in attempting to answer these questions in the decades since Johnson's paper appeared, with significant progress; for instance, Theorem 1.4 shows that no clique algorithm of the kind Johnson mentions is possible unless $P = NP$.

Other books on approximation algorithms are available, including the textbooks of Ausiello, Crescenzi, Gambosi, Kann, Marchetti-Spaccamela, and Protasi [27] and of Vazirani [283], and the collection of surveys edited by Hochbaum [162]. Many books on algorithms and combinatorial optimization now contain sections on approximation algorithms, including the textbooks of Bertsimas and Tsitsiklis [47], Cook, Cunningham, Pulleyblank, and Schrijver [81], Cormen, Leiserson, Rivest, and Stein [82], Kleinberg and Tardos [198], and Korte and Vygen [203].

For solid introductions to linear programming, we suggest the books of Bertsimas and Tsitsiklis [47], Chvátal [79] and Ferris, Mangasarian, and Wright [112]. Bertsekas and Tsitsiklis [45], Durrett [93, 94], and Ross [256] provide basic introductions to probability theory; the first few chapters of the book of Mitzenmacher and Upfal [226] provide a brief introduction to probability theory in the context of computer algorithms.

The antivirus application of the set cover problem mentioned is due to Kephart, Sorkin, Arnold, Chess, Tesauro, and White [188].

Theorem 1.3 on the non-existence of approximation schemes for problems in MAX SNP is due to Arora, Lund, Motwani, Sudan, and Szegedy [19], building on earlier work of Feige, Goldwasser, Lovász, Safra, and Szegedy [108] and Arora and Safra [23]. Theorem 1.4 on the hardness of approximating the maximum clique problem is due to Håstad [158], with a strengthening due to Zuckerman [296].

The LP rounding algorithm of Section 1.3 and the dual rounding algorithm of Section 1.4 are due to Hochbaum [160]. The primal-dual algorithm of Section 1.5 is due to Bar-Yehuda and Even [35]. The greedy algorithm and the LP-based analysis of Section 1.6 are due to Chvátal [78]. The randomized rounding algorithm of Section 1.7 is apparently folklore. Johnson [179] and Lovász [218] give earlier greedy $O(\log n)$-approximation algorithms for the unweighted set cover problem.

Theorem 1.13 on the hardness of approximating the set cover problem is due to Lund and Yannakakis [220], with a strengthening due to Bellare, Goldwasser, Lund, and Russell [43]. Theorem 1.14 on the hardness of the set cover problem is due to Feige [107]. Theorem 1.15 on the hardness of the vertex cover problem is due to Dinur and Safra [91], while Theorem 1.16, which uses the unique games conjecture, is due to Khot and Regev [194].

Exercise 1.3 is an unpublished result of Kleinberg and Williamson. The algorithm in Exercise 1.4 is due to Hochbaum [161]. Nemhauser and Trotter [231] show that all extreme points of the linear programming relaxation of vertex cover have value $\{0, \frac{1}{2}, 1\}$ (used in Exercise 1.5). Exercise 1.6 is due to Klein and Ravi [196].

CHAPTER 2

Greedy Algorithms and Local Search

In this chapter, we will consider two standard and related techniques for designing algorithms and heuristics, namely, *greedy algorithms* and *local search algorithms*. Both algorithms work by making a sequence of decisions that optimize some local choice, though these local choices might not lead to the best overall solution.

In a greedy algorithm, a solution is constructed step by step, and at each step of the algorithm the next part of the solution is constructed by making some decision that is locally the best possible. In Section 1.6, we gave an example of a greedy algorithm for the set cover problem that constructs a set cover by repeatedly choosing the set that minimizes the ratio of its weight to the number of currently uncovered elements it contains.

A local search algorithm starts with an arbitrary feasible solution to the problem, and then checks if some small, local change to the solution results in an improved objective function. If so, the change is made. When no further change can be made, we have a *locally optimal solution*, and it is sometimes possible to prove that such locally optimal solutions have value close to that of the optimal solution. Unlike other approximation algorithm design techniques, the most straightforward implementation of a local search algorithm typically does not run in polynomial time. The algorithm usually requires some restriction to the local changes allowed in order to ensure that enough progress is made during each improving step so that a locally optimal solution is found in polynomial time.

Thus, while both types of algorithm optimize local choices, greedy algorithms are typically *primal infeasible* algorithms: they construct a solution to the problem during the course of the algorithm. Local search algorithms are *primal feasible* algorithms: they always maintain a feasible solution to the problem and modify it during the course of the algorithm.

Both greedy algorithms and local search algorithms are extremely popular choices for heuristics for NP-hard problems. They are typically easy to implement and have good running times in practice. In this chapter, we will consider greedy and local search algorithms for scheduling problems, clustering problems, and others, including the most famous problem in combinatorial optimization, the traveling salesman problem.

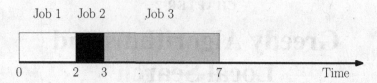

Figure 2.1. An instance of a schedule for the one-machine scheduling problem in which $p_1 = 2$, $r_1 = 0$, $p_2 = 1$, $r_2 = 2$, $p_3 = 4$, $r_3 = 1$. In this schedule, $C_1 = 2$, $C_2 = 3$, and $C_3 = 7$. If the deadlines for the jobs are such that $d_1 = -1$, $d_2 = 1$, and $d_3 = 10$, then $L_1 = 2 - (-1) = 3$, $L_2 = 3 - 1 = 2$, and $L_3 = 7 - 10 = -3$, so that $L_{max} = L_1 = 3$.

Because greedy and local search algorithms are natural choices for heuristics, some of these algorithms were among the very first approximation algorithms devised; in particular, the greedy algorithm for the parallel machine scheduling problem in Section 2.3 and the greedy algorithm for edge coloring in Section 2.7 were both given and analyzed in the 1960s, before the concept of NP-completeness was invented.

2.1 Scheduling Jobs with Deadlines on a Single Machine

One of the most common types of problems in combinatorial optimization is that of creating a schedule. We are given some type of work that must be done, and some resources to do the work, and from this we must create a schedule to complete the work that optimizes some objective; perhaps we want to finish all the work as soon as possible, or perhaps we want to make sure that the average time at which we complete the various pieces of work is as small as possible. We will often consider the problem of scheduling jobs (the work) on machines (the resources). We start this chapter by considering one of the simplest possible versions of this problem.

Suppose that there are n jobs to be scheduled on a single machine, where the machine can process at most one job at a time, and must process a job until its completion once it has begun processing; suppose that each job j must be processed for a specified p_j units of time, where the processing of job j may begin no earlier than a specified *release date* r_j, $j = 1, \ldots, n$. We assume that the schedule starts at time 0, and each release date is nonnegative. Furthermore, assume that each job j has a specified due date d_j, and if we complete its processing at time C_j, then its *lateness* L_j is equal to $C_j - d_j$; we are interested in scheduling the jobs so as to minimize the maximum lateness, $L_{max} = \max_{j=1,\ldots,n} L_j$. A sample instance of this problem is shown in Figure 2.1.

Unfortunately, this problem is NP-hard, and in fact, even deciding if there is a schedule for which $L_{max} \leq 0$ (i.e., deciding if all jobs can be completed by their due date) is strongly NP-hard (the reader unfamiliar with strong NP-hardness can consult Appendix B). Of course, this is a problem that we often encounter in everyday life, and many of us schedule our lives with the following simple greedy heuristic: focus on the task with the earliest due date. We will show that in certain circumstances this is a provably good thing to do. However, we first argue that as stated, this optimization problem is not particularly amenable to obtaining near-optimal solutions. If there were a ρ-approximation algorithm, then for any input with optimal value 0, the algorithm must still find a schedule of objective function value at most $\rho \cdot 0 = 0$, and hence (given the NP-hardness result stated above) this would imply that $P = NP$. (There is the further complication of what to do if the objective function of the optimal solution is negative!) One easy workaround to this is to assume that all due dates are negative, which implies that the optimal value is always positive. We shall give a 2-approximation algorithm for this special case.

We first provide a good lower bound on the optimal value for this scheduling problem. Let S denote a subset of jobs, and let $r(S) = \min_{j \in S} r_j$, $p(S) = \sum_{j \in S} p_j$, and $d(S) = \max_{j \in S} d_j$. Let $L^*_{\max}$ denote the optimal value.

Lemma 2.1. *For each subset S of jobs,*

$$L^*_{\max} \geq r(S) + p(S) - d(S).$$

Proof. Consider the optimal schedule, and view this simply as a schedule for the jobs in the subset S. Let job j be the last job in S to be processed. Since none of the jobs in S can be processed before $r(S)$, and in total they require $p(S)$ time units of processing, it follows that job j cannot complete any earlier than time $r(S) + p(S)$. The due date of job j is $d(S)$ or earlier, and so the lateness of job j in this schedule is at least $r(S) + p(S) - d(S)$; hence, $L^*_{\max} \geq r(S) + p(S) - d(S)$. $\square$

A job j is *available* at time t if its release date $r_j \leq t$. We consider the following natural algorithm: at each moment that the machine is idle, start processing next an available job with the earliest due date. This is known as the *earliest due date (EDD) rule*.

Theorem 2.2. *The EDD rule is a 2-approximation algorithm for the problem of minimizing the maximum lateness on a single machine subject to release dates with negative due dates.*

Proof. Consider the schedule produced by the EDD rule, and let job j be a job of maximum lateness in this schedule; that is, $L_{\max} = C_j - d_j$. Focus on the time C_j in this schedule; find the earliest point in time $t \leq C_j$ such that the machine was processing without any idle time for the entire period $[t, C_j)$. Several jobs may be processed in this time interval; we require only that the machine not be idle for some interval of positive length within it. Let S be the set of jobs that are processed in the interval $[t, C_j)$. By our choice of t, we know that just prior to t, none of these jobs were available (and clearly at least one job in S is available at time t); hence, $r(S) = t$. Furthermore, since only jobs in S are processed throughout this time interval, $p(S) = C_j - t = C_j - r(S)$. Thus, $C_j \leq r(S) + p(S)$; since $d(S) < 0$, we can apply Lemma 2.1 to get that

$$L^*_{\max} \geq r(S) + p(S) - d(S) \geq r(S) + p(S) \geq C_j. \tag{2.1}$$

On the other hand, by applying Lemma 2.1 with $S = \{j\}$,

$$L^*_{\max} \geq r_j + p_j - d_j \geq -d_j. \tag{2.2}$$

Adding inequalities (2.1) and (2.2), we see that the maximum lateness of the schedule computed is

$$L_{max} = C_j - d_j \leq 2L_{max}^*,$$

which completes the proof of the theorem. $\square$

2.2 The k-Center Problem

The problem of finding similarities and dissimilarities in large amounts of data is ubiquitous: companies wish to group customers with similar purchasing behavior, political consultants group precincts by their voting behavior, and search engines group webpages by their similarity of topic. Usually we speak of *clustering* data, and there has been extensive study of the problem of finding good clusterings.

Here we consider a particular variant of clustering, the k-center problem. In this problem, we are given as input an undirected, complete graph $G = (V, E)$, with a *distance* $d_{ij} \geq 0$ between each pair of vertices $i, j \in V$. We assume $d_{ii} = 0$, $d_{ij} = d_{ji}$ for each $i, j \in V$, and that the distances obey the *triangle inequality*: for each triple $i, j, l \in V$, it is the case that $d_{ij} + d_{jl} \geq d_{il}$. In this problem, distances model similarity: vertices that are closer to each other are more similar, whereas those farther apart are less similar. We are also given a positive integer k as input. The goal is to find k clusters, grouping together the vertices that are most similar into clusters together. In this problem, we will choose a set $S \subseteq V$, $|S| = k$, of k *cluster centers*. Each vertex will assign itself to its closest cluster center, grouping the vertices into k different clusters. For the k-center problem, the objective is to minimize the maximum distance of a vertex to its cluster center. Geometrically speaking, the goal is to find the centers of k different balls of the same radius that cover all points so that the radius is as small as possible. More formally, we define the distance of a vertex i from a set $S \subseteq V$ of vertices to be $d(i, S) = \min_{j \in S} d_{ij}$. Then the corresponding radius for S is equal to $\max_{i \in V} d(i, S)$, and the goal of the k-center problem is to find a set of size k of minimum radius.

In later chapters we will consider other objective functions, such as minimizing the *sum* of distances of vertices to their cluster centers, that is, minimizing $\sum_{i \in V} d(i, S)$. This is called the k-median problem, and we will consider it in Sections 7.7 and 9.2. We shall also consider another variant on clustering called correlation clustering in Section 6.4.

We give a greedy 2-approximation algorithm for the k-center problem that is simple and intuitive. Our algorithm first picks a vertex $i \in V$ arbitrarily, and puts it in our set S of cluster centers. Then it makes sense for the next cluster center to be as far away as possible from all the other cluster centers. Hence, while $|S| < k$, we repeatedly find a vertex $j \in V$ that determines the current radius (or in other words, for which the distance $d(j, S)$ is maximized) and add it to S. Once $|S| = k$, we stop and return S. Our algorithm is given in Algorithm 2.1.

An execution of the algorithm is shown in Figure 2.2.

We will now prove that the algorithm is a good approximation algorithm.

Theorem 2.3. *Algorithm 2.1 is a 2-approximation algorithm for the k-center problem.*

$$
\begin{aligned}
&\text{Pick arbitrary } i \in V \\
&S \leftarrow \{i\} \\
&\textbf{while } |S| < k \textbf{ do} \\
&\qquad j \leftarrow \arg\max_{j \in V} d(j, S) \\
&\qquad S \leftarrow S \cup \{j\}
\end{aligned}
$$

Algorithm 2.1. A greedy 2-approximation algorithm for the *k*-center problem.

Proof. Let $S^* = \{j_1, \ldots, j_k\}$ denote the optimal solution, and let r^* denote its radius. This solution partitions the nodes V into clusters $V_1, \ldots, V_k$, where each point $j \in V$ is placed in V_i if it is closest to j_i among all of the points in S^* (and ties are broken arbitrarily). Each pair of points j and j' in the same cluster V_i are at most $2r^*$ apart: by the triangle inequality, the distance $d_{jj'}$ between them is at most the sum of d_{jj_i}, the distance from j to the center j_i, plus $d_{j_i j'}$, the distance from the center j_i to j' (that is, $d_{jj'} \leq d_{jj_i} + d_{j_i j'}$); since d_{jj_i} and $d_{j'j_i}$ are each at most r^*, we see that $d_{jj'}$ is at most $2r^*$.

Now consider the set $S \subseteq V$ of points selected by the greedy algorithm. If one center in S is selected from each cluster of the optimal solution S^*, then every point in V is clearly within $2r^*$ of some selected point in S. However, suppose that the algorithm selects two points within the same cluster. That is, in some iteration, the algorithm selects a point $j \in V_i$, even though the algorithm had already selected a point $j' \in V_i$ in an earlier iteration. Again, the distance between these two points is at most $2r^*$. The algorithm selects j in this iteration because it is currently the furthest from the points already in S. Hence, all points are within a distance of at most $2r^*$ of some center already selected for S. Clearly, this remains true as the algorithm adds more centers in subsequent iterations, and we have proved the theorem. The instance in Figure 2.2 shows that this analysis is tight. □

We shall argue next that this result is the best possible; if there exists a ρ-approximation algorithm with $\rho < 2$, then P = NP. To see this, we consider the *dominating set problem*, which is NP-complete. In the dominating set problem, we are given a graph $G = (V, E)$ and an integer k, and we must decide if there exists a set $S \subseteq V$ of size k such that each vertex is either in S, or adjacent to a vertex in S. Given an instance

Figure 2.2. An instance of the *k*-center problem where $k = 3$ and the distances are given by the Euclidean distances between points. The execution of the greedy algorithm is shown; the nodes 1, 2, 3 are the nodes selected by the greedy algorithm, whereas the nodes 1*, 2*, 3* are the three nodes in an optimal solution.

of the dominating set problem, we can define an instance of the k-center problem by setting the distance between adjacent vertices to 1, and nonadjacent vertices to 2: there is a dominating set of size k if and only if the optimal radius for this k-center instance is 1. Furthermore, any ρ-approximation algorithm with $\rho < 2$ must always produce a solution of radius 1 if such a solution exists, since any solution of radius $\rho < 2$ must actually be of radius 1. This implies the following theorem.

Theorem 2.4. *There is no α-approximation algorithm for the k-center problem for $\alpha < 2$ unless* $P = NP$.

2.3 Scheduling Jobs on Identical Parallel Machines

In Section 2.1, we considered the problem of scheduling jobs on a single machine to minimize lateness. Here we consider a variation on that problem, in which we now have multiple machines and no release dates, but our goal is to minimize the time at which all jobs are finished. Suppose that there are n jobs to be processed, and there are m identical machines (running in parallel) to which each job may be assigned. Each job $j = 1, \ldots, n$, must be processed on one of these machines for p_j time units without interruption, and each job is available for processing at time 0. Each machine can process at most one job at a time. The aim is to complete all jobs as soon as possible; that is, if job j completes at a time C_j (presuming that the schedule starts at time 0), then we wish to minimize $C_{\max} = \max_{j=1,\ldots,n} C_j$, which is often called the *makespan* or *length* of the schedule. An equivalent view of the same problem is as a load-balancing problem: there are n items, each of a given weight p_j, and they are to be distributed among m machines; the aim is to assign each item to one machine so to minimize the maximum total weight assigned to one machine.

This scheduling problem has the property that even the simplest algorithms compute reasonably good solutions. In particular, we will show that both a local search algorithm and a very simple greedy algorithm find solutions that have makespan within a factor of 2 of the optimum. In fact, the analyses of these two algorithms are essentially identical.

Local search algorithms are defined by a set of local changes or local moves that change one feasible solution to another. The simplest local search procedure for this scheduling problem works as follows: Start with any schedule; consider the job ℓ that finishes last; check whether or not there exists a machine to which it can be reassigned that would cause this job to finish earlier. If so, transfer job ℓ to this other machine. We can determine whether to transfer job ℓ by checking if there exists a machine that finishes its currently assigned jobs earlier than $C_\ell - p_\ell$. The local search algorithm repeats this procedure until the last job to complete cannot be transferred. An illustration of this local move is shown in Figure 2.3.

In order to analyze the performance of this local search algorithm, we first provide some natural lower bounds on the length of an optimal schedule, $C_{\max}^*$. Since each job must be processed, it follows that

$$C_{\max}^* \geq \max_{j=1,\ldots,n} p_j. \tag{2.3}$$

On the other hand, there is, in total, $P = \sum_{j=1}^n p_j$ units of processing to accomplish, and only m machines to do this work. Hence, on average, a machine will be assigned

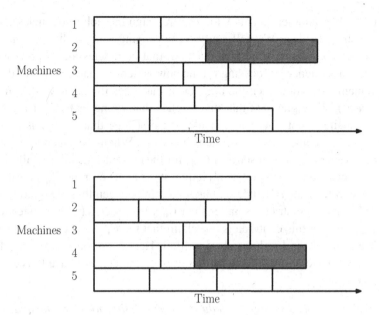

Figure 2.3. An example of a local move in the local search algorithm for scheduling jobs on parallel machines. The gray job on machine 2 finishes last in the schedule on the top, but the schedule can be improved by moving the gray job to machine 4. No further local moves are possible after this one since again the gray job finishes last.

P/m units of work, and consequently, there must exist one machine that is assigned at least that much work. Thus,

$$C^*_{\max} \geq \sum_{j=1}^{n} p_j/m. \tag{2.4}$$

Consider the solution produced by the local search algorithm. Let ℓ be a job that completes last in this final schedule; the completion time of job ℓ, C_ℓ, is equal to this solution's objective function value. By the fact that the algorithm terminated with this schedule, every other machine must be busy from time 0 until the start of job ℓ at time $S_\ell = C_\ell - p_\ell$. We can partition the schedule into two disjoint time intervals, from time 0 until S_ℓ, and the time during which job ℓ is being processed. By (2.3), the latter interval has length at most $C^*_{\max}$. Now consider the former time interval; we know that each machine is busy processing jobs throughout this period. The total amount of work being processed in this interval is mS_ℓ, which is clearly no more than the total work to be done, $\sum_{j=1}^{n} p_j$. Hence,

$$S_\ell \leq \sum_{j=1}^{n} p_j/m. \tag{2.5}$$

By combining this with (2.4), we see that $S_\ell \leq C^*_{\max}$. But now, we see that the length of the schedule before the start of job ℓ is at most $C^*_{\max}$, as is the length of the schedule afterward; in total, the makespan of the schedule computed is at most $2C^*_{\max}$.

Now consider the running time of this algorithm. This local search procedure has the property that the value of $C_{\max}$ for the sequence of schedules produced, iteration by iteration, never increases (it can remain the same, but then the number of machines that achieve the maximum value decreases). One natural assumption to make is that when we transfer a job to another machine, then we reassign that job to the machine that is currently finishing earliest. We will analyze the running time of this variant instead. Let $C_{\min}$ be the completion time of a machine that completes all its processing the earliest. One consequence of focusing on the new variant is that $C_{\min}$ never decreases (and if it remains the same, then the number of machines that achieve this minimum value decreases). We argue next that this implies that we never transfer a job twice. Suppose this claim is not true, and consider the first time that a job j is transferred twice, say, from machine i to i', and later then to i^*. When job j is reassigned from machine i to machine i', it then starts at $C_{\min}$ for the current schedule. Similarly, when job j is reassigned from machine i' to i^*, it then starts at the current $C'_{\min}$. Furthermore, no change occurred to the schedule on machine i' in between these two moves for job j. Hence, $C'_{\min}$ must be strictly smaller than $C_{\min}$ (in order for the transfer to be an improving move), but this contradicts our claim that the $C_{\min}$ value is non-decreasing over the iterations of the local search algorithm. Hence, no job is transferred twice, and after at most n iterations, the algorithm must terminate. We have thus shown the following theorem.

Theorem 2.5. *The local search procedure for scheduling jobs on identical parallel machines is a 2-approximation algorithm.*

In fact, it is not hard to see that the analysis of the approximation ratio can be refined slightly. In deriving the inequality (2.5), we included job ℓ among the work to be done *prior to the start of job ℓ*. Hence, we actually derived that

$$S_\ell \le \sum_{j \ne \ell} p_j / m,$$

and hence the total length of the schedule produced is at most

$$p_\ell + \sum_{j \ne \ell} p_j / m = \left(1 - \frac{1}{m}\right) p_\ell + \sum_{j=1}^{n} p_j / m.$$

By applying the two lower bounds (2.3) and (2.4) to these two terms, we see that the schedule has length at most $\left(2 - \frac{1}{m}\right) C^*_{\max}$. Of course, the difference between this bound and 2 is significant only if there are very few machines.

Another natural algorithm to compute a schedule is a greedy algorithm that assigns the jobs as soon as there is machine availability to process them: whenever a machine becomes idle, then one of the remaining jobs is assigned to start processing on that machine. This algorithm is often called the *list scheduling algorithm*, since one can equivalently view the algorithm as first ordering the jobs in a list (arbitrarily), and the next job to be processed is the one at the top of the list. Another viewpoint, from the load-balancing perspective, is that the next job on the list is assigned to the machine that is currently the least heavily loaded. It is in this sense that one can view the algorithm as a greedy algorithm. The analysis of this algorithm is now quite trivial; if one uses this schedule as the starting point for the local search procedure, that algorithm would immediately declare that the solution cannot be improved! To see this, consider a job ℓ that is (one of the jobs) last to complete its processing. Each machine is busy until $C_\ell - p_\ell$, since otherwise we would have assigned job ℓ to that other machine. Hence, no transfers are possible.

Theorem 2.6. *The list scheduling algorithm for the problem of minimizing the makespan on m identical parallel machines is a 2-approximation algorithm.*

It is not hard to obtain a stronger result by improving this list scheduling algorithm. Not all lists yield the same schedule, and it is natural to use an additional greedy rule that first sorts the jobs in non-increasing order. One way to view the results of Theorems 2.5 and 2.6 is that the relative error in the length of the schedule produced is entirely due to the length of the last job to finish. If that job is short, then the error is not too big. This greedy algorithm is called the *longest processing time rule*, or LPT.

Theorem 2.7. *The longest processing time rule is a 4/3-approximation algorithm for scheduling jobs to minimize the makespan on identical parallel machines.*

Proof. Suppose that the theorem is false, and consider an input that provides a counterexample to the theorem. For ease of notation, assume that $p_1 \geq \cdots \geq p_n$. First, we can assume that the last job to complete is indeed the last (and smallest) job in the list. This follows without loss of generality: any counterexample for which the last job ℓ to complete is not the smallest can yield a smaller counterexample, simply by omitting all of the jobs $\ell + 1, \ldots, n$; the length of the schedule produced is the same, and the optimal value of the reduced input can be no larger. Hence, the reduced input is also a counterexample.

So we know that the last job to complete in the schedule is job n. If this is a counterexample, what do we know about $p_n (= p_\ell)$? If $p_\ell \leq C^*_{\max}/3$, then the analysis of Theorem 2.6 implies that the schedule length is at most $(4/3)C^*_{\max}$, and so this is not a counterexample. Hence, we know that in this purported counterexample, job n (and therefore all of the jobs) has a processing requirement strictly greater than $C^*_{\max}/3$. This has the following simple corollary. In the optimal schedule, each machine may process at most two jobs (since otherwise the total processing assigned to that machine is more than $C^*_{\max}$).

However, we have now reduced our assumed counterexample to the point where it simply cannot exist. For inputs of this structure, we have the following lemma.

Lemma 2.8. *For any input to the problem of minimizing the makespan on identical parallel machines for which the processing requirement of each job is more than one-third the optimal makespan, the longest processing time rule computes an optimal schedule.*

This lemma can be proved by some careful case checking, and we defer this to an exercise (Exercise 2.2). However, the consequence of the lemma is clear; no counterexample to the theorem can exist, and hence the theorem must be true.   □

In Section 3.2, we will see that it is possible to give a polynomial-time approximation scheme for this problem.

2.4 The Traveling Salesman Problem

In the *traveling salesman problem*, or TSP, there is a given set of cities $\{1, 2, \ldots, n\}$, and the input consists of a symmetric n by n matrix $C = (c_{ij})$ that specifies the cost of traveling from city i to city j. By convention, we assume that the cost of traveling from any city to itself is equal to 0, and costs are nonnegative; the fact that the matrix is symmetric means that the cost of traveling from city i to city j is equal to the cost of traveling from j to i. (The *asymmetric traveling salesman problem*, where the restriction that the cost matrix be symmetric is relaxed, has already made an appearance in Exercise 1.3.) If we instead view the input as an undirected complete graph with a cost associated with each edge, then a feasible solution, or *tour*, consists of a Hamiltonian cycle in this graph; that is, we specify a cyclic permutation of the cities or, equivalently, a traversal of the cities in the order $k(1), k(2), \ldots, k(n)$, where each city j is listed as a unique image $k(i)$. The cost of the tour is equal to

$$c_{k(n)k(1)} + \sum_{i=1}^{n-1} c_{k(i)k(i+1)}.$$

Observe that each tour has n distinct representations, since it does not matter which city is selected as the one in which the tour starts.

The traveling salesman problem is one of the most well-studied combinatorial optimization problems, and this is certainly true from the point of view of approximation algorithms as well. There are severe limits on our ability to compute near-optimal tours, and we start with a discussion of these results. It is NP-complete to decide whether a given undirected graph $G = (V, E)$ has a Hamiltonian cycle. An approximation algorithm for the TSP can be used to solve the Hamiltonian cycle problem in the following way: Given a graph $G = (V, E)$, form an input to the TSP by setting, for each pair i, j, the cost c_{ij} equal to 1 if $(i, j) \in E$, and equal to $n + 2$ otherwise. If there is a Hamiltonian cycle in G, then there is a tour of cost n, and otherwise each tour costs at least $2n + 1$. If there were to exist a 2-approximation algorithm for the TSP, then we could use this algorithm to distinguish graphs with Hamiltonian cycles from those without any: run the approximation algorithm on the new TSP input, and if the tour computed has cost at most $2n$, then there exists a Hamiltonian cycle in G, and otherwise there does not. Of course, there is nothing special about setting the cost for the "non-edges" to be $n + 2$; setting the cost to be $\alpha n + 2$ has a similarly inflated consequence, and we obtain an input to the TSP of polynomial size provided that, for example, $\alpha = O(2^n)$. As a result, we obtain the following theorem.

Theorem 2.9. *For any $\alpha > 1$, there does not exist an α-approximation algorithm for the traveling salesman problem on n cities, provided $P \neq NP$. In fact, the existence of an $O(2^n)$-approximation algorithm for the TSP would similarly imply that $P = NP$.*

But is this the end of the story? Clearly not. A natural assumption to make about the input to the TSP is to restrict attention to those inputs that are *metric*; that is, for each triple $i, j, k \in V$, we have that the triangle inequality

$$c_{ik} \leq c_{ij} + c_{jk}$$

holds. This assumption rules out the construction used in the reduction for the Hamiltonian cycle problem above; the non-edges can be given cost at most 2 if we want the triangle inequality to hold, and this value is too small to yield a nontrivial nonapproximability result. We next give three approximation algorithms for this *metric traveling salesman problem*.

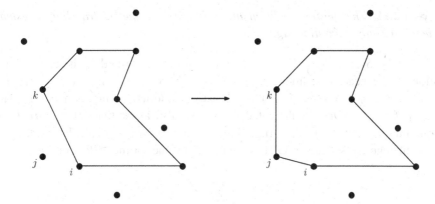

Figure 2.4. Illustration of a greedy step of the nearest addition algorithm.

Here is a natural greedy heuristic to consider for the traveling salesman problem; this is often referred to as the *nearest addition algorithm*. Find the two closest cities, say, i and j, and start by building a tour on that pair of cities; the tour consists of going from i to j and then back to i again. This is the first iteration. In each subsequent iteration, we extend the tour on the current subset S by including one additional city, until we include the full set of cities. In each iteration, we find a pair of cities $i \in S$ and $j \notin S$ for which the cost c_{ij} is minimum; let k be the city that follows i in the current tour on S. We add j to S, and insert j into the current tour between i and k. An illustration of this algorithm is shown in Figure 2.4.

The crux of the analysis of this algorithm is the relationship of this algorithm to Prim's algorithm for the minimum spanning tree in an undirected graph. A *spanning tree* of a connected graph $G = (V, E)$ is a minimal subset of edges $F \subseteq E$ such that each pair of nodes in G is connected by a path using edges only in F. A *minimum spanning tree* is a spanning tree for which the total edge cost is minimized. Prim's algorithm computes a minimum spanning tree by iteratively constructing a set S along with a tree T, starting with $S = \{v\}$ for some (arbitrarily chosen) node $v \in V$ and $T = (S, F)$ with $F = \emptyset$. In each iteration, it determines the edge (i, j) such that $i \in S$ and $j \notin S$ is of minimum cost, and adds the edge (i, j) to F. Clearly, this is the same sequence of vertex pairs identified by the nearest addition algorithm. Furthermore, there is another important relationship between the minimum spanning tree problem and the traveling salesman problem.

Lemma 2.10. *For any input to the traveling salesman problem, the cost of the optimal tour is at least the cost of the minimum spanning tree on the same input.*

Proof. The proof is quite simple. For any input with $n \geq 2$, start with the optimal tour. Delete any one edge from the tour. The result is a spanning tree (albeit a very special one), and this costs no more than the optimal tour. But the minimum spanning tree must cost no more than this special tree. Hence, the cost of the minimum spanning tree is at most the cost of the optimal tour. □

By combining these observations, we can obtain the following result with just a bit more work.

Theorem 2.11. *The nearest addition algorithm for the metric traveling salesman problem is a 2-approximation algorithm.*

Proof. Let $S_2, S_3, \ldots, S_n = \{1, \ldots, n\}$ be the subsets identified at the end of each iteration of the nearest addition algorithm (where $|S_\ell| = \ell$), and let $F = \{(i_2, j_2), (i_3, j_3), \ldots, (i_n, j_n)\}$, where (i_ℓ, j_ℓ) is the edge identified in iteration $\ell - 1$ (with $i_\ell \in S_{\ell-1}$, $\ell = 3, \ldots, n$). As indicated above, we also know that $(\{1, \ldots, n\}, F)$ is a minimum spanning tree for the original input, when viewed as a complete undirected graph with edge costs. Thus, if OPT is the optimal value for the TSP input, then

$$\text{OPT} \geq \sum_{\ell=2}^{n} c_{i_\ell j_\ell}.$$

The cost of the tour on the first two nodes i_2 and j_2 is exactly $2c_{i_2 j_2}$. Consider an iteration in which a city j is inserted between cities i and k in the current tour. How much does the length of the tour increase? An easy calculation gives $c_{ij} + c_{jk} - c_{ik}$. By the triangle inequality, we have that $c_{jk} \leq c_{ji} + c_{ik}$ or, equivalently, $c_{jk} - c_{ik} \leq c_{ji}$. Hence, the increase in cost in this iteration is at most $c_{ij} + c_{ji} = 2c_{ij}$. Thus, overall, we know that the final tour has cost at most

$$2\sum_{\ell=2}^{n} c_{i_\ell j_\ell} \leq 2\,\text{OPT},$$

and the theorem is proved. □

In fact, this algorithm can be viewed from another perspective. Although this new perspective deviates from viewing the algorithm as a "greedy" procedure, this approach ultimately leads to a better algorithm. First, we need some graph-theoretic preliminaries. A graph is said to be *Eulerian* if there exists a permutation of its edges of the form $(i_0, i_1), (i_1, i_2), \ldots, (i_{k-1}, i_k), (i_k, i_0)$; we will call this permutation a *traversal* of the edges, since it allows us to visit every edge exactly once. A graph is Eulerian if and only if it is connected and each node has even degree (where the degree of a node v is the number of edges with v as one of its endpoints). Furthermore, if a graph is Eulerian, one can easily construct the required traversal of the edges, given the graph.

To find a good tour for a TSP input, suppose that we first compute a minimum spanning tree (for example, by Prim's algorithm). Suppose that we then replace each edge by two copies of itself. The resulting (multi)graph has cost at most $2\,\text{OPT}$ and is Eulerian. We can construct a tour of the cities from the Eulerian traversal of the edges, $(i_0, i_1), (i_1, i_2), \ldots, (i_{k-1}, i_k), (i_k, i_0)$. Consider the sequence of nodes, $i_0, i_1, \ldots, i_k$, and remove all but the first occurrence of each city in this sequence. This yields a tour containing each city exactly once (assuming we then return to i_0 at the end). To bound the length of this tour, consider two consecutive cities in this tour, i_ℓ and i_m. We have omitted $i_{\ell+1}, \ldots, i_{m-1}$ because these cities have already been visited "earlier" in the tour. However, by the triangle inequality, the cost of the edge c_{i_ℓ, i_m} can be upper bounded by the total cost of the edges traversed in the Eulerian traversal between i_ℓ and i_m, that is, the total cost of the edges $(i_\ell, i_{\ell+1}), \ldots, (i_{m-1}, i_m)$. In total, the cost of the tour is at most the total cost of all of the edges in the Eulerian graph, which is at most $2\,\text{OPT}$. Hence, we have also analyzed this *double-tree algorithm*.

Theorem 2.12. *The double-tree algorithm for the metric traveling salesman problem is a 2-approximation algorithm.*

This technique of "skipping over" previously visited cities and bounding the cost of the resulting tour in terms of the total cost of all the edges is sometimes called *shortcutting.*

The bigger message of the analysis of the double-tree algorithm is also quite useful; if we can efficiently construct an Eulerian subgraph of the complete input graph, for which the total edge cost is at most α times the optimal value of the TSP input, then we have derived an α-approximation algorithm as well. This strategy can be carried out to yield a 3/2-approximation algorithm.

Consider the output from the minimum spanning tree computation. This graph is certainly not Eulerian, since any tree must have nodes of degree one, but it is possible that not many nodes have odd degree. Let O be the set of odd-degree nodes in the minimum spanning tree. For any graph, the sum of its node degrees must be even, since each edge in the graph contributes 2 to this total. The total degree of the even-degree nodes must also be even (since we are adding a collection of even numbers), but then the total degree of the odd-degree nodes must also be even. In other words, we must have an even number of odd-degree nodes; $|O| = 2k$ for some positive integer k.

Suppose that we pair up the nodes in O: $(i_1, i_2), (i_3, i_4), \ldots, (i_{2k-1}, i_{2k})$. Such a collection of edges that contain each node in O exactly once is called a *perfect matching* of O. One of the classic results of combinatorial optimization is that given a complete graph (on an even number of nodes) with edge costs, it is possible to compute the perfect matching of minimum total cost in polynomial time. Given the minimum spanning tree, we identify the set O of odd-degree nodes with even cardinality, and then compute a minimum-cost perfect matching on O. If we add this set of edges to our minimum spanning tree, we have constructed an Eulerian graph on our original set of cities: it is connected (since the spanning tree is connected) and has even degree (since we added a new edge incident to each node of odd degree in the spanning tree). As in the double-tree algorithm, we can shortcut this graph to produce a tour of no greater cost. This algorithm is known as *Christofides' algorithm.*

Theorem 2.13. *Christofides' algorithm for the metric traveling salesman problem is a 3/2-approximation algorithm.*

Proof. We want to show that the edges in the Eulerian graph produced by the algorithm have total cost at most $\frac{3}{2}$ OPT. We know that the minimum spanning tree edges have total cost at most OPT. So we need only show that the perfect matching on O has cost at most OPT/2. This is surprisingly simple.

First observe that there is a tour on just the nodes in O of total cost at most OPT. This again uses the shortcutting argument. Start with the optimal tour on the entire set of cities, and if for two cities i and j, the optimal tour between i and j contains only cities that are not in O, then include edge (i, j) in the tour on O. Each edge in the tour corresponds to disjoint paths in the original tour, and hence by the triangle inequality, the total length of the tour on O is no more than the length of the original tour.

Now consider this "shortcut" tour on the node set O. Color these edges red and blue, alternating colors as the tour is traversed. This partitions the edges into two sets, the red set and the blue set; each of these is a perfect matching on the node set O.

In total, these two edge sets have cost at most OPT. Thus, the cheaper of these two sets has cost at most OPT/2. Hence, there is a perfect matching on O of cost at most OPT/2. Therefore, the algorithm to find the minimum-cost perfect matching must find a matching of cost at most OPT/2, and this completes the proof of the theorem. □

Remarkably, no better approximation algorithm for the metric traveling salesman problem is known. However, substantially better algorithms might yet be found, since the strongest negative result is as follows.

Theorem 2.14. *Unless* P $=$ NP, *for any constant* $\alpha < \frac{220}{219} \approx 1.0045$, *no* α-*approximation algorithm for the metric TSP exists.*

We can give better approximation algorithms for the problem in special cases. In Section 10.1, we will see that it is possible to obtain a polynomial-time approximation scheme in the case that cities correspond to points in the Euclidean plane and the cost of traveling between two cities is equal to the Euclidean distance between the corresponding two points.

2.5 Maximizing Float in Bank Accounts

In the days before quick electronic check clearing, it was often advantageous for large corporations to maintain checking accounts in various locations in order to maximize float. The *float* is the time between making a payment by check and the time that the funds for that payment are deducted from the company's banking account. During that time, the company can continue to accrue interest on the money. Float can also be used by scam artists for *check kiting*: covering a deficit in the checking account in one bank by writing a check against another account in another bank that also has insufficient funds – then a few days later covering this deficit with a check written against the first account.

We can model the problem of maximizing float as follows. Suppose we wish to open up to k bank accounts so as to maximize our float. Let B be the set of banks where we can potentially open accounts, and let P be the set of payees to whom we regularly make payments. Let $v_{ij} \geq 0$ be the value of the float created by paying payee $j \in P$ from bank account $i \in B$; this may take into account the amount of time it takes for a check written to j to clear at i, the interest rate at bank i, and other factors. Then we wish to find a set $S \subseteq B$ of banks at which to open accounts such that $|S| \leq k$. Clearly we will pay payee $j \in P$ from the account $i \in S$ that maximizes v_{ij}. So we wish to find $S \subseteq B$, $|S| \leq k$, that maximizes $\sum_{j \in P} \max_{i \in S} v_{ij}$. We define $v(S)$ to be the value of this objective function for $S \subseteq B$.

A natural greedy algorithm is as follows: we start with $S = \emptyset$, and while $|S| < k$, find the bank $i \in B$ that most increases the objective function, and add it to S. This algorithm is summarized in Algorithm 2.2.

We will show that this algorithm has a performance guarantee of $1 - \frac{1}{e}$. To do this, we require the following lemma. We let O denote an optimal solution, so that $O \subseteq B$ and $|O| \leq k$.

$$S \leftarrow \emptyset$$

while $|S| < k$ **do**

$\quad i \leftarrow \arg\max_{i \in B} v(S \cup \{i\}) - v(S)$

$\quad S \leftarrow S \cup \{i\}$

return S

Algorithm 2.2. A greedy approximation algorithm for the float maximization problem.

Lemma 2.15. *Let S be the set of banks at the start of some iteration of Algorithm 2.2, and let $i \in B$ be the bank chosen in the iteration. Then*

$$v(S \cup \{i\}) - v(S) \geq \frac{1}{k}(v(O) - v(S)).$$

To get some intuition of why this is true, consider the optimal solution O. We can allocate shares of the value of the objective function $v(O)$ to each bank $i \in O$: the value v_{ij} for each $j \in P$ can be allocated to a bank $i \in O$ that attains the maximum of $\max_{i \in O} v_{ij}$. Since $|O| \leq k$, some bank $i \in O$ is allocated at least $v(O)/k$. So after choosing the first bank i to add to S, we have $v(\{i\}) \geq v(O)/k$. Intuitively speaking, there is also another bank $i' \in O$ that is allocated at least a $1/k$ fraction of whatever wasn't allocated to the first bank, so that there is an i' such that $v(S \cup \{i'\}) - v(S) \geq \frac{1}{k}(v(O) - v(S))$, and so on.

Given the lemma, we can prove the performance guarantee of the algorithm.

Theorem 2.16. *Algorithm 2.2 gives a $\left(1 - \frac{1}{e}\right)$-approximation algorithm for the float maximization problem.*

Proof. Let S^t be our greedy solution after t iterations of the algorithm, so that $S^0 = \emptyset$ and $S = S^k$. Let O be an optimal solution. We set $v(\emptyset) = 0$. Note that Lemma 2.15 implies that $v(S^t) \geq \frac{1}{k}v(O) + \left(1 - \frac{1}{k}\right)v(S^{t-1})$. By applying this inequality repeatedly, we have

$$
\begin{aligned}
v(S) = v(S^k) \\
\geq \frac{1}{k}v(O) + \left(1 - \frac{1}{k}\right)v(S^{k-1}) \\
\geq \frac{1}{k}v(O) + \left(1 - \frac{1}{k}\right)\left(\frac{1}{k}v(O) + \left(1 - \frac{1}{k}\right)v(S^{k-2})\right) \\
\geq \frac{v(O)}{k}\left(1 + \left(1 - \frac{1}{k}\right) + \left(1 - \frac{1}{k}\right)^2 + \cdots + \left(1 - \frac{1}{k}\right)^{k-1}\right) \\
= \frac{v(O)}{k} \cdot \frac{1 - \left(1 - \frac{1}{k}\right)^k}{1 - \left(1 - \frac{1}{k}\right)} \\
= v(O)\left(1 - \left(1 - \frac{1}{k}\right)^k\right) \\
\geq v(O)\left(1 - \frac{1}{e}\right),
\end{aligned}
$$

where in the final inequality we use the fact that $1 - x \leq e^{-x}$, setting $x = 1/k$. $\qquad \square$

To prove Lemma 2.15, we first prove the following.

Lemma 2.17. *For the objective function v, for any $X \subseteq Y$ and any $\ell \notin Y$,*

$$v(Y \cup \{\ell\}) - v(Y) \leq v(X \cup \{\ell\}) - v(X).$$

Proof. Consider any payee $j \in P$. Either j is paid from the same bank account in both $X \cup \{\ell\}$ and X, or it is paid by ℓ from $X \cup \{\ell\}$ and some other bank in X. Consequently,

$$v(X \cup \{\ell\}) - v(X) = \sum_{j \in P} \left(\max_{i \in X \cup \{\ell\}} v_{ij} - \max_{i \in X} v_{ij} \right) = \sum_{j \in P} \max \left\{ 0, \left(v_{\ell j} - \max_{i \in X} v_{ij} \right) \right\}. \tag{2.6}$$

Similarly,

$$v(Y \cup \{\ell\}) - v(Y) = \sum_{j \in P} \max \left\{ 0, \left(v_{\ell j} - \max_{i \in Y} v_{ij} \right) \right\}. \tag{2.7}$$

Now since $X \subseteq Y$ for a given $j \in P$, $\max_{i \in Y} v_{ij} \geq \max_{i \in X} v_{ij}$, so that

$$\max \left\{ 0, \left(v_{\ell j} - \max_{i \in Y} v_{ij} \right) \right\} \leq \max \left\{ 0, \left(v_{\ell j} - \max_{i \in X} v_{ij} \right) \right\}.$$

By summing this inequality over all $j \in P$ and using the equalities (2.6) and (2.7), we obtain the desired result. $\qquad \Box$

The property of the value function v that we have just proved is one that plays a central role in a number of algorithmic settings, and is often called *submodularity*, though the usual definition of this property is somewhat different (see Exercise 2.10). This definition captures the intuitive property of decreasing marginal benefits: as the set includes more elements, the marginal value of adding a new element decreases.

Finally, we prove Lemma 2.15.

Proof of Lemma 2.15. Let $O - S = \{i_1, \ldots, i_p\}$. Note that since $|O - S| \leq |O| \leq k$, then $p \leq k$. Since adding more bank accounts can only increase the overall value of the solution, we have that

$$v(O) \leq v(O \cup S),$$

and a simple rewriting gives

$$v(O \cup S) = v(S) + \sum_{j=1}^{p} \left[v(S \cup \{i_1, \ldots, i_j\}) - v(S \cup \{i_1, \ldots, i_{j-1}\}) \right].$$

By applying Lemma 2.17, we can upper bound the right-hand side by

$$v(S) + \sum_{j=1}^{p} \left[v(S \cup \{i_j\}) - v(S) \right].$$

Since the algorithm chooses $i \in B$ to maximize $v(S \cup \{i\}) - v(S)$, we have that for any j, $v(S \cup \{i\}) - v(S) \geq v(S \cup \{i_j\}) - v(S)$. We can use this bound to see that

$$v(O) \leq v(O \cup S) \leq v(S) + p[v(S \cup \{i\}) - v(S)] \leq v(S) + k[v(S \cup \{i\}) - v(S)].$$

This inequality can be rewritten to yield the inequality of the lemma, and this completes the proof.   □

This greedy approximation algorithm and its analysis can be extended to similar problems in which the objective function $v(S)$ is given by a set of items S, and is monotone and submodular. We leave the definition of these terms and the proofs of the extensions to Exercise 2.10.

2.6 Finding Minimum-Degree Spanning Trees

We now turn to a local search algorithm for the problem of minimizing the maximum degree of a spanning tree. The problem we consider is the following: given a graph $G = (V, E)$ we wish to find a spanning tree T of G so as to minimize the maximum degree of nodes in T. We will call this the *minimum-degree spanning tree problem*. This problem is NP-hard. A special type of spanning tree of a graph is a path that visits all nodes of the graph; this is called a *Hamiltonian path*. A spanning tree has maximum degree two if and only if it is a Hamiltonian path. Furthermore, deciding if a graph G has a Hamiltonian path is NP-complete. Thus, we have the following theorem.

Theorem 2.18. *It is* NP-*complete to decide whether or not a given graph has a minimum-degree spanning tree of maximum degree two.*

For a given graph G, let T^* be the spanning tree that minimizes the maximum degree, and let OPT be the maximum degree of T^*. We will give a polynomial-time local search algorithm that finds a tree T with maximum degree at most $2\,\text{OPT} + \lceil \log_2 n \rceil$, where $n = |V|$ is the number of vertices in the graph. To simplify notation, throughout this section we will let $\ell = \lceil \log_2 n \rceil$.

The local search algorithm starts with an arbitrary spanning tree T. We will give a local move to change T into another spanning tree in which the degree of some vertex has been reduced. Let $d_T(u)$ be the degree of u in T. The local move picks a vertex u and tries to reduce its degree by looking at all edges (v, w) that are not in T but if added to T create a cycle C containing u. Suppose $\max(d_T(v), d_T(w)) \leq d_T(u) - 2$. For example, consider the graph in Figure 2.5, in which the edges of the tree T are shown in bold. In this case, the degree of node u is 5, but those of v and w are 3. Let T' be the result of adding (v, w) and removing an edge from C incident to u. In the example, if we delete edge (u, y), then the degrees of u, v, and w will all be 4 after the move. The conditions ensure that this move provides improvement in general; the degree of u is reduced by one in T' (that is, $d_{T'}(u) = d_T(u) - 1$) and the degrees of v and w in T' are not greater than the reduced degree of u; that is, $\max(d_{T'}(v), d_{T'}(w)) \leq d_{T'}(u)$.

The local search algorithm carries out local moves on nodes that have high degree. It makes sense for us to carry out a local move to reduce the degree of any node, since it is possible that if we reduce the degree of a low-degree node, it may make possible another local move that reduces the degree of a high-degree node. However, we do not know how to show that such an algorithm terminates in polynomial time. To get a polynomial-time algorithm, we apply the local moves only to nodes whose degree is relatively high. Let $\Delta(T)$ be the maximum degree of T; that is, $\Delta(T) = \max_{u \in V} d_T(u)$.

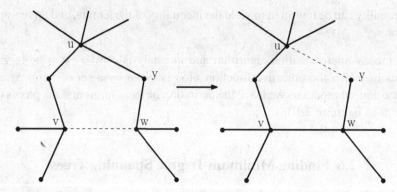

Figure 2.5. Illustration of a local move for minimizing the maximum degree of a spanning tree. The bold solid lines are in the tree, and the dashed lines are graph edges not in the tree.

The algorithm picks a node in T that has degree at least $\Delta(T) - \ell$ and attempts to reduce its degree using the local move. If there is no move that can reduce the degree of any node having degree between $\Delta(T) - \ell$ and $\Delta(T)$, then the algorithm stops. We say that the algorithm has found a *locally optimal* tree. By applying local moves only to nodes whose degree is between $\Delta(T) - \ell$ and $\Delta(T)$, we will be able to show that the algorithm runs in polynomial time.

We now need to prove two things. First, we need to show that any locally optimal tree has maximum degree at most $2 \text{OPT} + \ell$. Second, we need to show that we can find a locally optimal tree in polynomial time. For most approximation algorithms, the proof that the algorithm runs in polynomial time is relatively straightforward, but this is often not the case for local search algorithms. In fact, we usually need to restrict the set of local moves in order to prove that the algorithm converges to a locally optimal solution in polynomial time. Here we do this by restricting the local moves to apply only to nodes with high degree.

Theorem 2.19. *Let T be a locally optimal tree. Then $\Delta(T) \leq 2 \text{OPT} + \ell$, where $\ell = \lceil \log_2 n \rceil$.*

Proof. We first explain how we will obtain a lower bound on OPT. Suppose that we remove k edges of the spanning tree. This breaks the tree into $k + 1$ different connected components. Suppose we also find a set of nodes S such that each edge in G connecting two of the $k + 1$ connected components is incident on a node in S. For example, consider the graph in Figure 2.6 that shows the connected components remaining after the bold edges are deleted, along with an appropriate choice of the set S. Observe that any spanning tree of the graph must have at least k edges with endpoints in different components. Thus, the average degree of nodes in S is at least $k/|S|$ for any spanning tree, and $\text{OPT} \geq k/|S|$.

Now we show how to find the set of edges to remove and the set of nodes S so that we can apply this lower bound. Let S_i be the nodes of degree at least i in the locally optimal tree T. We claim that for each S_i, where $i \geq \Delta(T) - \ell + 1$, there are at least $(i - 1)|S_i| + 1$ distinct edges of T incident on the nodes of S_i, and after removing these edges, each edge that connects distinct connected components is incident on a node of S_{i-1}. Furthermore, we claim there exists an i such that $|S_{i-1}| \leq 2|S_i|$, so that the value

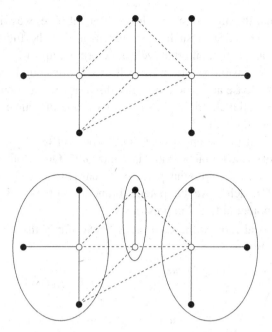

Figure 2.6. Illustration of lower bound on OPT. The vertices in S have white centers. If the bold edges are deleted, every potential edge for joining the resulting connected components has an endpoint in S.

of OPT implied by removing these edges with $S = S_{i-1}$ is

$$\text{OPT} \geq \frac{(i-1)|S_i|+1}{|S_{i-1}|} \geq \frac{(i-1)|S_i|+1}{2|S_i|} > (i-1)/2 \geq (\Delta(T)-\ell)/2.$$

Rearranging terms proves the desired inequality.

We turn to the proofs of the claims. We first show that there must exist some $i \geq \Delta(T) - \ell + 1$ such that $|S_{i-1}| \leq 2|S_i|$. Suppose not. Then clearly $|S_{\Delta(T)-\ell}| > 2^\ell |S_{\Delta(T)}|$ or $|S_{\Delta(T)-\ell}| > n|S_{\Delta(T)}| \geq n$ since $|S_{\Delta(T)}| \geq 1$. This is a contradiction, since any S_i can have at most n nodes.

Now we show that there are at least $(i-1)|S_i|+1$ distinct edges of T incident on the nodes of S_i, and after removing these edges, any edge connecting different connected components is incident on a node of S_{i-1}. Figure 2.6 gives an example of this construction for $i = 4$. Each edge that connects distinct connected components after removing the edges of T incident on nodes of S_i either must be one of the edges of T incident on S_i, or must close a cycle C in T containing some node in S_i. Because the tree is locally optimal, it must be the case that at least one of the endpoints has degree at least $i-1$, and so is in S_{i-1}. In removing the edges in T incident on nodes in S_i, there are at least $i|S_i|$ edges incident on nodes in S_i, since each node has degree at least i. At most $|S_i| - 1$ such edges can join two nodes in S_i since T is a spanning tree. Thus, there are at least $i|S_i| - (|S_i| - 1)$ distinct edges of T incident on the nodes S_i, and this proves the claim. $\qquad\square$

Theorem 2.20. *The algorithm finds a locally optimal tree in polynomial time.*

Proof. To prove that the algorithm runs in polynomial time, we will use a *potential function* argument. The idea of such an argument is that the function captures the current state of the algorithm, and that we can determine upper and lower bounds on this function for any feasible solution, as well as a lower bound on the amount that the function must decrease after each move. In this way, we can bound the number of moves possible before the algorithm must terminate, and of course, the resulting tree must therefore be locally optimal.

For a tree T, we let the potential of T, $\Phi(T)$, be $\Phi(T) = \sum_{v \in V} 3^{d_T(v)}$. Note that $\Phi(T) \leq n3^{\Delta(T)}$, and so the initial potential is at most $n3^n$. On the other hand, the lowest possible potential is for a Hamiltonian path, which has potential $2 \cdot 3 + (n-2)3^2 > n$. We will show that for each move, the potential function of the resulting tree is at most $1 - \frac{2}{27n^3}$ times the potential function previously.

After $\frac{27}{2}n^4 \ln 3$ local moves, the conditions above imply that the potential of the resulting tree is at most

$$\left(1 - \frac{2}{27n^3}\right)^{\frac{27}{2}n^4 \ln 3} \cdot (n3^n) \leq e^{-n \ln 3} \cdot (n3^n) = n,$$

using the fact that $1 - x \leq e^{-x}$. Since the potential of a tree is greater than n, after $O(n^4)$ local moves there must be no further local moves possible, and the tree must be locally optimal.

We must still prove the claimed potential reduction in each iteration. Suppose the algorithm reduces the degree of a vertex u from i to $i - 1$, where $i \geq \Delta(T) - \ell$, and adds an edge (v, w). Then the increase in the potential function due to increasing the degree of v and w is at most $2 \cdot (3^{i-1} - 3^{i-2}) = 4 \cdot 3^{i-2}$, since the degree of v and w can be increased to at most $i - 1$. The decrease in the potential function due to decreasing the degree of u is $3^i - 3^{i-1} = 2 \cdot 3^{i-1}$. Observe that

$$3^\ell \leq 3 \cdot 3^{\log_2 n} \leq 3 \cdot 2^{2 \log_2 n} = 3n^2.$$

Therefore, the overall decrease in the potential function is at least

$$2 \cdot 3^{i-1} - 4 \cdot 3^{i-2} = \frac{2}{9}3^i \geq \frac{2}{9}3^{\Delta(T)-\ell} \geq \frac{2}{27n^2}3^{\Delta(T)} \geq \frac{2}{27n^3}\Phi(T).$$

Thus, for the resulting tree T' we have that $\Phi(T') \leq (1 - \frac{2}{27n^3})\Phi(T)$. This completes the proof. $\qquad\square$

By slightly adjusting the parameters within the same proof outline, we can actually prove a stronger result. Given some constant $b > 1$, suppose we perform local changes on nodes of degree at least $\Delta(T) - \lceil \log_b n \rceil$. Then it is possible to show the following.

Corollary 2.21. *The local search algorithm runs in polynomial time and results in a spanning tree T such that $\Delta(T) \leq b\,\mathrm{OPT} + \lceil \log_b n \rceil$.*

In Section 9.3, we will prove a still stronger result: we can give a polynomial-time algorithm that finds a spanning tree T with $\Delta(T) \leq \mathrm{OPT} + 1$. Given that it is NP-hard to determine whether a spanning tree has degree exactly OPT, this is clearly the best possible result that can be obtained. In the next section, we give another result of this type for the edge coloring problem. In Section 11.2, we will show that there are

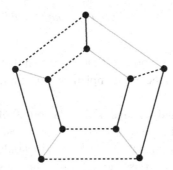

Figure 2.7. A graph with a 3-edge-coloring.

interesting extensions of these results to the case of spanning trees with costs on the edges.

2.7 Edge Coloring

To conclude this chapter, we give an algorithm that has the elements of both a greedy algorithm and a local search algorithm: it attempts to make progress in a greedy way, but when blocked it makes local changes until progress can be made again.

The algorithm is for the problem of finding an *edge coloring* of a graph. An undirected graph is *k-edge-colorable* if each edge can be assigned exactly one of k colors in such a way that no two edges with the same color share an endpoint. We call the assignment of colors to edges a *k-edge-coloring*. For example, Figure 2.7 shows a graph with a 3-edge-coloring. An analogous notion of *vertex coloring* will be discussed in Sections 5.12, 6.5, and 13.2.

For a given graph, we would like to obtain a k-edge-coloring with k as small as possible. Let Δ be the maximum degree of a vertex in the given graph. Clearly, we cannot hope to find a k-edge-coloring with $k < \Delta$, since at least Δ different colors must be incident to any vertex of maximum degree. Note that this shows that the coloring given in Figure 2.7 is optimal. On the other hand, consider the example in Figure 2.8, which is called the *Petersen graph*; it is not too hard to show that this graph is not 3-edge-colorable, and yet it is easy to color it with four colors. Furthermore, the following has been shown.

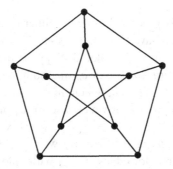

Figure 2.8. The Petersen graph. This graph is not 3-edge-colorable.

Theorem 2.22. *For graphs with* $\Delta = 3$, *it is* NP-*complete to decide whether the graph is 3-edge-colorable or not.*

In this section, we give a polynomial-time algorithm that will find a $(\Delta + 1)$-edge-coloring for any graph. Given the NP-completeness result, it is clearly the best we can hope to do unless $P = NP$.

We give the algorithm and its analysis in the proof of the theorem below. We repeatedly find an uncolored edge (u, v) and attempt to color it with one of the $\Delta + 1$ colors. If no color is available such that coloring (u, v) would result in a $(\Delta + 1)$-edge-coloring, then we show that it is possible to locally change some of the edge colors in such a way that we can correctly color (u, v).

Theorem 2.23. *There is a polynomial-time algorithm to find a* $(\Delta + 1)$-*edge-coloring of a graph.*

Proof. Our algorithm will start with a completely uncolored graph. In each iteration of the algorithm we will take some uncolored edge and color it. This will be done in such a way that the algorithm maintains a *legal* coloring of the graph at the beginning of each iteration of the main loop; that is, for any vertex v in the graph, no two colored edges incident on v have the same color, and at most $\Delta + 1$ distinct colors have been used. Clearly this is true initially, when the entire graph is uncolored. We show that this invariant is maintained throughout the course of each iteration. In the argument that follows, we say that a vertex v *lacks* color c if an edge of color c is not incident on v.

We summarize the algorithm in Algorithm 2.3, and now explain it in detail. Let (u, v_0) be the selected uncolored edge. We then construct a sequence of edges $(u, v_0), (u, v_1), \ldots$ and colors $c_0, c_1, \ldots$. We will use this sequence to do some local recoloring of edges so that we can correctly color the uncolored edge. Note that since we are maintaining a legal coloring of $\Delta + 1$ colors, and the maximum degree is Δ, each vertex must lack at least one of the $\Delta + 1$ colors. To build this sequence of edges, consider the current vertex v_i, starting initially with v_0; if v_i lacks a color that u also lacks, then we let c_i be this color, and the sequence is complete. If not, then choose the color c_i arbitrarily from among those that v_i lacks; note that u will not lack this color. If this color has not appeared in the sequence $c_0, c_1, \ldots$ to this point, then we let v_{i+1} be the vertex such that (u, v_{i+1}) is the edge incident to u of color c_i, and this extends our sequence (sometimes called a *fan sequence*) one edge further. If we have that $c_i = c_j$, where $j < i$, then we also stop building our sequence. (See Figure 2.9 for an example of this construction.)

We need to argue that this process terminates either in the case that u and v_i lack the same color c_i, or that we have $c_i = c_j$ for some $j < i$. Let d be the number of edges incident to u that are currently colored. Suppose the sequence reaches vertex v_d without terminating. If there is no color c_d that both u and v_d lack, then any color that v_d lacks is one that u does not lack, which must be one of the colors on the edges $(u, v_1), \ldots, (u, v_{d-1})$. Hence, the color we choose for c_d must be the same as one of the previous colors $c_0, \ldots, c_{d-1}$.

Suppose we complete the sequence because we find some c_i that both u and v_i lack. This case is easy: we recolor edges (u, v_j) with color c_j for $j = 0, \ldots, i$; call this *shifting recoloring*. This situation and the resulting recoloring are depicted in

while G is not completely colored **do**
    Pick uncolored edge (u, v_0)
    $i \leftarrow -1$
    repeat // Build fan sequence
        $i \leftarrow i + 1$
        if there is a color v_i lacks and u lacks **then**
            Let c_i be this color
        else
            Pick some color c_i that v_i lacks
            Let v_{i+1} be the edge (u, v_{i+1}) of color c_i
    until c_i is a color u lacks or $c_i = c_j$ for some $j < i$
    if u and v_i lack color c_i **then**
        Shift uncolored edge to (u, v_i) and color (u, v_i) with c_i
    else
        Let $j < i$ be such that $c_i = c_j$
        Shift uncolored edge to (u, v_j)
        Pick color c_u that u lacks
        Let $c = c_i$
        Let E' be edges colored c or c_u
        if u and v_j in different connected components of (V, E') **then**
            Switch colors c_u and c in component containing u of (V, E')
            Color (u, v_j) with color c
        else // u and v_i in different components of (V, E')
            Shift uncolored edge to (u, v_i)
            Switch colors c_u and c in component containing u of (V, E')
            Color (u, v_i) with color c

Algorithm 2.3. A greedy algorithm to compute a $(\Delta + 1)$-edge-coloring of a graph.

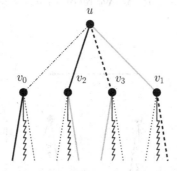

Figure 2.9. An example of building the fan sequence. Edge (u, v_0) is uncolored. Vertex v_0 lacks gray, but u does not lack gray due to (u, v_1), so c_0 is gray. Vertex v_1 lacks black, but u does not lack black due to (u, v_2), so c_1 is black. Vertex v_2 lacks the dashed color, but u does not lack dashed due to (u, v_3), so c_2 is dashed. Vertex v_3 lacks black, so c_3 is black, and the sequence repeats a color.

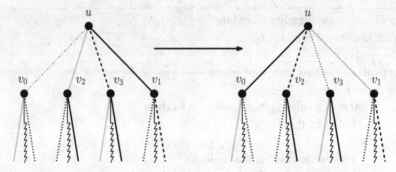

Figure 2.10. A slightly different fan sequence and its recoloring. As before, edge (u, v_0) is uncolored. Vertex v_0 lacks black, but u does not lack black due to (u, v_1), so c_0 is black. Vertex v_1 lacks gray, but u does not lack gray due to (u, v_2), so c_1 is gray. Vertex v_2 lacks dashed, but u does not lack dashed due to (u, v_3), so c_2 is dashed. Vertex v_3 lacks dotted, and u also lacks dotted, and thus c_3 is dotted. Therefore, we shift colors as shown and color the edge (u, v_3) with dotted.

Figure 2.10. In effect, we shift the uncolored edge to (u, v_i) and color it with c_i since both u and v_i lack c_i. The recoloring is correct since we know that each v_j lacks c_j and for $j < i$, c_j was incident on u previously via the edge (u, v_{j+1}), which we now give another color.

Now consider the remaining case, where we complete the sequence because $c_i = c_j$ for some $j < i$. This situation and its recoloring are given in Figure 2.11. We shift the uncolored edge to (u, v_j) by recoloring edges (u, v_k) with color c_k for $0 \le k < j$ and uncoloring edge (u, v_j); this is correct by the same argument as above. Now v_i and v_j lack the same color $c = c_i = c_j$. We let c_u be a color that u lacks; by our selection (and the fact that we did not fall in the first case), we know that both v_i and v_j do not lack c_u.

Consider the subgraph induced by taking all of the edges with colors c and c_u; since we have a legal coloring, this subgraph must be a collection of paths and simple cycles. Since each of u, v_i, and v_j has exactly one of these two colors incident to it, each is an endpoint of one of the path components, and since a path has only two endpoints, at least one of v_i and v_j must be in a different component than u. Suppose that v_j is in a different component than u. Suppose we recolor every edge of color c with color c_u

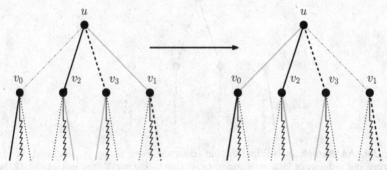

Figure 2.11. The fan sequence from Figure 2.9. We start by shifting the uncolored edge to (u, v_1). Now both v_1 and v_3 lack black. The dotted color can be the color c_u that u lacks but that v_1 and v_3 do not lack.

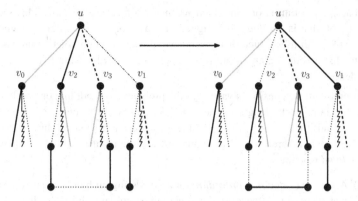

Figure 2.12. The example of Figure 2.11 continued, now showing the components of black and dotted edges containing u, v_1, and v_3. Since u and v_3 are at endpoints of the same black/dotted path, we switch the colors black and dotted on this path, then color (u, v_1) black.

and every edge of color c_u with color c in the component containing u; call this *path recoloring*. Afterward, u now lacks c (and this does not affect the colors incident to v_j at all), and so we may color the uncolored edge (u, v_j) with c. See Figure 2.12 for an example. Finally, suppose that u and v_j are endpoints of the same path, and so v_i must be in a different component. In this case, we can apply the previous shifting recoloring technique to first uncolor the edge (u, v_i). We then apply the path recoloring technique on the u-v_j path to make u lack c; this does not affect any of the colors incident on v_i, and it allows us to color edge (u, v_i) with c.

Clearly we color a previously uncolored edge in each iteration of the algorithm, and each iteration can be implemented in polynomial time. □

Exercises

2.1 The *k-suppliers* problem is similar to the *k*-center problem given in Section 2.2. The input to the problem is a positive integer k, and a set of vertices V, along with distances d_{ij} between any two vertices i, j that obey the same properties as in the *k*-center problem. However, now the vertices are partitioned into *suppliers* $F \subseteq V$ and *customers* $D = V - F$. The goal is to find k suppliers such that the maximum distance from a supplier to a customer is minimized. In other words, we wish to find $S \subseteq F, |S| \leq k$, that minimizes $\max_{j \in D} d(j, S)$.

    (a) Give a 3-approximation algorithm for the *k*-suppliers problem.
    (b) Prove that there is no α-approximation algorithm for $\alpha < 3$ unless P = NP.

2.2 Prove Lemma 2.8: show that for any input to the problem of minimizing the makespan on identical parallel machines for which the processing requirement of each job is more than one-third the optimal makespan, the longest processing time rule computes an optimal schedule.

2.3 We consider scheduling jobs on identical machines as in Section 2.3, but jobs are now subject to *precedence constraints*. We say $i \prec j$ if in any feasible schedule, job i must be completely processed before job j begins processing. A natural variant on the list scheduling algorithm is one in which whenever a machine becomes idle, then any remaining job that is *available* is assigned to start processing on that machine. A job j is available if all jobs i such that $i \prec j$ have already been completely processed. Show that this list scheduling algorithm is a 2-approximation algorithm for the problem with precedence constraints.

2.4   In this problem, we consider a variant of the problem of scheduling on parallel machines so as to minimize the length of the schedule. Now each machine i has an associated speed s_i, and it takes p_j/s_i units of time to process job j on machine i. Assume that machines are numbered from 1 to m and ordered such that $s_1 \geq s_2 \geq \cdots \geq s_m$. We call these *related* machines.

   (a) A ρ-*relaxed decision procedure* for a scheduling problem is an algorithm such that given an instance of the scheduling problem and a deadline D either produces a schedule of length at most $\rho \cdot D$ or correctly states that no schedule of length D is possible for the instance. Show that given a polynomial-time ρ-relaxed decision procedure for the problem of scheduling related machines, one can produce a ρ-approximation algorithm for the problem.

   (b) Consider the following variant of the list scheduling algorithm, now for related machines. Given a deadline D, we label every job j with the slowest machine i such that the job could complete on that machine in time D; that is, $p_j/s_i \leq D$. If there is no such machine for a job j, it is clear that no schedule of length D is possible. If machine i becomes idle at a time D or later, it stops processing. If machine i becomes idle at a time before D, it takes the next job of label i that has not been processed, and starts processing it. If no job of label i is available, it looks for jobs of label $i + 1$; if no jobs of label $i + 1$ are available, it looks for jobs of label $i + 2$, and so on. If no such jobs are available, it stops processing. If not all jobs are processed by this procedure, then the algorithm states that no schedule of length D is possible.
   Prove that this algorithm is a polynomial-time 2-relaxed decision procedure.

2.5   In the *minimum-cost Steiner tree problem*, we are given as input a complete, undirected graph $G = (V, E)$ with nonnegative costs $c_{ij} \geq 0$ for all edges $(i, j) \in E$. The set of vertices is partitioned into *terminals* R and *nonterminals* (or *Steiner vertices*) $V - R$. The goal is to find a minimum-cost tree containing all terminals.

   (a) Suppose initially that the edge costs obey the triangle inequality; that is, $c_{ij} \leq c_{ik} + c_{kj}$ for all $i, j, k \in V$. Let $G[R]$ be the graph induced on the set of terminals; that is, $G[R]$ contains the vertices in R and all edges from G that have both endpoints in R. Consider computing a minimum spanning tree in $G[R]$. Show that this gives a 2-approximation algorithm for the minimum-cost Steiner tree problem.

   (b) Now we suppose that edge costs do not obey the triangle inequality, and that the input graph G is connected but not necessarily complete. Let c'_{ij} be the cost of the shortest path from i to j in G using input edge costs c. Consider running the algorithm above in the complete graph G' on V with edge costs c' to obtain a tree T'. To compute a tree T in the original graph G, for each edge $(i, j) \in T'$, we add to T all edges in a shortest path from i to j in G using input edge costs c. Show that this is still a 2-approximation algorithm for the minimum-cost Steiner tree problem on the original (incomplete) input graph G. G' is sometimes called the *metric completion* of G.

2.6 Prove that there can be no α-approximation algorithm for the minimum-degree spanning tree problem for $\alpha < 3/2$ unless P = NP.

2.7 Suppose that an undirected graph G has a Hamiltonian path. Give a polynomial-time algorithm to find a path of length at least $\Omega(\log n/(\log \log n))$.

2.8 Consider the local search algorithm of Section 2.6 for finding a minimum-degree spanning tree, and suppose we apply a local move to a node whenever it is possible to do so; that is, we don't restrict local moves to nodes with degrees between $\Delta(T) - \ell$ and $\Delta(T)$. What kind of performance guarantee can you obtain for a locally optimal tree in this case?

2.9 As given in Exercise 2.5, in the Steiner tree problem we are given an undirected graph $G = (V, E)$ and a set of terminals $R \subseteq V$. A Steiner tree is a tree in G in which all the terminals are connected; a nonterminal need not be spanned. Show that the local search algorithm of Section 2.6 can be adapted to find a Steiner tree whose maximum degree is at most $2\,\text{OPT} + \lceil \log_2 n \rceil$, where OPT is the maximum degree of a minimum-degree Steiner tree.

2.10 Let E be a set of items, and for $S \subseteq E$, let $f(S)$ give the value of the subset S. Suppose we wish to find a maximum value subset of E of at most k items. Furthermore, suppose that $f(\emptyset) = 0$, and that f is *monotone* and *submodular*. We say that f is *monotone* if for any S and T with $S \subseteq T \subseteq E$, then $f(S) \leq f(T)$. We say that f is *submodular* if for any $S, T \subseteq E$, then

$$f(S) + f(T) \geq f(S \cup T) + f(S \cap T).$$

Show that the greedy $(1 - \frac{1}{e})$-approximation algorithm of Section 2.5 extends to this problem.

2.11 In the *maximum coverage problem*, we have a set of elements E, and m subsets of elements $S_1, \ldots, S_m \subseteq E$, each with a nonnegative weight $w_j \geq 0$. The goal is to choose k elements such that we maximize the weight of the subsets that are covered. We say that a subset is covered if we have chosen some element from it. Thus, we want to find $S \subseteq E$ such that $|S| = k$ and that we maximize the total weight of the subsets j such that $S \cap S_j \neq \emptyset$.

(a) Give a $(1 - \frac{1}{e})$-approximation algorithm for this problem.

(b) Show that if an approximation algorithm with performance guarantee better than $1 - \frac{1}{e} + \epsilon$ exists for the maximum coverage problem for some constant $\epsilon > 0$, then every NP-complete problem has an $O(n^{O(\log \log n)})$ time algorithm. (Hint: Recall Theorem 1.13.)

2.12 A *matroid* $(E, \mathcal{I})$ is a set E of ground elements together with a collection $\mathcal{I}$ of subsets of E; that is, if $S \in \mathcal{I}$, then $S \subseteq E$. A set $S \in \mathcal{I}$ is said to be *independent*. The independent sets of a matroid obey the following two axioms:

• If S is independent, then any $S' \subseteq S$ is also independent.
• If S and T are independent, and $|S| < |T|$, then there is some $e \in T - S$ such that $S \cup \{e\}$ is also independent.

An independent set S is a *base* of the matroid if no set strictly containing it is also independent.

(a) Given an undirected graph $G = (V, E)$, show that the forests of G form a matroid; that is, show that if E is the ground set, and $\mathcal{I}$ the set of forests of G, then the matroid axioms are obeyed.

    (b) Show that for any matroid, every base of the matroid has the same number of ground elements.

    (c) For any given matroid, suppose that for each $e \in E$, we have a nonnegative weight $w_e \geq 0$. Give a greedy algorithm for the problem of finding a maximum-weight base of a matroid.

2.13 Let $(E, \mathcal{I})$ be a matroid as defined in Exercise 2.12, and let f be a monotone, submodular function as defined in Exercise 2.10 such that $f(\emptyset) = 0$. Consider the following local search algorithm for finding a maximum-value base of the matroid: First, start with an arbitrary base S. Then consider all pairs $e \in S$ and $e' \notin S$. If $S \cup \{e\} - \{e'\}$ is a base, and $f(S \cup \{e'\} - \{e\}) > f(S)$, then set $S \leftarrow S \cup \{e'\} - \{e\}$. Repeat until a locally optimal solution is reached. The goal of this problem is to show that a locally optimal solution has value at least half the optimal value.

    (a) We begin with a simple case: Suppose that the matroid is a *uniform matroid*; that is, $S \subseteq E$ is independent if $|S| \leq k$ for some fixed k. Prove that for a locally optimal solution S, $f(S) \geq \frac{1}{2}$ OPT.

    (b) To prove the general case, it is useful to know that for any two bases of a matroid, X and Y, there exists a bijection $g : X \to Y$ such that for any $e \in X$, $S - \{e\} \cup \{g(e)\}$ is independent. Use this to prove that for any locally optimal solution S, $f(S) \geq \frac{1}{2}$ OPT.

    (c) For any $\epsilon > 0$, give a variant of this algorithm that is a $(\frac{1}{2} - \epsilon)$-approximation algorithm.

2.14 In the *edge-disjoint paths* problem in directed graphs, we are given as input a directed graph $G = (V, A)$ and k source-sink pairs $s_i, t_i \in V$. The goal of the problem is to find edge-disjoint paths so that as many source-sink pairs as possible have a path from s_i to t_i. More formally, let $S \subseteq \{1, \dots, k\}$. We want to find S and paths P_i for all $i \in S$ such that $|S|$ is as large as possible and for any $i, j \in S$, $i \neq j$, P_i and P_j are edge-disjoint ($P_i \cap P_j = \emptyset$).

    Consider the following greedy algorithm for the problem. Let ℓ be the maximum of $\sqrt{m}$ and the diameter of the graph (where $m = |A|$ is the number of input arcs). For each i from 1 to k, we check to see if there exists an s_i-t_i path of length at most ℓ in the graph. If there is such a path P_i, we add i to S and remove the arcs of P_i from the graph.

    Show that this greedy algorithm is an $\Omega(1/\ell)$-approximation algorithm for the edge-disjoint paths problem in directed graphs.

2.15 Prove that there is no α-approximation algorithm for the edge coloring problem for $\alpha < 4/3$ unless P = NP.

2.16 Let $G = (V, E)$ be a bipartite graph; that is, V can be partitioned into two sets A and B, such that each edge in E has one endpoint in A and the other in B. Let Δ be the maximum degree of a node in G. Give a polynomial-time algorithm for finding a Δ-edge-coloring of G.

Chapter Notes

As discussed in the introduction to this chapter, greedy algorithms and local search algorithms are very popular choices for heuristics for discrete optimization problems. Thus, it is not surprising that they are among the earliest algorithms analyzed for a performance guarantee. The greedy edge coloring algorithm in Section 2.7 is from a 1964 paper due to Vizing [284]. To the best of our knowledge, this is the earliest polynomial-time algorithm known for a combinatorial optimization problem that proves that its performance is close to optimal, with an additive performance guarantee. In 1966, Graham [142] gave the list scheduling algorithm for scheduling identical parallel machines found in Section 2.3. To our knowledge, this is the first appearance of a polynomial-time algorithm with a relative performance guarantee. The longest processing time algorithm and its analysis is from a 1969 paper of Graham [143].

Other early examples of the analysis of greedy approximation algorithms include a 1977 paper of Cornuejols, Fisher, and Nemhauser [83], who introduce the float maximization problem of Section 2.5, as well as the algorithm presented there. The analysis of the algorithm presented follows that given in Nemhauser and Wolsey [232]. The earliest due date rule given in Section 2.1 is from a 1955 paper of Jackson [174], and is sometimes called *Jackson's rule*. The analysis of the algorithm in the case of negative due dates was given by Kise, Ibaraki, and Mine [195] in 1979. The nearest addition algorithm for the metric traveling salesman problem given in Section 2.4 and the analysis of the algorithm are from a 1977 paper of Rosenkrantz, Stearns, and Lewis [255]. The double-tree algorithm from that section is folklore, while Christofides' algorithm is due, naturally enough, to Christofides [73]. The hardness result of Theorem 2.9 is due to Sahni and Gonzalez [257] while the result of Theorem 2.14 is due to Papadimitriou and Vempala [239].

There is an enormous literature on the traveling salesman problem. For book-length treatments of the problem, see the book edited by Lawler, Lenstra, Rinnooy Kan, and Shmoys [210] and the book of Applegate, Bixby, Chvátal, and Cook [9].

Of course, greedy algorithms for polynomial-time solvable discrete optimization problems have also been studied for many years. The greedy algorithm for finding a maximum-weight base of a matroid in Exercise 2.12 was given by Rado [246] in 1957, Gale [121] in 1968, and Edmonds [96] in 1971; matroids were first defined by Whitney [285].

Analysis of the performance guarantees of local search algorithms has been relatively rare, at least until some work on facility location problems from the late 1990s and early 2000s that will be discussed in Chapter 9. The local search algorithm for scheduling parallel machines given in Section 2.3 is a simplification of a local search algorithm given in a 1979 paper of Finn and Horowitz [113]; Finn and Horowitz show that their algorithm has performance guarantee of at most 2. The local search algorithm for finding a maximum-value base of Exercise 2.13 was given by Fisher, Nemhauser, and Wolsey [114] in 1978. The local search algorithm for finding a minimum-degree spanning tree in Section 2.6 is from 1992 and can be found in Fürer and Raghavachari [118].

Now to discuss the other results presented in the chapter: The algorithm and analysis of the k-center problem in Section 2.2 is due to Gonzalez [141]. An alternative 2-approximation algorithm for the problem is due to Hochbaum and Shmoys [163]. Theorem 2.4, which states that getting a performance guarantee better than 2 is NP-hard, is due to Hsu and Nemhauser [172]. Theorem 2.22, which states that deciding if a graph is 3-edge-colorable or not is NP-complete, is due to Holyer [170].

The k-supplier problem of Exercise 2.1, as well as a 3-approximation algorithm for it, were introduced in Hochbaum and Shmoys [164]. The list scheduling variant for problems with precedence constraints in Exercise 2.3 is due to Graham [142]. The idea of a ρ-relaxed decision procedure in Exercise 2.4 is due to Hochbaum and Shmoys [165]; the 2-relaxed decision procedure for related machines in that exercise is due to Shmoys, Wein, and Williamson [265]. Exercise 2.7 was suggested to us by Nick Harvey. Exercise 2.9 is due to Fürer and Raghavachari [118]. Exercises 2.10 and 2.11 are due to Nemhauser, Wolsey, and Fisher [233]. The hardness result of Exercise 2.11 is due to Feige [107]; Feige also shows that the same result can be obtained under the assumption that $P \neq NP$. Kleinberg [199] gives the greedy algorithm for the edge-disjoint paths problem in directed graphs given in Exercise 2.14. Kőnig [201] shows that it is possible to Δ-edge-color a bipartite graph as in Exercise 2.16.

CHAPTER 3

Rounding Data and Dynamic Programming

Dynamic programming is a standard technique in algorithm design in which an optimal solution for a problem is built up from optimal solutions for a number of subproblems, normally stored in a table or multidimensional array. Approximation algorithms can be designed using dynamic programming in a variety of ways, many of which involve rounding the input data in some way.

For instance, sometimes weakly NP-hard problems have dynamic programming algorithms that run in time polynomial in the input size if the input is represented in unary rather than in binary (so, for example, the number 7 would be encoded as 1111111). If so, we say that the algorithm is *pseudopolynomial*. Then by rounding the input values so that the number of distinct values is polynomial in the input size and an error parameter $\epsilon > 0$, this pseudopolynomial algorithm can be made to run in time polynomial in the size of the original instance. We can often show that the rounding does not sacrifice too much in the quality of the solution produced. We will use this technique in discussing the knapsack problem in Section 3.1.

For other problems, such as scheduling problems, we can often make distinctions between "large" and "small" parts of the input instance; for instance, in scheduling problems, we distinguish between jobs that have large and small processing times. We can then show that by rounding the sizes of the large inputs so that, again, the number of distinct, large input values is polynomial in the input size and an error parameter, we can use dynamic programming to find an optimal solution on just the large inputs. Then this solution must be augmented to a solution for the whole input by dealing with the small inputs in some way. Using these ideas, we will devise polynomial-time approximation schemes for the problem of scheduling parallel machines introduced in the last chapter, and for a new problem of packing bins.

3.1 The Knapsack Problem

A traveler with a knapsack comes across a treasure hoard. Unfortunately, his knapsack can hold only so much. What items should he place in his knapsack in order to

$A(1) \leftarrow \{(0, 0), (s_1, w_1)\}$
for $j \leftarrow 2$ to n **do**
   $A(j) \leftarrow A(j - 1)$
   for each $(t, w) \in A(j - 1)$ **do**
     if $t + s_j \leq B$ **then**
       Add $(t + s_j, w + v_j)$ to $A(j)$
   Remove dominated pairs from $A(j)$
return $\max_{(t, w) \in A(n)} w$

Algorithm 3.1. A dynamic programming algorithm for the knapsack problem.

maximize the value of the items he takes away? This unrealistic scenario gives the name to the *knapsack problem*. In the knapsack problem, we are given a set of n items $I = \{1, \ldots, n\}$, where each item i has a value v_i and a size s_i. All sizes and values are positive integers. The knapsack has capacity B, where B is also a positive integer. The goal is to find a subset of items $S \subseteq I$ that maximizes the value $\sum_{i \in S} v_i$ of items in the knapsack subject to the constraint that the total size of these items is no more than the capacity; that is, $\sum_{i \in S} s_i \leq B$. We assume that we consider only items that could actually fit in the knapsack (by themselves), so that $s_i \leq B$ for each $i \in I$. Although the application stated above is unlikely to be useful in real life, the knapsack problem is well studied because it is a simplified model of a problem that arises in many realistic scenarios.

We now argue that we can use dynamic programming to find the optimal solution to the knapsack problem. We maintain an array entry $A(j)$ for $j = 1, \ldots, n$. Each entry $A(j)$ is a list of pairs (t, w). A pair (t, w) in the list of entry $A(j)$ indicates that there is a set S from the first j items that uses space exactly $t \leq B$ and has value exactly w; that is, there exists a set $S \subseteq \{1, \ldots, j\}$, such that $\sum_{i \in S} s_i = t \leq B$ and $\sum_{i \in S} v_i = w$. Each list does not contain all possible such pairs, but instead keeps track of only the most efficient ones. To do this, we introduce the notion of one pair *dominating* another one; a pair (t, w) dominates another pair (t', w') if $t \leq t'$ and $w \geq w'$; that is, the solution indicated by the pair (t, w) uses no more space than (t', w'), but has at least as much value. Note that domination is a transitive property; that is, if (t, w) dominates (t', w') and (t', w') dominates (t'', w''), then (t, w) also dominates (t'', w''). We will ensure that in any list, no pair dominates another one; this means that we can assume each list $A(j)$ is of the form $(t_1, w_1), \ldots, (t_k, w_k)$ with $t_1 < t_2 < \cdots < t_k$ and $w_1 < w_2 < \cdots < w_k$. Since the sizes of the items are integers, this implies that there are at most $B + 1$ pairs in each list. Furthermore, if we let $V = \sum_{i=1}^{n} v_i$ be the maximum possible value for the knapsack, then there can be at most $V + 1$ pairs in the list. Finally, we ensure that for each feasible set $S \subseteq \{1, \ldots, j\}$ (with $\sum_{i \in S} s_i \leq B$), the list $A(j)$ contains some pair (t, w) that dominates $(\sum_{i \in S} s_i, \sum_{i \in S} v_i)$.

In Algorithm 3.1, we give the dynamic program that constructs the lists $A(j)$ and solves the knapsack problem. We start out with $A(1) = \{(0, 0), (s_1, w_1)\}$. For each $j = 2, \ldots, n$, we do the following. We first set $A(j) \leftarrow A(j - 1)$, and for each $(t, w) \in A(j - 1)$, we also add the pair $(t + s_j, w + v_j)$ to the list $A(j)$ if $t + s_j \leq B$. We finally remove from $A(j)$ all dominated pairs by sorting the list with respect to their space component, retaining the best value for each space total possible, and removing any larger space total that does not have a corresponding larger value. One way to view this process is to generate two lists, $A(j - 1)$ and the one augmented by (s_j, w_j), and then perform a type of merging of these two lists. We return the pair (t, w) from $A(n)$ of maximum value as our solution. Next we argue that this algorithm is correct.

Theorem 3.1. *Algorithm 3.1 correctly computes the optimal value of the knapsack problem.*

Proof. By induction on j we prove that $A(j)$ contains all non-dominated pairs corresponding to feasible sets $S \subseteq \{1, \ldots, j\}$. Certainly this is true in the base case by setting $A(1)$ to $\{(0, 0), (s_1, w_1)\}$. Now suppose it is true for $A(j - 1)$. Let $S \subseteq \{1, \ldots, j\}$, and let $t = \sum_{i \in S} s_i \leq B$ and $w = \sum_{i \in S} v_i$. We claim that there is some pair $(t', w') \in A(j)$ such that $t' \leq t$ and $w' \geq w$. First, suppose that $j \notin S$. Then the claim follows by the induction hypothesis and by the fact that we initially set $A(j)$ to $A(j - 1)$ and only removed dominated pairs. Now suppose $j \in S$. Then for $S' = S - \{j\}$, by the induction hypothesis, there is some $(\hat{t}, \hat{w}) \in A(j - 1)$ that dominates $(\sum_{i \in S'} s_i, \sum_{i \in S'} v_i)$, so that $\hat{t} \leq \sum_{i \in S'} s_i$ and $\hat{w} \geq \sum_{i \in S'} v_i$. Then the algorithm will add the pair $(\hat{t} + s_j, \hat{w} + v_j)$ to $A(j)$, where $\hat{t} + s_j \leq t \leq B$ and $\hat{w} + v_j \geq w$. Thus, there will be some pair $(t', w') \in A(j)$ that dominates (t, w). $\square$

Algorithm 3.1 takes $O(n \min(B, V))$ time. This is not a polynomial-time algorithm, since we assume that all input numbers are encoded in binary; thus, the size of the input number B is essentially $\log_2 B$, and so the running time $O(nB)$ is exponential in the size of the input number B, not polynomial. If we were to assume that the input is given in unary, then $O(nB)$ would be a polynomial in the size of the input. It is sometimes useful to make this distinction between problems.

Definition 3.2. *An algorithm for a problem* Π *is said to be* pseudopolynomial *if its running time is polynomial in the size of the input when the numeric part of the input is encoded in unary.*

If the maximum possible value V were some polynomial in n, then the running time would indeed be a polynomial in the input size. We now show how to get a polynomial-time approximation scheme for the knapsack problem by rounding the values of the items so that V is indeed a polynomial in n. The rounding induces some loss of precision in the value of a solution, but we will show that this does not affect the final value by too much. Recall the definition of an approximation scheme from Chapter 1.

Definition 3.3. *A* polynomial-time approximation scheme (PTAS) *is a family of algorithms* $\{A_\epsilon\}$, *where there is an algorithm for each* $\epsilon > 0$, *such that* A_ϵ *is a* $(1 + \epsilon)$-*approximation algorithm (for minimization problems) or a* $(1 - \epsilon)$-*approximation algorithm (for maximization problems).*

Note that the running time of the algorithm A_ϵ is allowed to depend arbitrarily on $1/\epsilon$: this dependence could be exponential in $1/\epsilon$, or worse. We often focus attention

$M \leftarrow \max_{i \in I} v_i$

$\mu \leftarrow \epsilon M/n$

$v_i' \leftarrow \lfloor v_i/\mu \rfloor$ for all $i \in I$

Run Algorithm 3.1 for knapsack instance with values v_i'

Algorithm 3.2. An approximation scheme for the knapsack problem.

on algorithms for which we can give a good bound of the dependence of the running time of A_ϵ on $1/\epsilon$. This motivates the following definition.

Definition 3.4. *A* fully polynomial-time approximation scheme (FPAS, FPTAS) *is an approximation scheme such that the running time of A_ϵ is bounded by a polynomial in $1/\epsilon$.*

We can now give a fully polynomial-time approximation scheme for the knapsack problem. Suppose that we measure value in (integer) multiples of μ (where we shall set μ below), and convert each value v_i by rounding down to the nearest integer multiple of μ; more precisely, we set v_i' to be $\lfloor v_i/\mu \rfloor$ for each item i. We can then run the dynamic programming algorithm of Figure 3.1 on the items with sizes s_i and values v_i', and output the optimal solution for the rounded data as a near-optimal solution for the true data. The main idea here is that we wish to show that the accuracy we lose in rounding is not so great, and yet the rounding enables us to have the algorithm run in polynomial time. Let us first do a rough estimate; if we used values $\tilde{v}_i = v_i' \mu$ instead of v_i, then each value is inaccurate by at most μ, and so each feasible solution has its value changed by at most $n\mu$. We want the error introduced to be at most ϵ times a lower bound on the optimal value (and so be sure that the true relative error is at most ϵ). Let M be the maximum value of an item; that is, $M = \max_{i \in I} v_i$. Then M is a lower bound on OPT, since one possible solution is to pack the most valuable item in the knapsack by itself. Thus, it makes sense to set μ so that $n\mu = \epsilon M$ or, in other words, to set $\mu = \epsilon M/n$.

Note that with the modified values, $V' = \sum_{i=1}^{n} v_i' = \sum_{i=1}^{n} \lfloor \frac{v_i}{\epsilon M/n} \rfloor = O(n^2/\epsilon)$. Thus, the running time of the algorithm is $O(n \min(B, V')) = O(n^3/\epsilon)$ and is bounded by a polynomial in $1/\epsilon$. We can now prove that the algorithm returns a solution whose value is at least $(1 - \epsilon)$ times the value of an optimal solution.

Theorem 3.5. *Algorithm 3.2 is a fully polynomial-time approximation scheme for the knapsack problem.*

Proof. We need to show that the algorithm returns a solution whose value is at least $(1 - \epsilon)$ times the value of an optimal solution. Let S be the set of items returned by the algorithm. Let O be an optimal set of items. Certainly $M \leq$ OPT, since one possible solution is to put the most valuable item in a knapsack by itself. Furthermore, by the definition of v_i', $\mu v_i' \leq v_i \leq \mu(v_i' + 1)$, so that $\mu v_i' \geq v_i - \mu$. Applying the definitions of the rounded data, along with the fact that S is an optimal solution for the values v_i', we can derive the following chain of inequalities:

$$\sum_{i \in S} v_i \geq \mu \sum_{i \in S} v_i'$$

$$\geq \mu \sum_{i \in O} v_i'$$

$$\geq \sum_{i \in O} v_i - |O|\mu$$

$$\geq \sum_{i \in O} v_i - n\mu$$

$$= \sum_{i \in O} v_i - \epsilon M$$

$$\geq \mathrm{OPT} - \epsilon\, \mathrm{OPT} = (1 - \epsilon)\,\mathrm{OPT}. \qquad \square$$

3.2 Scheduling Jobs on Identical Parallel Machines

We return to the problem of scheduling a collection of n jobs on m identical parallel machines; in Section 2.3 we presented a result that by first sorting the jobs in order of non-increasing processing requirement, and then using a list scheduling rule, we find a schedule of length guaranteed to be at most 4/3 times the optimum. In this section, we will show that this result contains the seeds of a polynomial-time approximation scheme: for any given value of $\rho > 1$, we give an algorithm that runs in polynomial time and finds a solution of objective function value at most ρ times the optimal value.

As in Section 2.3, we let the processing requirement of job j be p_j, $j = 1, \ldots, n$, and let $C_{\max}$ denote the length (or makespan) of a given schedule with job completion times C_j, $j = 1, \ldots, n$; the optimal value is denoted $C_{\max}^*$. We shall assume that each processing requirement is a positive integer. The key idea of the analysis of the list scheduling rule was that its error can be upper bounded by the processing requirement of the last job to complete. The 4/3-approximation algorithm was based on this fact, combined with the observation that when each job's processing requirement is more than $C_{\max}^*/3$, this natural greedy-type algorithm actually finds the optimal solution. We present an approximation scheme for this problem based on a similar principle: we focus on a specified subset of the longest jobs, and compute the optimal schedule for that subset; then we extend that partial schedule by using list scheduling on the remaining jobs. We will show that there is a trade-off between the number of long jobs and the quality of the solution found.

More precisely, let k be a fixed positive integer; we will derive a family of algorithms, and focus on the algorithm A_k among them. Suppose that we partition the job set into two parts: the *long* jobs and the *short* jobs, where a job ℓ is considered short if $p_\ell \leq \frac{1}{km} \sum_{j=1}^{n} p_j$. Note that this implies that there are at most km long jobs. Enumerate all possible schedules for the long jobs, and choose one with the minimum makespan. Extend this schedule by using list scheduling for the short jobs; that is, given an arbitrary order of the short jobs, schedule these jobs in order, always assigning the next job to the machine currently least loaded.

Consider the running time of algorithm A_k. To specify a schedule for the long jobs, we simply indicate to which of the m machines each long job is assigned; thus, there are at most m^{km} distinct assignments (since the order of processing on each machine is unimportant). If we focus on the special case of this problem in which the number of machines is a constant (say, 100, 1,000, or even 1,000,000), then this number is also a constant, not depending on the size of the input. Thus, we can check each schedule, and determine the optimal length schedule in polynomial time in this special case.

As in the analysis of the local search algorithm in Section 2.3, we focus on the last job ℓ to finish. Recall that we derived the equality that

$$C_{\max} \le p_\ell + \sum_{j \ne \ell} p_j/m; \tag{3.1}$$

the validity of this inequality relied only on the fact that each machine is busy up until the time that job ℓ starts. To analyze the algorithm that starts by finding the optimal schedule for the long jobs, we distinguish now between two cases. If the last job to finish (in the entire schedule), job ℓ, is a short job, then this job was scheduled by the list scheduling rule, and it follows that inequality (3.1) holds. Since job ℓ is short, and hence $p_\ell \le \sum_{j=1}^n p_j/(mk)$, it also follows that

$$C_{\max} \le \sum_{j=1}^n p_j/(mk) + \sum_{j \ne \ell} p_j/m \le \left(1 + \frac{1}{k}\right) \sum_{j=1}^n p_j/m \le \left(1 + \frac{1}{k}\right) C_{\max}^*.$$

If job ℓ is a long job, then the schedule delivered by the algorithm is optimal, since its makespan is equal to the length of the optimal schedule for just the long jobs, which is clearly no more than $C_{\max}^*$ for the entire input. The algorithm A_k can easily be implemented to run in polynomial time (treating m as a constant), and hence we have obtained the following theorem.

Theorem 3.6. *The family of algorithms $\{A_k\}$ is a polynomial-time approximation scheme for the problem of minimizing the makespan on any constant number of identical parallel machines.*

Of course, it is a significant limitation of this theorem that the number of machines is restricted to be a constant. In fact, it is not too hard to extend these techniques to obtain a polynomial-time approximation scheme even if the number of machines is allowed to be an input parameter (and hence the algorithm must also have running time polynomially bounded in the number of machines m). The key idea is that we didn't really need the schedule for the long jobs to be optimal. We used the optimality of the schedule for the long jobs only when the last job to finish was a long job. If we had found a schedule for the long jobs that had makespan at most $1 + \frac{1}{k}$ times the optimal value, then that clearly would have been sufficient. We will show how to obtain this near-optimal schedule for long jobs by rounding input sizes and dynamic programming, as we saw in the previous section on the knapsack problem.

It will be convenient to first set a target length T for the schedule. As before, we also fix a positive integer k; we will design a family of algorithms $\{B_k\}$ where B_k either proves that no schedule of length T exists, or else finds a schedule of length $(1 + \frac{1}{k})T$. Later we will show how such a family of algorithms also implies the existence of a polynomial-time approximation scheme. We can assume that $T \geq \frac{1}{m} \sum_{j=1}^{n} p_j$, since otherwise no feasible schedule exists.

The algorithm B_k is quite simple. We again partition the jobs into *long* and *short* jobs, but in this case, we require that $p_j > T/k$ for job j to be considered long. We round down the processing requirement of each long job to its nearest multiple of T/k^2. We will determine in polynomial time whether or not there is a feasible schedule for these rounded long jobs that completes within time T. If there is such a schedule, we then interpret it as a schedule for the long jobs with their original processing requirements. If not, we conclude that no feasible schedule of length T exists for the original input. Finally, we extend this schedule to include the short jobs by using the list scheduling algorithm for the short jobs.

We need to prove that the algorithm B_k always produces a schedule of length at most $(1 + \frac{1}{k})T$ whenever there exists a schedule of length at most T. When the original input has a schedule of length T, then so does the reduced input consisting only of the rounded long jobs (which is why we rounded down the processing requirements); in this case, the algorithm does compute a schedule for the original input. Suppose that a schedule is found. It starts with a schedule of length at most T for the rounded long jobs. Let S be the set of jobs assigned by this schedule to one machine. Since each job in S is long, and hence has rounded size at least T/k, it follows that $|S| \leq k$. Furthermore, for each job $j \in S$, the difference between its true processing requirement and its rounded one is at most T/k^2. Hence,

$$\sum_{j \in S} p_j \leq T + k(T/k^2) = \left(1 + \frac{1}{k}\right)T.$$

Now consider the effect of assigning the short jobs: each job ℓ, in turn, is assigned to a machine for which the current load is smallest. Since $\sum_{j=1}^{n} p_j/m \leq T$, we also know that $\sum_{j \neq \ell} p_j/m < T$. Since the average load assigned to a machine is less than T, there must exist a machine that is currently assigned jobs of total processing requirement less than T. So, when we choose the machine that currently has the lightest load, and then add job ℓ, this machine's new load is at most

$$p_\ell + \sum_{j \neq \ell} p_j/m < T/k + T = \left(1 + \frac{1}{k}\right)T.$$

Hence, the schedule produced by list scheduling will also be of length at most $(1 + \frac{1}{k})T$.

To complete the description of the algorithm B_k, we must still show that we can use dynamic programming to decide if there is a schedule of length T for the rounded long jobs. Clearly if there is a rounded long job of size greater than T, then there is no such schedule. Otherwise, we can describe an input by a k^2-dimensional vector, where the ith component specifies the number of long jobs of rounded size equal to iT/k^2, for each $i = 1, \ldots, k^2$. (In fact, we know that for $i < k$, there are no such jobs, since that would imply that their original processing requirement was less than T/k, and hence not long.) So there are at most n^{k^2} distinct inputs – a polynomial number!

How many distinct ways are there to feasibly assign long jobs to one machine? Each rounded long job still has processing time at least T/k. Hence, at most k jobs are assigned to one machine. Again, an assignment to one machine can be described by a k^2-dimensional vector, where again the ith component specifies the number of long jobs of rounded size equal to iT/k^2 that are assigned to that machine. Consider the vector $(s_1, s_2, \ldots, s_{k^2})$; we shall call it a *machine configuration* if

$$\sum_{i=1}^{k^2} s_i \cdot iT/k^2 \leq T.$$

Let $\mathcal{C}$ denote the set of all machine configurations. Note that there are at most $(k+1)^{k^2}$ distinct configurations, since each machine must process a number of rounded long jobs that is in the set $\{0, 1, \ldots, k\}$. Since k is fixed, this means that there are a constant number of configurations.

Let $\mathrm{OPT}(n_1, \ldots, n_{k^2})$ denote the minimum number of (identical) machines sufficient to schedule this arbitrary input. This value is governed by the following recurrence relation, based on the idea that a schedule consists of assigning some jobs to one machine, and then using as few machines as possible for the rest:

$$\mathrm{OPT}(n_1, \ldots, n_{k^2}) = 1 + \min_{(s_1, \ldots, s_{k^2}) \in \mathcal{C}} \mathrm{OPT}(n_1 - s_1, \ldots, n_{k^2} - s_{k^2}).$$

This can be viewed as a table with a polynomial number of entries (one for each possible input type), and to compute each entry, we need to find the minimum over a constant number of previously computed values. The desired schedule exists exactly when the corresponding optimal value is at most m.

Finally, we need to show that we can convert the family of algorithms $\{B_k\}$ into a polynomial-time approximation scheme. Fix the relative error $\epsilon > 0$. We use a bisection search procedure to determine a suitable choice of the target value T (which is required as part of the input for each algorithm B_k). We know that the optimal makespan for our scheduling input is within the interval $[L_0, U_0]$, where

$$L_0 = \max \left\{ \left\lceil \sum_{j=1}^{n} p_j/m \right\rceil, \max_{j=1, \ldots, n} p_j \right\}$$

and

$$U_0 = \left\lceil \sum_{j=1}^{n} p_j/m \right\rceil + \max_{j=1, \ldots, n} p_j.$$

(We strengthen the lower bound with the $\lceil \cdot \rceil$ by relying on the fact that the processing requirements are integral.) Throughout the bisection search, we maintain such an interval $[L, U]$, with the algorithmic invariants (1) that $L \leq C^*_{\max}$, and (2) that we can compute a schedule with makespan at most $(1 + \epsilon)U$. This is clearly true initially: by the arguments of Section 2.3, L_0 is a lower bound on the length of an optimal schedule, and using a list scheduling algorithm we can compute a schedule of length at most U_0.

In each iteration where the current interval is $[L, U]$, we set $T = \lfloor (L + U)/2 \rfloor$, and run the algorithm B_k, where $k = \lceil 1/\epsilon \rceil$. If the algorithm B_k produces a schedule, then update $U \leftarrow T$; otherwise, update $L \leftarrow T + 1$. The bisection continues until $L = U$, at which point the algorithm outputs the schedule associated with U (of length at most $(1 + \epsilon)U$).

It is easy to see that the claimed invariant is maintained: (1) when we update the lower limit L, the algorithm B_k has just shown that no feasible schedule of length T exists, and by the integrality of the processing times, we know then that $T + 1$ is a valid lower bound; (2) when we update the upper limit U, the algorithm B_k has just produced the schedule of length at most $(1 + \epsilon)T$, which is exactly what is required to justify this update.

The difference between the upper and lower limits is initially at most $\max_{j=1,\dots,n} p_j$, and is halved in each iteration. Hence, after a polynomial number of iterations, the difference becomes less than 1 and, by integrality, is therefore 0. Since both invariants must still hold for this trivial interval $[L, L]$, then we know that $C^*_{\max} \geq L$, and that the final schedule output by the algorithm is of length at most $(1 + \epsilon)L \leq (1 + \epsilon)C^*_{\max}$. The algorithm is a $(1 + \epsilon)$-approximation algorithm.

Theorem 3.7. *There is a polynomial-time approximation scheme for the problem of minimizing the makespan on an input number of identical parallel machines.*

Note that since we consider $(k + 1)^{k^2}$ configurations and $k = \lceil 1/\epsilon \rceil$, the running time in the worst case is exponential in $O(1/\epsilon^2)$. Thus, in this case, we did not obtain a fully polynomial-time approximation scheme (in contrast to the knapsack problem). This is for a fundamental reason. This scheduling problem is strongly NP-complete; that is, even if we require that the processing times be restricted to *values* at most $q(n)$, a polynomial function of the number of jobs, this special case is still NP-complete. We claim that if a fully polynomial-time approximation scheme exists for this problem, it could be used to solve this special case in polynomial time, which would imply that $P = NP$.

How can we use a fully polynomial-time approximation scheme to solve the special case with polynomially bounded processing times? Let P be the maximum processing time for an input satisfying this special structure. This implies that the optimal makespan is at most $nP \leq nq(n)$. If there were a fully polynomial-time approximation scheme $\{A_k\}$, suppose that we use the algorithm A_k that guarantees a solution with relative error at most $1/k$ where $k = \lceil 2nq(n) \rceil$. This implies that the algorithm finds a solution of makespan at most

$$\left(1 + \frac{1}{k}\right) C^*_{\max} \leq C^*_{\max} + \frac{1}{2}.$$

But since any feasible schedule is simply an assignment of jobs to machines, the makespan is clearly integer, and hence the algorithm must find the optimal assignment. We know that $q(n)$ is a polynomial; the requirements of a fully polynomial-time approximation scheme imply that the running time must be bounded by a polynomial in k, and hence we have computed this optimal schedule in polynomial time. Therefore, the existence of such a scheme implies that $P = NP$. This result is one special case of a much more general result; we know that (with very mild assumptions on the nature of the objective function) for any optimization problem, if the problem is strongly

NP-complete, then it does not have a fully polynomial-time approximation scheme. We give this as an exercise (Exercise 3.9).

3.3 The Bin-Packing Problem

In the *bin-packing problem*, we are given n pieces (or items) with specified sizes $a_1, a_2, \ldots, a_n$, such that

$$1 > a_1 \geq a_2 \geq \cdots \geq a_n > 0;$$

we wish to pack the pieces into bins, where each bin can hold any subset of pieces of total size at most 1, so as to minimize the number of bins used.

The bin-packing problem is related to a decision problem called the *partition problem*. In the partition problem, we are given n positive integers $b_1, \ldots, b_n$ whose sum $B = \sum_{i=1}^{n} b_i$ is even, and we wish to know if we can partition the set of indices $\{1, \ldots, n\}$ into sets S and T such that $\sum_{i \in S} b_i = \sum_{i \in T} b_i$. The partition problem is well known to be NP-complete. Notice that we can reduce this problem to a bin-packing problem by setting $a_i = 2b_i/B$ and checking whether we can pack all the pieces into two bins or not. This gives the following theorem.

Theorem 3.8. *Unless* $P = NP$, *there cannot exist a ρ-approximation algorithm for the bin-packing problem for any $\rho < 3/2$.*

However, consider the First-Fit-Decreasing algorithm, where the pieces are packed in order of non-increasing size, and the next piece is always packed into the first bin in which it fits; that is, we first open bin 1, and we start bin $k + 1$ only when the current piece does not fit into any of the bins $1, \ldots, k$. If FFD(I) denotes the number of bins used by this algorithm on input I, and OPT(I) denotes the number of bins used in the optimal packing, then a celebrated classic result shows that that FFD(I) $\leq (11/9)$ OPT(I) $+ 4$ for any input I.

Thus, significantly stronger results can be obtained by relaxing the notion of the performance guarantee to allow for small additive terms. In fact, it is completely consistent with our current understanding of complexity theory that there is an algorithm that always produces a packing with at most OPT(I) $+ 1$ bins.

Why is it that we have bothered to mention hardness results of the form "there does not exist a ρ-approximation algorithm unless $P = NP$" if such a result can be so easily circumvented? The reason is that for all of the weighted problems that we have discussed, any distinction between the two types of guarantees disappears; any algorithm guaranteed to produce a solution of value at most ρ OPT $+ c$ can be converted to a ρ-approximation algorithm. Each of these problems has a natural *rescaling property*: for any input I and any value κ, we can construct an essentially identical instance I' such that the objective function value of any feasible solution is rescaled by κ. For example, for the scheduling problem of Section 3.2, if one simply multiplies each processing time p_j by κ, one can accomplish this rescaling, or for a combinatorial problem such as the unweighted vertex cover problem, one can consider an input with κ disjoint copies of the original input graph. Such rescaling makes it possible to blunt the effect of any small additive term $c < \kappa$ in the guarantee, and make it effectively 0. Observe that the bin-packing problem does not have this rescaling property; there is no obvious way to "multiply" the instance in a way that does not blur the combinatorial structure of the original input. (Think about what happens if you construct a new input that contains two copies of each piece of I!) Thus, whenever we consider designing approximation algorithms for a new combinatorial optimization problem, it is important to consider first whether the problem does have the rescaling property, since that will indicate what sort of performance guarantee one might hope for.

Although we will not prove the performance guarantee for the First-Fit-Decreasing algorithm for the bin-packing problem, we shall show that an exceedingly simple algorithm does perform reasonably well. Consider the First-Fit algorithm, which works exactly as First-Fit-Decreasing, except that we don't first sort the pieces in non-increasing size order. We can analyze its performance in the following way. If we pair up bins 1 and 2, then 3 and 4, and so forth, then any such pair must have the property that the total piece size in them is at least 1: in fact, the first item placed in bin $2k$ is put there only because it did not fit in bin $2k - 1$. Thus, if we used ℓ bins, then the total size of the pieces in the input, $\text{SIZE}(I) = \sum_{i=1}^{n} a_i$, is at least $\lfloor \ell/2 \rfloor$. However, it is clear that $\text{OPT}(I) \geq \text{SIZE}(I)$, and hence, the number of bins used by First-Fit is $\text{FF}(I) = \ell \leq 2\,\text{SIZE}(I) + 1 \leq 2\,\text{OPT}(I) + 1$. Of course, this analysis did not use practically any information about the algorithm; we used only that there should not be two bins whose contents can be feasibly combined into one bin.

We shall present a family of polynomial-time approximation algorithms parameterized by $\epsilon > 0$, where each algorithm has the performance guarantee of computing a packing with at most $(1 + \epsilon)\,\text{OPT}(I) + 1$ bins for each input I. Throughout this discussion, we shall view ϵ as a positive constant. Note that this family of algorithms does not meet the definition of a polynomial-time approximation scheme because of the additive constant. This motivates the following definition.

Definition 3.9. *An* asymptotic polynomial-time approximation scheme (APTAS) *is a family of algorithms* $\{A_\epsilon\}$ *along with a constant c where there is an algorithm A_ϵ for each $\epsilon > 0$ such that A_ϵ returns a solution of value at most $(1 + \epsilon)\,\text{OPT} + c$ for minimization problems.*

One of the key ingredients of this asymptotic polynomial-time approximation scheme is the dynamic programming algorithm used in the approximation scheme for scheduling jobs on identical parallel machines, which was presented in Section 3.2. As stated earlier, that algorithm computed the minimum number of machines needed to assign jobs, so that each machine was assigned jobs of total processing requirement at most T. However, by rescaling each processing time by dividing by T, we have an input for the bin-packing problem. The dynamic programming algorithm presented solves the bin-packing problem in polynomial time in the special case in which there are only a constant number of distinct piece sizes, and only a constant number of pieces can fit into one bin. Starting with an arbitrary input to the bin-packing problem, we first construct a simplified input of this special form, which we then solve by dynamic programming. The simplified input will also have the property that we can transform the resulting packing into a packing for the original input, without introducing too many additional bins.

As in the scheduling result of Section 3.2, the first key observation is that one may ignore *small* pieces of size less than any given threshold, and can analyze its effect in a relatively simple way.

Lemma 3.10. *Any packing of all pieces of size greater than γ into ℓ bins can be extended to a packing for the entire input with at most* $\max\{\ell, \frac{1}{1-\gamma}\, \text{SIZE}(I) + 1\}$ *bins.*

Proof. Suppose that one uses the First-Fit algorithm, starting with the given packing, to compute a packing that also includes these small pieces. If First-Fit never starts a new bin in packing the small pieces, then clearly the resulting packing has ℓ bins. If it does start a new bin, then each bin in the resulting packing (with the lone exception of the last bin started) must not have been able to fit one additional small piece. Let $k + 1$ denote the number of bins used in this latter case. In other words, each of the first k bins must have pieces totaling at least $1 - \gamma$, and hence $\text{SIZE}(I) \geq (1 - \gamma)k$. Equivalently, $k \leq \text{SIZE}(I)/(1 - \gamma)$, which completes the proof of the lemma. $\quad\square$

Suppose that we were aiming to design an algorithm with a performance guarantee that is better than the one proved for First-Fit (which is truly a modest goal); in particular, we are trying to design an algorithm with performance guarantee $1 + \epsilon$ with $\epsilon < 1$. If we apply Lemma 3.10 by setting $\gamma = \epsilon/2$, then since $1/(1 - \epsilon/2) \leq 1 + \epsilon$, we see that the composite algorithm produces a packing with at most $\max\{\ell, (1 + \epsilon)\,\text{OPT}(I) + 1\}$ bins.

The elimination of the small pieces from the input also enforces one of our requirements for the special case solvable by dynamic programming: if each piece has size greater than $\epsilon/2$, then each bin must contain fewer than $2/\epsilon$ pieces in total. We shall assume for the rest of the discussion that our input I does not have such small pieces to begin with.

The last element of the algorithm is a technique to reduce the number of distinct piece sizes, which is accomplished by a *linear grouping scheme*. This scheme works as follows, and is based on a parameter k, which will be set later. Group the pieces of the given input I as follows: the first group consists of the k largest pieces, the next group consists of the next k largest pieces, and so on, until all pieces have been placed in a group. The last group contains h pieces, where $h \leq k$. The rounded instance I' is constructed by discarding the first group, and for each other group, rounding the size of its pieces up to the size of its largest piece. An input I and its transformed version I' are shown in Figure 3.1. We can prove the following lemma relating the optimal number of bins needed to pack I to the optimal number of bins needed to pack I'.

Lemma 3.11. *Let I' be the input obtained from an input I by applying linear grouping with group size k. Then*

$$\text{OPT}(I') \leq \text{OPT}(I) \leq \text{OPT}(I') + k,$$

and furthermore, any packing of I' can be used to generate a packing of I with at most k additional bins.

Proof. For the first inequality, observe that any packing of the input I yields a packing of the input I': for I', pack its k largest pieces wherever the k largest pieces of I were packed. (There is a one-to-one correspondence between these two sets of k pieces, and

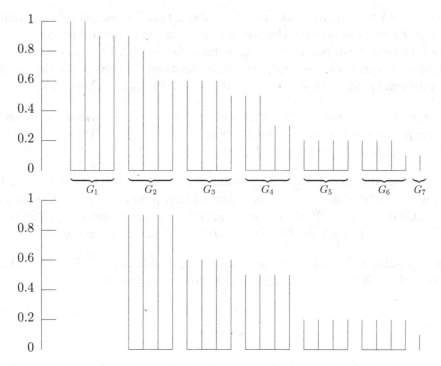

Figure 3.1. An input before and after linear grouping with group size $k = 4$.

each piece in the group from I' is no larger than the piece to which it corresponds in I.) The second k largest pieces of I' are packed wherever the second group of I were packed, and so forth. It is clear that this yields a feasible packing of I', and the first inequality follows.

To obtain the second inequality, we show how to take a packing of I', and use it to obtain a packing of I. This is also quite simple. To pack I, we pack each of the k largest pieces in its own bin. Now, the next largest group of k pieces in I can be packed wherever the largest group of pieces in I' are packed. Again, to do this, we use the fact that one can construct a one-to-one mapping between these two sets of k pieces, where each piece in I is no larger than its corresponding piece in I'. The fact that this last inequality is proved algorithmically is important, since this means that if we do obtain a good packing for I', then we can use it to obtain an "almost-as-good" packing for I. □

It is relatively straightforward to complete the derivation of an asymptotic polynomial-time approximation scheme for the bin-packing problem. If we consider the input I', then the number of distinct piece sizes is at most n/k, where n is the number of pieces in I. Since there are no small pieces in I, $\text{SIZE}(I) \geq \epsilon n/2$. If we set $k = \lfloor \epsilon \, \text{SIZE}(I) \rfloor$, then we see that $n/k \leq 2n/(\epsilon \, \text{SIZE}(I)) \leq 4/\epsilon^2$, where we crudely bound $\lfloor \alpha \rfloor \geq \alpha/2$ when $\alpha \geq 1$; we can assume $\epsilon \, \text{SIZE}(I) \geq 1$ since otherwise there are at most $(1/\epsilon)/(\epsilon/2) = 2/\epsilon^2$ (large) pieces and we could apply the dynamic programming algorithm to solve the input optimally without applying the linear grouping scheme. Consequently, after performing the linear grouping, we are left with a bin-packing input in which there are a constant number of distinct piece sizes, and only a constant number of pieces can fit in each bin; hence, we can obtain an optimal packing for the input I' by the dynamic programming algorithm of Section 3.2. This packing for I' can then be used to get a packing for the ungrouped input, and then be extended to include all of the small pieces with at most $(1 + \epsilon) \text{OPT}(I) + 1$ bins, as we show next.

Theorem 3.12. *For any $\epsilon > 0$, there is a polynomial-time algorithm for the bin-packing problem that computes a solution with at most $(1 + \epsilon) \text{OPT}(I) + 1$ bins; that is, there is an APTAS for the bin-packing problem.*

Proof. As we discussed earlier, the algorithm will open $\max\{\ell, (1 + \epsilon) \text{OPT}(I) + 1\}$ bins, where ℓ is the number of bins used to pack the large pieces. By Lemma 3.11, we use at most $\text{OPT}(I') + k \leq \text{OPT}(I) + k$ bins to pack these pieces, where $k = \lfloor \epsilon \text{ SIZE}(I) \rfloor$, so that $\ell \leq \text{OPT}(I) + \epsilon \text{ SIZE}(I) \leq (1 + \epsilon) \text{OPT}(I)$, which completes the proof. $\square$

It is possible to improve both the running time of this general approach, and its performance guarantee; we shall return to this problem in Section 4.6.

Exercises

3.1 Consider the following greedy algorithm for the knapsack problem. We initially sort all the items in order of non-increasing ratio of value to size so that $v_1/s_1 \geq v_2/s_2 \geq \cdots \geq v_n/s_n$. Let i^* be the index of an item of maximum value so that $v_{i^*} = \max_{i \in I} v_i$. The greedy algorithm puts items in the knapsack in index order until the next item no longer fits; that is, it finds k such that $\sum_{i=1}^{k} s_i \leq B$ but $\sum_{i=1}^{k+1} s_i > B$. The algorithm returns either $\{1, \ldots, k\}$ or $\{i^*\}$, whichever has greater value. Prove that this algorithm is a 1/2-approximation algorithm for the knapsack problem.

3.2 One key element in the construction of the fully polynomial-time approximation scheme for the knapsack problem was the ability to compute lower and upper bounds for the optimal value that are within a factor of n of each other (using the maximum value piece that fits in the knapsack to get the lower bound). Use the result of the previous exercise to derive a refined approximation scheme that eliminates one factor of n in the running time of the algorithm.

3.3 Consider the following scheduling problem: there are n jobs to be scheduled on a single machine, where each job j has a processing time p_j, a weight w_j, and a due date d_j, $j = 1, \ldots, n$. The objective is to schedule the jobs so as to maximize the total weight of the jobs that complete by their due date. First prove that there always exists an optimal schedule in which all on-time jobs complete before all late jobs, and the on-time jobs complete in an earliest due date order; use this structural result to show how to solve this problem using dynamic programming in $O(nW)$ time, where $W = \sum_j w_j$. Now use this result to derive a fully polynomial-time approximation scheme.

3.4 Instead of maximizing the total weight of the on-time set of jobs, as in the previous exercise, one could equivalently minimize the total weight of the set of jobs that complete late. This equivalence is only valid when one thinks of optimization, not approximation, since if only one job needs to be late then our approximation for the minimization problem can make only a small error, whereas for the maximization problem the situation is quite different. Or even worse, suppose that all jobs can complete on time. The good news is that there is an $O(n^2)$ algorithm to solve the following problem: minimize the weight of the maximum-weight job that completes late. First devise this algorithm, and then show how to use it to derive a fully polynomial-time approximation scheme for the problem of minimizing the total weight of the jobs that complete late.

3.5 Consider the following scheduling problem: there are n jobs to be scheduled on a constant number of machines m, where each job j has a processing time p_j and a weight w_j, $j = 1, \ldots, n$; once started, each job must be processed to completion on that machine without interruption. For a given schedule, let C_j denote the completion time of job j, $j = 1, \ldots, n$, and the objective is to minimize $\sum_j w_j C_j$ over all possible schedules. First show that there exists an optimal schedule where, for each machine, the jobs are scheduled in non-decreasing p_j/w_j order. Then use this property to derive a dynamic programming algorithm that can then be used to obtain a fully polynomial-time approximation scheme.

3.6 Suppose we are given a directed acyclic graph with specified source node s and sink node t, and each arc e has an associated cost c_e and length ℓ_e. We are also given a length bound L. Give a fully polynomial-time approximation scheme for the problem of finding a minimum-cost path from s to t of total length at most L.

3.7 In the proof of Theorem 3.7, we rounded down each processing time to the nearest multiple of T/k^2. Suppose that instead of constructing identical length intervals that get rounded to the same value, we have intervals that are geometrically increasing in length. Design an alternative polynomial-time approximation scheme, where the term in the running that is $O(n^{(1/k)^2})$ is reduced to $O(n^{(1/k)\log(1/k)})$.

3.8 The makespan minimization problem discussed in Section 3.2 can be viewed as minimizing the L_∞ norm of the machine loads. One can instead minimize the L_2 norm of the machine loads or, equivalently, the sum of the squares of the machine loads. To extend the framework discussed for the makespan objective, first give a dynamic programming algorithm that solves, in polynomial time, the special case in which there are only a constant number of job lengths, and each job length is at least a constant fraction of the average machine load (that is, $\sum_j p_j/m$, where m is the number of machines). Then use this to derive a polynomial-time approximation scheme. (One additional idea might be useful: for some notion of a "small" job, clump the small jobs into relatively "small" clumps of jobs that are then assigned to machines together.)

3.9 Suppose we have a strongly NP-hard minimization problem Π with the following two properties. First, any feasible solution has a nonnegative, integral objective function value. Second, there is a polynomial p, such that if it takes n bits to encode the input instance I in unary, $\text{OPT}(I) \leq p(n)$. Prove that if there is a fully polynomial-time approximation scheme for Π, then there is a pseudopolynomial algorithm for Π. Since there is no pseudopolynomial algorithm for a strongly NP-hard problem unless P = NP, conclude that this would imply P = NP.

Chapter Notes

The approach to describing the dynamic program for the knapsack problem in Section 3.1 is due to Lawler [211], as is Exercise 3.2. The approximation scheme is due to Ibarra and Kim [173]. Exercises 3.3 and 3.5 are due to Sahni [258]. Gens and Levner [129] proved the result stated in Exercise 3.4. Throughout the 1970s much of the work in this area was being done in parallel in both the United States and the Soviet

Union (although not recognized at the time); Gens and Levner [128] give a detailed comparison of the evolution of this area at that time. Exercise 3.6 is due to Hassin [157].

The approximation scheme for scheduling parallel machines with a constant number of machines given in Section 3.2 is due to Graham [143]. The approximation scheme for the case in which the number of machines is part of the input is due to Hochbaum and Shmoys [165]. Exercise 3.8 is due to Alon, Azar, Woeginger, and Yadid [6].

Fernandez de la Vega and Lueker [111] gave the first approximation scheme for the bin-packing problem. The approximation scheme given here is a variant of theirs. The analysis of the First-Fit-Decreasing algorithm, showing it to be an 11/9-approximation algorithm, is in the Ph.D. thesis of Johnson [178]. The analysis of First-Fit we give is also in this thesis, although we use the analysis there of another algorithm called Next-Fit.

Exercise 3.9 is due to Garey and Johnson [122].

CHAPTER 4

Deterministic Rounding
of Linear Programs

In the introduction, we said that one of the principal theses of this book is the central role played by linear programming in the design and analysis of approximation algorithms. In the previous two chapters, we have not used linear programming at all, but starting with this chapter we will be using it extensively.

In this chapter, we will look at one of the most straightforward uses of linear programming. Given an integer programming formulation of a problem, we can relax it to a linear program. We solve the linear program to obtain a fractional solution, then round it to an integer solution via some process.

The easiest way to round the fractional solution to an integer solution in which all values are 0 or 1 is to take variables with relatively large values and round them up to 1, while rounding all other variables down to 0. We saw this technique in Section 1.3 applied to the set cover problem, in which we chose sets whose corresponding linear programming variables were sufficiently large. We will see another application of this technique when we introduce the prize-collecting Steiner tree problem in Section 4.4. We will revisit this problem several times in the course of the book. For this problem we give an integer programming relaxation in which there are 0-1 variables for both nodes and edges. We round up the node variables that are sufficiently large in order to decide which nodes should be spanned in a solution; we then find a tree spanning these nodes.

In Sections 4.1 and 4.2, we consider a single-machine scheduling problem, and see another way of rounding fractional solutions to integer solutions. We will see that by solving a relaxation, we are able to get information on how the jobs might be ordered. Then we construct a solution in which we schedule jobs in the same order as given by the relaxation, and we are able to show that this leads to a good solution. In the first section, we use a relaxation of the problem to a preemptive scheduling problem, rather than a linear program. The analysis of this algorithm gives some ideas for an algorithm in the next section that uses a linear programming relaxation for a scheduling problem with a more general objective function.

In Section 4.5, we introduce the uncapacitated facility location problem, another problem that we will revisit several times in the course of this book. In this problem we

73

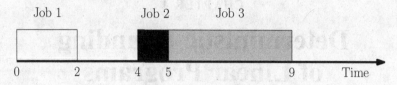

Figure 4.1. An example of a nonpreemptive schedule, in which $p_1 = 2, r_1 = 0, p_2 = 1, r_2 = 4$, $p_3 = 4, r_3 = 1$. In this schedule, $C_1 = 2, C_2 = 5$, and $C_3 = 9$, so that $\sum_j C_j = 2 + 5 + 9 = 16$.

have clients and facilities; we must choose a subset of facilities to open, and every client must be assigned to some open facility. Here the rounding procedure is much more complex than simply choosing large values and rounding up. The fractional values indicate to us which facilities we might consider opening and which assignments we might think about making.

Finally, in Section 4.6, we revisit the bin-packing problem. We give an integer programming formulation in which we have an integer variable to indicate how many bins should be packed in a certain way. Then we round variables *down*, in the sense that we take the integer part of each variable and pack bins as indicated, then take all the pieces corresponding to the fractional part and iterate.

In several cases in this chapter and later in the book, we will need to solve very large linear programs in which the number of constraints is exponential in the input size of the problem. These linear programs can be solved in polynomial time using an algorithm called the ellipsoid method. We introduce the ellipsoid method in Section 4.3, and discuss the cases in which it can be used to solve exponentially large linear programs in polynomial time.

4.1 Minimizing the Sum of Completion Times on a Single Machine

In this section, we consider the problem of scheduling jobs on a single machine so as to minimize the sum of the job completion times. In particular, we are given as input n jobs, each of which has a processing time p_j and release date r_j. The values p_j and r_j are integers such that $r_j \geq 0$ and $p_j > 0$. We must construct a schedule for these jobs on a single machine such that at most one job is processed at each point in time, no job is processed before its release date, and each job must be processed *nonpreemptively*; that is, once a job begins to be processed, it must be processed completely before any other job begins its processing. See Figure 4.1 for an example. If C_j denotes the time at which job j is finished processing, then the goal is to find the schedule that minimizes $\sum_{j=1}^{n} C_j$. Observe that this objective is equivalent to the problem of minimizing the average completion time, since the average completion time just rescales the objective function for each feasible solution by a factor of $1/n$.

Below we will show that we can convert any *preemptive* schedule into a nonpreemptive schedule in such a way that the completion time of each job at most doubles. In a preemptive schedule, we can still schedule only one job at a time on the machine, but we do not need to complete each job's required processing consecutively; we can

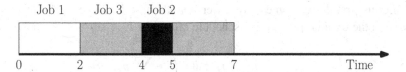

Figure 4.2. An example of a preemptive schedule created using the SRPT rule, with the same instance as in Figure 4.1. In this schedule, $C_1 = 2$, $C_2 = 5$, and $C_3 = 7$, so that $\sum_j C_j = 2 + 5 + 7 = 14$. Note that we do not interrupt the processing of job 1 when job 3 arrives at time 1, since job 1 has less remaining processing time, but we do interrupt the processing of job 3 when job 2 arrives.

interrupt the processing of a job with the processing of other jobs. In the *preemptive version* of this problem, the goal is to find a preemptive schedule that minimizes the sum of the completion times.

An optimal solution to the preemptive version of the scheduling problem can be found in polynomial time via the *shortest remaining processing time* (SRPT) rule, which is as follows. We start at time 0 and schedule the job with the smallest amount of remaining processing time as long as the job is past its release date and we have not already completed it. We schedule it until either it is completed or a new job is released. We then iterate. See Figure 4.2 for an example.

Let C_j^P be the completion time of job j in an optimal preemptive schedule, and let OPT be the sum of completion times in an optimal nonpreemptive schedule. We have the following observation.

Observation 4.1.

$$\sum_{j=1}^n C_j^P \le \text{OPT}.$$

Proof. This immediately follows from the fact that an optimal nonpreemptive schedule is feasible for the preemptive scheduling problem. $\square$

Now consider the following scheduling algorithm. Find an optimal preemptive schedule using SRPT. We schedule the jobs nonpreemptively in the same order that they complete in this preemptive schedule. To be more precise, suppose that the jobs are indexed such that $C_1^P \le C_2^P \le \cdots \le C_n^P$. Then we schedule job 1 from its release date r_1 to time $r_1 + p_1$. We schedule job 2 to start as soon as possible after job 1; that is, we schedule it from $\max(r_1 + p_1, r_2)$ to $\max(r_1 + p_1, r_2) + p_2$. The remaining jobs are scheduled analogously. If we let C_j^N denote the completion time of job j in the nonpreemptive schedule that we construct, for $j = 1, \ldots, n$, then job j is processed from $\max\{C_{j-1}^N, r_j\}$ to $\max\{C_{j-1}^N, r_j\} + p_j$.

We show below that scheduling nonpreemptively in this way does not delay the jobs by too much.

Lemma 4.2. *For each job* $j = 1, \ldots, n$,

$$C_j^N \le 2C_j^P.$$

Proof. Let us first derive some easy lower bounds on C_j^P. Since we know that j is processed in the optimal preemptive schedule after jobs $1, \ldots, j-1$, we have

$$C_j^P \geq \max_{k=1,\ldots,j} r_k \text{ and } C_j^P \geq \sum_{k=1}^{j} p_k.$$

By construction it is also the case that

$$C_j^N \geq \max_{k=1,\ldots,j} r_k.$$

Consider the nonpreemptive schedule constructed by the algorithm, and focus on any period of time that the machine is idle; idle time occurs only when the next job to be processed has not yet been released. Consequently, in the time interval from $\max_{k=1,\ldots,j} r_k$ to C_j^N, there cannot be any point in time at which the machine is idle. Therefore, this interval can be of length at most $\sum_{k=1}^{j} p_k$ since otherwise we would run out of jobs to process. This implies that

$$C_j^N \leq \max_{k=1,\ldots,j} r_k + \sum_{k=1}^{j} p_k \leq 2C_j^P,$$

where the last inequality follows from the two lower bounds on C_j^P derived above. $\square$

This leads easily to the following theorem.

Theorem 4.3. *Scheduling in order of the completion times of an optimal preemptive schedule is a 2-approximation algorithm for scheduling a single machine with release dates to minimize the sum of completion times.*

Proof. We have that

$$\sum_{j=1}^{n} C_j^N \leq 2 \sum_{j=1}^{n} C_j^P \leq 2\,\text{OPT},$$

where the first inequality follows by Lemma 4.2 and the second by Observation 4.1. $\square$

4.2 Minimizing the Weighted Sum of Completion Times on a Single Machine

We now consider a generalization of the problem from the previous section. In this generalization, each job has a weight $w_j \geq 0$, and our goal is to minimize the weighted sum of completion times. If C_j denotes the time at which job j is finished processing, then the goal is to find a schedule that minimizes $\sum_{j=1}^{n} w_j C_j$. We will call the problem of the previous section the *unweighted* case, and the problem in this section the *weighted* case.

Unlike the unweighted case, it is NP-hard to find an optimal schedule for the preemptive version of the weighted case. Although the algorithm and analysis of the previous section give us a way to round any preemptive schedule to one whose sum of weighted completion times is at most twice more, we cannot use the same technique of finding a lower bound on the cost of the optimal nonpreemptive schedule by finding an optimal preemptive schedule.

Nevertheless, we can still get a constant approximation algorithm for this problem by using some of the ideas from the previous section. To obtain the 2-approximation algorithm in the previous section, we used that $C_j^N \leq 2C_j^P$; if we look at the proof of Lemma 4.2, to prove this inequality we used only that the completion times C_j^P satisfied $C_j^P \geq \max_{k=1,\ldots,j} r_k$ and $C_j^P \geq \sum_{k=1}^{j} p_k$ (assuming that jobs are indexed such that $C_1^P \leq C_2^P \leq \cdots \leq C_n^P$). Furthermore, in order to obtain an approximation algorithm, we needed that $\sum_{j=1}^{n} C_j^P \leq \text{OPT}$. We will show below that we can give a linear programming relaxation of the problem with variables C_j such that these inequalities hold within a constant factor, which in turn will lead to a constant factor approximation algorithm for the problem.

To construct our linear programming relaxation, we will let the variable C_j denote the completion time of job j. Then our objective function is clear: we want to minimize $\sum_{j=1}^{n} w_j C_j$. We now need to give constraints. The first set of constraints is easy: for each job $j = 1, \ldots, n$, job j cannot complete before it is released and processed, so that $C_j \geq r_j + p_j$.

In order to introduce the second set of constraints, consider some set $S \subseteq \{1, \ldots, n\}$ of jobs. Consider the sum $\sum_{j \in S} p_j C_j$. This sum is minimized when all the jobs in S have a release date of zero and all the jobs in S finish first in the schedule. Assuming these two conditions hold, then any completion time C_j for $j \in S$ is equal to p_j plus the sum of all the processing times of the jobs in S that preceded j in the schedule. Then in the product $p_j C_j$, p_j multiplies itself and the processing times of all jobs in S preceding j in the schedule. The sum $\sum_{j \in S} p_j C_j$ must contain the term $p_j p_k$ for all pairs $j, k \in S$, since either k precedes j or j precedes k in the schedule. Thus,

$$\sum_{j \in S} p_j C_j = \sum_{j,k \in S: j \leq k} p_j p_k = \frac{1}{2} \left(\sum_{j \in S} p_j \right)^2 + \frac{1}{2} \sum_{j \in S} p_j^2 \geq \frac{1}{2} \left(\sum_{j \in S} p_j \right)^2.$$

Simplifying notation somewhat, let $N = \{1, \ldots, n\}$, and let $p(S) = \sum_{j \in S} p_j$, so that the inequality above becomes $\sum_{j \in S} p_j C_j \geq \frac{1}{2} p(S)^2$. As we said above, the sum $\sum_{j \in S} p_j C_j$ can be greater only if the jobs in S have a release date greater than zero or do not finish first in the schedule, so the inequality must hold unconditionally for any $S \subseteq N$. Thus, our second set of constraints is

$$\sum_{j \in S} p_j C_j \geq \frac{1}{2} p(S)^2$$

for each $S \subseteq N$.

This gives our linear programming relaxation for the scheduling problem:

$$\text{minimize} \sum_{j=1}^{n} w_j C_j \tag{4.1}$$

$$\text{subject to} \qquad C_j \geq r_j + p_j, \qquad \forall j \in N, \tag{4.2}$$

$$\sum_{j \in S} p_j C_j \geq \frac{1}{2} p(S)^2, \qquad \forall S \subseteq N. \tag{4.3}$$

By the arguments above, this LP is a relaxation of the problem, so that for an optimal LP solution C^*, $\sum_{j=1}^{n} w_j C_j^* \leq$ OPT, where OPT denotes the value of the optimal solution to the problem. There are an exponential number of the second type of constraint (4.3), but we will show in Section 4.3 that we can use an algorithm called the ellipsoid method to solve this linear program in polynomial time.

Let C^* be an optimal solution for the relaxation that we obtain in polynomial time. Our algorithm is then almost the same as in the previous section: we schedule the jobs nonpreemptively in the same order as of the completion times of C^*. That is, suppose that the jobs are reindexed so that $C_1^* \leq C_2^* \leq \cdots \leq C_n^*$. Then, as in the previous section, we schedule job 1 from its release date r_1 to time $r_1 + p_1$. We schedule job 2 to start as soon as possible after job 1; that is, we schedule it from $\max(r_1 + p_1, r_2)$ to $\max(r_1 + p_1, r_2) + p_2$. The remaining jobs are scheduled similarly. We claim that this gives a 3-approximation algorithm for the problem.

Theorem 4.4. *Scheduling in order of the completion time of C^* is a 3-approximation algorithm for scheduling jobs on a single machine with release dates to minimize the sum of weighted completion times.*

Proof. Again, assume that the jobs are reindexed so that $C_1^* \leq C_2^* \leq \cdots \leq C_n^*$. Let C_j^N be the completion time of job j in the schedule we construct. We will show that $C_j^N \leq 3C_j^*$ for each $j = 1, \ldots, n$. Then we have that $\sum_{j=1}^{n} w_j C_j^N \leq 3 \sum_{j=1}^{n} w_j C_j^* \leq$ 3 OPT, which gives the desired result.

As in the proof of Lemma 4.2, there cannot be any idle time between $\max_{k=1,\ldots,j} r_k$ and C_j^N, and therefore it must be the case that $C_j^N \leq \max_{k=1,\ldots,j} r_k + \sum_{k=1}^{j} p_k$. Let $\ell \in \{1, \ldots, j\}$ be the index of the job that maximizes $\max_{k=1,\ldots,j} r_k$ so that $r_\ell = \max_{k=1,\ldots,j} r_k$. By the indexing of the jobs, $C_j^* \geq C_\ell^*$, and $C_\ell^* \geq r_\ell$ by the LP constraint (4.2); thus, $C_j^* \geq \max_{k=1,\ldots,j} r_k$. Let $[j]$ denote the set $\{1, \ldots, j\}$. We will argue that $C_j^* \geq \frac{1}{2} p([j])$, and from these simple facts, it follows that

$$C_j^N \leq p([j]) + \max_{k=1,\ldots,j} r_k \leq 2C_j^* + C_j^* = 3C_j^*.$$

Let $S = [j]$. From the fact that C^* is a feasible LP solution, we know that

$$\sum_{k \in S} p_k C_k^* \geq \frac{1}{2} p(S)^2.$$

However, by our relabeling, $C_j^* \geq \cdots \geq C_1^*$, and hence

$$C_j^* \sum_{k \in S} p_k = C_j^* \cdot p(S) \geq \sum_{k \in S} p_k C_k^*.$$

By combining these two inequalities and rewriting, we see that

$$C_j^* \cdot p(S) \geq \frac{1}{2} p(S)^2.$$

Dividing both sides by $p(S)$ shows that $C_j^* \geq \frac{1}{2} p(S) = \frac{1}{2} p([j])$. $\square$

In Section 5.9, we will show how randomization can be used to obtain a 2-approximation algorithm for this problem.

4.3 Solving Large Linear Programs in Polynomial Time via the Ellipsoid Method

We now turn to the question of how to solve the linear program (4.1) in polynomial time. The most popular and practical algorithm for solving linear programs is known as the simplex method. Although the simplex method is quite fast in practice, there is no known variant of the algorithm that runs in polynomial time. Interior-point methods are a class of algorithms for solving linear programs; while typically not as fast or as popular as the simplex method, interior-point methods do solve linear programs in polynomial time. However, this isn't sufficient for solving the linear program above because the size of the linear program is exponential in the size of the input scheduling instance. Therefore, we will use a linear programming algorithm called the *ellipsoid method*. Because we will use this technique frequently, we will discuss the general technique before turning to how to solve our particular linear program.

Suppose we have the following general linear program:

$$\text{minimize} \quad \sum_{j=1}^{n} d_j x_j \tag{4.4}$$

$$\text{subject to} \quad \sum_{j=1}^{n} a_{ij} x_j \geq b_i, \qquad i = 1, \ldots, m,$$

$$x_j \geq 0, \qquad \forall j.$$

Suppose that we can give a bound ϕ on the number of bits needed to encode any inequality $\sum_{j=1}^{n} a_{ij} x_j \geq b_i$. Then the ellipsoid method for linear programming allows us to find an optimal solution to the linear program in time polynomial in n (the number of variables) and ϕ, given a polynomial-time *separation oracle* (which we will define momentarily). It is sometimes desirable for us to obtain an optimal solution that has an additional property of being a basic solution; we do not define basic solutions here, but the ellipsoid method will return such basic optimal solutions (see Chapter 11 or Appendix A for a definition). Note that this running time *does not depend on m*, the number of constraints of the linear program. Thus, as in the case of the previous linear program for the single-machine scheduling problem, we can solve linear programs with exponentially many constraints in polynomial time given that we have a polynomial-time separation oracle.

A separation oracle takes as input a supposedly feasible solution x to the linear program, and either verifies that x is indeed a feasible solution to the linear program or, if it is infeasible, produces a constraint that is violated by x. That is, if it is not the case that $\sum_{j=1}^{n} a_{ij} x_j \geq b_i$ for each $i = 1, \ldots, m$, then the separation oracle returns some constraint i such that $\sum_{j=1}^{n} a_{ij} x_j < b_i$.

In the notes at the end of the chapter, we sketch how a polynomial-time separation oracle leads to a polynomial-time algorithm for solving LPs with exponentially many constraints. It is truly remarkable that such LPs are efficiently solvable. Here, however, efficiency is a relative term: the ellipsoid method is not a practical algorithm. For exponentially large LPs that we solve via the ellipsoid method, it is sometimes the case that the LP can be written as a polynomially sized LP, but it is more convenient to discuss the larger LP. We will indicate when this is the case. Even if there is no known way of rewriting the exponentially sized LP, one can heuristically find an optimal solution to the LP by repeatedly using any LP algorithm (typically the simplex method) on a small subset of the constraints and using the separation oracle to check if the current solution is feasible. If it is feasible, then we have solved the LP, but if not, we add the violated constraints to the LP and resolve. Practical experience shows that this approach is much more efficient than can be theoretically justified, and should be in the algorithm designer's toolkit.

We now turn to the scheduling problem at hand, and give a polynomial-time separation oracle for the constraints (4.3). Given a solution C, let us reindex the variables so that $C_1 \leq C_2 \leq \cdots \leq C_n$. Let $S_1 = \{1\}$, $S_2 = \{1, 2\}$, ..., $S_n = \{1, \ldots, n\}$. We claim that it is sufficient to check whether the constraints are violated for the n sets $S_1, \ldots, S_n$. If any of these n constraints are violated, then we return the set as a violated constraint. If not, we show below that all constraints are satisfied.

Lemma 4.5. *Given variables C_j, if constraints (4.3) are satisfied for the n sets $S_1, \ldots, S_n$, then they are satisfied for all $S \subseteq N$.*

Proof. Let S be a constraint that is not satisfied; that is, $\sum_{j \in S} p_j C_j < \frac{1}{2} p(S)^2$. We will show that then there must be some set S_i that is also not satisfied. We do this by considering changes to S that decrease the difference $\sum_{j \in S} p_j C_j - \frac{1}{2} p(S)^2$. Any such change will result in another set S' that also does not satisfy the constraint. Note that removing a job k from S decreases this difference if

$$-p_k C_k + p_k p(S - k) + \frac{1}{2} p_k^2 < 0,$$

or if $C_k > p(S - k) + \frac{1}{2} p_k$. Adding a job k to S decreases this difference if

$$p_k C_k - p_k p(S) - \frac{1}{2} p_k^2 < 0,$$

or if $C_k < p(S) + \frac{1}{2} p_k$.

Now let ℓ be the highest indexed job in S. We remove ℓ from S if $C_\ell > p(S - \ell) + \frac{1}{2} p_\ell$; by the reasoning above the resulting set $S - \ell$ also does not satisfy the corresponding constraint (4.3). We continue to remove the highest indexed job in the resulting set until finally we have a set S' such that its highest indexed job ℓ has $C_\ell \leq p(S' - \ell) + \frac{1}{2} p_\ell < p(S')$ (using $p_\ell > 0$). Now suppose $S' \neq S_\ell = \{1, \ldots, \ell\}$. Then there is some $k < \ell$ such that $k \notin S'$. Then since $C_k \leq C_\ell < p(S') < p(S') + \frac{1}{2} p_k$, adding k to S' can only decrease the difference. Thus, we can add all $k < \ell$ to S', and the resulting set S_ℓ will also not satisfy the constraint (4.3). $\square$

4.4 The Prize-Collecting Steiner Tree Problem

We now turn to a variation of the Steiner tree problem introduced in Exercise 2.5. This variation is called the *prize-collecting Steiner tree problem*. As input, we are given an undirected graph $G = (V, E)$, an edge cost $c_e \geq 0$ for each $e \in E$, a selected *root vertex* $r \in V$, and a penalty $\pi_i \geq 0$ for each $i \in V$. The goal is to find a tree T that contains the root vertex r so as to minimize the cost of the edges in the tree plus the penalties of all vertices not in the tree. In other words, if $V(T)$ is the set of vertices in the tree T, the goal is to minimize $\sum_{e \in T} c_e + \sum_{i \in V - V(T)} \pi_i$. The Steiner tree problem of Exercise 2.5 is a special case of the problem in which for every $i \in V$ either $\pi_i = \infty$ (and thus i must be included in the tree) or $\pi_i = 0$ (and thus i may be omitted from the tree with no penalty). The vertices that must be included in the solution in the Steiner tree problem are called *terminals*.

One application of the prize-collecting Steiner tree problem is deciding how to extend cable access to new customers. In this case, each vertex represents a potential new customer, the cost of edge (i, j) represents the cost of connecting i to j by cable, the root vertex r represents a site that is already connected to the cable network, and the "penalties" π_i represent the potential profit to be gained by connecting customer i to the network. Thus, the goal is to minimize the total cost of connecting new customers to the network plus the profits lost by leaving the unconnected customers out of the network.

The prize-collecting Steiner tree problem can be modeled as an integer program. We use a 0-1 variable y_i for each $i \in V$ and x_e for each $e \in E$. Variable y_i is set to 1 if i is in the solution tree and 0 if it is not, while x_e is set to 1 if e is in the solution tree and 0 if it is not. Obviously, then, the objective function is

$$\text{minimize} \sum_{e \in E} c_e x_e + \sum_{i \in V} \pi_i (1 - y_i).$$

We now need constraints to enforce that the tree connects the root r to each vertex i with $y_i = 1$. Given a nonempty set of vertices $S \subset V$, let $\delta(S)$ denote the set of edges in the *cut* defined by S; that is, $\delta(S)$ is the set of all edges with exactly one endpoint in S. We will introduce the constraints

$$\sum_{e \in \delta(S)} x_e \geq y_i$$

for each $i \in S$, and each $S \subseteq V - r$. To see that these constraints enforce that the tree connects the root to each vertex i with $y_i = 1$, take any feasible solution x and consider the graph $G' = (V, E')$ with $E' = \{e \in E : x_e = 1\}$. Pick any i such that $y_i = 1$. The constraints ensure that for any r-i cut S, there must be at least one edge of E' in $\delta(S)$: that is, the size of the minimum r-i cut in G' must be at least one. Thus, by the max-flow/min-cut theorem the maximum r-i flow in G' is at least one, which implies that there is a path from r to i in G'. Similarly, if x is not feasible, then there is some r-i cut S for which there are no edges of E' in $\delta(S)$, which implies that the size of minimum r-i cut is zero, and thus the maximum r-i flow is zero. Hence, there is a path from r to i with $y_i = 1$ if and only if these constraints are satisfied, and if they are all satisfied, there will be a tree connecting r to all i such that $y_i = 1$. Thus, the following integer program models the prize-collecting Steiner tree problem:

$$\text{minimize} \sum_{e \in E} c_e x_e + \sum_{i \in V} \pi_i (1 - y_i)$$

$$\text{subject to} \sum_{e \in \delta(S)} x_e \geq y_i, \qquad \forall S \subseteq V - r, S \neq \emptyset, \forall i \in S, \qquad (4.5)$$

$$y_r = 1,$$

$$y_i \in \{0, 1\}, \qquad \forall i \in V,$$

$$x_e \in \{0, 1\}, \qquad \forall e \in E.$$

> Solve LP, get optimal primal solution (x^*, y^*)
> $U \leftarrow \{i \in V : y_i^* \geq \alpha\}$
> Use algorithm of Exercise 7.6 to build tree T on U
> **return** T

Algorithm 4.1. Deterministic rounding algorithm for the prize-collecting Steiner tree problem.

In order to apply deterministic rounding to the problem, we relax the integer programming formulation to a linear programming relaxation by replacing the constraints $y_i \in \{0, 1\}$ and $x_e \in \{0, 1\}$ with $y_i \geq 0$ and $x_e \geq 0$. We can now apply the ellipsoid method, introduced in Section 4.3, to solve the linear program in polynomial time. The separation oracle for the constraints $\sum_{e \in \delta(S)} x_e \geq y_i$ is as follows: given a solution (x, y), we construct a network flow problem on the graph G in which the capacity of each edge e is set to x_e. For each vertex i, we check whether the maximum flow from i to the root r is at least y_i. If not, then the minimum cut S separating i from r gives a violated constraint such that $\sum_{e \in \delta(S)} x_e < y_i$ for $i \in S, S \subseteq V - r$. If the flow is at least y_i, then for all cuts S separating i from r, $i \in S, S \subseteq V - r$, $\sum_{e \in \delta(S)} x_e \geq y_i$ by the max-flow/min-cut theorem. Hence, given a solution (x, y), we can find a violated constraint, if any exists, in polynomial time.

Given an optimal solution (x^*, y^*) to the linear programming relaxation, there is a very simple deterministic rounding algorithm for the problem, which we give in Algorithm 4.1. It is similar to the deterministic rounding algorithm for the set cover problem given in Section 1.3: for some value $\alpha \in [0, 1)$, let U be the set of all vertices such that $y_i \geq \alpha$. Since $y_r = 1$, the root r is in U. Now build a tree on the vertices in U in the graph G. Since we want to build a tree with cost as low as possible, this is just a Steiner tree problem on the graph G in which the terminals are the set U. We could apply the algorithm given in Exercise 2.5. Instead, we use another algorithm, given in Exercise 7.6 of Chapter 7, whose analysis will be very easy once we have studied the primal-dual method of that chapter. Let T be the tree produced by that algorithm.

We now begin the analysis of the algorithm in terms of the parameter α. Later we will fix the value of α to give the best possible performance guarantee for the deterministic rounding algorithm. We will analyze the cost of the constructed tree T and the penalties on the vertices not in T separately, comparing them to their contribution to the objective function of the linear programming relaxation. We use the result of Exercise 7.6 to analyze the cost of the tree T.

Lemma 4.6 (Exercise 7.6). *The tree T returned by the algorithm of Exercise 7.6 has cost*

$$\sum_{e \in T} c_e \leq \frac{2}{\alpha} \sum_{e \in E} c_e x_e^*.$$

The analysis for the penalties is simple.

Lemma 4.7.

$$\sum_{i \in V - V(T)} \pi_i \leq \frac{1}{1 - \alpha} \sum_{i \in V} \pi_i (1 - y_i^*).$$

Proof. If i is not in the tree T, then clearly it was not in the set of vertices U, and so $y_i^* < \alpha$. Thus, $1 - y_i^* > 1 - \alpha$, and $\frac{1-y_i^*}{1-\alpha} > 1$. The lemma statement follows. $\square$

Combining the two lemmas immediately gives the following theorem and corollary.

Theorem 4.8. *The cost of the solution produced by Algorithm 4.1 is*

$$\sum_{e \in T} c_e + \sum_{i \in V - V(T)} \pi_i \leq \frac{2}{\alpha} \sum_{e \in E} c_e x_e^* + \frac{1}{1-\alpha} \sum_{i \in V} \pi_i (1 - y_i^*).$$

Corollary 4.9. *Using Algorithm 4.1 with $\alpha = \frac{2}{3}$ gives a 3-approximation algorithm for the prize-collecting Steiner tree problem.*

Proof. Clearly the algorithm runs in polynomial time. We can bound the performance guarantee by the $\max\{2/\alpha, 1/(1-\alpha)\}$. We can minimize this maximum by setting $\frac{2}{\alpha} = \frac{1}{1-\alpha}$; thus, we obtain $\alpha = \frac{2}{3}$. Then by Theorem 4.8, the cost of the tree obtained is

$$\sum_{e \in T} c_e + \sum_{i \in V - V(T)} \pi_i \leq 3 \left(\sum_{e \in E} c_e x_e^* + \sum_{i \in V} \pi_i (1 - y_i^*) \right) \leq 3\,\mathrm{OPT},$$

since $\sum_{e \in E} c_e x_e^* + \sum_{i \in V} \pi_i (1 - y_i^*)$ is the objective function of the linear programming relaxation of the problem. $\square$

In Algorithm 4.1, we choose a set of vertices U such that $y_i^* \geq \alpha = 2/3$ and construct a Steiner tree on that set of vertices. A very natural idea is to try all possible values α: since there are $|V|$ variables y_i^*, there are at most $|V|$ distinct values of y_i^*. Thus, we can construct $|V|$ sets $U_j = \{i \in V : y_i^* \geq y_j^*\}$. For each $j \in V$, construct a Steiner tree T_j on the vertices U_j, and return the best overall solution out of the $|V|$ solutions constructed. Unfortunately, we do not know how to analyze such an algorithm directly. However, we will see in Chapter 5 that this algorithm can be analyzed as a deterministic variant of a randomized algorithm. We will return to the prize-collecting Steiner tree problem in Section 5.7.

4.5 The Uncapacitated Facility Location Problem

We now start our consideration of the *uncapacitated facility location problem*. We will return to this problem many times, since many of the techniques we discuss in this book are useful for devising approximation algorithms for this problem. In the uncapacitated facility location problem, we have a set of *clients* or *demands* D and a set of *facilities* F. For each client $j \in D$ and facility $i \in F$, there is a cost c_{ij} of assigning client j to facility i. Furthermore, there is a cost f_i associated with each facility $i \in F$. The goal of the problem is to choose a subset of facilities $F' \subseteq F$ so as to minimize the total cost of the facilities in F' and the cost of assigning each client $j \in D$ to the nearest facility in F'. In other words, we wish to find F' so as to minimize $\sum_{i \in F'} f_i + \sum_{j \in D} \min_{i \in F'} c_{ij}$. We call the first part of the cost the *facility cost* and the second part of the cost the *assignment cost* or *service cost*. We say that we *open* the facilities in F'.

The uncapacitated facility location problem is a simplified variant of a problem that arises in many different contexts. In one large computer company, a version

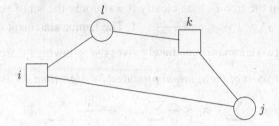

Figure 4.3. An illustration of the inequality obeyed by the assignment costs. The circles represent clients, and the squares represent facilities. For clients j, l and facilities i, k, $c_{ij} \leq c_{il} + c_{kl} + c_{kj}$.

of this problem occurs in deciding where to build or lease facilities to warehouse expensive parts needed for computer repair. The clients represent customers with service agreements that might require the use of the part. The facility cost is the cost of building or leasing the warehouse, and the assignment cost is the distance from the warehouse to the customer. In this problem it is also important to ensure that almost all of the customers are within a four-hour trip of a facility containing the needed part. Other typical complications include limits on the number of clients that can be served by a given facility (the *capacitated* facility location problem), and multiple types of facilities (for example, both distribution centers and warehouses, with clients assigned to warehouses, and warehouses assigned to distribution centers).

In its full generality, the uncapacitated facility location problem is as hard to approximate as the set cover problem (see Exercise 1.4). However, it is relatively common for facilities and clients to be points in a metric space, with assignment costs c_{ij} representing the distance from facility i to client j. For this reason, we will from here on consider the *metric* uncapacitated facility location problem, in which clients and facilities correspond to points in a metric space, and assignment costs obey the triangle inequality. More precisely, given clients j, l and facilities i, k, we have that $c_{ij} \leq c_{il} + c_{kl} + c_{kj}$ (see Figure 4.3). Since the clients and facilities correspond to points in a metric space, we assume that we have distances $c_{ii'}$ between two facilities i and i', and $c_{jj'}$ between two clients j and j'; we will not need this assumption in this section, but it will prove useful in later sections. We are able to give much better approximation algorithms for the metric version of the problem than we can for the more general version.

Our first approach to this problem will be to apply a deterministic rounding technique, from which we will get a 4-approximation algorithm. In subsequent chapters we will get improved performance guarantees by applying randomized rounding, the primal-dual method, local search, and greedy techniques. We begin by defining an integer programming formulation for the problem. We will have decision variables $y_i \in \{0, 1\}$ for each facility $i \in F$; if we decide to open facility i, then $y_i = 1$ and $y_i = 0$ otherwise. We also introduce decision variables $x_{ij} \in \{0, 1\}$ for all $i \in F$ and all $j \in D$; if we assign client j to facility i, then $x_{ij} = 1$ while $x_{ij} = 0$ otherwise. Then the objective function is relatively simple: we wish to minimize the total facility cost plus the total assignment cost. This can be expressed as

$$\text{minimize} \sum_{i \in F} f_i y_i + \sum_{i \in F, j \in D} c_{ij} x_{ij}.$$

We need to ensure that each client $j \in D$ is assigned to exactly one facility. This can be expressed via the following constraint:

$$\sum_{i \in F} x_{ij} = 1.$$

Finally, we need to make sure that clients are assigned to facilities that are open. We achieve this by introducing the constraint $x_{ij} \leq y_i$ for all $i \in F$ and $j \in D$; this ensures that whenever $x_{ij} = 1$ and client j is assigned to facility i, then $y_i = 1$ and the facility is open. Thus, the integer programming formulation of the uncapacitated facility location problem can be summarized as follows:

$$\text{minimize} \sum_{i \in F} f_i y_i + \sum_{i \in F, j \in D} c_{ij} x_{ij} \tag{4.6}$$

$$\text{subject to} \quad \sum_{i \in F} x_{ij} = 1, \qquad \forall j \in D, \tag{4.7}$$

$$x_{ij} \leq y_i, \qquad \forall i \in F, j \in D, \tag{4.8}$$

$$x_{ij} \in \{0, 1\}, \qquad \forall i \in F, j \in D,$$

$$y_i \in \{0, 1\}, \qquad \forall i \in F.$$

As usual, we obtain a linear programming relaxation from the integer program by replacing the constraints $x_{ij} \in \{0, 1\}$ and $y_i \in \{0, 1\}$ with $x_{ij} \geq 0$ and $y_i \geq 0$.

It will be useful for us to consider the dual of the linear programming relaxation. Although one can derive the dual in a purely mechanical way, we will instead motivate it as a natural lower bound on the uncapacitated facility location problem. The most trivial lower bound for this problem is to ignore the facility costs entirely (that is, to pretend that the cost $f_i = 0$, for each $i \in F$). In that case, the optimal solution is to open all facilities and to assign each client to its nearest facility: if we set $v_j = \min_{i \in F} c_{ij}$, then this lower bound is $\sum_{j \in D} v_j$. How can this be improved? Suppose that each facility takes its cost f_i, and divides it into shares apportioned among the clients: $f_i = \sum_{j \in D} w_{ij}$, where each $w_{ij} \geq 0$. The meaning of this share is that client j needs to pay this share only if it uses facility i. In this way, we no longer charge explicitly for opening a facility, but still recoup some of its cost. But in this way, we still have the situation that all of the (explicit) facility costs are 0, and so the optimal solution is to assign each client to the facility where the net cost is minimum; that is, we now can set $v_j = \min_{i \in F}(c_{ij} + w_{ij})$, and then $\sum_{j \in D} v_j$ is a lower bound on the true optimal value. Of course, we did not specify a way to determine each client's share of facility cost f_i; we can make this an optimization problem by setting the shares so as to maximize the value of the resulting lower bound. If we allow v_j to be any value for which $v_j \leq c_{ij} + w_{ij}$ and maximize $\sum_{j \in D} v_j$, then at the optimum v_j will be set to the smallest such right-hand side. Thus, we have derived the following form for this lower bound, which is the dual linear program for the primal linear program (4.6):

$$\text{maximize} \quad \sum_{j \in D} v_j$$

$$\text{subject to} \quad \sum_{j \in D} w_{ij} \leq f_i, \qquad \forall i \in F,$$

$$v_j - w_{ij} \leq c_{ij}, \qquad \forall i \in F, j \in D,$$

$$w_{ij} \geq 0, \qquad \forall i \in F, j \in D.$$

If Z_{LP}^* is the optimal value of the primal linear program (4.6) and OPT is the value of the optimal solution to the instance of the uncapacitated facility location problem, then for any feasible solution (v, w) to the dual linear program, by weak duality we have that $\sum_{j \in D} v_j \leq Z_{LP}^* \leq$ OPT.

Of course, as with any primal-dual linear programming pair, we have a correspondence between primal constraints and dual variables, and vice versa. For example, the dual variable w_{ij} corresponds to the primal constraint $x_{ij} \leq y_i$, and the primal variable x_{ij} corresponds to the dual constraint $v_j - w_{ij} \leq c_{ij}$.

We would like to use the information from an optimal solution (x^*, y^*) to the primal LP to determine a low-cost integral solution. In particular, if a client j is fractionally assigned to some facility i – that is, $x_{ij}^* > 0$ – then perhaps we should also consider assigning j to i. We formalize this by saying that i is a *neighbor* of j (see Figure 4.4).

Definition 4.10. *Given an LP solution* x^*, *we say that facility* i *neighbors client* j *if* $x_{ij}^* > 0$. *We let* $N(j) = \{i \in F : x_{ij}^* > 0\}$.

The following lemma shows a connection between the cost of assigning j to a neighboring facility and the value of the dual variables.

Lemma 4.11. *If* (x^*, y^*) *is an optimal solution to the facility location LP and* (v^*, w^*) *is an optimal solution to its dual, then* $x_{ij}^* > 0$ *implies* $c_{ij} \leq v_j^*$.

Proof. By complementary slackness, $x_{ij}^* > 0$ implies $v_j^* - w_{ij}^* = c_{ij}$. Furthermore, since $w_{ij}^* \geq 0$, we have that $c_{ij} \leq v_j^*$.   □

The following is an intuitive argument about why neighboring facilities are useful. If we open a set of facilities S such that for all clients $j \in D$, there exists an open facility $i \in N(j)$, and then the cost of assigning j to i is no more than v_j^* by Lemma 4.11. Thus, the total assignment cost is no more than $\sum_{j \in D} v_j^* \leq$ OPT, since this is the dual objective function.

Unfortunately, such a set of facilities S might have a very high facility cost. What can we do to have a good facility cost? Here is an idea: suppose we can partition some subset $F' \subseteq F$ of the facilities into sets F_k such that each $F_k = N(j_k)$ for some client j_k. Then if we open the cheapest facility i_k in $N(j_k)$, we can bound the cost of i_k by

$$f_{i_k} = f_{i_k} \sum_{i \in N(j_k)} x_{ij_k}^* \leq \sum_{i \in N(j_k)} f_i x_{ij_k}^*,$$

where the equality follows from constraint (4.7) of the linear program, and the inequality follows from the choice of i_k as the cheapest facility in F_k. Using the LP constraints (4.8) that $x_{ij} \leq y_i$, we see that

$$f_{i_k} \leq \sum_{i \in N(j_k)} f_i x_{ij_k}^* \leq \sum_{i \in N(j_k)} f_i y_i^*.$$

If we sum this inequality over all facilities that we open, then we have

$$\sum_k f_{i_k} \leq \sum_k \sum_{i \in N(j_k)} f_i y_i^* = \sum_{i \in F'} f_i y_i^* \leq \sum_{i \in F} f_i y_i^*,$$

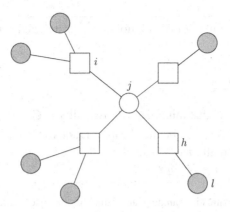

Figure 4.4. A representation of the neighborhoods $N(j)$ and $N^2(j)$. The circles represent clients, the squares represent facilities, and the edges are drawn between facilities i and clients k such that $x_{ik} > 0$. The central client is j. The surrounding facilities are the facilities $N(j)$. The shaded clients are in $N^2(j)$.

where the equality follows since the $N(j_k)$ partition F'. This scheme bounds the facility costs of open facilities by the facility cost of the linear programming solution.

Opening facilities in this way does not guarantee us that every client will be a neighbor of an open facility. However, we can take advantage of the fact that assignment costs obey the triangle inequality and make sure that clients are not too far away from an open facility. We first define an augmented version of neighborhood (see also Figure 4.4).

Definition 4.12. *Let $N^2(j)$ denote all neighboring clients of the neighboring facilities of client j; that is, $N^2(j) = \{k \in D : \text{client } k \text{ neighbors some facility } i \in N(j)\}$.*

Consider Algorithm 4.2. The algorithm loops until all clients are assigned to some facility. In each loop it picks the client j_k that minimizes v_j^*; we will see in a little bit why this is helpful. It then opens the cheapest facility i_k in the neighborhood of $N(j_k)$, and assigns j_k and all previously unassigned clients in $N^2(j_k)$ to i_k. Note that by assigning the clients in $N^2(j_k)$ to i_k, we ensure that the neighborhoods $N(j_k)$ form a partition of a subset of the facilities: because no client in the neighborhood of any facility of $N(j_k)$ is unassigned after iteration k, no facility of $N(j_k)$ is a neighbor of some client j_l chosen in later iterations ($l > k$).

We can now analyze the performance of this algorithm.

Theorem 4.13. *Algorithm 4.2 is a 4-approximation algorithm for the uncapacitated facility location problem.*

Proof. We have shown above that $\sum_k f_{i_k} \leq \sum_{i \in F} f_i y_i^* \leq \text{OPT}$. Fix an iteration k, and let $j = j_k$ and $i = i_k$. By Lemma 4.11, the cost of assigning j to i is $c_{ij} \leq v_j^*$. As depicted in Figure 4.4, consider the cost of assigning an unassigned client $l \in N^2(j)$ to facility i, where client l neighbors facility h that neighbors client j; then, applying the triangle inequality and Lemma 4.11, we see that

$$c_{il} \leq c_{ij} + c_{hj} + c_{hl} \leq v_j^* + v_j^* + v_l^*.$$

> Solve LP, get optimal primal solution (x^*, y^*) and dual solution (v^*, w^*)
> $C \leftarrow D$
> $k \leftarrow 0$
> **while** $C \neq \emptyset$ **do**
> $k \leftarrow k + 1$
>   Choose $j_k \in C$ that minimizes v_j^* over all $j \in C$
>   Choose $i_k \in N(j_k)$ to be the cheapest facility in $N(j_k)$
>   Assign j_k and all unassigned clients in $N^2(j_k)$ to i_k
> $C \leftarrow C - \{j_k\} - N^2(j_k)$

Algorithm 4.2. Deterministic rounding algorithm for the uncapacitated facility location problem.

Recall that we have selected client j in this iteration because, among all currently unassigned clients, it has the smallest dual variable v_j^*. However, l is also still unassigned, and so we know that $v_j^* \leq v_l^*$. Thus, we can conclude that $c_{il} \leq 3v_l^*$. Combining all of these bounds, we see that the solution constructed has facility cost at most OPT and assignment cost at most $3 \sum_{j \in D} v_j^* \leq 3$ OPT (by weak duality), for an overall cost of at most 4 times optimal. $\square$

In Section 5.8, we will see how randomization can help us improve this algorithm to a 3-approximation algorithm. In subsequent chapters we will improve the performance guarantee still further. The following is known about the hardness of approximating the metric uncapacitated facility location problem via a reduction from the set cover problem.

Theorem 4.14. *There is no α-approximation algorithm for the metric uncapacitated facility location problem with constant $\alpha < 1.463$ unless each problem in NP has an $O(n^{O(\log \log n)})$ time algorithm.*

We will prove this theorem in Section 16.2.

4.6 The Bin-Packing Problem

We return to the bin-packing problem, for which we gave an asymptotic polynomial-time approximation scheme in Section 3.3. Recall that in the bin-packing problem, we are given a collection of n items (or pieces), where item j is of size $a_j \in (0, 1]$, $j = 1, \ldots, n$, and we wish to assign each item to a bin, so that the total size assigned to each bin is at most 1; the objective is to use as few bins as possible. We showed previously that for each $\epsilon > 0$, there is a polynomial-time algorithm that computes a solution with at most $(1 + \epsilon) \text{OPT}_{BP}(I) + 1$ bins, where $\text{OPT}_{BP}(I)$ is the optimal value for instance I of the problem. We shall improve on that result significantly; we shall give a polynomial-time algorithm that finds a solution that uses at most $\text{OPT}_{BP}(I) + O(\log^2(\text{OPT}_{BP}(I)))$ bins. In obtaining this new bound, there will be three key components: an integer programming formulation to replace the dynamic programming formulation, and the integer program will be approximately solved by rounding its LP relaxation; an improved grouping scheme, which we call the harmonic grouping scheme; and an ingenious recursive application of the previous two components.

We first present the integer programming formulation on which the new algorithm will be based. Suppose that we group pieces of identical size, so that there are b_1 pieces of the largest size s_1, b_2 of the second largest size $s_2, \ldots, b_m$ pieces of the smallest size s_m. Consider the ways in which a single bin can be packed. The contents of each bin can be described by an m-tuple $(t_1, \ldots, t_m)$, where t_i indicates the number of pieces of size s_i that are included. We shall call such an m-tuple a *configuration* if $\sum_i t_i s_i \leq 1$; that is, the total size of the contents of the bin is at most 1, and so each configuration corresponds to one feasible way to pack a bin. There might be an exponential number of configurations. Let N denote the number of configurations, and let $T_1, \ldots, T_N$ be a complete enumeration of them, where t_{ij} denotes the ith component of T_j. We introduce a variable x_j for each T_j that specifies the number of bins packed according to configuration T_j; that is, x_j is an integer variable. The total number of bins used can be computed by summing these variables. If we pack x_j bins according to configuration T_j, then this packs $t_{ij}x_j$ pieces of size s_i, $i = 1, \ldots, m$. In this way, we can restrict attention to feasible solutions by requiring that we pack at least b_i pieces of size s_i, in total. This leads to the following integer programming formulation of the bin-packing problem; this is sometimes called the *configuration* integer program:

$$\text{minimize} \quad \sum_{j=1}^{N} x_j \tag{4.9}$$

$$\text{subject to} \sum_{j=1}^{N} t_{ij}x_j \geq b_i, \qquad i = 1, \ldots, m,$$

$$x_j \in \mathbf{N}, \qquad j = 1, \ldots, N.$$

This formulation was introduced in the context of designing practical algorithms to find optimal solutions to certain bin-packing problems.

Our algorithm is based on solving the linear programming relaxation of this integer program; we let $\text{OPT}_{LP}(I)$ denote the optimal value of this linear program. If we recall that $\text{SIZE}(I) = \sum_{i=1}^{m} s_i b_i$, then clearly we have that

$$\text{SIZE}(I) \leq \text{OPT}_{LP}(I) \leq \text{OPT}_{BP}(I).$$

Recall from Section 4.3 that the ellipsoid method is a polynomial-time algorithm for linear programs that have a polynomial number of variables, and for which there is a polynomial-time separation oracle to find a violated constraint. The configuration LP has few constraints, but an exponential number of variables. However, its dual linear program will then have m variables and an exponential number of constraints, and is as follows:

$$\text{maximize} \quad \sum_{i=1}^{m} b_i y_i$$

$$\text{subject to} \sum_{i=1}^{m} t_{ij}y_i \leq 1, \qquad j = 1, \ldots, N,$$

$$y_i \geq 0, \qquad i = 1, \ldots, m.$$

We observe that the problem of deciding whether or not there is a violated dual constraint given dual variables y is simply a knapsack problem. If we view y_i as the value of piece i, then the dual constraints say that for all possible ways of packing pieces into a bin (or knapsack) of size 1, the total value is at most 1. Hence, to obtain a separation oracle, we can use an algorithm for the knapsack problem to decide, given values y, whether or not there is a way of packing pieces into a bin of size 1 that has value more than 1; such a packing will correspond to a violated dual constraint. Since the knapsack problem is NP-hard, it would seem that it is not possible to obtain a polynomial-time separation oracle. However, by delving deeper into the analysis of the ellipsoid method, one can show that a fully polynomial-time approximation scheme for the knapsack problem (as given in Section 3.1) is sufficient to ensure the polynomial-time convergence of the ellipsoid method; we defer the details of how this can be done until Section 15.3, after which we give the problem as an exercise (Exercise 15.8). Hence, one can approximately solve the configuration linear program, within an additive error of 1, in time bounded by a polynomial in m and $\log(n/s_m)$.

In Section 3.3, one of the key ingredients for the asymptotic polynomial-time approximation scheme is a result that enables us to ignore pieces smaller than a given threshold γ. By applying this result, Lemma 3.10, we can assume, without loss of generality, that the smallest piece size $s_m \geq 1/\text{SIZE}(I)$, since smaller pieces can again be packed later without changing the order of magnitude of the additive error.

The *harmonic grouping scheme* works as follows: process the pieces in order of decreasing size, close the current group whenever its total size is at least 2, and then start a new group with the next piece. Let r denote the number of groups, let G_i denote the ith group, and let n_i denote the number of pieces in G_i. Observe that since we sort the pieces from largest to smallest, it follows that for $i = 2, \ldots, r - 1$, we have that $n_i \geq n_{i-1}$. (For $i = r$, the group G_r need not have total size at least 2.) As in the proof of Lemma 3.11, from a given input I we form a new instance I', where a number of pieces are discarded and packed separately. For each $i = 2, 3, \ldots, r - 1$, we put n_{i-1} pieces in I' of size equal to the largest piece in G_i and discard the remaining pieces. In effect, we discard G_1, G_r, and the $n_i - n_{i-1}$ smallest pieces in G_i, $i = 2, \ldots, r - 1$, while increasing the size of the remaining pieces in a group to be equal to the largest one. Figure 4.5 shows the effect of the harmonic grouping on one input.

First of all, it should be clear that any packing of the rounded instance I' can be used to pack those pieces of the original instance that were not discarded; there is a natural mapping from any nondiscarded piece in the original instance to a piece at least as large in I'. The following lemma gives two key properties of the harmonic grouping scheme.

Lemma 4.15. *Let I' be the bin-packing input obtained from an input I by applying the harmonic grouping scheme. The number of distinct piece sizes in I' is at most $\text{SIZE}(I)/2$; the total size of all discarded pieces is $O(\log \text{SIZE}(I))$.*

Proof. The first claim of the lemma is easy: each distinct piece size in I' corresponds to one of the groups $G_2, \ldots, G_{r-1}$; each of these groups has size at least 2, and so there are at most $\text{SIZE}(I)/2$ of them. To prove the second property, suppose, for the moment, that each group G_i has at most one more piece than the previous group G_{i-1}, $i = 2, \ldots, r - 1$. Consequently, we discard at most one item from each of the groups $G_2, \ldots, G_{r-1}$. To bound the total size of the discarded pieces, the total

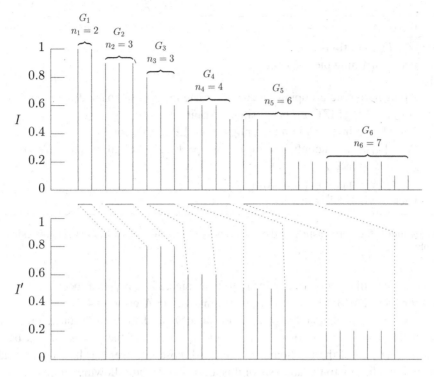

Figure 4.5. An input before and after harmonic grouping.

size of each group is at most 3, and so the total size of G_1 and G_r is at most 6. Furthermore, the size of the smallest piece in group G_i is at most $3/n_i$. Since we discard a piece from G_i, $i = 2, \ldots, r - 1$, only when G_i is the first group that has n_i pieces and we discard its smallest piece, the total size of these discarded pieces is at most $\sum_{j=1}^{n_r} 3/j$. Recall from Section 1.6 that the kth harmonic number, H_k, is defined to be $H_k = 1 + \frac{1}{2} + \frac{1}{3} + \cdots + \frac{1}{k}$ and that $H_k = O(\log k)$. Since each piece has size at least $1/\text{SIZE}(I)$, we have that $n_r \leq 3\,\text{SIZE}(I)$, and so we see that the total size of the discarded pieces is $O(\log \text{SIZE}(I))$.

Now consider the general case in which each group need not be only one larger than the previous one. Consider any group G_i that contains more pieces than G_{i-1}, $i = 2, \ldots, r - 1$; more precisely, suppose that it contains $k = n_i - n_{i-1}$ more pieces. The k discarded pieces are of size at most $3(k/n_i)$ since they are the k smallest of n_i pieces of total at most 3. We can upper bound this value by adding k terms, each of which is at least $3/n_i$; that is, the total size of these discarded pieces is at most $\sum_{j=n_{i-1}+1}^{n_i} 3/j$. Adding these terms together (for all groups), we get that the total size of the discarded pieces is at most $\sum_{j=1}^{n_r} 3/j$, which we have already seen is $O(\log \text{SIZE}(I))$. $\square$

The harmonic grouping scheme can be used to design an approximation algorithm that always finds a packing with $\text{OPT}_{LP}(I) + O(\log^2(\text{SIZE}(I)))$ bins. This algorithm uses the harmonic scheme recursively. The algorithm applies the grouping scheme, packs the discarded pieces using the First-Fit algorithm (or virtually any other simple algorithm), and solves the linear program for the rounded instance. The fractional variables of the LP are rounded down to the nearest integer to obtain a packing of a subset of the pieces. This leaves some pieces unpacked, and these are handled by a

---

BinPack(I)
if SIZE(I) < 10 then
    Pack remaining pieces using First Fit
else
    Apply harmonic grouping scheme to create instance I'; pack discards in
          $O(\log \text{SIZE}(I))$ bins using First Fit
    Let x be optimal solution to configuration LP for instance I'
    Pack $\lfloor x_j \rfloor$ bins in configuration T_j for $j = 1, \ldots, N$; call the packed pieces
          instance I_1
    Let I_2 be remaining pieces from I'
    Pack I_2 via BinPack(I_2)

Algorithm 4.3. Deterministic rounding algorithm for packing large pieces of the bin-packing problem.

recursive call until the total size of the remaining pieces is less than a specified constant (say, for example, 10). The algorithm is summarized in Algorithm 4.3.

We shall use I to denote the original instance, I' to denote the instance on which the first linear program is solved, and I_1 and I_2 to denote the pieces packed based on the integer part of the fractional solution and those left over for the recursive call, respectively. The key to the analysis of this algorithm is the following lemma.

Lemma 4.16. *For any bin-packing input I, from which the harmonic grouping scheme produces an input I', which is then partitioned into I_1 and I_2, based on the integer and fractional parts of an optimal solution to the configuration linear program, we have that*

$$\text{OPT}_{LP}(I_1) + \text{OPT}_{LP}(I_2) \leq \text{OPT}_{LP}(I') \leq \text{OPT}_{LP}(I). \qquad (4.10)$$

Proof. The crucial property of the harmonic grouping scheme is that each piece in the input I' can be mapped to a distinct piece in the original input I of no lesser size. By inverting this mapping, any feasible solution for I can be interpreted as a feasible solution for I' (where each piece in I that is not the image of a piece in I' is simply deleted). Hence, the optimal value for the bin-packing problem for I' is at most the optimal value for I. Similarly, each configuration for I induces a corresponding configuration for I', and so we see that

$$\text{OPT}_{LP}(I') \leq \text{OPT}_{LP}(I).$$

By definition, if x is an optimal solution to the configuration LP for I' used to construct I_1 and I_2, we have that $\lfloor x_j \rfloor$, $j = 1, \ldots, N$, is a feasible solution for the configuration LP for I_1 (which is even integer!), and $x_j - \lfloor x_j \rfloor$, $j = 1, \ldots, N$, is a feasible solution for the configuration LP for I_2. Hence, the sum of the optimal values for these two LPs is at most $\sum_{j=1}^{N} x_j = \text{OPT}_{LP}(I')$. In fact, one can prove that $\text{OPT}_{LP}(I_1) + \text{OPT}_{LP}(I_2) = \text{OPT}_{LP}(I')$, but this is not needed. $\qquad \square$

Each level of the recursion partitions the pieces into one of three sets: those pieces packed by the integer part of the LP solution, those pieces packed after having been discarded by the grouping scheme, and those pieces packed by a recursive call of the algorithm. (So, for the top level of the recursion, the first corresponds to I_1 and the last corresponds to I_2.) If one focuses on those pieces that fall in the first category over all recursive calls of the algorithm, the inequality (4.10) implies that the sum of the LP values of these inputs is at most $\text{OPT}_{LP}(I)$.

This implies that the only error introduced in each level of recursion is caused by the discarded pieces. We have bounded the total size of the pieces discarded in one level of recursion, and so we need to bound the number of levels of recursion. We will do this by showing that the total size of the input called in the recursive call is at most half the total size of the original input.

The recursive input I_2 is the leftover that corresponds to the fractional part of the optimal configuration LP solution x; hence, we can bound its total size by the sum of the fractions $\sum_{j=1}^{N} x_j - \lfloor x_j \rfloor$. A very crude upper bound on this sum is to count the number of nonzeroes in the optimal LP solution x. We claim that the number of nonzeroes in the optimal solution x can be bounded by the number of constraints in the configuration LP. We leave this as an exercise to the reader (Exercise 4.5), though it follows directly from the properties of basic optimal solutions, which we discuss in Chapter 11 and Appendix A. The number of constraints is the number of distinct piece sizes in I'. By Lemma 4.15, this is at most $\text{SIZE}(I)/2$.

By combining all of these arguments, we see that the total size of I_2, that is, $\text{SIZE}(I_2)$, is at most $\text{SIZE}(I)/2$. Hence, the size of the instance decreases by a factor of 2 in each level of recursion; the recursion terminates when the total size remaining is less than 10, and so there are $O(\log \text{SIZE}(I))$ levels. In each of these levels, we use $O(\log \text{SIZE}(I))$ bins to pack the discarded pieces; since $\text{SIZE}(I) \leq \text{OPT}_{LP}(I) \leq \text{OPT}_{BP}(I)$, we obtain the following theorem.

Theorem 4.17. *The recursive application of the harmonic grouping scheme yields a polynomial-time approximation algorithm for the bin-packing problem that uses* $\text{OPT}_{BP}(I) + O(\log^2(\text{OPT}_{BP}(I)))$ *bins.*

It is an important open question whether this result can be improved; it is possible that the bin-packing problem can be approximated within an additive error of 1; however, showing that this is impossible would also be a striking advance.

Exercises

4.1 The following problem arises in telecommunications networks, and is known as the *SONET ring loading problem*. The network consists of a cycle on n nodes, numbered 0 through $n - 1$ clockwise around the cycle. Some set C of calls is given; each call is a pair (i, j) originating at node i and destined to node j. The call can be routed either clockwise or counterclockwise around the ring. The objective is to route the calls so as to minimize the total *load* on the network. The load L_i on link $(i, i + 1(\text{mod } n))$ is the number of calls routed through link $(i, i + 1(\text{mod } n))$, and the total load is $\max_{1 \leq i \leq n} L_i$.

Give a 2-approximation algorithm for the SONET ring loading problem.

4.2 Consider the scheduling problem of Section 4.2, but without release dates. That is, we must schedule jobs nonpreemptively on a single machine to minimize the weighted sum of completion times $\sum_{j=1}^{n} w_j C_j$. Suppose that jobs are indexed such that $\frac{w_1}{p_1} \geq \frac{w_2}{p_2} \geq \cdots \geq \frac{w_n}{p_n}$. Then show it is optimal to schedule job 1 first, job 2 second, and so on. This scheduling rule is called *Smith's rule*.

4.3 Recall from Exercise 2.3 the concept of *precedence constraints* between jobs in a scheduling problem: We say $i \prec j$ if in any feasible schedule, job i must be completely processed before job j begins processing. Consider a variation of the single-machine scheduling problem from Section 4.2 in which we have precedence constraints but no release dates. That is, we are given n jobs with processing times $p_j > 0$ and weights $w_j \geq 0$, and the goal is to find a nonpreemptive schedule on a single machine that is feasible with respect to the precedence constraints $\prec$ and that minimizes the weighted sum of completed times $\sum_{j=1}^{n} w_j C_j$. Use the ideas of Section 4.2 to give a 2-approximation algorithm for this problem.

4.4 In the algorithm for the bin-packing problem, we used *harmonic grouping* in each iteration of the algorithm to create an instance I' from I. Consider the following grouping scheme: for $i = 0, \ldots, \lceil \log_2 \text{SIZE}(I) \rceil$, create a group G_i such that all pieces from I of size $(2^{-(i+1)}, 2^{-i}]$ are placed in group G_i. In each group G_i, create subgroups $G_{i,1}, G_{i,2}, \ldots, G_{i,k_i}$ by arranging the pieces in G_i from largest to smallest and putting the $4 \cdot 2^i$ largest in the first subgroup, the next $4 \cdot 2^i$ in the next subgroup, and so on. Now create instance I' from I in the following manner: for each $i = 0, \ldots, \lceil \log_2 \text{SIZE}(I) \rceil$, discard subgroups $G_{i,1}$ and G_{i,k_i} (i.e., the first and last subgroups of G_i), and for $j = 2, \ldots, k_i - 1$ round each piece of subgroup $G_{i,j}$ to the size of the largest piece in $G_{i,j}$.

Prove that by using this grouping scheme within the bin-packing algorithm, we obtain an algorithm that uses at most $\text{OPT}_{BP}(I) + O(\log^2(\text{OPT}_{BP}(I)))$ for all instances I.

4.5 Show that there exists an optimal solution x to the linear programming relaxation of the integer program (4.9) that has at most m nonzero entries, where m is the number of different piece sizes.

4.6 Let $G = (A, B, E)$ be a bipartite graph; that is, each edge $(i, j) \in E$ has $i \in A$ and $j \in B$. Assume that $|A| \leq |B|$ and that we are given nonnegative costs $c_{ij} \geq 0$ for each edge $(i, j) \in E$. A *complete matching* of A is a subset of edges $M \subseteq E$ such that each vertex in A has exactly one edge of M incident on it, and each vertex in B has at most one edge of M incident on it. We wish to find a minimum-cost complete matching. We can formulate an integer program for this problem in which we have an integer variable $x_{ij} \in \{0, 1\}$ for each edge $(i, j) \in E$, where $x_{ij} = 1$ if (i, j) is in the matching, and 0 otherwise. Then the integer program is as follows:

$$\text{minimize} \quad \sum_{(i,j) \in E} c_{ij} x_{ij}$$

$$\text{subject to} \quad \sum_{j \in B: (i,j) \in E} x_{ij} = 1, \qquad \forall i \in A,$$

$$\sum_{i \in A: (i,j) \in E} x_{ij} \leq 1, \qquad \forall j \in B,$$

$$x_{ij} \in \{0, 1\}, \qquad \forall (i, j) \in E.$$

Consider the linear programming relaxation of the integer program in which we replace the integer constraints $x_{ij} \in \{0, 1\}$ with $x_{ij} \geq 0$ for all $(i, j) \in E$.

(a) Show that given any fractional solution to the linear programming relaxation, it is possible to find in polynomial time an integer solution that costs no more than the fractional solution. (Hint: Given a set of fractional variables, find a way to modify their values repeatedly such that the solution stays feasible, the overall cost does not increase, and at least one additional fractional variable becomes 0 or 1.) Conclude that there is a polynomial-time algorithm for finding a minimum-cost complete matching.

(b) Show that any extreme point of the linear programming relaxation has the property that $x_{ij} \in \{0, 1\}$ for all $(i, j) \in E$. (Recall that an extreme point x is a feasible solution that cannot be expressed as $\lambda x^1 + (1 - \lambda)x^2$ for $0 < \lambda < 1$ and feasible solutions x^1 and x^2 distinct from x.)

4.7 This exercise introduces a deterministic rounding technique called *pipage rounding*, which builds on ideas similar to those used in Exercise 4.6. To illustrate this technique, we will consider the problem of finding a maximum cut in a graph with a constraint on the size of each part. In the maximum cut problem, we are given as input an undirected graph $G = (V, E)$ with nonnegative weights $w_{ij} \geq 0$ for all $(i, j) \in E$. We wish to partition the vertex set into two parts U and $W = V - U$ so as to maximize the weight of the edges whose two endpoints are in different parts. We will also assume that we are given an integer $k \leq |V|/2$, and we must find a partition such that $|U| = k$ (we will consider the maximum cut problem without this constraint in Sections 5.1 and 6.2).

(a) Show that the following *nonlinear* integer program models the maximum cut problem with a constraint on the size of the parts:

$$\text{maximize} \sum_{(i,j)\in E} w_{ij}(x_i + x_j - 2x_i x_j)$$

$$\text{subject to} \sum_{i\in V} x_i = k,$$

$$x_i \in \{0, 1\}, \qquad \forall i \in V.$$

(b) Show that the following linear program is a relaxation of the problem:

$$\text{maximize} \sum_{(i,j)\in E} w_{ij} z_{ij}$$

$$\text{subject to } z_{ij} \leq x_i + x_j, \qquad \forall (i, j) \in E,$$

$$z_{ij} \leq 2 - x_i - x_j, \qquad \forall (i, j) \in E,$$

$$\sum_{i\in V} x_i = k,$$

$$0 \leq z_{ij} \leq 1, \qquad \forall (i, j) \in E,$$

$$0 \leq x_i \leq 1, \qquad \forall i \in V.$$

(c) Let $F(x) = \sum_{(i,j)\in E} w_{ij}(x_i + x_j - 2x_i x_j)$ be the objective function from the nonlinear integer program. Show that for any (x, z) that is a feasible solution to the linear programming relaxation, $F(x) \geq \frac{1}{2} \sum_{(i,j)\in E} w_{ij} z_{ij}$.

(d) Argue that given a fractional solution x, for two fractional variables x_i and x_j, it is possible to increase one by $\epsilon > 0$ and decrease the other by ϵ such that $F(x)$ does not decrease and one of the two variables becomes integer.

(e) Use the arguments above to devise a $\frac{1}{2}$-approximation algorithm for the maximum cut problem with a constraint on the size of the parts.

Chapter Notes

Early deterministic LP rounding algorithms include the set cover algorithm given in Section 1.3 due to Hochbaum [160] and the bin-packing algorithm of Section 4.6 due to Karmarkar and Karp [187]. Both of these papers appeared in 1982. Work on deterministic rounding approximation algorithms did not precede this date by much because the first polynomial-time algorithms for solving linear programs did not appear until the late 1970s with the publication of the ellipsoid method.

As discussed in the introduction to the chapter, the easiest way to round a fractional solution is to round some variables up to 1 and others down to 0. This is the case for the prize-collecting Steiner tree problem introduced in Section 4.4. The prize-collecting Steiner tree problem is a variant of a problem introduced by Balas [31]. This version of the problem and the algorithm of this section are due to Bienstock, Goemans, Simchi-Levi, and Williamson [48].

The ellipsoid method discussed in Section 4.3 as a polynomial-time algorithm for solving linear programs was first given by Khachiyan [189], building on earlier work for nonlinear programs by Shor [267]. The algorithm that uses a separation oracle for solving linear programs with an exponential number of constraints is due to Grötschel, Lovász, and Schrijver [144]. An extended treatment of the topic can be found in the book of Grötschel, Lovász, and Schrijver [145]; a survey-level treatment can be found in Bland, Goldfarb, and Todd [50].

At a high level, the ellipsoid method works as follows. Suppose we are trying to solve the linear program (4.4) from Section 4.3. Initially, the algorithm finds an ellipsoid in $\Re^n$ containing all basic feasible solutions for the linear program (see Chapter 11 or Appendix A for discussion of basic feasible and basic optimal solutions). Let $\tilde{x}$ be the center of the ellipsoid. The algorithm calls the separation oracle with $\tilde{x}$. If $\tilde{x}$ is feasible, it creates a constraint $\sum_{j=1}^{n} d_j x_j \leq \sum_{j=1}^{n} d_j \tilde{x}_j$, since a basic optimal solution must have objective function value no greater than the feasible solution $\tilde{x}$ (this constraint is sometimes called an *objective function cut*). If $\tilde{x}$ is not feasible, the separation oracle returns a constraint $\sum_{j=1}^{n} a_{ij} x_j \geq b_i$ that is violated by $\tilde{x}$. In either case, we have a hyperplane through $\tilde{x}$ such that a basic optimal solution to the linear program (if one exists) must lie on one side of the hyperplane; in the case of a feasible $\tilde{x}$ the hyperplane is $\sum_{j=1}^{n} d_j x_j \leq \sum_{j=1}^{n} d_j \tilde{x}_j$, and in the case of an infeasible $\tilde{x}$ the hyperplane is $\sum_{j=1}^{n} a_{ij} x_j \geq \sum_{j=1}^{n} a_{ij} \tilde{x}_j$. The hyperplane containing $\tilde{x}$ splits the ellipsoid in two. The algorithm then finds a new ellipsoid containing the appropriate half of the original ellipsoid, and then considers the center of the new ellipsoid. This process repeats until the ellipsoid is sufficiently small that it can contain at most one basic feasible solution, if any; this then must be a basic optimal solution if one exists. The key to the proof of the running time of the algorithm is to show that after $O(n)$ iterations, the volume of the ellipsoid has dropped by a constant factor; then by relating the size of the initial to the final ellipsoid, the polynomial bound on the running time can be obtained.

As we saw in the chapter, sometimes rounding algorithms are more sophisticated than simply choosing large fractional variables and rounding up. The algorithm for the unweighted single-machine scheduling problem in Section 4.1 is due to Phillips, Stein, and Wein [241]. The algorithm for the weighted case in Section 4.2 is due to

Hall, Schulz, Shmoys, and Wein [155]; the linear programming formulation used in the section was developed by Wolsey [292] and Queyranne [243], and the separation oracle for the linear program in Section 4.3 is due to Queyranne [243]. The algorithm for the uncapacitated facility location problem in Section 4.5 is due to Chudak and Shmoys [77], building on earlier work of Shmoys, Tardos, and Aardal [264]. The hardness result of Theorem 4.14 is due to Guha and Khuller [146]. The pipage rounding technique in Exercise 4.7 for the maximum cut problem with size constraints is due to Ageev and Sviridenko [2, 3].

Smith's rule in Exercise 4.2 is due to Smith [270]. The result of Exercise 4.3 is due to Hall, Schulz, Shmoys, and Wein [155]. Exercise 4.4 is due to Karmarkar and Karp [187]. Exercise 4.6 is essentially due to Birkhoff [49].

CHAPTER 5

Random Sampling and Randomized Rounding of Linear Programs

Sometimes it turns out to be useful to allow our algorithms to make random choices; that is, the algorithm can flip a coin, or flip a biased coin, or draw a value uniformly from a given interval. The performance guarantee of an approximation algorithm that makes random choices is then the *expected* value of the solution produced relative to the value of an optimal solution, where the expectation is taken over the random choices of the algorithm.

At first this might seem like a weaker class of algorithm. In what sense is there a performance guarantee if it holds only in expectation? However, in most cases we will be able to show that randomized approximation algorithms can be *derandomized*: that is, we can use a certain algorithmic technique known as the method of conditional expectations to produce a deterministic version of the algorithm that has the same performance guarantee as the randomized version. Of what use then is randomization? It turns out that it is often much simpler to state and analyze the randomized version of the algorithm than to state and analyze the deterministic version that results from derandomization. Thus, randomization gains us simplicity in our algorithm design and analysis, while derandomization ensures that the performance guarantee can be obtained deterministically.

In a few cases, it is easy to state the deterministic, derandomized version of an algorithm, but we know how to analyze only the randomized version. Here the randomized algorithm allows us to analyze an algorithm that we are unable to analyze otherwise. We will see an example of this when we revisit the prize-collecting Steiner tree problem in Section 5.7.

It is also sometimes the case that we can prove that the performance guarantee of a randomized approximation algorithm holds with high probability. By this we mean that the probability that the performance guarantee does not hold is one over some polynomial in the input size of the problem. Usually we can make this polynomial as large as we want (and thus the probability as small as we want) by weakening the performance guarantee by some constant factor. Here derandomization is less necessary, though sometimes still possible by using more sophisticated techniques.

We begin the chapter by looking at very simple randomized algorithms for two problems, the maximum satisfiability problem and the maximum cut problem. Here we show that sampling a solution uniformly at random from the set of all possible solutions gives a good randomized approximation algorithm. For the maximum satisfiability problem, we are able to go still further and show that biasing our choice yields a better performance guarantee. We then revisit the idea of using randomized rounding of linear programming relaxations introduced in Section 1.7, and show that it leads to still better approximation algorithms for the maximum satisfiability problem, as well as better algorithms for other problems we have seen previously, such as the prize-collecting Steiner tree problem, the uncapacitated facility location problem, and a single-machine scheduling problem.

We then give Chernoff bounds, which allow us to bound the probability that a sum of random variables is far away from its expected value. We show how these bounds can be applied to an integer multicommodity flow problem, which is historically the first use of randomized rounding. We end with a much more sophisticated use of drawing a random sample, and show that this technique can be used to 3-color certain kinds of dense 3-colorable graphs with high probability.

5.1 Simple Algorithms for MAX SAT and MAX CUT

Two problems will play an especially prominent role in our discussion of randomization in the design and analysis of approximation algorithms: the maximum satisfiability problem and the maximum cut problem. The former will be highlighted in this chapter, whereas the central developments for the latter will be deferred to the next chapter. However, in this section we will give a simple randomized $\frac{1}{2}$-approximation algorithm for each problem.

In the maximum satisfiability problem (often abbreviated as MAX SAT), the input consists of n Boolean variables $x_1, \ldots, x_n$ (each of which may be set to either true or false), m clauses $C_1, \ldots, C_m$ (each of which consists of a disjunction (that is, an "or") of some number of the variables and their negations – for example, $x_3 \vee \bar{x}_5 \vee x_{11}$, where $\bar{x}_i$ is the negation of x_i), and a nonnegative weight w_j for each clause C_j. The objective of the problem is to find an assignment of true/false to the x_i that maximizes the weight of the *satisfied* clauses. A clause is said to be satisfied if one of the unnegated variables is set to true, or one of the negated variables is set to false. For example, in the clause $x_3 \vee \bar{x}_5 \vee x_{11}$, the clause is not satisfied only if x_3 is set to false, x_5 to true, and x_{11} to false.

Some terminology will be useful in discussing the MAX SAT problem. We say that a variable x_i or a negated variable $\bar{x}_i$ is a *literal*, so that each clause consists of some number of literals. A variable x_i is called a *positive* literal, and a negated variable $\bar{x}_i$ is called a *negative* literal. The number of literals in a clause is called its *size* or *length*. We will denote the length of a clause C_j by l_j. Clauses of length one are sometimes called *unit* clauses. Without loss of generality, we assume that no literal is repeated in a clause (since this does not affect the satisfiability of the instance), and that at most one of x_i and $\bar{x}_i$ appears in a clause (since if both x_i and $\bar{x}_i$ are in a clause, it is trivially satisfiable). Finally, it is natural to assume that the clauses are distinct, since we can simply sum the weights of two identical clauses.

A very straightforward use of randomization for MAX SAT is to set each x_i to true independently with probability $1/2$. An alternative perspective on this algorithm is that we choose a setting of the variables uniformly at random from the space of all possible settings. It turns out that this gives a reasonable approximation algorithm for this problem.

Theorem 5.1. *Setting each x_i to* true *with probability $1/2$ independently gives a randomized $\frac{1}{2}$-approximation algorithm for the maximum satisfiability problem.*

Proof. Consider a random variable Y_j such that Y_j is 1 if clause j is satisfied and 0 otherwise. Let W be a random variable that is equal to the total weight of the satisfied clauses, so that $W = \sum_{j=1}^{m} w_j Y_j$. Let OPT denote the optimum value of the MAX SAT instance. Then, by linearity of expectation, and the definition of the expectation of a 0-1 random variable, we know that

$$E[W] = \sum_{j=1}^{m} w_j E[Y_j] = \sum_{j=1}^{m} w_j \Pr[\text{clause } C_j \text{ satisfied}].$$

For each clause C_j, $j = 1, \ldots, n$, the probability that it is not satisfied is the probability that each positive literal in C_j is set to false and each negative literal in C_j is set to true, each of which happens with probability $1/2$ independently; hence,

$$\Pr[\text{clause } C_j \text{ satisfied}] = \left(1 - \left(\frac{1}{2}\right)^{l_j}\right) \geq \frac{1}{2},$$

where the last inequality is a consequence of the fact that $l_j \geq 1$. Hence,

$$E[W] \geq \frac{1}{2} \sum_{j=1}^{m} w_j \geq \frac{1}{2} \text{OPT},$$

where the last inequality follows from the fact that the total weight is an easy upper bound on the optimal value, since each weight is assumed to be nonnegative. $\square$

Observe that if $l_j \geq k$ for each clause j, then the analysis above shows that the algorithm is a $\left(1 - \left(\frac{1}{2}\right)^k\right)$-approximation algorithm for such instances. Thus, the performance of the algorithm is better on MAX SAT instances consisting of long clauses. This observation will be useful to us later.

Although this seems like a pretty naive algorithm, a hardness theorem shows that this is the best that can be done in some cases. Consider the case in which $l_j = 3$ for all clauses j; this restriction of the problem is sometimes called MAX E3SAT, since there are exactly three literals in each clause. The analysis above shows that the randomized algorithm gives an approximation algorithm with performance guarantee $\left(1 - \left(\frac{1}{2}\right)^3\right) = \frac{7}{8}$. A truly remarkable result shows that nothing better is possible for these instances unless P = NP.

Theorem 5.2. *If there is a $(\frac{7}{8} + \epsilon)$-approximation algorithm for MAX E3SAT for any constant $\epsilon > 0$, then $\mathrm{P} = \mathrm{NP}$.*

We discuss this result further in Section 16.3.

In the maximum cut problem (sometimes abbreviated MAX CUT), the input is an undirected graph $G = (V, E)$, along with a nonnegative weight $w_{ij} \geq 0$ for each edge $(i, j) \in E$. The goal is to partition the vertex set into two parts, U and $W = V - U$, so as to maximize the weight of the edges whose two endpoints are in different parts, one in U and one in W. We say that an edge with endpoints in both U and W is *in the cut*. In the case $w_{ij} = 1$ for each edge $(i, j) \in E$, we have an *unweighted* MAX CUT problem.

It is easy to give a $\frac{1}{2}$-approximation algorithm for the MAX CUT problem along the same lines as the previous randomized algorithm for MAX SAT. Here we place each vertex $v \in V$ into U independently with probability $1/2$. As with the MAX SAT algorithm, this can be viewed as sampling a solution uniformly from the space of all possible solutions.

Theorem 5.3. *If we place each vertex $v \in V$ into U independently with probability $1/2$, then we obtain a randomized $\frac{1}{2}$-approximation algorithm for the maximum cut problem.*

Proof. Consider a random variable X_{ij} that is 1 if the edge (i, j) is in the cut, and 0 otherwise. Let Z be the random variable equal to the total weight of edges in the cut, so that $Z = \sum_{(i,j) \in E} w_{ij} X_{ij}$. Let OPT denote the optimal value of the maximum cut instance. Then, as before, by linearity of expectation and the definition of expectation of a 0-1 random variable, we get that

$$E[Z] = \sum_{(i,j) \in E} w_{ij} E[X_{ij}] = \sum_{(i,j) \in E} w_{ij} \Pr[\text{Edge } (i, j) \text{ in cut}].$$

In this case, the probability that a specific edge (i, j) is in the cut is easy to calculate: since the two endpoints are placed in the sets independently, they are in different sets with probability equal to $\frac{1}{2}$. Hence,

$$E[Z] = \frac{1}{2} \sum_{(i,j) \in E} w_{ij} \geq \frac{1}{2} \text{OPT},$$

where the inequality follows directly from the fact that the sum of the (nonnegative) weights of all edges is obviously an upper bound on the weight of the edges in an optimal cut. $\square$

We will show in Section 6.2 that by using more sophisticated techniques we can get a substantially better performance guarantee for the MAX CUT problem.

5.2 Derandomization

As we mentioned in the introduction to the chapter, it is often possible to *derandomize* a randomized algorithm, that is, to obtain a deterministic algorithm whose solution value is as good as the expected value of the randomized algorithm.

To illustrate, we will show how the algorithm of the preceding section for the maximum satisfiability problem can be derandomized by replacing the randomized decision of whether to set x_i to true with a deterministic one that will preserve the expected value of the solution. These decisions will be made sequentially: the value of x_1 is determined first, then x_2, and so on.

How should x_1 be set so as to preserve the expected value of the algorithm? Assume for the moment that we will make the choice of x_1 deterministically, but all other variables will be set true with probability $1/2$ as before. Then the best way to set x_1 is that which will maximize the expected value of the resulting solution; that is, we should determine the expected value of W, the weight of satisfied clauses, given that x_1 is set to true, and the expected weight of W given that x_1 is set to false, and set x_1 to whichever value maximizes the expected value of W. It makes intuitive sense that this should work, since the maximum is always greater than an average, and the expected value of W is the average of its expected value given the two possible settings of x_1. In this way, we maintain an algorithmic invariant that the expected value is at least half the optimum, while having fewer random variables left.

More formally, if $E[W|x_1 \leftarrow \text{true}] \geq E[W|x_1 \leftarrow \text{false}]$, then we set x_1 true; otherwise, we set it to false. Since by the definition of conditional expectations,

$$E[W] = E[W|x_1 \leftarrow \text{true}]\Pr[x_1 \leftarrow \text{true}] + E[W|x_1 \leftarrow \text{false}]\Pr[x_1 \leftarrow \text{false}]$$
$$= \frac{1}{2}\left(E[W|x_1 \leftarrow \text{true}] + E[W|x_1 \leftarrow \text{false}]\right),$$

if we set x_1 to truth value b_1 so as to maximize the conditional expectation, then $E[W|x_1 \leftarrow b_1] \geq E[W]$; that is, the deterministic choice of how to set x_1 guarantees an expected value no less than the expected value of the completely randomized algorithm.

Assuming for the moment that we can compute these conditional expectations, the deterministic decision of how to set the remaining variables is similar. Assume that we have set variables $x_1, \dots, x_i$ to truth values $b_1, \dots, b_i$, respectively. How shall we set variable x_{i+1}? Again, assume that the remaining variables are set randomly. Then the best way to set x_{i+1} is so as to maximize the expected value given the previous settings of $x_1, \dots, x_i$. So if $E[W|x_1 \leftarrow b_1, \dots, x_i \leftarrow b_i, x_{i+1} \leftarrow \text{true}] \geq E[W|x_1 \leftarrow b_1, \dots, x_i \leftarrow b_i, x_{i+1} \leftarrow \text{false}]$, we set x_{i+1} to true (thus setting b_{i+1} to true); otherwise, we set x_{i+1} to false (thus setting b_{i+1} to false). Then since

$$E[W|x_1 \leftarrow b_1, \dots, x_i \leftarrow b_i]$$
$$= E[W|x_1 \leftarrow b_1, \dots, x_i \leftarrow b_i, x_{i+1} \leftarrow \text{true}]\Pr[x_{i+1} \leftarrow \text{true}]$$
$$+ E[W|x_1 \leftarrow b_1, \dots, x_i \leftarrow b_i, x_{i+1} \leftarrow \text{false}]\Pr[x_{i+1} \leftarrow \text{false}]$$
$$= \frac{1}{2}(E[W|x_1 \leftarrow b_1, \dots, x_i \leftarrow b_i, x_{i+1} \leftarrow \text{true}]$$
$$+ E[W|x_1 \leftarrow b_1, \dots, x_i \leftarrow b_i, x_{i+1} \leftarrow \text{false}]),$$

setting x_{i+1} to truth value b_{i+1} as described above ensures that

$$E[W|x_1 \leftarrow b_1, \ldots, x_i \leftarrow b_i, x_{i+1} \leftarrow b_{i+1}] \geq E[W|x_1 \leftarrow b_1, \ldots, x_i \leftarrow b_i].$$

By induction, this implies that $E[W|x_1 \leftarrow b_1, \ldots, x_i \leftarrow b_i, x_{i+1} \leftarrow b_{i+1}] \geq E[W]$.

We continue this process until all n variables have been set. Then since the conditional expectation given the setting of all n variables, $E[W|x_1 \leftarrow b_1, \ldots, x_n \leftarrow b_n]$, is simply the value of the solution given by the deterministic algorithm, we know that the value of the solution returned is at least $E[W] \geq \frac{1}{2} \text{OPT}$. Therefore, the algorithm is a $\frac{1}{2}$-approximation algorithm.

These conditional expectations are not difficult to compute. By definition,

$$E[W|x_1 \leftarrow b_1, \ldots, x_i \leftarrow b_i] = \sum_{j=1}^{m} w_j E[Y_j|x_1 \leftarrow b_1, \ldots, x_i \leftarrow b_i]$$

$$= \sum_{j=1}^{m} w_j \Pr[\text{clause } C_j \text{ satisfied}|x_1 \leftarrow b_1, \ldots, x_i \leftarrow b_i].$$

Furthermore, the probability that clause C_j is satisfied given that $x_1 \leftarrow b_1, \ldots, x_i \leftarrow b_i$ is easily seen to be 1 if the settings of $x_1, \ldots, x_i$ already satisfy the clause, and is $1 - (1/2)^k$ otherwise, where k is the number of literals in the clause that remain unset by this procedure. For example, consider the clause $x_3 \vee \bar{x}_5 \vee \bar{x}_7$. It is the case that

$$\Pr[\text{clause satisfied}|x_1 \leftarrow \text{true}, x_2 \leftarrow \text{false}, x_3 \leftarrow \text{true}] = 1,$$

since setting x_3 to true satisfies the clause. On the other hand,

$$\Pr[\text{clause satisfied}|x_1 \leftarrow \text{true}, x_2 \leftarrow \text{false}, x_3 \leftarrow \text{false}] = 1 - \left(\frac{1}{2}\right)^2 = \frac{3}{4},$$

since the clause will be unsatisfied only if x_5 and x_7 are set true, an event that occurs with probability 1/4.

This technique for derandomizing algorithms works with a wide variety of randomized algorithms in which variables are set independently and the conditional expectations are polynomial-time computable. It is sometimes called the *method of conditional expectations*, due to its use of conditional expectations. In particular, an almost identical argument leads to a derandomized version of the randomized $\frac{1}{2}$-approximation algorithm for the MAX CUT problem. Most of the randomized algorithms we discuss in this chapter can be derandomized via this method. The randomized versions of the algorithms are easier to present and analyze, and so we will frequently not discuss their deterministic variants.

5.3 Flipping Biased Coins

How might we improve the randomized algorithm for MAX SAT? We will show here that biasing the probability with which we set x_i is actually helpful; that is, we will set x_i true with some probability not equal to $1/2$. To do this, it is easiest to start by considering only MAX SAT instances with no unit clauses $\bar{x}_i$, that is, no negated unit clauses. We will later show that we can remove this assumption. Suppose now we set each x_i to be true independently with probability $p > 1/2$. As in the analysis of the previous randomized algorithm, we will need to analyze the probability that any given clause is satisfied.

Lemma 5.4. *If each x_i is set to* true *with probability $p > 1/2$ independently, then the probability that any given clause is satisfied is at least $\min(p, 1 - p^2)$ for MAX SAT instances with no negated unit clauses.*

Proof. If the clause is a unit clause, then the probability the clause is satisfied is p, since it must be of the form x_i, and the probability x_i is set true is p. If the clause has length at least two, then the probability that the clause is satisfied is $1 - p^a(1 - p)^b$, where a is the number of negated variables in the clause and b is the number of unnegated variables in the clause, so that $a + b = l_j \geq 2$. Since $p > \frac{1}{2} > 1 - p$, this probability is at least $1 - p^{a+b} = 1 - p^{l_j} \geq 1 - p^2$, and the lemma is proved. $\square$

We can obtain the best performance guarantee by setting $p = 1 - p^2$. This yields $p = \frac{1}{2}(\sqrt{5} - 1) \approx 0.618$. The lemma immediately implies the following theorem.

Theorem 5.5. *Setting each x_i to* true *with probability p independently gives a randomized $\min(p, 1 - p^2)$-approximation algorithm for MAX SAT instances with no negated unit clauses.*

Proof. This follows since

$$E[W] = \sum_{j=1}^{m} w_j \Pr[\text{clause } C_j \text{ satisfied}] \geq \min(p, 1 - p^2) \sum_{j=1}^{m} w_j$$
$$\geq \min(p, 1 - p^2) \, \text{OPT} . \qquad \square$$

We would like to extend this result to all MAX SAT instances. To do this, we will use a better bound on OPT than $\sum_{j=1}^{m} w_j$. Assume that for every i the weight of the unit clause x_i appearing in the instance is at least the weight of the unit clause $\bar{x}_i$; this is without loss of generality since we could negate all occurrences of x_i if the assumption is not true. Let v_i be the weight of the unit clause $\bar{x}_i$ if it exists in the instance, and let v_i be 0 otherwise.

Lemma 5.6. OPT $\leq \sum_{j=1}^{m} w_j - \sum_{i=1}^{n} v_i$.

Proof. For each i, the optimal solution can satisfy exactly one of x_i and $\bar{x}_i$. Thus, the weight of the optimal solution cannot include both the weight of the clause x_i and the clause $\bar{x}_i$. Since v_i is the smaller of these two weights, the lemma follows. $\square$

We can now extend the result.

Theorem 5.7. *We can obtain a randomized $\frac{1}{2}(\sqrt{5} - 1)$-approximation algorithm for MAX SAT.*

Proof. Let U be the set of indices of clauses of the instance excluding unit clauses of the form $\bar{x}_i$. As above, we assume without loss of generality that the weight of each clause

$\bar{x}_i$ is no greater than the weight of clause x_i. Thus, $\sum_{j \in U} w_j = \sum_{j=1}^{m} w_j - \sum_{i=1}^{n} v_i$. Then set each x_i to be true independently with probability $p = \frac{1}{2}(\sqrt{5} - 1)$. Then

$$E[W] = \sum_{j=1}^{m} w_j \Pr[\text{clause } C_j \text{ satisfied}]$$

$$\geq \sum_{j \in U} w_j \Pr[\text{clause } C_j \text{ satisfied}]$$

$$\geq p \cdot \sum_{j \in U} w_j \tag{5.1}$$

$$= p \cdot \left(\sum_{j=1}^{m} w_j - \sum_{i=1}^{n} v_i \right) \geq p \cdot \text{OPT},$$

where (5.1) follows by Theorem 5.5 and the fact that $p = \min(p, 1 - p^2)$. $\qquad \square$

This algorithm can be derandomized using the method of conditional expectations.

5.4 Randomized Rounding

The algorithm of the previous section shows that biasing the probability with which we set x_i true yields an improved approximation algorithm. However, we gave each variable the same bias. In this section, we show that we can do still better by giving each variable its own bias. We do this by returning to the idea of *randomized rounding*, which we examined briefly in Section 1.7 in the context of the set cover problem.

Recall that in randomized rounding, we first set up an integer programming formulation of the problem at hand in which there are 0-1 integer variables. In this case we will create an integer program with a 0-1 variable y_i for each Boolean variable x_i such that $y_i = 1$ corresponds to x_i set true. The integer program is relaxed to a linear program by replacing the constraints $y_i \in \{0, 1\}$ with $0 \leq y_i \leq 1$, and the linear programming relaxation is solved in polynomial time. Recall that the central idea of randomized rounding is that the fractional value y_i^* is interpreted as the probability that y_i should be set to 1. In this case, we set each x_i to true with probability y_i^* independently.

We now give an integer programming formulation of the MAX SAT problem. In addition to the variables y_i, we introduce a variable z_j for each clause C_j that will be 1 if the clause is satisfied and 0 otherwise. For each clause C_j, let P_j be the indices of the variables x_i that occur positively in the clause, and let N_j be the indices of the variables x_i that are negated in the clause. We denote the clause C_j by

$$\bigvee_{i \in P_j} x_i \vee \bigvee_{i \in N_j} \bar{x}_i.$$

Then the inequality

$$\sum_{i \in P_j} y_i + \sum_{i \in N_j} (1 - y_i) \geq z_j$$

must hold for clause C_j since if each variable that occurs positively in the clause is set to false (and its corresponding y_i is set to 0) and each variable that occurs negatively is set to true (and its corresponding y_i is set to 1), then the clause is not satisfied, and z_j must be 0. This inequality yields the following integer programming formulation of the MAX SAT problem:

$$\text{maximize} \sum_{j=1}^{m} w_j z_j$$

$$\text{subject to} \sum_{i \in P_j} y_i + \sum_{i \in N_j} (1 - y_i) \geq z_j, \qquad \forall C_j = \bigvee_{i \in P_j} x_i \vee \bigvee_{i \in N_j} \bar{x}_i,$$

$$y_i \in \{0, 1\}, \qquad i = 1, \dots, n,$$

$$0 \leq z_j \leq 1, \qquad j = 1, \dots, m.$$

If Z_{IP}^* is the optimal value of this integer program, then it is not hard to see that $Z_{IP}^* = \text{OPT}$.

The corresponding linear programming relaxation of this integer program is

$$\text{maximize} \sum_{j=1}^{m} w_j z_j$$

$$\text{subject to} \sum_{i \in P_j} y_i + \sum_{i \in N_j} (1 - y_i) \geq z_j, \qquad \forall C_j = \bigvee_{i \in P_j} x_i \vee \bigvee_{i \in N_j} \bar{x}_i,$$

$$0 \leq y_i \leq 1, \qquad i = 1, \dots, n,$$

$$0 \leq z_j \leq 1, \qquad j = 1, \dots, m.$$

If Z_{LP}^* is the optimal value of this linear program, then clearly $Z_{LP}^* \geq Z_{IP}^* = \text{OPT}$.

Let (y^*, z^*) be an optimal solution to the linear programming relaxation. We now consider the result of using randomized rounding, and setting x_i to true with probability y_i^* independently. Before we can begin the analysis, we will need two facts. The first is commonly called the *arithmetic-geometric mean inequality* because it compares the arithmetic and geometric means of a set of numbers.

Fact 5.8 (Arithmetic-geometric mean inequality). *For any nonnegative $a_1, \dots, a_k$,*

$$\left(\prod_{i=1}^{k} a_i \right)^{1/k} \leq \frac{1}{k} \sum_{i=1}^{k} a_i.$$

Fact 5.9. *If a function $f(x)$ is concave on the interval $[0, 1]$ (that is, $f''(x) \leq 0$ on $[0, 1]$), and $f(0) = a$ and $f(1) = b + a$, then $f(x) \geq bx + a$ for $x \in [0, 1]$ (see Figure 5.1).*

Theorem 5.10. *Randomized rounding gives a randomized $(1 - \frac{1}{e})$-approximation algorithm for MAX SAT.*

Proof. As in the analyses of the algorithms in the previous sections, the main difficulty is analyzing the probability that a given clause C_j is satisfied. Pick an arbitrary clause

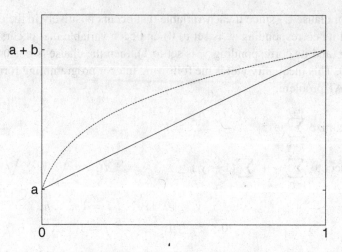

Figure 5.1. An illustration of Fact 5.9.

C_j. Then, by applying the arithmetic-geometric mean inequality, we see that

$$\Pr[\text{clause } C_j \text{ not satisfied}] = \prod_{i \in P_j}(1 - y_i^*) \prod_{i \in N_j} y_i^* \leq \left[\frac{1}{l_j}\left(\sum_{i \in P_j}(1 - y_i^*) + \sum_{i \in N_j} y_i^* \right) \right]^{l_j}.$$

By rearranging terms, we can derive that

$$\left[\frac{1}{l_j}\left(\sum_{i \in P_j}(1 - y_i^*) + \sum_{i \in N_j} y_i^* \right) \right]^{l_j} = \left[1 - \frac{1}{l_j}\left(\sum_{i \in P_j} y_i^* + \sum_{i \in N_j}(1 - y_i^*) \right) \right]^{l_j}.$$

By invoking the corresponding inequality from the linear program,

$$\sum_{i \in P_j} y_i^* + \sum_{i \in N_j}(1 - y_i^*) \geq z_j^*,$$

we see that

$$\Pr[\text{clause } C_j \text{ not satisfied}] \leq \left(1 - \frac{z_j^*}{l_j} \right)^{l_j}.$$

The function $f(z_j^*) = 1 - \left(1 - \frac{z_j^*}{l_j} \right)^{l_j}$ is concave for $l_j \geq 1$. Then by using Fact 5.9,

$$\Pr[\text{clause } C_j \text{ satisfied}] \geq 1 - \left(1 - \frac{z_j^*}{l_j} \right)^{l_j}$$

$$\geq \left[1 - \left(1 - \frac{1}{l_j} \right)^{l_j} \right] z_j^*.$$

Therefore, the expected value of the randomized rounding algorithm is

$$E[W] = \sum_{j=1}^{m} w_j \Pr[\text{clause } C_j \text{ satisfied}]$$

$$\geq \sum_{j=1}^{m} w_j z_j^* \left[1 - \left(1 - \frac{1}{l_j} \right)^{l_j} \right]$$

$$\geq \min_{k \geq 1} \left[1 - \left(1 - \frac{1}{k} \right)^{k} \right] \sum_{j=1}^{m} w_j z_j^*.$$

Note that $\left[1 - \left(1 - \frac{1}{k} \right)^{k} \right]$ is a non-increasing function in k and that it approaches $\left(1 - \frac{1}{e} \right)$ from above as k tends to infinity. Since $\sum_{j=1}^{m} w_j z_j^* = Z_{LP}^* \geq \text{OPT}$, we have that

$$E[W] \geq \min_{k \geq 1} \left[1 - \left(1 - \frac{1}{k} \right)^{k} \right] \sum_{j=1}^{m} w_j z_j^* \geq \left(1 - \frac{1}{e} \right) \text{OPT}. \qquad \square$$

This randomized rounding algorithm can be derandomized in the standard way using the method of conditional expectations.

5.5 Choosing the Better of Two Solutions

In this section we observe that choosing the better solution from the two given by the randomized rounding algorithm of the previous section and the unbiased randomized algorithm of the first section gives a better performance guarantee than that of either algorithm. This happens because, as we shall see, the algorithms have contrasting bad cases: when one algorithm is far from optimal, the other is close, and vice versa. This technique can be useful in other situations, and does not require using randomized algorithms.

In this case, consider a given clause C_j of length l_j. The randomized rounding algorithm of Section 5.4 satisfies the clause with probability at least $\left[1 - \left(1 - \frac{1}{l_j} \right)^{l_j} \right] z_j^*$, while the unbiased randomized algorithm of Section 5.1 satisfies the clause with probability $1 - 2^{-l_j} \geq (1 - 2^{-l_j}) z_j^*$. Thus, when the clause is short, it is very likely to be satisfied by the randomized rounding algorithm, though not by the unbiased randomized algorithm, and when the clause is long the opposite is true. This observation is made precise and rigorous in the following theorem.

Theorem 5.11. *Choosing the better of the two solutions given by the randomized rounding algorithm and the unbiased randomized algorithm yields a randomized $\frac{3}{4}$-approximation algorithm for MAX SAT.*

Proof. Let W_1 be a random variable denoting the value of the solution returned by the randomized rounding algorithm, and let W_2 be a random variable denoting the value

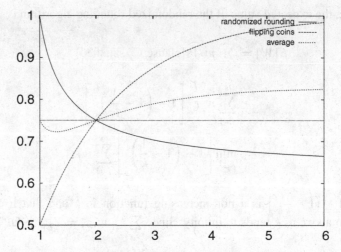

Figure 5.2. Illustration of the proof of Theorem 5.11. The "randomized rounding" line is the function $1 - (1 - \frac{1}{k})^k$. The "flipping coins" line is the function $1 - 2^{-k}$. The "average" line is the average of these two functions, which is at least $\frac{3}{4}$ for all integers $k \geq 1$.

of the solution returned by the unbiased randomized algorithm. Then we wish to show that

$$E[\max(W_1, W_2)] \geq \frac{3}{4} \text{OPT}.$$

To obtain this inequality, observe that

$$E[\max(W_1, W_2)] \geq E\left[\frac{1}{2}W_1 + \frac{1}{2}W_2\right]$$

$$= \frac{1}{2}E[W_1] + \frac{1}{2}E[W_2]$$

$$\geq \frac{1}{2}\sum_{j=1}^{m} w_j z_j^* \left[1 - \left(1 - \frac{1}{l_j}\right)^{l_j}\right] + \frac{1}{2}\sum_{j=1}^{m} w_j \left(1 - 2^{-l_j}\right)$$

$$\geq \sum_{j=1}^{m} w_j z_j^* \left[\frac{1}{2}\left(1 - \left(1 - \frac{1}{l_j}\right)^{l_j}\right) + \frac{1}{2}\left(1 - 2^{-l_j}\right)\right].$$

We claim that

$$\left[\frac{1}{2}\left(1 - \left(1 - \frac{1}{l_j}\right)^{l_j}\right) + \frac{1}{2}\left(1 - 2^{-l_j}\right)\right] \geq \frac{3}{4}$$

for all positive integers l_j. We will prove this shortly, but this can be seen in Figure 5.2. Given the claim, we have that

$$E[\max(W_1, W_2)] \geq \frac{3}{4}\sum_{j=1}^{m} w_j z_j^* = \frac{3}{4}Z_{LP}^* \geq \frac{3}{4}\text{OPT}.$$

Now to prove the claim. Observe that the claim holds for $l_j = 1$, since

$$\frac{1}{2} \cdot 1 + \frac{1}{2} \cdot \frac{1}{2} = \frac{3}{4},$$

and the claim holds for $l_j = 2$, since

$$\frac{1}{2} \cdot \left(1 - \left(\frac{1}{2}\right)^2\right) + \frac{1}{2}(1 - 2^{-2}) = \frac{3}{4}.$$

For all $l_j \geq 3$, $\left(1 - \left(1 - \frac{1}{l_j}\right)^{l_j}\right) \geq 1 - \frac{1}{e}$ and $\left(1 - 2^{-l_j}\right) \geq \frac{7}{8}$, and

$$\frac{1}{2}\left(1 - \frac{1}{e}\right) + \frac{1}{2} \cdot \frac{7}{8} \approx 0.753 \geq \frac{3}{4},$$

so the claim is proven. $\qquad\square$

Notice that taking the better solution of the two derandomized algorithms gives at least $\max(E[W_1], E[W_2]) \geq \frac{1}{2}E[W_1] + \frac{1}{2}E[W_2]$. The proof above shows that this quantity is at least $\frac{3}{4}$ OPT. Thus, taking the better solution of the two derandomized algorithms is a deterministic $\frac{3}{4}$-approximation algorithm.

5.6 Nonlinear Randomized Rounding

Thus far in our applications of randomized rounding, we have used the variable y_i^* from the linear programming relaxation as a probability to decide whether to set y_i to 1 in the integer programming formulation of the problem. In the case of the MAX SAT problem, we set x_i to true with probability y_i^*. There is no reason, however, that we cannot use some function $f : [0, 1] \to [0, 1]$ to set x_i to true with probability $f(y_i^*)$. Sometimes this yields approximation algorithms with better performance guarantees than using the identity function, as we will see in this section.

In this section we will show that a $\frac{3}{4}$-approximation algorithm for MAX SAT can be obtained directly by using randomized rounding with a nonlinear function f. In fact, there is considerable freedom in choosing such a function f: let f be any function such that $f : [0, 1] \to [0, 1]$ and

$$1 - 4^{-x} \leq f(x) \leq 4^{x-1}. \tag{5.2}$$

See Figure 5.3 for a plot of the bounding functions. We will see that this ensures that the probability a clause C_j is satisfied is at least $1 - 4^{-z_j^*} \geq \frac{3}{4}z_j^*$, which will give the $\frac{3}{4}$-approximation algorithm.

Theorem 5.12. *Randomized rounding with the function f is a randomized $\frac{3}{4}$-approximation algorithm for MAX SAT.*

Proof. Once again, it suffices to analyze the probability that a given clause C_j is satisfied. By the definition of f,

$$\Pr[\text{clause } C_j \text{ not satisfied}] = \prod_{i \in P_j}(1 - f(y_i^*)) \prod_{i \in N_j} f(y_i^*) \leq \prod_{i \in P_j} 4^{-y_i^*} \prod_{i \in N_j} 4^{y_i^* - 1}.$$

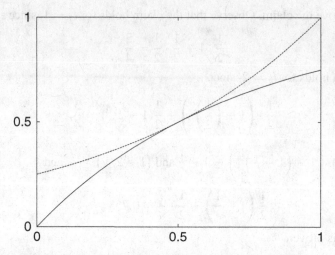

Figure 5.3. A plot of the functions of (5.2). The upper curve is 4^{x-1} and the lower curve is $1 - 4^{-x}$.

Rewriting the product and using the linear programming constraint for clause C_j gives us

$$\Pr[\text{clause } C_j \text{ not satisfied}] \leq \prod_{i \in P_j} 4^{-y_i^*} \prod_{i \in N_j} 4^{y_i^*-1} = 4^{-\left(\sum_{i \in P_j} y_i^* + \sum_{i \in N_j} (1-y_i^*)\right)} \leq 4^{-z_j^*}.$$

Then using Fact 5.9 and observing that the function $g(z) = 1 - 4^{-z}$ is concave on $[0,1]$, we have

$$\Pr[\text{clause } C_j \text{ satisfied}] \geq 1 - 4^{-z_j^*} \geq (1 - 4^{-1})z_j^* = \frac{3}{4}z_j^*.$$

It follows that the expected performance of the algorithm is

$$E[W] = \sum_{j=1}^{m} w_j \Pr[\text{clause } C_j \text{ satisfied}] \geq \frac{3}{4} \sum_{j=1}^{m} w_j z_j^* \geq \frac{3}{4} \text{OPT}. \qquad \square$$

Once again, the algorithm can be derandomized using the method of conditional expectations.

There are other choices of the function f that also lead to a $\frac{3}{4}$-approximation algorithm for MAX SAT. Some other possibilities are presented in the exercises at the end of the chapter.

Is it possible to get an algorithm with a performance guarantee better than $\frac{3}{4}$ by using some more complicated form of randomized rounding? It turns out that the answer is no, at least for any algorithm that derives its performance guarantee by comparing its value to that of the linear programming relaxation. To see this, consider the instance of the maximum satisfiability problem with two variables x_1 and x_2 and four clauses of weight 1 each, $x_1 \vee x_2$, $x_1 \vee \bar{x}_2$, $\bar{x}_1 \vee x_2$, and $\bar{x}_1 \vee \bar{x}_2$. Any feasible solution, including the optimal solution, satisfies exactly three of the four clauses. However, if we set $y_1 = y_2 = \frac{1}{2}$ and $z_j = 1$ for all four clauses C_j, then this solution is feasible for the linear program and has value 4. Thus, the value to any solution to the MAX SAT instance can be at most $\frac{3}{4} \sum_{j=1}^{m} w_j z_j^*$. We say that this integer programming formulation of the maximum satisfiability problem has an *integrality gap* of $\frac{3}{4}$.

Definition 5.13. *The* integrality gap *of an integer program is the worst-case ratio over all instances of the problem of the value of an optimal solution to the integer programming formulation to the value of an optimal solution to its linear programming relaxation.*

The example above shows that the integrality gap is at most $\frac{3}{4}$, whereas the proof of Theorem 5.12 shows that it is at least $\frac{3}{4}$. If an integer programming formulation has integrality gap ρ, then any algorithm for a maximization problem whose performance guarantee α is proven by showing that the value of its solution is at least α times the value of the linear programming relaxation can have performance guarantee at most ρ. A similar statement holds for minimization problems.

5.7 The Prize-Collecting Steiner Tree Problem

We now consider other problems for which randomized techniques are useful. In particular, in the next few sections, we revisit some of the problems we studied earlier in the book and show that we can obtain improved performance guarantees by using the randomized methods that we have developed in this chapter.

We start by returning to the prize-collecting Steiner tree problem we discussed in Section 4.4. Recall that in this problem we are given an undirected graph $G = (V, E)$, an edge cost $c_e \geq 0$ for each $e \in E$, a selected root vertex $r \in V$, and a penalty $\pi_i \geq 0$ for each $i \in V$. The goal is to find a tree T that contains the root vertex r so as to minimize $\sum_{e \in T} c_e + \sum_{i \in V - V(T)} \pi_i$, where $V(T)$ is the set of vertices in the tree. We used the following linear programming relaxation of the problem:

$$\text{minimize} \quad \sum_{e \in E} c_e x_e + \sum_{i \in V} \pi_i (1 - y_i)$$

$$\text{subject to} \quad \sum_{e \in \delta(S)} x_e \geq y_i, \qquad \forall S \subseteq V - r, S \neq \emptyset, \forall i \in S,$$

$$y_r = 1,$$

$$y_i \geq 0, \qquad \forall i \in V,$$

$$x_e \geq 0, \qquad \forall e \in E.$$

In the 3-approximation algorithm given in Section 4.4, we found an optimal LP solution (x^*, y^*), and for a specified value of α, we built a Steiner tree on all nodes such that $y_i^* \geq \alpha$. We claimed that the cost of the edges in the tree is within a factor of $2/\alpha$ of the fractional cost of the tree edges in the LP solution, while the cost of the penalties is within a factor of $1/(1 - \alpha)$ of the cost of the penalties in the LP solution. Thus, if α is close to 1, the cost of the tree edges is within a factor of 2 of the corresponding cost of the LP, while if α is close to 0, our penalty cost is close to the corresponding cost of the LP.

In the previous section we set $\alpha = 2/3$ to trade off the costs of the tree edges and the penalties, resulting in a performance guarantee of 3. Suppose instead that we choose the value of α randomly rather than considering just one value of α. We will see that this improves the performance guarantee from 3 to about 2.54.

Recall Lemma 4.6 from Section 4.4, which allowed us to bound the cost of the spanning tree T constructed in terms of α and the LP solution (x^*, y^*).

Lemma 5.14 (Lemma 4.6).

$$\sum_{e \in T} c_e \le \frac{2}{\alpha} \sum_{e \in E} c_e x_e^*.$$

Because the bound becomes infinite as α tends to zero, we don't want to choose α too close to zero. Instead, we will choose α uniformly from the range $[\gamma, 1]$, and will later decide how to set γ. Recall that in computing the expected value of a continuous random variable X, if that variable has a probability density function $f(x)$ over the domain $[a, b]$ (specifying the probability that $X = x$), then we compute the expectation of X by integrating $f(x)x\,dx$ over that interval. The probability density function for a uniform random variable over $[\gamma, 1]$ is the constant $1/(1 - \gamma)$. We can then analyze the expected cost of the tree for the randomized algorithm below.

Lemma 5.15.

$$E\left[\sum_{e \in T} c_e\right] \le \left(\frac{2}{1 - \gamma} \ln \frac{1}{\gamma}\right) \sum_{e \in E} c_e x_e^*.$$

Proof. Using simple algebra and calculus, we obtain

$$E\left[\sum_{e \in T} c_e\right] \le E\left[\frac{2}{\alpha} \sum_{e \in E} c_e x_e^*\right]$$

$$= E\left[\frac{2}{\alpha}\right] \sum_{e \in E} c_e x_e^*$$

$$= \left(\frac{1}{1 - \gamma} \int_\gamma^1 \frac{2}{x} dx\right) \sum_{e \in E} c_e x_e^*$$

$$= \left[\frac{2}{1 - \gamma} \ln x\right]_\gamma^1 \cdot \sum_{e \in E} c_e x_e^*$$

$$= \left(\frac{2}{1 - \gamma} \ln \frac{1}{\gamma}\right) \sum_{e \in E} c_e x_e^*. \qquad \square$$

The expected penalty for the vertices not in the tree is also easy to analyze.

Lemma 5.16.

$$E\left[\sum_{i \in V - V(T)} \pi_i\right] \le \frac{1}{1 - \gamma} \sum_{i \in V} \pi_i (1 - y_i^*).$$

Proof. Let $U = \{i \in V : y_i^* \ge \alpha\}$; any vertex not in the tree must not be in U, so we have that $\sum_{i \in V - V(T)} \pi_i \le \sum_{i \notin U} \pi_i$. Observe that if $y_i^* \ge \gamma$, then the probability that $i \notin U$ is $(1 - y_i^*)/(1 - \gamma)$. If $y_i^* < \gamma$, then $i \notin U$ with probability 1. But then $1 \le (1 - y_i^*)/(1 - \gamma)$, and so the lemma statement follows. $\qquad \square$

Thus, we have the following theorem and corollary.

Theorem 5.17. *The expected cost of the solution produced by the randomized algorithm is*

$$E\left[\sum_{e\in T} c_e + \sum_{i\in V - V(T)} \pi_i\right] \le \left(\frac{2}{1-\gamma} \ln\frac{1}{\gamma}\right)\sum_{e\in E} c_e x_e^* + \frac{1}{1-\gamma}\sum_{i\in V}\pi_i(1 - y_i^*).$$

Corollary 5.18. *Using the randomized rounding algorithm with $\gamma = e^{-1/2}$ gives a $(1 - e^{-1/2})^{-1}$-approximation algorithm for the prize-collecting Steiner tree problem, where $(1 - e^{-1/2})^{-1} \approx 2.54$.*

Proof. We want to ensure that the maximum of the coefficients of the two terms in the bound of Theorem 5.17 is as small as possible. The first coefficient is a decreasing function of γ, and the second is an increasing function. We can minimize the maximum by setting them equal. By setting $\frac{2}{1-\gamma}\ln\frac{1}{\gamma} = \frac{1}{1-\gamma}$, we obtain $\gamma = e^{-1/2}$. Then by Theorem 5.17, the expected cost of the tree obtained is no greater than

$$\frac{1}{1 - e^{-1/2}}\left(\sum_{e\in E} c_e x_e^* + \sum_{i\in V}\pi_i(1 - y_i^*)\right) \le \frac{1}{1 - e^{-1/2}}\cdot\text{OPT}. \qquad \square$$

The derandomization of the algorithm is straightforward: since there are $|V|$ variables y_i^*, there are at most $|V|$ distinct values of y_i^*. Thus, consider the $|V|$ sets $U_j = \{i \in V : y_i^* \ge y_j^*\}$. Any possible value of α corresponds to one of these $|V|$ sets. Thus, if a random choice of α has a certain expected performance guarantee, the algorithm that tries each set U_j and chooses the best solution generated will have a deterministic performance guarantee at least as good as that of the expectation of the randomized algorithm. Interestingly, the use of randomization allows us to analyze this natural deterministic algorithm, whereas we know of no means of analyzing the deterministic algorithm directly.

Recall from the end of the previous section that we defined the integrality gap of an integer programming formulation to be the worst-case ratio, over all instances of a problem, of the value of an optimal solution to the integer programming formulation to the value of an optimal solution to the linear programming relaxation. We also explained that the integrality gap bounds the performance guarantee that we can get via LP rounding arguments. Consider a graph G that is a cycle on n nodes, and let the penalty for each node be infinite and the cost of each edge be 1. Then there is a feasible solution to the linear programming relaxation of cost $n/2$ by setting each edge variable to $1/2$, while there is an optimal integral solution of cost $n - 1$ by taking every edge of the cycle except one (see Figure 5.4). Hence, the integrality gap for this instance of the problem is at least $(n - 1)/(n/2) = 2 - 2/n$. Thus, we cannot expect a performance guarantee for the prize-collecting Steiner tree problem better than $2 - \frac{2}{n}$ using LP rounding arguments with this formulation. In Chapter 14, we will return to the prize-collecting Steiner tree problem and show that the primal-dual method can be used to obtain a 2-approximation algorithm for the problem. The argument there will show that the integrality gap of the integer programming formulation is at most 2.

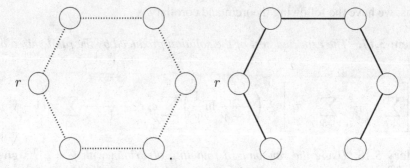

Figure 5.4. Example of the integrality gap of the integer programming formulation for the prize-collecting Steiner tree problem. On the left is a feasible solution for the linear program in which each edge has value $1/2$. On the right is an optimal solution for the integer programming formulation in which each edge shown has value 1.

5.8 The Uncapacitated Facility Location Problem

In this section, we revisit the metric uncapacitated facility location problem introduced in Section 4.5. Recall that in this problem we are given a set of clients D and a set of facilities F, along with facility costs f_i for all facilities $i \in F$, and assignment costs c_{ij} for all facilities $i \in F$ and clients $j \in D$. All clients and facilities are points in a metric space, and given clients j, l and facilities i, k, we have that $c_{ij} \leq c_{il} + c_{kl} + c_{kj}$. The goal of the problem is to select a subset of facilities to open and an assignment of clients to open facilities so as to minimize the total cost of the open facilities plus the assignment costs. We used the following linear programming relaxation of the problem:

$$\text{minimize} \quad \sum_{i \in F} f_i y_i + \sum_{i \in F, j \in D} c_{ij} x_{ij}$$

$$\text{subject to} \quad \sum_{i \in F} x_{ij} = 1, \qquad \forall j \in D,$$

$$x_{ij} \leq y_i, \qquad \forall i \in F, j \in D,$$

$$x_{ij} \geq 0, \qquad \forall i \in F, j \in D,$$

$$y_i \geq 0, \qquad \forall i \in F,$$

where the variable x_{ij} indicates whether client j is assigned to facility i, and the variable y_i indicates whether facility i is open or not. We also used the dual of the LP relaxation:

$$\text{maximize} \quad \sum_{j \in D} v_j$$

$$\text{subject to} \quad \sum_{j \in D} w_{ij} \leq f_i, \qquad \forall i \in F,$$

$$v_j - w_{ij} \leq c_{ij}, \qquad \forall i \in F, j \in D,$$

$$w_{ij} \geq 0, \qquad \forall i \in F, j \in D.$$

Solve LP, get optimal primal solution (x^*, y^*) and dual solution (v^*, w^*)
$C \leftarrow D$
$k \leftarrow 0$
while $C \neq \emptyset$ **do**
    $k \leftarrow k + 1$
    Choose $j_k \in C$ that minimizes $v_j^* + C_j^*$ over all $j \in C$
    Choose $i_k \in N(j_k)$ according to the probability distribution $x_{ij_k}^*$
    Assign j_k and all unassigned clients in $N^2(j_k)$ to i_k
    $C \leftarrow C - \{j_k\} - N^2(j_k)$

Algorithm 5.1. Randomized rounding algorithm for the uncapacitated facility location problem.

Finally, given an LP solution (x^*, y^*), we said that a client j neighbors a facility i if $x_{ij}^* > 0$. We denote the neighbors of j as $N(j) = \{i \in F : x_{ij}^* > 0\}$, and the neighbors of the neighbors of j as $N^2(j) = \{k \in D : \exists i \in N(j), x_{ik}^* > 0\}$. Recall that we showed in Lemma 4.11 that if (v^*, w^*) is an optimal dual solution and $i \in N(j)$ then the cost of assigning j to i is bounded by v_j^* (that is, $c_{ij} \leq v_j^*$).

We gave a 4-approximation algorithm in Algorithm 4.2 of Section 4.5 that works by choosing an unassigned client j that minimizes the value of v_j^* among all remaining unassigned clients, opening the cheapest facility in the neighborhood of $N(j)$, and then assigning j and all clients in $N^2(j)$ to this facility. We showed that for an optimal LP solution (x^*, y^*) and optimal dual solution v^*, this gave a solution of cost at most $\sum_{i \in F} f_i y_i^* + 3 \sum_{j \in D} v_j^* \leq 4 \cdot \text{OPT}$.

This analysis is a little unsatisfactory in the sense that we bound $\sum_{i \in F} f_i y_i^*$ by OPT, whereas we know that we have the stronger bound $\sum_{i \in F} f_i y_i^* + \sum_{i \in F, j \in D} c_{ij} x_{ij}^* \leq \text{OPT}$. In this section, we show that by using randomized rounding we can modify the algorithm of Section 4.5 slightly and improve the analysis to a 3-approximation algorithm.

The basic idea is that once we have selected a client j in the algorithm, instead of opening the cheapest facility in $N(j)$, we use randomized rounding to choose the facility, and open facility $i \in N(j)$ with probability x_{ij}^* (note that $\sum_{i \in N(j)} x_{ij}^* = 1$). This improves the analysis since in the previous version of the algorithm we had to make worst-case assumptions about how far away the cheapest facility would be from the clients assigned to it. In this algorithm we can amortize the costs over all possible choices of facilities in $N(j)$.

In order to get our analysis to work, we modify the choice of client selected in each iteration as well. We define $C_j^* = \sum_{i \in F} c_{ij} x_{ij}^*$; that is, the assignment cost incurred by client j in the LP solution (x^*, y^*). We now choose the unassigned client that minimizes $v_j^* + C_j^*$ over all unassigned clients in each iteration. Our new algorithm is given in Algorithm 5.1. Note that the only changes from the previous algorithm of Section 4.5 (Algorithm 4.2) are in the third from the last and second from the last lines.

We can now analyze this new algorithm.

Theorem 5.19. *Algorithm 5.1 is a randomized 3-approximation algorithm for the uncapacitated facility location problem.*

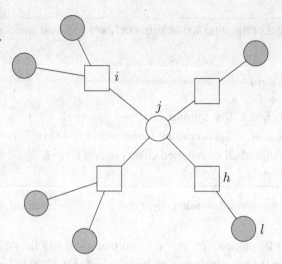

Figure 5.5. Illustration of proof of Theorem 5.19.

Proof. In an iteration k, the expected cost of the facility opened is

$$\sum_{i \in N(j_k)} f_i x_{ij_k}^* \le \sum_{i \in N(j_k)} f_i y_i^*,$$

using the LP constraint $x_{ij_k}^* \le y_i^*$. As we argued in Section 4.5, the neighborhoods $N(j_k)$ form a partition of a subset of the facilities so that the overall expected cost of facilities opened is at most

$$\sum_k \sum_{i \in N(j_k)} f_i y_i^* \le \sum_{i \in F} f_i y_i^*.$$

We now fix an iteration k and let j denote the client j_k selected and let i denote the facility i_k opened. The expected cost of assigning j to i is

$$\sum_{i \in N(j)} c_{ij} x_{ij}^* = C_j^*.$$

As can be seen from Figure 5.5, the expected cost of assigning an unassigned client $l \in N^2(j)$ to i, where the client l neighbors facility h, which neighbors client j, is at most

$$c_{hl} + c_{hj} + \sum_{i \in N(j)} c_{ij} x_{ij}^* = c_{hl} + c_{hj} + C_j^*.$$

By Lemma 4.11, $c_{hl} \le v_l^*$ and $c_{hj} \le v_j^*$, so that this cost is at most $v_l^* + v_j^* + C_j^*$. Then since we chose j to minimize $v_j^* + C_j^*$ among all unassigned clients, we know that $v_j^* + C_j^* \le v_l^* + C_l^*$. Hence, the expected cost of assigning l to i is at most

$$v_l^* + v_j^* + C_j^* \le 2v_l^* + C_l^*.$$

Thus, we have that our total expected cost is no more than

$$\sum_{i \in F} f_i y_i^* + \sum_{j \in D} (2v_j^* + C_j^*) = \sum_{i \in F} f_i y_i^* + \sum_{i \in F, j \in D} c_{ij} x_{ij}^* + 2 \sum_{j \in D} v_j^*$$
$$\leq 3 \, \text{OPT}. \qquad \square$$

Note that we were able to reduce the performance guarantee from 4 to 3 because the random choice of facility allows us to include the assignment cost C_j^* in the analysis; instead of bounding only the facility cost by OPT, we can bound both the facility cost and part of the assignment cost by OPT.

One can imagine a different type of randomized rounding algorithm: suppose we obtain an optimal LP solution (x^*, y^*) and open each facility $i \in F$ with probability y_i^*. Given the open facilities, we then assign each client to the closest open facility. This algorithm has the nice feature that the expected facility cost is $\sum_{i \in F} f_i y_i^*$. However, this simple algorithm clearly has the difficulty that with nonzero probability, the algorithm opens no facilities at all, and hence the expected assignment cost is unbounded. We consider a modified version of this algorithm later in the book, in Section 12.1.

5.9 Scheduling a Single Machine with Release Dates

In this section, we return to the problem considered in Section 4.2 of scheduling a single machine with release dates so as to minimize the weighted sum of completion times. Recall that we are given as input n jobs, each of which has a processing time $p_j > 0$, weight $w_j \geq 0$, and release date $r_j \geq 0$. The values p_j, r_j, and w_j are all nonnegative integers. We must construct a schedule for these jobs on a single machine such that at most one job is processed at any point in time, no job is processed before its release date, and once a job begins to be processed, it must be processed *nonpreemptively*; that is, it must be processed completely before any other job can be scheduled. If C_j denotes the time at which job j is finished processing, then the goal is to find the schedule that minimizes $\sum_{j=1}^n w_j C_j$.

In Section 4.2, we gave a linear programming relaxation of the problem. In order to apply randomized rounding, we will use a different integer programming formulation of this problem. In fact, we will not use an integer programming formulation of the problem, but an integer programming *relaxation*. Solutions in which jobs are scheduled preemptively are feasible; however, the contribution of job j to the objective function is less than $w_j C_j$ unless job j is scheduled nonpreemptively. Thus, the integer program is a relaxation since for any solution corresponding to a nonpreemptive schedule, the objective function value is equal to the sum of weighted completion times of the schedule.

Furthermore, although this relaxation is an integer program and has a number of constraints and variables exponential in the size of the problem instance, we will be able to find a solution to it in polynomial time.

We now give the integer programming relaxation. Let T equal $\max_j r_j + \sum_{j=1}^n p_j$, which is the latest possible time any job can be processed in any schedule that processes a job nonpreemptively whenever it can. We introduce variables y_{jt} for $j = 1, \ldots, n$, $t = 1, \ldots, T$, where

$$y_{jt} = \begin{cases} 1 & \text{if job } j \text{ is processed in time } [t-1, t), \\ 0 & \text{otherwise.} \end{cases}$$

We derive a series of constraints for the integer program to capture the constraints of the scheduling problem. Since at most one job can be processed at any point in time, for each time $t = 1, \ldots, T$ we impose the constraint

$$\sum_{j=1}^{n} y_{jt} \leq 1.$$

Since each job j must be processed for p_j units of time, for each job $j = 1, \ldots, n$ we impose the constraint

$$\sum_{t=1}^{T} y_{jt} = p_j.$$

Since no job j can be processed before its release date, we set

$$y_{jt} = 0$$

for each job $j = 1, \ldots, n$ and each time $t = 1, \ldots, r_j$. For $t = r_j + 1, \ldots, T$, obviously we want

$$y_{jt} \in \{0, 1\}.$$

Note that this integer program has size that is exponential in the size of the scheduling instance because T is exponential in the number of bits used to encode r_j and p_j.

Finally, we need to express the completion time of job j in terms of the variables y_{jt}, $j = 1, \ldots, n$. Given a nonpreemptive schedule, suppose that job j completes at time D. If we set the variables y_{jt} to indicate the times at which jobs are processed in the schedule, and so $y_{jt} = 1$ for $t = D - p_j + 1, \ldots, D$, whereas $y_{jt} = 0$ otherwise. Observe that if we take the average of the midpoints of each unit of time at which job j is processed ($t - \frac{1}{2}$ for $t = D - p_j + 1, \ldots, D$), we get the midpoint of the processing time of the job, namely, $D - \frac{p_j}{2}$. Thus,

$$\frac{1}{p_j} \sum_{t=D-p_j+1}^{D} \left(t - \frac{1}{2}\right) = D - \frac{p_j}{2}.$$

Given the settings of the variables y_{jt}, we can rewrite this as

$$\frac{1}{p_j} \sum_{t=1}^{T} y_{jt} \left(t - \frac{1}{2}\right) = D - \frac{p_j}{2}.$$

We wish to have variable C_j represent the completion time of job j. Rearranging terms, then, we set the variable C_j as follows:

$$C_j = \frac{1}{p_j} \sum_{t=1}^{T} y_{jt} \left(t - \frac{1}{2}\right) + \frac{p_j}{2}.$$

This variable C_j underestimates the completion time of job j when all of the variables y_{jt} that are set to 1 are not consecutive in time. To see this, first start with the case above in which $y_{jt} = 1$ for $t = D - p_j + 1, \ldots, D$ for a completion time D. By the arguments above, $C_j = D$. If we then modify the variables y_{jt} by successively setting $y_{jt} = 0$ for some $t \in [D - p_j + 1, D - 1]$ and $y_{jt} = 1$ for some $t \leq D - p_j$, it is clear that the variable C_j only decreases.

The overall *integer* programming relaxation of the problem we will use is

$$\text{minimize} \sum_{j=1}^{n} w_j C_j \tag{5.3}$$

$$\text{subject to} \sum_{j=1}^{n} y_{jt} \leq 1, \qquad\qquad t = 1, \ldots, T, \tag{5.4}$$

$$\sum_{t=1}^{T} y_{jt} = p_j, \qquad\qquad j = 1, \ldots, n, \tag{5.5}$$

$$y_{jt} = 0, \qquad\qquad j = 1, \ldots, n; t = 1, \ldots, r_j,$$

$$y_{jt} \in \{0, 1\}, \qquad\qquad j = 1, \ldots, n; t = 1, \ldots, T,$$

$$C_j = \frac{1}{p_j} \sum_{t=1}^{T} y_{jt} \left(t - \frac{1}{2} \right) + \frac{p_j}{2}, \quad j = 1, \ldots, n. \tag{5.6}$$

Even though we restrict the variables y_{jt} to take on integer values, the corresponding linear programming relaxation is well known to have optimal solutions for which these variables have integer values (for a simpler case of this phenomenon, see Exercise 4.6).

We can now consider a randomised rounding algorithm for this problem. Let (y^*, C^*) be an optimal solution to the integer programming relaxation. For each job j, let X_j be a random variable that is $t - \frac{1}{2}$ with probability y_{jt}^*/p_j; observe that by (5.5), $\sum_{t=1}^{T} \frac{y_{jt}^*}{p_j} = 1$ so that the y_{jt}^*/p_j give a probability distribution on time t for each job j. We defer for the moment a discussion on how to make this run in randomized polynomial time, since T is exponential in the input size and we need to solve the integer program in order to perform the randomized rounding. As in the algorithms of Sections 4.1 and 4.2 we now schedule the jobs as early as possible in the same relative order as the value of the X_j. Without loss of generality, suppose that $X_1 \leq X_2 \leq \cdots \leq X_n$. Then we schedule job 1 as early as possible (that is, not before r_1), then job 2, and in general we schedule job j to start at the maximum of the completion time of job $j - 1$ and r_j. Let $\hat{C}_j$ be a random variable denoting the completion time of job j in this schedule.

We begin the analysis of this algorithm by considering the expected value of $\hat{C}_j$ given a fixed value of X_j.

Lemma 5.20. $E[\hat{C}_j | X_j = x] \leq p_j + 2x$.

Proof. As we argued in the proof of Lemma 4.2, there cannot be any idle time between $\max_{k=1,\ldots,j} r_k$ and $\hat{C}_j$, and therefore it must be the case that $\hat{C}_j \leq \max_{k=1,\ldots,j} r_k + \sum_{k=1}^{j} p_j$. Because the ordering of the jobs results from randomized rounding, we let R be a random variable such that $R = \max_{k=1,\ldots,j} r_k$, and let random variable $P = \sum_{k=1}^{j-1} p_j$, so that the bound on $\hat{C}_j$ becomes $\hat{C}_j \leq R + P + p_j$.

First, we bound the value of R given that $X_j = x$. Note that since $y_{kt}^* = 0$ for $t \leq r_k$, it must be the case that $X_k \geq r_k + \frac{1}{2}$ for any job k. Thus,

$$R \leq \max_{k:X_k \leq X_j} r_k \leq \max_{k:X_k \leq X_j} X_k - \frac{1}{2} \leq X_j - \frac{1}{2} = x - \frac{1}{2}.$$

Now we bound the expected value of P given that $X_j = x$. We can bound it as follows:

$$E[P|X_j = x] = \sum_{k:k \neq j} p_k \Pr[\text{job } k \text{ is processed before } j | X_j = x]$$

$$= \sum_{k:k \neq j} p_k \Pr[X_k \leq X_j | X_j = x]$$

$$= \sum_{k:k \neq j} p_k \sum_{t=1}^{x+\frac{1}{2}} \Pr\left[X_k = t - \frac{1}{2}\right].$$

Since we set $X_k = t - \frac{1}{2}$ with probability y_{kt}^*/p_k, then

$$E[P|X_j = x] = \sum_{k:k \neq j} p_k \left(\sum_{t=1}^{x+\frac{1}{2}} \frac{y_{kt}^*}{p_k}\right) = \sum_{k:k \neq j} \sum_{t=1}^{x+\frac{1}{2}} y_{kt}^* = \sum_{t=1}^{x+\frac{1}{2}} \sum_{k:k \neq j} y_{kt}^*.$$

Constraint (5.4) of the integer programming relaxation imposes that $\sum_{k:k \neq j} y_{kt} \leq 1$ for all times t, so then

$$E[P|X_j = x] = \sum_{t=1}^{x+\frac{1}{2}} \sum_{k:k \neq j} y_{kt}^* \leq x + \frac{1}{2}.$$

Therefore,

$$E[\hat{C}_j|X_j = x] \leq p_j + E[R|X_j = x] + E[P|X_j = x]$$

$$\leq p_j + \left(x - \frac{1}{2}\right) + \left(x + \frac{1}{2}\right) = p_j + 2x. \qquad \square$$

Given the lemma above, we can prove the following theorem.

Theorem 5.21. *The randomized rounding algorithm is a randomized 2-approximation algorithm for the single-machine scheduling problem with release dates minimizing the sum of weighted completion times.*

Proof. Using the lemma above, we have that

$$E[\hat{C}_j] = \sum_{t=1}^{T} E\left[\hat{C}_j \,\Big|\, X_j = t - \frac{1}{2}\right] \Pr\left[X_j = t - \frac{1}{2}\right]$$

$$\leq p_j + 2\sum_{t=1}^{T}\left(t - \frac{1}{2}\right)\Pr\left[X_j = t - \frac{1}{2}\right]$$

$$= p_j + 2\sum_{t=1}^{T}\left(t - \frac{1}{2}\right)\frac{y_{jt}^*}{p_j}$$

$$= 2\left[\frac{p_j}{2} + \frac{1}{p_j}\sum_{t=0}^{T-1}\left(t - \frac{1}{2}\right)y_{jt}^*\right]$$

$$= 2C_j^*, \tag{5.7}$$

where equation (5.7) follows from the definition of C_j^* in the integer programming relaxation (equation (5.6)). Thus, we have that

$$E\left[\sum_{j=1}^{n} w_j\hat{C}_j\right] = \sum_{j=1}^{n} w_j E[\hat{C}_j] \leq 2\sum_{j=1}^{n} w_j C_j^* \leq 2\,\mathrm{OPT},$$

since $\sum_{j=1}^{n} w_j C_j^*$ is the objective function of the integer programming relaxation and thus a lower bound on OPT. $\qquad\square$

Unlike the previous randomized algorithms of the section, we do not know directly how to derandomize this algorithm, although a deterministic 2-approximation algorithm for this problem does exist.

We now show that the integer programming relaxation can be solved in polynomial time, and that the randomized rounding algorithm can be made to run in polynomial time. First, sort the jobs in order of non-increasing ratio of weight to processing time; we assume jobs are then indexed in this order so that $\frac{w_1}{p_1} \geq \frac{w_2}{p_2} \geq \cdots \geq \frac{w_n}{p_n}$. Now we use the following rule to create a (possibly preemptive) schedule: we always schedule the job of minimum index that is available but not yet completely processed. More formally, as t varies from 1 to T, let j be the smallest index such that $r_j \leq t - 1$ and $\sum_{z=1}^{t-1} y_{jz}^* < p_j$, if such a job j exists. Then set $y_{jt}^* = 1$ for job j and $y_{kt}^* = 0$ for all jobs $k \neq j$. If no such j exists, we set $y_{jt}^* = 0$ for all jobs j. Since in creating this schedule there are only n points in time corresponding to release dates r_j and n points in time at which a job has finished being processed, there are at most $2n$ points in time at which the index attaining the minimum might change. Thus, we can actually give the schedule as a sequence of at most $2n$ intervals of time, specifying which job (if any) is scheduled for each interval. It is not hard to see that we can compute this set of intervals in polynomial time without explicitly enumerating each time t. Furthermore, from the discussion above in which we explained how to express the variable C_j in terms of the y_{jt}, we know that if $y_{jt} = 1$ for $t = a + 1$ to b, then $\sum_{t=a+1}^{b} y_{jt}\left(t - \frac{1}{2}\right) = (b-a)(b - \frac{1}{2}(b-a))$, so that we can compute the values of the variables C_j^* from these intervals.

The randomized rounding algorithm can be made to run in polynomial time because it is equivalent to the following algorithm: for each job j, choose a value $\alpha_j \in [0, 1]$ independently and uniformly. Let X_j be the α_j-*point* of job j, that is, the time when $\alpha_j p_j$ units of job j have been processed in the preemptive schedule. Observe that it is easy to compute this point in time from the intervals describing the preemptive schedule. Then schedule the jobs according to the ordering of the X_j as in the randomized rounding algorithm. To see why this is equivalent to the original algorithm, consider the probability that $X_j \in [t - 1, t)$. This is simply the probability that $\alpha_j p_j$ units of job j have finished processing in this interval, which is the probability that

$$\sum_{s=1}^{t-1} y_{js}^* \leq \alpha_j p_j < \sum_{s=1}^{t} y_{js}^*.$$

This, then, is the probability that $\alpha_j \in [\frac{1}{p_j} \sum_{s=1}^{t-1} y_{js}^*, \frac{1}{p_j} \sum_{s=1}^{t} y_{js}^*)$; since α_j is chosen uniformly, this probability is y_{jt}^*/p_j. So the probability that $X_j \in [t - 1, t)$ in the α_j-point algorithm is the same as in the original algorithm, and the proof of the performance guarantee goes through with some small modifications.

Interestingly, one can also prove that if a single value of α is chosen uniformly from $[0, 1]$, and X_j is the α-point of job j, then scheduling jobs according to the ordering of the X_j is also a 2-approximation algorithm. Proving this fact is beyond the scope of this section. However, the algorithm in which a single value of α is chosen is easy to derandomize because it is possible to show that at most n different schedules can result from all possible choices of $\alpha \in [0, 1]$. Then to derive a deterministic 2-approximation algorithm, we need only enumerate the n different schedules, and choose the one that minimizes the weighted sum of the completion times.

It remains to show that the constructed solution (y^*, C^*) is in fact optimal. This is left to the reader to complete by a straightforward interchange argument in Exercise 5.11.

Lemma 5.22. *The solution (y^*, C^*) given above to the integer program is an optimal solution.*

5.10 Chernoff Bounds

This section introduces some theorems that are extremely useful for analyzing randomized rounding algorithms. In essence, the theorems say that it is very likely that the sum of n independent 0-1 random variables is not far away from the expected value of the sum. In the subsequent two sections, we will illustrate the usefulness of these bounds.

We begin by stating the main theorems.

Theorem 5.23. *Let $X_1, \ldots, X_n$ be n independent 0-1 random variables, not necessarily identically distributed. Then for $X = \sum_{i=1}^{n} X_i$ and $\mu = E[X]$, $L \leq \mu \leq U$, and $\delta > 0$,*

$$\Pr[X \geq (1 + \delta)U] < \left(\frac{e^{\delta}}{(1 + \delta)^{(1+\delta)}} \right)^U,$$

and

$$\Pr[X \le (1 - \delta)L] < \left(\frac{e^{-\delta}}{(1 - \delta)^{(1-\delta)}}\right)^L.$$

The second theorem generalizes the first by replacing 0-1 random variables with 0-a_i random variables, where $0 < a_i \le 1$.

Theorem 5.24. *Let $X_1, \ldots, X_n$ be n independent random variables, not necessarily identically distributed, such that each X_i takes either the value 0 or the value a_i for some $0 < a_i \le 1$. Then for $X = \sum_{i=1}^n X_i$ and $\mu = E[X]$, $L \le \mu \le U$, and $\delta > 0$,*

$$\Pr[X \ge (1 + \delta)U] < \left(\frac{e^{\delta}}{(1 + \delta)^{(1+\delta)}}\right)^U,$$

and

$$\Pr[X \le (1 - \delta)L] < \left(\frac{e^{-\delta}}{(1 - \delta)^{(1-\delta)}}\right)^L.$$

These theorems are generalizations of results due to Chernoff and are sometimes called *Chernoff bounds*, since they bound the probability that the sum of variables is far away from its mean.

To prove the bounds, we will need the following commonly used inequality known as *Markov's inequality*.

Lemma 5.25 (Markov's inequality). *If X is a random variable taking on nonnegative values, then $\Pr[X \ge a] \le E[X]/a$ for $a > 0$.*

Proof. Since X takes on nonnegative values, $E[X] \ge a \Pr[X \ge a]$, and the inequality follows. □

Now we can prove Theorem 5.24.

Proof of Theorem 5.24. We prove only the first bound in the theorem; the proof of the other bound is analogous. Note that if $E[X] = 0$, then $X = 0$ and the bound holds trivially, so we can assume $E[X] > 0$ and $E[X_i] > 0$ for some i. We ignore all i such that $E[X_i] = 0$ since $X_i = 0$ for such i. Let $p_i = \Pr[X_i = a_i]$. Since $E[X_i] > 0$, $p_i > 0$. Then $\mu = E[X] = \sum_{i=1}^n p_i a_i \le U$. For any $t > 0$,

$$\Pr[X \ge (1 + \delta)U] = \Pr[e^{tX} \ge e^{t(1+\delta)U}].$$

By Markov's inequality,

$$\Pr[e^{tX} \ge e^{t(1+\delta)U}] \le \frac{E[e^{tX}]}{e^{t(1+\delta)U}}. \tag{5.8}$$

Now

$$E[e^{tX}] = E\left[e^{t\sum_{i=1}^n X_i}\right] = E\left[\prod_{i=1}^n e^{tX_i}\right] = \prod_{i=1}^n E[e^{tX_i}], \tag{5.9}$$

where the equality follows by the independence of the X_i. Then for each i,

$$E[e^{tX_i}] = (1 - p_i) + p_i e^{ta_i} = 1 + p_i(e^{ta_i} - 1).$$

We will show that $e^{ta_i} - 1 \le a_i(e^t - 1)$ for $t > 0$, so that $E[e^{tX_i}] \le 1 + p_i a_i(e^t - 1)$. Using that $1 + x < e^x$ for $x > 0$, and that $t, a_i, p_i > 0$, we obtain

$$E[e^{tX_i}] < e^{p_i a_i(e^t - 1)}.$$

Plugging these back into equation (5.9), we have

$$E[e^{tX}] < \prod_{i=1}^n e^{p_i a_i(e^t - 1)} = e^{\sum_{i=1}^n p_i a_i(e^t - 1)} \le e^{U(e^t - 1)}.$$

Then putting this back into inequality (5.8) and setting $t = \ln(1 + \delta) > 0$, we see that

$$\Pr[X \ge (1 + \delta)U] \le \frac{E[e^{tX}]}{e^{t(1+\delta)U}}$$

$$< \frac{e^{U(e^t - 1)}}{e^{t(1+\delta)U}}$$

$$= \left(\frac{e^\delta}{(1 + \delta)^{(1+\delta)}} \right)^U,$$

as desired.

Finally, to see that $e^{a_i t} - 1 \le a_i(e^t - 1)$ for $t > 0$, let $f(t) = a_i(e^t - 1) - e^{a_i t} - 1$. Then $f'(t) = a_i e^t - a_i e^{a_i t} \ge 0$ for any $t \ge 0$ given that $0 < a_i \le 1$; thus, $f(t)$ is non-decreasing for $t \ge 0$. Since $f(0) = 0$ and the function f is non-decreasing, the inequality holds. $\qquad \square$

The right-hand sides of the inequalities in Theorems 5.23 and 5.24 are a bit complicated, and so it will be useful to consider variants of the results in which the right-hand side is simpler, at the cost of restricting the results somewhat.

Lemma 5.26. *For $0 \le \delta \le 1$, we have that*

$$\left(\frac{e^\delta}{(1 + \delta)^{(1+\delta)}} \right)^U \le e^{-U\delta^2/3},$$

and for $0 \le \delta < 1$, we have that

$$\left(\frac{e^{-\delta}}{(1 - \delta)^{(1-\delta)}} \right)^L \le e^{-L\delta^2/2}.$$

Proof. For the first inequality, we take the logarithm of both sides. We would like to show that

$$U(\delta - (1 + \delta) \ln(1 + \delta)) \le -U\delta^2/3.$$

We observe that the inequality holds for $\delta = 0$; if we can show that the derivative of the left-hand side is no more than that of the right-hand side for $0 \le \delta \le 1$, the inequality will hold for $0 \le \delta \le 1$. Taking derivatives of both sides, we need to show that

$$-U \ln(1 + \delta) \le -2U\delta/3.$$

Letting $f(\delta) = -U \ln(1 + \delta) + 2U\delta/3$, we need to show that $f(\delta) \le 0$ on $[0, 1]$. Note that $f(0) = 0$ and $f(1) \le 0$ since $-\ln 2 \approx -0.693 < -2/3$. As long as the function $f(\delta)$ is convex on $[0, 1]$ (that is, $f''(\delta) \ge 0$), we may conclude that $f(\delta) \le 0$ on $[0, 1]$, in the convex analog of Fact 5.9. We observe that $f'(\delta) = -U/(1 + \delta) + 2U/3$ and $f''(\delta) = U/(1 + \delta)^2$, so that $f''(\delta) \geq 0$ for $\delta \in [0, 1]$, and the inequality is shown.

We turn to the second inequality for the case $0 \leq \delta < 1$. Taking the logarithm of both sides, we would like to show that

$$L(-\delta - (1 - \delta)\ln(1 - \delta)) \leq -L\delta^2/2.$$

The inequality holds for $\delta = 0$, and will hold for $0 < \delta < 1$ if the derivative of the left-hand side is no more than the derivative of the right-hand side for $0 \leq \delta < 1$. Taking derivatives of both sides, we would like to show that

$$L \ln(1 - \delta) \leq -L\delta$$

for $0 \leq \delta < 1$. Again the inequality holds for $\delta = 0$ and will hold for $0 \leq \delta < 1$ if the derivative of the left-hand side is no more than the derivative of the right-hand side for $0 \leq \delta < 1$. Taking derivatives of both sides again, we obtain

$$-L/(1 - \delta) \leq -L,$$

which holds for $0 \leq \delta < 1$. $\qquad\qquad\qquad\qquad\qquad\qquad\qquad\qquad\square$

It will sometimes be useful to provide a bound on the probability that $X \leq (1 - \delta)L$ in the case $\delta = 1$. Notice that since the variables X_i are either 0-1 or 0-a_i this is asking for a bound on the probability that $X = 0$. We can give a bound as follows.

Lemma 5.27. *Let* $X_1, \ldots, X_n$ *be* n *independent random variables, not necessarily identically distributed, such that each* X_i *takes either the value 0 or the value* a_i *for some* $0 < a_i \leq 1$. *Then for* $X = \sum_{i=1}^n X_i$ *and* $\mu = E[X]$, $L \leq \mu$,

$$\Pr[X = 0] < e^{-L}.$$

Proof. We assume $\mu = E[X] > 0$ since otherwise $X = 0$ and $L \leq \mu = 0$ and the bound holds trivially. Let $p_i = \Pr[X_i = a_i]$. Then $\mu = \sum_{i=1}^n a_i p_i$ and

$$\Pr[X = 0] = \prod_{i=1}^n (1 - p_i).$$

Applying the arithmetic-geometric mean inequality from Fact 5.8, we get that

$$\prod_{i=1}^n (1 - p_i) \leq \left[\frac{1}{n} \sum_{i=1}^n (1 - p_i) \right]^n = \left[1 - \frac{1}{n} \sum_{i=1}^n p_i \right]^n.$$

Since each $a_i \leq 1$, we then obtain

$$\left[1 - \frac{1}{n} \sum_{i=1}^n p_i \right]^n \leq \left[1 - \frac{1}{n} \sum_{i=1}^n a_i p_i \right]^n = \left[1 - \frac{1}{n} \mu \right]^n.$$

Then using the fact that $1 - x < e^{-x}$ for $x > 0$, we get

$$\left[1 - \frac{1}{n} \mu \right]^n < e^{-\mu} \leq e^{-L}. \qquad\qquad\qquad\qquad\qquad\square$$

As a corollary, we can then extend the bound of Lemma 5.26 to the case $\delta = 1$. In fact, since the probability that $X < (1 - \delta)L$ for $\delta > 1$ and $L \geq 0$ is 0, we can extend the bound to any positive δ.

Corollary 5.28. *Let $X_1, \ldots, X_n$ be n independent random variables, not necessarily identically distributed, such that each X_i takes either the value 0 or the value a_i for some $a_i \leq 1$. Then for $X = \sum_{i=1}^{n} X_i$ and $\mu = E[X]$, $0 \leq L \leq \mu$, and $\delta > 0$,*

$$\Pr[X \leq (1 - \delta)L] < e^{-L\delta^2/2}.$$

5.11 Integer Multicommodity Flows

To see how Chernoff bounds can be used in the context of randomized rounding, we will apply them to the *minimum-capacity multicommodity flow problem*. In this problem, we are given as input an undirected graph $G = (V, E)$ and k pairs of vertices $s_i, t_i \in V$, $i = 1, \ldots, k$. The goal is to find, for each $i = 1, \ldots, k$, a single simple path from s_i to t_i so as to minimize the maximum number of paths containing the same edge. This problem arises in routing wires on chips. In this problem, k wires need to be routed, each wire from some point s_i on the chip to another point t_i on the chip. Wires must be routed through channels on the chip, which correspond to edges in a graph. The goal is to route the wires so as minimize the channel capacity needed, that is, the number of wires routed through the same channel. The problem as stated here is a special case of a more interesting problem, since often the wires must join up three or more points on a chip.

We give an integer programming formulation of the problem. Let $\mathcal{P}_i$ be the set of all possible simple paths P in G from s_i to t_i, where P is the set of edges in the path. We create a 0-1 variable x_P for each path $P \in \mathcal{P}_i$ to indicate when path P from s_i to t_i is used. Then the total number of paths using an edge $e \in E$ is simply $\sum_{P:e\in P} x_P$. We create another decision variable W to denote the maximum number of paths using an edge, so that our objective function is to minimize W. We have the constraint that

$$\sum_{P:e\in P} x_P \leq W$$

for each edge $e \in E$. Finally, we need to choose some path $P \in \mathcal{P}_i$ for every s_i-t_i pair, so that

$$\sum_{P\in\mathcal{P}_i} x_P = 1$$

for each $i = 1, \ldots, k$. This gives us the following integer programming formulation of the minimum-capacity multicommodity flow problem:

$$
\begin{aligned}
\text{minimize} \quad & W & & (5.10) \\
\text{subject to} \quad & \sum_{P\in\mathcal{P}_i} x_P = 1, & & i = 1, \ldots, k, \\
& \sum_{P:e\in P} x_P \leq W, & & e \in E, & (5.11) \\
& x_P \in \{0, 1\}, & & \forall P \in \mathcal{P}_i, i = 1, \ldots, k.
\end{aligned}
$$

The integer program can be relaxed to a linear program by replacing the constraints $x_P \in \{0, 1\}$ with $x_P \geq 0$. We claim for now that this linear program can be solved in polynomial time and that at most a polynomial number of variables x_P of an optimal solution can be nonzero.

We now apply randomized rounding to obtain a solution to the problem. For $i = 1, \ldots, k$, we choose exactly one path $P \in \mathcal{P}_i$ according to the probability distribution x_P^* on paths $P \in \mathcal{P}_i$, where x^* is an optimal solution of value W^*.

Assuming W^* is large enough, we can show that the total number of paths going through any edge is close to W^* by using the Chernoff bound from Theorem 5.23. Let n be the number of vertices in the graph. Recall that in Section 1.7 we said that a probabilistic event happens with high probability if the probability that it does not occur is at most n^{-c} for some $c \geq 1$.

Theorem 5.29. *If $W^* \geq c \ln n$ for some constant c, then with high probability, the total number of paths using any edge is at most $W^* + \sqrt{c W^* \ln n}$.*

Proof. For each $e \in E$, define random variables X_e^i, where $X_e^i = 1$ if the chosen s_i-t_i path uses edge e, and $X_e^i = 0$ otherwise. Then the number of paths using edge e is $Y_e = \sum_{i=1}^k X_e^i$. We want to bound $\max_{e \in E} Y_e$, and show that this is close to the LP value W^*. Certainly

$$E[Y_e] = \sum_{i=1}^k \sum_{P \in \mathcal{P}_i : e \in P} x_P^* = \sum_{P : e \in P} x_P^* \leq W^*,$$

by constraint (5.11) from the LP. For a fixed edge e, the random variables X_e^i are independent, so we can apply the Chernoff bound of Theorem 5.23. Set $\delta = \sqrt{(c \ln n)/W^*}$. Since $W^* \geq c \ln n$ by assumption, it follows that $\delta \leq 1$. Then by Theorem 5.23 and Lemma 5.26 with $U = W^*$,

$$\Pr[Y_e \geq (1 + \delta) W^*] < e^{-W^* \delta^2 / 3} = e^{-(c \ln n)/3} = \frac{1}{n^{c/3}}.$$

Also $(1 + \delta) W^* = W^* + \sqrt{c W^* \ln n}$. Since there can be at most n^2 edges,

$$\Pr\left[\max_{e \in E} Y_e \geq (1 + \delta) W^*\right] \leq \sum_{e \in E} \Pr[Y_e \geq (1 + \delta) W^*]$$

$$\leq n^2 \cdot \frac{1}{n^{c/3}} = n^{2 - c/3}.$$

For a constant $c \geq 12$, this ensures that the theorem statement fails to hold with probability at most $\frac{1}{n^2}$, and by increasing c we can make the probability as small as we like. $\qquad \square$

Observe that since $W^* \geq c \ln n$, the theorem above guarantees that the randomized algorithm produces a solution of no more than $2W^* \leq 2\,\mathrm{OPT}$. However, the algorithm might produce a solution considerably closer to optimal if $W^* \gg c \ln n$. We also observe the following corollary.

Corollary 5.30. *If $W^* \geq 1$, then with high probability, the total number of paths using any edge is $O(\log n) \cdot W^*$.*

Proof. We repeat the proof above with $U = (c \ln n) W^*$ and $\delta = 1$. $\qquad \square$

In fact, the statement of the corollary can be sharpened by replacing the $O(\log n)$ with $O(\log n / \log \log n)$ (see Exercise 5.13).

To solve the linear program in polynomial time, we show that it is equivalent to a polynomially sized linear program; we leave this as an exercise to the reader (Exercise 5.14, to be precise).

5.12 Random Sampling and Coloring Dense 3-Colorable Graphs

In this section we turn to another application of Chernoff bounds. We consider coloring a δ-dense 3-colorable graph. We say that a graph is *dense* if for some constant α the number of edges in the graph is at least $\alpha\binom{n}{2}$; in other words, some constant fraction of the edges that could exist in the graph do exist. A δ-*dense* graph is a special case of a dense graph. A graph is δ-dense if every node has at least δn neighbors for some constant δ; that is, every node has some constant fraction of the neighbors it could have. Finally, a graph is *k-colorable* if each of the nodes can be assigned exactly one of k colors in such a way that no edge has its two endpoints assigned the same color. In general, it is NP-complete to decide whether a graph is 3-colorable; in fact, the following is known.

Theorem 5.31. *It is NP-hard to decide if a graph can be colored with only three colors, or needs at least five colors.*

Theorem 5.32. *Assuming a variant of the unique games conjecture, for any constant $k > 3$, it is NP-hard to decide if a graph can be colored with only three colors, or needs at least k colors.*

In Sections 6.5 and 13.2 we will discuss approximation algorithms for coloring any 3-colorable graph. Here we will show that with high probability we can properly color any δ-dense 3-colorable graph in polynomial time. While this is not an approximation algorithm, it is a useful application of Chernoff bounds, which we will use again in Section 12.4.

In this case, we use the bounds to show that if we know the correct coloring for a small, randomly chosen sample of a δ-dense graph, we can give a polynomial-time algorithm that with high probability successfully colors the rest of the graph. This would seem to pose a problem, though, since we do not know the coloring for the sample. Nevertheless, if the sample is no larger than $O(\log n)$, we can enumerate all possible colorings of the sample in polynomial time, and run the algorithm above for each coloring. Since one of the colorings of the sample will be the correct one, for at least one of the possible colorings of the sample the algorithm will result in a correct coloring of the graph with high probability.

More specifically, given a δ-dense graph, we will select a random subset $S \subseteq V$ of $O((\ln n)/\delta)$ vertices by including each vertex in the subset with probability $(3c \ln n)/\delta n$ for some constant c. We will show first that the set size is no more than $(6c \ln n)/\delta$ with high probability, and then that with high probability, every vertex has at least one neighbor in S. Thus, given a correct coloring of S, we can use the information about the coloring of S to deduce the colors of the rest of the vertices. Since each vertex has a neighbor in S, its color is restricted to be one of the two remaining colors, and this turns out to be enough of a restriction that we can infer the remaining coloring. Finally, although we do not know the correct coloring of S we can run this algorithm for each of the $3^{(6c \ln n)/\delta} = n^{O(c/\delta)}$ possible colorings of S. One of the colorings of S will be the correct coloring, and thus in at least one run of the algorithm we will be able to color the graph successfully.

Lemma 5.33. *With probability at most $n^{-c/\delta}$, the set S has size $|S| \geq (6c \ln n)/\delta$.*

Proof. We use the Chernoff bound (Theorem 5.23 and Lemma 5.26). Let X_i be a 0-1 random variable indicating whether vertex i is included in S. Then since each vertex is included with probability $3c \ln n/\delta n$, $\mu = E[\sum_{i=1}^n X_i] = (3c \ln n)/\delta$. Applying the lemma with $U = (3c \ln n)/\delta$, the probability that $|S| \geq 2U$ is at most $e^{-\mu/3} = n^{-c/\delta}$. $\quad\square$

Lemma 5.34. *The probability that a given vertex $v \notin S$ has no neighbor in S is at most n^{-3c}.*

Proof. Let X_i be a 0-1 random variable indicating whether the ith neighbor of v is in S or not. Then $\mu = E[\sum_i X_i] \geq 3c \ln n$, since v has at least δn neighbors. Then applying Lemma 5.27 with $L = 3c \ln n$, the probability that v has no neighbors in S is no more than $\Pr[\sum_i X_i = 0] \leq e^{-L} = n^{-3c}$. $\quad\square$

Corollary 5.35. *With probability at least $1 - 2n^{-(c-1)}$, $|S| \leq (6c \ln n)/\delta$ and every $v \notin S$ has at least one neighbor in S.*

Proof. This follows from Lemmas 5.33 and 5.34. The probability that both statements of the lemma are true is at least one minus the sum of the probabilities that either statement is false. The probability that every $v \notin S$ has no neighbor in S is at worst n times the probability that a given vertex $v \notin S$ has no neighbor in S. Since $\delta \leq 1$, the overall probability that both statements are true is at least

$$1 - n^{-c/\delta} - n \cdot n^{-3c} \geq 1 - 2n^{-(c-1)}. \qquad \square$$

Now we assume we have some coloring of the vertices in S, not necessarily one that is consistent with the correct coloring of the graph. We also assume that every vertex not in S has at least one neighbor in S. We further assume that the coloring of S is such that every edge with both endpoints in S has differently colored endpoints, since otherwise this is clearly not a correct coloring of the graph. Assume we color the graph with colors $\{0, 1, 2\}$. Given a vertex $v \notin S$, because it has some neighbor in S colored with some color $n(v) \in \{0, 1, 2\}$, we know that v cannot be colored with color $n(v)$. Possibly v has other neighbors in S with colors other than $n(v)$. Either this forces the color of v or there is no way we can successfully color v; in the latter case our current coloring of S must not have been correct, and we terminate. If the color of v is not determined, then we create a binary variable $x(v)$, which if true indicates that we color v with color $n(v) + 1 \pmod 3$, and if false indicates that we color v with color $n(v) - 1 \pmod 3$. Now every edge $(u, v) \in E$ for $u, v \notin S$ imposes the constraint $n(u) \neq n(v)$. To capture this, we create an instance of the maximum satisfiability problem such that all clauses are satisfiable if and only if the vertices not in S can be correctly colored. For each possible setting of the Boolean variables $x(u)$

and $x(v)$ that would cause $n(u) = n(v)$, we create a disjunction of $x(u)$ and $x(v)$ that is false if it implies $n(u) = n(v)$; for example, if $x(u) = $ true and $x(v) = $ false implies that $n(u) = n(v)$, then we create a clause $(\overline{x(u)} \vee x(v))$. Since G is 3-colorable, given a correct coloring of S, there exists a setting of the variables $x(v)$ that satisfies all the clauses. Since each clause has two variables, it is possible to determine in polynomial time whether the instance is satisfiable or not; we leave it as an exercise to the reader to prove this (Exercise 6.3). Obviously if we find a setting of the variables that satisfies all constraints, this implies a correct coloring of the entire graph, whereas if the constraints are not satisfiable, our current coloring of S must not have been correct.

In Section 12.4, we'll revisit the idea from this section of drawing a small random sample of a graph and using it to determine the overall solution for the maximum cut problem in dense graphs.

Exercises

5.1 In the *maximum k-cut problem*, we are given an undirected graph $G = (V, E)$, and non-negative weights $w_{ij} \geq 0$ for all $(i, j) \in E$. The goal is to partition the vertex set V into k parts $V_1, \ldots, V_k$ so as to maximize the weight of all edges whose endpoints are in different parts (i.e., $\max_{(i,j) \in E : i \in V_a, j \in V_b, a \neq b} w_{ij}$).
Give a randomized $\frac{k-1}{k}$-approximation algorithm for the MAX k-CUT problem.

5.2 Consider the following greedy algorithm for the maximum cut problem. We suppose the vertices are numbered $1, \ldots, n$. In the first iteration, the algorithm places vertex 1 in U. In the kth iteration of the algorithm, we will place vertex k in either U or W. In order to decide which choice to make, we will look at all the edges F that have the vertex k as one endpoint and whose other endpoint is $1, \ldots, k - 1$, so that $F = \{(j, k) \in E : 1 \leq j \leq k - 1\}$. We choose to put vertex k in U or W depending on which of these two choices maximizes the number of edges of F being in the cut.

(a) Prove that this algorithm is a 1/2-approximation algorithm for the maximum cut problem.

(b) Prove that this algorithm is equivalent to the derandomization of the maximum cut algorithm of Section 5.1 via the method of conditional expectations.

5.3 In the *maximum directed cut problem* (sometimes called MAX DICUT), we are given as input a directed graph $G = (V, A)$. Each directed arc $(i, j) \in A$ has nonnegative weight $w_{ij} \geq 0$. The goal is to partition V into two sets U and $W = V - U$ so as to maximize the total weight of the arcs going from U to W (that is, arcs (i, j) with $i \in U$ and $j \in W$). Give a randomized $\frac{1}{4}$-approximation algorithm for this problem.

5.4 Consider the nonlinear randomized rounding algorithm for MAX SAT as given in Section 5.6. Prove that using randomized rounding with the linear function $f(y_i) = \frac{1}{2} y_i + \frac{1}{4}$ also gives a $\frac{3}{4}$-approximation algorithm for MAX SAT.

5.5 Consider the nonlinear randomized rounding algorithm for MAX SAT as given in Section 5.6. Prove that using randomized rounding with the piecewise linear function

$$f(y_i) = \begin{cases} \frac{3}{4} y_i + \frac{1}{4} & \text{for } 0 \leq y_i \leq \frac{1}{3} \\ 1/2 & \text{for } \frac{1}{3} \leq y_i \leq \frac{2}{3} \\ \frac{3}{4} y_i & \text{for } \frac{2}{3} \leq y_i \leq 1 \end{cases}$$

also gives a $\frac{3}{4}$-approximation algorithm for MAX SAT.

5.6 Consider again the maximum directed cut problem from Exercise 5.3.

(a) Show that the following integer program models the maximum directed cut problem:

$$\text{maximize} \sum_{(i,j)\in A} w_{ij} z_{ij}$$

$$\begin{aligned} \text{subject to} \quad z_{ij} &\le x_i, & \forall(i,j) \in A, \\ z_{ij} &\le 1 - x_j, & \forall(i,j) \in A, \\ x_i &\in \{0,1\}, & \forall i \in V, \\ 0 \le z_{ij} &\le 1, & \forall(i,j) \in A. \end{aligned}$$

(b) Consider a randomized rounding algorithm for the maximum directed cut problem that solves a linear programming relaxation of the integer program and puts vertex $i \in U$ with probability $1/4 + x_i/2$. Show that this gives a randomized $1/2$-approximation algorithm for the maximum directed cut problem.

5.7 In this exercise, we consider how to derandomize the randomized rounding algorithm for the set cover problem given in Section 1.7. We would like to apply the method of conditional expectations, but we need to ensure that at the end of the process we obtain a valid set cover. Let X_j be a random variable indicating whether set S_j is included in the solution. Then if w_j is the weight of set S_j, let W be the weight of the set cover obtained by randomized rounding, so that $W = \sum_{j=1}^m w_j X_j$. Let Z be a random variable such that $Z = 1$ if randomized rounding does not produce a valid set cover, and $Z = 0$ if it does. Then consider applying the method of conditional expectations to the objective function $W + \lambda Z$ for some choice of $\lambda \ge 0$. Show that for the proper choice of λ, the method of conditional expectations applied to the randomized rounding algorithm yields an $O(\ln n)$-approximation algorithm for the set cover problem that always produces a set cover.

5.8 Consider a variation of the maximum satisfiability problem in which all variables occur positively in each clause, and there is an additional nonnegative weight $v_i \ge 0$ for each Boolean variable x_i. The goal is now to set the Boolean variables to maximize the total weight of the satisfied clauses plus the total weight of variables set to be false. Give an integer programming formulation for this problem, with 0-1 variables y_i to indicate whether x_i is set true. Show that a randomized rounding of the linear program in which variable x_l is set true with probability $1 - \lambda + \lambda y_i^*$ gives a $2(\sqrt{2} - 1)$-approximation algorithm for some appropriate setting of λ; note that $2(\sqrt{2} - 1) \approx 0.828$.

5.9 Recall the maximum coverage problem from Exercise 2.11; in it, we are given a set of elements E, and m subsets of elements $S_1, \ldots, S_m \subseteq E$ with a nonnegative weight $w_j \ge 0$ for each subset S_j. We would like to find a subset $S \subseteq E$ of size k that maximizes the total weight of the subsets covered by S, where S covers S_j if $S \cap S_j \neq \emptyset$.

(a) Show that the following nonlinear integer program models the maximum coverage problem:

$$\text{maximize} \sum_{j\in[m]} w_j \left(1 - \prod_{e\in S_j}(1 - x_e) \right)$$

$$\text{subject to} \sum_{e\in E} x_e = k,$$

$$x_e \in \{0,1\}, \quad \forall e \in E.$$

(b) Show that the following linear program is a relaxation of the maximum coverage problem:

$$\text{maximize} \sum_{j \in [m]} w_j z_j$$

$$\text{subject to} \sum_{e \in S_j} x_e \geq z_j, \qquad \forall j \in [m],$$

$$\sum_{e \in E} x_e = k,$$

$$0 \leq z_j \leq 1, \qquad \forall j \in [m],$$

$$0 \leq x_e \leq 1, \qquad \forall e \in E.$$

(c) Using the pipage rounding technique from Exercise 4.7, give an algorithm that deterministically rounds the optimal LP solution to an integer solution and has a performance guarantee of $1 - \frac{1}{e}$.

5.10 In the *uniform labeling problem*, we are given a graph $G = (V, E)$, costs $c_e \geq 0$ for all $e \in E$, and a set of labels L that can be assigned to the vertices of V. There is a nonnegative cost $c_v^i \geq 0$ for assigning label $i \in L$ to vertex $v \in V$, and an edge $e = (u, v)$ incurs cost c_e if u and v are assigned different labels. The goal of the problem is to assign each vertex in V a label so as to minimize the total cost.

We give an integer programming formulation of the problem. Let the variable $x_v^i \in \{0, 1\}$ be 1 if vertex v is assigned label $i \in L$, and 0 otherwise. Let the variable z_e^i be 1 if exactly one of the two endpoints of the edge e is assigned label i, and 0 otherwise. Then the integer programming formulation is as follows:

$$\text{minimize} \frac{1}{2} \sum_{e \in E} c_e \sum_{i \in L} z_e^i + \sum_{v \in V, i \in L} c_v^i x_v^i$$

$$\text{subject to} \sum_{i \in L} x_v^i = 1, \qquad \forall v \in V,$$

$$z_e^i \geq x_u^i - x_v^i, \quad \forall (u, v) \in E, \forall i \in L,$$

$$z_e^i \geq x_v^i - x_u^i, \quad \forall (u, v) \in E, \forall i \in L,$$

$$z_e^i \in \{0, 1\}, \qquad \forall e \in E, \forall i \in L,$$

$$x_v^i \in \{0, 1\}, \qquad \forall v \in V, \forall i \in L.$$

(a) Prove that the integer programming formulation models the uniform labeling problem.

Consider now the following algorithm. First, the algorithm solves the linear programming relaxation of the integer program above. The algorithm then proceeds in phases. In each phase, it picks a label $i \in L$ uniformly at random, and a number $\alpha \in [0, 1]$ uniformly at random. For each vertex $v \in V$ that has not yet been assigned a label, we assign it label i if $\alpha \leq x_v^i$.

(b) Suppose that vertex $v \in V$ has not yet been assigned a label. Prove that the probability that v is assigned label $i \in L$ in the next phase is exactly $x_v^i / |L|$, and the probability that it is assigned a label in the next phase is exactly $1/|L|$. Further prove that the probability that v is assigned label i by the algorithm is exactly x_v^i.

(c) We say that an edge e is *separated by a phase* if both endpoints were not assigned labels prior to the phase, and exactly one of the endpoints is assigned a label in this phase. Prove that the probability that an edge e is separated by a phase is $\frac{1}{|L|} \sum_{i \in L} z_e^i$.

(d) Prove that the probability that the endpoints of edge e receive different labels is at most $\sum_{i \in L} z_e^i$.

(e) Prove that the algorithm is a 2-approximation algorithm for the uniform labeling problem.

5.11 Prove Lemma 5.22, and show that the integer programming solution (y^*, C^*) described at the end of Section 5.9 must be optimal for the integer program (5.3).

5.12 Using randomized rounding and First Fit, give a randomized polynomial-time algorithm for the bin-packing problem that uses $\rho \cdot \text{OPT}(I) + k$ bins for some $\rho < 2$ and some small constant k. One idea is to consider the linear program from Section 4.6.

5.13 Show that the $O(\log n)$ factor in Corollary 5.30 can be replaced with $O(\log n / \log \log n)$ by using Theorem 5.23.

5.14 Show that there is a linear programming relaxation for the integer multicommodity flow problem of Section 5.10 that is equivalent to the linear program (5.10) but has a number of variables and constraints that are bounded by a polynomial in the input size of the flow problem.

Chapter Notes

The textbooks of Mitzenmacher and Upfal [226] and Motwani and Raghavan [228] give more extensive treatments of randomized algorithms.

A 1967 paper of Erdős [99] on the maximum cut problem showed that sampling a solution uniformly at random as in Theorem 5.3 gives a solution whose expected value is at least half the sum of the edge weights. This is one of the first randomized approximation algorithms of which we are aware. This algorithm can also be viewed as a randomized version of a deterministic algorithm given by Sahni and Gonzalez [257] (the deterministic algorithm of Sahni and Gonzalez is given in Exercise 5.2).

Raghavan and Thompson [247] were the first to introduce the idea of the randomized rounding of a linear programming relaxation. The result for integer multicommodity flows in Section 5.11 is from their paper.

Random sampling and randomized rounding are most easily applied to unconstrained problems, such as the maximum satisfiability problem and the maximum cut problem, in which any solution is feasible. Even problems such as the prize-collecting Steiner tree problem and the uncapacitated facility location problem can be viewed as unconstrained problems: we need merely to select a set of vertices to span or facilities to open. Randomized approximation algorithms for constrained problems exist, but are much rarer.

The results for the maximum satisfiability problem in this chapter are due to a variety of authors. The simple randomized algorithm of Section 5.1 is given by Yannakakis [293] as a randomized variant of an earlier deterministic algorithm introduced by Johnson [179]. The "biased coins" algorithm of Section 5.3 is a similar randomization of an algorithm of Lieberherr and Specker [216]. The randomized rounding, "better of two," and nonlinear randomized rounding algorithms in Sections 5.4, 5.5, and 5.6, respectively, are due to Goemans and Williamson [137].

The derandomization of randomized algorithms is a major topic of study. The method of conditional expectations given in Section 5.2 is implicit in the work of Erdős and Selfridge [101], and has been developed by Spencer [271].

The randomized algorithm for the prize-collecting Steiner tree problem in Section 5.7 is an unpublished result of Goemans.

The algorithm of Section 5.8 for uncapacitated facility location is due to Chudak and Shmoys [77].

The scheduling algorithm of Section 5.9 is due to Schulz and Skutella [261]. The algorithm for solving the integer programming relaxation of this problem is due to Goemans [132], and the α-point algorithm that uses a single value of α is also due to Goemans [133].

Chernoff [71] gives the general ideas used in the proof of Chernoff bounds. Our proofs of these bounds follow those of Mitzenmacher and Upfal [226] and Motwani and Raghavan [228].

The randomized algorithm for 3-coloring a dense 3-colorable graph is due to Arora, Karger, and Karpinski [16]; a deterministic algorithm for the problem had earlier been given by Edwards [97]. Theorems 5.31 and 5.32 are due to Khanna, Linial, and Safra [190] (see also Guruswami and Khanna [152]) and Dinur, Mossel, and Regev [90], respectively.

Exercises 5.4 and 5.5 are due to Goemans and Williamson [137]. Exercise 5.6 is due to Trevisan [279, 280]. Exercise 5.7 is due to Norton [237]. Ageev and Sviridenko [1] gave the algorithm and analysis in Exercise 5.8, and Exercise 5.9 is also due to Ageev and Sviridenko [2, 3]. The algorithm for the uniform labeling problem in Exercise 5.10 is due to Kleinberg and Tardos [197]; the uniform labeling problem models a problem arising in image processing. Exercise 5.12 is an unpublished result of Williamson.

CHAPTER 6

Randomized Rounding of Semidefinite Programs

We now turn to a new tool that gives substantially improved performance guarantees for some problems. So far we have used linear programming relaxations to design and analyze various approximation algorithms. In this section, we show how nonlinear programming relaxations can give us better algorithms than we know how to obtain via linear programming; in particular we use a type of nonlinear program called a semidefinite program. Part of the power of semidefinite programming is that semidefinite programs can be solved in polynomial time.

We begin with a brief overview of semidefinite programming. Throughout the chapter we assume some basic knowledge of vectors and linear algebra; see the notes at the end of the chapter for suggested references on these topics. We then give an application of semidefinite programming to approximating the maximum cut problem. The algorithm for this problem introduces a technique of rounding the semidefinite program by choosing a random hyperplane. We then explore other problems for which choosing a random hyperplane, or multiple random hyperplanes, is useful, including approximating quadratic programs, approximating clustering problems, and coloring 3-colorable graphs.

6.1 A Brief Introduction to Semidefinite Programming

Semidefinite programming uses symmetric, positive semidefinite matrices, so we briefly review a few properties of these matrices. In what follows, X^T is the transpose of the matrix X, and vectors $v \in \Re^n$ are assumed to be column vectors, so that $v^T v$ is the inner product of v with itself, while vv^T is an n by n matrix.

Definition 6.1. *A matrix $X \in \Re^{n \times n}$ is positive semidefinite iff for all $y \in \Re^n$, $y^T X y \geq 0$.*

Sometimes we abbreviate "positive semidefinite" as "psd." Sometimes we will write $X \succeq 0$ to denote that a matrix X is positive semidefinite. Symmetric positive semidefinite matrices have some special properties that we list below. From here on, we will generally assume (unless otherwise stated) that any psd matrix X is also symmetric.

Fact 6.2. *If $X \in \Re^{n \times n}$ is a symmetric matrix, then the following statements are equivalent:*

1. *X is psd;*
2. *X has nonnegative eigenvalues;*
3. *$X = V^T V$ for some $V \in \Re^{m \times n}$ where $m \le n$;*
4. *$X = \sum_{i=1}^{n} \lambda_i w_i w_i^T$ for some $\lambda_i \ge 0$ and vectors $w_i \in \Re^n$ such that $w_i^T w_i = 1$ and $w_i^T w_j = 0$ for $i \ne j$.*

A *semidefinite program (SDP)* is similar to a linear program in that there is a linear objective function and linear constraints. In addition, however, a square symmetric matrix of variables can be constrained to be positive semidefinite. Below is an example in which the variables are x_{ij} for $1 \le i, j \le n$:

$$\text{maximize or minimize} \quad \sum_{i,j} c_{ij} x_{ij} \tag{6.1}$$

$$\text{subject to} \quad \sum_{i,j} a_{ijk} x_{ij} = b_k, \quad \forall k,$$

$$x_{ij} = x_{ji}, \quad \forall i, j,$$

$$X = (x_{ij}) \succeq 0.$$

Given some technical conditions, semidefinite programs can be solved to within an additive error of ϵ in time that is polynomial in the size of the input and $\log(1/\epsilon)$. We explain the technical conditions in more detail in the notes at the end of the chapter. We will usually ignore the additive error when discussing semidefinite programs and assume that the SDPs can be solved exactly, since the algorithms we will use do not assume exact solutions, and one can usually analyze the algorithm that has additive error in the same way with only a small loss in performance guarantee.

We will often use semidefinite programming in the form of *vector programming*. The variables of vector programs are vectors $v_i \in \Re^n$, where the dimension n of the space is the number of vectors in the vector program. The vector program has an objective function and constraints that are linear in the inner product of these vectors. We write the inner product of v_i and v_j as $v_i \cdot v_j$, or sometimes as $v_i^T v_j$. Below we give an example of a vector program:

$$\text{maximize or minimize} \quad \sum_{i,j} c_{ij} (v_i \cdot v_j) \tag{6.2}$$

$$\text{subject to} \quad \sum_{i,j} a_{ijk} (v_i \cdot v_j) = b_k, \quad \forall k,$$

$$v_i \in \Re^n, \quad i = 1, \ldots, n.$$

We claim that in fact the SDP (6.1) and the vector program (6.2) are equivalent. This follows from Fact 6.2; in particular, it follows since a symmetric X is psd if and only if $X = V^T V$ for some matrix V. Given a solution to the SDP (6.1), we can take the solution X, compute in polynomial time a matrix V for which $X = V^T V$ (to within small error, which we again will ignore), and set v_i to be the ith column of V. Then $x_{ij} = v_i^T v_j = v_i \cdot v_j$, and the v_i are a feasible solution of the same value to the vector program (6.2). Similarly, given a solution v_i to the vector program, we construct a matrix V whose ith column is v_i, and let $X = V^T V$. Then X is symmetric and psd, with $x_{ij} = v_i \cdot v_j$, so that X is a feasible solution of the same value for the SDP (6.1).

6.2 Finding Large Cuts

In this section, we show how to use semidefinite programming to find an improved approximation algorithm for the maximum cut problem, or MAX CUT problem, which we introduced in Section 5.1. Recall that for this problem, the input is an undirected graph $G = (V, E)$, and nonnegative weights $w_{ij} \geq 0$ for each edge $(i, j) \in E$. The goal is to partition the vertex set into two parts, U and $W = V - U$, so as to maximize the weight of the edges whose two endpoints are in different parts, one in U and one in W. In Section 5.1, we gave a $\frac{1}{2}$-approximation algorithm for the maximum cut problem.

We will now use semidefinite programming to give a 0.878-approximation algorithm for the problem in general graphs. We start by considering the following formulation of the maximum cut problem:

$$\text{maximize} \quad \frac{1}{2} \sum_{(i,j) \in E} w_{ij}(1 - y_i y_j) \tag{6.3}$$

$$\text{subject to } y_i \in \{-1, +1\}, \qquad i = 1, \ldots, n.$$

We claim that if we can solve this formulation, then we can solve the MAX CUT problem.

Lemma 6.3. *The program (6.3) models the maximum cut problem.*

Proof. Consider the cut $U = \{i : y_i = -1\}$ and $W = \{i : y_i = +1\}$. Note that if an edge (i, j) is in this cut, then $y_i y_j = -1$, while if the edge is not in the cut, $y_i y_j = 1$. Thus,

$$\frac{1}{2} \sum_{(i,j) \in E} w_{ij}(1 - y_i y_j)$$

gives the weight of all the edges in the cut. Hence, finding the setting of the y_i to ± 1 that maximizes this sum gives the maximum-weight cut. □

We can now consider the following vector programming relaxation of the program (6.3):

$$\text{maximize} \quad \frac{1}{2} \sum_{(i,j) \in E} w_{ij}(1 - v_i \cdot v_j) \tag{6.4}$$

$$\text{subject to } v_i \cdot v_i = 1, \qquad i = 1, \ldots, n,$$

$$v_i \in \Re^n, \qquad i = 1, \ldots, n.$$

This program is a relaxation of (6.3) since we can take any feasible solution y and produce a feasible solution to this program of the same value by setting

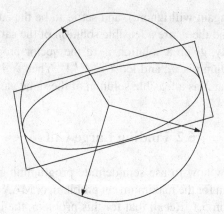

Figure 6.1. An illustration of a random hyperplane.

$v_i = (y_i, 0, 0, \ldots, 0)$: clearly $v_i \cdot v_i = 1$ and $v_i \cdot v_j = y_i y_j$ for this solution. Thus, if Z_{VP} is the value of an optimal solution to the vector program, it must be the case that $Z_{VP} \geq \text{OPT}$.

We can solve (6.4) in polynomial time. We would now like to round the solution to obtain a near-optimal cut. To do this, we introduce a form of randomized rounding suitable for vector programming. In particular, we pick a random vector $r = (r_1, \ldots, r_n)$ by drawing each component from $\mathcal{N}(0, 1)$, the normal distribution with mean 0 and variance 1. The normal distribution can be simulated by an algorithm that draws repeatedly from the uniform distribution on $[0, 1]$. Then given a solution to (6.4), we iterate through all the vertices and put $i \in U$ if $v_i \cdot r \geq 0$ and $i \in W$ otherwise.

Another way of looking at this algorithm is that we consider the hyperplane with normal r containing the origin. All vectors v_i lie on the unit sphere, since $v_i \cdot v_i = 1$ and they are unit vectors. The hyperplane with normal r containing the origin splits the sphere in half; all vertices in one half (the half such that $v_i \cdot r \geq 0$) are put into U, and all vertices in the other half are put into W (see Figure 6.1). As we will see below, the vector $r/\|r\|$ is uniform over the unit sphere, so this is equivalent to randomly splitting the unit sphere in half. For this reason, this technique is sometimes called *choosing a random hyperplane*.

To prove that this is a good approximation algorithm, we need the following facts.

Fact 6.4. *The normalization of r, $r/\|r\|$, is uniformly distributed over the n-dimensional unit sphere.*

Fact 6.5. *The projections of r onto two unit vectors e_1 and e_2 are independent and are normally distributed with mean 0 and variance 1 iff e_1 and e_2 are orthogonal.*

Corollary 6.6. *Let r' be the projection of r onto a 2-dimensional plane. Then the normalization of r', $r'/\|r'\|$, is uniformly distributed on a unit circle in the plane.*

We now begin the proof that choosing a random hyperplane gives a 0.878-approximation algorithm for the problem. We will need the following two lemmas.

Lemma 6.7. *The probability that edge (i, j) is in the cut is $\frac{1}{\pi} \arccos(v_i \cdot v_j)$.*

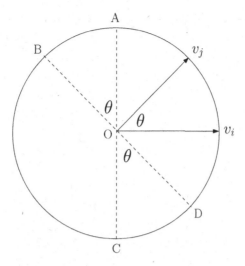

Figure 6.2. Figure for proof of Lemma 6.7.

Proof. Let r' be the projection of r onto the plane defined by v_i and v_j. If $r = r' + r''$, then r'' is orthogonal to both v_i and v_j, and $v_i \cdot r = v_i \cdot (r' + r'') = v_i \cdot r'$. Similarly, $v_j \cdot r = v_j \cdot r'$.

Consider Figure 6.2, where line AC is perpendicular to the vector v_i and line BD is perpendicular to the vector v_j. By Corollary 6.6, the vector r' with its tail at the origin O is oriented with respect to the vector v_i by an angle α chosen uniformly from $[0, 2\pi)$. If r' is to the right of the line AC, v_i will have a nonnegative inner product with r', otherwise not. If r' is above the line BD, v_j will have nonnegative inner product with r', otherwise not. Thus, we have $i \in W$ and $j \in U$ if r' is in the sector AB and $i \in U$ and $j \in W$ if r' is in the sector CD. If the angle formed by v_i and v_j is θ radians, then the angles $\angle AOB$ and $\angle COD$ are also θ radians. Hence, the fraction of values for which α, the angle of r', corresponds to the event in which (i, j) is in the cut is $2\theta/2\pi$. Thus, the probability that (i, j) is in the cut is $\frac{\theta}{\pi}$. We know that $v_i \cdot v_j = \|v_i\| \|v_j\| \cos\theta$. Since v_i and v_j are both unit length vectors, we have that $\theta = \arccos(v_i \cdot v_j)$, which completes the proof of the lemma. □

Lemma 6.8. *For $x \in [-1, 1]$,*

$$\frac{1}{\pi} \arccos(x) \geq 0.878 \cdot \frac{1}{2}(1 - x).$$

Proof. The proof follows from simple calculus. See Figure 6.3 for an illustration. □

Theorem 6.9. *Rounding the vector program (6.4) by choosing a random hyperplane is a 0.878-approximation algorithm for the maximum cut problem.*

Proof. Let X_{ij} be a random variable for edge (i, j) such that $X_{ij} = 1$ if (i, j) is in the cut given by the algorithm, and 0 otherwise. Let W be a random variable that gives the

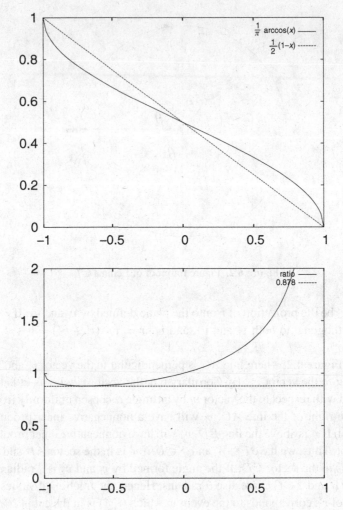

Figure 6.3. Illustration of Lemma 6.8. The upper figure shows plots of the functions $\frac{1}{\pi}\arccos(x)$ and $\frac{1}{2}(1-x)$. The lower figure shows a plot of the ratio of the two functions.

weight of the cut; that is, $W = \sum_{(i,j)\in E} w_{ij} X_{ij}$. Then by Lemma 6.7,

$$E[W] = \sum_{(i,j)\in E} w_{ij} \cdot \Pr[\text{edge } (i,j) \text{ is in cut}] = \sum_{(i,j)\in E} w_{ij} \cdot \frac{1}{\pi}\arccos(v_i \cdot v_j).$$

By Lemma 6.8, we can bound each term $\frac{1}{\pi}\arccos(v_i \cdot v_j)$ below by $0.878 \cdot \frac{1}{2}(1 - v_i \cdot v_j)$, so that

$$E[W] \geq 0.878 \cdot \frac{1}{2} \sum_{(i,j)\in E} w_{ij}(1 - v_i \cdot v_j) = 0.878 \cdot Z_{VP} \geq 0.878 \cdot \text{OPT}. \qquad \square$$

We know that $Z_{VP} \geq \text{OPT}$. The proof of the theorem above shows that there is a cut of value at least $0.878 \cdot Z_{VP}$, so that $\text{OPT} \geq 0.878 \cdot Z_{VP}$. Thus, we have that $\text{OPT} \leq Z_{VP} \leq \frac{1}{0.878} \text{OPT}$. It has been shown that there are graphs for which the upper inequality is met with equality. This implies that we can get no better performance guarantee for the maximum cut problem by using Z_{VP} as an upper bound on OPT. Currently, 0.878 is the best performance guarantee known for the maximum cut problem. The following theorems show that this is either close to, or exactly, the best performance guarantee that is likely attainable.

Theorem 6.10. *If there is an α-approximation algorithm for the maximum cut problem with $\alpha > \frac{16}{17} \approx 0.941$, then* P = NP.

Theorem 6.11. *Given the unique games conjecture, there is no α-approximation algorithm for the maximum cut problem with constant*

$$\alpha > \min_{-1 \leq x \leq 1} \frac{\frac{1}{\pi} \arccos(x)}{\frac{1}{2}(1 - x)} \geq 0.878$$

unless P = NP.

We sketch the proof of the second theorem in Section 16.5.

So far we have discussed only a randomized algorithm for the maximum cut problem. It is possible to derandomize the algorithm by using a sophisticated application of the method of conditional expectations that iteratively determines the various coordinates of the random vector. The derandomization incurs a loss in the performance guarantee that can be made as small as desired (by increasing the running time).

6.3 Approximating Quadratic Programs

We can extend the algorithm above for the maximum cut problem to the following more general problem. Suppose we wish to approximate the quadratic program below:

$$\text{maximize} \quad \sum_{1 \leq i, j \leq n} a_{ij} x_i x_j \tag{6.5}$$

$$\text{subject to} \quad x_i \in \{-1, +1\}, \qquad i = 1, \ldots, n.$$

We need to be slightly careful in this case since as stated it is possible that the value of an optimal solution is negative (for instance, if the values of a_{ii} are negative and all other a_{ij} are zero). Thus far we have restricted our attention to problems for which all feasible solutions have nonnegative value so that the definition of an α-approximation algorithm makes sense. To see that the definition might not make sense in the case of negative solution values, suppose we have an α-approximation algorithm for a maximization problem with $\alpha < 1$, and suppose we have a problem instance in which OPT is negative. Then the approximation algorithm guarantees the value of our solution is at least $\alpha \cdot$ OPT, which means that the value of our solution will be greater than that of OPT. In order to get around this difficulty, in this case we will restrict the objective function matrix $A = (a_{ij})$ in (6.5) to itself be positive semidefinite. Observe then that for any feasible solution x, the value of the objective function will be $x^T A x$ and will be nonnegative by the definition of positive semidefinite matrices.

As in the case of the maximum cut problem, we can then have the following vector programming relaxation:

$$\text{maximize} \quad \sum_{1 \leq i, j \leq n} a_{ij}(v_i \cdot v_j) \qquad (6.6)$$
$$\text{subject to} \quad v_i \cdot v_i = 1, \qquad i = 1, \ldots, n,$$
$$v_i \in \Re^n, \qquad i = 1, \ldots, n.$$

Let Z_{VP} be the value of an optimal solution for this vector program. By the same argument as in the previous section, $Z_{VP} \geq \text{OPT}$.

We can also use the same algorithm as we did for the maximum cut problem. We solve the vector program (6.6) in polynomial time and obtain vectors v_i. We choose a random hyperplane with normal r, and generate a solution $\bar{x}$ for the quadratic program (6.5) by setting $\bar{x}_i = 1$ if $r \cdot v_i \geq 0$ and $\bar{x}_i = -1$ otherwise. We will show below that this gives a $\frac{2}{\pi}$-approximation algorithm for the quadratic program (6.5).

Lemma 6.12.

$$E[\bar{x}_i \bar{x}_j] = \frac{2}{\pi} \arcsin(v_i \cdot v_j).$$

Proof. Recall from Lemma 6.7 that the probability v_i and v_j will be on different sides of the random hyperplane is $\frac{1}{\pi} \arccos(v_i \cdot v_j)$. Thus, the probability that $\bar{x}_i$ and $\bar{x}_j$ have different values is $\frac{1}{\pi} \arccos(v_i \cdot v_j)$. Observe that if $\bar{x}_i$ and $\bar{x}_j$ have different values, then their product must be -1, while if they have the same value, their product must be 1. Thus, the probability that the product is 1 must be $1 - \frac{1}{\pi} \arccos(v_i \cdot v_j)$. Hence,

$$E[\bar{x}_i \bar{x}_j] = \Pr[\bar{x}_i \bar{x}_j = 1] - \Pr[\bar{x}_i \bar{x}_j = -1]$$
$$= \left(1 - \frac{1}{\pi} \arccos(v_i \cdot v_j)\right) - \left(\frac{1}{\pi} \arccos(v_i \cdot v_j)\right)$$
$$= 1 - \frac{2}{\pi} \arccos(v_i \cdot v_j).$$

Using $\arcsin(x) + \arccos(x) = \frac{\pi}{2}$, we get

$$E[\bar{x}_i \bar{x}_j] = 1 - \frac{2}{\pi}\left[\frac{\pi}{2} - \arcsin(v_i \cdot v_j)\right] = \frac{2}{\pi} \arcsin(v_i \cdot v_j). \qquad \square$$

We would like to make the same argument as we did for the maximum cut problem in Theorem 6.9, but there is a difficulty with the analysis. Let

$$\alpha = \min_{-1 \leq x \leq 1} \frac{\frac{2}{\pi} \arcsin(x)}{x}.$$

Then we would like to argue that the expected value of the solution is

$$E\left[\sum_{i,j} a_{ij}\bar{x}_i\bar{x}_j\right] = \sum_{i,j} a_{ij}E[\bar{x}_i\bar{x}_j]$$

$$= \frac{2}{\pi}\sum_{i,j} a_{ij}\arcsin(v_i \cdot v_j)$$

$$\geq \alpha\sum_{i,j} a_{ij}(v_i \cdot v_j)$$

$$\geq \alpha \cdot \mathrm{OPT}$$

by the same reasoning as in Theorem 6.9. However, the penultimate inequality is not necessarily correct since it may be the case that some of the a_{ij} are negative. We are assuming that the inequality holds on a term-by-term basis, and this is not true when some of the $a_{ij} < 0$.

Thus, in order to analyze this algorithm, we will have to use a global analysis, rather than a term-by-term analysis. To do so, we will need the following fact, called the *Schur product theorem*, and the subsequent two corollaries.

Fact 6.13 (Schur product theorem). *For matrices $A = (a_{ij})$ and $B = (b_{ij})$, define $A \circ B = (a_{ij}b_{ij})$. If $A \succeq 0$ and $B \succeq 0$, then $A \circ B \succeq 0$.*

Corollary 6.14. *If $A \succeq 0$ and $B \succeq 0$, then $\sum_{i,j} a_{ij}b_{ij} \geq 0$.*

Proof. By Fact 6.13, we know that $A \circ B \succeq 0$, so that for the vector $\vec{1}$ of all ones, $\sum_{i,j} a_{ij}b_{ij} = \vec{1}^T(A \circ B)\vec{1} \geq 0$, by the definition of psd matrices. □

Corollary 6.15. *If $X \succeq 0$, $|x_{ij}| \leq 1$ for all i, j, and $Z = (z_{ij})$ such that $z_{ij} = \arcsin(x_{ij}) - x_{ij}$, then $Z \succeq 0$.*

Proof. We recall that the Taylor series expansion for $\arcsin x$ around zero is

$$\arcsin x = x + \frac{1}{2 \cdot 3}x^3 + \frac{1 \cdot 3}{2 \cdot 4 \cdot 5}x^5 + \cdots + \frac{1 \cdot 3 \cdot 5 \cdots (2n+1)}{2 \cdot 4 \cdot 6 \cdots 2n \cdot (2n+1)}x^{2n+1} + \cdots,$$

and it converges for $|x| \leq 1$. Since the matrix $Z = (z_{ij})$ where $z_{ij} = \arcsin(x_{ij}) - x_{ij}$, we can express it as

$$Z = \frac{1}{2 \cdot 3}((X \circ X) \circ X) + \frac{1 \cdot 3}{2 \cdot 4 \cdot 5}((((X \circ X) \circ X) \circ X) \circ X) + \cdots.$$

By Fact 6.13, because $X \succeq 0$, each term on the right-hand side is a positive semidefinite matrix, and therefore their sum will be also. □

We can now show the following theorem.

Theorem 6.16. *Rounding the vector program (6.6) by choosing a random hyperplane is a $\frac{2}{\pi}$-approximation algorithm for the quadratic program (6.5) when the objective function matrix A is positive semidefinite.*

Proof. We want to show that

$$E\left[\sum_{i,j} a_{ij}\bar{x}_i\bar{x}_j\right] \ge \frac{2}{\pi}\sum_{i,j} a_{ij}(v_i \cdot v_j) \ge \frac{2}{\pi} \cdot \text{OPT}.$$

We know that

$$E\left[\sum_{i,j} a_{ij}\bar{x}_i\bar{x}_j\right] = \frac{2}{\pi}\sum_{i,j} a_{ij}\arcsin(v_i \cdot v_j).$$

Thus, we need to show that

$$\frac{2}{\pi}\sum_{i,j} a_{ij}\arcsin(v_i \cdot v_j) - \frac{2}{\pi}\sum_{i,j} a_{ij}(v_i \cdot v_j) \ge 0.$$

By setting $x_{ij} = v_i \cdot v_j$ and letting θ_{ij} denote the angle between the two vectors, we obtain that $X = (x_{ij}) \succeq 0$ and $|x_{ij}| \le 1$ since

$$|v_i \cdot v_j| = \|v_i\|\|v_j\|\cos\theta_{ij}| = |\cos\theta_{ij}| \le 1.$$

Thus, we want to show that

$$\frac{2}{\pi}\sum_{i,j} a_{ij}(\arcsin(x_{ij}) - x_{ij}) \ge 0.$$

If we set $z_{ij} = \arcsin(x_{ij}) - x_{ij}$, then it is equivalent to show that

$$\frac{2}{\pi}\sum_{i,j} a_{ij}z_{ij} \ge 0.$$

This follows since $Z = (z_{ij}) \succeq 0$ by Corollary 6.15, and thus $\sum_{i,j} a_{ij}z_{ij} \ge 0$ by Corollary 6.14 since $A \succeq 0$. □

6.4 Finding a Correlation Clustering

In this section, we show that semidefinite programming can be used to obtain a good *correlation clustering* in an undirected graph. In this problem we are given an undirected graph in which each edge $(i, j) \in E$ is given two nonnegative weights, $w_{ij}^+ \ge 0$ and $w_{ij}^- \ge 0$. The goal is to *cluster* the vertices into sets of similar vertices; the degree to which i and j are similar is given by w_{ij}^+, and the degree to which they are different is given by w_{ij}^-. We represent a clustering of the vertices by a partition S of the vertex set into nonempty subsets. Let $\delta(S)$ be the set of edges that have endpoints in different sets of the partition, and let $E(S)$ be the set of edges that have both endpoints in the same part of the partition. Then the goal of the problem is to find a partition S that maximizes the total w^+ weight of edges inside the sets of the partition plus the total w^- weight of edges between sets of the partition; in other words, we find S to maximize

$$\sum_{(i,j)\in E(S)} w_{ij}^+ + \sum_{(i,j)\in\delta(S)} w_{ij}^-.$$

Observe that it is easy to get a $\frac{1}{2}$-approximation algorithm for this problem. If we put all the vertices into a single cluster (that is, $\mathcal{S} = \{V\}$), then the value of this solution is $\sum_{(i,j)\in E} w_{ij}^+$. If we make each vertex its own cluster (that is, $\mathcal{S} = \{\{i\} : i \in V\}$), then the value of this solution is $\sum_{(i,j)\in E} w_{ij}^-$. Since OPT $\leq \sum_{(i,j)\in E}(w_{ij}^+ + w_{ij}^-)$, at least one of these two solutions has a value of at least $\frac{1}{2}$ OPT.

We now show that we can obtain a $\frac{3}{4}$-approximation algorithm by using semidefinite programming. Here we model the problem as follows. Let e_k be the kth unit vector; that is, it has a one in the kth coordinate and zeros elsewhere. We will have a vector x_i for each vertex $i \in V$; we set $x_i = e_k$ if i is in the kth cluster. The model of the problem then becomes

$$\text{maximize} \sum_{(i,j)\in E} \left(w_{ij}^+(x_i \cdot x_j) + w_{ij}^-(1 - x_i \cdot x_j) \right)$$

$$\text{subject to } x_i \in \{e_1, \ldots, e_n\}, \qquad \forall i,$$

since $e_k \cdot e_l = 1$ if $k = l$ and 0 otherwise. We can then relax this model to the following vector program:

$$\text{maximize} \sum_{(i,j)\in E} \left(w_{ij}^+(v_i \cdot v_j) + w_{ij}^-(1 - v_i \cdot v_j) \right) \qquad (6.7)$$

$$\text{subject to } v_i \cdot v_i = 1, \qquad \forall i,$$

$$v_i \cdot v_j \geq 0, \qquad \forall i, j,$$

$$v_i \in \Re^n, \qquad \forall i.$$

Let Z_{CC} be the value of an optimal solution for the vector program. Observe that the vector program is a relaxation, since any feasible solution to the model above is feasible for the vector program and has the same value. Thus, $Z_{CC} \geq$ OPT.

In the previous two sections, we chose a random hyperplane to partition the vectors into two sets; in the case of the maximum cut problem, this gave the two sides of the cut, and in the case of quadratic programming, this gave the variables of value $+1$ and -1. In this case, we will choose two random hyperplanes, with two independent random vectors r_1 and r_2 as their normals. This partitions the vertices into $2^2 = 4$ sets: in particular, we partition the vertices into the sets

$$R_1 = \{i \in V : r_1 \cdot v_i \geq 0, r_2 \cdot v_i \geq 0\}$$
$$R_2 = \{i \in V : r_1 \cdot v_i \geq 0, r_2 \cdot v_i < 0\}$$
$$R_3 = \{i \in V : r_1 \cdot v_i < 0, r_2 \cdot v_i \geq 0\}$$
$$R_4 = \{i \in V : r_1 \cdot v_i < 0, r_2 \cdot v_i < 0\}.$$

We will show that the solution consisting of these four clusters, with $\mathcal{S} = \{R_1, R_2, R_3, R_4\}$, comes within a factor of $\frac{3}{4}$ of the optimal value. We first need the following lemma.

Lemma 6.17. *For $x \in [0, 1]$,*

$$\frac{(1 - \frac{1}{\pi}\arccos(x))^2}{x} \geq 0.75$$

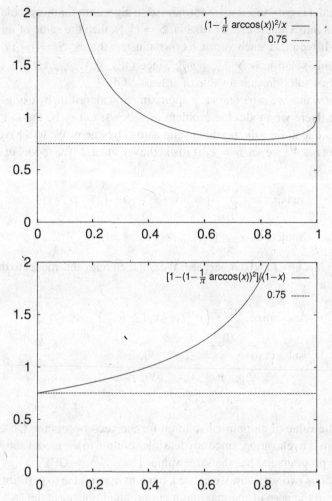

Figure 6.4. Illustration of Lemma 6.17. The upper figure shows a plot of $(1 - \frac{1}{\pi} \arccos(x))^2/x$, and the lower figure shows a plot of $[1 - (1 - \frac{1}{\pi} \arccos(x))^2]/(1 - x)$.

and

$$\frac{1 - (1 - \frac{1}{\pi} \arccos(x))^2}{(1 - x)} \geq 0.75.$$

Proof. These statements follow by simple calculus. See Figure 6.4 for an illustration.   □

We can now give the main theorem.

Theorem 6.18. *Rounding the vector program (6.7) by using two random hyperplanes as above gives a $\frac{3}{4}$-approximation algorithm for the correlation clustering problem.*

Proof. Let X_{ij} be a random variable that is 1 if vertices i and j end up in the same cluster, and is 0 otherwise. Note that the probability that a single random hyperplane has the vectors v_i and v_j on different sides of the hyperplane is $\frac{1}{\pi} \arccos(v_i \cdot v_j)$ by

Lemma 6.7. Then the probability that v_i and v_j are on the same side of a single random hyperplane is $1 - \frac{1}{\pi} \arccos(v_i \cdot v_j)$. Furthermore, the probability that the vectors are both on the same sides of the two random hyperplanes defined by r_1 and r_2 is $(1 - \frac{1}{\pi} \arccos(v_i \cdot v_j))^2$, since r_1 and r_2 are chosen independently. Thus, $E[X_{ij}] = (1 - \frac{1}{\pi} \arccos(v_i \cdot v_j))^2$.

Let W be a random variable denoting the weight of the partition. Observe that

$$W = \sum_{(i,j) \in E} \left(w_{ij}^+ X_{ij} + w_{ij}^- (1 - X_{ij}) \right).$$

Thus,

$$E[W] = \sum_{(i,j) \in E} \left(w_{ij}^+ E[X_{ij}] + w_{ij}^- (1 - E[X_{ij}]) \right)$$

$$= \sum_{(i,j) \in E} \left[w_{ij}^+ \left(1 - \frac{1}{\pi} \arccos(v_i \cdot v_j) \right)^2 \right.$$

$$\left. + w_{ij}^- \left(1 - \left(1 - \frac{1}{\pi} \arccos(v_i \cdot v_j) \right)^2 \right) \right].$$

We now want to use Lemma 6.17 to bound each term in the sum from below; we can do so because the constraints of the vector program imply that $v_i \cdot v_j \in [0, 1]$. Thus,

$$E[W] \geq 0.75 \sum_{(i,j) \in E} \left(w_{ij}^+ (v_i \cdot v_j) + w_{ij}^- (1 - v_i \cdot v_j) \right) = 0.75 \cdot Z_{CC} \geq 0.75 \cdot \text{OPT}.$$

$\square$

6.5 Coloring 3-Colorable Graphs

In Section 5.12, we saw that with high probability we can 3-color a δ-dense 3-colorable graph. The situation for arbitrary 3-colorable graphs is much worse, however. We will give a quite simple algorithm that colors a 3-colorable graph $G = (V, E)$ with $O(\sqrt{n})$ colors, where $n = |V|$. Then by using semidefinite programming, we will obtain an algorithm that uses $\tilde{O}(n^{0.387})$ colors where $\tilde{O}$ is defined below.

Definition 6.19. *A function $g(n) = \tilde{O}(f(n))$ if there exists some constant $c \geq 0$ and some n_0 such that for all $n \geq n_0$, $g(n) = O(f(n) \log^c n)$.*

The best known algorithm does not use much fewer than $\tilde{O}(n^{0.387})$ colors. Graph coloring is one of the most difficult problems to approximate.

Some coloring problems are quite simple: it is known that a 2-colorable graph can be 2-colored in polynomial time, and that an arbitrary graph with maximum degree Δ can be $(\Delta + 1)$-colored in polynomial time. We leave these results as exercises (Exercise 6.4).

Given these results, it is quite simple to give an algorithm that colors a 3-colorable graph with $O(\sqrt{n})$ colors. As long as there exists a vertex in the graph with degree at least $\sqrt{n}$, we pick three new colors, color the vertex with one of the new colors, and use the 2-coloring algorithm to 2-color the neighbors of the vertex with the other two new colors; we know that we can do this because the graph is 3-colorable. We remove

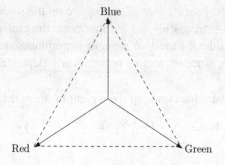

Figure 6.5. Proof of Lemma 6.21.

all these vertices from the graph and repeat. When we have no vertices in the graph of degree at least $\sqrt{n}$, we use the algorithm that colors a graph with $\Delta + 1$ colors to color the remaining graph with $\sqrt{n}$ new colors.

We can prove the following.

Theorem 6.20. *The algorithm above colors any 3-colorable graph with at most $4\sqrt{n}$ colors.*

Proof. Each time the algorithm finds a vertex of degree at least $\sqrt{n}$, we use three new colors. This can happen at most $n/\sqrt{n}$ times, since we remove at least $\sqrt{n}$ vertices from the graph each time we do this. Hence, this loop uses at most $3\sqrt{n}$ colors. The final step uses an additional $\sqrt{n}$ colors. $\square$

We now turn to semidefinite programming to help improve our coloring algorithms. We will use the following vector program in which we have a vector v_i for each $i \in V$:

$$\text{minimize} \quad \lambda \tag{6.8}$$
$$\text{subject to } v_i \cdot v_j \le \lambda, \qquad \forall (i, j) \in E,$$
$$v_i \cdot v_i = 1, \qquad \forall i \in V,$$
$$v_i \in \Re^n, \qquad \forall i \in V.$$

The lemma below suggests why the vector program will be useful in deriving an algorithm for coloring 3-colorable graphs.

Lemma 6.21. *For any 3-colorable graph, there is a feasible solution to (6.8) with $\lambda \le -\frac{1}{2}$.*

Proof. Consider an equilateral triangle, and associate the unit vectors for all the vertices with the three different colors with the three different vertices of the triangle (see Figure 6.5). Note that the angle between any two vectors of the same color is 0, while the angle between vectors of different colors is $2\pi/3$. Then for v_i, v_j such that $(i, j) \in E$, we have

$$v_i \cdot v_j = \|v_i\| \|v_j\| \cos\left(\frac{2\pi}{3}\right) = -\frac{1}{2}.$$

Since we have given a feasible solution to the vector program with $\lambda = -1/2$, it must be the case that for the optimal solution $\lambda \le -1/2$. $\square$

Note that the proof of the lemma has actually shown the following corollary; this will be useful later.

Corollary 6.22. *For any 3-colorable graph, there is a feasible solution to (6.8) such that $v_i \cdot v_j = -1/2$ for all edges $(i, j) \in E$.*

To achieve our result, we will show how to obtain a randomized algorithm that produces a *semicoloring*. A semicoloring is a coloring of nodes such that at most $n/4$ edges have endpoints with the same color. This implies that at least $n/2$ vertices are colored such that any edge between them has endpoints that are colored differently. We claim that an algorithm for producing a semicoloring is sufficient, for if we can semicolor a graph with k colors, then we can color the entire graph with $k \log n$ colors in the following way. We first semicolor the graph with k colors, and take the vertices that are colored correctly. We then semicolor the vertices left over (no more than $n/2$) with k new colors, take the vertices that are colored correctly, and repeat. This takes $\log n$ iterations, after which the entire graph is colored correctly with $k \log n$ colors.

Now we give the randomized algorithm for producing a semicoloring. The basic idea is similar to that used in the correlation clustering algorithm in Section 6.4. We solve the vector program (6.8), and choose $t = 2 + \log_3 \Delta$ random vectors $r_1, \ldots, r_t$, where Δ is the maximum degree of any vertex in the graph. The t random vectors define 2^t different regions into which the vectors v_i can fall: one region for each distinct possibility of whether $r_j \cdot v_i \geq 0$ or $r_j \cdot v_i < 0$ for all $j = 1, \ldots, t$. We then color the vectors in each region with a distinct color.

Theorem 6.23. *This coloring algorithm produces a semicoloring of $4\Delta^{\log_3 2}$ colors with probability at least 1/2.*

Proof. Since we used 2^t colors for $t = 2 + \log_3 \Delta$, we use $4 \cdot 2^{\log_3 \Delta} = 4\Delta^{\log_3 2}$ colors.

We now need to show that this produces a semicoloring with probability at least 1/2. First, we consider the probability that vertices i and j get the same color for a given edge (i, j). This probability is the probability that both i and j fall into the same region, that is, the probability that none of the t random hyperplanes separate i and j. Note that by Lemma 6.7, the probability that a single random hyperplane separates i and j is $\frac{1}{\pi} \arccos(v_i \cdot v_j)$. Therefore, the probability that t independently chosen hyperplanes fail to separate i and j is $(1 - \frac{1}{\pi} \arccos(v_i \cdot v_j))^t$. Thus,

$$\Pr[i \text{ and } j \text{ get the same color for edge } (i, j)]$$
$$= \left(1 - \frac{1}{\pi} \arccos(v_i \cdot v_j)\right)^t \leq \left(1 - \frac{1}{\pi} \arccos(\lambda)\right)^t,$$

where the last inequality follows from the inequalities of the vector program (6.8) and since arccos is a non-increasing function. Then by Lemma 6.21,

$$\left(1 - \frac{1}{\pi} \arccos(\lambda)\right)^t \leq \left(1 - \frac{1}{\pi} \arccos(-1/2)\right)^t.$$

Finally, using some simple algebra and the definition of t,

$$\left(1 - \frac{1}{\pi} \arccos(-1/2)\right)^t = \left(1 - \frac{1}{\pi} \frac{2\pi}{3}\right)^t = \left(\frac{1}{3}\right)^t \leq \frac{1}{9\Delta}.$$

Therefore,

$$\Pr[i \text{ and } j \text{ get the same color for edge } (i, j)] \leq \frac{1}{9\Delta}.$$

If m denotes the number of edges in the graph, then $m \leq n\Delta/2$. Thus, the expected number of edges that have both endpoints colored the same is no more than $m/9\Delta$, which is at most $n/18$. Let X be a random variable denoting the number of edges that have both endpoints colored the same. By Markov's inequality (Lemma 5.25), the probability that there are more than $n/4$ edges that have both endpoints colored the same is at most

$$\Pr[X \geq n/4] \leq \frac{E[X]}{n/4} \leq \frac{n/18}{n/4} \leq \frac{1}{2}. \qquad \square$$

If we use n as a bound on the maximum degree Δ, then we obtain an algorithm that produces a semicoloring with $O(n^{\log_3 2})$ colors and thus a coloring with $\tilde{O}(n^{\log_3 2})$ colors. Since $\log_3 2 \approx 0.631$, this is worse than the algorithm we presented at the beginning of the section that uses $O(n^{1/2})$ colors. However, we can use some ideas from that algorithm to do better. Let σ be some parameter we will choose later. As long as there is a vertex in the graph of degree at least σ, we pick three new colors, color the vertex with one of the new colors, and use the 2-coloring algorithm to 2-color the neighbors of the vertex with the other two new colors; we know that we can do this because the graph is 3-colorable. We remove all these vertices from the graph and repeat. When we have no vertices in the graph of degree at least σ, we use the algorithm above to semicolor the remaining graph with $O(\sigma^{\log_3 2})$ new colors. We can now show the following.

Theorem 6.24. *The algorithm above semicolors a 3-colorable graph with $O(n^{0.387})$ colors with probability at least 1/2.*

Proof. The first part of this algorithm uses $3n/\sigma$ colors in total, since we remove at least σ vertices from the graph each time. To balance the two parts of the algorithm, we set σ such that $\frac{n}{\sigma} = \sigma^{\log_3 2}$, which gives $\sigma = n^{\log_6 3}$, or $\sigma \approx n^{0.613}$. Thus, both parts use $O(n^{0.387})$ colors, which gives the theorem. $\qquad \square$

From the theorem we get an overall algorithm that colors a graph with $\tilde{O}(n^{0.387})$ colors.

In Section 13.2, we will show how to use semidefinite programming to obtain an algorithm that 3-colors a graph with $\tilde{O}(\Delta^{1/3}\sqrt{\ln \Delta})$ colors. Using the same ideas as above, this can be converted into an algorithm that colors using $\tilde{O}(n^{1/4})$ colors.

Exercises

6.1 As with linear programs, semidefinite programs have duals. The dual of the MAX CUT SDP (6.4) is

$$\text{minimize} \quad \frac{1}{2}\sum_{i<j} w_{ij} + \frac{1}{4}\sum_i \gamma_i$$

$$\text{subject to} \quad W + diag(\gamma) \succeq 0,$$

where the matrix W is the symmetric matrix of the edge weights w_{ij} and $diag(\gamma)$ is the matrix of zeroes with γ_i as the ith entry on the diagonal. Show that the value of any feasible solution for this dual is an upper bound on the cost of any cut.

6.2 Semidefinite programming can also be used to give improved approximation algorithms for the maximum satisfiability problem. First we start with the MAX 2SAT problem, in which every clause has at most two literals.

(a) As in the case of the maximum cut problem, we'd like to express the MAX 2SAT problem as an "integer quadratic program" in which the only constraints are $y_i \in \{-1, 1\}$ and the objective function is quadratic in the y_i. Show that the MAX 2SAT problem can be expressed this way. (Hint: It may help to introduce a variable y_0 that indicates whether the value -1 or 1 is "TRUE.")

(b) Derive a 0.878-approximation algorithm for the MAX 2SAT problem.

(c) Use this 0.878-approximation algorithm for MAX 2SAT to derive a $(\frac{3}{4} + \epsilon)$-approximation algorithm for the maximum satisfiability problem, for some $\epsilon > 0$. How large an ϵ can you get?

6.3 Given a MAX 2SAT instance as defined in Exercise 6.2, prove that it is possible to decide in polynomial time whether all the clauses can be satisfied or not.

6.4 Give polynomial-time algorithms for the following:

(a) Coloring a 2-colorable graph with two colors.

(b) Coloring a graph of maximum degree Δ with $\Delta + 1$ colors.

6.5 An important quantity in combinatorial optimization is called the *Lovász theta function*. The theta function is defined on undirected graphs $G = (V, E)$. One of its many definitions is given below as a semidefinite program:

$$\vartheta(\bar{G}) = \text{maximize} \quad \sum_{i,j} b_{ij}$$

$$\text{subject to} \quad \sum_i b_{ii} = 1,$$

$$b_{ij} = 0, \qquad \forall i \neq j, (i, j) \notin E,$$

$$B = (b_{ij}) \succeq 0, \qquad B \text{ symmetric.}$$

Lovász showed that $\omega(G) \leq \vartheta(\bar{G}) \leq \chi(G)$, where $\omega(G)$ is the size of the largest clique in G and $\chi(G)$ is the minimum number of colors needed to color G.

(a) Show that $\omega(G) \leq \vartheta(\bar{G})$.

(b) The following is a small variation in the vector program we used for graph coloring:

$$\text{minimize} \quad \alpha$$

$$\text{subject to } v_i \cdot v_j = \alpha, \qquad \forall (i, j) \in E,$$

$$v_i \cdot v_i = 1, \qquad \forall i \in V,$$

$$v_i \in \Re^n, \qquad \forall i \in V.$$

Its dual is

$$\text{maximize} -\sum_i u_i \cdot u_i$$

$$\text{subject to} \quad \sum_{i \neq j} u_i \cdot u_j \geq 1,$$

$$u_i \cdot u_j = 0, \qquad \forall (i, j) \notin E, i \neq j,$$

$$u_i \in \Re^n, \qquad \forall i \in V.$$

Show that the value of the dual is $1/(1 - \vartheta(\bar{G}))$. By strong duality, this is also the value of the primal; however, see the chapter notes for a discussion of conditions under which strong duality holds.

The value of this vector program is sometimes called the *strict vector chromatic number* of the graph, and the value of original vector programming relaxation (6.8) is the *vector chromatic number* of the graph.

6.6 Recall the maximum directed cut problem from Exercises 5.3 and 5.6: We are given as input a directed graph $G = (V, A)$, with a nonnegative weight $w_{ij} \geq 0$ for all arcs $(i, j) \in A$. The goal is to partition V into two sets U and $W = V - U$ so as to maximize the total weight of the arcs going from U to W (that is, arcs (i, j) with $i \in U$ and $j \in W$).

(a) As in the case of the maximum cut problem, we'd like to express the maximum directed cut problem as an integer quadratic program in which the only constraints are $y_i \in \{-1, 1\}$ and the objective function is quadratic in y_i. Show that the maximum directed cut problem can be expressed in this way. (Hint: As is the case for MAX 2SAT in Exercise 6.2, it may help to introduce a variable y_0 that indicates whether the value -1 or 1 means that y_i is in the set U.)

(b) Find an α-approximation algorithm for the maximum directed cut problem using a vector programming relaxation of the integer quadratic program above. Find the best value of α that you can.

6.7 Recall the MAX 2SAT problem from Exercise 6.2. We consider a variant, called MAX E2SAT, in which every clause has exactly two literals in it; that is, there are no unit clauses. We say that a MAX E2SAT instance is *balanced* if for each i, the weight of clauses in which x_i appears is equal to the weight of the clauses in which $\bar{x}_i$ appears. Give a β-approximation algorithm for balanced MAX E2SAT instances, where

$$\beta = \min_{x: -1 \leq x \leq 1} \frac{\frac{1}{2} + \frac{1}{2\pi} \arccos x}{\frac{3}{4} - \frac{1}{4}x} \approx 0.94394.$$

6.8 Consider again the maximum directed cut problem given in Exercise 6.6. We say that an instance of the directed cut problem is *balanced* if for each vertex $i \in V$, the total weight of arcs entering i is equal to the total weight of arcs leaving i. Give an α-approximation algorithm for balanced maximum directed cut instances where α is the same performance guarantee as for the maximum cut problem; that is,

$$\alpha = \min_{x: -1 \leq x \leq 1} \frac{\frac{1}{\pi} \arccos(x)}{\frac{1}{2}(1 - x)}.$$

Chapter Notes

Strang [273, 274] provides introductions to linear algebra that are useful in the context of our discussion of semidefinite programming and various operations on vectors and matrices.

A 1979 paper of Lovász [219] gives an early application of SDP to combinatorial optimization with his ϑ-number for graphs (see Exercise 6.5). The algorithmic implications of the ϑ-number were highlighted in the work of Grötschel, Lovász, and Schrijver [144]; they showed that the ellipsoid method could be used to solve the associated semidefinite program for the ϑ-number, and that in general the ellipsoid method could be used to solve convex programs in polynomial time given a polynomial-time separation oracle. Alizadeh [5] and Nesterov and Nemirovskii [236] showed that polynomial-time interior-point methods for linear programming could be extended to SDP. A good overview of SDP can be found in the edited volume of Wolkowicz, Saigal, and Vandenberghe [290].

Unlike linear programs, the most general case of semidefinite programs is not solvable in polynomial time without additional assumptions. There are examples of SDPs in which the coefficients of all variables are either 1 or 2, but whose optimal value is doubly exponential in the number of variables (see [5, Section 3.3]), and so no polynomial-time algorithm is possible. Even when SDPs are solvable in polynomial time, they are solvable only to within an additive error of ϵ; this is in part due to the fact that exact solutions can be irrational, and thus are not expressible in polynomial space. To show that an SDP is solvable in polynomial time to within an additive error of ϵ, it is sufficient for the feasible region to be nonempty and to be contained in a polynomially sized ball centered on the origin. These conditions are met for the problems we discuss. Weak duality always holds for semidefinite programs. If there are points in the interior of the feasible region of the primal and dual (called the "Slater conditions"), strong duality also holds. As a quick way to see the solvability of semidefinite programs in polynomial time, we observe that the constraint $X \succeq 0$ is equivalent to the infinite family of constraints $y^T X y \geq 0$ for all $y \in \Re^n$. Suppose we compute the minimum eigenvalue λ and corresponding eigenvector v of the matrix X. If $\lambda \geq 0$, then X is positive semidefinite, whereas if $\lambda < 0$, then $v^T(Xv) = v^T(\lambda v) = \lambda v^T v < 0$ gives a violated constraint. Thus, we have a separation oracle and can apply the ellipsoid method to find an approximate solution assuming the initial feasible region can be bounded by a polynomially sized ellipsoid and assuming that we can carry out the eigenvalue and eigenvector computation to reasonable precision in polynomial time. Grötschel, Lovász, and Schrijver [144] avoid the issue of computing an eigenvector in polynomial time by giving a polynomial-time separation oracle that computes a basis of the columns of X, and then computes determinants to check whether X is positive semidefinite and to return a constraint $y^T X y < 0$ if not.

The SDP-based algorithm of Section 6.2 for the maximum cut problem is due to Goemans and Williamson [139]; they gave the first use of semidefinite programming for approximation algorithms. Knuth [200, Section 3.4.1C] gives algorithms for sampling from the normal distribution via samples from the uniform [0, 1] distribution. Fact 6.4 is from Knuth [200, pp. 135–136] and Fact 6.5 is a paraphrase of Theorem IV.16.3 of Rényi [251]. Feige and Schechtman [109] give graphs for which $Z_{VP} = \frac{1}{0.878}$ OPT.

Theorem 6.10 is due to Håstad [159]. Theorem 6.11 is due to Khot, Kindler, Mossel, and O'Donnell [193] together with a result of Mossel, O'Donnell, and Oleszkiewicz [227]. The derandomization of the maximum cut algorithm is due to Mahajan and Ramesh [222]. This derandomization technique works for many of the randomized algorithms in this chapter that use random hyperplanes.

Subsequent to the work of Goemans and Williamson, Nesterov [235] gave the algorithm for quadratic programs found in Section 6.3, Swamy [277] gave the algorithm of Section 6.4 on correlation clustering, and Karger, Motwani, and Sudan [182] gave the SDP-based algorithm for coloring 3-colorable graphs in Section 6.5. The $O(\sqrt{n})$-approximation algorithm for coloring 3-colorable graphs given at the beginning of Section 6.5 is due to Wigderson [286].

Fact 6.13 is known as the Schur product theorem; see, for example, Theorem 7.5.3 of Horn and Johnson [171].

Exercises 6.1, 6.2, and 6.6 are from Goemans and Williamson [139]. Exercise 6.3 has been shown by Even, Itai, and Shamir [104], who also point to previous work on the 2SAT problem. Exercise 6.5 is due to Tardos and Williamson as cited in [182]. Exercises 6.7 and 6.8 on balanced MAX 2SAT and balanced maximum directed cut problem instances are due to Khot, Kindler, Mossel, and O'Donnell [193].

CHAPTER 7

The Primal-Dual Method

We introduced the primal-dual method in Section 1.5, and showed how it gave an approximation algorithm for the set cover problem. Although there it did not give a better performance guarantee than various LP rounding algorithms, we observed that in practice the primal-dual method gives much faster algorithms than those that require solving a linear program.

In this chapter, we will cover primal-dual algorithms in more depth. We begin by reviewing the primal-dual algorithm for the set cover problem from Section 1.5. We then apply the primal-dual method to a number of problems, gradually developing a number of principles in deciding how to apply the technique so as to get good performance guarantees. In discussing the feedback vertex set problem in Section 7.2, we see that it is sometimes useful to focus on increasing particular dual variables that correspond to small or minimal constraints not satisfied by the current primal solution. In Section 7.3, we discuss the shortest s-t path problem, and see that to obtain a good performance guarantee it is sometimes necessary to remove unneeded elements in the primal solution returned by the algorithm. In Section 7.4 we introduce the generalized Steiner tree problem (also known as the Steiner forest problem), and show that to obtain a good performance guarantee it can be helpful to increase multiple dual variables at the same time. In Section 7.5, we see that it can be useful to consider alternative integer programming formulations in order to obtain improved performance guarantees. We conclude the chapter with an application of the primal-dual method to the uncapacitated facility location problem, and an extension of this algorithm to the related k-median problem. For the latter problem, we use a technique called Lagrangean relaxation to obtain the appropriate relaxation for the approximation algorithm.

7.1 The Set Cover Problem: A Review

We begin by reviewing the primal-dual algorithm and its analysis for the set cover problem from Section 1.5. Recall that in the set cover problem, we are given as input a ground set of elements $E = \{e_1, \ldots, e_n\}$, some subsets of those elements

$y \leftarrow 0$
$I \leftarrow \emptyset$
while there exists $e_i \notin \bigcup_{j \in I} S_j$ **do**
    Increase the dual variable y_i until there is some ℓ such that $\sum_{j:e_j \in S_\ell} y_j = w_\ell$
    $I \leftarrow I \cup \{\ell\}$
return I

Algorithm 7.1. Primal-dual algorithm for the set cover problem.

$S_1, S_2, \ldots, S_m \subseteq E$, and a nonnegative weight w_j for each subset S_j. The goal is to find a minimum-weight collection of subsets that covers all of E; that is, we wish to find an $I \subseteq \{1, \ldots, m\}$ that minimizes $\sum_{j \in I} w_j$ subject to $\bigcup_{j \in I} S_j = E$.

We observed in Section 1.5 that the set cover problem can be modeled as the following integer program:

$$\text{minimize} \sum_{j=1}^{m} w_j x_j \tag{7.1}$$

$$\text{subject to} \sum_{j:e_i \in S_j} x_j \geq 1, \qquad i = 1, \ldots, n, \tag{7.2}$$

$$x_j \in \{0, 1\}, \qquad j = 1, \ldots, m. \tag{7.3}$$

If we relax the integer program to a linear program by replacing the constraints $x_j \in \{0, 1\}$ with $x_j \geq 0$, and take the dual, we obtain

$$\text{maximize} \sum_{i=1}^{n} y_i$$

$$\text{subject to} \sum_{i:e_i \in S_j} y_i \leq w_j, \qquad j = 1, \ldots, m,$$

$$y_i \geq 0, \qquad i = 1, \ldots, n.$$

We then gave the following algorithm, which we repeat in Algorithm 7.1. We begin with the dual solution $y = 0$; this is a feasible solution since $w_j \geq 0$ for all j. We also have an infeasible primal solution $I = \emptyset$. As long as there is some element e_i not covered by I, we look at all the sets S_j that contain e_i, and consider the amount by which we can increase the dual variable y_i associated with e_i and still maintain dual feasibility. This amount is $\epsilon = \min_{j:e_i \in S_j}(w_j - \sum_{k:e_k \in S_j} y_k)$ (note that possibly this is zero). We then increase y_i by ϵ. This will cause some dual constraint associated with some set S_ℓ to become *tight*; that is, after increasing y_i we will have for this set S_ℓ

$$\sum_{k:e_k \in S_\ell} y_k = w_\ell.$$

We add the set S_ℓ to our cover (by adding ℓ to I) and continue until all elements are covered.

In Section 1.5, we argued that this algorithm is an f-approximation algorithm for the set cover problem, where $f = \max_i |\{j : e_i \in S_j\}|$. We repeat the analysis here, since there are several features of the analysis that are used frequently in analyzing primal-dual approximation algorithms.

Theorem 7.1. *Algorithm 7.1 is an f-approximation algorithm for the set cover problem.*

Proof. For the cover I constructed by the algorithm, we would like to show that $\sum_{j \in I} w_j \leq f \cdot \text{OPT}$. Let Z_{LP}^* be the optimal value of the linear programming relaxation of (7.1). It is sufficient to show that $\sum_{j \in I} w_j \leq f \cdot \sum_{i=1}^{n} y_i$ for the final dual solution y, since by weak duality we know that for any dual feasible solution y, $\sum_{i=1}^{n} y_i \leq Z_{LP}^*$, and since the LP is a relaxation, $Z_{LP}^* \leq \text{OPT}$.

Because we added a set S_j to our cover only when its corresponding dual inequality was tight, we know that for any $j \in I$, $w_j = \sum_{i:e_i \in S_j} y_i$. Thus, we have that

$$\sum_{j \in I} w_j = \sum_{j \in I} \sum_{i:e_i \in S_j} y_i$$

$$= \sum_{i=1}^{n} y_i \cdot |\{j \in I : e_i \in S_j\}|,$$

where the second equality comes from rewriting the double sum. We then observe that since $|\{j \in I : e_i \in S_j\}| \leq f$, we get that

$$\sum_{j \in I} w_j < f \cdot \sum_{i=1}^{n} y_i \leq f \cdot \text{OPT}. \qquad \square$$

We'll be using several features of the algorithm and the analysis repeatedly in this chapter. In particular, we maintain a feasible dual solution, and increase dual variables until a dual constraint becomes tight. This indicates an object that we need to add to our primal solution (a set, in this case). When we analyze the cost of the primal solution, each object in the solution was given by a tight dual inequality. Thus, we can rewrite the cost of the primal solution in terms of the dual variables. We then compare this cost with the dual objective function and show that the primal cost is within a certain factor of the dual objective, which shows that we are close to the value of an optimal solution.

In this case, we increase dual variables until $w_j = \sum_{i:e_i \in S_j} y_i$ for some set S_j, which we then add to our primal solution. When we have a feasible primal solution I, we can rewrite its cost in terms of the dual variables by using the tight dual inequalities, so that

$$\sum_{j \in I} w_j = \sum_{j \in I} \sum_{i:e_i \in S_j} y_i.$$

By exchanging the double summation, we have that

$$\sum_{j \in I} w_j = \sum_{i=1}^{n} y_i \cdot |\{j \in I : e_i \in S_j\}|.$$

Then by bounding the value of $|\{j \in I : e_i \in S_j\}|$ by f, we get that the cost is at most f times the dual objective function, proving a performance guarantee on the algorithm.

Because we will use this form of analysis frequently in this chapter, we will call it the *standard primal-dual analysis*.

This method of analysis is strongly related to the complementary slackness conditions discussed at the end of Section 1.4. Let I be the set cover returned by the primal-dual algorithm, and consider an integer primal solution x^* for the integer programming formulation (7.1) of the set cover problem in which we set $x_j^* = 1$ for each set $j \in I$. Then we know that whenever $x_j^* > 0$, the corresponding dual inequality is tight, so this part of the complementary slackness conditions is satisfied. If it were also the case that whenever $y_i^* > 0$, the corresponding primal inequality were tight (namely, $\sum_{j:e_i \in S_j} x_j^* = 1$), then the complementary slackness conditions would imply that x^* is an optimal solution. This is not the case, but we have an *approximate* form of the complementary slackness condition that holds; namely, whenever $y_i^* > 0$,

$$\sum_{j:e_i \in S_j} x_j^* = |\{j \in I : e_i \in S_j\}| \leq f.$$

Whenever we can show that these complementary slackness conditions hold within a factor of α, we can then obtain an α-approximation algorithm.

Recall from Section 5.6 that we defined the integrality gap of an integer programming formulation to be the worst-case ratio over all instances of the problem of the optimal value of the integer program to the optimal value of the linear programming relaxation. Standard primal-dual algorithms construct a primal integer solution and a solution to the dual of the linear programming relaxation, and the performance guarantee of the algorithm gives an upper bound on the ratio of these two values over all possible instances of the problem. Therefore, the performance guarantee of a primal-dual algorithm provides an upper bound on the integrality gap of an integer programming formulation. However, the opposite is also true: the integrality gap gives a lower bound on the performance guarantee that can be achieved via a standard primal-dual algorithm and analysis, or indeed any algorithm that compares the value of its solution with the value of the linear programming relaxation. In this chapter we will sometimes be able to show limits on primal-dual algorithms that use particular integer programming formulations due to an instance of the problem with a bad integrality gap.

7.2 Choosing Variables to Increase: The Feedback Vertex Set Problem in Undirected Graphs

In the *feedback vertex set problem in undirected graphs*, we are given an undirected graph $G = (V, E)$ and nonnegative weights $w_i \geq 0$ for vertices $i \in V$. The goal is to choose a minimum-cost subset of vertices $S \subseteq V$ such that every cycle C in the graph contains some vertex of S. We sometimes say that S *hits* every cycle of the graph. Another way to view the problem is that the goal is to find a minimum-cost subset of vertices S such that removing S from the graph leaves the graph acyclic. Let $G[V - S]$ be the graph on the set of vertices $V - S$ with the edges from G that have both endpoints in $V - S$; we say that $G[V - S]$ is the graph *induced* by $V - S$. A third way to view the problem is to find a minimum-cost set of vertices S such that the induced graph $G[V - S]$ is acyclic.

We will give a primal-dual algorithm for this problem. In the case of the set cover problem, it did not matter which dual variable was increased; we could increase any variable y_i corresponding to an uncovered element e_i and obtain the same performance guarantee. However, it is often helpful to carefully select the dual variable to increase, and we will see this principle in the course of devising an algorithm for the feedback vertex set problem.

If we let $\mathcal{C}$ denote the set of all cycles C in the graph, we can formulate the feedback vertex set problem in undirected graphs as the following integer program:

$$\text{minimize} \sum_{i \in V} w_i x_i \tag{7.4}$$

$$\text{subject to} \quad \sum_{i \in C} x_i \geq 1, \qquad \forall C \in \mathcal{C},$$

$$x_i \in \{0, 1\}, \qquad \forall i \in V.$$

Initially this might not seem like such a good choice of a formulation: the number of cycles in the graph can be exponential in the size of the graph. However, with the primal-dual method we do not actually need to solve either the integer program or its linear programming relaxation; our use of the linear program and the dual only guides the algorithm and its analysis, so having an exponential number of constraints is not problematic.

If we relax the integer program to a linear program by replacing the constraints $x_i \in \{0, 1\}$ with $x_i \geq 0$, and take its dual, we obtain

$$\text{maximize} \quad \sum_{C \in \mathcal{C}} y_C$$

$$\text{subject to} \quad \sum_{C \in \mathcal{C}: i \in C} y_C \leq w_i, \qquad \forall i \in V,$$

$$y_C \geq 0, \qquad \forall C \in \mathcal{C}.$$

Again, it might seem worrisome that we now have an exponential number of dual variables, since the primal-dual method maintains a feasible dual solution. In the course of the algorithm, however, only a polynomial number of these will become nonzero, so we need to keep track of only these nonzero variables.

By analogy with the primal-dual algorithm for the set cover problem, we obtain Algorithm 7.2. We start with the dual feasible solution in which all y_C are set to zero, and with the primal infeasible solution $S = \emptyset$. We see if there is any cycle C left in the induced graph $G[V - S]$. If there is, then we determine the amount by which we can increase the dual variable y_C while still maintaining dual feasibility. This amount is $\epsilon = \min_{i \in C} \left(w_i - \sum_{C': i \in C'} y_{C'} \right)$. Increasing y_C causes a dual inequality to become tight for some vertex $\ell \in C$; in particular, it becomes tight for a vertex $\ell \in C$ that attains the minimum in the expression for ϵ. We add this vertex ℓ to our solution S, and we remove ℓ from the graph. We also repeatedly remove any vertices of degree one from the graph (since they cannot be in any cycle) until we are left with a graph that contains only vertices of degree two or higher. Let $n = |V|$ be the number of vertices in

$y \leftarrow 0$
$S \leftarrow \emptyset$
while there exists a cycle C in G **do**
    Increase y_C until there is some $\ell \in C$ such that $\sum_{C' \in \mathcal{C}: \ell \in C'} y_{C'} = w_\ell$
    $S \leftarrow S \cup \{\ell\}$
    Remove ℓ from G
    Repeatedly remove vertices of degree one from G
return S

Algorithm 7.2. Primal-dual algorithm for the feedback vertex set problem (first attempt).

the graph. Then note that we can add at most n vertices to our solution, so that we only go through the main loop at most n times, and at most n dual variables are nonzero.

Suppose we now analyze the algorithm as we did for the set cover problem. Let S be the final set of vertices chosen. We know that for any $i \in S$, $w_i = \sum_{C: i \in C} y_C$. Thus, we can write the cost of our chosen solution as

$$\sum_{i \in S} w_i = \sum_{i \in S} \sum_{C: i \in C} y_C = \sum_{C \in \mathcal{C}} |S \cap C| y_C.$$

Note that $|S \cap C|$ is simply the number of vertices of the solution S in the cycle C. If we can show that $|S \cap C| \leq \alpha$ whenever $y_C > 0$, then we will have $\sum_{i \in S} w_i \leq \alpha \sum_{C \in \mathcal{C}} y_C \leq \alpha \cdot \text{OPT}$.

Unfortunately, if in the main loop of the algorithm we choose an arbitrary cycle C and increase its dual variable y_C, it is possible that $|S \cap C|$ can be quite large. In order to do better, we need to make a careful choice of cycle C. If we can always choose a short cycle, with $|C| \leq \alpha$, then certainly we will have $|S \cap C| \leq |C| \leq \alpha$. This isn't always possible either: the graph itself can be one large cycle through all n vertices. In such a case, however, it suffices to choose one vertex from the cycle in order to have a feasible solution. This leads to the following observation.

Observation 7.2. *For any path P of vertices of degree two in graph G, Algorithm 7.2 will choose at most one vertex from P; that is, $|S \cap P| \leq 1$ for the final solution S given by the algorithm.*

Proof. Once S contains a vertex of P, we remove that vertex from the graph. Its neighbors in P will then have degree one and be removed. Iteratively, the entire path P will be removed from the graph, and so no further vertices of P will be added to S. $\square$

Suppose that in the main loop of Algorithm 7.2 we choose the cycle C that minimizes the number of vertices that have degree three or higher. Note that in such a cycle, vertices of degree three or more alternate with paths of vertices of degree two (possibly paths of a single edge). Thus, by Observation 7.2, the value of $|S \cap C|$ for the final solution S will be at most twice the number of vertices of degree three or higher in C. The next

```
y ← 0
S ← ∅
Repeatedly remove vertices of degree one from G
while there exists a cycle in G do
    Find cycle C with at most 2⌈log₂ n⌉ vertices of degree three or more
    Increase y_C until there is some ℓ ∈ C such that ∑_{C'∈𝒞:ℓ∈C'} y_{C'} = w_ℓ
    S ← S ∪ {ℓ}
    Remove ℓ from G
    Repeatedly remove vertices of degree one from G
return S
```

Algorithm 7.3. Primal-dual algorithm for the feedback vertex set problem (second attempt).

lemma shows us that we can find a cycle C with at most $O(\log n)$ vertices of degree three or higher.

Lemma 7.3. *In any graph G that has no vertices of degree one, there is a cycle with at most $2\lceil \log_2 n \rceil$ vertices of degree three or more, and it can be found in linear time.*

Proof. If G has only vertices of degree two, then the statement is trivially true. Otherwise, pick an arbitrary vertex of degree three or higher. We start a variant of a breadth-first search from this vertex, in which we treat every path of vertices of degree two as a single edge joining vertices of degree three or more; note that since there are no degree one vertices, every such path joins vertices of degree at least three. Thus, each level of the breadth-first search tree consists only of vertices of degree three or more. This implies that the number of vertices at each level is at least twice the number of vertices of the previous level. Observe then that the depth of the breadth-first search can be at most $\lceil \log_2 n \rceil$: once we reach level $\lceil \log_2 n \rceil$, we have reached all n vertices of the graph. We continue the breadth-first search until we close a cycle; that is, we find a path of vertices of degree two from a node on the current level to a previously visited node. This cycle has at most $2\lceil \log_2 n \rceil$ vertices of degree three or more, since at worst the cycle is closed by an edge joining two vertices at depth $\lceil \log_2 n \rceil$. □

We give the revised algorithm in Algorithm 7.3. We can now show the following theorem.

Theorem 7.4. *Algorithm 7.3 is a $(4\lceil \log_2 n \rceil)$-approximation algorithm for the feedback vertex set problem in undirected graphs.*

Proof. As we showed above, the cost of our final solution S is

$$\sum_{i \in S} w_i = \sum_{i \in S} \sum_{C:i \in C} y_C = \sum_{C \in \mathcal{C}} |S \cap C| y_C.$$

By construction, $y_C > 0$ only when C contains at most $2\lceil \log_2 n \rceil$ vertices of degree three or more in the graph at the time we increased y_C. Note that at this time $S \cap C = \emptyset$. By Observation 7.2, each path of vertices of degree two joining two vertices of degree three or more in C can contain at most one vertex of S. Thus, if C has at most $2\lceil \log_2 n \rceil$ vertices of degree three or more, it can have at most $4\lceil \log_2 n \rceil$ vertices of S overall:

possibly each vertex of degree three or more is in S, and then at most one of the vertices in the path joining adjacent vertices of degree three or more can be in S. Since as the algorithm proceeds, the degree of a vertex can only go down, we obtain that whenever $y_C > 0$, $|S \cap C| \leq 4\lceil \log_2 n \rceil$. Thus, we have that

$$\sum_{i \in S} w_i = \sum_{C \in \mathcal{C}} |S \cap C| y_C \leq (4\lceil \log_2 n \rceil) \sum_{C \in \mathcal{C}} y_C \leq (4\lceil \log_2 n \rceil) \text{OPT}. \qquad \square$$

The important observation of this section is that in order to get a good performance guarantee, one must choose carefully the dual variable to increase, and it is frequently useful to choose a dual variable that is small or minimal in some sense.

The integrality gap of the integer programming formulation (7.4) is known to be $\Omega(\log n)$, and so a performance guarantee of $O(\log n)$ is the best we can hope for from a primal-dual algorithm using this formulation. However, this does not rule out obtaining a better performance guarantee by a primal-dual algorithm using a different integer programming formulation of the problem. In Section 14.2, we will show that we can obtain a primal-dual 2-approximation algorithm for the feedback vertex set problem in undirected graphs by considering a more sophisticated integer programming formulation of the problem.

7.3 Cleaning Up the Primal Solution: The Shortest s-t Path Problem

In the *shortest s-t path problem*, we are given an undirected graph $G = (V, E)$, nonnegative costs $c_e \geq 0$ on all edges $e \in E$, and a pair of distinguished vertices s and t. The goal is to find the minimum-cost path from s to t. It is well known that the optimal solution can be found in polynomial time; for instance, Dijkstra's algorithm finds an optimal solution in polynomial time. However, it is instructive to think about applying the primal-dual method to this problem, in part because it gives us insight into using the primal-dual method for related problems that are NP-hard; we will see this in the next section. Additionally, the algorithm we find using the primal-dual method turns out to be equivalent to Dijkstra's algorithm.

Let $\mathcal{S} = \{S \subseteq V : s \in S, t \notin S\}$; that is, $\mathcal{S}$ is the set of all s-t cuts in the graph. Then we can model the shortest s-t path problem with the following integer program:

$$\text{minimize} \sum_{e \in E} c_e x_e$$

$$\text{subject to} \sum_{e \in \delta(S)} x_e \geq 1, \qquad \forall S \in \mathcal{S},$$

$$x_e \in \{0, 1\}, \qquad \forall e \in E,$$

where $\delta(S)$ is the set of all edges that have one endpoint in S and the other endpoint not in S. To see that this integer program models the shortest s-t path problem, take any feasible solution x and consider the graph $G' = (V, E')$ with $E' = \{e \in E : x_e = 1\}$. The constraints ensure that for any s-t cut S, there must be at least one edge of E' in $\delta(S)$: that is, the size of the minimum s-t cut in G' must be at least one. Thus, by the

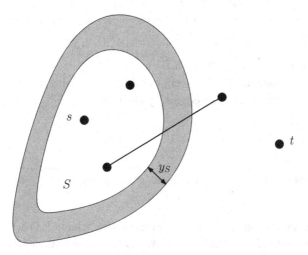

Figure 7.1. An illustration of a moat separating s from t. The moat contains the nodes in S, and its width is y_S.

max-flow/min-cut theorem the maximum s-t flow in G' is at least one, which implies that there is a path from s to t in G'. Similarly, if x is not feasible, then there is some s-t cut S for which there are no edges of E' in $\delta(S)$, which implies that the size of minimum s-t cut is zero, and thus the maximum s-t flow is zero. Hence, there is no path from s to t in G'.

Once again the number of constraints in the integer program is exponential in the size of the problem, and as with the feedback vertex set problem in Section 7.2, this is not problematic since we use the formulation only to guide the algorithm and its analysis.

If we replace the constraints $x_e \in \{0, 1\}$ with $x_e \geq 0$ to obtain a linear programming relaxation and take the dual of this linear program, we obtain

$$
\begin{aligned}
\text{maximize} \quad & \sum_{S \in \mathcal{S}} y_S \\
\text{subject to} \quad & \sum_{S \in \mathcal{S}: e \in \delta(S)} y_S \leq c_e, \qquad \forall e \in E, \\
& y_S \geq 0, \qquad \forall S \in \mathcal{S}.
\end{aligned}
$$

The dual variables y_S have a nice geometric interpretation; they can be interpreted as "moats" surrounding the set S of width y_S; see Figure 7.1 for an illustration. Any path from s to t must cross this moat, and hence must have cost at least y_S. Moats must be nonoverlapping, and thus for any edge e, we cannot have edge e crossing moats of total width more than c_e – thus the dual constraint that $\sum_{S:e \in \delta(S)} y_S \leq c_e$. We can have many moats, and any s-t path must cross them all, and have total length at most $\sum_{S \in \mathcal{S}} y_S$.

We now give a primal-dual algorithm for the shortest s-t path problem in Algorithm 7.4 that follows the general lines of the primal-dual algorithms we have given previously for the set cover and feedback vertex set problems. We start with a dual feasible solution $y = 0$ and the primal infeasible solution of $F = \emptyset$. While we don't yet have a feasible solution, we increase the dual variable y_C associated with an s-t cut C

$y \leftarrow 0$
$F \leftarrow \emptyset$
while there is no s-t path in (V, F) **do**
    Let C be the connected component of (V, F) containing s
    Increase y_C until there is an edge $e' \in \delta(C)$ such that $\sum_{S \in S: e' \in \delta(S)} y_S = c_{e'}$
    $F \leftarrow F \cup \{e'\}$
Let P be an s-t path in (V, F)
return P

Algorithm 7.4. Primal-dual algorithm for the shortest s-t path problem.

that the current solution does not satisfy, that is, for which $F \cap \delta(C) = \emptyset$. We call such constraints *violated constraints*. Following the lesson of the previous section, we carefully choose the "smallest" such constraint: we let C be the set of vertices of the connected component containing s in the set of edges F. Because F does not contain an s-t path, we know that $t \notin C$, and by the definition of a connected component we know that $\delta(C) \cap F = \emptyset$. We increase the dual variable y_C until some constraint of the dual becomes tight for some edge $e' \in E$, and we add e' to F.

Once our primal solution F is feasible and contains an s-t path, we end the main loop. Now we do something slightly different than we did before: we don't return the solution F, but rather a subset of F. Let P be any s-t path such that $P \subseteq F$. Our algorithm returns P. We do this since it may be too expensive to return all the edges in F, so we effectively delete any edge we do not need and return only the edges in P.

We begin the analysis by showing that the set of edges F found by the algorithm forms a tree; this implies that the s-t path P is unique.

Lemma 7.5. *At any point in Algorithm 7.4, the set of edges in F forms a tree containing the vertex s.*

Proof. We prove this by induction on the number of edges added to F. In each step of the main loop, we consider the connected component C of (V, F) containing s, and add an edge e' from the set $\delta(C)$ to our solution F. Since exactly one endpoint of e' is in C, e' cannot close a cycle in the tree F, and causes F to span a new vertex not previously spanned. $\qquad \Box$

We can now show that this algorithm gives an optimal algorithm for the shortest s-t path problem.

Theorem 7.6. *Algorithm 7.4 finds a shortest path from s to t.*

Proof. We prove this using the standard primal-dual analysis. As usual, since for every edge $e \in P$, we have that $c_e = \sum_{S: e \in \delta(S)} y_S$, and we know that

$$\sum_{e \in P} c_e = \sum_{e \in P} \sum_{S: e \in \delta(S)} y_S = \sum_{S: s \in S, t \notin S} |P \cap \delta(S)| y_S.$$

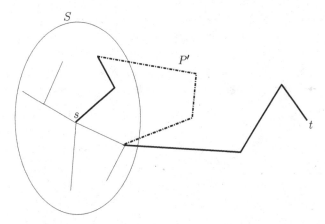

Figure 7.2. Proof of Theorem 7.6. The heavy line is the path P; the dotted heavy line is the subpath P'.

If we can now show that whenever $y_S > 0$, we have $|P \cap \delta(S)| = 1$, then we will show that

$$\sum_{e \in P} c_e = \sum_{S: s \in S, t \notin S} y_S \leq \text{OPT}$$

by weak duality. But of course since P is an s-t path of cost no less than OPT, it must have cost exactly OPT.

We now show that if $y_S > 0$, then $|P \cap \delta(S)| = 1$. Suppose otherwise, and $|P \cap \delta(S)| > 1$. Then there must be a subpath P' of P joining two vertices of S such that the only vertices of P' in S are its start and end vertices; see Figure 7.2. Since $y_S > 0$, we know that at the time we increased y_S, F was a tree spanning just the vertices in S. Thus, $F \cup P'$ must contain a cycle. Since P is a subset of the final set of edges F, this implies that the final F contains a cycle, which contradicts Lemma 7.5. Thus, it must be the case that $|P \cap \delta(S)| = 1$. $\qquad\square$

As we stated previously, one can show that this algorithm behaves in exactly the same way as Dijkstra's algorithm for solving the shortest s-t path problem; proving this equivalence is given as Exercise 7.1.

7.4 Increasing Multiple Variables at Once: The Generalized Steiner Tree Problem

We now turn to a problem known as the *generalized Steiner tree problem* or the *Steiner forest problem*. In this problem we are given an undirected graph $G = (V, E)$, nonnegative costs $c_e \geq 0$ for all edges $e \in E$, and k pairs of vertices $s_i, t_i \in V$. The goal is to find a minimum-cost subset of edges $F \subseteq E$ such that every s_i-t_i pair is connected in the set of selected edges; that is, s_i and t_i are connected in (V, F) for all i.

Figure 7.3. Illustration of moats for the generalized Steiner tree problem. Each of s_1, s_2, and t_3 has a white moat surrounding just that node; additionally, there is a grey moat depicting $y_{\{s_1,s_2,t_3\}} = \delta$.

Let $\mathcal{S}_i$ be the subsets of vertices separating s_i and t_i; that is, $\mathcal{S}_i = \{S \subseteq V : |S \cap \{s_i, t_i\}| = 1\}$. Then we can model this problem with the following integer program:

$$\text{minimize} \sum_{e \in E} c_e x_e \tag{7.5}$$

$$\text{subject to} \sum_{e \in \delta(S)} x_e \geq 1, \qquad \forall S \subseteq V : S \in \mathcal{S}_i \text{ for some } i,$$

$$x_e \in \{0, 1\}, \qquad e \in E.$$

The set of constraints enforce that for any s_i-t_i cut S with $s_i \in S$, $t_i \notin S$ or vice versa, we must select one edge from $\delta(S)$. The argument that this models the generalized Steiner tree problem is similar to that for the shortest s-t path problem in the previous section. Given the linear programming relaxation obtained by dropping the constraints $x_e \in \{0, 1\}$ and replacing them with $x_e \geq 0$, the dual of this linear program is

$$\text{maximize} \sum_{S \subseteq V : \exists i, S \in \mathcal{S}_i} y_S$$

$$\text{subject to} \sum_{S : e \in \delta(S)} y_S \leq c_e, \qquad \forall e \in E,$$

$$y_S \geq 0, \qquad \exists i : S \in \mathcal{S}_i.$$

As in the case of the shortest s-t path problem, the dual has a natural geometric interpretation as moats. In this case, however, we can have moats around any set of vertices $S \in \mathcal{S}_i$ for any i. See Figure 7.3 for an illustration.

Our initial attempt at a primal-dual algorithm is given in Algorithm 7.5, and is similar to the shortest s-t path algorithm given in the previous section. In every iteration, we choose some connected component C such that $|C \cap \{s_i, t_i\}| = 1$ for some i. We increase the dual variable y_C associated with C until the dual inequality associated with some edge $e' \in \delta(C)$ becomes tight, and we add this edge to our primal solution F.

$y \leftarrow 0$
$F \leftarrow \emptyset$
while not all s_i-t_i pairs are connected in (V, F) **do**
    Let C be a connected component of (V, F) such that $|C \cap \{s_i, t_i\}| = 1$ for
      some i
    Increase y_C until there is an edge $e' \in \delta(C)$ such that $\sum_{S \in \mathcal{S}: e' \in \delta(S)} y_S = c_{e'}$
    $F \leftarrow F \cup \{e'\}$
return F

Algorithm 7.5. Primal-dual algorithm for the generalized Steiner tree problem (first attempt).

Using the standard primal-dual analysis, we can analyze the cost of the final solution F as follows:

$$\sum_{e \in F} c_e = \sum_{e \in F} \sum_{S: e \in \delta(S)} y_S = \sum_S |\delta(S) \cap F| y_S.$$

In order to compare the term $\sum_S |\delta(S) \cap F| y_S$ with the dual objective function $\sum_S y_S$, we will need to show that $|\delta(S) \cap F| \leq \alpha$ for some α whenever $y_S > 0$.

Unfortunately, it is possible to give an example showing that $|\delta(S) \cap F| = k$ (where k is the number of s_i-t_i pairs) for $y_S > 0$ no matter what connected component is chosen in the main loop of Algorithm 7.5. To see this, consider the complete graph on $k + 1$ vertices. Let each edge have cost 1, let one vertex correspond to all s_i, and let the remaining k vertices be $t_1, \ldots, t_k$ (see Figure 7.4). The algorithm must choose one of the $k + 1$ vertices initially for the set C. The dual y_C gets value $y_C = 1$, and this is the only nonzero dual at the end of the algorithm. The final solution F has edges from the vertex chosen for C to all k other vertices, giving $|\delta(C) \cap F| = k$. However, observe that in the final solution if we take the average of $|\delta(C) \cap F|$ over all the $k + 1$ vertices we could have chosen for the initial set C, we get $2k/(k + 1) \approx 2$ since $\sum_{j \in V} |\delta(\{j\}) \cap F| = 2k$.

This observation suggests that perhaps we should increase the dual variables for several sets C at once. We present this variation in Algorithm 7.6. Let $\mathcal{C}$ be the set of *all* the connected components C such that $|C \cap \{s_i, t_i\}| = 1$. We increase associated

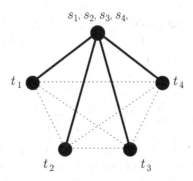

Figure 7.4. Bad example for Algorithm 7.5. If the algorithm chooses the vertex $s_1, \ldots, s_4$ as its initial connected component C, then it will eventually add all solid edges to F, and $|\delta(C) \cap F| = 4$.

$$y \leftarrow 0$$
$$F \leftarrow \emptyset$$
$$\ell \leftarrow 0$$
while not all s_i-t_i pairs are connected in (V, F) **do**
    $\ell \leftarrow \ell + 1$
    Let $\mathcal{C}$ be the set of all connected components C of (V, F) such that
        $|C \cap \{s_i, t_i\}| = 1$ for some i
    Increase y_C for all C in $\mathcal{C}$ uniformly until for some $e_\ell \in \delta(C')$, $C' \in \mathcal{C}$,
        $c_{e_\ell} = \sum_{S: e_\ell \in \delta(S)} y_S$
    $F \leftarrow F \cup \{e_\ell\}$
$F' \leftarrow F$
for $k \leftarrow \ell$ downto 1 **do**
    if $F' - e_k$ is a feasible solution **then**
        Remove e_k from F'
return F'

Algorithm 7.6. Primal-dual algorithm for the generalized Steiner tree problem (second attempt).

dual variables y_C for all $C \in \mathcal{C}$ at the same rate until a dual inequality becomes tight for some edge $e \in \delta(C)$ for a set C whose dual we increased. We then add e to our solution F and continue. Additionally, we index the edges we add as we go along: e_1 is added in the first iteration, e_2 in the second, and so on. Once we have a feasible solution F such that all s_i-t_i pairs are connected in F, we go through the edges in the reverse of the order in which they were added, from the edge added in the last iteration to the edge added in the first iteration. If the edge can be removed without affecting the feasibility of the solution, it is deleted. The final set of edges returned after this "reverse deletion" step is F'. This reverse deletion step is solely to simplify our analysis; in Exercise 7.4 the reader is asked to show that removing all unnecessary edges in any order gives an equally good approximation algorithm.

Given the geometric interpretation of the dual variables as moats, we can give an illustration of the algorithm in Figure 7.5.

We can now show that our intuition gathered from the bad example in Figure 7.4 is essentially correct, and that the algorithm is a 2-approximation algorithm for the generalized Steiner tree problem. In order to do this, we first state a lemma, whose proof we defer for a moment.

Lemma 7.7. *For any $\mathcal{C}$ in any iteration of the algorithm,*

$$\sum_{C \in \mathcal{C}} |\delta(C) \cap F'| \leq 2|\mathcal{C}|.$$

In terms of the geometric interpretation, we wish to show that the number of times that the edges in the solution cross a moat is at most twice the number of moats; see Figure 7.6. The main intuition of the proof is that the degree of nodes in a tree is at most twice the number of nodes, where we treat each connected component C as a node of the tree and the edges in $\delta(C)$ as the edges of the tree. The proof is slightly

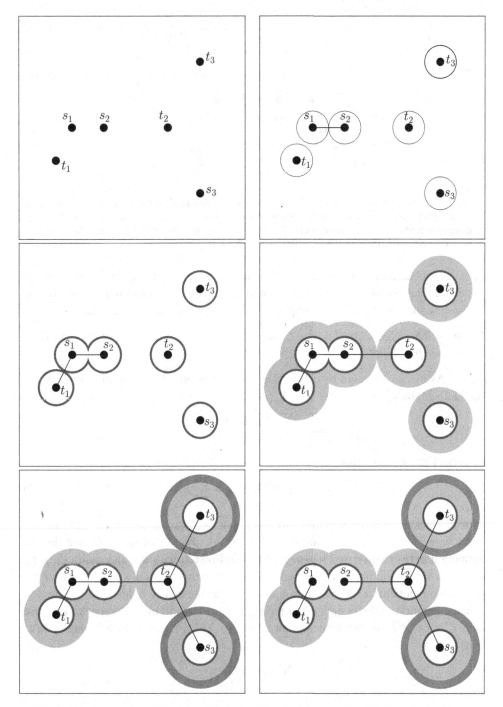

Figure 7.5. Illustration of the primal-dual algorithm for the generalized Steiner tree problem. Two edges go tight simultaneously in the last iteration before the deletion step. The deletion step removes the edge (s_1, s_2) added in the first iteration. The final set of edges is shown in the last panel.

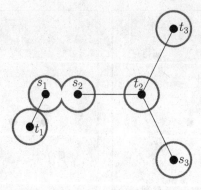

Figure 7.6. Illustration of Lemma 7.7. Consider the five thin dark moats. The edges of F' cross these moats eight times (twice each by the edges joining s_1-t_1, s_2-t_2, t_2-t_3, and t_2-s_3). Each moat corresponds to a connected component $C \in \mathcal{C}$ in the iteration in which the corresponding duals y_C were increased. Thus, in this iteration we see that $8 = \sum_{C \in \mathcal{C}} |\delta(C) \cap F'| \leq 2|\mathcal{C}| = 10$.

more complicated than this because only some components C are in $\mathcal{C}$, but we show that every "leaf" of the tree is a component in $\mathcal{C}$ and this is sufficient to prove the result.

We now show that the lemma implies the desired performance guarantee.

Theorem 7.8. *Algorithm 7.6 is a 2-approximation algorithm for the generalized Steiner tree problem.*

Proof. As usual, we begin by expressing the cost of our primal solution in terms of the dual variables:

$$\sum_{e \in F'} c_e = \sum_{e \in F'} \sum_{S:e \in \delta(S)} y_S = \sum_S |F' \cap \delta(S)| y_S.$$

We would like to show that

$$\sum_S |F' \cap \delta(S)| y_S \leq 2 \sum_S y_S, \tag{7.6}$$

since by weak duality, this will imply that the algorithm is a 2-approximation algorithm. As is suggested by the bad example in Figure 7.4, we cannot simply prove this by showing that $|F' \cap \delta(S)| \leq 2$ whenever $y_S > 0$. Instead, we show inequality (7.6) by induction on the number of iterations of the algorithm. Initially all dual variables $y_S = 0$, so inequality (7.6) holds. Suppose that the inequality holds at the beginning of some iteration of the main loop of the algorithm. Then in this iteration we increase each y_C for $C \in \mathcal{C}$ by the same amount (call it ϵ). This increases the left-hand side of (7.6) by

$$\epsilon \sum_{C \in \mathcal{C}} |F' \cap \delta(C)|$$

and the right-hand side by

$$2\epsilon |\mathcal{C}|.$$

However, by the inequality of Lemma 7.7, this means that the increase in the left-hand side is no greater than the increase in the right-hand side. Thus, if the inequality held before the increase of the dual variables in this iteration, it will also hold afterward. □

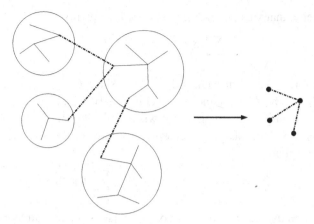

Figure 7.7. Proof of Lemma 7.7. On the left is the current set of connected components, with the edges in H shown in dashed lines. The right side shows the contracted graph.

We now turn to the proof of Lemma 7.7. We first need an observation.

Observation 7.9. *At any point in the algorithm, the set of edges F is a forest.*

Proof. We prove the statement by induction on the number of iterations of the algorithm. The set $F = \emptyset$ is initially a forest. Any time we add an edge to the solution, it has at most one endpoint in any given connected component of $\mathcal{C}$. Thus, it joins two connected components of the forest F, and the forest remains a forest. □

Proof of Lemma 7.7. Consider the iteration in which edge e_i is added to F. Let F_i be the edges already in F at this point; that is, $F_i = \{e_1, \ldots, e_{i-1}\}$. Let $H = F' - F_i$. Observe that $F_i \cup H = F_i \cup F'$ is a feasible solution to the problem, since F' by itself is a feasible solution to the problem. We claim also that if we remove any edge $e \in H$ from $F_i \cup H$, it will not be a feasible solution. This follows from the deletion procedure at the end of the algorithm: at the time we consider edge e_{i-1} for deletion, the edges in F' at that point in the procedure are exactly those in $F_i \cup H$. Hence, it must be the case that any edge already considered and remaining in F' is necessary for the solution to be feasible. These edges are exactly the edges in H.

We form a new graph by contracting each connected component of (V, F_i) to a single vertex. Let V' be this new set of vertices. Observe that since at any point F is a forest, once we have contracted all the edges in F_i into vertices V', no edge in H can have both endpoints corresponding to the same vertex in V'. Thus, we can consider the forest of edges H on the set of vertices V', where each edge in H is connected to the two vertices in V' corresponding to the two connected components it joined in (V, F_i). See Figure 7.7 for an illustration. We let $\deg(v)$ for $v \in V'$ represent the degree of vertex v in this forest. We also color the vertices in V' with two different colors, red and blue. The red vertices in V' are those connected components C of (V, F_i) that are in the set $\mathcal{C}$ in this iteration (that is, for some j, $|C \cap \{s_j, t_j\}| = 1$). The blue vertices are all the other vertices of V'. Let R denote the set of red vertices in V' and B the set of blue vertices v that have $\deg(v) > 0$.

We now observe that we can rewrite the desired inequality

$$\sum_{C \in \mathcal{C}} |\delta(C) \cap F'| \le 2|\mathcal{C}|$$

in terms of this forest. The right-hand side is $2|R|$. Since $F' \subseteq F_i \cup H$ and no edge of F_i can appear in $\delta(C)$ for $C \in \mathcal{C}$ (since C is a connected component of F_i), the left-hand side is no greater than $\sum_{v \in R} \deg(v)$. So we wish to prove that $\sum_{v \in R} \deg(v) \le 2|R|$.

To prove this, we claim that no blue vertex can have degree exactly one. If this is true, then we have that

$$\sum_{v \in R} \deg(v) = \sum_{v \in R \cup B} \deg(v) - \sum_{v \in B} \deg(v).$$

Then since the total degree of a forest is no more than twice the number of vertices in it, and since all blue vertices of nonzero degree have degree at least two by the claim, we have that

$$\sum_{v \in R} \deg(v) \le 2(|R| + |B|) - 2|B| = 2|R|,$$

as desired.

It remains to prove that no blue vertex can have degree one. Suppose otherwise, and let $v \in V'$ be a blue vertex of degree one, let C be the connected component of the uncontracted graph corresponding to v, and let $e \in H$ be the incident edge. By our initial discussion, e must be necessary for the feasibility of the solution. Thus, it must be on some path between s_j and t_j for some j, and $|C \cap \{s_j, t_j\}| = 1$. But in this case, C must be in $\mathcal{C}$, and v must be red, which is a contradiction. $\qquad \square$

Since the proof shows that the algorithm finds a solution to the integer programming formulation (7.5) of cost at most twice the value of a dual solution to the dual of the linear programming relaxation, the proof implies that the integrality gap of the formulation is at most 2. We can use the integrality gap instance for the prize-collecting Steiner tree problem in Section 5.7 (see Figure 5.4) to show that the integrality gap for this formulation is essentially 2, so that no better performance guarantee can be obtained by using a primal-dual algorithm with this formulation.

In Section 16.4, we will consider a directed version of the generalized Steiner tree problem, and we will show that it is substantially more difficult to approximate the directed version of the problem.

7.5 Strengthening Inequalities: The Minimum Knapsack Problem

In this section, we turn to a minimization version of the knapsack problem introduced in Section 3.1. As in the previous version of the knapsack problem, we are given a set I of n items, $I = \{1, 2, \ldots, n\}$. Each item has a value v_i and a size s_i. In the previous version of the problem, we additionally had a knapsack capacity B, and the goal was to find the maximum-value subset of items such that the total size of the items was at most the capacity of the knapsack. In the minimization version of the problem, we are given a demand D, and the goal of the problem is to find a subset of items having minimum total size such that the total value is at least the demand. That is, we try to find a subset $X \subseteq I$ of items minimizing $s(X) = \sum_{i \in X} s_i$ subject to the constraint that $v(X) = \sum_{i \in X} v_i \geq D$.

We can formulate the problem as the following integer program, in which the primal variable x_i indicates whether item i is chosen to be in the solution or not:

$$\text{minimize} \quad \sum_{i \in I} s_i x_i$$
$$\text{subject to} \quad \sum_{i \in I} v_i x_i \geq D,$$
$$x_i \in \{0, 1\}, \qquad \forall i \in I.$$

We obtain a linear programming relaxation for the problem by replacing the constraints $x_i \in \{0, 1\}$ with linear constraints $0 \leq x_i \leq 1$ for all $i \in I$. However, this linear programming relaxation is not a particularly good one, in the sense that it has a bad integrality gap. Consider a two-item set $I = \{1, 2\}$, where $v_1 = D - 1$, $v_2 = D$, $s_1 = 0$, and $s_2 = 1$. The only feasible integer solutions require us to take item 2 ($x_2 = 1$), for a total size of 1. But the solution $x_1 = 1$, $x_2 = 1/D$ is feasible for the linear programming relaxation and has total size $1/D$. This example shows that the integrality gap of this formulation is at least $1/(1/D) = D$.

To get a primal-dual algorithm with a reasonable performance guarantee, we must use a different integer programming formulation of the same problem, one with a better integrality gap. We introduce a new set of constraints, one for every subset $A \subseteq I$ of items such that $v(A) < D$. Let $D_A = D - v(A)$; we can think of D_A as the demand left over if the items in A are added to the knapsack. Notice that even if we select every item in the set A, we must still choose additional items of total value at least D_A. Given the set A, this is simply another minimum knapsack problem on the set of items $I - A$, where the desired demand is now D_A. Given A, we can also reduce the value of each item in $I - A$ to be the minimum of its value and D_A; since the desired demand is D_A, we don't need the value of the item to be any larger. We let $v_i^A = \min(v_i, D_A)$. Then for any $A \subseteq I$ and any set of items $X \subseteq I$ such that $v(X) \geq D$, it is the case that $\sum_{i \in X - A} v_i^A \geq D_A$. We can then give the following integer programming formulation of the problem:

$$\text{minimize} \quad \sum_{i \in I} s_i x_i$$
$$\text{subject to} \quad \sum_{i \in I - A} v_i^A x_i \geq D_A, \qquad \forall A \subseteq I,$$
$$x_i \in \{0, 1\}, \qquad \forall i \in I.$$

As we argued above, any integer solution corresponding to a knapsack of value at least D is a feasible solution to the integer program, and thus the integer program models the minimum knapsack problem.

$y \leftarrow 0$
$A \leftarrow \emptyset$
while $v(A) < D$ **do**
    Increase y_A until for some $i \in I - A$, $\sum_{B \subseteq I : i \notin B} v_i^B y_B = s_i$
    $A \leftarrow A \cup \{i\}$
return A

Algorithm 7.7. Primal-dual algorithm for the minimum knapsack problem.

We now consider the linear programming relaxation of the integer program above, replacing the constraints $x_i \in \{0, 1\}$ with $x_i \geq 0$:

$$\text{minimize} \quad \sum_{i \in I} s_i x_i$$
$$\text{subject to} \quad \sum_{i \in I - A} v_i^A x_i \geq D_A, \quad \forall A \subseteq I,$$
$$x_i \geq 0, \quad \forall i \in I.$$

Observe that for the instance that gave a bad integrality gap for the previous integer programming formulation, the given LP solution is no longer feasible. In that example, we had $I = \{1, 2\}$, with $v_1 = D - 1$, $v_2 = D$, $s_1 = 0$, and $s_2 = 1$. Now consider the constraint corresponding to $A = \{1\}$. We have $D_A = D - v_1 = 1$, and $v_2^A = \min(v_2, D_A) = 1$, so that the constraint $\sum_{i \in I - A} v_i^A x_i \geq D_A$ is $x_2 \geq 1$ for this choice of A. The constraint forces us to take item 2; we cannot take a $1/D$ fraction of item 2 to meet the missing single unit of demand.

The dual of the linear programming relaxation is

$$\text{maximize} \quad \sum_{A : A \subseteq I} D_A y_A$$
$$\text{subject to} \quad \sum_{A \subseteq I : i \notin A} v_i^A y_A \leq s_i, \quad \forall i \in I,$$
$$y_A \geq 0, \quad \forall A \subset I.$$

We can now consider a primal-dual algorithm for the problem using the primal and dual formulations as given above. We start with an empty set of selected items, and a dual solution $y_A = 0$ for all $A \subseteq I$. Now we must select some dual variable to increase. Which one should it be? Following the idea introduced previously of choosing a variable corresponding to a minimal object of some sort, we increase the dual variable $y_\emptyset$. A dual constraint will become tight for some item $i \in I$, and we will add this to our set of selected items. Which variable should we increase next? Notice that in order to maintain dual feasibility, it will have to be a variable y_A for some set A such that $i \in A$; if $i \notin A$, then we cannot increase y_A without violating the tight dual constraint for i. The most natural choice is to increase y_A for $A = \{i\}$. We continue in this fashion, letting A be our set of selected items; whenever a dual constraint becomes tight for some new item $j \in I$, we add j to A, and in the next iteration increase the dual variable y_A. The algorithm is given in Algorithm 7.7. The algorithm terminates when $v(A) \geq D$.

We can now show that the algorithm is a 2-approximation algorithm for the minimum knapsack problem.

Theorem 7.10. *Algorithm 7.7 is a 2-approximation algorithm for the minimum knapsack problem.*

Proof. Let ℓ be the final item selected by the algorithm, and let X be the set of items returned at the end of the algorithm. We know that $v(X) \geq D$; since item ℓ was added to X, it must be the case that before ℓ was added, the total value of the set of items was less than D, so that $v(X - \ell) < D$.

Following the standard primal-dual analysis, we know that

$$\sum_{i \in X} s_i = \sum_{i \in X} \sum_{A \subseteq I : i \notin A} v_i^A y_A.$$

Reversing the double sum, we have that

$$\sum_{i \in X} \sum_{A \subseteq I : i \notin A} v_i^A y_A = \sum_{A \subseteq I} y_A \sum_{i \in X - A} v_i^A.$$

Note that in any iteration of the algorithm except the last one, adding the next item i to the current set of items A did not cause the value of the knapsack to become at least D; that is, $v_i < D - v(A) = D_A$ at that point in the algorithm. Thus, for all items $i \in X$ except ℓ, $v_i^A = \min(v_i, D_A) = v_i$ for the point in the algorithm at which A was the current set of items. Thus, we can rewrite

$$\sum_{i \in X - A} v_i^A = v_\ell^A + \sum_{i \in X - A : i \neq \ell} v_i^A = v_\ell^A + v(X - \ell) - v(A).$$

Note that $v_\ell^A \leq D_A$ by definition, and as argued at the beginning of the proof $v(X - \ell) < D$ so that $v(X - \ell) - v(A) < D - v(A) = D_A$; thus, we have that

$$v_\ell^A + v(X - \ell) - v(A) < 2D_A.$$

Therefore,

$$\sum_{i \in X} s_i = \sum_{A \subseteq I} y_A \sum_{i \in X - A} v_i^A < 2 \sum_{A : A \subseteq I} D_A y_A \leq 2\,\text{OPT},$$

where the final inequality follows by weak duality since $\sum_{A : A \subseteq I} D_A y_A$ is the dual objective function. $\square$

The proof of the performance guarantee of the algorithm shows that the integrality gap of the new integer programming formulation must be at most 2.

7.6 The Uncapacitated Facility Location Problem

We now return to the uncapacitated facility location problem introduced in Section 4.5 for which we gave a randomized approximation algorithm in Section 5.8. Recall that the input to the problem is a set of clients D and a set of facilities F, with facility costs f_i for all facilities $i \in F$, and assignment costs c_{ij} for all facilities $i \in F$ and clients $j \in D$. The goal is to select a subset of facilities to open and an assignment of clients to open facilities so as to minimize the total cost of the open facilities plus the assignment costs. As before, we consider the *metric* uncapacitated facility location and assume that the clients and facilities are points in a metric space, and the assignment cost c_{ij} is the distance between client j and facility i. In particular, given clients j, l and facilities i, k, we have that $c_{ij} \leq c_{il} + c_{kl} + c_{kj}$ by the triangle inequality.

We will now give a primal-dual approximation algorithm for the problem. Recall the linear programming relaxation of the problem we used in previous sections:

$$\text{minimize} \sum_{i \in F} f_i y_i + \sum_{i \in F, j \in D} c_{ij} x_{ij}$$

$$\text{subject to} \sum_{i \in F} x_{ij} = 1, \qquad \forall j \in D,$$

$$x_{ij} \leq y_i, \qquad \forall i \in F, j \in D,$$

$$x_{ij} \geq 0, \qquad \forall i \in F, j \in D,$$

$$y_i \geq 0, \qquad \forall i \in F,$$

in which variable x_{ij} indicates whether client j is assigned to facility i, and variable y_i indicates whether facility i is open or not. The dual of the LP relaxation is

$$\text{maximize} \quad \sum_{j \in D} v_j$$

$$\text{subject to} \quad \sum_{j \in D} w_{ij} \leq f_i, \qquad \forall i \in F,$$

$$v_j - w_{ij} \leq c_{ij}, \qquad \forall i \in F, j \in D,$$

$$w_{ij} \geq 0, \qquad \forall i \in F, j \in D.$$

It is also useful to recall the intuition for the dual that we gave in Section 4.5. We can view the dual variables v_j as the amount that each client j will pay toward its part of the cost of the solution. If facility costs are all zero, then $v_j = \min_{i \in F} c_{ij}$. To handle nonzero facility costs, the cost f_i is split into nonnegative cost shares w_{ij} apportioned among the clients, so that $\sum_{j \in D} w_{ij} \leq f_i$. A client j needs to pay this share only if it uses facility i. In this way, we no longer charge explicitly for opening a facility, but still recover some of its cost. Each client j is willing to pay the lowest cost over all facilities of its service cost and its share of the facility cost, so that $v_j = \min_{i \in F}(c_{ij} + w_{ij})$. By allowing v_j to be any value for which $v_j \leq c_{ij} + w_{ij}$, the objective function maximizing $\sum_{j \in D} v_j$ forces v_j to be equal to the smallest right-hand side over all facilities $i \in F$. Thus, any feasible solution to the dual is a lower bound on the cost of an optimal solution to the facility location problem.

To get some intuition for why a primal-dual analysis will be useful for this problem, let us first consider a dual feasible solution (v^*, w^*) that is *maximal*; that is, we cannot increase any v_j^* by any positive amount and then derive a set of w_{ij}^* that gives a dual feasible solution. Such a dual solution has some very nice structure. To discuss this further, we modify a definition used in previous sections, and introduce a new one.

Definition 7.11. *Given a dual solution* (v^*, w^*), *we say that a client* j *neighbors a facility* i *(or that* i *neighbors* j*) if* $v_j^* \geq c_{ij}$. *We let* $N(j) = \{i \in F : v_j^* \geq c_{ij}\}$ *be the neighbors of a client* j *and* $N(i) = \{j \in D : v_j^* \geq c_{ij}\}$ *be the neighbors of a facility* i.

Definition 7.12. *Given a dual solution* (v^*, w^*), *we say that a client* j *contributes to a facility* i *if* $w_{ij}^* > 0$.

In other words, a client j contributes to facility i if it has a nonzero cost share w_{ij}^* for that facility.

We observe that given dual variables v^*, we can derive a feasible set of cost shares w^* (if they exist) by setting $w_{ij}^* = \max(0, v_j^* - c_{ij})$. Observe that if we derive w^* in this way and client j contributes to facility i, then j neighbors i ($j \in N(i)$), since $w_{ij}^* > 0$ implies $v_j^* > c_{ij}$. Furthermore, if $j \in N(i)$, then $v_j^* = c_{ij} + w_{ij}^*$.

Let T be the set of all facilities such that the sum of the cost shares is equal to the cost of the facility; in other words, the corresponding dual inequality is tight. Then $T = \{i \in F : \sum_{j \in D} w_{ij}^* = f_i\}$. First we claim that in a maximal dual solution (v^*, w^*), every client must neighbor some facility in T. To see this we claim that in a maximal dual solution, it must be the case that $v_j^* = \min_{i \in F}(c_{ij} + w_{ij}^*)$, and some facility $i \in F$ attaining the minimum must be in T. Then for this facility i, $v_j^* \geq c_{ij}$, and j neighbors $i \in T$. To see the claim, clearly if $v_j^* < \min_{i \in F}(c_{ij} + w_{ij}^*)$, we can feasibly increase v_j^* and the solution is not maximal. If $v_j^* = \min_{i \in F}(c_{ij} + w_{ij}^*)$ and all facilities i attaining the minimum are not in T, then since $\sum_{k \in D} w_{ik}^* < f_i$ for these facilities i we can feasibly increase v_j^* and w_{ij}^* for these facilities i, and once again the solution is not maximal.

Given some facility $i \in T$, the cost of the facility plus the cost of assigning the neighbors $N(i)$ to i is exactly equal to the sum of the dual variables of the neighboring clients; that is,

$$f_i + \sum_{j \in N(i)} c_{ij} = \sum_{j \in N(i)} (w_{ij}^* + c_{ij}) = \sum_{j \in N(i)} v_j^*,$$

where the first equality follows since $w_{ij}^* > 0$ implies that $j \in N(i)$ and the second equality follows since $j \in N(i)$ implies that $w_{ij}^* + c_{ij} = v_j^*$. Since all clients have a neighbor in T, it would then seem that we could get an optimal algorithm by opening all facilities in T and assigning each client to its neighbor in T. The difficulty with this approach is that a given client j might neighbor several facilities in T and might contribute to many of them; we then use v_j^* multiple times to pay for the cost of these facilities. We can fix this by opening only a subset T' of T such that each client contributes to the cost of at most one facility in T'. If we do this in such a way that clients not neighboring a facility in T' are nonetheless not too far away from a facility in T', we can get a good performance guarantee for the algorithm.

We now give the primal-dual algorithm in Algorithm 7.8. We generate a maximal dual solution by increasing the dual variables v_j. We let S be the set of clients whose duals we are increasing, and T be the set of facilities whose dual inequality is tight. Initially $S = D$ and $T = \emptyset$. We increase v_j uniformly for all $j \in S$. Once $v_j = c_{ij}$ for some i, we increase w_{ij} uniformly with v_j. We increase v_j until one of two things happens: either j becomes a neighbor of a facility in T, or a dual inequality becomes tight for some facility i. In the first case, we remove j from S, and in the second case

$v \leftarrow 0, w \leftarrow 0$
$S \leftarrow D$
$T \leftarrow \emptyset$
while $S \neq \emptyset$ **do** // While not all clients neighbor a facility in T
    Increase v_j for all $j \in S$ and w_{ij} for all $i \in N(j)$, $j \in S$ uniformly until some
        $j \in S$ neighbors some $i \in T$ or some $i \notin T$ has a tight dual inequality
    if some $j \in S$ neighbors some $i \in T$ **then**
        $S \leftarrow S - \{j\}$
    if $i \notin T$ has a tight dual inequality **then**
        // facility i is added to T
        $T \leftarrow T \cup \{i\}$
        $S \leftarrow S - N(i)$
$T' \leftarrow \emptyset$
while $T \neq \emptyset$ **do**
    Pick $i \in T$; $T' \leftarrow T' \cup \{i\}$
    // remove all facilities h if some client j contributes to h and i
    $T \leftarrow T - \{h \in T : \exists j \in D, w_{ij} > 0 \text{ and } w_{hj} > 0\}$

Algorithm 7.8. Primal-dual algorithm for the uncapacitated facility location problem.

we add i to T and remove all neighboring clients $N(i)$ from S. Once S is empty and every client neighbors a facility in T, we select a subset T' of T by iteratively picking an arbitrary $i \in T$, then deleting all facilities i' in T such that there exists some client j that contributes to both i and i'. We then open all facilities in T' and assign every client to the closest open facility.

We claim the following lemma about the set of facilities T' and the dual solution (v, w) produced by the algorithm. It shows that if a client does not have a neighbor in T', then it is not far away from a facility in T'.

Lemma 7.13. *If a client j does not have a neighbor in T', then there exists a facility $i \in T'$ such that $c_{ij} \leq 3v_j$.*

The intuition is that if a client j does not have a neighbor in T', then it must have neighbored some tight facility $h \notin T'$ such that some other client k contributed both to h and another facility $i \in T'$ (see Figure 7.8). By applying triangle inequality we obtain the factor of 3. We defer the proof of the lemma for the moment and show that it implies a performance guarantee of 3 for the algorithm.

Theorem 7.14. *Algorithm 7.8 is a 3-approximation algorithm for the uncapacitated facility location problem.*

Proof. For any client that contributes to a facility in T', we assign it to this facility. Note that by construction of the algorithm, any client contributes to at most one facility in T', so this assignment is unique. For clients that neighbor facilities in T' but do not contribute to any of them, assign each to some arbitrary neighboring facility in T'. Let $A(i) \subseteq N(i)$ be the neighboring clients assigned to a facility $i \in T'$. Then as discussed above, the cost of opening the facilities in T' plus the cost of assigning the neighboring clients is

$$\sum_{i \in T'} \left(f_i + \sum_{j \in A(i)} c_{ij} \right) = \sum_{i \in T'} \sum_{j \in A(i)} (w_{ij} + c_{ij}) = \sum_{i \in T'} \sum_{j \in A(i)} v_j,$$

where the first equality holds because $i \in T'$ implies $\sum_{j \in D} w_{ij} = f_i$ and $w_{ij} > 0$ implies $j \in A(i)$. Let Z be the set of all clients not neighboring a facility in T', so that $Z = D - \bigcup_{i \in T'} A(i)$. We have by Lemma 7.13 that the cost of assigning any $j \in Z$ to some facility in T' is at most $3v_j$. Thus, the total assignment cost for these clients is at most

$$3 \sum_{j \in Z} v_j.$$

Putting everything together, we have that the cost of the solution is at most

$$\sum_{i \subset T'} \sum_{j \subset A(i)} v_j + 3 \sum_{j \in Z} v_j \leq 3 \sum_{j \in D} v_j \leq 3 \, \mathrm{OPT},$$

where the final inequality follows by weak duality. $\square$

Now we finish the proof of the lemma.

Proof of Lemma 7.13. Let j be an arbitrary client that does not neighbor a facility in T'. During the course of the algorithm, we stopped increasing v_j because j neighbored some $h \in T$. Obviously $h \notin T'$, since otherwise j would neighbor a facility in T'. The facility h must have been removed from T' during the final phase of the algorithm because there exists another client k such that k contributes to both h and another facility $i \in T'$. See Figure 7.8. We would now like to show that the cost of assigning j to this facility i is at most $3v_j$. In particular, we will show that each of the three terms in $c_{hj} + c_{hk} + c_{ik}$ is no more than v_j, which will then prove by the triangle inequality that $c_{ij} \leq 3v_j$.

We know that $c_{hj} \leq v_j$ simply because j neighbors h. Now consider the point in the algorithm at which we stop increasing v_j. By our choice of h, at this point in the algorithm either h is already in T or the algorithm adds h to T. Because client k contributes to facility h, it must be the case that either v_k has already stopped increasing or we stop increasing it at the same point that we stop increasing v_j. Because the dual variables are increased uniformly, we must have that $v_j \geq v_k$. Since client k contributes to both facilities h and i, we know that $v_k \geq c_{hk}$ and $v_k \geq c_{ik}$. Thus, $v_j \geq v_k \geq c_{hk}$ and $v_j \geq v_k \geq c_{ik}$, as claimed. $\square$

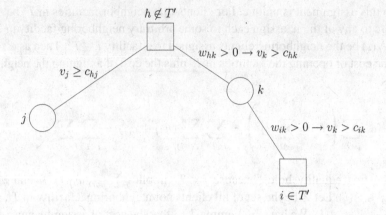

Figure 7.8. Proof of Lemma 7.13.

7.7 Lagrangean Relaxation and the k-Median Problem

In this section, we look at a variant of the uncapacitated facility location problem called the *k-median problem*. As in the uncapacitated facility location problem, we are given as input a set of clients D and a set of facilities F, with assignment costs c_{ij} for all facilities $i \in F$ and clients $j \in D$. However, there are no longer costs for opening facilities; instead, we are given as input a positive integer k that is an upper bound on the number of facilities that can be opened. The goal is to select a subset of facilities of at most k facilities to open and an assignment of clients to open facilities so as to minimize the total assignment costs. As before, we assume that the clients and facilities are points in a metric space, and the assignment cost c_{ij} is the distance between client j and facility i. Since the facilities are points in a metric space, we also have distances between pairs of facilities, a fact we will use in our algorithm. For facilities $h, i \in F$, let c_{hi} denote the distance between h and i.

An alternative perspective on the k-median problem is that it is a type of clustering problem. In Section 2.2, we saw the k-center problem, in which we wished to find k clusters of a set of vertices. Each cluster was defined by a cluster center; each vertex assigned itself to the closest cluster center, and the goal was to find a set of k cluster centers such that the maximum distance of a vertex to its cluster center was minimized. In the k-median problem, the facilities correspond to potential cluster centers, and the clients correspond to vertices. As in the k-center problem, we choose k cluster centers, and each vertex assigns itself to the closest cluster center. However, rather than trying to minimize the maximum distance of a vertex to its cluster center, we minimize the sum of the distances of the vertices to their cluster centers. For the rest of this section, we will discuss the k-median problem in terms of a facility location problem; since the clustering problem is completely equivalent, this is just a choice of terminology.

We can formulate the k-median problem as an integer program very similar to the one used for the uncapacitated facility location in Section 4.5. If we let $y_i \in \{0, 1\}$ indicate whether we open facility i, then in order to limit the number of open facilities to k, we introduce the constraint $\sum_{i \in F} y_i \leq k$. This gives the following integer programming formulation:

$$\text{minimize} \quad \sum_{i \in F, j \in D} c_{ij} x_{ij}$$

$$\text{subject to} \quad \sum_{i \in F} x_{ij} = 1, \qquad \forall j \in D,$$

$$x_{ij} \le y_i, \qquad \forall i \in F, j \in D,$$

$$\sum_{i \in F} y_i \le k,$$

$$x_{ij} \in \{0, 1\}, \qquad \forall i \in F, j \in D,$$

$$y_i \in \{0, 1\}, \qquad \forall i \in F.$$

The only differences from the uncapacitated facility location integer program of Section 4.5 is the extra constraint and the objective function, which has no facility costs.

We use the idea of *Lagrangean relaxation* to reduce the k-median problem to the uncapacitated facility location problem. In Lagrangean relaxation, we eliminate complicating constraints but add penalties for their violation to the objective function. For example, consider the linear programming relaxation of the integer program for the k-median problem:

$$\text{minimize} \quad \sum_{i \in F, j \in D} c_{ij} x_{ij} \tag{7.7}$$

$$\text{subject to} \quad \sum_{i \in F} x_{ij} = 1, \qquad \forall j \in D,$$

$$x_{ij} \le y_i, \qquad \forall i \in F, j \in D,$$

$$\sum_{i \in F} y_i \le k,$$

$$x_{ij} \ge 0, \qquad \forall i \in F, j \in D,$$

$$y_i \ge 0, \qquad \forall i \in F.$$

To make the problem more closely resemble the uncapacitated facility location problem, we would like to get rid of the constraint $\sum_{i \in F} y_i \le k$. To do this, we add a penalty $\lambda \left(\sum_{i \in F} y_i - k \right)$ to the objective function for some constant $\lambda \ge 0$. The penalty term favors solutions that obey the constraint. So our new linear program is then

$$\text{minimize} \quad \sum_{i \in F, j \in D} c_{ij} x_{ij} + \sum_{i \in F} \lambda y_i - \lambda k \tag{7.8}$$

$$\text{subject to} \quad \sum_{i \in F} x_{ij} = 1, \qquad \forall j \in D,$$

$$x_{ij} \le y_i, \qquad \forall i \in F, j \in D,$$

$$x_{ij} \ge 0, \qquad \forall i \in F, j \in D,$$

$$y_i \ge 0, \qquad \forall i \in F.$$

First, observe that any feasible solution for the linear programming relaxation (7.7) of the k-median problem is also feasible for this linear program (7.8). Also, for any $\lambda \geq 0$, any feasible solution for the linear programming relaxation of the k-median problem (7.7) has an objective function value in this linear program (7.8) at most that of its value in (7.7). Therefore, this linear program (7.8) gives a lower bound on the cost of an optimal solution to the k-median problem. We will denote the optimum cost of the k-median problem as OPT_k. Observe that except for the constant term of $-\lambda k$, the linear program now looks exactly like the linear programming relaxation of the uncapacitated facility location problem in which each facility cost $f_i = \lambda$. If we take the dual of this linear program, we obtain

$$\text{maximize} \quad \sum_{j \in D} v_j - \lambda k \tag{7.9}$$

$$\text{subject to} \quad \sum_{j \in D} w_{ij} \leq \lambda, \qquad \forall i \in F,$$

$$v_j - w_{ij} \leq c_{ij}, \qquad \forall i \in F, j \in D,$$

$$w_{ij} \geq 0, \qquad \forall i \in F, j \in D.$$

Again, this is the same as the dual of the linear programming relaxation of the uncapacitated facility location problem except that each facility cost is λ and there is an extra constant term of $-\lambda k$ in the objective function.

We would like to use the primal-dual algorithm for the uncapacitated facility location problem from the previous section in which all facility costs f_i are set to λ for some choice of $\lambda \geq 0$. While this will open some set of facilities, how can we then obtain a performance guarantee? In the previous section, we showed that the algorithm opens a set S of facilities and constructs a feasible dual (v, w) so that

$$\sum_{j \in D} \min_{i \in S} c_{ij} + \sum_{i \in S} f_i \leq 3 \sum_{j \in D} v_j.$$

For notational convenience, let $c(S) = \sum_{j \in D} \min_{i \in S} c_{ij}$. In Exercise 7.8, we observe that this claim can be strengthened slightly to

$$c(S) + 3 \sum_{i \in S} f_i \leq 3 \sum_{j \in D} v_j.$$

Substituting $f_i = \lambda$, and rearranging, gives us

$$c(S) \leq 3 \left(\sum_{j \in D} v_j - \lambda |S| \right). \tag{7.10}$$

Note that if, by chance, the algorithm opens a set of facilities S such that $|S| = k$, we then have that

$$c(S) \leq 3 \left(\sum_{j \in D} v_j - \lambda k \right) \leq 3 \cdot \mathrm{OPT}_k.$$

This follows since (v, w) is a feasible solution to the dual program (7.9), which is a lower bound on the cost of an optimal solution to the k-median problem, and since $\sum_{j \in D} v_j - \lambda k$ is the dual objective function.

A natural idea is to try to find some value of λ such that the facility location algorithm opens a set of facilities S with $|S| = k$. We will do this via a bisection search. To initialize the search, we need two initial values of λ, one for which the facility location algorithm opens at least k facilities, and one for which it opens at most k facilities. Consider what happens with the facility location algorithm when $\lambda = 0$. If the algorithm opens fewer than k facilities, then we can open an additional $k - |S|$ facilities at no cost, and apply the previous reasoning to get a solution of cost at most $3 \, \mathrm{OPT}_k$. So we assume that with $\lambda = 0$, the algorithm opens more than k facilities. It is also not hard to show that if $\lambda = \sum_{j \in D} \sum_{i \in F} c_{ij}$, then the algorithm opens a single facility.

Thus, we can run the bisection search on λ as follows. We initially set $\lambda_1 = 0$ and $\lambda_2 = \sum_{j \in D} \sum_{i \in F} c_{ij}$; as discussed above, these two values of λ return solutions S_1 and S_2 (respectively) in which $|S_1| > k$ and $|S_2| < k$. We run the algorithm on the value $\lambda = \frac{1}{2}(\lambda_1 + \lambda_2)$. If the algorithm returns a solution S with exactly k facilities, then by the arguments above, we are done, and we have a solution of cost at most $3 \, \mathrm{OPT}_k$. If S has more than k facilities, then we set $\lambda_1 = \lambda$ and $S_1 = S$; otherwise, S has fewer than k facilities and we set $\lambda_2 = \lambda$ and $S_2 = S$. We then repeat until either the algorithm finds a solution with exactly k facilities or the interval $\lambda_2 - \lambda_1$ becomes suitably small, at which point we will be able to obtain a solution to the k-median problem by appropriately combining the solutions from S_1 and S_2. If we let $c_{\min}$ be the smallest nonzero assignment cost, we run the bisection search until either the algorithm finds a solution with exactly k facilities, or $\lambda_2 - \lambda_1 \leq \epsilon c_{\min}/|F|$. In the latter case, we will use S_1 and S_2 to obtain a solution S in polynomial time such that $|S| = k$ and $c(S) \leq 2(3 + \epsilon) \, \mathrm{OPT}_k$. This will give us a $2(3 + \epsilon)$-approximation algorithm for the k-median problem.

If we have not terminated with a solution with exactly k facilities, the algorithm terminates with solutions S_1 and S_2 and corresponding dual solutions (v^1, w^1) and (v^2, w^2) such that $|S_1| > k > |S_2|$ and $c(S_\ell) \leq 3(\sum_{j \in D} v_j^\ell - \lambda_\ell k)$ for $\ell = 1, 2$ by inequality (7.10). Also, by the termination condition, $\lambda_2 - \lambda_1 \leq \epsilon c_{\min}/|F|$. Without loss of generality, we can assume that $0 < c_{\min} \leq \mathrm{OPT}_k$, since otherwise $\mathrm{OPT}_k = 0$; we leave it as an exercise to show that we can find an optimal solution to the k-median problem in polynomial time if $\mathrm{OPT}_k = 0$ (Exercise 7.9). Note that the binary search on λ makes $O(\log \frac{|F| \sum c_{ij}}{\epsilon c_{\min}})$ calls to the facility location algorithm, and thus the overall algorithm runs in polynomial time.

We will now show how we can use the two solutions S_1 and S_2 to obtain a solution S in polynomial time such that $|S| = k$ and $c(S) \leq 2(3 + \epsilon) \, \mathrm{OPT}_k$. To do this, we first need to relate the costs of the two solutions to OPT_k. Let α_1 and α_2 be such that $\alpha_1 |S_1| + \alpha_2 |S_2| = k$ and $\alpha_1 + \alpha_2 = 1$, with $\alpha_1, \alpha_2 \geq 0$. Note that this implies that

$$\alpha_1 = \frac{k - |S_2|}{|S_1| - |S_2|} \text{ and } \alpha_2 = \frac{|S_1| - k}{|S_1| - |S_2|}.$$

We can then get a dual solution $(\tilde{v}, \tilde{w})$ by letting $\tilde{v} = \alpha_1 v^1 + \alpha_2 v^2$ and $\tilde{w} = \alpha_1 w^1 + \alpha_2 w^2$. Note that $(\tilde{v}, \tilde{w})$ is feasible for the dual linear program (7.9) with facility costs

λ_2 since it is a convex combination of two feasible dual solutions. We can now prove the following lemma, which states that the convex combination of the costs of S_1 and S_2 must be close to the cost of an optimal solution.

Lemma 7.15.

$$\alpha_1 c(S_1) + \alpha_2 c(S_2) \leq (3 + \epsilon) \operatorname{OPT}_k.$$

Proof. We first observe that

$$c(S_1) \leq 3 \left(\sum_{j \in D} v_j^1 - \lambda_1 |S_1| \right)$$

$$= 3 \left(\sum_{j \in D} v_j^1 - (\lambda_1 + \lambda_2 - \lambda_2)|S_1| \right)$$

$$= 3 \left(\sum_{j \in D} v_j^1 - \lambda_2 |S_1| \right) + (\lambda_2 - \lambda_1)|S_1|$$

$$\leq 3 \left(\sum_{j \in D} v_j^1 - \lambda_2 |S_1| \right) + \epsilon \operatorname{OPT}_k,$$

where the last inequality follows from our bound on the difference $\lambda_2 - \lambda_1$.

Now if we take the convex combination of the inequality above and our bound on $c(S_2)$, we obtain

$$\alpha_1 c(S_1) + \alpha_2 c(S_2) \leq 3\alpha_1 \left(\sum_{j \in D} v_j^1 - \lambda_2 |S_1| \right) + \alpha_1 \epsilon \operatorname{OPT}_k$$

$$+ 3\alpha_2 \left(\sum_{j \in D} v_j^2 - \lambda_2 |S_2| \right).$$

Recalling that $\tilde{v} = \alpha_1 v^1 + \alpha_2 v^2$ is a dual feasible solution for facility costs λ_2, that $\alpha_1 |S_1| + \alpha_2 |S_2| = k$, and that $\alpha_1 \leq 1$, we have that

$$\alpha_1 c(S_1) + \alpha_2 c(S_2) \leq 3 \left(\sum_{j \in D} \tilde{v}_j - \lambda_2 k \right) + \alpha_1 \epsilon \cdot \operatorname{OPT}_k \leq (3 + \epsilon) \operatorname{OPT}_k. \qquad \square$$

Our algorithm then splits into two cases, a simple case when $\alpha_2 \geq \frac{1}{2}$ and a more complicated case when $\alpha_2 < \frac{1}{2}$. If $\alpha_2 \geq \frac{1}{2}$, we return S_2 as our solution. Note that $|S_2| < k$, and thus is a feasible solution. Using $\alpha_2 \geq \frac{1}{2}$ and Lemma 7.15, we obtain

$$c(S_2) \leq 2\alpha_2 c(S_2) \leq 2 (\alpha_1 c(S_1) + \alpha_2 c(S_2)) \leq 2(3 + \epsilon) \operatorname{OPT}_k,$$

as desired.

Before we give our algorithm for the remaining case, we let $c(j, S) = \min_{i \in S} c_{ij}$, so that $\sum_{j \in D} c(j, S) = c(S)$. Now for each facility $i \in S_2$, we open the closest facility $h \in S_1$; that is, the facility $h \in S_1$ that minimizes c_{ih}. If this doesn't open $|S_2|$ facilities

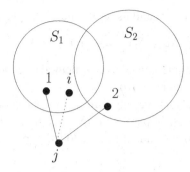

Figure 7.9. The bad case of assigning clients. Client j is closest to 1 in S_1, is closest to 2 in S_2, but gets assigned to i in S_1 since this is the closest facility in S_1 to 2 in S_2.

of S_1 because some facilities in S_2 are close to the same facility in S_1, we open some arbitrary facilities in S_1 so that exactly $|S_2|$ are opened. We then choose a random subset of $k - |S_2|$ of the $|S_1| - |S_2|$ facilities of S_1 remaining, and open these. Let S be the resulting set of facilities opened.

We now show the following lemma.

Lemma 7.16. *If $\alpha_2 < \frac{1}{2}$, then opening the facilities as above has cost $E[c(S)] \leq 2(3 + \epsilon)\mathrm{OPT}_k$.*

Proof. To prove the lemma, we consider the expected cost of assigning a given client $j \in D$ to a facility opened by the randomized algorithm. Let us suppose that the facility $1 \in S_1$ is the open facility in S_1 closest to j; that is, $c_{1j} = c(j, S_1)$; similarly, let $2 \in S_2$ be the open facility in S_2 closest to j. Note that with probability $\frac{k - |S_2|}{|S_1| - |S_2|} = \alpha_1$, the facility $1 \in S_1$ is opened in the randomized step of the algorithm if it has not already been opened by the first step of the algorithm. Thus, with probability at least α_1, the cost of assigning j to the closest open facility in S is at most $c_{1j} = c(j, S_1)$. With probability at most $1 - \alpha_1 = \alpha_2$, the facility 1 is not opened. In this case, we can at worst assign j to a facility opened in the first step of the algorithm; in particular, we assign j to the facility in S_1 closest to $2 \in S_2$. Let $i \in S_1$ be the closest facility to $2 \in S_2$; see Figure 7.9. Then

$$c_{ij} \leq c_{i2} + c_{2j}$$

by triangle inequality. We know that $c_{i2} \leq c_{12}$ since i is the closest facility in S_1 to 2, so that

$$c_{ij} \leq c_{12} + c_{2j}.$$

Finally, by triangle inequality $c_{12} \leq c_{1j} + c_{2j}$, so that we have

$$c_{ij} \leq c_{1j} + c_{2j} + c_{2j} = c(j, S_1) + 2c(j, S_2).$$

Thus, the expected cost of assigning j to the closest facility in S is

$$E[c(j, S)] \leq \alpha_1 c(j, S_1) + \alpha_2 (c(j, S_1) + 2c(j, S_2)) = c(j, S_1) + 2\alpha_2 c(j, S_2).$$

By the assumption $\alpha_2 < \frac{1}{2}$, so that $\alpha_1 = 1 - \alpha_2 > \frac{1}{2}$, we obtain

$$E[c(j, S)] \leq 2(\alpha_1 c(j, S_1) + \alpha_2 c(j, S_2)).$$

Then summing over all $j \in D$ and using Lemma 7.15, we obtain

$$E[c(S)] \le 2(\alpha_1 c(S_1) + \alpha_2 c(S_2)) \le 2(3 + \epsilon) \mathrm{OPT}_k . \qquad \square$$

This algorithm can be derandomized by the method of conditional expectations; we leave this as an exercise (Exercise 7.10).

In Chapter 9, we will see improved algorithms for the k-median problem using local search and greedy algorithms. In particular, in Section 9.4, we will see a dual fitting greedy algorithm for the uncapacitated facility location problem that opens a set S of facilities such that

$$c(S) + 2 \sum_{i \in S} f_i \le 2 \sum_{j \in D} v_j,$$

where v is a feasible solution to the dual of the linear programming relaxation of the uncapacitated facility location problem. Then we will be able to follow the same logic as the algorithm above to get a $2(2 + \epsilon)$-approximation algorithm for the k-median problem.

Note that it is crucial for the analysis that we have an uncapacitated facility location algorithm that returns a solution S such that

$$c(S) + \alpha \sum_{i \in S} f_i \le \alpha \sum_{j \in D} v_j$$

for some α. If this is the case, then when we set $f_i = \lambda$, we are able to derive that

$$c(S) \le \alpha \left(\sum_{j \in D} v_j - \lambda |S| \right),$$

which then allows us to use as a bound the objective function of the dual of the Lagrangean relaxation. Such algorithms are called *Lagrangean multiplier preserving*. In Chapter 14, we will see another example of a Lagrangean multiplier preserving algorithm: a primal-dual 2-approximation algorithm for the prize-collecting Steiner tree problem.

The following hardness result is known for the k-median problem via a reduction from the set cover problem. We discuss this result further in Section 16.2.

Theorem 7.17. *There is no α-approximation algorithm for the k-median problem with constant $\alpha < 1 + \frac{2}{e} \approx 1.736$ unless each problem in NP has an $O(n^{O(\log \log n)})$ time algorithm.*

Exercises

7.1 Prove that the shortest s-t path algorithm in Section 7.3 is equivalent to Dijkstra's algorithm: that is, in each step, it adds the same edge that Dijkstra's algorithm would add.

7.2 Consider the *multicut problem in trees*. In this problem, we are given a tree $T = (V, E)$, k pairs of vertices s_i-t_i, and costs $c_e \ge 0$ for each edge $e \in E$. The goal is to find a minimum-cost set of edges F such that for all i, s_i and t_i are in different connected components of $G' = (V, E - F)$.

Let P_i be the set of edges in the unique path in T between s_i and t_i. Then we can formulate the problem as the following integer program:

$$\text{minimize} \sum_{e \in E} c_e x_e$$

$$\text{subject to} \sum_{e \in P_i} x_e \geq 1, \qquad 1 \leq i \leq k,$$

$$x_e \in \{0, 1\}, \qquad e \in E.$$

Suppose we root the tree at an arbitrary vertex r. Let $depth(v)$ be the number of edges on the path from v to r. Let $lca(s_i, t_i)$ be the vertex v on the path from s_i to t_i whose depth is minimum. Suppose we use the primal-dual method to solve this problem, where the dual variable we increase in each iteration corresponds to the violated constraint that maximizes $depth(lca(s_i, t_i))$.

Prove that this gives a 2-approximation algorithm for the multicut problem in trees.

7.3 The *local ratio* technique is another technique that is highly related to the primal-dual method; however, its use of duality is implicit. Consider the following local ratio algorithm for the set cover problem. As with the primal-dual algorithm, we compute a collection I of indices of a set cover, where I is initially empty. In each iteration, we find some element e_i not covered by the current collection I. Let ϵ be the minimum weight of any set containing e_i. We subtract ϵ from the weight of each set containing e_i; some such set now has weight zero, and we add the index of this set to I.

We now analyze the performance of this algorithm. To do this, let ϵ_j be the value of ϵ from the jth iteration of the algorithm,

   (a) Show that the cost of the solution returned is at most $f \sum_j \epsilon_j$, where $f = \max_i |\{j : e_i \in S_j\}|$.
   (b) Show that the cost of the optimal solution must be at least $\sum_j \epsilon_j$.
   (c) Conclude that the algorithm is an f-approximation algorithm.

In its most general application, the local ratio technique depends upon the *local ratio theorem*, stated below. For a minimization problem Π with weights w, we say that a feasible solution F is α-*approximate with respect to* w if the weight of F is at most α times the weight of an optimal solution given weights w. Then the local ratio theorem states that if we have nonnegative weights w such that $w = w^1 + w^2$, where w^1 and w^2 are also nonnegative weights, and we have a feasible solution F such that F is α-approximate with respect to both w^1 and w^2, then F is α-approximate with respect to w.

   (d) Prove the local ratio theorem.
   (e) Explain how the set cover algorithm above can be analyzed in terms of the local ratio theorem to prove that it is an f-approximation algorithm.

Most of the algorithms in this chapter have local ratio variants.

7.4 In the 2-approximation algorithm for the generalized Steiner tree problem that we gave in Section 7.4, we first add certain edges, then remove unnecessary edges in the order opposite of the order in which they were added.

Prove that one can in fact remove unnecessary edges in *any* order and still obtain a 2-approximation algorithm for the problem. That is, we replace the edge removal steps in Algorithm 7.6 with a step that checks if there exists any edge e in F' such that $F' - e$

is feasible. If so, e is removed from F', and if not, F' is returned as the final solution. Prove that $\sum_{e \in F'} c_e \leq 2 \sum_S y_S$ for the dual y generated by the algorithm.

7.5 In the *minimum-cost branching problem* we are given a directed graph $G = (V, A)$, a root vertex $r \in V$, and weights $w_{ij} \geq 0$ for all $(i, j) \in A$. The goal of the problem is to find a minimum-cost set of arcs $F \subseteq A$ such that for every $v \in V$, there is exactly one directed path in F from r to v. Use the primal-dual method to give an optimal algorithm for this problem.

7.6 Recall that in our algorithms of Sections 4.4 and 5.7 for the prize-collecting Steiner tree problem, we used the following linear programming relaxation of the problem:

$$\text{minimize} \quad \sum_{e \in E} c_e x_e + \sum_{i \in V} \pi_i (1 - y_i)$$

$$\text{subject to} \quad \sum_{e \in \delta(S)} x_e \geq y_i, \qquad \forall i \in S, \forall S \subseteq V - r, S \neq \emptyset,$$

$$y_r = 1,$$

$$y_i \geq 0, \qquad \forall i \in V,$$

$$x_e \geq 0, \qquad \forall e \in E.$$

Given an optimal solution (x^*, y^*) to the linear program, we then selected a set of vertices U such that $U = \{i \in V : y_i^* \geq \alpha\}$ for some value of $\alpha > 0$.

Give a primal-dual algorithm that finds a Steiner tree T on the set of terminals U such that

$$\sum_{e \in T} c_e \leq \frac{2}{\alpha} \sum_{e \in E} c_e x_e^*.$$

(Hint: You should not need to design a new primal-dual algorithm.)

7.7 In the *k-path partition problem*, we are given a complete, undirected graph $G = (V, E)$ with edge costs $c_e \geq 0$ that obey the triangle inequality (that is, $c_{(u,v)} \leq c_{(u,w)} + c_{(w,v)}$ for all $u, v, w \in V$), and a parameter k such that $|V|$ is a multiple of k. The goal is to find a minimum-cost collection of paths of k vertices such that each vertex is on exactly one path.

A related problem is that of partitioning a graph into $0(\text{mod } k)$-trees. The input to this problem is the same as that above, except that the graph is not necessarily complete and edge costs do not necessarily obey the triangle inequality. The goal is to find a minimum-cost collection of trees such that each tree has $0(\text{mod } k)$ vertices, and each vertex is in exactly one tree.

(a) Given an α-approximation algorithm for the second problem, produce a $2\alpha(1 - \frac{1}{k})$-approximation algorithm for the first.

(b) Use the primal-dual method to give a 2-approximation algorithm for the second problem.

(c) Give a $4(1 - \frac{1}{k})$-approximation algorithm for the problem of partitioning a graph into *cycles* of length exactly k.

7.8 Show that the performance guarantee of the primal-dual algorithm for the uncapacitated facility location algorithm in Section 7.6 can be strengthened in the following way. Suppose that the algorithm opens the set T' of facilities and constructs the dual solution

(v, w). Show that

$$\sum_{j \in D} \min_{i \in T'} c_{ij} + 3 \sum_{i \in T'} f_i \leq 3 \sum_{j \in D} v_j.$$

7.9 Show that for the k-median problem as defined in Section 7.7, the optimal solution can be found in polynomial time if the optimum cost $OPT_k = 0$.

7.10 By using the method of conditional expectations, show that the randomized algorithm for choosing k facilities in the k-median algorithm of Section 7.7 can be made deterministic.

Chapter Notes

The primal-dual method for approximation algorithms is a generalization of the primal-dual method used for linear programming and combinatorial optimization problems such as the shortest s-t path problem, the maximum flow problem, the assignment problem, the minimum-cost branching problem, and others. For an overview of the primal-dual method and its application to these problems, see Papadimitriou and Steiglitz [238]. Edmonds [95] gives the primal-dual algorithm for the minimum-cost branching problem in Exercise 7.5. The idea of Section 7.3 that the shortest s-t path problem can be solved by an algorithm that greedily increases dual variables is due to Hoffman [168]. Dijkstra's algorithm for the same problem is due, of course, to Dijkstra [88].

The first use of the primal-dual method for approximation algorithms is due to Bar-Yehuda and Even [35]; they gave the algorithm of Section 7.1 for the set cover problem. Work in primal-dual approximation algorithms was revived by work on the generalized Steiner tree problem of Section 7.4. The first 2-approximation algorithm for the generalized Steiner tree problem is due to Agrawal, Klein, and Ravi [4], and the algorithm presented in Section 7.4 is essentially that of [4]. The use of linear programming and LP duality in the algorithm was made explicit by Goemans and Williamson [138], who extended the technique to other problems (such as the k-path partition problem of Exercise 7.7). The idea of depicting dual variables as moats is due to Jünger and Pulleyblank [180].

Several uses of the primal-dual method for approximation algorithms then followed. Bar-Yehuda, Geiger, Naor, and Roth [37] gave the feedback vertex set algorithm of Section 7.2, using Lemma 7.3, which is due to Erdős and Pósa [100]. Jain and Vazirani [177] developed the primal-dual algorithm for the uncapacitated facility location problem and the use of Lagrangean relaxation for the k-median problem in Sections 7.6 and 7.7. Carnes and Shmoys [61] gave the primal-dual algorithm for the minimum knapsack problem in Section 7.5; their algorithm uses an integer programming formulation of the problem due to Carr, Fleischer, Leung, and Phillips [62], who gave an LP-rounding 2-approximation algorithm for the problem based on their formulation.

Surveys of the primal-dual method for approximation algorithms are given by Bertsimas and Teo [46], Goemans and Williamson [140], and Williamson [288].

The local ratio technique of Exercise 7.3 is due to Bar-Yehuda and Even [36]. All of the algorithms in Sections 7.1 through 7.4 are known to have local ratio equivalents. A formal proof of the equivalence of the primal-dual method and the local ratio technique for a defined set of problems is given in Bar-Yehuda and Rawitz [38]. Surveys of the local ratio technique have been given by Bar-Yehuda [33], Bar-Yehuda, Bendel, Freund, and Rawitz [34], and Bar-Yehuda and Rawitz [38].

The hardness result for the k-median problem in Theorem 7.17 is due to Jain, Mahdian, Markakis, Saberi, and Vazirani [176], following work of Guha and Khuller [146] for the hardness of the uncapacitated facility location problem. The result of Exercise 7.2 is due to Garg, Vazirani, and Yannakakis [127]. The results of Exercises 7.4 and 7.7 are from Goemans and Williamson [138]. The result of Exercise 7.8 is from Jain and Vazirani [177]; Exercise 7.10 is also from this paper.

CHAPTER 8

Cuts and Metrics

In this chapter, we think about problems involving *metrics*. A metric (V, d) on a set of vertices V gives a distance d_{uv} for each pair of vertices $u, v \in V$ such that three properties are obeyed: (1) $d_{uv} = 0$ if and only if $v = u$; (2) $d_{uv} = d_{vu}$ for all $u, v \in V$; and (3) $d_{uv} \leq d_{uw} + d_{wv}$ for all $u, v, w \in V$. The final property is sometimes called the *triangle inequality*. We will sometimes simply refer to the metric d instead of (V, d) if the set of vertices V is clear from the context. A concept related to a metric is a *semimetric* (V, d), in which properties (2) and (3) are obeyed, but not necessarily (1), so that if $d_{uv} = 0$, then possibly $u \neq v$ (a semimetric maintains that $d_{uu} = 0$). We may sometimes ignore this distinction between metrics and semimetrics, and call them both metrics.

Metrics turn out to be a useful way of thinking about graph problems involving cuts. Many important problems in discrete optimization require finding cuts in graphs of various types. To see the connection between cuts and metrics, note that for any cut $S \subseteq V$, we can define d where $d_{uv} = 1$ if $u \in S$ and $v \notin S$, and $d_{uv} = 0$ otherwise. Note that (V, d) is then a semimetric; it is sometimes called the *cut semimetric* associated with S. Then a problem in a graph $G = (V, E)$ in which we are trying to find a cut to minimize or maximize the sum of weights w_e of the edges e in the cut becomes one of finding a cut semimetric that minimizes or maximizes $\sum_{e=(u,v) \in E} w_e d_{uv}$. In several examples in this chapter, we set up a linear programming relaxation with variables d_{uv} in which we have constraints on d corresponding to the properties of a semimetric. Then we use the metric properties of d_{uv} to help find the desired cut. In many cases, we consider for some vertex $s \in V$ all the vertices within some small distance r of s (using the LP variables d_{uv} as distances) and put them on the same side of the cut and all other vertices on the other side; we view this as taking a ball of radius r around s. This is a technique we will use extensively.

We will also consider the notion of approximating a given metric (V, d) by a metric of a simpler form. In particular, we will consider tree metrics; tree metrics are metrics that are defined by the shortest paths in a tree. Sometimes we wish to approximate problems involving distances in a graph, in which the problem becomes straightforward in a tree metric. We can sometimes get good approximation algorithms by first approximating the graph distances by a tree metric, then solving the problem easily in the tree metric.

We begin the chapter by considering a number of different cut problems. We start in Section 8.1 with the multiway cut problem, and first show that a simple algorithm involving finding a number of minimum s-t cuts gives a 2-approximation algorithm. We then show that the randomized rounding of an LP solution along the lines described above improves this to a $\frac{3}{2}$-approximation algorithm. We consider the multicut problem in Section 8.3, which also uses an LP relaxation and a rounding technique as described above. For this problem, we introduce an important technique called "region growing" that relates the edges in the cut formed by a ball to the value of the LP solution on edges inside the ball. In the following section, we apply the region-growing technique to the problem of finding small balanced cuts; balanced cuts are ones in which the two parts of the cut have roughly equal numbers of vertices. The final three sections of the chapter discuss the technique of approximating metrics by tree metrics, and present applications of this technique to the buy-at-bulk network design problem and the linear arrangement problem.

8.1 The Multiway Cut Problem and a Minimum-Cut-Based Algorithm

We begin by considering a simple variety of cut problem, and give an approximation algorithm that does not require using a linear programming relaxation. We then show that using a linear programming relaxation and treating its solution as a metric on the set of vertices gives a better performance guarantee. The problem is known as the *multiway cut* problem. We are given an undirected graph $G = (V, E)$, costs $c_e \geq 0$ for all edges $e \in E$, and k distinguished vertices $s_1, \ldots, s_k$. The goal is to remove a minimum-cost set of edges F such that no pair of distinguished vertices s_i and s_j for $i \neq j$ are in the same connected component of $(V, E - F)$.

One application of this problem arises in distributed computing. Each vertex represents an object, and an edge e between them of cost c_e represents the amount of communication between the objects. The objects need to be partitioned to reside on k different machines, with special object s_i needing to reside on the ith machine. The goal is to partition the objects onto the k machines in such a way that communication between the machines is minimized.

Our algorithm for the multiway cut problem begins with some observations about the structure of any feasible solution F. Given a feasible F, let C_i be the set of vertices reachable in $(V, E - F)$ from each distinguished vertex s_i. Let $F_i = \delta(C_i)$, where $\delta(S)$ is the set of all edges in E with exactly one endpoint in S. Observe that each F_i is a cut separating s_i from $s_1, \ldots, s_{i-1}, s_{i+1}, \ldots, s_k$. We call F_i an *isolating cut*: it isolates s_i from the other distinguished vertices. Observe also that some edges might appear in two different F_i: an edge e can have one endpoint in C_i and the other in C_j for some $j \neq i$, so that $e \in F_i$ and $e \in F_j$.

Our algorithm will compute a *minimum* isolating cut F_i between s_i and $s_1, \ldots, s_{i-1}, s_{i+1}, \ldots, s_k$ for each i: we can do this by adding a sink vertex t to the graph with infinite cost edges from the distinguished vertices (other than s_i) to the sink, and then computing a minimum s_i-t cut. We return as our solution $\bigcup_{i=1}^{k} F_i$.

Theorem 8.1. *The algorithm of computing a minimum cut between each s_i and the other distinguished vertices is a 2-approximation algorithm for the multiway cut problem.*

Proof. As above, let F_i be the minimum isolating cut between s_i and the other distinguished vertices. Let F^* be an optimal solution, and let F_i^* be the isolating cut in the optimal solution for s_i. For a subset of edges $A \subseteq E$, let $c(A) = \sum_{e \in A} c_e$. Because F_i is a minimum isolating cut for s_i, we know that $c(F_i) \leq c(F_i^*)$. Hence, the cost of the solution of the algorithm is at most $\sum_{i=1}^{k} c(F_i) \leq \sum_{i=1}^{k} c(F_i^*)$. We observed above that each edge in the optimal solution F^* can be in at most two F_i^*, so that

$$\sum_{i=1}^{k} c(F_i) \leq \sum_{i=1}^{k} c(F_i^*) \leq 2c(F^*) = 2\,\text{OPT}.$$ □

By being only slightly cleverer, we can improve the performance guarantee a little bit. Without loss of generality, let F_k be the costliest cut of $F_1, \ldots, F_k$. Note that the union of the first $k - 1$ isolating cuts, $F = \bigcup_{i=1}^{k-1} F_i$, is also a feasible solution for the problem: if s_k can reach any other distinguished vertex s_i in $(V, E - F)$, then F_i was not an isolating cut for s_i. Then we have the following.

Corollary 8.2. *The algorithm of returning the cheapest $k - 1$ minimum isolating cuts is a $(2 - \frac{2}{k})$-approximation algorithm for the multiway cut problem.*

Proof. We use the same notation as in the proof of the theorem above. Observe that the cost of our new solution F is at most $(1 - \frac{1}{k}) \sum_{i=1}^{k} c(F_i)$. Thus, its cost is at most

$$\left(1 - \frac{1}{k}\right) \sum_{i=1}^{k} c(F_i) \leq \left(1 - \frac{1}{k}\right) \sum_{i=1}^{k} c(F_i^*) \leq 2\left(1 - \frac{1}{k}\right)\text{OPT}.$$ □

8.2 The Multiway Cut Problem and an LP Rounding Algorithm

We now show that one can obtain a better approximation algorithm for the multiway cut problem via LP rounding.

First, we need to strengthen some of our observations above. We noted that for any feasible solution F to the problem, we can compute sets C_i of vertices reachable from each distinguished vertex s_i. We claim for any minimal solution F, the C_i must be a partition of the vertices V. To see this, suppose we are given some solution F such that the corresponding sets C_i do not partition V. Let S be all vertices not reachable from any s_i. Pick some j arbitrarily and add S to C_j. Let the new solution be $F' = \bigcup_{i=1}^{k} \delta(C_i)$. Then we claim that $F' \subseteq F$. Observe that for any $i \neq j$, $\delta(C_i)$ is in F. Furthermore, any edge $e \in \delta(C_j)$ must have some endpoint in some C_i with $i \neq j$. Thus, $e \in \delta(C_i)$ and is in F also.

Therefore, another way of looking at the multiway cut problem is finding an optimal partition of V into sets C_i such that $s_i \in C_i$ for all i and such that the cost of $F = \bigcup_{i=1}^{k} \delta(C_i)$ is minimized. Given this perspective, we formulate the problem as an integer program. For each vertex $u \in V$, we have k different variables, x_u^i. The variable $x_u^i = 1$ if u is assigned to the set C_i and is 0 otherwise. We create a variable z_e^i, which will be 1 if $e \in \delta(C_i)$ and 0 otherwise. Since if $e \in \delta(C_i)$, it is also the case that $e \in \delta(C_j)$ for some $j \neq i$, the objective function of the integer program is then

$$\frac{1}{2} \sum_{e \in E} c_e \sum_{i=1}^{k} z_e^i;$$

this will give exactly the cost of the edges in the solution $F = \bigcup_{i=1}^{k} \delta(C_i)$ for the assignment of vertices to sets C_i given by the variables x_u^i. Now we consider constraints for the program. Obviously s_i must be assigned to C_i, so we have $x_{s_i}^i = 1$ for all i. To enforce that $z_e^i = 1$ when $e \in \delta(C_i)$ for $e = (u, v)$, we add constraints $z_e^i \geq x_u^i - x_v^i$ and $z_e^i \geq x_v^i - x_u^i$; this enforces that $z^i \geq |x_u^i - x_v^i|$. Since the integer program will minimize the objective function and z_e^i appears with a nonnegative coefficient in the objective function, at optimality we will have $z_e^i = |x_u^i - x_v^i|$. Thus, $z_e^i = 1$ if one of the two endpoints of the edge $e = (u, v)$ is assigned to the set C_i and the other is not. Then the overall integer program is as follows:

$$\text{minimize} \quad \frac{1}{2} \sum_{e \in E} c_e \sum_{i=1}^{k} z_e^i \tag{8.1}$$

$$\text{subject to} \quad \sum_{i=1}^{k} x_u^i = 1, \qquad \forall u \in V, \tag{8.2}$$

$$z_e^i \geq x_u^i - x_v^i, \qquad \forall e = (u, v) \in E,$$

$$z_e^i \geq x_v^i - x_u^i, \qquad \forall e = (u, v) \in E,$$

$$x_{s_i}^i = 1, \qquad i = 1, \ldots, k,$$

$$x_u^i \in \{0, 1\}, \qquad \forall u \in V, i = 1, \ldots, k.$$

The linear programming relaxation of this integer program is closely connected with the ℓ_1 metric for measuring distances in Euclidean space. Let $x, y \in \mathfrak{R}^n$, and suppose that x^i, y^i are the ith coordinates of x and y. Then the ℓ_1 metric is as follows.

Definition 8.3. *Given $x, y \in \mathfrak{R}^n$, the ℓ_1-metric is a metric such that the distance between x and y is $\|x - y\|_1 = \sum_{i=1}^{n} |x^i - y^i|$.*

We relax the integer program above to a linear program by replacing the integrality condition $x_u^i \in \{0, 1\}$ with $x_u^i \geq 0$. Observe then that the linear program can be given a much more compact formulation. The variable x_u^i is the ith coordinate of a vector x_u. Each $x_u \in \mathfrak{R}^k$; in fact, because of constraint (8.2), each x_u lies in the k-simplex Δ_k, where $\Delta_k = \{x \in \mathfrak{R}^k : \sum_{i=1}^{k} x^i = 1\}$. Each distinguished vertex s_i has $x_{s_i} = e_i$, where e_i is the vector with 1 in the ith coordinate and zeroes elsewhere. Finally, we observe that $\sum_{i=1}^{k} z_e^i = \sum_{i=1}^{k} |x_u^i - x_v^i| = \|x_u - x_v\|_1$, which is just the distance between the points x_u and x_v under the ℓ_1 metric. Thus, the linear programming relaxation

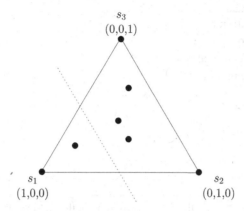

Figure 8.1. A geometric representation of an LP solution for $k = 3$. The distinguished vertices s_1, s_2, and s_3 are given by the coordinates $(1, 0, 0)$, $(0, 1, 0)$, and $(0, 0, 1)$, respectively. Any other vertex lies in the triangle defined by these three coordinates. The dotted line represents a ball around s_1.

becomes

$$\text{minimize } \frac{1}{2} \sum_{e=(u,v)\in E} c_e \|x_u - x_v\|_1 \tag{8.3}$$

$$\text{subject to } x_{s_i} = e_i, \qquad i = 1, \ldots, k,$$

$$x_u \in \Delta_k, \qquad \forall u \in V.$$

In Figure 8.1, we give a geometric representation of an instance with $k = 3$.

We will give an approximation algorithm by the randomized rounding of the solution of the linear program. In particular, we will take all vertices that are close to the distinguished vertex s_i in the LP solution and put them in C_i. For any $r \geq 0$ and $1 \leq i \leq k$, let $B(e_i, r)$ be the set of vertices corresponding to the points x_u in a ball of radius r in the ℓ_1 metric around e_i; that is, $B(e_i, r) = \{u \in V : \frac{1}{2}\|e_i - x_u\|_1 \leq r\}$. We will sometimes write $B(s_i, r)$ instead of $B(e_i, r)$. We include the factor of $1/2$ in the

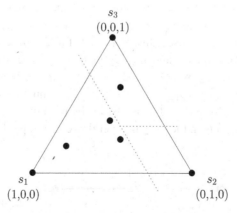

Figure 8.2. A geometric representation of the algorithm for $k = 3$. The random permutation is 1,3,2. The ball around s_3 assigns to C_3 all vertices in the ball not already assigned to C_1.

Let x be an LP solution to (8.3)
for all $1 \leq i \leq k$ **do** $C_i \leftarrow \emptyset$
Pick $r \in (0, 1)$ uniformly at random
Pick a random permutation π of $\{1, \ldots, k\}$
$X \leftarrow \emptyset$ // X keeps track of all currently assigned vertices
for $i \leftarrow 1$ to $k - 1$ **do**
$\quad C_{\pi(i)} \leftarrow B(s_{\pi(i)}, r) - X$
$\quad X \leftarrow X \cup C_{\pi(i)}$
$C_{\pi(k)} \leftarrow V - X$
return $F = \bigcup_{i=1}^{k} \delta(C_i)$

Algorithm 8.1. Randomized rounding algorithm for the multiway cut problem.

definition so that all vertices are within a ball of radius 1: $B(e_i, 1) = V$ for all i. See Figure 8.1 for an illustration.

We now consider Algorithm 8.1. The algorithm selects $r \in (0, 1)$ uniformly at random, and a random permutation π of the indices $\{1, \ldots, k\}$. The algorithm proceeds through the indices in the order given by the permutation. For index $\pi(i)$ in the ordering, the algorithm assigns all previously unassigned vertices in $B(s_{\pi(i)}, r)$ to $C_{\pi(i)}$. At the end of the order, any unassigned vertices are assigned to $C_{\pi(k)}$. See Figure 8.2 for an example.

Before we get into the details of the proof, let's look at an example that will show why picking a random radius and a random permutation π is useful in giving a good performance guarantee. To simplify matters, suppose that k is large, and suppose we have an edge (u, v) where $x_v = (0, 1, 0, 0, \ldots)$ and $x_u = (\frac{1}{2}, \frac{1}{2}, 0, 0, \ldots)$; see Figure 8.3 for an illustration. We suppose that $x_{s_1} = (1, 0, 0, \ldots)$ and $x_{s_2} = (0, 1, 0, \ldots)$. Note that in this case, u can be only in the balls $B(s_1, r)$ or $B(s_2, r)$ since $r < 1$ and $\frac{1}{2}\|e_i - x_u\|_1 = 1$ for $i \neq 1, 2$. Thus, u can be assigned only to C_1, C_2, or $C_{\pi(k)}$, with the last case occurring if $x_u \notin B(s_1, r)$ and $x_u \notin B(s_2, r)$. Somewhat similarly, v can be assigned only to C_1 or C_2; in this case, x_v is always in $B(s_2, r)$ since $r > 0$ and $\|e_2 - x_v\|_1 = 0$.

Now, suppose we have a fixed permutation π. If the permutation orders s_1 before s_2, and s_2 is not last in the permutation, then we claim (u, v) enters the cut with probability $\|x_u - x_v\|_1 = 1$. To see this, note that if $1/2 \leq r < 1$, then $u \in B(s_1, r)$, but $v \notin B(s_1, r)$, so that $u \in C_1$ and $v \in C_2$. If $0 < r < 1/2$, then $v \in B(s_2, r)$, but $u \notin B(s_2, r)$, so that $v \in C_2$; we observed above that u can be assigned only to C_1, C_2, and $C_{\pi(k)}$, so that if $u \notin B(s_2, r)$ and $\pi(k) \neq 2$, it must be the case that $u \notin C_2$ and (u, v) is in the cut. Note that if s_2 is last in the permutation, this can only lower the probability that (u, v) is in the cut. In general, we can upper bound the probability

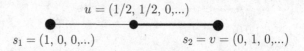

$$u = (1/2, 1/2, 0, \ldots)$$

$s_1 = (1, 0, 0, \ldots) \qquad\qquad s_2 = v = (0, 1, 0, \ldots)$

Figure 8.3. An illustration of the ideas of the analysis.

that an edge (u, v) ends up in the cut by $\|x_u - x_v\|_1$, but analyzing the algorithm with this probability is only good enough to give a performance guarantee of 2, since the contribution of edge $e = (u, v)$ to the objective function is $\frac{1}{2}c_e\|x_u - x_v\|_1$. However, if the permutation π orders s_2 before s_1, then the edge is in the cut if $0 < r < 1/2$, since $v \in C_2$ but $u \notin C_2$ as before, while if $r > 1/2$, then the edge cannot end up in the cut at all because both u and v are in $B(s_2, r)$ and hence both are assigned to C_2. Since the probability that s_2 is ordered before s_1 is $1/2$ in a random permutation, the overall probability that (u, v) is in the cut is at most

$$\Pr[(u, v) \text{ in cut } |s_1 \text{ before } s_2] \Pr[s_1 \text{ before } s_2]$$
$$+ \Pr[(u, v) \text{ in cut } |s_2 \text{ before } s_1] \Pr[s_2 \text{ before } s_1]$$
$$\leq \|x_u - x_v\|_1 \cdot \frac{1}{2} + \frac{1}{2}\|x_u - x_v\|_1 \cdot \frac{1}{2}$$
$$= \frac{3}{2} \cdot \frac{1}{2}\|x_u - x_v\|_1,$$

which will give us a performance guarantee of $3/2$.

To start the analysis, we need some lemmas that will be helpful later. The first lemma observes that any coordinate accounts for at most half of the ℓ_1 distance. The second lemma gives us a condition under which a vertex is in a ball of radius r.

Lemma 8.4. *For any index ℓ and any two vertices $u, v \in V$,*

$$|x_u^\ell - x_v^\ell| \leq \frac{1}{2}\|x_u - x_v\|_1.$$

Proof. Without loss of generality, assume that $x_u^\ell \geq x_v^\ell$. Then

$$|x_u^\ell - x_v^\ell| = x_u^\ell - x_v^\ell = \left(1 - \sum_{j \neq \ell} x_u^j\right) - \left(1 - \sum_{j \neq \ell} x_v^j\right)$$
$$= \sum_{j \neq \ell}(x_v^j - x_u^j) \leq \sum_{j \neq \ell}|x_u^j - x_v^j|.$$

By adding $|x_u^\ell - x_v^\ell|$ to both sides, we have

$$2|x_u^\ell - x_v^\ell| \leq \|x_u - x_v\|_1,$$

which gives the lemma. $\square$

Lemma 8.5. $u \in B(s_i, r)$ *if and only if $1 - x_u^i \leq r$.*

Proof. We have $u \in B(s_i, r)$ if and only if $\frac{1}{2}\|e_i - x_u\|_1 \leq r$. This is equivalent to $\frac{1}{2}\sum_{\ell=1}^{k}|e_i^\ell - x_u^\ell| \leq r$, which is equivalent to $\frac{1}{2}\sum_{\ell \neq i}x_u^\ell + \frac{1}{2}(1 - x_u^i) \leq r$. Since $\sum_{\ell \neq i}x_u^\ell = 1 - x_u^i$, this is equivalent to $1 - x_u^i \leq r$. $\square$

Theorem 8.6. *Algorithm 8.1 is a randomized $\frac{3}{2}$-approximation algorithm for the multiway cut problem.*

Proof. Pick an arbitrary edge $(u, v) \in E$. We claim that the probability that the endpoints lie in different parts of the partition is at most $\frac{3}{4}\|x_u - x_v\|_1$. Let W be a random variable denoting the value of the cut, and let Z_{uv} be a 0-1 random variable that is 1 if

u and v are in different parts of the partition, so that $W = \sum_{e=(u,v)\in E} c_e Z_{uv}$. Given the claim, we have

$$E[W] = E\left[\sum_{e=(u,v)\in E} c_e Z_{uv}\right]$$

$$= \sum_{e=(u,v)\in E} c_e E[Z_{uv}]$$

$$= \sum_{e=(u,v)\in E} c_e \cdot \Pr[(u, v) \text{ in cut}]$$

$$\leq \sum_{e=(u,v)\in E} c_e \cdot \frac{3}{4}\|x_u - x_v\|_1$$

$$= \frac{3}{2} \cdot \frac{1}{2} \sum_{e=(u,v)\in E} c_e\|x_u - x_v\|_1$$

$$\leq \frac{3}{2}\,\text{OPT},$$

where the final inequality follows since $\frac{1}{2}\sum_{e=(u,v)\in E} c_e\|x_u - x_v\|_1$ is the objective function of the LP relaxation.

Now to prove the claim. We say that an index i *settles* edge (u, v) if i is the first index in the random permutation such that at least one of $u, v \in B(s_i, r)$. We say that index i *cuts* edge (u, v) if exactly one of $u, v \in B(s_i, r)$. Let S_i be the event that i settles (u, v) and X_i be the event that i cuts (u, v). Note that S_i depends on the random permutation, while X_i is independent of the random permutation. In order for (u, v) to be in the multiway cut, there must be some index i that both settles and cuts (u, v); if this happens, then $(u, v) \in \delta(C_i)$. Thus, the probability that edge (u, v) is in the multiway cut is at most $\sum_{i=1}^{k} \Pr[S_i \wedge X_i]$. We will now show that $\sum_{i=1}^{k} \Pr[S_i \wedge X_i] \leq \frac{3}{4}\|x_u - x_v\|_1$.

By Lemma 8.5,

$$\Pr[X_i] = \Pr[\min(1 - x_u^i, 1 - x_v^i) \leq r < \max(1 - x_u^i, 1 - x_v^i)] = |x_u^i - x_v^i|.$$

Let ℓ be the index that minimizes $\min_i(\min(1 - x_u^i, 1 - x_v^i))$; in other words, s_ℓ is the distinguished vertex that is closest to one of the two endpoints of (u, v). We claim that index $i \neq \ell$ cannot settle edge (u, v) if ℓ is ordered before i in the random permutation π: by Lemma 8.5 and the definition of ℓ, if at least one of $u, v \in B(e_i, r)$, then at least one of $u, v \in B(e_\ell, r)$. Note that the probability that ℓ occurs after i in the random permutation π is $1/2$. Hence, for $i \neq \ell$,

$$\Pr[S_i \wedge X_i] = \Pr[S_i \wedge X_i | \ell \text{ occurs after } i \text{ in } \pi] \cdot \Pr[\ell \text{ occurs after } i \text{ in } \pi]$$

$$+ \Pr[S_i \wedge X_i | \ell \text{ occurs before } i \text{ in } \pi] \cdot \Pr[\ell \text{ occurs before } i \text{ in } \pi]$$

$$\leq \Pr[X_i | \ell \text{ occurs after } i \text{ in } \pi] \cdot \frac{1}{2} + 0.$$

Since the event X_i is independent of the choice of random permutation, $\Pr[X_i | \ell \text{ occurs after } i \text{ in } \pi] = \Pr[X_i]$, and therefore for $i \neq \ell$

$$\Pr[S_i \wedge X_i] \leq \Pr[X_i] \cdot \frac{1}{2} = \frac{1}{2}|x_u^i - x_v^i|.$$

We also have that $\Pr[S_\ell \wedge X_\ell] \leq \Pr[X_\ell] \leq |x_u^\ell - x_v^\ell|$. Therefore, we have that the probability that (u, v) is in the multiway cut is

$$\sum_{i=1}^{k} \Pr[S_i \wedge X_i] \leq |x_u^\ell - x_v^\ell| + \frac{1}{2} \sum_{i \neq \ell} |x_u^i - x_v^i|$$

$$= \frac{1}{2}|x_u^\ell - x_v^\ell| + \frac{1}{2}\|x_u - x_v\|_1.$$

Using Lemma 8.4, $\frac{1}{2}|x_u^\ell - x_v^\ell| \leq \frac{1}{4}\|x_u - x_v\|_1$, so that

$$\sum_{i=1}^{k} \Pr[S_i \wedge X_i] \leq \frac{3}{4}\|x_u - x_v\|_1,$$

as desired. □

With only slightly more work, the performance guarantee of the algorithm can be improved to $\frac{3}{2} - \frac{1}{k}$; this is left to Exercise 8.1. One can also obtain a $\frac{3}{2}$-approximation algorithm by choosing between two fixed permutations; we explore this in Exercise 8.2. The idea of partitioning vertices by taking balls of fixed radius in the order given by a random permutation is a useful one that we will apply again in Section 8.5.

8.3 The Multicut Problem

In this section, we consider a slightly different cut problem, called the *multicut problem*. Rather than having a set of distinguished vertices $s_1, \ldots, s_k$, we now have a set of distinguished source-sink pairs of vertices $(s_1, t_1), \ldots, (s_k, t_k)$. Given an undirected graph $G = (V, E)$ with nonnegative costs $c_e \geq 0$ for all $e \in E$, our goal is to find a minimum-cost set of edges F whose removal disconnects all pairs; that is, for every $i, 1 \leq i \leq k$, there is no path connecting s_i and t_i in $(V, E - F)$. Unlike the previous problem, there can be paths connecting s_i and s_j or s_i and t_j for $i \neq j$. We previously considered a special case of the multicut problem in trees in Exercise 7.2.

Given a graph G, let $\mathcal{P}_i$ be the set of all paths P joining s_i and t_i. Then an integer programming formulation of the problem is

$$\text{minimize} \sum_{e \in E} c_e x_e$$

$$\text{subject to} \quad \sum_{e \in P} x_e \geq 1, \qquad \forall P \in \mathcal{P}_i, 1 \leq i \leq k,$$

$$x_e \in \{0, 1\}, \qquad \forall e \in E.$$

The constraints ensure that for each i, for each path $P \in \mathcal{P}_i$, some edge is selected from P.

To obtain a linear programming relaxation, we replace the constraints $x_e \in \{0, 1\}$ with $x_e \geq 0$. Although the formulation is exponential in the size of the input (since there could be an exponential number of paths $P \in \mathcal{P}_i$), we can solve the linear program in polynomial time by using the ellipsoid method described in Section 4.3. The separation oracle works as follows: Given a solution x, we consider the graph G in which the

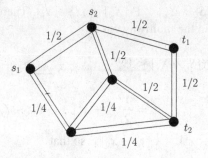

Figure 8.4. An illustration of a pipe system. The width of the pipe corresponds to its cost c_e, and the number next to it gives its length. The distance between each source-sink pair is at least 1 along any path.

length of each edge e is x_e. For each i, $1 \leq i \leq k$, we compute the length of the shortest path between s_i and t_i. If for some i, the length of the shortest path P is less than 1, we return it as a violated constraint, since we have $\sum_{e \in P} x_e < 1$ for $P \in \mathcal{P}_i$. If for each i, the length of the shortest path between s_i and t_i is at least 1, then the length of every path $P \in \mathcal{P}_i$ is at least 1, and the solution is feasible. Thus, we have a polynomial-time separation oracle for the linear program. Alternatively, it is possible to give an equivalent, polynomially sized linear program that can be solved directly in polynomial time, and whose solution can be transformed into a solution of this linear program in polynomial time; we leave this as an exercise (Exercise 8.4).

As in the LP rounding algorithm for the multiway cut problem, we will build our solution by taking balls around the vertex s_i for each i. In order to do this, we must define a notion of distance. Given an optimal solution x to the LP, we will let x_e denote the length of edge e for the purposes of our algorithm. We then let $d_x(u, v)$ denote the length of the shortest path from vertex u to v using x_e as edge lengths. Observe that d_x will obey the triangle inequality by the definition of shortest paths. Also, in any feasible LP solution we have $d_x(s_i, t_i) \geq 1$ for all i. Let $B_x(s_i, r) = \{v \in V : d_x(s_i, v) \leq r\}$ be the ball of radius r around vertex s_i using these distances.

Additionally, it will be useful to think of each edge $e \in E$ as being a pipe with length x_e and cross-sectional area c_e. Then the product $c_e x_e$ gives the volume of edge e. The LP produces the minimum-volume system of pipes such that $d_x(s_i, t_i) \geq 1$ for all i. See Figure 8.4 for an illustration of the pipe system, and Figure 8.5 for an illustration of a ball in the pipe system. Given an optimal solution x to the LP, we let $V^* = \sum_{e \in E} c_e x_e$ be the total volume of the pipes. We know that $V^* \leq \text{OPT}$. Let $V_x(s_i, r)$ be the volume of pipes within distance r of s_i plus an extra V^*/k term; that is,

$$V_x(s_i, r) = \frac{V^*}{k} + \sum_{e=(u,v):u,v \in B_x(s_i,r)} c_e x_e + \sum_{e=(u,v):u \in B_x(s_i,r), v \notin B_x(s_i,r)} c_e(r - d_x(s_i, u)).$$

The first term ensures that $V_x(s_i, 0)$ is nonzero, and that the sum of $V(s_i, 0)$ over all s_i is V^*; it will later be clear why this is useful. The second term adds up the volume of all edges (u, v) such that both u and v are inside the ball of distance r around s_i, while the third term adds up the volume of pipes that fall partially within the ball. Let $\delta(S)$ be the set of all edges that have exactly one endpoint in the set of vertices S.

Let x be an optimal solution to the LP
$F \leftarrow \emptyset$
for $i \leftarrow 1$ to k **do**
    if s_i and t_i are connected in $(V, E - F)$ **then**
        Choose radius $r < 1/2$ around s_i as in Lemma 8.7
        $F \leftarrow F \cup \delta(B_x(s_i, r))$
        Remove $B_x(s_i, r)$ and incident edges from graph
return F

Algorithm 8.2. Algorithm for the multicut problem.

For a given radius r, let $c(\delta(B_x(s_i, r)))$ be the cost of the edges in $\delta(B_x(s_i, r))$; that is, $c(\delta(B_x(s_i, r))) = \sum_{e \in \delta(B_x(s_i,r))} c_e$. We will first claim that it is always possible to find some radius $r < 1/2$ such that the cost $c(\delta(B_x(s_i, r)))$ of the cut induced by the ball of radius r around s_i is not much more than the volume of the ball; finding a ball of this sort is sometimes called *region growing*.

Lemma 8.7. *Given a feasible solution to the linear program x, for any s_i one can find in polynomial time a radius $r < 1/2$ such that*

$$c(\delta(B_x(s_i, r))) \leq (2\ln(k + 1))V_x(s_i, r).$$

This leads to the following algorithm, which is summarized in Algorithm 8.2. We start out with an empty set of edges F, and we sequence through each i from 1 to k. If s_i and t_i are not already separated by the cut F, we invoke Lemma 8.7 to find an appropriate radius $r < 1/2$ around s_i. We then add the edges of $\delta(B_x(s_i, r))$ to F. We remove all the vertices of $B_x(s_i, r)$ and all incident edges from the graph and continue. We note that in any iteration, the balls $B_x(s_i, r)$ and volumes $V_x(s_i, r)$ are taken with respect to the edges and vertices remaining in the current graph.

We first show that the algorithm produces a feasible solution.

Lemma 8.8. *Algorithm 8.2 produces a feasible solution for the multicut problem.*

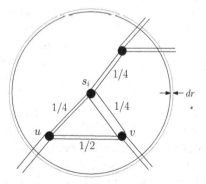

Figure 8.5. An illustration of a ball in a pipe system. The ball has radius $3/8$ around s_i. Note that the volume of the ball will jump from radius $r = 1/4 - \epsilon$ to $r = 1/4$ due to the presence of edge (u, v). Observe also that if we consider a second ball of radius $r + dr$ for sufficiently small dr, then the volume of the difference of the two balls is just the cross-sectional area of the pipes with one endpoint inside the ball and one outside; that is, it is $c(\delta_x(B_x(s_i, r)))dr$.

Proof. The only possible way in which the solution might not be feasible is if we have some s_j-t_j pair in the ball $B_x(s_i, r)$ when the vertices in the ball get removed from the graph. However, if $s_j, t_j \in B_x(s_i, r)$ for $r < 1/2$, then $d_x(s_i, s_j) < 1/2$ and $d_x(s_i, t_j) < 1/2$ so that $d_x(s_j, t_j) < 1$. This contradicts the feasibility of the LP solution x. So it must be the case that whenever we remove the vertices in a ball $B_x(s_i, r)$ from the graph, it can contain at most one of the pair of vertices s_j, t_j for all j.   □

Assuming Lemma 8.7, we can now prove that the algorithm is a good approximation algorithm for the multicut problem.

Theorem 8.9. *Algorithm 8.2 is a $(4 \ln(k + 1))$-approximation algorithm for the multicut problem.*

Proof. Let B_i be the set of vertices in the ball $B_x(s_i, r)$ chosen by the algorithm when the pair s_i-t_i are selected for separation; we set $B_i = \emptyset$ if no ball is chosen for i. Let F_i be the edges in $\delta(B_i)$ when B_i and its incident edges are removed from the graph (where $F_i = \emptyset$ if $B_i = \emptyset$). Then $F = \bigcup_{i=1}^{k} F_i$. Let V_i be the total volume of edges removed when the vertices of B_i and its incident edges are removed from the graph. Note that $V_i \geq V_x(s_i, r) - \frac{V^*}{k}$ since V_i contains the full volume of edges in F_i, while $V_x(s_i, r)$ contains only part of the volume of these edges, but has an extra term of V^*/k. Note that by the choice of r in Lemma 8.7, we have that $c(F_i) \leq (2 \ln(k + 1))V_x(s_i, r) \leq (2 \ln(k + 1)) \left(V_i + \frac{V^*}{k} \right)$. Further, observe that the volume of each edge belongs to at most one V_i; once the edge is part of V_i it is removed from the graph and cannot be part of the volume of a ball B_j removed in a later iteration. This observation implies that $\sum_{i=1}^{k} V_i \leq V^*$.

Putting all of this together, we have that

$$\sum_{e \in F} c_e = \sum_{i=1}^{k} \sum_{e \in F_i} c_e \leq (2 \ln(k + 1)) \sum_{i=1}^{k} \left(V_i + \frac{V^*}{k} \right)$$
$$\leq (4 \ln(k + 1))V^* \leq (4 \ln(k + 1)) \text{OPT}. \qquad \square$$

We finally turn to the proof of Lemma 8.7.

Proof of Lemma 8.7. For simplicity we write $V(r) = V_x(s_i, r)$ and $c(r) = c(\delta(B_x(s_i, r)))$. Our proof will show that for r chosen uniformly at random from $[0, 1/2)$, the expected value of $c(r)/V(r)$ is no more than $2 \ln(k + 1)$. This implies that for some value of r, we have that $c(r) \leq (2 \ln(k + 1))V(r)$. We will then show how we can quickly find such a value of r deterministically.

To set up the computation of the expectation, we need the following observations. For any value of r such that $V(r)$ is differentiable, note that the derivative is exactly the cost of the edges in the cut given by the ball of radius r around s_i; that is, $\frac{dV}{dr} = c(r)$ (see Figure 8.5). We observe that the points at which $V(r)$ is not differentiable are values of r such that $B_x(s_i, r)$ changes, that is, at values of r such that $d_x(s_i, v) = r$ for some vertex v. Furthermore, $V(r)$ may not even be continuous for these values: if there are two vertices u and v such that there is an edge (u, v) of positive volume $\delta > 0$ and $d_x(s_i, u) = d_x(s_i, v) = r$, then $V(r) - V(r - \epsilon) \geq \delta$ as $\epsilon \downarrow 0$ (see Figure 8.5). Nevertheless, note that $V(r)$ is non-decreasing in r.

Essentially we would now like to invoke the mean value theorem from calculus. Recall that the mean value theorem states that for a function f continuous on an interval $[a, b]$ and differentiable on (a, b), there exists some $c \in (a, b)$ such that $f'(c) = \frac{f(b)-f(a)}{b-a}$. If we set $f(r) = \ln V(r)$, we note that

$$f'(r) = \frac{\frac{d}{dr} V(r)}{V(r)} = \frac{c(r)}{V(r)}.$$

Observe that $V(1/2) \le V^* + \frac{V^*}{k}$ since $V(1/2)$ cannot be more than the entire volume plus V^*/k, and $V(0)$ is exactly V^*/k. Following the mean value theorem, we want to show that there is some $r \in (0, 1/2)$ such that

$$f'(r) \le \frac{\ln V(1/2) - \ln V(0)}{1/2 - 0} = 2 \ln \left(\frac{V(1/2)}{V(0)} \right) \le 2 \ln \left(\frac{V^* + \frac{V^*}{k}}{V^*/k} \right) = 2 \ln(k + 1).$$

(8.4)

However, the mean value theorem doesn't apply since as we noticed earlier $V(r)$ may not be continuous and differentiable in $(0, 1/2)$. Nevertheless, we show a form of the mean value theorem still holds in this case.

We now sort and label the vertices in $B_x(s_i, 1/2)$ according to their distance from s_i; let $r_j = d_x(s_i, v_j)$ be such that $0 = r_0 \le r_1 \le \cdots \le r_{l-1} \le 1/2$. Then the vertices are labeled $s_i = v_0, v_1, v_2, \ldots, v_{l-1}$. For notational simplicity define $r_l = 1/2$. Let r_j^- be a value infinitesimally smaller than r_j.

The expected value of $c(r)/V(r)$ for r chosen uniformly from $[0, 1/2)$ is then

$$\frac{1}{1/2} \sum_{j=0}^{l-1} \int_{r_j}^{r_{j+1}^-} \frac{c(r)}{V(r)} dr = 2 \sum_{j=0}^{l-1} \int_{r_j}^{r_{j+1}^-} \frac{1}{V(r)} \frac{dV}{dr} dr$$

$$= 2 \sum_{j=0}^{l-1} [\ln V(r)]_{r_j}^{r_{j+1}^-}$$

$$= 2 \sum_{j=0}^{l-1} \left[\ln V(r_{j+1}^-) - \ln V(r_j) \right].$$

Since $V(r)$ is non-decreasing, this last sum is at most

$$2 \sum_{j=0}^{l-1} \left[\ln V(r_{j+1}) - \ln V(r_j) \right].$$

Then the sum telescopes so that

$$2 \sum_{j=0}^{l-1} \left[\ln V(r_{j+1}) - \ln V(r_j) \right] = 2 \left(\ln V(1/2) - \ln V(0) \right),$$

and this can be bounded above by $2 \ln(k + 1)$ as shown in (8.4).

Thus, it must be the case that there exists $r \in [0, 1/2)$ such that $c(r) \le (2 \ln(k + 1)) V(r)$. How can we find this value of r quickly? Observe that for $r \in [r_j, r_{j+1}^-]$, $c(r)$ stays constant (since $B_x(s_i, r)$ is unchanged), while $V(r)$ is non-decreasing. Thus, if the inequality holds at any point in this interval, it must also hold at r_{j+1}^-. Therefore, we need to check the inequality only at r_{j+1}^- for $j = 0, \ldots, l - 1$; by the argument above, the inequality must hold for some value of j.   □

While no better approximation algorithm for the multicut problem is known, given the unique games conjecture, we cannot do significantly better.

Theorem 8.10. *Assuming the unique games conjecture, for any constant $\alpha \geq 1$, there is no α-approximation algorithm for the multicut problem unless $P = NP$.*

We will prove this theorem in Section 16.5.

It will be useful in later sections to have a slight generalization of Lemma 8.7. We observe that by modifying the proof of Lemma 8.7 one can get the following corollary.

Corollary 8.11. *Given lengths x_e on edges $e \in E$ and a vertex u, one can find in polynomial time a radius $r \in [a, b)$ such that*

$$c(\delta(B_x(u, r))) \leq \frac{1}{b - a} \ln \left(\frac{V_x(u, b)}{V_x(u, a)} \right) V_x(u, r).$$

8.4 Balanced Cuts

We now turn to the graph cut problem that most commonly arises in practice. We say that a set of vertices S is a *b-balanced cut* for $b \in (0, 1/2]$ if $\lfloor bn \rfloor \leq |S| \leq \lceil (1 - b)n \rceil$, where $n = |V|$. Given an undirected graph $G = (V, E)$ with nonnegative edge costs $c_e \geq 0$ for all edges $e \in E$, and a $b \in (0, 1/2]$, the goal is to find a b-balanced cut S that minimizes the cost of the edges with exactly one endpoint in S. The case when $b = 1/2$ is sometimes called the *minimum bisection problem*.

Finding b-balanced cuts arises in divide-and-conquer schemes used in a variety of applications: the cut S is found, some graph problem is solved on S and $V - S$, then the solution is the result of combining the two solutions in S and $V - S$ via the edges between them. If the cut has low cost, then the combining step becomes easier. Furthermore, if S and $V - S$ have approximately the same size, then the algorithm can be applied recursively to each side, and the total depth of the recursion will be $O(\log n)$.

In this section, we will not give an approximation algorithm for the balanced cut problem, settling instead for a *pseudo*-approximation algorithm; by this we mean that our algorithm will find a b-balanced cut whose cost is within an $O(\log n)$ factor of the cost of the optimal b'-balanced cut for $b' \neq b$. Let $\text{OPT}(b)$ denote the value of the minimum-cost b-balanced cut. In particular, we will show how to find a $\frac{1}{3}$-balanced cut of value at most $O(\log n) \text{OPT}(1/2)$. Note first of all that $\text{OPT}(1/3) \leq \text{OPT}(1/2)$, since any $\frac{1}{2}$-balanced cut is also a $\frac{1}{3}$-balanced cut. However, $\text{OPT}(1/2)$ could be substantially larger than $\text{OPT}(1/3)$: in fact, if the graph consists of a clique on $\frac{2}{3}n$ nodes connected by a single edge to a clique on $\frac{1}{3}n$ nodes, and all edges have weight 1, $\text{OPT}(1/3) = 1$ while $\text{OPT}(1/2) = \Omega(n^2)$. Thus, the algorithm is not a true approximation algorithm since we compare the cost of the solution found by the algorithm with the optimum $\text{OPT}(1/2)$ for a problem that could be much larger than the optimum $\text{OPT}(1/3)$ of the problem for which the algorithm finds a solution. While we give an algorithm to find a $\frac{1}{3}$-balanced cut of cost at most $O(\log n)\,\text{OPT}(1/2)$, the discussion that follows can be generalized to give a b-balanced cut of cost at most $O(\frac{1}{b'-b}\log n)\,\text{OPT}(b')$ for $b \leq 1/3$ and $b < b'$.

Our approach to the problem follows that used for the multicut problem in the previous section. We claim that the following is a linear programming relaxation of the minimum bisection problem; we will shortly prove that this is true. Given a graph G, let $\mathcal{P}_{uv}$ be the set of all paths between u and v in G. Consider the following linear program:

$$\text{minimize} \sum_{e \in E} c_e x_e$$

$$\text{subject to} \quad d_{uv} \leq \sum_{e \in P} x_e, \qquad \forall u, v \in V, \forall P \in \mathcal{P}_{uv},$$

$$\sum_{v \in S} d_{uv} \geq \left(\frac{2}{3} - \frac{1}{2}\right)n, \qquad \forall S \subseteq V : |S| \geq \left\lceil \frac{2}{3}n \right\rceil + 1, \forall u \in S,$$

$$d_{uv} \geq 0, \qquad \forall u, v \in V,$$

$$x_e \geq 0, \qquad \forall e \in E.$$

In this relaxation, we have a variable d_{uv} that is intended to denote the distance between u and v using edge lengths x_e; if we let $d_x(u, v)$ be the actual shortest path length between u and v using edge lengths x_e, then $d_{uv} \leq d_x(u, v)$.

To solve the linear program in polynomial time, we once again apply the ellipsoid method as described in Section 4.3. Given a solution (d, x), we can first check if the first set of constraints is obeyed by computing the shortest path distance between u and v using edge lengths x_e, and ensuring that $d_{uv} \leq d_x(u, v)$. For each vertex u, we find the closest $\lceil \frac{2}{3}n \rceil + 1$ vertices using distances d_{uv}; this will include u itself since $d_{uu} = 0$. Let $u = v_0, v_1, v_2, \ldots, v_{\lceil \frac{2}{3}n \rceil}$ be the $\lceil \frac{2}{3}n \rceil + 1$ vertices that minimize d_{uv}. If $\sum_{j=0}^{\lceil \frac{2}{3}n \rceil} d_{uv_j} < (\frac{2}{3} - \frac{1}{2})n$, then clearly the constraint is violated for $S = \{v_0, \ldots, v_{\lceil \frac{2}{3}n \rceil}\}$ and this choice of u. Note that if $\sum_{j=0}^{\lceil \frac{2}{3}n \rceil} d_{uv_j} \geq (\frac{2}{3} - \frac{1}{2})n$, then there is no other set S with $|S| \geq \lceil \frac{2}{3}n \rceil + 1$ and $u \in S$ such that the constraint is violated, since any S containing $v_0, \ldots, v_{\lceil \frac{2}{3}n \rceil}$ can only give rise to a larger sum, and since these vertices were chosen to make the sum as small as possible. Thus, in polynomial time we can check whether (d, x) is a feasible solution and find a violated constraint if it is not feasible.

We now argue that the linear program is a relaxation.

Lemma 8.12. *The linear program above is a relaxation of the minimum bisection problem.*

Proof. Given an optimal bisection S, we construct a solution $(\bar{d}, \bar{x})$ for the linear program by setting $\bar{x}_e = 1$ if $e \in \delta(S)$ and $\bar{x}_e = 0$ otherwise. We then set $\bar{d}_{uv} = 1$ for all $u \in S$, $v \notin S$, and $\bar{d}_{uv} = 0$ otherwise. We argue that this solution is feasible, which is sufficient to prove the lemma. Clearly the first set of constraints is obeyed, since any path P from $u \in S$ to $v \notin S$ must use an edge $e \in \delta(S)$.

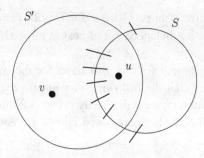

Figure 8.6. An illustration of the proof of Lemma 8.12. At least $(\frac{2}{3} - \frac{1}{2})n$ vertices must be in both $S \cap S'$ and $S' - S$, so for any $u \in S'$, there must be at least $(\frac{2}{3} - \frac{1}{2})n$ vertices v that lie on the other side of the bisection S.

Now consider any set S' such that $|S'| \geq \lceil \frac{2}{3}n \rceil + 1$. Notice that $|S' - S| \geq \lceil \frac{2}{3}n \rceil + 1 - \lceil \frac{1}{2}n \rceil \geq (\frac{2}{3} - \frac{1}{2})n$ and $|S' \cap S| \geq \lceil \frac{2}{3}n \rceil + 1 - \lceil \frac{1}{2}n \rceil \geq (\frac{2}{3} - \frac{1}{2})n$; call $S' - S$ and $S' \cap S$ the two parts of S'. See Figure 8.6. One part (namely, $S' \cap S$) is contained in S and the other (namely, $S' - S$) has no vertices of S, so for u and v in different parts, $\bar{d}_{uv} = 1$. Pick any $u \in S'$. Since u is in one of the two parts of S', there are at least $(\frac{2}{3} - \frac{1}{2})n$ vertices v in the other part of S' that does not contain u. Thus, $\sum_{v \in S'} \bar{d}_{uv} \geq (\frac{2}{3} - \frac{1}{2})n$. $\qquad \square$

Given an optimal solution (d, x) to the linear program, let $B_x(u, r)$ be the set of vertices in the ball of radius r around u; that is, $B_x(u, r) = \{v \in V : d_x(u, v) \leq r\}$. As with the multicut problem, we let $V^* = \sum_{e \in E} c_e x_e$, so that we know $V^* \leq \text{OPT}(1/2)$ by Lemma 8.12. We define the volume of the ball of radius r around a vertex u as we did in the previous section:

$$V_x(u, r) = \frac{V^*}{n} + \sum_{e=(v,w):v,w \in B_x(u,r)} c_e x_e + \sum_{e=(v,w):v \in B_x(u,r), w \notin B_x(u,r)} c_e(r - d_x(u, v)).$$

As before, define $c(\delta(B_x(u, r)))$ to be the cost of the edges with exactly one endpoint in $B_x(u, r)$. We can then prove the following lemma, which is analogous to Lemma 8.7.

Lemma 8.13. *Given a feasible solution to the linear program (d, x) and two vertices u and v such that $d_x(u, v) \geq 1/12$, one can find in polynomial time a radius $r < 1/12$ such that*

$$c(\delta(B_x(u, r))) \leq (12 \ln(n + 1)) V_x(u, r).$$

Proof. We apply Corollary 8.11 to the interval $[0, 1/12)$, and observe that

$$\ln\left(\frac{V_x(u, 1/12)}{V_x(u, 0)}\right) \leq \ln\left(\frac{V^* + V^*/n}{V^*/n}\right) = \ln(n + 1). \qquad \square$$

Our algorithm for the $\frac{1}{3}$-balanced cut problem is given in Algorithm 8.3. We let S be the set of vertices that will be in the cut; S is initially empty. We let F be a superset of the edges in the cut, and it is also initially empty. Our final solution requires that $\lfloor \frac{1}{3}n \rfloor \leq |S| \leq \lceil \frac{2}{3}n \rceil$. As long as $|S| < \lfloor \frac{1}{3}n \rfloor$, we will show that there must exist two vertices $u, v \notin S$ such that $d_x(u, v) \geq \frac{1}{6}$. We apply Lemma 8.13 to find balls of radius less than $1/12$ around both u and v. We take the ball of smaller cardinality, add it to S,

Let (d, x) be an optimal solution to the LP relaxation
$F \leftarrow \emptyset; S \leftarrow \emptyset$
while $|S| < \lfloor \frac{1}{3}n \rfloor$ **do**
    Choose some $u, v \notin S$ such that $d_x(u, v) \geq 1/6$
    Choose radius $r < 1/12$ around u as in Lemma 8.13
    Choose radius $r' < 1/12$ around v as in Lemma 8.13
    if $|B_x(u, r)| \leq |B_x(v, r')|$ **then**
        $S \leftarrow S \cup B_x(u, r)$
        $F \leftarrow F \cup \delta(B_x(u, r))$
        Remove $B_x(u, r)$ and incident edges from graph
    else
        $S \leftarrow S \cup B_x(v, r')$
        $F \leftarrow F \cup \delta(B_x(v, r'))$
        Remove $B_x(v, r')$ and incident edges from graph
return S

Algorithm 8.3. Algorithm for the $\frac{1}{3}$-balanced cut problem.

add the corresponding cut to F, and remove the ball and its incident edges from the graph.

We now need to prove that the algorithm is correct, and returns a $\frac{1}{3}$-balanced cut.

Lemma 8.14. *For any iteration of the algorithm in which* $|S| < \lfloor \frac{1}{3}n \rfloor$, *there exist* $u, v \notin S$ *such that* $d_x(u, v) \geq 1/6$.

Proof. Consider $S' = V - S$. Then $|S'| \geq \lceil \frac{2}{3}n \rceil + 1$. Then by the linear programming constraint, for any $u \in S'$, $\sum_{v \in S'} d_{uv} \geq (\frac{2}{3} - \frac{1}{2})n = \frac{1}{6}n$. Since there are at most n vertices in S', it must be the case that for some $v \in S'$, $d_{uv} \geq 1/6$. Finally, we know that $d_x(u, v) \geq d_{uv}$. $\quad\square$

Lemma 8.15. *The algorithm returns S such that* $\lfloor \frac{1}{3}n \rfloor \leq |S| \leq \lceil \frac{2}{3}n \rceil$.

Proof. By construction of the algorithm, $|S| \geq \lfloor \frac{1}{3}n \rfloor$. Thus, it suffices to show that $|S| \leq \lceil \frac{2}{3}n \rceil$. Let $\hat{S}$ be the contents of S at the beginning of the iteration before the algorithm terminated. Then $|\hat{S}| < \lfloor \frac{1}{3}n \rfloor$, and we added the smaller of the two balls around u and v to $\hat{S}$ to obtain the final solution S. Since we considered $B_x(u, r)$ and $B_x(v, r')$ for $r < 1/12$, $r' < 1/12$, and $d_x(u, v) \geq 1/6$, it must be the case that these two balls are disjoint; that is, $B_x(u, r) \cap B_x(v, r') = \emptyset$. Since we chose the smaller ball to add to $\hat{S}$, this implies that the size of the ball added to $\hat{S}$ had no more than half the remaining vertices, or no more than $\frac{1}{2}(n - |\hat{S}|)$ vertices. Thus,

$$|S| = |\hat{S}| + \min(|B_x(u, r)|, |B_x(v, r')|) \leq |\hat{S}| + \frac{1}{2}(n - |\hat{S}|) = \frac{1}{2}n + \frac{1}{2}|\hat{S}| \leq \left\lceil \frac{2}{3}n \right\rceil,$$

since $|\hat{S}| < \lfloor \frac{1}{3}n \rfloor$. $\quad\square$

The proof of the performance guarantee is nearly the same as that for the multicut algorithm, and so we omit it.

Theorem 8.16. *Algorithm 8.3 returns a $\frac{1}{3}$-balanced cut of cost no more than* $(24\ln(n+1))V^* \leq (24\ln(n+1))\,\mathrm{OPT}(1/2)$.

As mentioned previously, the algorithm above can be generalized to give a b-balanced cut of cost at most $O(\frac{1}{b'-b}\log n)\,\mathrm{OPT}(b')$ for $b \leq 1/3$ and $b < b'$.

In Section 15.3, we will give an $O(\log n)$-approximation algorithm for the minimum bisection problem; this algorithm is not a pseudo-approximation algorithm, but is an algorithm that produces a bisection of cost at most $O(\log n)\,\mathrm{OPT}(1/2)$.

8.5 Probabilistic Approximation of Metrics by Tree Metrics

In this section, we introduce the idea of *tree metrics*, which we will consider for the remainder of the chapter. Tree metrics have become an important tool for devising approximation algorithms for a wide variety of problems.

We use tree metrics to approximate a given distance metric d on a set of vertices V. A tree metric (V', T) for a set of vertices V is a tree T defined on some set of vertices $V' \supseteq V$, together with nonnegative lengths on each edge of T. The distance T_{uv} between vertices $u, v \in V'$ is the length of the unique shortest path between u and v in T. We would like to have a tree metric (V', T) that approximates d on V in the sense that $d_{uv} \leq T_{uv} \leq \alpha \cdot d_{uv}$ for all $u, v \in V$ for some value of α. The parameter α is called the *distortion* of the embedding of d into the tree metric (V', T).

Given a low-distortion embedding, we can often reduce problems on general metric spaces to problems on tree metrics with a loss of a factor of α in the performance guarantee. It is often much easier to produce an algorithm for a tree metric than for a general metric. We will see examples of this in the following two sections, in which we discuss the buy-at-bulk network design problem and the linear arrangement problem. Further examples can be found in the exercises.

Unfortunately, it can be shown that for a cycle on n vertices, no tree metric has distortion less than $(n-1)/8$ (see Exercise 8.7 for a restricted proof of this). However, we can give a randomized algorithm for producing a tree T such that for each $u, v \in V$, $d_{uv} \leq T_{uv}$ and $E[T_{uv}] \leq O(\log n)d_{uv}$; that is, the expected distortion is $O(\log n)$. Another way to view this is that we can give a probability distribution on trees such that the expected distortion is $O(\log n)$. We refer to this as the *probabilistic approximation* of the metric d by a tree metric.

Theorem 8.17. *Given a distance metric (V, d), such that $d_{uv} \geq 1$ for all $u \neq v$, $u, v \in V$, there is a randomized, polynomial-time algorithm that produces a tree metric (V', T), $V \subseteq V'$, such that for all $u, v \in V$, $d_{uv} \leq T_{uv}$ and $E[T_{uv}] \leq O(\log n)d_{uv}$.*

It is known that there exist metrics such that any probabilistic approximation of the metric by tree metrics must have distortion $\Omega(\log n)$, so the result above is the best possible to within constant factors.

We now begin to give the details of how the algorithm of Theorem 8.17 works. The tree is constructed via a *hierarchical cut decomposition* of the metric d. Let Δ be the

Level $\log_2 \Delta$

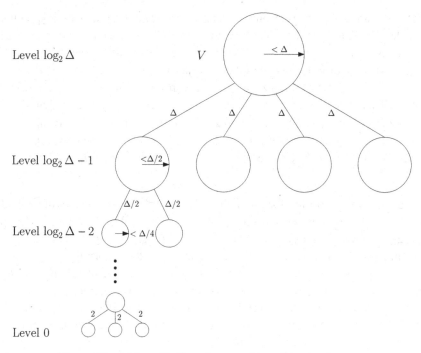

Level $\log_2 \Delta - 1$

Level $\log_2 \Delta - 2$

Level 0

Figure 8.7. A hierarchical cut decomposition of the metric space.

smallest power of 2 greater than $2 \max_{u,v} d_{uv}$. The hierarchical cut decomposition is a rooted tree with $\log_2 \Delta + 1$ levels. The nodes at each level of the tree correspond to some partitioning of the vertex set V: the root node (at level $\log_2 \Delta$) corresponds to V itself, while each leaf of the tree (at level 0) corresponds to a single vertex of V. A given node at level i corresponds to some subset S of vertices V; the children of the node corresponding to S correspond to a partitioning of S. For a given node at level i that corresponds to a set S, the vertices in S will be the vertices in a ball of radius less than 2^i and at least 2^{i-1} centered on some vertex. Notice that each leaf of the tree at level 0 is in a ball of radius less than $2^0 = 1$ centered on some vertex u, and so u is in the ball by itself since $d_{uv} \geq 1$ for all $v \neq u$. Observe also that by the definition of Δ, the set V is contained in a ball of radius Δ centered on any vertex, since the radius of the ball at level $\log_2 \Delta$ is at least $\frac{1}{2}\Delta \geq \max_{u,v} d_{uv}$. The length of the tree edge joining the children at level $i - 1$ to their parent at level i is 2^i. See Figure 8.7 for an illustration of the hierarchical cut decomposition.

Each node of the tree will be a vertex in V', so that the tree is a tree on the vertices in V'. We let each leaf correspond to the unique $v \in V$ that it contains, so that the leaves are the vertex set V, while the internal vertices are the remaining nodes in V', and $V \subseteq V'$.

Before we state precisely how to obtain the decomposition, we observe the following properties of the tree obtained in this way.

Lemma 8.18. *Any tree T obtained via the hierarchical cut decomposition of metric d as above has $T_{uv} \geq d_{uv}$ for all pairs of vertices $u, v \in V$. Furthermore, if the least common ancestor of $u, v \in V$ is at level i, then $T_{uv} \leq 2^{i+2}$.*

Proof. The distance d_{uv} between any pair of vertices u and v in a set S corresponding to a node at level i of the tree is less than 2^{i+1}, since the radius of the ball containing S is less than 2^i. Thus, vertices u and v cannot belong to the same node at level $\lfloor \log_2 d_{uv} \rfloor - 1$, since otherwise the distance between them would be less than $2^{\lfloor \log_2 d_{uv} \rfloor} \leq d_{uv}$, a contradiction. The lowest level at which u and v can belong to the same node is thus $\lfloor \log_2 d_{uv} \rfloor$. Therefore, the distance $T_{uv} \geq 2 \sum_{j=1}^{\lfloor \log_2 d_{uv} \rfloor} 2^j \geq d_{uv}$ since the length of the tree edge joining level $j - 1$ to j is 2^j, and the path from u to v in T starts at u at level 0, goes through a node of level at least $\lfloor \log_2 d_{uv} \rfloor$, and returns to v at level 0.

If the least common ancestor of $u, v \in V$ is at level i, then $T_{uv} = 2 \sum_{j=1}^{i} 2^j = 2^{i+2} - 4 \leq 2^{i+2}$. $\qquad\square$

The randomized algorithm for producing a tree metric begins by picking a random permutation π of the vertices and setting a radius r_i for all balls at level i. We pick $r_0 \in [1/2, 1)$ uniformly at random, and set $r_i = 2^i r_0$ for i, $1 \leq i \leq \log_2 \Delta$. We observe that this implies that for any i, r_i is distributed in $[2^{i-1}, 2^i)$ uniformly.

In order to show how to produce the tree metric, it suffices to specify how to obtain the children of a node corresponding to a set S at level i in the hierarchical cut decomposition. The partitioning of S into children on level $i - 1$ is performed as follows: we go through all the vertices of V in the order given by the permutation, starting with $\pi(1)$. For a vertex $\pi(j)$ we consider the ball $B(\pi(j), r_{i-1})$: if $B(\pi(j), r_{i-1}) \cap S = \emptyset$, we go on to vertex $\pi(j + 1)$; otherwise, we make $B(\pi(j), r_{i-1}) \cap S$ a child node of S, remove the vertices of $B(\pi(j), r_{i-1})$ from S, and go on to vertex $\pi(j + 1)$ with the remaining nodes of S (if there are any). An alternative perspective of this procedure is that for each $u \in S$, we assign u to the first $\pi(j)$ in the permutation such that $u \in B(\pi(j), r_{i-1})$; all the vertices of S assigned to the same $\pi(j)$ are put in the same set of the partition. Note that all vertices in S are accounted for by this procedure, since every vertex in S is a member of the ball centered on itself. Observe also that a child node of S can have as its center a vertex $\pi(j)$ that is not in S, or a vertex $\pi(j)$ that is in another, previously formed part of the partition. See Figure 8.8 for an illustration of the partitioning, and see Algorithm 8.4 for a summary of the algorithm.

We now prove that the constructed tree probabilistically approximates the metric d. We restate the theorem here for convenience.

Theorem 8.17. *Given a distance metric (V, d), such that $d_{uv} \geq 1$ for all $u \neq v$, $u, v \in V$, there is a randomized, polynomial-time algorithm that produces a tree metric (V', T), $V \subseteq V'$, such that for all $u, v \in V$, $d_{uv} \leq T_{uv}$ and $E[T_{uv}] \leq O(\log n)d_{uv}$.*

Proof. Lemma 8.18 shows that for tree T, $T_{uv} \geq d_{uv}$. Now to show the other inequality, pick a particular pair of vertices $u, v \in V$. The lemma also shows that the length T_{uv} depends on the level of the least common ancestor of u and v, and if this level is level $i + 1$, $T_{uv} \leq 2^{i+3}$. For this least common ancestor to be at level $i + 1$, u and v must be in different sets on level i. In order for this to happen, there must be some vertex w such that exactly one of u and v is in the set corresponding to the ball centered on w on level i. As in the proof of Theorem 8.6, we say that w *settles* the pair u, v on level i if w is the first vertex in the random permutation of vertices such that at least one of u, v is in the ball $B(w, r_i)$. We say that w *cuts* the pair u, v on level i if exactly one of u and v is in $B(w, r_i)$. Let X_{iw} be the event that w cuts (u, v) on level i, and let S_{iw} be

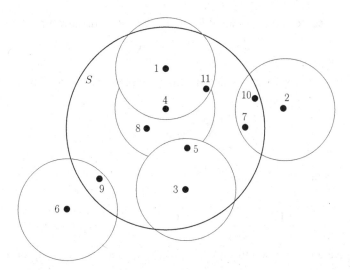

Figure 8.8. An example of the partitioning of set $S = \{1, 3, 4, 5, 7, 8, 9, 10, 11\}$ in the hierarchical cut decomposition. Suppose that the random permutation is the identity. The ball centered on 1 contains 1, 4, and 11, and $\{1, 4, 11\}$ forms a child node. The ball centered on 2 contains 7 and 10, and $\{7, 10\}$ forms a child node. The ball centered on 3 contains 3 and 5, and $\{3, 5\}$ forms a child node. The ball centered on 4 contains 8, and $\{8\}$ forms a child node; note that the ball centered on 4 also contains 4, 1, and 11, but these have already been put into the first child node. The ball centered on 5 contains no elements of S that are not already in child nodes. The ball centered on 6 contains 9, and $\{9\}$ forms a child node, so all elements of S are accounted for. Thus, S is partitioned into sets $\{1, 4, 11\}$, $\{3, 5\}$, $\{7, 10\}$, $\{8\}$, and $\{9\}$.

Pick a random permutation π of V
Set Δ to the smallest power of 2 greater than $2 \max_{u,v} d_{uv}$
Pick $r_0 \in [1/2, 1)$ uniformly at random; set $r_i = 2^i r_0$ for all $i : 1 \le i \le \log_2 \Delta$
// $\mathcal{C}(i)$ will be the sets corresponding to the nodes at level i;
    the sets partition V
$\mathcal{C}(\log_2 \Delta) = \{V\}$
Create tree node corresponding to V
for $i \leftarrow \log_2 \Delta$ downto 1 **do**
    $\mathcal{C}(i - 1) \leftarrow \emptyset$
    for all $C \in \mathcal{C}(i)$ **do**
        $S \leftarrow C$
        for $j \leftarrow 1$ to n **do**
            if $B(\pi(j), r_{i-1}) \cap S \neq \emptyset$ **then**
                Add $B(\pi(j), r_{i-1}) \cap S$ to $\mathcal{C}(i - 1)$
                Remove $B(\pi(j), r_{i-1}) \cap S$ from S
    Create tree nodes corresponding to all sets in $\mathcal{C}(i - 1)$ that are subsets of C
    Join these nodes to node corresponding to C by edge of length 2^i

Algorithm 8.4. Algorithm to create a hierarchical tree decomposition.

the event that w settles (u, v) on level i. Then if $\mathbf{1}$ is the indicator function,

$$T_{uv} \leq \max_{i=0,\ldots,\log \Delta - 1} \mathbf{1}(\exists w \in V : X_{iw} \wedge S_{iw}) \cdot 2^{i+3}.$$

We can simplify slightly by replacing the maximum and the existential quantifier with sums, so that

$$T_{uv} \leq \sum_{w \in V} \sum_{i=0}^{\log \Delta - 1} \mathbf{1}(X_{iw} \wedge S_{iw}) \cdot 2^{i+3}.$$

Taking the expectation, we obtain

$$E[T_{uv}] \leq \sum_{w \in V} \sum_{i=0}^{\log \Delta - 1} \Pr[X_{iw} \wedge S_{iw}] \cdot 2^{i+3}.$$

We will give an upper bound b_w on $\Pr[S_{iw}|X_{iw}]$ that depends only on w, and will show that $\sum_{i=1}^{\log \Delta} \Pr[X_{iw}] \cdot 2^{i+3} \leq 16 d_{uv}$. Then

$$\begin{aligned}
E[T_{uv}] &\leq \sum_{w \in V} \sum_{i=0}^{\log \Delta - 1} \Pr[X_{iw} \wedge S_{iw}] \cdot 2^{i+3} \\
&= \sum_{w \in V} \sum_{i=0}^{\log \Delta - 1} \Pr[S_{iw}|X_{iw}] \Pr[X_{iw}] \cdot 2^{i+3} \\
&\leq \sum_{w \in V} b_w \sum_{i=0}^{\log \Delta - 1} \Pr[X_{iw}] \cdot 2^{i+3} \\
&\leq 16 d_{uv} \sum_{w \in V} b_w.
\end{aligned}$$

In particular, we will show that $\sum_{w \in V} b_w = O(\log n)$, which will give the result.

First we show that $\sum_{i=0}^{\log \Delta - 1} \Pr[X_{iw}] \cdot 2^{i+3} \leq 16 d_{uv}$. Suppose without loss of generality that $d_{uw} \leq d_{vw}$. Then the probability that w cuts (u, v) on level i is the probability that $u \in B(w, r_i)$ and $v \notin B(w, r_i)$, or that $d_{uw} \leq r_i < d_{vw}$. Since $r_i \in [2^{i-1}, 2^i)$ uniformly at random, this probability is simply $1/(2^i - 2^{i-1})$ times the length of the intersection of the intervals $[2^{i-1}, 2^i)$ and $[d_{uw}, d_{vw})$, so that

$$\Pr[X_{iw}] = \frac{|[2^{i-1}, 2^i) \cap [d_{uw}, d_{vw})|}{|[2^{i-1}, 2^i)|} = \frac{|[2^{i-1}, 2^i) \cap [d_{uw}, d_{vw})|}{2^{i-1}}.$$

Then

$$2^{i+3} \Pr[X_{iw}] = \frac{2^{i+3}}{2^{i-1}} |[2^{i-1}, 2^i) \cap [d_{uw}, d_{vw})| = 16|[2^{i-1}, 2^i) \cap [d_{uw}, d_{vw})|.$$

Since the intervals $[2^{i-1}, 2^i)$ for $i = 0$ to $\log_2 \Delta - 1$ partition the interval $[1/2, \Delta/2)$, it follows that

$$\sum_{i=0}^{\log_2 \Delta - 1} \Pr[X_{iw}] \cdot 2^{i+3} \leq 16|[d_{uw}, d_{vw})| = 16(d_{vw} - d_{uw}) \leq 16 d_{uv},$$

where the final inequality follows by the triangle inequality.

> Set P_i to be the unique s_i-t_i path in T
>
> Set $c_e = \sum_{i:e \in P_i} d_i$ for all $e \in T$

Algorithm 8.5. Algorithm for the buy-at-bulk network design problem in a tree T.

Now to bound $\Pr[S_{iw}|X_{iw}]$. We order the vertices $w \in V$ in order of their distance to the pair u, v; that is, we order the vertices $w \in V$ by $\min(d_{uw}, d_{vw})$. Note that if event X_{iw} happens, then one of u and v is in the ball $B(w, r_i)$. Thus, any vertex z closer to the pair u, v than w will also have at least one of u and v in the ball $B(z, r_i)$. So in order for w to settle the pair u, v given that it cuts u, v on level i, it must come before all closer vertices z in the random permutation of vertices. If w is the jth closest vertex to u, v, this happens with probability at most $1/j$. Thus, $\Pr[S_{iw}|X_{iw}] \leq 1/j$ if w is the jth closest vertex to the pair u, v. We can then define the bound b_w on this probability as $1/j$. Since for each j, $1 \leq j \leq n$, there is some vertex w that is the jth closest to the pair u, v, we have that $\sum_{w \in V} b_w = \sum_{j=1}^{n} \frac{1}{j} = O(\log n)$, as desired. $\qquad\square$

8.6 An Application of Tree Metrics: Buy-at-Bulk Network Design

To get a sense of the kinds of problems for which we can obtain approximation algorithms using probabilistic approximation by tree metrics, we consider the *buy-at-bulk network design problem*. In this problem, we are given an undirected graph $G = (V, E)$ with lengths $\ell_e \geq 0$ for each $e \in E$. There are k source-sink pairs s_i-t_i, with $s_i, t_i \in V$, and each pair has an associated demand d_i. We can purchase a capacity u on any edge at a cost of $f(u)$ per unit distance. We assume that $f(0) = 0$ and that f is non-decreasing; as we purchase more capacity, the total cost does not go down. We further assume that the function f obeys economies of scale: the cost per unit of capacity does not increase as the desired capacity increases. Note that this implies that f is *subadditive*: $f(u_1 + u_2) \leq f(u_1) + f(u_2)$ (see Exercise 8.9 for an alternative assumption about how capacity is purchased). The goal of the problem is to find a path P_i from s_i to t_i for each i and a minimum-cost set of capacities c_e for all edges $e \in E$ such that a multicommodity flow can be routed in the graph of nonzero capacities, that is, such that we can send d_i units of commodity i from s_i to t_i on path P_i for all i using the capacities c_e. The cost of the solution is $\sum_{e \in E} f(c_e)\ell_e$.

Observe that the problem is easy to solve in a tree metric T; let T_{uv} be the length of the unique path in T between u and v. Because there is only one path P_i in T between any s_i and t_i, the desired capacity on a given edge in the tree is simply the sum of the demands of the commodities whose unique path uses the edge. This algorithm is summarized in Algorithm 8.5. Thus, given the algorithm of the previous section that approximates general metrics d by tree metrics, a straightforward idea presents itself. Let d_{uv} be the length of the shortest path in G between u and v using lengths ℓ_e. Use the algorithm to probabilistically approximate d by a tree metric T, then run the algorithm on the tree T. There is a slight problem in that since the tree metric is over a set of vertices $V' \supseteq V$, it is not clear how we translate a result on the tree metric (V', T) back into one on the original graph. To do this, we will use the following theorem.

> Apply Corollary 8.20 to find tree metric (V, T') that approximates input metric d
>
> Find shortest path P_{xy} in G for each $(x, y) \in T'$
>
> Let $P'_{s_i t_i}$ be the unique s_i-t_i path in T' for all i
>
> Let P_i be concatenation of paths P_{xy} for all $(x, y) \in P'_{s_i t_i}$ for all i
>
> Set $c_e = \sum_{i:e \in P_i} d_i$ for all $e \in E$

Algorithm 8.6. Algorithm for the buy-at-bulk network design problem for general metrics d.

Theorem 8.19. *For any tree metric (V', T) with $V \subseteq V'$ defined by a hierarchical cut decomposition, with the vertices in V as the leaves of T, we can find in polynomial time another tree metric (V, T') such that $T_{uv} \leq T'_{uv} \leq 4T_{uv}$.*

Proof. Pick any $v \in V$ such that the parent w of v in the tree T is not in V (that is, $w \in V' - V$). We contract the edge (v, w), merging the subtree at v into its parent w, and identify the newly merged node as v. Repeat this process until every vertex in the tree is a vertex of V. Finally, multiply the length of every remaining edge by four. Let T' denote the resulting tree.

Clearly $T'_{uv} \leq 4T_{uv}$ since the distance between u and v could have only decreased during the contraction of edges, and then increased by a factor of 4 when the edge lengths were multiplied. Now suppose that the least common ancestor of u and v in the original tree T was a node w at level i so that $T_{uv} = 2^{i+2} - 4$, as shown in the proof of Lemma 8.18. Then since the contraction process only moves u and v upward in T, and does not identify the nodes u and v, the distance T'_{uv} in T' must be at least 4 times the length of the edge from w to one of its children, which is $4 \cdot 2^i = 2^{i+2}$. Thus, $T'_{uv} \geq T_{uv}$. $\square$

We thus obtain the following corollary from Theorem 8.17.

Corollary 8.20. *Given a distance metric (V, d), such that $d_{uv} \geq 1$ for all $u \neq v$, $u, v \in V$, there is a randomized, polynomial-time algorithm that produces a tree metric (V, T'), such that for all $u, v \in V$, $d_{uv} \leq T'_{uv}$ and $E[T'_{uv}] \leq O(\log n)d_{uv}$.*

Proof. By the proof of Lemma 8.18, the least common ancestor of u and v in the tree T obtained from a hierarchical cut decomposition must be on level $\lfloor \log_2 d_{uv} \rfloor$ or higher. By the proof of Theorem 8.19, the distance $T'_{uv} \geq 2^{i+2}$ for vertices in u and v that have their least common ancestor at level i in tree T. Thus, $T'_{uv} \geq d_{uv}$. The other statements follow immediately. $\square$

Thus, our algorithm now uses the algorithm of Corollary 8.20 to find a tree metric T', then uses Algorithm 8.5 to solve the buy-at-bulk problem on T'. For each edge $(x, y) \in T'$, we find a corresponding shortest path P_{xy} in our input graph G. Then our output path P_i from s_i to t_i in our input metric is the concatenation of the paths P_{xy} for all edges $(x, y) \in T'$ on the path from s_i to t_i in the tree T'. Given the paths P_i, we set the capacity of edge e to be the sum of the demands routed on paths that use e, so that $c_e = \sum_{i:e \in P_i} d_i$. This algorithm is summarized in Algorithm 8.6. Thus, the cost of our solution is $\sum_{e \in E} \ell_e f(c_e)$.

We will now show in a sequence of lemmas that Algorithm 8.6 is an $O(\log n)$-approximation algorithm for the buy-at-bulk network design problem. We do this by relating both the cost of our algorithm's solution and the cost of an optimal solution to the cost of a solution in T'. First, we give a bit of notation. Let P_{uv} denote the set of edges in a fixed shortest path from u to v in G, and let P'_{xy} denote the set of edges in the unique path from x to y in T'. Let c'_{xy} for edges $(x, y) \in T'$ be the capacity used by our algorithm on edge (x, y) of the tree T'; that is, $c'_{xy} = \sum_{i:(x,y)\in P'_{s_i t_i}} d_i$.

Recall that our algorithm first finds a solution in T', then translates the solution into G. We first show that the cost of the solution can only decrease with this translation.

Lemma 8.21. *The cost of the solution given by the algorithm is at most* $\sum_{(x,y)\in T'} T'_{xy} f(c'_{xy})$.

Proof. For each $(x, y) \in T'$, our algorithm finds a shortest x-y path in G, P_{xy}. We know that every demand i that uses (x, y) in T' will send its demand in G along this path, so that c'_{xy} demand is sent along this path at a cost of $d_{xy} f(c'_{xy}) \leq T'_{xy} f(c'_{xy})$. Note that it is possible that some edge e in G is contained in more than one shortest path corresponding to edges from T'; for example, e might be contained in P_{xy} and P_{vw} corresponding to two edges (x, y) and (v, w) from T'. Then we will route demand $c'_{xy} + c'_{vw}$ across e. However, by the subadditivity of f, we know that routing multiple paths on e cannot increase the total cost of the solution since $f(c'_{xy} + c'_{vw}) \leq f(c'_{xy}) + f(c'_{vw})$. Thus, we claim that the cost of the solution in T' does not increase when mapped to G.

Arguing more precisely, we have that

$$\sum_{(x,y)\in T'} T'_{xy} f(c'_{xy}) \geq \sum_{(x,y)\in T'} d_{xy} f(c'_{xy})$$

$$= \sum_{(x,y)\in T'} f(c'_{xy}) \sum_{e\in P_{xy}} \ell_e$$

$$= \sum_{e\in E} \ell_e \sum_{(x,y)\in T': e\in P_{xy}} f(c'_{xy})$$

$$\geq \sum_{e\in E} \ell_e f\left(\sum_{(x,y)\in T': e\in P_{xy}} c'_{xy} \right)$$

$$= \sum_{e\in E} \ell_e f(c_e),$$

as desired. □

Now suppose that an optimal solution uses paths P_i^* in G. Then the optimal solution uses capacity $c_e^* = \sum_{i:e\in P_i^*} d_i$ on edge e, and has cost $\text{OPT} = \sum_{e\in E} \ell_e f(c_e^*)$. In order to compare the cost of the optimal solution with the cost for our solution with the tree T', we think about how to translate the optimal solution in G to a solution on T'. For each edge $e = (u, v) \in E$, we'll install c_e^* units of capacity on all edges in the unique u-v path in T'. We now show that the cost of this translated optimal solution on T' must cost at least as much as our solution on T'.

Lemma 8.22. *The cost of the optimal solution in G translated to T' is at least* $\sum_{(x,y)\in T'} T'_{xy} f(c'_{xy})$.

Proof. To see this, we observe that for any edge $(x, y) \in T'$, our solution uses capacity c'_{xy}, which is exactly equal to the demands of all s_i-t_i pairs that would be separated in T' if we removed (x, y) from T'. Any other solution in T' sending d_i units of demand from s_i to t_i for every i must use capacity at least this much, so the translation of the optimal solution must use capacity at least c'_{xy} on edge (x, y). Thus, since f is non-decreasing, and the translation into T' of the optimal solution uses capacity at least c'_{xy} on edge $(x, y) \in T'$ for all $(x, y) \in T'$, the cost of the optimal solution in G translated to T' must be at least $\sum_{(x,y)\in T'} T'_{xy} f(c'_{xy})$. $\qquad\square$

We can now prove the main theorem.

Theorem 8.23. *The above randomized algorithm gives an $O(\log n)$-approximation algorithm for the buy-at-bulk network design problem.*

Proof. By combining Lemmas 8.21 and 8.22, we see that the cost of the solution given by the algorithm is at most the cost of the optimal solution in G translated to T'. We now need to show that this cost, in expectation, is $O(\log n)$ OPT.

We first claim that the cost of the optimal solution in G translated to T' is at most $\sum_{e=(u,v)\in E} f(c^*_e) T'_{uv}$. Given the claim, the theorem follows since then the expected cost of the solution is at most

$$E\left[\sum_{e=(u,v)\in E} f(c^*_e) T'_{uv}\right] \leq O(\log n) \sum_{e=(u,v)\in E} f(c^*_e) d_{uv} \leq O(\log n) \sum_{e\in E} f(c^*_e) \ell_e$$

$$= O(\log n)\, \text{OPT}.$$

Now to show the claim. The capacity that the translated solution needs for any edge $(x, y) \in T'$ is $\sum_{e=(u,v)\in E:(x,y)\in P'_{uv}} c^*_e$. Then by subadditivity, the cost of the optimal solution translated to T' is

$$\sum_{(x,y)\in T'} T'_{xy} \cdot f\left(\sum_{e=(u,v)\in E:(x,y)\in P'_{uv}} c^*_e\right) \leq \sum_{(x,y)\in T'} T'_{xy} \sum_{e=(u,v)\in E:(x,y)\in P'_{uv}} f(c^*_e)$$

$$= \sum_{e=(u,v)\in E} f(c^*_e) \sum_{(x,y)\in P'_{uv}} T'_{xy}$$

$$= \sum_{e=(u,v)\in E} f(c^*_e) T'_{uv}. \qquad\square$$

8.7 Spreading Metrics, Tree Metrics, and Linear Arrangement

We turn to one more problem that can be approximated using tree metrics. We consider the *linear arrangement problem*. In the linear arrangement problem, we are given an undirected graph $G = (V, E)$ and nonnegative weights $w_e \geq 0$ for all edges $e \in E$. A feasible solution is a one-to-one mapping f of the vertices to the numbers $\{1, 2, \ldots, n\}$, where $n = |V|$. The goal is to find the mapping that minimizes the sum $\sum_{e=(u,v)\in E} w_e |f(u) - f(v)|$. Intuitively, we are mapping a graph to points on the line so that we do not stretch the edges by too much; an example of the problem is shown in Figure 8.9. To find a solution to the problem, we first give an LP relaxation using a

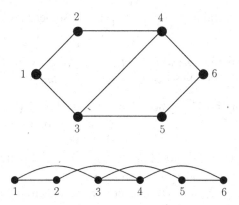

Figure 8.9. An example of the linear arrangement problem. We can map the vertices of the graph on the top of the figure to $\{1, \ldots, 6\}$ as shown on the bottom of the figure. Assuming the edges all have unit weight, this mapping gives a solution of cost $1 + 1 + 1 + 2 + 2 + 2 + 2 = 11$.

kind of metric called a spreading metric. Then we approximate the spreading metric by a tree metric. Finally, since we will be trying to minimize a sum of distances, we show that we can deterministically find a good tree metric.

We claim that the following linear program is a relaxation of the linear arrangement problem:

$$\text{minimize} \quad \sum_{e=(u,v)\in E} w_e d_{uv}$$

$$\text{subject to} \quad \sum_{v\in S} d_{uv} \geq \frac{1}{4}|S|^2, \qquad \forall S \subseteq V, u \notin S,$$

$$d_{uv} = d_{vu}, \qquad \forall u, v \in V,$$

$$d_{uv} \leq d_{uw} + d_{wv}, \qquad \forall u, v, w \in V,$$

$$d_{uv} \geq 1, \qquad \forall u, v \in V, u \neq v,$$

$$d_{uu} = 0, \qquad \forall u \in V.$$

To see that this is a relaxation, given a one-to-one mapping $f : V \to \{1, \ldots, n\}$, let d_{uv} be the distance between u and v under the mapping f, so that $d_{uv} = |f(u) - f(v)|$. Clearly the value of the solution is the cost of the linear arrangement. It is easy to see that then $d_{uv} = d_{vu}$, $d_{uv} \leq d_{uw} + d_{wv}$, $d_{uv} \geq 1$ if $u \neq v$, and $d_{uu} = 0$. To see that the final set of constraints is obeyed, note that for any set of vertices S and any $u \notin S$, there can be at most two vertices in S at distance 1 from $f(u)$ (namely, the vertices mapped to $f(u) + 1$ and $f(u) - 1$), at most two at distance 2, and so on. Thus,

$$\sum_{v\in S} d_{uv} \geq \frac{|S|}{2} \cdot \left(\frac{|S|}{2} + 1\right) \geq \frac{1}{4}|S|^2.$$

The variables d arising from the solution to the LP are a metric (V, d) since they obey the three properties of a metric as defined at the beginning of the chapter. This metric is sometimes called a *spreading metric*, since the constraint on sets $S \subseteq V$ enforces that for any set S and any $u \notin S$, there is a $v \in S$ that is far from u. Indeed, for any $S \subseteq V$ and any $u \notin S$, let $z = \max_{v\in S} d_{uv}$. Then observe that $z|S| \geq \sum_{v\in S} d_{uv} \geq \frac{1}{4}|S|^2$ implies that $z \geq \frac{1}{4}|S|$. The constraint $\sum_{v \in S} d_{uv} \geq \frac{1}{4}|S|^2$ is sometimes called the *spreading constraint*.

Observation 8.24. *For the spreading metric d defined as above, for any subset of vertices S and vertex $u \notin S$, there exists vertex v such that $d_{uv} \geq \frac{1}{4}|S|$.*

The linear program above can be solved in polynomial time by using the ellipsoid method given in Section 4.3. There are a polynomial number of constraints excepting the spreading constraints. The polynomial-time separation oracle for the spreading constraints is as follows. For each $u \in V$ we sort the remaining vertices in order of their distance from u, from smallest to largest: let $v_1, \ldots, v_{n-1}$ be such that $d_{uv_1} \leq d_{uv_2} \leq \cdots \leq d_{uv_{n-1}}$. We then check the constraint for each of the sets $\{v_1\},\{v_1, v_2\},\ldots,\{v_1,\ldots,v_{n-1}\}$. We claim that if the constraint is not violated for any of these sets for any u, then no constraint is violated. Suppose the constraint is violated for some S and some $u \notin S$. Then clearly the sum $\sum_{v \in S} d_{uv}$ is at least as large as $\sum_{i=1}^{|S|} d_{uv_i}$, so if the constraint is violated for S and $u \notin S$, it will also be violated for u and the set $\{v_1, \ldots, v_{|S|}\}$.

To get an approximation algorithm for the problem, we use a tree metric to approximate the metric d_{uv} obtained by solving the LP. However, here we will show that we can deterministically obtain a tree metric with the desired properties. In particular, we will show below that for any metric d, and any set of nonnegative costs $c_{uv} \geq 0$ on pairs of vertices $u, v \in V$, one can find in polynomial time a tree metric (V', T) such that $T_{uv} \geq d_{uv}$ and

$$\sum_{u,v \in V} c_{uv}T_{uv} \leq O(\log n) \sum_{u,v \in V} c_{uv}d_{uv}.$$

Observe that the results of Section 8.5 give a randomized algorithm such that

$$E[\sum_{u,v \in V} c_{uv}T_{uv}] \leq O(\log n) \sum_{u,v \in V} c_{uv}d_{uv}.$$

Since this inequality holds over the random choices of the trees from the randomized algorithm, there must exist some tree T generated by the algorithm such that the inequality holds. In fact, we can easily give a randomized algorithm to find such a tree metric (see Exercise 8.12). However, in the rest of this section we will deterministically find a hierarchical cut decomposition, leading to a tree metric, such that the inequality above holds.

We now show how finding a tree metric to approximate d applies to the linear arrangement problem. We will need the tree metric T to have some additional properties: first, T is a rooted tree with all the vertices of V at the leaves of the tree; and second, if vertex $z \in V$ belongs to the smallest subtree containing vertices $u, v \in V$, then $T_{uv} \geq T_{uz}$. Note that these additional properties are satisfied by trees resulting from a hierarchical cut decomposition. We claim that we can find such a tree efficiently.

Theorem 8.25. *Given a metric d_{uv} on vertices V and nonnegative costs c_{uv} for all $u, v \in V$, in polynomial time we can compute a tree metric (V', T) on a set of vertices $V' \supseteq V$ such that $T_{uv} \geq d_{uv}$ for all $u, v \in V$ and $\sum_{u,v \in V} c_{uv}T_{uv} \leq O(\log n) \sum_{u,v \in V} c_{uv}d_{uv}$. Furthermore, T is a rooted tree with all vertices of V at its* *leaves, and if vertex $z \in V$ belongs to the smallest subtree containing vertices $u, v \in V$, then $T_{uv} \geq T_{uz}$.*

Our algorithm for linear arrangement is as follows. We solve the linear programming relaxation above to obtain the metric d, and use the theorem to obtain a tree metric (V', T); we do so with costs $c_{uv} = w_e$ for $e = (u, v) \in E$ and $c_{uv} = 0$ otherwise. We then assign each leaf of the tree T a number from 1 to n; intuitively, we number them consecutively from left to right. Then each subtree in T has leaves that are numbered consecutively. Since each vertex of V is a leaf of the tree, the process assigns each $v \in V$ a number from 1 to n.

Theorem 8.26. *The algorithm given above is an $O(\log n)$-approximation algorithm for the linear arrangement problem.*

Proof. Let f be the one-to-one mapping produced by the algorithm. For any given edge $e = (u, v)$, consider the smallest subtree in the tree T that contains both u and v. This subtree is assigned some range of integers $[a, b]$. Since the leaves of the subtree are numbered consecutively, there are $b - a + 1$ leaves in the subtree. At worst, we can have one endpoint of the edge assigned to a and the other to b; hence, $|f(u) - f(v)| \leq b - a$. Let S be the set of leaves in the subtree other than u; we have $|S| = b - a$. By Observation 8.24, we know there is some other vertex $z \in S$ such that $d_{uz} \geq \frac{1}{4}(b - a)$. Therefore, by the property of the tree metric in Theorem 8.25, $T_{uv} \geq T_{uz} \geq d_{uz} \geq \frac{1}{4}(b - a)$, since z belongs to the smallest subtree containing u and v. Hence, we have $|f(u) - f(v)| \leq 4 \cdot T_{uv}$. By Theorem 8.25, we can then bound the cost of the solution f as follows:

$$\sum_{e=(u,v)\in E} w_e |f(u) - f(v)| \leq 4 \sum_{e=(u,v)\in E} w_e T_{uv} \leq O(\log n) \sum_{e=(u,v)\in E} w_e d_{uv}$$

$$\leq O(\log n)\,\mathrm{OPT},$$

where the final inequality follows since $\sum_{e=(u,v)\in E} w_e d_{uv}$ is the objective function of the linear programming relaxation of the linear arrangement problem.   □

We now begin our proof of Theorem 8.25. As we have mentioned previously, we will construct our tree via a hierarchical cut decomposition, as in Section 8.5. To give the decomposition, we need to explain how to partition a set S corresponding to a node at level i of the tree so as to obtain its children at level $i - 1$. As in the previous sections, we need to define the concept of a ball and the volume of a ball. For a given metric d, let $B_d(u, r)$ be the set of vertices within distance r of u, so that $B_d(u, r) = \{v \in V : d_{uv} \leq r\}$. Let $V^* = \sum_{u,v \in V} c_{uv} d_{uv}$. We define the volume $V_d(u, r)$ as in the previous sections, with

$$V_d(u, r) = \frac{V^*}{n} + \sum_{v,w \in B_d(u,r)} c_{vw} d_{vw} + \sum_{v \in B_d(u,r), w \notin B_d(u,r)} c_{vw}(r - d_{uv}).$$

We define $c(\delta(B_d(u, r)))$ to be the cost of the pairs of vertices with exactly one vertex in $B_d(u, r)$, so that $c(\delta(B_d(u, r))) = \sum_{v \in B_d(u,r), w \notin B_d(u,r)} c_{vw}$. We let $c_d(u, r)$ be shorthand for $c(\delta(B_d(u, r)))$.

Note that in Section 8.5, we made a random choice of the radii r_i for the balls at level i. Here we note that we can make good deterministic choices via the region-growing technique that relates the cost $c_d(u, r)$ to the volume of the ball.

Lemma 8.27. *In polynomial time it is possible to find a value r for any $u \in V$ and i, $0 \leq i \leq \log_2 \Delta$, such that $2^{i-1} \leq r < 2^i$ and*

$$c_d(u, r) \leq 2^{1-i} \ln \left(\frac{V_d(u, 2^i)}{V_d(u, 2^{i-1})} \right) V_d(u, r).$$

Proof. This follows from Corollary 8.11 applied to the interval $[2^{i-1}, 2^i)$.   □

The partitioning of a node corresponding to S at level i into children at level $i - 1$ is performed as follows. Rather than using a random ordering on the vertices, we find a vertex $u \in S$ that maximizes the volume $V_d(u, 2^{i-2})$, and find a ball of radius r, $2^{i-2} \leq r < 2^{i-1}$, around u via Lemma 8.27. We make a child node of S corresponding to all the vertices of $B_d(u, r)$ in S, remove these vertices from S, and repeat as long as $S \neq \emptyset$. Note that the ball has radius less than 2^{i-1} as required.

We can now prove the main theorem, which we restate here for convenience.

Theorem 8.25. *Given a metric d_{uv} on vertices V and nonnegative costs c_{uv} for all $u, v \in V$, in polynomial time we can compute a tree metric (V', T) on a set of vertices $V' \supseteq V$ such that $T_{uv} \geq d_{uv}$ for all $u, v \in V$ and $\sum_{u,v \in V} c_{uv} T_{uv} \leq O(\log n) \sum_{u,v \in V} c_{uv} d_{uv}$. Furthermore, T is a rooted tree with all vertices of V at its leaves, and if vertex $z \in V$ belongs to the smallest subtree containing vertices $u, v \in V$, then $T_{uv} \geq T_{uz}$.*

Proof. It follows from the properties of a hierarchical cut decomposition that each leaf of T corresponds to a single vertex $v \in V$. Furthermore, by Lemma 8.18, the distance between u and v depends solely on the level of the least common ancestor containing u and v; namely, if it is at level i, then $T_{uv} = 2 \sum_{j=1}^{i} 2^j = 2^{i+2} - 4$. Thus, if z is in the smallest subtree containing u and v, clearly the least common ancestor of u and z is at level at most i, so that $T_{uv} \geq T_{uz}$.

We now need to argue that $\sum_{u,v \in V} c_{uv} T_{uv} \leq O(\log n) \sum_{u,v \in V} c_{uv} d_{uv}$. For a given pair of vertices $u, v \in V$, let $i + 1$ be the level of the least common ancestor in the tree T containing both u and v. As shown in Lemma 8.18, then $T_{uv} \leq 2^{i+3}$. Let E_{i+1} be the pairs of vertices (u, v) with $u, v \in V$ whose least common ancestor in the tree T is at level $i + 1$. Thus,

$$\sum_{u,v \in V} c_{uv} T_{uv} \leq \sum_{i=0}^{\log_2 \Delta - 1} \sum_{(u,v) \in E_{i+1}} 2^{i+3} \cdot c_{uv}.$$

Note that $(u, v) \in E_{i+1}$ implies that there is a node at level i of the tree T corresponding to a ball such that exactly one of u and v is inside the ball. Thus, $\sum_{(u,v) \in E_{i+1}} c_{uv}$ is at most the sum of the cuts created when we formed the children at level i, and by Lemma 8.27, we can relate these cuts to the volume of these children.

Let C_i be the set of the centers of the balls corresponding to the nodes of level i of the tree T, and for $z \in C_i$, let r_{zi} be the radius of the ball around z we chose via

Lemma 8.27. Then for any level i, $\sum_{(u,v)\in E_{i+1}} c_{uv} \le \sum_{z\in C_i} c_d(z, r_{zi})$. By Lemma 8.27, we know that $c_d(z, r_{zi}) \le 2^{1-i} \ln \left(\frac{V_d(z, 2^i)}{V_d(z, 2^{i-1})}\right) V_d(z, r_{zi})$. Thus,

$$\sum_{u,v\in V} c_{uv} T_{uv} \le \sum_{i=0}^{\log_2 \Delta - 1} \sum_{(u,v)\in E_{i+1}} 2^{i+3} \cdot c_{uv}$$

$$\le \sum_{i=0}^{\log_2 \Delta - 1} \sum_{z\in C_i} 2^{i+3} \cdot c_d(z, r_i)$$

$$\le 16 \sum_{i=0}^{\log_2 \Delta - 1} \sum_{z\in C_i} \ln \left(\frac{V_d(z, 2^i)}{V_d(z, 2^{i-1})}\right) V_d(z, r_{iz}).$$

To bound this final term, we need to somehow relate the sum to the overall volume. To do this, let $g(v)$ be the volume of all the edges incident on vertex v plus V^*/n; that is, $g(v) = \frac{V^*}{n} + \sum_{u\in V} c_{uv} d_{uv}$. Then certainly the volume of the set associated with any node in the tree is at most the sum of the $g(v)$ of all the vertices v in the set; that is, for a set S corresponding to a node at level i generated by a ball around a center z of radius r_{iz}, $V_d(z, r_{iz}) \le \sum_{v\in S} g(v)$. Pick any $v \in S$. Since $r_{iz} < 2^i$, any edge or part of an edge contributing volume to the ball of radius r_{iz} in S must also be in a ball of radius 2^{i+1} around v. Thus, $V_d(z, r_{iz}) \le V_d(v, 2^{i+1})$. By construction of the algorithm, if z is a center of a ball corresponding to a node of level i in the tree, it must be the case that $V_d(z, 2^{i-1}) \ge V_d(v, 2^{i-1})$ for any other $v \in S$ since we chose $z \in S$ to maximize the volume $V_d(z, 2^{i-1})$. Putting all of these together, for any level i and set S corresponding to a node on level i, with z as its corresponding center, we have that

$$\ln \left(\frac{V_d(z, 2^i)}{V_d(z, 2^{i-1})}\right) V_d(z, r_{zi}) \le \sum_{v\in S} \ln \left(\frac{V_d(z, 2^i)}{V_d(z, 2^{i-1})}\right) g(v) \le \sum_{v\in S} \ln \left(\frac{V_d(v, 2^{i+1})}{V_d(v, 2^{i-1})}\right) g(v).$$

Substituting this into the inequality above and using the fact that the nodes at level i partition V, we have

$$\sum_{u,v\in V} c_{uv} T_{uv} \le 16 \sum_{i=0}^{\log_2 \Delta - 1} \sum_{v\in V} \ln \left(\frac{V_d(v, 2^{i+1})}{V_d(v, 2^{i-1})}\right) g(v)$$

$$= 16 \sum_{v\in V} \sum_{i=0}^{\log_2 \Delta - 1} \ln \left(\frac{V_d(v, 2^{i+1})}{V_d(v, 2^{i-1})}\right) g(v).$$

For each $v \in V$ the sum telescopes to $\ln(V_d(v, \Delta)) + \ln(V_d(v, \Delta/2)) - \ln(V_d(v, 1)) - \ln(V_d(v, 1/2))$, which can be bounded above by $2(\ln(V_d(v, \Delta)) - \ln(V_d(v, 0)))$. Thus, this sum is at most

$$32 \sum_{v\in V} \ln \left(\frac{V_d(v, \Delta)}{V_d(v, 0)}\right) g(v).$$

Then since $V_d(v, \Delta)$ is at most V^*, the entire volume, plus the extra V^*/n term, while $V_d(v, 0) = V^*/n$,

$$32 \sum_{v \in V} \ln \left(\frac{V_d(v, \Delta)}{V_d(v, 0)} \right) g(v) \leq 32 \sum_{v \in V} \ln \left(\frac{V^* + V^*/n}{V^*/n} \right) g(v) = 32 \ln(n+1) \sum_{v \in V} g(v).$$

Using the definition of $g(v)$, we have that

$$32 \ln(n+1) \sum_{v \in V} g(v) = 32 \ln(n+1) \sum_{v \in V} \left(\frac{V^*}{n} + \sum_{u \in V} c_{uv} d_{uv} \right)$$

$$= 96 \ln(n+1) \sum_{u,v \in V} c_{uv} d_{uv},$$

so that

$$\sum_{u,v \in V} c_{uv} T_{uv} \leq O(\log n) \sum_{u,v \in V} c_{uv} d_{uv},$$

as desired.   □

While we have gone to considerable lengths to give a deterministic algorithm to find a tree metric T such that $\sum_{u,v \in V} c_{uv} T_{uv} \leq O(\log n) \sum_{u,v \in V} c_{uv} d_{uv}$, we can quite simply obtain a randomized algorithm that finds such a tree metric with high probability given a randomized algorithm for probabilistically approximating a metric by a tree metric with distortion $O(\log n)$. We give this as an exercise (Exercise 8.12). The reverse direction can also be shown; given any deterministic algorithm to find a tree metric T such that $\sum_{u,v \in V} c_{uv} T_{uv} \leq O(\log n) \sum_{u,v \in V} c_{uv} d_{uv}$, we can obtain a randomized algorithm that can probabilistically approximate d by a tree metric with distortion $O(\log n)$. We give the latter problem as an exercise later in the book, once we have a bit more experience with the ellipsoid method (Exercise 15.9).

Exercises

8.1 Prove that the analysis of the performance guarantee of the multiway cut algorithm of Section 8.2 can be improved to $\frac{3}{2} - \frac{1}{k}$.

8.2 Consider the following two permutations π_1 and π_2, where $\pi_1(1) = 1, \pi_1(2) = 2, \ldots, \pi_1(k) = k$, while $\pi_2(1) = k, \pi_2(2) = k - 1, \ldots, \pi_2(k) = 1$. Consider a modification of Algorithm 8.1 in which we do not choose a random permutation π, but rather choose $\pi = \pi_1$ with probability $1/2$ and $\pi = \pi_2$ with probability $1/2$. Show that the modified algorithm is still a $\frac{3}{2}$-approximation algorithm for the multiway cut problem.

8.3 In the *Steiner k-cut problem*, we are given an undirected graph $G = (V, E)$, costs $c_e \geq 0$ for all $e \in E$, a set of terminals $T \subseteq V$, and a positive integer $k \leq |T|$. The goal of the problem is to partition the vertices into k sets $S_1, \ldots, S_k$ such that each set contains at least one terminal (that is, $S_i \cap T \neq \emptyset$ for $i = 1, \ldots, k$) and to minimize the weight of the edges with endpoints in different parts. Given a partition $\mathcal{P} = \{S_1, \ldots, S_k\}$, let $c(\mathcal{P})$ be the total cost of the edges that have endpoints in different parts of the partition.

Consider the following greedy algorithm for the Steiner k-cut problem: We start with $\mathcal{P} = \{V\}$. As long as $\mathcal{P}$ does not have k parts, we consider each set $S \in \mathcal{P}$ with $|S \cap T| \geq 2$, consider each pair of terminals in $S \cap T$, and compute the minimum-cost cut between that pair of terminals. We then choose the minimum-cost cut found overall by this procedure; note that this breaks some set $S \in \mathcal{P}$ into two parts. We replace S in $\mathcal{P}$ with these two new parts, and continue.

(a) Let $\mathcal{P}_i$ be the contents of the partition found by the algorithm when it has i parts. Let $\hat{\mathcal{P}} = \{V_1, V_2, \ldots, V_i\}$ be any valid partition into i parts (that is, $V_j \cap T \neq \emptyset$ for $j = 1, \ldots, i$). Show that

$$c(\mathcal{P}_i) \leq \sum_{j=1}^{i-1} \sum_{e \in \delta(V_j)} c_e.$$

(b) Use the above to show that this greedy algorithm is a $\left(2 - \frac{2}{k}\right)$-approximation algorithm for the Steiner k-cut problem.

8.4 Give a linear programming relaxation for the minimum multicut problem of Section 8.3 whose number of variables and constraints can be bounded by a polynomial in the size of the input graph G. Show that it is equivalent to the linear programming relaxation of Section 8.3, and show that any optimal solution to your linear program can be transformed to an optimal solution of the other linear program in polynomial time.

8.5 In the *minimum-cut linear arrangement problem*, we are given an undirected graph $G = (V, E)$ and costs $c_e \geq 0$ for all $e \in E$. As in the linear arrangement problem, a feasible solution is a one-to-one mapping f of the vertices to the numbers $\{1, 2, \ldots, n\}$. In this problem, however, the goal is to minimize the cost of the cut $\{f(1), \ldots, f(i)\}$ over all i; that is, we wish to minimize

$$\max_{1 \leq i < n} \sum_{e=(u,v): f(u) \leq i, f(v) > i} c_e.$$

Show that by using the balanced cut pseudo-approximation algorithm of Section 8.4, one can obtain an $O(\log^2 n)$-approximation algorithm for this problem.

8.6 In the *sparsest cut problem*, we are given an undirected graph $G = (V, E)$, costs $c_e \geq 0$ for all $e \in E$, and k pairs of vertices s_i, t_i, each pair with an associated positive integer demand d_i. We want to find a set of vertices S that minimizes

$$\frac{\sum_{e \in \delta(S)} c_e}{\sum_{i:|S \cap \{s_i, t_i\}|=1} d_i}.$$

That is, the sparsest cut problem finds a cut that minimizes the ratio of the cost of the edges in the cut to demands separated by the cut. Let $\mathcal{P}_i$ denote the set of all paths P from s_i to t_i.

(a) Prove that it is equivalent to find a minimum-cost set of edges F that minimizes

$$\frac{\sum_{e \in F} c_e}{\sum_{i \in s(F)} d_i},$$

where $s(F)$ is the set of indices i such that s_i and t_i are not connected in the graph $(V, E - F)$.

(b) Prove that the following LP is a linear programming relaxation of the sparsest cut problem.

$$\text{minimize} \sum_{e \in E} c_e x_e$$

$$\text{subject to} \sum_{i=1}^{k} d_i y_i = 1,$$

$$\sum_{e \in P} x_e \geq y_i, \qquad \forall P \in \mathcal{P}_i, 1 \leq i \leq k,$$

$$y_i \geq 0, \qquad 1 \leq i \leq k,$$

$$x_e \geq 0.$$

(c) Prove that the linear program can be solved in polynomial time.

(d) Let (x^*, y^*) be an optimal solution to the linear program, and suppose that $y_1^* \geq y_2^* \geq \cdots \geq y_k^*$. Let $D_i = \sum_{j=1}^{i} d_j$, and $H_n = 1 + \frac{1}{2} + \cdots + \frac{1}{n}$. Show that there exists i, $1 \leq i \leq k$, such that

$$y_i^* \geq \frac{1}{D_i \cdot H_{D_k}}.$$

(e) Use the preceding discussion to get an $O(\log k \cdot H_{D_k})$-approximation algorithm for the sparsest cut problem. Since $H_n = O(\log n)$, this is an $O(\log k \cdot \log D_k)$-approximation algorithm.

8.7 Let $C_n = (V, E)$ be a cycle on n vertices, and let d_{uv} be the distance between $u, v \in V$ on C_n. Show that for any tree metric (V, T) on the same set of vertices V, there must exist a pair of vertices $u, v \in V$ such that $d_{uv} = 1$, but $T_{uv} \geq n - 1$. To do this, suppose that of all trees T with optimal distortion, T has the minimum total length. Show that T must be a path of vertices of degree two, then conclude the statement above.

8.8 In the *universal traveling salesman problem*, we are given as input a metric space (V, d) and must construct a tour π of the vertices. Let π_S be the tour of the vertices $S \subseteq V$ given by visiting them in the order given by the tour π. Let OPT_S be the value of an optimal tour on the metric space induced by the vertices $S \subseteq V$. The goal of the problem is to find a tour π that minimizes π_S / OPT_S over all $S \subseteq V$; in other words, we'd like to find a tour such that for any subset $S \subseteq V$, visiting the vertices of S in the order given by the tour is close in value to the optimal tour of S.

Show that if (V, d) is a tree metric, then it is possible to find a tour π such that $\pi_S = \text{OPT}_S$ for all $S \subseteq V$.

8.9 A typical variant of the buy-at-bulk problem discussed in Section 8.6 is to assume that cables come in different types: cable type i costs c_i and has capacity u_i. We must choose the type and number of cables to install on each edge given the demand to be supported on the edge. Show that given a demand d to be supported on an edge, installing enough copies of a single cable type i (e.g., $\lceil d/u_i \rceil$ copies for some i) is a 2-approximation algorithm for this problem.

8.10 Consider a slight variant of the k-median problem given in Section 7.7: We are given as input a set of locations N in a metric space, and a parameter k. Let c_{ij} be the distance between i and j for $i, j \in N$. We wish to select a subset $S \subseteq N$ of k centers to minimize the sum of the distances of each location to the nearest center; that is, we wish to select $S \subseteq N$ with $|S| = k$ to minimize $\sum_{j \in N} \min_{i \in S} c_{ij}$.

(a) Give a polynomial-time algorithm for the problem in the case that the metric c_{ij} comes from a tree metric (N, T). You can assume you know the tree T. (Hint: Use dynamic programming on the structure of the tree. It might help to assume that the tree is a rooted binary tree such that each internal node has at most two children; show that this assumption is without loss of generality.)

(b) Give a randomized $O(\log |N|)$-approximation algorithm for this variant of the k-median problem.

8.11 In the *capacitated dial-a-ride problem*, we are given a metric (V, d), a vehicle of capacity C, a starting point $r \in V$, and k source-sink pairs s_i-t_i for $i = 1, \ldots, k$, where $s_i, t_i \in V$. At each source s_i there is an item that must be delivered to the sink t_i by the vehicle. The vehicle can carry at most C items at a time. The goal is to find the shortest possible tour for the vehicle that starts at r, delivers each item from its source to its destination without exceeding the vehicle capacity, then returns to r; note that such a tour may visit a node of V multiple times. We assume that the vehicle is allowed to temporarily leave items at any node in V.

(a) Suppose that the metric (V, d) is a tree metric (V, T). Give a 2-approximation algorithm for this case. (Hint: How many times must each edge $(u, v) \in T$ be traversed going from u to v, and going from v to u? Give an algorithm that traverses each edge at most twice as many times as it needs to.)

(b) Give a randomized $O(\log |V|)$-approximation algorithm for the capacitated dial-a-ride problem in the general case.

8.12 Suppose we have a metric (V, d) and costs c_{uv} for all $u, v \in V$. Suppose we are also given a randomized algorithm that finds a tree metric (V', T) with $V' \supseteq V$ such that $d_{uv} \leq T_{uv}$ and $E[T_{uv}] \leq O(\log n)d_{uv}$ for all $u, v \in V$. Obtain a randomized algorithm that with high probability obtains a tree metric (V'', T') with $V'' \supseteq V$ such that $d_{uv} \leq T'_{uv}$ and $\sum_{u,v \in V} c_{uv} T'_{uv} \leq O(\log n) \sum_{u,v \in V} c_{uv} d_{uv}$.

Chapter Notes

Most early work on approximation algorithms for NP-hard cut problems used polynomial-time algorithms for finding a minimum s-t cut as a subroutine. The isolating cut algorithm for the multiway cut problem in Section 8.1 is an example of such an algorithm; this algorithm is due to Dahlhaus, Johnson, Papadimitriou, Seymour, and Yannakakis [86]. The application mentioned of assigning objects to machines is due to Hogstedt, Kimelman, Rajan, Roth, and Wegman [169]. Although it is of relatively recent vintage, the Steiner k-cut algorithm of Exercise 8.3 is another example of reducing a cut problem to repeated applications of a minimum s-t cut algorithm. The Steiner k-cut problem was independently introduced by Chekuri, Guha, and Naor [70] and Maeda, Nagamochi, and Ibaraki [221]. The algorithm given in the exercise is due to Zhao, Nagamochi, and Ibaraki [295] based on earlier algorithms for other problems. The analysis of the exercise is due to an unpublished result of Chekuri. The problem itself generalizes the k-cut problem; in the k-cut problem, the goal is to remove edges of minimum total cost so that the graph has at least k components. The k-cut problem is a special case of the Steiner k-cut problem in which $T = V$; a 2-approximation algorithm for the k-cut problem due to Saran and Vazirani [259] was previously known.

Leighton and Rao [213, 214] wrote a highly influential paper that used solutions to linear programming relaxations as metrics and rounded the LP solutions to obtain solutions to cut problems. The idea of region growing appeared in this paper, in the context of obtaining an $O(\log n)$-approximation algorithm for a variant of the sparsest cut problem (discussed in Exercise 8.6) called the *uniform* sparsest cut problem; in the uniform sparsest cut problem, each pair of vertices $u, v \in V$ is an s_i-t_i pair with demand $d_i = 1$. The first pseudo-approximation algorithm for the balanced cut problem (as discussed in Section 8.4) was given in this paper. Several applications of these techniques to cut and arrangement problems also appeared in this paper, including the result for the minimum cut linear arrangement problem given in Exercise 8.5.

Subsequent work on treating LP solutions as metrics includes the multicut algorithm of Section 8.3 (due to Garg, Vazirani, and Yannakakis [126]), the pseudo-approximation algorithm given in Section 8.4 for the balanced cut problem (due to Even, Naor, Rao, and Schieber [102]), and the LP rounding algorithm for the multiway cut problem (due to Călinescu, Karloff, and Rabani [60]). Karger, Klein, Stein, Thorup, and Young [185] give a more sophisticated LP rounding algorithm for the same LP relaxation of the multiway cut problem and obtain somewhat better performance guarantees.

Bartal [39] defined the notion of the probabilistic approximation of metrics by tree metrics we use here, although his work was inspired by earlier unpublished work of Karp and work of Alon, Karp, Peleg, and West [7]. Bartal [39, 40] also gave the first algorithms for finding such tree metrics. Bartal [39] shows the existence of a metric for which any probabilistic approximation by tree metrics must have distortion $\Omega(\log n)$; the graph is one in which every cycle in the graph has at least $\Omega(\log n)$ vertices. The algorithm of Section 8.5 for the probabilistic approximation of metrics by tree metrics is due to Fakcharoenphol, Rao, and Talwar [106]. The tree metric algorithm from Section 8.7 is also from this paper. As mentioned in the section, many approximation algorithms use probabilistic approximation of metrics by tree metrics as a subroutine. The application of tree metrics to the buy-at-bulk network design problem in Section 8.6 was made by Awerbuch and Azar [28]; Theorem 8.19 in that section is due to Konjevod, Ravi, and Sibel Salman [202]. Even, Naor, Rao, and Schieber [103] introduce spreading metrics and their application to the linear arrangement problem. The application of tree metrics to this problem in Section 8.7 follows a survey of Fakcharoenphol, Rao, and Talwar [105]. For some time, the k-median approximation algorithm of Exercise 8.10 was the best approximation algorithm known for the problem; approximation algorithms with constant performance guarantees are discussed in Sections 7.7 and 9.2. Polynomial-time algorithms for the k-median problem in tree metrics are due to Kariv and Hakimi [186] and Tamir [278]. The capacitated dial-a-ride algorithm of Exercise 8.11 is due to Charikar and Raghavachari [66].

Exercises 8.1 and 8.2 are due to Călinescu, Karloff, and Rabani [60]. The algorithm and analysis for the sparsest cut problem given in Exercise 8.6 are due to Kahale [181]. Exercise 8.8 is due to Schalekamp and Shmoys [260]. Exercise 8.7 is due to Gupta [147]. Exercise 8.9 can be found in Awerbuch and Azar [28].

PART TWO

Further Uses of the Techniques

CHAPTER 9

Further Uses of Greedy and Local Search Algorithms

We have now concluded our initial introduction to the various techniques for designing approximation algorithms. In this second part of the book, we revisit each of these techniques and give additional applications of them. In some cases, these applications are recent or more advanced, but in others they are just a bit more technically involved, or are in some other way "nonintroductory." Hence, this second part covers "further uses" of each technique, rather than "advanced uses" or "recent uses."

In this chapter, we look again at greedy and local search algorithms. We revisit the problem of minimizing the maximum degree of a spanning tree, and show that a variant of the local search algorithm described in Section 2.6 in which the local moves are carefully ordered results in a spanning tree whose maximum degree is within 1 of the optimum. When we revisit the technique of deterministic rounding in Chapter 11, we will show a similar result for a version of the problem in which there are costs on the edges.

The bulk of this chapter is spent on greedy and local search algorithms for the uncapacitated facility location problem and the k-median problem. Simple local search algorithms for these problems have been known since the early 1960s. It is only relatively recently, however, that it has been shown that these algorithms produce provably near-optimal solutions. In Section 9.1, we show that a local search algorithm for the uncapacitated facility location problem gives a $(3 + \epsilon)$-approximation algorithm for that problem. Then by using a technique called scaling, in which we artificially scale the facility costs by a certain factor before running the local search algorithm, we show that we can obtain a $(1 + \sqrt{2} + \epsilon)$-approximation algorithm for the same problem, where $1 + \sqrt{2} \approx 2.414$. In Section 9.2, we show that a simple local search algorithm for the k-median problem gives a $(5 + \epsilon)$-approximation algorithm for the problem. Finally, in Section 9.4, we give a greedy algorithm for the uncapacitated facility location problem that is analogous to the greedy algorithm for the set cover problem we discussed in Section 1.6. By using a dual fitting analysis similar to the one for the set cover problem, we are able to show that the greedy algorithm is a 2-approximation algorithm for the uncapacitated facility location problem. Furthermore, the algorithm is Lagrangean multiplier preserving in the sense mentioned at the end of Section 7.7, and thus leads to a $2(2 + \epsilon)$-approximation algorithm for the k-median problem.

9.1 A Local Search Algorithm for the Uncapacitated Facility Location Problem

In this section, we turn to a local search algorithm for the uncapacitated facility location problem that we have considered previously several times. We will show that we can obtain a somewhat better performance guarantee by a local search algorithm than we did with the primal-dual algorithm in Section 7.6. Recall that the input to the problem is a set of clients D and a set of facilities F, with a facility cost f_i for each facility $i \in F$, and an assignment cost c_{ij} for each facility $i \in F$ and each client $j \in D$. The goal is to select a subset of facilities to open and an assignment of clients to open facilities so as to minimize the total cost of the open facilities plus the assignment costs. As before, we will assume that the set of clients and potential facility locations are in a metric space; that is, for each $i, j \in F \cup D$, we have a value c_{ij}, and for each $i, j, k \in F \cup D$, we have that $c_{ij} + c_{jk} \geq c_{ik}$. Note that whenever we consider a distance between $i \in F$ and $j \in D$, we will maintain the convention that it is referred to as c_{ij}.

The local search algorithm for the problem will maintain a (nonempty) set of open facilities $S \subseteq F$ and an assignment σ of clients to facilities in S; that is, $\sigma(j) = i$ if client j is assigned to facility $i \in S$. The algorithm that we first consider is perhaps the most natural local search algorithm, in that we permit three types of changes to the current solution: we can open one additional facility (an "add" move), we can close one facility that is currently open (a "delete" move), and we can do both of these simultaneously (a "swap" move). Of course, we must also update the current assignment of clients to open facilities. The algorithm will always maintain that each client is assigned to its nearest open facility. We repeatedly check if any of these changes to the current solution reduces the total cost; if so, we make the change to the current solution. Once no further change decreases the total cost, we stop; the current solution is said to be a *locally optimal solution*.

We first analyze the quality of the solution found by this procedure. In fact, we will first focus not on an algorithmic statement but instead on proving that *any* locally optimal solution is near-optimal. In essence, we show that for any locally optimal solution, the absence of any improving add move implies that the total assignment cost of the current solution is relatively small. Then we show that the absence of improving swap and delete moves implies that the total facility cost is relatively small. Together, this yields an upper bound on the cost of any locally optimal solution. We focus on a particular optimal solution; let S^* be its open facilities and let σ^* denote the corresponding optimal assignment of clients to open facilities. To compare the cost of this optimal solution to the current, locally optimal solution of the algorithm, we let F and F^* denote, respectively, the total facility cost of the current solution and the optimal one, and similarly let C and C^* denote their respective total assignment costs. The optimal value OPT is clearly $F^* + C^*$. Note that now F stands for both the set of facilities and the facility cost of the current solution, but the meaning at any given point should be clear from the context.

The strategy in proving this guarantee is to focus on a particular subset of possible moves; each move consists of an update to S and an update to σ. We know that each such move can generate an inequality based on the fact that the change in cost must be nonnegative. In fact, the update to the assignment σ need not be the optimal one relative to the new choice of open facilities; since the corresponding change in cost is greater than or equal to the change if we updated the assignment optimally, we are free to consider this suboptimal assignment update, and still conclude that the overall change in cost is nonnegative.

Lemma 9.1. *Let S and σ be a locally optimal solution. Then*

$$C \leq F^* + C^* = \text{OPT}. \tag{9.1}$$

Proof. Since S is a locally optimal solution, we know that adding any facility to S does not improve the solution (with respect to the best possible updated assignment). In this way, we will focus on a few potential changes to the current solution, and analyze their change in cost. Note that we consider the changes only for the sake of analysis, and we do not actually change the solution.

Consider some facility $i^* \in S^* - S$, and suppose that we open the additional facility i^*, and reassign to that facility all of the clients that were assigned to i^* in the optimal solution: that is, we reassign all clients j such that $\sigma^*(j) = i^*$. Since our current solution S and σ is locally optimal, we know that the additional facility cost of i^* is at least as much as the improvement in cost that would result from reassigning each client optimally to its nearest open facility; hence, f_{i^*} must also be more than the improvement resulting from our specific reassignment; that is,

$$f_{i^*} \geq \sum_{j:\sigma^*(j)=i^*} (c_{\sigma(j)j} - c_{\sigma^*(j)j}). \tag{9.2}$$

Consider also a facility i^* that is in both S and S^*; although it might seem a bit odd, observe that the same inequality (9.2) must hold for such a facility i^*, since the local optimality of S and σ implies that each client j is currently assigned to its closest open facility, and so each term in the summation on the right-hand side of the inequality must be nonpositive. Consequently, we can add inequality (9.2) for each $i^* \in S^*$, to obtain

$$\sum_{i^* \in S^*} f_{i^*} \geq \sum_{i^* \in S^*} \sum_{j:\sigma^*(j)=i^*} (c_{\sigma(j)j} - c_{\sigma^*(j)j}).$$

The left-hand side of this inequality is clearly equal to F^*. For the right-hand side, since each client j is assigned to exactly one facility $i^* \in S^*$ by σ^*, the double summation is the same as summing over all possible clients $j \in F$. Hence, the first right-hand-side terms (corresponding to $c_{\sigma(j)j}$) sum to C, whereas the second terms sum to C^*. It follows that $F^* \geq C - C^*$, and the lemma has been proved. □

The argument to show that a local optimum has a small total facility cost is somewhat more complicated. As in the proof of the previous lemma, we will consider a set of changes to the solution S, each of which will generate a corresponding inequality. For any move that deletes a facility $i \in S$ (either a delete move or a swap move that "swaps out" facility i), we must reassign each of the clients that are assigned to i. If we were

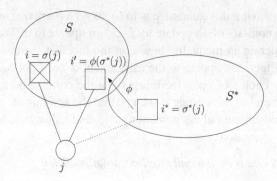

Figure 9.1. The reassignment of a client j to $i' = \phi(\sigma^*(j))$ when facility $i = \sigma(j)$ is closed.

simply deleting i, then each such client must be reassigned to a facility in $S - \{i\}$. One natural way to determine this facility is as follows: For each client j, it is assigned to a facility $i^* = \sigma^*(j)$ in our fixed optimal solution. For each $i^* \in S^*$, let $\phi(i^*)$ be the facility in S closest to i^*; for each client j, if $i \neq i'$, where $i' = \phi(\sigma^*(j))$, then it seems reasonable to reassign client j to i' (see Figure 9.1). In fact, the following lemma proves this intuition correct.

Lemma 9.2. *Consider any client j for which $\sigma(j) = i$ is not equal to $i' = \phi(\sigma^*(j))$. Then the increase in cost of reassigning client j to i' (instead of to i) is at most $2c_{\sigma^*(j)j}$.*

Proof. Consider a client j currently being served by i, where its facility in S^*, $i^* = \sigma^*(j)$, is such that i^*'s nearest facility in S, $\phi(i^*)$, is not the facility i. Let $i' = \phi(i^*)$. What can we conclude about the assignment cost $c_{i'j}$? Consider Figure 9.1. By the triangle inequality,

$$c_{i'j} \leq c_{i'i^*} + c_{i^*j}.$$

By the choice of i', we see that $c_{i'i^*} \leq c_{ii^*}$, from which we can conclude that

$$c_{i'j} \leq c_{ii^*} + c_{i^*j}.$$

But now we also know that $c_{ii^*} \leq c_{ij} + c_{i^*j}$ by the triangle inequality, and hence we have that

$$c_{i'j} \leq c_{ij} + 2c_{i^*j}. \tag{9.3}$$

Note that by subtracting c_{ij} from both sides, we can reinterpret this inequality as saying that the increase in the assignment cost of client j by this reassignment is at most $2c_{\sigma^*(j)j}$. $\square$

We will apply this lemma both when i is deleted and when i is swapped out of the solution.

Lemma 9.3. *Let S and σ be a locally optimal solution. Then*

$$F \leq F^* + 2C^*. \tag{9.4}$$

Proof. As in the proof of Lemma 9.1, we will prove this by considering a set of changes to the solution S, and by deriving an inequality based on each change. Because S is locally optimal, we know that any delete, swap, or add move must result in a nonnegative change in total cost. Again, we consider these moves solely for the sake of analysis. In this construction, we will give a set of moves that either deletes or swaps out every facility in S (once each) and either adds or swaps in every facility in S^* (again once each). Since the change in cost for each of these local moves is nonnegative, this will allow us to bound the facility cost F in terms of the facility cost F^* and additional terms that we will bound by twice the optimal assignment cost.

Suppose that we want to delete a facility $i \in S$. Each client j that is currently served by i must be reassigned to one of the remaining open facilities in $S - \{i\}$. If we are to apply Lemma 9.2, then we need that for each client j such that $\sigma(j) = i$, we also have that $\phi(\sigma^*(j)) \neq i$. We shall call a facility i *safe* if for *every* facility $i^* \in S^*$, the facility $\phi(i^*) \in S$ closest to i^* is different from i. As this name suggests, for any safe facility i, we can consider the local move of closing facility i, since we can safely reassign each of its clients j to $\phi(\sigma^*(j))$, and apply Lemma 9.2 to bound the resulting increase in the assignment cost for reassigned client j. Again, since S is locally optimal, we know that this local change cannot decrease the overall cost, and hence the savings obtained by closing the safe facility i must be no more than the increase in assignment costs incurred by reassigning all of the clients assigned to i. That is,

$$f_i \leq \sum_{j:\sigma(j)=i} 2c_{\sigma^*(j)j},$$

or equivalently,

$$- f_i + \sum_{j:\sigma(j)=i} 2c_{\sigma^*(j)j} \geq 0. \tag{9.5}$$

Consider a facility i that is not safe (or, in other words, is unsafe), and let $R \subseteq S^*$ be the (nonempty) set of facilities $i^* \in S^*$ such that $\phi(i^*) = i$; among those facilities in R, let i' be the one closest to i. We will derive one inequality for each member of R, based on an add move for each member of $R - \{i'\}$, plus one swap move closing the facility at i, while opening a facility at i'.

First let us derive an inequality for each add move corresponding to $i^* \in R - \{i'\}$. As in the proof of Lemma 9.3, we open a facility at i^*, and for each client j that is assigned to i in the locally optimal solution and is assigned to i^* in the optimal solution, we reassign client j to i^*. The change in cost caused by this move must also be nonnegative, and we derive the inequality

$$f_{i^*} + \sum_{j:\sigma(j)=i \ \& \ \sigma^*(j)=i^*} (c_{\sigma^*(j)j} - c_{\sigma(j)j}) \geq 0. \tag{9.6}$$

Next, we derive an inequality based on the swap move that closes the facility at i but opens a facility at i'. Of course, in order for this to make sense as a swap move, we need that $i' \neq i$. However, we will see that the ultimate inequality derived from this move also holds if $i' = i$, and so this will turn out to be unimportant. To make this swap move precise, we will also specify a (suboptimal) reassignment of the clients assigned to i by σ: each client j for which $\sigma^*(j) \notin R$ is reassigned to $\phi(\sigma^*(j))$, and the rest are reassigned to i'.

Let us consider the change in cost incurred by this swap move. Clearly, the change in cost of the facilities is $f_{i'} - f_i$. To bound the reassignment cost for the clients, consider the two cases of the reassignment rule. For any client j reassigned to $\phi(\sigma^*(j))$, we are in the case governed by Lemma 9.2, and hence the increase in the assignment cost is at most $2c_{\sigma^*(j)j}$. If j is assigned to i', then the change in the assignment cost is exactly $c_{i'j} - c_{ij}$. Combining all of these pieces, we obtain an upper bound on the total change in cost of this swap move (where it is an upper bound both because we are focusing on a potentially suboptimal reassignment, and because we are only computing an upper bound on the increase in that reassignment cost). Again, we know that the true change in cost is nonnegative, and hence

$$f_{i'} - f_i + \sum_{j:\sigma(j)=i \ \& \ \sigma^*(j)\notin R} 2c_{\sigma^*(j)j} + \sum_{j:\sigma(j)=i \ \& \ \sigma^*(j)\in R} (c_{i'j} - c_{ij}) \geq 0. \qquad (9.7)$$

Again, suppose that $i' = i$; this inequality reduces to the essentially trivial inequality that

$$\sum_{j:\sigma(j)=i \ \& \ \sigma^*(j)\notin R} 2c_{\sigma^*(j)j} \geq 0.$$

For this unsafe facility i, let us consider the net effect of combining all of these inequalities (that is, the one (9.7) derived from the swap move, and the remaining ones (9.6) from add moves). Adding these, we get that

$$-f_i + \sum_{i^*\in R} f_{i^*} + \sum_{j:\sigma(j)=i \ \& \ \sigma^*(j)\notin R} 2c_{\sigma^*(j)j} + \sum_{j:\sigma(j)=i \ \& \ \sigma^*(j)\in R} (c_{i'j} - c_{ij})$$
$$+ \sum_{j:\sigma(j)=i \ \& \ \sigma^*(j)\in R-\{i'\}} (c_{\sigma^*(j)j} - c_{\sigma(j)j}) \geq 0.$$

We will simplify this expression by combining the final two summations, and by showing that for each client j that appears in either summation, we can upper bound its total contribution by $2c_{\sigma^*(j)j}$. If $\sigma^*(j) = i'$, then this is quite simple, since in that case, the contribution for client j is $c_{i'j} - c_{ij}$, which is no more than $2c_{i'j}$. Next consider any client j for which $\sigma(j) = i$ and $\sigma^*(j) \in R - \{i'\}$; its total contribution is $c_{i'j} + c_{\sigma^*(j)j} - 2c_{ij}$. By the triangle inequality, $c_{i'j} \leq c_{i'i} + c_{ij}$. Furthermore, by the choice of i' among R, $c_{i'i} \leq c_{\sigma^*(j)i}$. Finally, again by the triangle inequality, $c_{\sigma^*(j)i} \leq c_{\sigma^*(j)j} + c_{ij}$. Combining these three inequalities, we see that $c_{i'j} \leq c_{\sigma^*(j)j} + 2c_{ij}$, which proves our claim that the total contribution of j is at most $2c_{\sigma^*(j)j}$. Consequently, we see that

$$- f_i + \sum_{i^*\in R} f_{i^*} + \sum_{j:\sigma(j)=i} 2c_{\sigma^*(j)j} \geq 0. \qquad (9.8)$$

Finally, suppose we add inequality (9.5) for each safe facility $i \in S$, and inequality (9.8) for each unsafe facility $i \in S$; note that as we consider each of the unsafe facilities, each facility $i^* \in S^*$ occurs in exactly one corresponding set R. Hence we see that

$$\sum_{i^*\in S^*} f_{i^*} - \sum_{i\in S} f_i + \sum_{j\in D} 2c_{\sigma^*(j)j} \geq 0. \qquad (9.9)$$

Thus, $F^* - F + 2C^* \geq 0$, and we have proved the lemma. $\qquad\square$

By adding the inequalities of these two lemmas, we obtain directly the following theorem.

Theorem 9.4. *Let S and σ be a locally optimal solution for the uncapacitated facility location problem. Then this solution has a total cost that is at most* 3 OPT.

This theorem is not quite the ultimate result in two ways: first, we really proved a stronger result, that the cost is at most $3C^* + 2F^*$, and this will allow us to improve the guarantee slightly, and second, we did not prove that the corresponding local search algorithm terminates in polynomial time, and hence it is not a 3-approximation algorithm. In the latter case, if the cost of the solution improves by 1 with each local move, then the algorithm could take time exponential in the size of the input.

The first of these issues is the simpler of the two. Suppose that we rescaled the facility costs by dividing each f_i by a factor μ. For an input in which the optimal solution had assignment cost C^* and facility cost F^*, there now must exist a solution of assignment cost C^* and facility cost F^*/μ. By Lemmas 9.3 and 9.1, the resulting solution found by local search must therefore have assignment cost at most $C^* + F^*/\mu$, and (rescaled) facility cost at most $2C^* + F^*/\mu$. (To be more careful, we should note that the proof of these lemmas did not actually use the fact that the fixed optimal solution was optimal, merely that there was a feasible solution with the particular facility and assignment costs.) Reinterpreting this solution in terms of the original costs (that is, multiplying the facility costs by μ), we obtain a solution of total cost at most $(1 + 2\mu)C^* + (1 + 1/\mu)F^*$. If we set μ so that the maximum of these two coefficients is as small as possible (by setting them equal), we want that $\mu = \sqrt{2}/2$, and the resulting performance guarantee is $1 + \sqrt{2} \approx 2.414$.

The idea behind ensuring that the local search algorithm runs in polynomial time is simple, but the details in analyzing that the idea works involve some calculation. To speed up the algorithm, rather than just requiring any decrease in cost, suppose that we insist that the cost decreases in each iteration by some factor $1 - \delta$ that is strictly less than 1. If the objective function value is initially equal to M, and the input data are integral (and hence so is any feasible objective function value), then if k is chosen such that $(1 - \delta)^k M < 1$, we can be sure that k iterations suffice for the algorithm to terminate. Suppose that the algorithm stopped whenever the current solution was nearly locally optimal, in the sense that each possible move did not decrease the cost of the solution by a factor of $1 - \delta$. Consider the proof of Lemma 9.1; in order to derive equation (9.2), we use the fact that there are no improving moves. Now we must rely only on the fact any move does not improve the solution too much, and so we may only conclude that

$$f_i - \sum_{j:\sigma^*(j)=i} (c_{\sigma(j)j} - c_{\sigma^*(j)j}) \geq -\delta(C + F). \tag{9.10}$$

As we trace through the rest of the proof of Lemma 9.1, we add at most $|F|$ such inequalities. Hence, if we let $m = |F|$, we can conclude that

$$F^* - C + C^* \geq -m\delta(C + F).$$

Similarly, in the proof of Lemma 9.3, we derive the result by adding the inequalities (9.5), (9.7), and (9.6). Again, there are at most m inequalities, and if we require that a move produces a solution that is a factor of $1 - \delta$ cheaper, this would result in each right-hand side being $-\delta(C + F)$ rather than 0. Hence, we can still derive that

$$F^* - F + 2C^* \geq -m\delta(C + F).$$

Adding these two inequalties, we obtain the inequality that

$$(1 - 2m\delta)(C + F) \leq 3C^* + 2F^* \leq 3\,\text{OPT}.$$

Hence, the "bigger step" local search algorithm has a performance guarantee of $\frac{3}{1-2m\delta}$.

We will show that if we set $\delta = \epsilon/(4m)$, then we both have a polynomial-time algorithm, and achieve a performance guarantee of $3(1 + \epsilon)$. For the first, $(1 - \epsilon/(4m))^{4m/\epsilon} \leq 1/e$, and so $(4m \ln M)/\epsilon$ iterations suffice, where M could be $\sum_{i \in F} f_i + \sum_{i \in F, j \in D} c_{ij}$ (by starting with the solution in which all facilities are open), and so this is a polynomial bound on the number of iterations. A straightforward calculation shows that $\frac{1}{1-\epsilon/2} \leq 1 + \epsilon$ (provided $\epsilon \leq 1$). Hence, we can convert the local search algorithm into a polynomial-time algorithm, losing an arbitrarily small factor in the performance guarantee, by requiring these bigger steps. And finally, it is easy to see that one could combine the rescaling idea with the big steps to yield the following theorem.

Theorem 9.5. *For any constant $\rho > 1 + \sqrt{2}$, the rescaled local search algorithm using bigger steps yields a ρ-approximation algorithm for the uncapacitated facility location problem.*

9.2 A Local Search Algorithm for the k-Median Problem

In this section, we shall consider again the *k-median problem* originally considered in Section 7.7; however, we shall consider a slightly simpler variant in which we have a set of locations N, each of which is both a client and a potential facility location. For each pair of locations i and j, there is a cost c_{ij} of assigning location j to a facility at location i. We can select at most k locations at which to open facilities, where k is part of the input. The goal is to find a set of locations S at which to open a facility, where $|S| \leq k$, such that the assignment cost is minimized: $\sum_{j \in N} \min_{i \in S} c_{ij}$. Without loss of generality, we can assume that $|S| = k$. In other words, this problem can be viewed as the min-sum analogue of the k-center problem, previously considered in Section 2.2, which is a min-max problem. As in the k-center problem, we shall assume that the distance matrix is symmetric, satisfies the triangle inequality, and has zeros on the diagonal (i.e., $c_{ii} = 0$ for each $i \in N$).

We will give a local search algorithm for the k-median problem. We will let $S \subseteq N$ denote the set of open facilities for the current solution, and let $S^* \subseteq N$ denote the set of open facilities in a fixed optimal solution. For each of these two solutions, each client j is assigned to its nearest open facility (breaking ties arbitrarily); we let this mapping be denoted $\sigma(j)$ and $\sigma^*(j)$, respectively, for these two assignments. Analogously, we let C and C^* denote, respectively, the total cost of the current and optimal solutions.

The local search algorithm that we shall consider is the most natural one. Each current solution is specified by a subset $S \subseteq N$ of exactly k locations. To move from

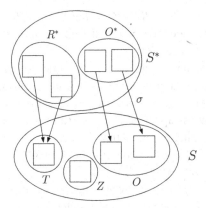

Figure 9.2. The mapping of locations in S^* to S used to construct the crucial swaps.

one feasible solution to a neighboring one, we *swap* two locations; that is, we select one location $i \in S$ to delete from the current set, and choose one location $i' \in N - S$ to add to the current set of facilities. Afterward, we reassign each client to its nearest open facility. In our local search procedure, we repeatedly check to see if any swap move yields a solution of lower cost; if so, the resulting solution is our new current solution. We repeat this step until, from the current solution, no swap move decreases the cost. The current solution at this point is said to be locally optimal.

We shall prove the following theorem.

Theorem 9.6. *For any input to the k-median problem, any feasible solution S that is locally optimal with respect to the pairwise swap move has a cost that is at most 5 times the optimal value.*

Proof. The proof will focus on first constructing a set of k special swaps, which we shall call the *crucial swaps*. Since the current solution S is locally optimal, we know that each of these swaps does not improve the objective function of the resulting solution. These swaps will all be constructed by swapping into the solution one location i^* in S^* and swapping out of the solution one location i in S. Each $i^* \in S^*$ will participate in exactly one of these k swaps, and each $i \in S$ will participate in at most 2 of these k swaps. (We will allow the possibility that $i^* = i$, and hence the swap move is degenerate, but clearly such a "change" would also not improve the objective function of the current solution, even if we change the corresponding assignment.) Observe that the current solution provides a mapping from each facility $i^* \in S^*$ to a facility $\sigma(i^*) \in S$.

As Figure 9.2 shows, this mapping allows us to categorize the facilities in S:

- let $O \subseteq S$ consist of those facilities $i \in S$ that have exactly one facility $i^* \in S^*$ with $\sigma(i^*) = i$;
- let $Z \subseteq S$ consist of those facilities $i \in S$ for which none of the facilities $i^* \in S^*$ have $\sigma(i^*) = i$;
- and let $T \subseteq S$ consist of those facilities $i \in S$ such that i has at least two locations in S^* assigned to it in the current solution.

We make a few simple observations. The mapping σ provides a matching between a subset $O^* \subseteq S^*$ and the set $O \subseteq S$ (by the definition of O). Hence, if ℓ denotes the number of locations in $R^* = S^* - O^*$, then ℓ must also equal $|Z \cup T|$ (since $|S^*| = |S| = k$). Since each location in T is the image of at least two locations in R^*, it follows that $|T| \leq \ell/2$. Hence, $|Z| \geq \ell/2$.

We now construct the crucial swaps as follows: first, for each $i^* \in O^*$, we swap i^* with $\sigma(i^*)$; second, we build a collection of ℓ swaps, each of which swaps into the solution a distinct location in R^*, and swaps out a location in Z, where each location in Z appears in at most two swaps. For the swaps involving locations in R^* and Z, we are free to choose any mapping provided that each element of R^* is swapped in exactly once, and each element of Z is swapped out once or twice.

Consider one crucial swap, where $i^* \in S^*$ and $i \in S$ denote the swapped locations; we analyze the change of cost incurred by no longer opening a facility at location $i \in S$, and using i^* instead. Let S' denote the set of selected locations after this swap; that is, $S' = S - \{i\} \cup \{i^*\}$. To complete the analysis, we also specify the assignment of each location in N to an open facility in S'. For each location j such that $\sigma^*(j) = i^*$, we assign j to i^* (since i^* is in S'). For each location j such that $\sigma^*(j) \neq i^*$, but $\sigma(j) = i$, then we need a new facility to serve j, and we now assign it to $\sigma(\sigma^*(j))$. All other locations j remain served by $\sigma(j)$.

One must argue that $\sigma(\sigma^*(j)) \neq i$ when $\sigma^*(j) \neq i^*$ (since we need that this location must remain in S'). Assume, for a contradiction, that $\sigma(\sigma^*(j)) = i$; then $i \in O$ (since each location swapped out by a crucial swap is in either Z or O, and the former is clearly not possible by the definition of Z). Since $i \in O$, it is σ's image of exactly one element in O^*, and we build a crucial swap by swapping i with that one element. Hence, $\sigma^*(j) = i^*$, but this is a contradiction.

We have now constructed a new set of facilities S' and an assignment of each location in N to one of the facilities in S'. There may be some location j that is not served by its closest point in S' by this assignment. However, since there are no improving swaps from the current solution S, any swap combined with a suboptimal assignment must also not decrease the overall cost; hence, the change to S' along with the specified assignment also must not improve over using S with the assignment given by function σ.

What is the change of cost for this swap? By focusing only on the clients j for which $\sigma^*(j) = i^*$, or both $\sigma^*(j) \neq i^*$ and $\sigma(j) = i$, we can compute the change in the cost to be

$$\sum_{j:\sigma^*(j)=i^*} (c_{\sigma^*(j)j} - c_{\sigma(j)j}) + \sum_{j:\sigma^*(j)\neq i^* \ \& \ \sigma(j)=i} (c_{\sigma(\sigma^*(j))j} - c_{\sigma(j)j}).$$

We can simplify the terms in the second summation by considering Figure 9.3. By the triangle inequality, we have that

$$c_{\sigma(\sigma^*(j))j} \leq c_{\sigma(\sigma^*(j))\sigma^*(j)} + c_{\sigma^*(j)j}.$$

In the current solution S, $\sigma^*(j)$ is assigned to $\sigma(\sigma^*(j))$ instead of to $\sigma(j)$, and so we know that

$$c_{\sigma(\sigma^*(j))\sigma^*(j)} \leq c_{\sigma(j)\sigma^*(j)}.$$

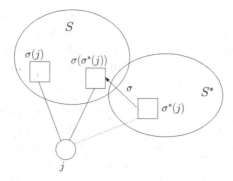

Figure 9.3. Bounding the length of the edge from j to $\sigma(\sigma^*(j))$.

Once again, we can apply the triangle inequality to get that

$$c_{\sigma(j)\sigma^*(j)} \leq c_{\sigma^*(j)j} + c_{\sigma(j)j},$$

and so, putting these pieces together, we have that

$$c_{\sigma(\sigma^*(j))j} \leq 2c_{\sigma^*(j)j} + c_{\sigma(j)j},$$

or equivalently,

$$c_{\sigma(\sigma^*(j))j} - c_{\sigma(j)j} \leq 2c_{\sigma^*(j)j}.$$

(In fact, a little reflection indicates that we had already proved this, in Lemma 9.2, where now σ plays the same role as ϕ.) This yields a more compact upper bound on the change in the cost, which we know must be nonnegative; that is, for each crucial swap i^* and i, we have that

$$0 \leq \sum_{j:\sigma^*(j)=i^*} (c_{\sigma^*(j)j} - c_{\sigma(j)j}) + \sum_{j:\sigma^*(j)\neq i^* \ \& \ \sigma(j)=i} 2c_{\sigma^*(j)j}. \qquad (9.11)$$

Now we add inequality (9.11) over all k crucial swaps. Consider the contribution for each of the two terms in the first summation. Recall that each $i^* \in S^*$ participates in exactly one crucial swap. For the first term, we add $c_{\sigma^*(j)j}$ over all clients j for which $\sigma^*(j) - i^*$, and this sum is then added for each choice of i^* in S^*. Each client j has a unique facility $\sigma^*(j) \in S^*$ to which it is assigned by the fixed optimal solution, and so the net effect is to compute the sum $\sum_{j\in N} c_{\sigma^*(j)j} = C^*$. However, the same is true for the second term; the double summation is merely the sum over all possible locations j, and so the second terms contribute a total of $-\sum_{j\in N} c_{\sigma(j)j} = -C$. Now consider the second summation in (9.11). We can upper bound this expression by

$$\sum_{j:\sigma(j)=i} 2c_{\sigma^*(j)j}.$$

What is the effect of adding this summation over all crucial swaps? Each facility $i \in S$ occurs in 0, 1, or 2 crucial swaps; let n_i be the number of swaps in which each $i \in S$ occurs. Thus, we can upper bound the double summation as follows:

$$\sum_{i\in S} \sum_{j:\sigma(j)=i} 2n_i c_{\sigma^*(j)j} \leq 4 \sum_{i\in S} \sum_{j:\sigma(j)=i} c_{\sigma^*(j)j}.$$

But now we can apply the same reasoning as above; each location j is served in the current solution by a unique facility location $\sigma(j) \in S$, and hence the effect of the double summation is merely to sum over each j in N. That is, we have now deduced that this term is at most $4 \sum_{j \in N} c_{\sigma^*(j)j} = 4C^*$. Furthermore, we have concluded that $0 \leq 5C^* - C$, and hence $C \leq 5C^*$. □

Finally, we observe that the same idea used in the previous section to obtain a polynomial-time algorithm can be applied here. The central ingredients to that proof are that if we restrict attention to moves (in this case, swap moves) in which we improve the total cost by a factor of $1 - \delta$, then provided the analysis is based on a polynomial number of moves (each of which generates an inequality that the change in cost from this move is nonnegative), we can set δ so that we can obtain a polynomial-time bound, while degrading the performance guarantee by an arbitrarily small constant.

Theorem 9.7. *For any constant $\rho > 5$, the local search algorithm for the k-median problem that uses bigger improving swaps yields a ρ-approximation algorithm.*

9.3 Minimum-Degree Spanning Trees

In this section we return to the minimum-degree spanning tree problem introduced in Section 2.6. Recall that the problem is to find a spanning tree T in a graph $G = (V, E)$ that minimizes the maximum degree. If T^* is an optimal tree that minimizes the maximum degree, let OPT be the maximum degree of T^*. In Section 2.6, we showed that a particular local search algorithm finds a locally optimal tree of maximum degree at most $2\,\mathrm{OPT} + \lceil \log_2 n \rceil$ in polynomial time. In this section, we will show that another variation on the local search algorithm finds a locally optimal tree of maximum degree at most $\mathrm{OPT} + 1$ in polynomial time. As we discussed in Section 2.6, since it is NP-hard to minimize the maximum degree of a spanning tree, this is the best result possible unless $P = NP$.

As in the algorithm of Section 2.6, we start with an arbitrary spanning tree T, and we will make local changes to it in order to decrease the degree of nodes in the tree. Let $d_T(u)$ be the degree of u in T. We pick a node u and attempt to reduce its degree by adding an edge (v, w) to T that creates a cycle C containing u, then removing an edge of the cycle C incident on u. Let $\Delta(T) = \max_{v \in V} d_T(v)$ be the maximum degree of the current tree T. We will make local changes in a way that is driven by the following lemma, which gives us a condition under which the current tree T has $\Delta(T) \leq \mathrm{OPT} + 1$.

Lemma 9.8. *Let $k = \Delta(T)$, let D_k be any nonempty subset of nodes of tree T with degree k, and let D_{k-1} be any subset of nodes of tree T with degree $k - 1$. Let F be the edges of T incident on nodes in $D_k \cup D_{k-1}$, and let $\mathcal{C}$ be the collection of $|F| + 1$ connected components formed by removing the edges of F from T. If each edge of graph G that connects two different components in $\mathcal{C}$ has at least one endpoint in $D_k \cup D_{k-1}$, then $\Delta(T) \leq \mathrm{OPT} + 1$.*

Proof. See Figure 9.4 for an illustration of the terms. We use the same idea as in the proof of Theorem 2.19 to obtain a lower bound on OPT. Since any spanning tree

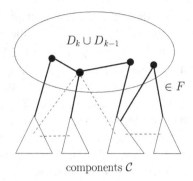

Figure 9.4. Illustration of the terms used in the statement of Lemma 9.8. The edges in F are shown in bold. Some edges in G that are not in the tree T are shown as dotted lines; note that they are not all incident on nodes in $D_k \cup D_{k-1}$. The components $\mathcal{C}$ are the components of the tree T remaining after the edges in F are removed.

in G will need $|F|$ edges of G to connect the components in $\mathcal{C}$, the average degree of the nodes in $D_k \cup D_{k-1}$ in any spanning tree is at least $|F|/|D_k \cup D_{k-1}|$. Thus, OPT $\geq \lceil |F|/|D_k \cup D_{k-1}| \rceil$.

We now bound $|F|$ in order to prove the lemma. The sum of the degrees of the nodes in D_k and D_{k-1} must be $|D_k|k + |D_{k-1}|(k-1)$. However, this sum of degrees may double count some edges of F that have both endpoints in $D_k \cup D_{k-1}$. Because T is acyclic, there can be at most $|D_k| + |D_{k-1}| - 1$ such edges. Hence, $|F| \geq |D_k|k + |D_{k-1}|(k-1) - (|D_k| + |D_{k-1}| - 1)$. Thus,

$$
\begin{aligned}
\text{OPT} &\geq \left\lceil \frac{|D_k|k + |D_{k-1}|(k-1) - (|D_k| + |D_{k-1}| - 1)}{|D_k| + |D_{k-1}|} \right\rceil \\
&\geq \left\lceil k - 1 - \frac{|D_{k-1}| - 1}{|D_k| + |D_{k-1}|} \right\rceil \\
&\geq k - 1,
\end{aligned}
$$

implying that $k = \Delta(T) \leq \text{OPT} + 1$. $\qquad\qquad\square$

The goal of the local search algorithm is to continue to reduce the degree of the nodes of degree $\Delta(T)$ while trying to attain the conditions of Lemma 9.8. The algorithm works in a sequence of phases, with each phase divided into subphases. At the beginning of the phase, for the current tree T, let $k = \Delta(T)$. At the beginning of a subphase, we let D_k be all the degree k vertices in T, let D_{k-1} be all the degree $k - 1$ vertices in T, let F be the edges of T incident to $D_k \cup D_{k-1}$, and let $\mathcal{C}$ be the components of T formed if F is removed from T. The goal of each phase is to make local moves to remove all nodes of degree k from the tree; the goal of each subphase is to make local moves to remove a single vertex of degree k. In the process of executing a subphase, we discover nodes of degree $k - 1$ in D_{k-1} for which we can make a local move to reduce their degree. We do not yet execute these moves, but we mark the nodes as *reducible* via the particular local move, remove them from D_{k-1}, and update F and $\mathcal{C}$ accordingly by removing edges from F and merging components in $\mathcal{C}$. The algorithm is summarized in Algorithm 9.1, and we now discuss its details.

In a subphase, we consider all edges of G that connect any two components of $\mathcal{C}$. If all such edges have an endpoint in $D_k \cup D_{k-1}$, we meet the condition of Lemma 9.8, and the algorithm terminates with a tree T such that $\Delta(T) \leq \text{OPT} + 1$. If there is some such edge (v, w) without an endpoint in $D_k \cup D_{k-1}$, then consider the cycle formed by adding (v, w) to T. Because (v, w) connects two different components of $\mathcal{C}$, it must be the case that the cycle includes some node $u \in D_k \cup D_{k-1}$. Note that if we desire, we can make a local move to reduce the degree of u by adding (v, w) to the tree T and removing a tree edge incident to u. If the cycle contains nodes of D_{k-1} only, then we do not yet make the local move, but we make a note that for any of the nodes in D_{k-1} on the cycle, we could do so if necessary. We label these nodes in D_{k-1} on the cycle as reducible via the edge (v, w), remove them from D_{k-1}, update F to be the tree edges incident on the current set of $D_k \cup D_{k-1}$, and update $\mathcal{C}$ accordingly. Note that since we removed all nodes on the cycle from D_{k-1}, this only removes edges from F and merges components in $\mathcal{C}$; in particular, the two components connected by (v, w) will be merged in the updated $\mathcal{C}$. If, on the other hand, the cycle includes a node of $u \in D_k$, we go ahead and reduce its degree by adding (v, w) to the tree and removing an edge incident on u. Decreasing the degree of u decreases the number of nodes of degree k in the tree, but we want to ensure that we do not increase the degree of nodes v and w to k. Note that this could happen only if the degree of v or w in the tree is $k - 1$ and at some previous point in the subphase the node was removed from D_{k-1} and labeled reducible. In this case, we carry out the local move that allows us to reduce the degree of reducible node to $k - 2$, then add (v, w) to the tree and remove an edge incident to u from the tree. It is possible that carrying out the local move to reduce the degree of the reducible node to $k - 2$ might cause a cascade of local moves; for instance, if v has degree $k - 1$, and we can reduce its degree by adding edge (x, y), potentially x also has degree $k - 1$ and is reducible, and so on; we will show that it is possible to carry out all these moves, and reduce the degree of u to $k - 1$ without creating any new nodes of degree k. We say that we are able to *propagate* the local move for u. Once we reduce the degree of u from k to $k - 1$, we start a new subphase. If there are no further nodes of degree k, we start a new phase.

We can now prove that the algorithm is correct and runs in polynomial time.

Theorem 9.9. *Algorithm 9.1 returns a spanning tree T with $\Delta(T) \leq \text{OPT} + 1$ in polynomial time.*

Proof. Because the algorithm terminates only when it meets the conditions of Lemma 9.8, it returns a tree T with $\Delta(T) \leq \text{OPT} + 1$ if it does indeed terminate. We claim that in each subphase, we can propagate local moves to reduce the degree of a reducible node in a component in $\mathcal{C}$ without creating any new nodes of degree k. Then either the algorithm terminates or in each subphase, we find some node u of degree k whose degree can be reduced to $k - 1$ by making a local move with an edge (v, w). Since v and w must be in separate components of $\mathcal{C}$, either their degree is less than $k - 1$ or they have degree $k - 1$ and are reducible, and by the claim we can propagate local moves to reduce their degree. Thus, we can reduce the degree of u from k to $k - 1$ without creating any new nodes of degree k, and so each phase eliminates all nodes of degree k. Since we cannot have a feasible spanning tree with $\Delta(T) = 1$, the algorithm must eventually terminate. Clearly the algorithm runs in polynomial time.

Let T be an arbitrary spanning tree of $G = (V, E)$
while true **do**
    $k \leftarrow \Delta(T)$ // Start a new phase
    while there are nodes of degree k in T **do**   // Start a new subphase
        $D_k \leftarrow$ all nodes of degree k in T
        $D_{k-1} \leftarrow$ all nodes of degree $k - 1$ in T
        $F \leftarrow$ all edges of T incident on nodes in $D_k \cup D_{k-1}$
        $\mathcal{C} \leftarrow$ all components formed by removing F from T
        All nodes $u \in D_{k-1}$ are unlabeled
        if for all $(v, w) \in E$ connecting two components in $\mathcal{C}$: either v or w in
            $D_k \cup D_{k-1}$ **then**
            return T
        for all $(v, w) \in E$ connecting two components in $\mathcal{C}$: $v, w \notin D_k \cup D_{k-1}$ **do**
            Let C be a cycle created by adding (v, w) to T
            if $C \cap D_k = \emptyset$ **then**
                Mark all $u \in C \cap D_{k-1}$ reducible via (v, w)
                Remove $C \cap D_{k-1}$ from D_{k-1}
                Update F and $\mathcal{C}$
        else
            if $u \in C \cap D_k$ **then**
                if v or w marked reducible **then**
                    Reduce degree of v and/or w via local move and propagate
                      local moves if necessary
                Reduce degree of u via local move with (v, w)
                Break for loop   // Start new subphase

Algorithm 9.1. Local search algorithm for the minimum-degree spanning tree problem.

We now prove the claim by showing that at any iteration of the subphase, we can propagate local moves to reduce the degree of a reducible node in a component in $\mathcal{C}$. We prove this by induction on the number of iterations in the subphase. In the first iteration, no nodes are marked reducible and the claim is trivially true. Now suppose we are at some iteration $i > 1$ of the subphase, and let u be labeled reducible in this iteration. The node u is currently reducible because we have a local move with a non-tree edge (v, w) that will reduce the degree of u from $k - 1$ to $k - 2$; furthermore, the components in $\mathcal{C}$ containing v and w are disjoint in the current iteration. If v is reducible, it was labeled such in an iteration $j < i$, and by induction we can carry out local moves to ensure that its degree is at most $k - 2$. The same is true for w, and by induction we can carry out the local moves for both v and w because they are in separate components in $\mathcal{C}$. In the next iteration the components containing v and w are merged into a single component that also contains u. Since the only changes that can happen to components in $\mathcal{C}$ during a subphase is that components are merged, u, v, and w remain in the same component of $\mathcal{C}$ through the rest of the subphase, and the local moves of adding (v, w) and reducing the degree of u remain available. $\square$

In Section 11.2, we will consider a version of the problem in which there are costs on the edges and specified bounds on the degrees of the nodes. If a tree with the given degree bounds exists, we will show how to find a minimum-cost tree such that the degree bounds are exceeded by at most one.

9.4 A Greedy Algorithm for the
Uncapacitated Facility Location Problem

In this section, we give yet another approximation algorithm for the uncapacitated facility location problem. We will give a greedy algorithm for the problem, then use dual fitting to analyze it; this is similar to what we did in Theorem 1.12 for the set cover problem.

A very natural greedy algorithm is to repeatedly choose a facility and some clients to assign to that facility. We open the facility, assign the clients to the facility, remove the facility and clients from further consideration, and repeat. For a greedy algorithm, we would somehow like to find a facility and set of clients that minimizes total cost for the amount of progress made. To do this, we use the same criterion we used for the greedy set cover algorithm in Section 1.6: we maximize the bang for the buck by minimizing the ratio of the total cost per client assigned. To be more precise, let X be the set of facilities opened so far, and let S be the set of clients that are not connected to facilities in X so far. We pick some $i \in F - X$ and $Y \subseteq S$ that minimizes the ratio

$$\frac{f_i + \sum_{j \in Y} c_{ij}}{|Y|}.$$

We then add i to X, remove Y from S, and repeat. Note that to find the appropriate set $Y \subseteq S$, for any given facility i, we can sort the clients in S by their distance from i, from nearest to farthest, and the set Y minimizing the ratio for i will be some prefix of this ordering.

We now add two simple improvements to this proposed algorithm. The first is that once we select facility i, rather than removing it from the set of facilities that can be chosen in the future, we instead allow it to be chosen again and set its facility cost to zero. The intuition here is that in future iterations it may be more cost-effective to assign some clients to i rather than opening another facility to serve them, and since i has already been opened, we should treat its facility cost as zero. The second idea is that rather than assigning clients to a facility and fixing that assignment from then on, we consider switching assignments to other facilities we open later. We include the savings gained by switching assignments when trying to choose the facility to open. Let $c(j, X) = \min_{i \in X} c_{ij}$, and let $(a)_+ = \max(a, 0)$. Then if we have already assigned the clients in $D - S$ to some facilities in X, and we are considering opening facility i, we can decrease assignment costs for all clients $j \notin S$ such that $c(j, X) > c_{ij}$ by reassigning them from X to i. The savings achieved is $\sum_{j \notin S}(c(j, X) - c_{ij})_+$. Thus, in every step we pick some $i \in F$ and $Y \subseteq S$ that minimizes the ratio

$$\frac{f_i - \sum_{j \notin S}(c(j, X) - c_{ij})_+ + \sum_{j \in Y} c_{ij}}{|Y|}.$$

Our revised greedy algorithm is given in Algorithm 9.2.

$S \leftarrow D$
$X \leftarrow \emptyset$
while $S \neq \emptyset$ **do**
    Choose $i \in F$ and $Y \subseteq D - S$
        minimizing $(f_i - \sum_{j \notin S}(c(j, X) - c_{ij})_+ + \sum_{j \in Y} c_{ij})/|Y|$
    $f_i \leftarrow 0; S \leftarrow S - Y$
Open all facilities in X, assign client j to closest facility in X

Algorithm 9.2. Greedy algorithm for the uncapacitated facility location problem.

To analyze this algorithm, we will use a dual fitting analysis: we will construct an infeasible solution to the dual of the linear programming relaxation such that the cost of the primal solution is equal to the value of the dual objective. Then we show that scaling the dual solution by a factor of 2 makes it feasible. This implies that the cost of the primal solution is at most twice the value of a solution to the dual of the linear programming relaxation, which implies that the algorithm is a 2-approximation algorithm.

First, recall the dual of the linear programming relaxation of the uncapacitated facility location problem that we introduced in Section 4.5:

$$\text{maximize} \quad \sum_{j \in D} v_j$$
$$\text{subject to} \quad \sum_{j \in D} w_{ij} \leq f_i, \qquad \forall i \in F,$$
$$v_j - w_{ij} \leq c_{ij}, \qquad \forall i \in F, j \in D,$$
$$w_{ij} \geq 0, \qquad \forall i \in F, j \in D.$$

We claim that the greedy algorithm above can be restated in the following way. Each facility will make a bid α_j toward its share of the service and facility costs. We increase the bids of clients uniformly until each client is connected to a facility whose cost is paid for by the bids. A client j that is not connected to a facility i bids the difference of α_j and the service cost toward the cost of facility i; that is, it bids $(\alpha_j - c_{ij})_+$ toward the cost of facility i. When the total of the bids on a facility i equals its facility cost f_i, we open the facility i. We also allow connected clients to bid the difference in service costs toward the facility cost of a closer facility; that is, if client j is currently connected to a facility in X, it bids $(c(j, X) - c_{ij})_+$ toward the facility cost of i. If facility i is opened, then client j connects itself to facility i instead, decreasing its service cost by exactly $(c(j, X) - c_{ij})_+$. Once every client is connected to some open facility, the algorithm terminates.

We summarize the algorithm in Algorithm 9.3. For ease of proofs, it turns out to be better to have the algorithm use facility costs $\hat{f}_i = 2f_i$. As in the statement of the greedy algorithm, let the set $S \subseteq D$ keep track of which clients have not yet been connected to an open facility, and let $X \subseteq F$ keep track of the currently open facilities.

We leave it as an exercise (Exercise 9.1) to prove that the two algorithms are equivalent. The basic idea is that the value of client j's bid α_j is the value of the ratio $(f_i - \sum_{j \notin S}(c(j, X) - c_{ij})_+ + \sum_{j \in Y} c_{ij})/|Y|$ when j is first connected to a facility.

$\alpha \leftarrow 0$
$S \leftarrow D$
$X \leftarrow \emptyset$
$\hat{f}_i = 2 f_i$ for all $i \in F$
while $S \neq \emptyset$ **do**   // While not all clients neighbor a facility in X
    Increase α_j for all $j \in S$ uniformly until $[\exists j \in S, i \in X$ such that $\alpha_j = c_{ij}]$ or
        $[\exists i \in F - X : \sum_{j \in S}(\alpha_j - c_{ij})_+ + \sum_{j \notin S}(c(j, X) - c_{ij})_+ = \hat{f}_i]$
    if $\exists j \in S, i \in X$ such that $\alpha_j = c_{ij}$ **then**
        // j becomes a neighbor of an existing facility i in X
        $S \leftarrow S - \{j\}$
    else
        // facility i is added to X
        $X \leftarrow X \cup \{i\}$
        for all $j \in S$ such that $\alpha_j \geq c_{ij}$ **do**
            $S \leftarrow S - \{j\}$
Open all facilities in X, assign client j to closest facility in X

Algorithm 9.3. Dual fitting algorithm for the uncapacitated facility location problem.

We observe in passing that there are some strong similarities between Algorithm 9.3 and the primal-dual algorithm for the uncapacitated facility location problem in Section 7.6. Here we are increasing a bid α_j uniformly for all unconnected clients, while in the primal-dual algorithm, we increase a dual variable v_j for each client uniformly until the dual inequality associated with a facility becomes tight, or until a client connects to a temporarily opened facility. However, in that algorithm, we open only a subset of the temporarily opened facilities, and in order to remain dual feasible we need that $\sum_j (v_j - c_{ij})_+ \leq f_i$ for facilities i, where the sum is over all clients j. In this algorithm we allow $\sum_{j \in S}(\alpha_j - c_{ij})_+ + \sum_{j \notin S}(c(j, X) - c_{ij})_+ \leq f_i$. In this algorithm, the clients j not in S contribute only $(c(j, X) - c_{ij})_+$ toward the sum, while in the primal-dual algorithm they contribute the potentially larger amount of $(v_j - c_{ij})_+$. For this reason, the bids α are not in general feasible for the dual linear program.

We will shortly prove the following two lemmas. Let α be the final set of bids from Algorithm 9.3, and let X be the set of facilities opened by the algorithm. The first lemma says that the total bids of all clients equals the cost of the solution with facility costs $\hat{f}$. The second lemma says that $\alpha/2$ is dual feasible.

Lemma 9.10. *For α and X given by Algorithm 9.3,*

$$\sum_{j \in D} \alpha_j = \sum_{j \in D} c(j, X) + 2 \sum_{i \in X} f_i.$$

Lemma 9.11. *Let $v_j = \alpha_j/2$, and let $w_{ij} = (v_j - c_{ij})_+$. Then (v, w) is a feasible solution to the dual.*

From these two lemmas, it is easy to show the following theorem.

Theorem 9.12. *Algorithm 9.3 is a 2-approximation algorithm for the uncapacitated facility location problem.*

Proof. Combining Lemmas 9.10 and 9.11, we have that

$$\sum_{j\in D} c(j, X) + \sum_{i\in X} f_i \le \sum_{j\in D} c(j, X) + 2\sum_{i\in X} f_i$$

$$= \sum_{j\in D} \alpha_j$$

$$= 2\sum_{j\in D} v_j$$

$$\le 2\,\mathrm{OPT},$$

where the final inequality follows since $\sum_{j\in D} v_j$ is the dual objective function, and by weak duality is a lower bound on the cost of the optimal integer solution. $\square$

Note that we actually prove that

$$\sum_{j\in D} c(j, X) + 2\sum_{i\in X} f_i \le 2\sum_{j\in D} v_j$$

for the feasible dual solution (v, w). Thus, the algorithm is Lagrangean multiplier preserving as we defined it at the end of Section 7.7. As we argued there, plugging this algorithm into the algorithm for the k-median problem given in that section results in a $2(2 + \epsilon)$-approximation algorithm for the k-median problem for any $\epsilon > 0$.

We now turn to the proofs of Lemmas 9.10 and 9.11.

Proof of Lemma 9.10. We will prove by induction on the algorithm that at the beginning of each execution of the main loop,

$$\sum_{j\in D-S} \alpha_j = \sum_{j\in D-S} c(j, X) + 2\sum_{i\in X} f_i.$$

Since at the end of the algorithm $S = \emptyset$, this implies the lemma.

The equality is initially true since initially $S = D$ and $X = \emptyset$. In each execution of the loop, either we connect some $j \in S$ to a facility i already in X or we open a new facility in X. In the first case, we have that $\alpha_j = c(j, X)$, and we remove j from S. Thus, the left-hand side of the equality increases by α_j and the right-hand side by $c(j, X)$, so the equality continues to hold. In the second case, we have that $\sum_{j\in S}(\alpha_j - c_{ij})_+ + \sum_{j\notin S}(c(j, X) - c_{ij})_+ = \hat{f}_i$, and i is added to X. The algorithm removes from S all $j \in S$ such that $\alpha_j - c_{ij} \ge 0$. Let S' represent this subset of S. Thus, the left-hand side of the equality increases by $\sum_{j\in S'} \alpha_j$. Let S'' be the set of all $j \notin S$ that make positive bids for facility i; that is, $(c(j, X) - c_{ij})_+ > 0$ for $j \in S''$. Note that all of the clients in S'' are exactly those closer to i than any other facility in X, so when i is added to X, $c(j, X \cup \{i\}) = c_{ij}$ for all $j \in S''$. Thus, the change in the cost of the right-hand side is

$$2f_i + \sum_{j\in S'} c_{ij} + \sum_{j\in S''}(c(j, X \cup \{i\}) - c(j, X)) = 2f_i + \sum_{j\in S:\alpha_j\ge c_{ij}} c_{ij} - \sum_{j\notin S}(c(j, X) - c_{ij})_+.$$

Using the fact that $2f_i = \hat{f}_i = \sum_{j \in S}(\alpha_j - c_{ij})_+ + \sum_{j \notin S}(c(j, X) - c_{ij})_+$, and substituting this for $2f_i$ in the above, we obtain that the change in cost of the right-hand side is $\sum_{j \in S: \alpha_j \geq c_{ij}} \alpha_j = \sum_{j \in S'} \alpha_j$, which is exactly the change in cost of the left-hand side. Thus, the equality continues to hold.   □

To prove Lemma 9.11, we first prove a sequence of lemmas. In proving these lemmas, we use a notion of time in the algorithm. The algorithm starts at time 0, and uniformly increases all α_j with $j \in S$. At time t, any client j not yet connected to a facility (and thus $j \in S$) has $\alpha_j = t$.

Lemma 9.13. *Consider the time α_j at which j first connects to some facility. Then the bid of client k on facility i at that time, for any client k such that $\alpha_k \leq \alpha_j$, is at least $\alpha_j - c_{ij} - 2c_{ik}$.*

Proof. Either client k connects to a facility at the same time as j and $\alpha_k = \alpha_j$, or it connects to a facility at an earlier time than j, and $\alpha_k < \alpha_j$.

If k connects to a facility at the same time as j, then $\alpha_j = \alpha_k$ and at time α_j its bid on facility i is $(\alpha_k - c_{ik})_+ = (\alpha_j - c_{ik})_+ \geq \alpha_j - c_{ij} - 2c_{ik}$.

Now suppose k connects to a facility at an earlier time than j. Let h be the facility that client k is connected to at time α_j. Then at time α_j, the bid that k offers facility i is $(c_{hk} - c_{ik})_+$. By the triangle inequality, we know that $c_{hj} \leq c_{ij} + c_{ik} + c_{hk}$. Furthermore, since j first connects to a facility at a time later than α_k, it must be the case that j did not earlier connect to h, and so $\alpha_j \leq c_{hj}$. Thus, we have $\alpha_j \leq c_{ij} + c_{ik} + c_{hk}$. So the bid of client k on facility i at time α_j is $(c_{hk} - c_{ik})_+ \geq c_{hk} - c_{ik} \geq \alpha_j - c_{ij} - 2c_{ik}$, as claimed.   □

Lemma 9.14. *Let $A \subseteq D$ be any subset of clients. Reindex the clients of A so that $A = \{1, \ldots, p\}$ and $\alpha_1 \leq \cdots \leq \alpha_p$. Then for any $j \in A$,*

$$\sum_{k=1}^{j-1}(\alpha_j - c_{ij} - 2c_{ik}) + \sum_{k=j}^{p}(\alpha_j - c_{ik}) \leq \hat{f}_i.$$

Proof. We know that at any time, the sum of the bids on facility i is at most the facility cost $\hat{f}_i$. By Lemma 9.13 at time α_j, for all clients k with $k < j$, the bid of k for facility i is at least $\alpha_j - c_{ij} - 2c_{ik}$. For all clients $k \geq j$, since $\alpha_k \geq \alpha_j$, at any time just before α_j, they have not connected to a facility, so their bid on facility i at time α_j is $(\alpha_j - c_{ik})_+ \geq \alpha_j - c_{ik}$. Putting these together gives the lemma statement.   □

Lemma 9.15. *Let $A \subseteq D$ be any subset of clients. Reindex the clients of A so that $A = \{1, \ldots, p\}$ and $\alpha_1 \leq \cdots \leq \alpha_p$. Then*

$$\sum_{j \in A}(\alpha_j - 2c_{ij}) \leq \hat{f}_i.$$

Proof. If we sum the inequality of Lemma 9.14 over all $j \in A$, we obtain

$$\sum_{j=1}^{p}\left(\sum_{k=1}^{j-1}(\alpha_j - c_{ij} - 2c_{ik}) + \sum_{k=j}^{p}(\alpha_j - c_{ik})\right) \leq p\hat{f}_i.$$

This is equivalent to

$$p \sum_{j=1}^{p} \alpha_j - \sum_{k=1}^{p}(k-1)c_{ik} - p\sum_{k=1}^{p}c_{ik} - \sum_{k=1}^{p}(p-k)c_{ik} \le p\hat{f}_i,$$

which implies

$$\sum_{j=1}^{p}(\alpha_j - 2c_{ij}) \le \hat{f}_i. \qquad \Box$$

We can finally prove that $v_j = \alpha_j/2$ gives a feasible dual solution.

Proof of Lemma 9.11. Let $v_j = \alpha_j/2$, and let $w_{ij} = (v_j - c_{ij})_+$. Then certainly $v_j - w_{ij} \le c_{ij}$. Now we must show that for all $i \in F$, $\sum_{j \in D} w_{ij} \le f_i$. To do this, pick an arbitrary $i \in F$, and let $A = \{j \in D : w_{ij} > 0\}$, so that it is sufficient to prove that $\sum_{j \in A} w_{ij} \le f_i$. We have from Lemma 9.15 that

$$\sum_{j \in A}(\alpha_j - 2c_{ij}) \le \hat{f}_i.$$

Rewriting, we obtain

$$\sum_{j \in A}(2v_j - 2c_{ij}) \le 2f_i.$$

Dividing both sides by 2, we get

$$\sum_{j \in A}(v_j - c_{ij}) \le f_i.$$

Finally, by the definition of A and w we have that $w_{ij} = v_j - c_{ij}$ for $j \in A$, and we are done. $\qquad \Box$

A significantly more involved analysis of this algorithm shows that its performance guarantee is 1.61; see the notes at the end of the chapter for more details.

Exercises

9.1 Prove that the uncapacitated facility location algorithms in Algorithm 9.2 and Algorithm 9.3 are equivalent.

9.2 The *locality gap* of a local search algorithm for an optimization problem is the worst-case ratio of the cost of a locally optimal solution to the cost of an optimal solution, where the ratio is taken over all instances of the problem and over all locally optimal solutions to the instance. One can think of the locality gap as an analog of the integrality gap of a linear programming relaxation.

We consider the locality gap of the local search algorithm for the uncapacitated facility location problem in Section 9.1. Consider the instance shown in Figure 9.5, where the facilities $F = \{1, \ldots, n, 2n+1\}$, and the clients $D = \{n+1, \ldots, 2n\}$. The cost of each facility $1, \ldots, n$ is 1, while the cost of facility $2n+1$ is $n-1$. The cost of each edge in the figure is 1, and the assignment cost c_{ij} is the shortest path distance in the graph between

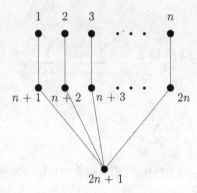

Figure 9.5. Instance for Exercise 9.2 showing a bad locality gap for the local search algorithm of Section 9.1.

$i \in F$ and $j \in D$. Use the instance to show that the locality gap is at least $3 - \epsilon$ for any $\epsilon > 0$.

9.3 Show that the local search algorithm of Section 9.3 can be adapted to find a Steiner tree whose maximum degree is at most $OPT + 1$, where OPT is the maximum degree of a minimum-degree Steiner tree.

9.4 Recall the uniform labeling problem from Exercise 5.10: We are given a graph $G = (V, E)$, costs $c_e \geq 0$ for all $e \in E$, and a set of labels L that can be assigned to the vertices of V. There is a nonnegative cost $c_v^i \geq 0$ for assigning label $i \in L$ to vertex $v \in V$, and an edge $e = (u, v)$ incurs cost c_e if u and v are assigned different labels. The goal of the problem is to assign each vertex in V a label so as to minimize the total cost. In Exercise 5.10, we gave a randomized rounding 2-approximation algorithm for the problem; here we give a local search algorithm with a performance guarantee of $(2 + \epsilon)$.

Our local search algorithm will use the following local move. Given a current assignment of labels to vertices in V, it picks some label $i \in L$ and considers the minimum-cost i-*expansion* of the label i; that is, it considers the minimum-cost assignment of labels to vertices in V in which each vertex either keeps its current label or is relabeled with label i (note that all vertices currently with label i do not change their label). If the cost of the labeling from the i-expansion is cheaper than the current labeling, then we switch to the labeling from the i-expansion. We continue until we find a locally optimal solution; that is, an assignment of labels to vertices such that the minimum-cost i-expansion for each $i \in L$ costs no less than the current assignment.

(a) Prove that for any given label $i \in L$, we can compute the minimum-cost i-expansion in polynomial time. (Hint: Find a minimum s-t cut in a graph where s corresponds to the label i and t corresponds to all other labels.)

(b) Prove that any locally optimal assignment has cost at most twice the optimal cost.

(c) Show that for any constant $\epsilon > 0$, we can obtain a $(2 + \epsilon)$-approximation algorithm.

9.5 The *online facility location problem* is a variant of the uncapacitated facility location problem in which clients arrive over time and we do not know in advance which clients will want service. As before, let F be the set of facilities that can be opened, and let D be a set of potential clients. Let f_i be the cost of opening facility $i \in F$ and c_{ij} the cost of assigning a client $j \in D$ to facility $i \in F$. We assume that the assignment costs obey the triangle inequality. At each time step t, a new set $D_t \subseteq D$ of clients arrive, and they must be connected to open facilities. We are allowed to open new facilities in each time step; once a client is assigned to a facility, it cannot be reassigned if a closer facility opens later. For each time step t, we wish to minimize the total cost (facility plus assignment) incurred by all clients that have arrived up to and including time t. We compare this cost with the optimal cost of the uncapacitated facility location problem on the total set of clients that have arrived up to and including time t. The ratio of these two costs gives the *competitive ratio* of the algorithm for the online problem.

Consider the following variation on Algorithm 9.3. As before, we let S be the set of clients that have not yet been connected to some facility, and let X be the set of currently open facilities. At each time step t, we sequence through the clients j in D_t. We increase the client's bid α_j from zero until either it connects to some previously open facility ($\alpha_j = c_{ij}$ for some $i \in X$), or some facility receives enough bids to allow it to open. As in the greedy algorithm, we allow previously connected clients j to bid toward facility i the difference between the cost $c(j, X)$ of connecting to the closest open facility and the cost of connecting to facility i; that is, j bids $(c(j, X) - c_{ij})_+$ toward the facility i. Thus, facility i is opened when $(\alpha_j - c_{ij})_+ + \sum_{j \notin S}(c(j, X) - c_{ij})_+ = f_i$. Note that even if facility i is opened and is closer to some client j than previously opened facilities in X, we do not reassign j to i (per the requirements of the problem).

(a) Prove that at the end of each time step t, the cost of the current solution is at most twice the sum of the client bids $\sum_{j \in D} \alpha_j$.

(b) Consider two clients j and k such that we increase the bid for j before that of k. Let X be the set of facilities open when we increase α_k. Prove that for any facility i, $c(X, j) - c_{ij} \geq \alpha_k - c_{ik} - 2c_{ij}$.

(c) For any time step t, pick any subset A of clients that have arrived so far and any facility i. Let $A = \{1, \dots, p\}$, where we increase the bids for the clients in A in order of the indices.

    (i) Prove that for any $\ell \in A$, $\ell(\alpha_\ell - c_{i\ell}) - 2\sum_{j < \ell} c_{ij} \leq f_i$.

    (ii) Use the above to prove that $\sum_{\ell=1}^{p}(\alpha_\ell - 2H_p c_{i\ell}) \leq H_p f_i$, where $H_p = 1 + \frac{1}{2} + \cdots + \frac{1}{p}$.

(d) Prove that $v_j = \alpha_j / 2H_n$ is a dual feasible solution for the uncapacitated facility location problem at time t, where n is the number of clients that have arrived up to and including time t.

(e) Use the above to conclude that the algorithm has a competitive ratio of $4H_n$.

Chapter Notes

As was discussed in Chapter 2, local search algorithms are an extremely popular form of heuristic and have been used for some time; for instance, a local search algorithm for the uncapacitated facility location problem was proposed in 1963 by Kuehn and Hamburger [206]. However, not many approximation algorithms based on local search were known until recently. A paper by Korupolu, Plaxton, and Rajaraman [205] in 2000 touched off recent research on approximation algorithms using local search. The paper gave the first performance guarantees for local search algorithms for the uncapacitated facility location problem and the k-median problem, although their k-median algorithm opened up to $2k$ facilities rather than only k. Charikar and Guha [64] first proved a performance guarantee of 3 for a local search algorithm for the uncapacitated facility location problem; they also introduced the idea of rescaling to show that the performance guarantee could be improved to $1 + 2\sqrt{2}$. The analysis we use here is due to Gupta and Tangwongsan [151]. Arya, Garg, Khandekar, Meyerson, Munagala, and Pandit [24] first proved a performance guarantee of 5 for a local search algorithm for the k-median problem. The result in Section 9.2 is a modification of their analysis due to Gupta and Tangwongsan [151]. Exercise 9.2 is due to Arya et al.

Although not many local search approximation algorithms were known until the recent work on location problems, the algorithm for finding a minimum-degree spanning tree of Section 9.3 is an exception; this work appeared in 1994 and is due to Fürer and Raghavachari [119]. Exercise 9.3 is also from this paper.

The greedy/dual-fitting algorithm for the uncapacitated facility location problem given in Section 9.4 is due to Jain, Mahdian, Markakis, Saberi, and Vazirani [176]. As was mentioned at the end of the section, a much more careful analysis of this algorithm shows that it has a performance guarantee of 1.61. This analysis involves the use of *factor-revealing LPs*: for any given facility $i \in F$, we consider the bids α_j of the clients as LP variables, and set up constraints on the variables stating that the total bid on the facility can be at most the sum of the bids, and other inequalities such as those resulting from Lemma 9.13. Subject to these constraints, we then maximize the ratio of the sum of the bids over the cost of the facility i plus the cost of connecting the clients to facility i. If we divide the α_j by this ratio, we obtain a feasible solution v for the dual of the LP relaxation for the uncapacitated facility location problem. Hence, this LP "reveals" the performance guarantee of the algorithm. The technical difficulty of the analysis is determining the value of the LP for any number of clients.

Exercise 9.4 is a result from Boykov, Veksler, and Zabih [57]. Exercise 9.5 gives an algorithm for the online facility location problem due to Fotakis [116]. The analysis used is due to Nagarajan and Williamson [229].

CHAPTER 10

Further Uses of Rounding Data and Dynamic Programming

In this chapter, we return to the technique of applying dynamic programming via rounding data. We look at two, more technically difficult, applications of this technique to find polynomial-time approximation schemes for two different problems.

First, we consider the traveling salesman problem, introduced in Section 2.4, for instances in which the cities are points in the Euclidean plane and the cost of traveling between two cities is the Euclidean distance between the corresponding points. In this case the dynamic program works by recursively dividing the plane into squares. Starting with the smallest squares, we compute the least-cost set of paths for visiting all the cities in the squares, then use these to compute solutions for larger squares. We can show that the optimal tour can be modified at low cost such that it doesn't enter and exit any square too many times; this "rounding" of the optimal tour makes it possible to solve the dynamic program in polynomial time. This technique turns out to be widely applicable to problems in the Euclidean plane, including the Steiner tree problem and the k-median problem for Euclidean instances.

Second, we consider the maximum independent set problem in planar graphs. We show that the maximum independent set problem is easy to solve on trees, and can be solved in graphs that are "treelike." We can measure how close a graph is to being a tree via a parameter called its treewidth, and we give an algorithm to solve the maximum independent set problem in time that is polynomial in the number of vertices and exponential in the treewidth of the input graph. Planar graphs don't necessarily have low treewidth, but we show a way to partition the vertices of the planar graph into k parts such that removing any one of the parts from the graph yields a low-treewidth graph. Then since at least one of the k parts must have at most a $\frac{1}{k}$ fraction of the weight of an optimal solution, we can from this get a $\left(1 - \frac{1}{k}\right)$-approximation algorithm for the maximum independent set problem in planar graphs, and we can use this to obtain a PTAS for the problem.

10.1 The Euclidean Traveling Salesman Problem

To see a more sophisticated use of dynamic programming for approximation algorithms, we return to the traveling salesman problem (TSP) introduced in Section 2.4 and show how we can use dynamic programming to obtain a polynomial-time approximation scheme for a certain class of TSP instances. In these TSP instances, each city i is defined by a point (x_i, y_i) in the Euclidean plane, and the cost c_{ij} for traveling from city i to city j is simply the Euclidean distance between (x_i, y_i) and (x_j, y_j) (namely, $c_{ij} = \sqrt{(x_i - x_j)^2 + (y_i - y_j)^2}$). We call such instances of the TSP *Euclidean TSP* instances. Note that the input of the Euclidean TSP is simply a list of the points (x_i, y_i) for each of the n cities; the distances c_{ij} are not part of the input.

The basic idea of the algorithm is to recursively subdivide the plane into squares and show that there is a tour that costs only slightly more than OPT such that it doesn't cross the boundary of any square too many times. Given that such a tour exists, we can apply dynamic programming to find it: we start by finding the cheapest ways to visit the nodes inside the smallest squares, then combine these partial solutions to find the cheapest ways to visit the nodes inside next larger squares, and so on. In the end we find the cheapest overall tour with this structure.

The overall proof strategy is then as follows. First, we show that it is sufficient to design a PTAS for Euclidean instances that have certain nice properties. Second, we recursively divide the plane into squares as mentioned above; we introduce some randomization in how we do this. Third, we show that with probability at least $\frac{1}{2}$, a tour of cost at most $(1 + \epsilon)$ OPT exists for the nice instances with respect to the random subdivision of the plane; this tour has the property that it doesn't cross the squares of the subdivision too many times. Last, we use dynamic programming to find the least expensive tour with the given property. This results in the PTAS.

We begin by showing that it is sufficient to obtain a PTAS for a subclass of Euclidean TSP instances. We will say that a Euclidean TSP instance is *nice* for constant $\epsilon > 0$ if the minimum nonzero distance between points is at least 4, and all coordinates x_i, y_i are integers in $[0, O(n)]$, where n is the number of points.

Lemma 10.1. *Given a polynomial-time approximation scheme for nice Euclidean TSP instances, we obtain a polynomial-time approximation scheme for all Euclidean TSP instances.*

Proof. We will show how to transform any instance into a nice instance such that the cost of any tour in the transformed instance doesn't differ by much from that of the original instance. This will allow us to prove the lemma.

Let L be the length of a side of the smallest axis-aligned square containing all of the points of the instance; thus, $L = \max(\max_i x_i - \min_i x_i, \max_i y_i - \min_i y_i)$. Note that since there are two points at least distance L apart, it is the case that $L \leq$ OPT. Let $\epsilon > 0$ be a constant parameter that we specify later. To get a nice instance, we create a grid of horizontal and vertical lines where the spacing between the lines is $\epsilon L/2n$; see Figure 10.1. We then move each point of the original instance to the nearest grid point (that is, the nearest intersection of a horizontal and a vertical grid line). Because we end up moving any point by a distance of at most $\epsilon L/2n$, the distance between any

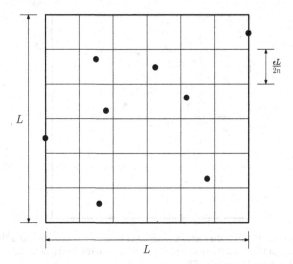

Figure 10.1. An example of the smallest square containing all the points of the instance, and the grid of lines spaced $\epsilon L/2n$ apart.

two points changes by at most $\pm 2\epsilon L/2n$. Thus, the overall cost of any tour changes by at most $\pm \epsilon L$.

We now increase the grid spacing by a factor of $8n/\epsilon L$, so that the spacing between any two grid lines is $\frac{\epsilon L}{2n} \cdot \frac{8n}{\epsilon L} = 4$, and translate the bounding square so the lower left-hand corner is on the origin. This enforces that each point in the modified instance is now at nonnegative integer coordinates and that the minimum nonzero distance between any two points is at least 4. Furthermore, the maximum distance between any two points before increasing the grid spacing was at most $2L$; after increasing grid spacing it is at most $2L \cdot \frac{8n}{\epsilon L} = O(n)$, so that each x, y coordinate is in the range $[0, O(n)]$. Thus, for any tour in the original instance of cost C, its cost in the nice instance is at least $\frac{8n}{\epsilon L}(C - \epsilon L)$ and at most $\frac{8n}{\epsilon L}(C + \epsilon L)$.

Let OPT be the cost of an optimal tour in the original instance, OPT$'$ the cost of an optimal tour in the corresponding nice instance, C' the cost of the tour returned by the PTAS on the nice instance, and C the cost of the corresponding tour in the original instance. We know that $C' \le (1 + \epsilon)$ OPT$'$. Furthermore, it must be the case that OPT$'$ is no more than the cost of the optimal tour of the original instance in the corresponding nice instance, so that OPT$' \le \frac{8n}{\epsilon L}(\text{OPT} + \epsilon L)$. Putting everything together, we have that

$$\frac{8n}{\epsilon L}(C - \epsilon L) \le C' \le (1 + \epsilon)\,\text{OPT}' \le (1 + \epsilon)\frac{8n}{\epsilon L}(\text{OPT} + \epsilon L),$$

or

$$C - \epsilon L \le (1 + \epsilon)(\text{OPT} + \epsilon L).$$

Recalling that $L \le \text{OPT}$, we have that

$$C \le (1 + 3\epsilon + \epsilon^2)\,\text{OPT}.$$

Choosing ϵ suitably small will allow us to obtain a tour of cost at most $(1 + \epsilon')$ OPT for any choice of ϵ'. $\qquad \square$

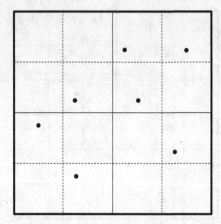

Figure 10.2. An example of a dissection. The level 0 square is outlined in a thick black line, the level 1 squares in thin black lines, and the level 2 squares in dashed lines. The thin black lines are level 1 lines, and the dashed lines are level 2 lines.

From here on, we assume we have a nice Euclidean TSP instance, and we show how to obtain a PTAS for such instances.

In order to perform dynamic programming on nice instances, we need to structure the problem so that we can build up a solution from smaller subproblems. To do this, we are going to recursively divide the plane into squares in a way that involves randomization. First, we will describe the recursive division without randomization, and then we will introduce the randomization.

As in the proof of Lemma 10.1, we let L be the length of a side of the smallest square containing all the points of the instance. Let L' be the smallest power of 2 that is at least $2L$. We will take a square of side length L' around the points of the instance, divide it into four equal-size squares, then recursively divide each of these squares into four equal-size squares, and so on; see Figure 10.2. We stop the process when each square has side length 1. We call this division of the instance into squares a *dissection*. It will be useful to refer to the level of a given square of the dissection; we say that the top-level square of side length L' is at level 0, the four squares dividing the top-level square are at level 1, and so on. Since the maximum distance between points in a nice instance is $O(n)$, we know that $L' = O(n)$. Therefore, the level of the smallest squares of the dissection (of side length 1) is $O(\log n)$. Since the minimum nonzero distance between any two points is 4, we know that in the smallest squares of side length 1, there can be at most one distinct point.

So far we have not completely specified how to create the dissection because there are many squares of side length L' that contain all the points of the instance. In fact, any translation of the square that has its lower left-hand coordinates at (a, b) for $a, b \in (-L'/2, 0]$ will work. It will be useful for us to choose this translation randomly by choosing integers a and b from $(-L'/2, 0]$ uniformly at random. We will call such a dissection after a and b are chosen an (a, b)-*dissection*. We will give an intuitive explanation for the randomization in a moment.

Now, to further help construct a dynamic program for the problem, we will consider tours that enter and exit the squares of the dissection only at prespecified points called *portals*. For each square of level i, we place portals at all four corners, then $m - 1$

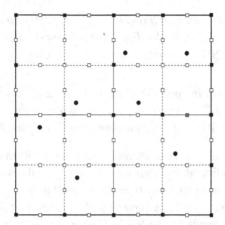

Figure 10.3. Portals added to the squares of the dissection with portal parameter $m = 2$. The black squares are portals for both the level 1 and level 2 squares; the white squares are portals for the level 2 squares.

additional portals equally spaced along each side, for m some power of 2. We will call m the *portal parameter*. Note that since m is a power of 2, each portal on the sides of a level $i - 1$ square are at the same location as a portal on the side of some level i square contained in the level $i - 1$ square. See Figure 10.3 for an illustration of portals.

We now consider *p-tours*, which are tours that optionally include portals; as in the case of the Steiner tree problem (from Exercise 2.5), the tour must include the points of the TSP instance, but may include portals. We say that a p-tour is *portal respecting* if for every square of the dissection, the tour enters and exits the square only via a portal for that square. See Figure 10.4 for an example of a portal-respecting p-tour. We'll say that a portal-respecting p-tour is *r-light* if for every square of the dissection it crosses each side of the square at most r times.

We can now state two central theorems in obtaining an approximation scheme for Euclidean TSP instances. The second builds on the first and is somewhat more complicated to prove.

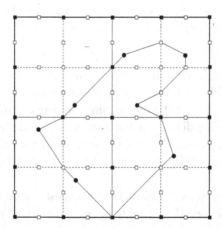

Figure 10.4. A portal-respecting p-tour. Note that only black portals are used to enter or exit the level 1 squares, while the portals on the level 2 squares are used to enter or exit the level 2 squares.

Theorem 10.2. *If we pick integers a and b from $(-L'/2, 0]$ uniformly at random, then with probability at least 1/2, the (a, b)-dissection has an r-light portal-respecting p-tour of cost at most $(1 + \epsilon)$ OPT for portal parameter $m = O(\frac{1}{\epsilon} \log L')$ and $r = 2m + 4$.*

Theorem 10.3. *If we pick integer a and b from $(-L'/2, 0]$ uniformly at random, then with probability at least 1/2, the (a, b)-dissection has an r-light portal-respecting p-tour of cost at most $(1 + \epsilon)$ OPT for portal parameter $m = O(\frac{1}{\epsilon} \log L')$ and $r = O(\frac{1}{\epsilon})$.*

We will give the proofs of these theorems in a moment; the essential idea is that we will be able to modify an optimal tour to be a portal-respecting p-tour without increasing the cost by too much. Any time the optimal tour crosses a square at a point that is not a portal for that square, we move it to the nearest portal; the distance we need to move the crossing depends on the level of the square, which given the randomized choice of the (a, b)-dissection will trade off nicely with the probability that the square is of any given level. Similarly, if the tour crosses a side of a square too many times, we will be able to modify it so that it crosses fewer times at a cost proportional to the length of the side of the square; again, given the randomized choice of the (a, b)-dissection, this cost trades off nicely with the probability that the square is of a given level.

Before we show how this can be done, we first show that for a nice Euclidean instance, we can find a tour of cost at most $(1 + \epsilon)$ OPT in polynomial time, given the theorems, where the running time depends on the portal parameter and how many times the tour crosses each side of each square in the dissection.

Theorem 10.4. *With probability at least 1/2, we can find a tour of cost at most $(1 + \epsilon)$ OPT in $O(m^{O(r)} n \log n)$ time for nice Euclidean TSP instances.*

Recalling that $L' = O(n)$, that $m = O(\frac{1}{\epsilon} \log L') = O(\frac{1}{\epsilon} \log n)$, and that $(\log n)^{\log n} = n^{\log \log n}$, we get the following corollaries.

Corollary 10.5. *For the choice of m and r as in Theorem 10.2, the running time is $O(n^{O(\log \log n)})$ for constant $\epsilon > 0$.*

Corollary 10.6. *For the choice of m and r as in Theorem 10.3, the running time is $O(n \log^{O(1/\epsilon)} n)$ for constant $\epsilon > 0$.*

Proof of Theorem 10.4. From both Theorems 10.2 and 10.3, we know that with probability at least 1/2, with a, b chosen as in the theorem, there is an (a, b)-dissection with an r-light portal-respecting p-tour of cost at most $(1 + \epsilon)$ OPT for $m = O(\frac{1}{\epsilon} \log L') = O(\frac{1}{\epsilon} \log n)$; the only distinction between the two theorems is the value of r. For a given (a, b)-dissection, we'll show that we can find the cheapest r-light portal-respecting p-tour in $O(m^{O(r)} n \log n)$ time, given the values of m and r. Note than any p-tour can be converted to a standard tour of no greater cost by shortcutting the portals.

As we mentioned before, we will find the cheapest such p-tour by dynamic programming. Consider any portal-respecting p-tour of the given instance. Then for any given square in the (a, b)-dissection, the p-tour may enter the square, visit some of the points inside it, then exit, visit points outside the square, then reenter the square, and so on. We call the part of the p-tour inside the square a *partial p-tour*; note that a partial

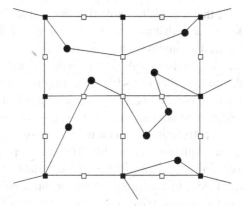

Figure 10.5. Partial p-tour inside a square.

p-tour visits all of the points of the TSP instance inside the square; see Figure 10.5. Because the p-tour is r-light, we know that the p-tour crosses each side of the square at most r times, and so it uses at most $4r$ portals on the sides of the square. Furthermore, we can pair up the portals used by the p-tour into pairs, where each pair represents a portal through which the p-tour entered the square and a portal through which the p-tour then left the square. The goal of our dynamic program will be to compute for every square in the dissection, for every choice of up to r portals per side, and for every pairing of the portals into entry/exit pairs, the cheapest partial p-tour that visits all the points of the TSP instance inside the square. Clearly if we can do this, we can find the cheapest overall r-light portal-respecting p-tour by considering the entry in the dynamic programming table for the level 0 square that does not use any of the portals on the boundary of the square.

To begin discussion of the dynamic program, we start by computing the number of entries in the table that we will need. Note that for any given level of squares in the dissection, there are at most n that contain any points of the TSP instance. For any square that contains no points of the instance, it suffices to consider one square of any given size. Since there are $O(\log L') = O(\log n)$ levels of the dissection, there are at most $O(n \log n)$ squares that we must consider. For each square of level i, there are $4m$ portals on the square and thus at most $(4m + 1)^{4r}$ choices for the up to r portals on each side of the square (including not choosing any portals) through which an r-light portal-respecting p-tour could cross. Finally, there are at most $(4r)!$ possible pairings of the selected portals into entry/exit pairs. With $r = O(m)$, the total number of entries in the table is

$$O(n \log n) \times (4m + 1)^{4r} \times (4r)! = O(m^{O(r)} n \log n).$$

Now we discuss how to build up the entries in the table. For each distinct point, we find the largest square in the dissection that contains only that point. The case for each such square is straightforward; for each choice of portals and pairings of portals, we find the shortest paths that enter/exit the square in the designated way and visit the one distinct point inside the square. We now build up the solutions to other entries in the table from previous entries, working our way up from smaller squares of the dissection to larger squares. We construct solutions for a square S from the solutions for the four smaller squares $s_1, \ldots, s_4$ that it contains. Note that any partial p-tour for S might use portals on the four sides of the s_i that are not also on a side of S. Let's call these sides the *internal* sides of the s_i. To combine solutions from the s_i to get a solution for the square S, we enumerate over all the portals on the internal sides that the partial p-tour for S might have used, and the order in which the partial p-tour visited these portals, and pick the best solution found. Notice that specifying a set of portals used on the internal sides and an order in which they are used implies for each s_i a set of portals that are used, as well as an entry/exit pairing on the portals, so we will be able to look up the best solution for each square s_i in our table. Therefore, given a square S, a set of portals of S that are used, and entry/exit pairings of the portals, we enumerate over all · the portals on the internal sides that a partial p-tour for this configuration might have used, and an ordering on the portals. We can pick up to r portals from each of the four internal sides, each of which has $m + 1$ portals, so that there are no more than $(m + 2)^{4r}$ possibilities (including not choosing any portal). Since the partial p-tour inside S uses at most $4r$ portals on the sides of S, there can be at most $2r$ paths entering and exiting S; thus, we need to specify on which of these $2r$ paths the portals on the internal sides lie. This gives another $(2r)^{4r}$ possibilities. Finally, there are at most $(4r)!$ ways to order the portals along the paths. Thus, if we enumerate over the

$$(m + 2)^{4r} \times (2r)^{4r} \times (4r)! = O(m^{O(r)})$$

possibilities, we will find the best solution for the table entry consisting of the square S, the chosen portals from S, and the entry/exit pairing of the portals. This takes $O(m^{O(r)})$ time. Since we do the computation for $O(m^{O(r)}n \log n)$ dynamic programming table entries, the total time taken is $O(m^{O(r)}n \log n)$. □

We now turn to the proof of Theorem 10.2. As we mentioned previously, the proof works by showing that with reasonable probability, an optimal tour can be modified to a portal-respecting p-tour without increasing the cost by too much. Notice that an r-light tour with $r = 2m + 2$ is implied by a tour that crosses the side of any square at most twice at any portal. If the tour crosses three or more times at a portal, it can be shortcut to cross at most twice; see Figure 10.6. Thus, it suffices to show that modifying the tour to be portal respecting does not increase the cost by more than ϵ OPT. To prove this, we first need some notation and a lemma. We will use ℓ to denote either a vertical line $x = i$ or a horizontal line $y = i$ for some integer i. Given an optimal tour, let $t(\ell)$ be the number of times that the optimal tour crosses the line ℓ. Let T be the sum of $t(\ell)$ over all such horizontal and vertical lines ℓ.

Lemma 10.7. *For nice Euclidean instances, $T \leq 2 \, \text{OPT}$.*

Proof. Consider an edge in the optimal tour from point (x_1, y_1) to point (x_2, y_2). The edge contributes at most $|x_1 - x_2| + |y_1 - y_2| + 2$ to T, and has a length $s = \sqrt{(x_1 - x_2)^2 + (y_1 - y_2)^2}$. Recall that for a nice instance the minimum nonzero distance between points of the instance is at least 4, so that $s \geq 4$. If we let $x = |x_1 - x_2|$ and $y = |y_1 - y_2|$, then since $(x - y)^2 \geq 0$, we have that $x^2 + y^2 \geq 2xy$, or $2x^2 + 2y^2 \geq x^2 + 2xy + y^2 = (x + y)^2$, or $\sqrt{2(x^2 + y^2)} \geq x + y$. Thus, we can bound the

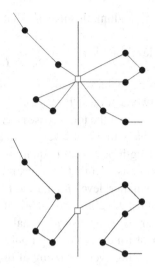

Figure 10.6. Illustration of shortcutting a portal.

contribution of the edge to T as follows:

$$x + y + 2 = |x_1 - x_2| + |y_1 - y_2| + 2$$
$$\leq \sqrt{2[(x_1 - x_2)^2 + (y_1 - y_2)^2]} + 2$$
$$\leq \sqrt{2s^2} + 2$$
$$\leq 2s,$$

where the last inequality follows since $s \geq 4$. Thus, summing over all edges in the tour, we obtain that $T \leq 2\,\mathrm{OPT}$. $\qquad\qquad\square$

Now we can give the proof of Theorem 10.2, which we restate here for convenience.

Theorem 10.2. *If we pick integers a and b from $(-L'/2, 0]$ uniformly at random, then with probability at least $1/2$, the (a, b)-dissection has an r-light portal respecting p-tour of cost at most $(1 + \epsilon)\,\mathrm{OPT}$ for portal parameter $m = O(\frac{1}{\epsilon} \log L')$ and $r = 2m + 4$.*

Proof. As described earlier, the general idea of the proof is that we modify the optimal tour to ensure that it crosses any square of the dissection at a portal for that square. When we move the crossing of the optimal tour, we increase it by an amount that depends on the distance between the portals for that square. As the level of a square gets smaller, this distance is greater, but the probability that any given line ℓ belongs to a square of that level also gets smaller, so that the overall expected distance we need to move the tour will depend only on $t(\ell)$ and m, which we can relate to the cost of the, optimal tour by Lemma 10.7.

To show this formally, define the *level* of line ℓ to be the minimum level over all squares of the (a, b)-dissection such that ℓ contains the side of the square. Observe that to split the level i squares into level $i + 1$ squares, we draw 2^i horizontal and 2^i vertical lines that are then level $i + 1$ lines; see Figure 10.2 for an illustration. Because we choose a and b uniformly at random, this implies that

$$\Pr[\text{level of } \ell \text{ is } i] \leq \frac{2^{i-1}}{L'/2} = \frac{2^i}{L'}.$$

Thus, for instance, the probability that a vertical line ℓ is the single level 1 vertical line splitting the bounding box in two is at most $1/(L'/2)$.

We modify the optimal tour so that the tour crosses any square of the dissection at a portal for that square. Consider any line ℓ of level i. Since it contains the boundary of a level i square, and the side length of a level i square is $L'/2^i$, the distance between portals is at most $L'/2^i m$. Observe also that by construction the portal for a level i square is also a portal for any smaller, level j square for $j > i$. Thus, if we move any crossing of a level i line ℓ at most $L'/2^i m$, any square of the dissection whose side is contained in ℓ will have the tour crossing at some portal for that square. Recall that we defined $t(\ell)$ to be the number of times that the optimal tour crosses line ℓ. Thus, the expected increase in cost for moving every crossing of line ℓ to the nearest portal is at most

$$\sum_{i=1}^{\log L'} \Pr[\text{level of } \ell \text{ is } i] \cdot t(\ell) \cdot \frac{L'}{2^i m} \leq \sum_{i=1}^{\log L'} \frac{2^i}{L'} \cdot t(\ell) \cdot \frac{L'}{2^i m}$$

$$= \frac{t(\ell)}{m} \log L'.$$

We choose the portal parameter m to be the smallest power of 2 that is at least $\frac{4}{\epsilon} \log L'$. Then the total expected increase is at most $\frac{\epsilon}{4} t(\ell)$.

Recall that we defined T to be the sum over all lines ℓ of $t(\ell)$. Thus, the total expected cost of what we have done in moving the crossings to portals as above is

$$\sum_{\text{lines } \ell} \frac{\epsilon}{4} t(\ell) = \frac{\epsilon}{4} T.$$

Lemma 10.7 shows that $T \leq 2\,\mathrm{OPT}$ for nice Euclidean instances. Then we have that the expected increase in cost is at most $\frac{\epsilon}{4} T \leq \frac{\epsilon}{2}\,\mathrm{OPT}$. If the random variable X represents the expected increase in cost, then by Markov's inequality (Lemma 5.25), $\Pr[X \geq \epsilon\,\mathrm{OPT}] \leq E[X]/(\epsilon\,\mathrm{OPT}) = (\frac{\epsilon}{2}\,\mathrm{OPT})/(\epsilon\,\mathrm{OPT}) = 1/2$. Thus, we obtain that the increase in cost is at most $\epsilon\,\mathrm{OPT}$ with probability at least $1/2$. $\square$

To prove Theorem 10.3, we additionally need to show that if a tour crosses a given line too many times, we can modify it at a small increase in cost to a tour that doesn't cross the line too many times. We will call the following lemma the *Patching lemma*.

Lemma 10.8 (Patching lemma). *Given a line segment R of length l, if a tour crosses R three or more times, we can increase the length of the tour by no more than $6l$ to get a closed path that contains the previous tour and crosses R at most twice.*

Proof. Suppose the tour crosses the line segment k times. We take the tour, and break it at the k points at which it crosses line R. We add $2k$ new points by adding k new points on either side of R where the tour crossed R; see Figure 10.7.

We now add a cycle and a matching to the new points on each side of the lines; if k is odd, the matching matches the first $k - 1$ points on each side. If k is odd, we

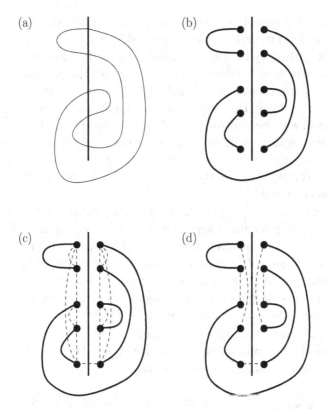

Figure 10.7. Illustration of the Patching lemma: (a) the original tour; (b) breaking the tour at the points at which it crosses the line; (c) adding a tour and a matching to both sides of the line; (d) shortcutting to a closed path.

add an edge connecting the last pair of new points, while if k is even we add two edges connecting the last two pairs of new points. This results in an Eulerian graph that contains the points of the tour and crosses R at most twice. Each of the two cycles added has cost at most $2l$, and each of the two matchings has cost l, for an overall cost of $6l$. A traversal of the Eulerian graph contains all points of the tour. We can shortcut the traversal to obtain a closed path that contains all points of the tour. $\qquad\square$

We can now prove Theorem 10.3, which we restate here for convenience

Theorem 10.3. *If we pick integer a and b from $(-L'/2, 0]$ uniformly at random, then with probability at least 1/2, the (a, b)-dissection has an r-light portal-respecting p-tour of cost at most $(1 + \epsilon)$ OPT for portal parameter $m = O(\frac{1}{\epsilon} \log L')$ and $r = O(\frac{1}{\epsilon})$.*

Proof. The basic idea is to apply the Patching lemma repeatedly so that the side of each square is not crossed more than r times. The cost of the patching depends on the side length of the square, which is larger for squares of smaller level; however, the probability that any line ℓ contains a side of a square of that level is smaller for smaller levels. Once again, these quantities trade off so that the expected cost for patching a line ℓ is proportional to $t(\ell)$ and inversely proportional to r, so that for a good choice of r, we can relate the patching cost to the optimal cost via Lemma 10.7.

Now we begin the formal proof. Consider a level i line ℓ. We invoke the Patching lemma (Lemma 10.8) to ensure that for every side of every square that ℓ contains, that side is not crossed by the tour more than r times. However, we must apply the Patching lemma carefully. We do the following: We start with the sides of the smallest squares whose sides are contained in ℓ, and apply the lemma if the side of any square is crossed more than r times. Then we do the same for the next smallest squares, and so on, until we finish with the level i squares; since ℓ is a level i line, it contains no square side for any larger square. In other words, we perform a loop, setting j to $\log L'$ and decrementing j down to i. In each iteration of the loop, we consider all level j squares that have a side contained in ℓ. If the side is crossed more than r times, we apply the Patching lemma to that side.

To bound the cost of applying the Patching lemma, we let c_j denote the number of times that the Patching lemma is applied when considering squares of level j. Then $\sum_{j \geq 1} c_j \leq t(\ell)/(r - 1)$, since each time the Patching lemma is invoked, it replaces at least $r + 1$ crossings with at most 2. By the Patching lemma, the cost of replacing at least r crossings of the side of a level j square with at most two crossings is at most 6 times the side length of a level j square; thus, the cost is at most $6L'/2^j$. Thus, if ℓ is level i, the total cost of applying the Patching lemma as given above is $\sum_{j=i}^{\log L'} c_j(6L'/2^j)$. Since the level of line ℓ depends on the random choices of a and b at the beginning of the algorithm, we have that the expected increase in cost of applying the Patching lemma as discussed above is at most

$$\sum_{i=1}^{\log L'} \Pr[\text{level of } \ell \text{ is } i] \sum_{j=i}^{\log L'} c_j \frac{6L'}{2^j} \leq \sum_{i=1}^{\log L'} \frac{2^i}{L'} \sum_{j=i}^{\log L'} c_j \frac{6L'}{2^j}$$

$$= 6 \sum_{j=1}^{\log L'} \frac{c_j}{2^j} \sum_{i=1}^{j} 2^i$$

$$\leq 6 \sum_{j=1}^{\log L'} 2c_j$$

$$\leq 12t(\ell)/(r - 1).$$

As in the proof of Theorem 10.2, we can modify the tour to cross the line ℓ only at portals with an expected increase in cost of at most $\frac{t(\ell)}{m} \log L'$. Choosing m to be the smallest power of 2 that is at least $(r - 1) \log L'$, this expected increase becomes at most $t(\ell)/(r - 1)$. Recall that we defined T to be the sum over all lines ℓ of $t(\ell)$. Thus, the total expected increase in cost of moving the crossings to portals as above is

$$\sum_{\text{lines } \ell} 13t(\ell)/(r - 1) = \frac{13}{r - 1} T.$$

Setting $r = \frac{52}{\epsilon} + 1$ and recalling from Lemma 10.7 that $T \leq 2\,\text{OPT}$ for nice Euclidean instances, we have that the expected increase in cost is at most $\frac{\epsilon}{4} T \leq \frac{\epsilon}{2}\,\text{OPT}$. As we argued at the end of the proof of Theorem 10.2, this implies that we obtain that the increase in cost is at most $\epsilon\,\text{OPT}$ with probability at least $1/2$.

To conclude, we need to argue that we have successfully made the tour into an r-light portal-respecting p-tour. This becomes somewhat complicated, because it could be the case that in reducing the number of crossings for a vertical line ℓ we may increase the number of crossings for a horizontal line ℓ' that intersects it. We note that the additional vertical crossings of ℓ' introduced by the Patching lemma in reducing the crossings of ℓ are immediately on either side of ℓ, and thus go through the portal corresponding to the intersection of ℓ and ℓ'. We can apply the Patching lemma again to ensure that the number of times ℓ' is crossed at this point is at most twice at no increase in cost (because the crossings all occur at a single geometric point). Thus, reducing the crossings of vertical lines ℓ may increase the number of crossings at the corners of the squares of dissections by at most 4; we get 2 from each application of the Patching Lemma on each side of ℓ; this increases the number of crossings on a side of a square by at most 8 (4 for each corner). Thus, we get an $(r + 8)$-light portal-respecting p-tour, which is sufficient for the purposes of the theorem.   □

The idea of this algorithm for the Euclidean TSP can be applied to many other standard problems in a Euclidean setting, such as the Steiner tree problem, the k-median problem, and others.

10.2 The Maximum Independent Set Problem in Planar Graphs

Given an undirected graph $G = (V, E)$, an *independent set* of vertices $S \subseteq V$ is one such that no two vertices of S are joined by an edge; that is, for all $i, j \in S, (i, j) \notin E$. If we are given nonnegative weights $w_i \geq 0$ for all vertices $i \in V$, then the *maximum independent set problem* is that of finding an independent set S of maximum weight $w(S) = \sum_{i \in S} w_i$. Sometimes we are interested in the *unweighted* version of the problem, in which $w_i = 1$ for all vertices $i \in V$; then we are interested in finding an independent set of maximum cardinality.

The maximum independent set problem is essentially identical to another problem introduced at the very beginning of the book: the *maximum clique problem*. A *clique* of vertices $S \subseteq V$ is one such that *every* pair $i, j \in S$ has an edge connecting it; that is, for all $i, j \in S, (i, j) \in E$. Given nonnegative weights $w_i \geq 0$ for all vertices $i \in V$, the maximum clique problem is that of finding a clique of maximum weight. As in the case of the maximum independent set problem, we can consider an unweighted version in which we are interested in finding a clique of maximum cardinality. To see the connection between the maximum clique and maximum independent set problems, let $\bar{G} = (V, \bar{E})$ be the *complement* of graph $G = (V, E)$ where $\bar{E}$ is the set of all pairs of vertices (i, j) that are not edges in E, so that $\bar{E} = \{(i, j) : i, j \in V, i \neq j, (i, j) \notin E\}$. Now notice that any clique S in G is an independent set in $\bar{G}$ of the same weight and vice versa. Thus, given any approximation algorithm for the maximum independent set problem, we can convert it to an approximation algorithm of the same performance guarantee for the maximum clique problem simply by running it on the complement graph, and similarly if we have an approximation algorithm for the maximum clique problem.

We recall Theorem 1.4 from Chapter 1, which says that the unweighted version of the maximum clique problem is very hard to approximate.

Theorem 10.9 (Theorem 1.4). *Let n denote the number of vertices in an input graph, and consider any constant $\epsilon > 0$. Then there does not exist an $O(n^{\epsilon-1})$-approximation algorithm for the unweighted maximum clique problem, unless* $\mathrm{P} = \mathrm{NP}$.

Thus, the maximum independent set problem is very hard to approximate as well.

Nevertheless, for some special classes of graphs, it is possible to do better – in fact, much better. We observe that it is relatively easy to find the maximum independent set in a tree in polynomial time via a dynamic programming algorithm. We suppose that the tree T is rooted at some node. The dynamic program will work in a bottom-up fashion, starting with the leaves and working up to the root. Let T_u be the subtree of T rooted at a node u. The dynamic programming table will have two entries for each node u in the tree, $I(T_u, u)$ and $I(T_u, \emptyset)$: $I(T_u, u)$ is the weight of a maximum independent set of T_u that includes u, and $I(T_u, \emptyset)$ is the weight of the maximum independent set of T_u that excludes u. If u is a leaf, we can easily compute the two entries for u. Now suppose that u is an internal node, with k children $v_1, \ldots, v_k$, and suppose we have already computed the entries for each child. We can then compute the two entries for u. Clearly if u is included in the independent set for T_u, then $v_1, \ldots, v_k$ must be excluded, so the maximum independent set for T_u including u is u plus the union of the maximum independent sets for the T_{v_i} excluding v_i; that is,

$$I(T_u, u) = w_u + \sum_{i=1}^{k} I(T_{v_i}, \emptyset).$$

If u is excluded from the independent set for T_u, then we have the choice for each child v_i about whether we should take the maximum independent set of T_{v_i} including v_i or excluding v_i. Since there are no edges from any T_{v_i} to T_{v_j} for $i \neq j$, the decision for T_{v_i} can be made independently from that for T_{v_j} and we can choose either possibility; we simply pick the set of largest weight for each v_i, and this gives the maximum independent set for T_u excluding u. Thus, $I(T_u, \emptyset) = \sum_{i=1}^{k} \max(I(T_{v_i}, v_i), I(T_{v_i}, \emptyset))$. Once we have computed both entries for the root vertex r, we take the entry that has largest weight, and this gives the maximum independent set for the entire tree.

Trees are a very restricted class of graphs; we would like to be able to devise good algorithms for larger classes of graphs. In this section, we will show that for planar graphs, it is possible to get a polynomial-time approximation scheme for the maximum independent set problem. *Planar graphs* are graphs that can be drawn in the Euclidean plane without crossing edges. More precisely, we correspond each vertex of the graph to some Euclidean point in the plane, and each edge (i, j) of the graph to a curve in the plane joining the points corresponding to i and j. The graph is planar if it is possible to do this such that no two curves corresponding to edges intersect. The mapping of the graph G to points and curves is called a planar *embedding* for planar graphs G. A graph G is *outerplanar* if it has a planar embedding such that all the vertices lie on the exterior face of the embedding; roughly speaking, they are all on the "outside" of the drawing of the graph. See Figure 10.8 for examples of planar and outerplanar graphs.

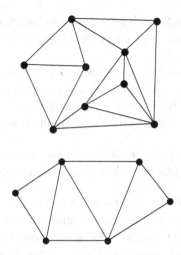

Figure 10.8. Illustration of planar embeddings of planar graphs. Both graphs are planar, but only the bottom graph is outerplanar.

To obtain the PTAS for planar graphs, we will need to define the concept of a *k-outerplanar graph*. Given a planar embedding of a graph G, we say that all the vertices on the exterior face are level 1 vertices of the graph. Then in general the level i vertices of the graph are all the vertices on the exterior face of the same planar embedding of G after removing all level $1, \ldots, i - 1$ vertices and incident edges. A graph G is k-outerplanar if there exists a planar embedding of G such that all the vertices of the graph are level k or less; see Figure 10.9 for examples of k-outerplanar graphs. It is possible to determine whether a graph G is k-outerplanar in time polynomial in k and n, but the proof of this is outside the scope of this book.

The central theorem we will need to prove the PTAS for planar graphs is the following.

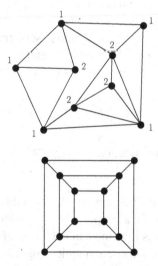

Figure 10.9. A 2-outerplanar graph and a 3-outerplanar graph. The levels of the vertices in the 2-outerplanar graph are labeled.

Theorem 10.10. *There is a dynamic programming algorithm for finding the maximum independent set in k-outerplanar graphs with running time $O(2^{O(k)}n^2)$.*

The key to proving this theorem is to show that k-outerplanar graphs can be decomposed into a treelike structure, so that we can run a dynamic programming algorithm similar to the one given above for trees.

Given the theorem, it is relatively simple to obtain the approximation scheme.

Theorem 10.11. *There is a polynomial-time approximation scheme for the maximum independent set problem in planar graphs running in time $O(2^{O(1/\epsilon)}n^2)$.*

Proof. Given a planar graph G with a planar embedding of G, we let L_i denote all the level i vertices of G. Observe that by the definition of level, it cannot be the case that an edge has endpoints that differ in level by two or more, since then in the embedding the curve corresponding to the edge would intersect the curves corresponding to edges connecting intermediate-level vertices.

If we want a $(1 - \epsilon)$-approximation algorithm, let k be the smallest positive integer such that $1/k \leq \epsilon$. Let S_i be the set of all vertices whose level is $i(\bmod k)$, for $i = 0, \ldots, k - 1$. Now consider the graphs G_i induced on all vertices *except* those in S_i; that is, $G_i = G[V - S_i]$. For each $i = 0, \ldots, k - 1$, by removing all the vertices in S_i and edges incident on it we obtain a graph G_i for which each connected component is a k-outerplanar graph. For instance, in G_0, we remove vertices from levels $k, 2k, 3k$, and so on. Thus, the vertices in $L_1, \ldots, L_{k-1}$ are disconnected from all other vertices in G_i, and these form a k-outerplanar graph. Similarly, the vertices in $L_{k+1}, \ldots, L_{2k-1}$ are also disconnected from other vertices in G_i, and these also form a k-outerplanar graph, and so on. We use the algorithm of Theorem 10.10 to find a maximum independent set for each connected component of G_i separately, and the union of these independent sets gives a maximum independent set X_i for G_i. The running time is $O(2^{O(1/\epsilon)}n^2)$. Note that any independent set X_i for G_i is also independent for the original graph G. Then we return as our solution the independent set X_i whose weight is the largest.

Let O be a maximum independent set for G, so that $w(O) = \text{OPT}$. We observe that since the S_i partition all the vertices in V into k sets, there exists some j such that $w(O \cap S_j) \leq w(O)/k$. Since $O - S_j$ is an independent set for G_j, the weight of the independent set X_j found by the algorithm for G_j must be at least

$$w(O - S_j) = w(O) - w(O \cap S_j) \geq \left(1 - \frac{1}{k}\right)w(O) \geq (1 - \epsilon)\text{OPT}.$$

Thus, the algorithm will return a solution of weight at least $(1 - \epsilon)\text{OPT}$ in $O(2^{O(1/\epsilon)}n^2)$ time. $\square$

We now turn to the proof of Theorem 10.10. To do this, we shall introduce another concept, called the *treewidth* of a graph. The treewidth of a graph in some sense measures how close the graph is to being a tree. Our proof agenda then will be to show that any graph with treewidth t has a dynamic programming algorithm to solve the maximum independent set problem in time exponential in t but polynomial in n, and to show that k-outerplanar graphs have treewidth at most $3k + 2$.

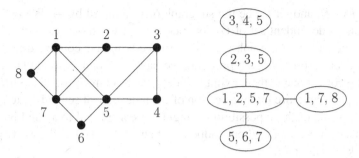

Figure 10.10. An example of a tree decomposition of a graph; the graph is on the left and the tree decomposition on the right. The treewidth of this tree decomposition is 3.

Given an undirected graph $G = (V, E)$, a *tree decomposition* of G is a spanning tree T on a new set of nodes V', where each $i \in V'$ corresponds to a subset X_i of vertices of V. The tree decomposition has the following three properties:

1. for every vertex $u \in V$, there is some $i \in V'$ such that $u \in X_i$;
2. for every edge $(u, v) \in E$, there is some $i \in V'$ such that both $u, v \in X_i$; and
3. for $i, j, k \in V'$, if j lies on the path in T from i to k, then $X_i \cap X_k \subseteq X_j$.

As an example, suppose that the original graph G is itself a tree. Then we can make a tree decomposition of G by creating a node i_u in V' for each node $u \in V$ and a node i_e for each edge in $e \in E$. The tree T will have edges (i_u, i_e) for all $u \subset V$ and $e \in E$ such that u is an endpoint of e; note that this gives a tree since G itself is a tree. The node $i_u \in V'$ will have corresponding subset $X_{i_u} = \{u\}$, and the node $i_e \in V'$ for edge $e = (u, v) \in E$ will have corresponding subset $X_{i_e} = \{u, v\}$. It can then be seen that this decomposition obeys all three properties of a tree decomposition. See Figure 10.10 for an example of a tree decomposition of a graph.

The *treewidth* of a tree decomposition of G is the maximum over all $i \in V'$ of $|X_i| - 1$, and the treewidth of a graph G is the minimum treewidth over all tree decompositions of G. One might wonder about the -1 term in the definition, but note that given the tree decomposition of a tree given above, this definition yields that trees have a treewidth of 1; since the second property of tree decomposition requires that each edge of the graph have both endpoints in some subset of the decomposition, no smaller treewidth is possible unless the graph has no edges.

We can now show that we can find the maximum independent set in a graph with low treewidth in time exponential in the treewidth. The algorithm is simply a generalization of the dynamic program for finding a maximum independent set in a tree.

Theorem 10.12. *Given a tree decomposition of a graph $G = (V, E)$ with nodes V' and treewidth t, we can find a maximum independent set in G in time $O(2^{O(t)}|V'|)$ via dynamic programming.*

Proof. Given the tree decomposition T of graph $G = (V, E)$ with nodes V' and sets $X_i \subseteq V$ for all $i \in V'$, we root the tree T. As in the dynamic program for trees, our algorithm will work bottom-up on the tree T. Now for each $i \in V'$, let T_i be the subtree of T rooted at i. Let V_i be the set of vertices given by taking the union of all the

X_j for all j in T_i, and let G_i be the subgraph of G induced by V_i. We will compute the maximum independent set of G_i for each $i \in V'$; when we reach the root vertex r of the rooted tree T, the graph $G_r = G$, and we will have computed its maximum independent set. In our dynamic program, we have $2^{|X_i|}$ entries in the table for each $i \in V'$; these correspond to the maximum independent set in G_i for all possible subsets $U \subseteq X_i$ where we require the intersection of the independent set and X_i to be exactly U. Note that some of these possibilities might not correspond to a valid independent set (for instance, if we include both endpoints of an edge of G_i), and these table entries will be marked "not valid."

If i is a leaf vertex of T, then $V_i = X_i$. Then since each table entry for i dictates whether each vertex of X_i is included or excluded, it suffices to check whether the given inclusions/exclusions yield a valid independent set to compute the entry.

Now suppose that i is an interior node of the tree. To handle this case, we must first establish two claims: (1) for any two distinct children j, k of i, $V_j \cap V_k \subseteq X_i$; (2) any edge of G_i must have either both endpoints in X_i or both endpoints in V_j for some child j of i. To see claim (1), suppose that there is some $u \in V_j \cap V_k$. We have $u \in V_j$ because $u \in X_p$ for some node p in the subtree T_j and $u \in V_k$ since $u \in X_q$ for some q in the subtree T_k. Now since i is on the path from p to q in the tree T, by the third property of a tree decomposition, it must be the case that $u \in X_p \cap X_q \subseteq X_i$. To see claim (2), pick any edge (u, v) in G_i. By the second property of a tree decomposition, there is some node ℓ in the tree such that both $u, v \in X_\ell$. If $\ell = i$, then $u, v \in X_i$. If ℓ is in the subtree T_i, but $\ell \neq i$, then ℓ is in the subtree T_j for some child j of i, and both $u, v \in V_j$. Now suppose ℓ is not in the subtree T_i. Since u and v are in G_i, there must be nodes p and q in the subtree T_i such that $u \in X_p$ and $v \in X_q$. The node i is on the path from p to ℓ in the decomposition tree T, and is also on the path from q to ℓ in T. Therefore, by the third property of the tree, $u \in X_p \cap X_\ell \subseteq X_i$ and $v \in X_q \cap X_\ell \subseteq X_i$, so both $u, v \in X_i$.

We can now show how to compute the table entries for i when i is an interior node of the tree. For any given valid set $U \subseteq X_i$, and any child j of i, consider an entry $W \subseteq X_j$ for j. We say that the entry W for the child j is *compatible* with the entry U for i if U and W agree on $X_i \cap X_j$ (that is, $U \cap X_i \cap X_j = W \cap X_i \cap X_j$). Then to compute the entry for i for set $U \subseteq X_i$, for each child j of i, we find the compatible entry of maximum weight; call this independent set S_j. We claim that U together with the union of the S_j over all children j is the maximum independent set for G_i whose intersection with X_i is exactly U; call this set $S = U \cup \bigcup_j S_j$. Note that by claim (1), $V_j - X_i$ are disjoint over all children j of i, so S is well defined. By induction, the S_j are maximum independent sets compatible with U, so if S is an independent set, there cannot be one of larger weight. Also, S is an independent set since by claim (2) any edge (u, v) in G_i must have either both endpoints in X_i or both endpoints in V_j for some child j of i. It cannot be the case that both u and v are in the independent set, since then either both of them were in U and U was not valid, or both of them were in S_j and S_j was not a valid independent set.

For each node in $|V'|$, there are 2^{t+1} entries we must compute. We compute these by checking for compatible entries at the child nodes; each of the 2^{t+1} entries of a child is checked once by the parent node for each entry of the parent node. Hence, the overall time taken is $O(2^{O(t)}|V'|)$.   □

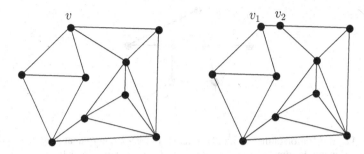

Figure 10.11. Splitting vertex v into v_1 and v_2, and maintaining k-outerplanarity.

We now turn to showing that k-outerplanar graphs have low treewidth. It will be useful for us to consider k-outerplanar graphs with maximum degree at most three; we will show that these have treewidth at most $3k + 1$. We show below that this is in fact general since any k-outerplanar graph G can be transformed into a k-outerplanar graph G' of maximum degree three, such that we can compute a tree decomposition of G from that of G' and the treewidth of G is bounded above by the treewidth of G'.

Lemma 10.13. *For any k-outerplanar graph G there is a k-outerplanar graph G' of maximum degree three such that given a tree decomposition of G' we can compute a tree decomposition of G of no greater treewidth.*

Proof. Given the k-outerplanar graph G with some vertex v of degree d greater than three, we can create a new graph G' by splitting v into two vertices v_1 and v_2 joined by an edge of degree three and degree $d - 1$, respectively. This can be done in such a way that the graph remains k-outerplanar; see Figure 10.11. Given a tree decomposition T' of G', we can create a new tree decomposition T of G by taking any subset X'_i containing either v_1 or v_2 and replacing it with v; that is, set $X_i = \left(X'_i - \{v_1, v_2\}\right) \cup \{v\}$ if X'_i contains v_1 or v_2; otherwise, $X_i = X'_i$. Then T is a valid tree decomposition of G given that T' is a valid tree decomposition of G', and clearly the treewidth of the decomposition of G is no greater than that of G'.

Given any k-outerplanar graph G of maximum degree greater than three, we can use the transformation above to create a sequence of new graphs $G_1, G_2, \ldots, G_z$ such that G_z has maximum degree at most three and then, from a tree decomposition of G_z, work backward to create a sequence of decompositions of $G_{z-1}, \ldots, G_1, G$ such that the treewidth of the decomposition of G is at most that of G_z. $\square$

Given a maximum spanning forest (V, F) of a graph G, consider any edge $e \in E - F$. The *fundamental cycle* of e is the cycle closed in the forest by adding e to F. We say that the *load* of a vertex $v \in V$ is the number of fundamental cycles in which it participates over all $e \in E - F$. Similarly, the load of a tree edge $e \in F$ is the number of fundamental cycles in which it participates over all $e \in E - F$. The *maximum load* of a maximum spanning forest (V, F) for a graph G is the maximum over all $v \in V$ and $e \in F$ of the loads of v and e.

Lemma 10.14. *Every k-outerplanar graph with maximum degree three has a maximum spanning forest (V, F) of maximum load $3k$.*

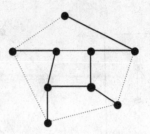

Figure 10.12. Illustration of the proof of Lemma 10.14 for a 2-outerplanar graph. The edges of the maximum spanning forest F, adding edges from R, are shown in thick lines. The remaining edges of R are dotted.

Proof. We show the result by induction on k. Suppose $k = 1$, and the graph G is outerplanar. Let R be the set of edges on the exterior face of the embedding of G. Note that after removing the edges of R the resulting graph must be acyclic since G is outerplanar; extend $E - R$ to a maximum spanning forest F of G by adding as many edges of R as possible. Then any edge of $E - F$ is on the exterior face; adding it to F creates a unique interior face of the embedding of G. Since any edge of G bounds at most two interior faces of the embedding, and any vertex bounds a number of interior faces at most its degree, each edge has load at most two and each vertex has load at most three.

Now suppose we have a k-outerplanar graph for $k > 1$. Again, let R be all the edges on the exterior face of the embedding of G. If we remove all the edges in R, then since the graph has degree three, the vertices on the exterior face will have degree at most one, and so the remaining graph will be at most $(k - 1)$-outerplanar. By induction, we know that we can find a maximum spanning forest F' of the graph $(V, E - R)$ such that the maximum load is at most $3(k - 1)$. We extend F' to a maximum spanning forest F of G by adding as many edges of R as possible. As above, adding any edge of $R - F$ closes a unique interior face of a planar graph $(V, F \cup R)$, and thus the additional load imposed on any edge of F by edges in $R - F$ is at most two, and the additional load imposed on any vertex v by edges in $R - F$ is at most three. See Figure 10.12 for an illustration. Hence, the maximum load of the forest (V, F) for G is at most $3k$.   □

Lemma 10.15. *If a graph G of maximum degree three has a maximum spanning forest (V, F) such that the maximum load of F is at most ℓ, then G has treewidth at most $\ell + 1$.*

Proof. Given $G = (V, E)$, we start by giving a tree decomposition of the forest F as shown previously in the discussion of tree decompositions: that is, we create a node i_u for each $u \in V$, and a node i_e for each edge e in the forest F. We start by setting $X_{i_u} = \{u\}$ and $X_{i_e} = \{u, v\}$ for $e = (u, v)$, and the decomposition tree T has edges (i_u, i_e) whenever u is an endpoint of an edge e in the forest F. This decomposition obeys the first and third properties of tree decompositions, but not the second because there may be edges in $E - F$ that do not have both endpoints in the same subset of the decomposition. We now update the tree for each $(u, v) \in E - F$ to fix this problem. Given an edge $e = (u, v) \in E - F$, we choose one of the endpoints arbitrarily, say, u. Consider the fundamental cycle of e. For every vertex $w \neq v$ in this cycle, we add u to the set X_{i_w}, and for every edge $e' \neq e$ in the cycle, we add u to the set $X_{i_{e'}}$.

We claim this gives a tree decomposition of G. The first property is satisfied, as is the second for every edge $e \in F$. For any edge $e = (u, v) \in E - F$, consider the fundamental cycle of e; there must be an edge $(w, v) \in F$ in this cycle incident on v. We added u to $X_{(w,v)}$ and this set already included v, so the second property is satisfied for all edges of E. The third property is also satisfied: it was satisfied in the initial decomposition of the spanning tree F, and then whenever we added a vertex u to subsets in the decomposition, we added it to all the subsets along a path in the decomposition tree T. Thus, for nodes i, j, k in the tree decomposition, if j is on the path from i to k in the decomposition tree T, $X_i \cap X_k \subseteq X_j$.

Note that initially every set in the decomposition has size at most two, and we add to each subset X_{i_u} a number of vertices that is at most the load of $u \in V$, and we add to each subset X_{i_e} a number of vertices that is at most the load of $e \in E$. Thus, the treewidth of this decomposition is at most $\ell + 1$. $\square$

We can finally summarize the discussion above in the following theorem.

Theorem 10.16. *There is a dynamic programming algorithm to find a maximum independent set in a k-outerplanar graph in $O(2^{O(k)}n^2)$ time.*

Proof. We will use the fact that a planar graph of n vertices has at most $m \le 3n - 6$ edges. We begin by noting that the arguments of Lemmas 10.13, 10.14, and 10.15 can be made algorithmic. We can apply Lemma 10.13 to create a k-outerplanar graph of maximum degree at most three; we create from the original graph of n vertices and m edges a graph with n' vertices and m' edges, where n' is at most the sum of the degrees of the original graph. Thus, $n' \le 2m = O(n)$, and $m' \le 3n' - 6 = O(n)$. We then use Lemma 10.14 to compute the appropriate maximum spanning forest of the degree three graph in $O(m') = O(n)$ time, and apply Lemma 10.15 to create a tree decomposition in $O(m'n') = O(n^2)$ time of size $|V'| = O(m' + n') = O(n)$. Then we invoke Lemma 10.13 again in $O(m'|V'|) = O(n^2)$ time to get the tree decomposition of the original graph. Note that the tree decomposition of the original graph is still on the vertex set V' with $|V'| = O(n)$. Using Theorem 10.12 then finds the maximum independent set. $\square$

Many hard combinatorial optimization problems on graphs have algorithms whose running time is polynomial in the size of the graph and exponential in the treewidth of the graph. We give some examples in the exercises below.

Exercises

10.1 In the *Euclidean Steiner tree problem*, we are given as input a set T of points in the plane called terminals. We are allowed to choose any other set N of points in the plane; we call these points nonterminals. For any pair of points $i, j \in T \cup N$, the cost of an edge connecting i and j is the Euclidean distance between the points. The goal is to find a set N of nonterminals such that the cost of the minimum spanning tree on $T \cup N$ is minimized.

Show that the polynomial-time approximation scheme for the Euclidean TSP can be adapted to give a polynomial-time approximation scheme for the Euclidean Steiner tree problem.

10.2 In this problem, we consider a Euclidean variant of the k-median problem from Section 9.2. We are given a set N of points in the plane that are clients and potential locations for facilities. We must find a subset $S \subseteq N$ with $|S| \leq k$ of facilities to open so as to minimize $\sum_{j \in N} \min_{i \in S} c_{ij}$, where c_{ij} is the Euclidean distance between $i, j \in N$. Using the techniques of Section 10.1, give a polynomial-time approximation scheme for the Euclidean k-median problem. (Extended hint: Several aspects of the proof must be adapted. For the Euclidean TSP, the side length L of the smallest square containing all points of the instance is a lower bound on the cost of an optimal solution, and then can be used in modifying the instance to be a nice instance. For the Euclidean k-median problem, L isn't necessarily a lower bound on the cost of an optimal solution. What can be used instead? In the dynamic program, for each square of side length s, it will be useful to keep track of the number of facilities opened in the square. Also for each portal of the square we may wish to keep track of two estimates: first, the distance from the portal to the nearest open facility inside the square (if any) in increments of s/m (where m is the number of portals on a side); and second, the distance of the portal to the nearest open facility outside the square, also in increments of s/m. Note that for two adjacent portals, both estimates should differ by at most one increment of s/m.)

10.3 Recall the vertex cover problem defined in Section 1.2. In the problem we are given an undirected graph $G = (V, E)$ and a nonnegative weight w_i for each vertex $i \in V$. The goal is to find a minimum-weight subset of vertices $C \subseteq V$ such that for each edge $(i, j) \in E$, either $i \in C$ or $j \in C$.

Show that the polynomial-time approximation scheme for the maximum independent set problem in planar graphs can be adapted to give a polynomial-time approximation scheme for the vertex cover problem in planar graphs.

10.4 Recall from Section 5.12 that we say a graph $G = (V, E)$ is k-colorable if we can assign each vertex one of k colors such that for any edge $(i, j) \in E$, i and j are assigned different colors. Suppose that G has a tree decomposition T of treewidth t, for constant t. Prove that for any k, one can decide in polynomial time whether the graph is k-colorable.

10.5 In the *graphical traveling salesman problem*, we are given a graph $G = (V, E)$ with edge costs $c_e \geq 0$ for all $e \in E$. The goal is to find a minimum-cost multiset of edges F such that (V, F) is Eulerian. One can view this as a variant of the traveling salesman problem in which cities can be visited multiple times, but it is not possible to travel directly from city i to city j when $(i, j) \notin E$. In this problem, we will show that we can compute the optimal solution to the graphical TSP when the graph G has low branchwidth, a concept related to treewidth.

Given an undirected graph $G = (V, E)$, a *branch decomposition* of G is a spanning tree T on a new set of nodes V' such that the degree of each internal node of T is exactly three, and T has exactly $|E|$ leaves; each edge e of G maps to a unique leaf of T. Removing an edge of the tree T therefore partitions the edges of G into two parts A and B corresponding to the leaves in the two connected components of T after the edge has been removed. The width of the separation is the number of vertices of G that have edges from both A and B incident on them. The width of the branch decomposition is the maximum width of the separation over all edges in the tree T. The *branchwidth* of G is the smallest width of a branch decomposition over all branch decompositions of G.

Suppose we are given an instance of the graphical traveling salesman problem, and a branch decomposition T of the input graph $G = (V, E)$ of branchwidth t. We can root the tree T by removing an arbitrary edge (a, b) and replacing it with two edges (a, r) and (r, b). Show that by using dynamic programming, there is a polynomial-time algorithm for the graphical TSP when the branchwidth t is a constant.

Chapter Notes

Approximation schemes for Euclidean instances of the traveling salesman problem and some other geometric problems were discovered independently by Arora [11] and Mitchell [225]. Arora's scheme also generalizes to Euclidean problems in higher dimensions, as long as the dimension d is $o(\log \log n)$. The algorithm and presentation given in Section 10.1 are due to Arora [11], somewhat following a survey of Arora [12]. As mentioned in the introduction, this technique turns out to be widely applicable to optimization problems in the Euclidean plane, including the Steiner tree problem (discussed in both [11] and [225]), given in Exercise 10.1, and the k-median problem (due to Arora, Raghavan, and Rao [20]), given in Exercise 10.2.

The approximation scheme of Section 10.2 for the maximum independent set in planar graphs is due to Baker [30], although we give a different presentation here. The result for the vertex cover problem in Exercise 10.3 is also from Baker [30]. The concept of the treewidth of a graph was introduced by Robertson and Seymour [252]; other equivalent concepts were introduced independently in the literature. For one such concept, *partial k-trees*, Arnborg and Proskurowski [10] give a "linear time" dynamic program for finding the maximum independent set. Bodlaender [52] shows that k-outerplanar graphs have treewidth at most $3k - 1$; we adapt (and weaken slightly) his presentation. The concept of branchwidth in Exercise 10.5 was introduced by Robertson and Seymour [253]; they showed that a graph of branchwidth t has treewidth at most $3t/2$, and a graph with treewidth k has branchwidth at most $k + 1$. The graphical traveling salesman problem was introduced by Cornuéjols, Fonlupt, and Naddef [84], and the dynamic programming algorithm of Exercise 10.5 is due to Cook and Seymour [80].

CHAPTER 11

Further Uses of Deterministic Rounding of Linear Programs

In this chapter, we return to the technique of deterministically rounding linear programs. We begin with a generalization of the problem of scheduling jobs on identical machines that we introduced in Section 2.3. In this general case, not only does a job j take different amounts of processing time depending on which machine i it is assigned to, but also a job j incurs a cost c_{ij} when assigned to machine i. If there is any feasible schedule of cost C in which the jobs are completed by time T, we show that by rounding a linear programming relaxation we can in polynomial time produce a schedule of cost at most C in which all jobs finish by time $2T$.

For the remaining applications, we use the fact that there is always a *basic* optimal solution to a linear program, and that algorithms for solving linear programs return such a solution. Suppose we have a linear program with n variables x_j in which there is a constraint $x_j \geq 0$ for each variable x_j. Then the number of constraints $m \geq n$, since there is at least one constraint per variable. Let a_i be a vector and b_i be a scalar giving the ith constraint, $a_i^T x \geq b_i$. A feasible solution $\bar{x}$ is a *basic feasible solution* if there are n linearly independent vectors a_i such that the corresponding constraints are met with equality; that is, $a_i^T \bar{x} = b_i$. Observe that this linear system uniquely defines $\bar{x}$. Basic feasible solutions are equivalent to extreme points of the geometric region of feasible solutions defined by the linear program; recall that an extreme point is a feasible solution that cannot be expressed as the convex combination of two other feasible solutions (see, for example, Exercise 1.5). There is always an optimal solution to the linear program that is a basic feasible solution, and we call such a solution a *basic optimal solution*.

The structure of basic solutions is very useful in designing approximation algorithms. In Section 11.2, we consider a version of the minimum-degree spanning tree problem introduced in Section 2.6: Here we have costs on the edges and bounds b_v on the degree of each vertex $v \in V$. We show that if there exists a spanning tree of cost at most C such that the degree of each vertex is at most b_v, we can in polynomial time find a spanning tree of cost at most C in which each vertex v has degree at most $b_v + 1$. The algorithm uses the properties of basic optimal solutions to generate a sequence of linear programming relaxations of the problem, where each LP in the sequence is defined on a smaller graph and has fewer constraints than the previous LPs. The final LP in the sequence returns a spanning tree with the desired properties.

In Section 11.3, we consider a generalization of the generalized Steiner tree problem introduced in Section 7.4 in which we must find a minimum-cost subgraph with several edge-disjoint paths between certain pairs of vertices. We show a remarkable theorem that any basic feasible solution to the linear programming relaxation of this problem must have some variable of value at least 1/2. We round this variable up to 1, then iterate on the remaining problem; this technique is called *iterated rounding*, and it gives a 2-approximation algorithm for the problem. This theorem can be viewed as a weakening of a statement we proved about a linear programming relaxation for the vertex cover problem in Exercise 1.5, in which *all* variables in a basic feasible solution have value 0, 1, or 1/2. Here we show only that *some* variable will have value at least 1/2, but this is sufficient to give a good approximation algorithm.

11.1 The Generalized Assignment Problem

In the *generalized assignment problem*, we are given a collection of n jobs to be assigned to m machines. Each job $j = 1, \ldots, n$ is to be assigned to exactly one machine; if it is assigned to machine i, then it requires p_{ij} time units of processing, and incurs a cost of c_{ij}. Furthermore, we are given a time bound T that limits the total processing of each machine $i = 1, \ldots, m$. The aim is to find a feasible assignment of minimum total cost.

If we write this problem as an integer program, and introduce a 0-1 variable x_{ij}, $i = 1, \ldots, m$, $j = 1, \ldots, n$, to indicate whether job j is assigned to machine i, then we obtain

$$\text{minimize} \quad \sum_{i=1}^{m} \sum_{j=1}^{n} c_{ij} x_{ij} \tag{11.1}$$

$$\text{subject to} \quad \sum_{i=1}^{m} x_{ij} = 1, \qquad j = 1, \ldots, n, \tag{11.2}$$

$$\sum_{j=1}^{n} p_{ij} x_{ij} \le T, \qquad i = 1, \ldots, m, \tag{11.3}$$

$$x_{ij} \in \{0, 1\}, \qquad i = 1, \ldots, m, \quad j = 1, \ldots, n. \tag{11.4}$$

It is not hard to see that just deciding whether there is a feasible solution to the integer program is strongly NP-hard; for instance, checking whether there is a feasible solution to the integer program captures the problem of minimizing the makespan on identical parallel machines (the case in which $p_{ij} = p_j$, $i = 1, \ldots, m$ for each job $j = 1, \ldots, n$). Nonetheless, we shall see that a rather strong approximation result is possible: for a given input, we either prove that no feasible solution exists, or else output a solution of total cost no greater than the optimum, but violate feasibility by allowing each machine to process jobs for a total time no greater than $2T$.

We shall give an LP rounding algorithm to find the near-optimal schedule. However, the linear programming relaxation of the integer program (11.1)–(11.4) in which the constraints (11.4) are replaced by

$$x_{ij} \geq 0, \qquad i = 1, \ldots, m, \quad j = 1, \ldots, n, \qquad (11.5)$$

does not provide a sufficiently strong bound on which to base the algorithm. Instead, we will strengthen this linear program in a seemingly trivial way; we add the constraints that

$$x_{ij} = 0 \text{ if } p_{ij} > T, \qquad (11.6)$$

which clearly hold for any feasible integer solution.

In carrying out the rounding of the fractional solution x, we shall rely heavily on a beautiful well-known result from matching theory (or more generally, from the theory of network flows). Suppose we are given a bipartite graph with two disjoint sets of nodes V and W, and an edge set F where each edge has one endpoint in each of V and W; let $B = (V, W, F)$ denote such a graph. We say that $M \subseteq F$ is a *complete matching* for V in this graph if (a) for each node $v \in V$, there is exactly one edge of M incident to v, and (b) for each node $w \in W$, there is at most one edge of M incident to w. (We shall assume that $|V| \leq |W|$, since otherwise no such matching is possible.)

Deciding whether a given bipartite graph $B = (V, W, F)$ has a complete matching is equivalent to deciding whether the following integer program has a feasible solution, where the 0-1 variable y_{vw} indicates that edge (v, w) is in the matching.

$$\sum_{v:(v,w)\in F} y_{vw} \leq 1, \qquad \forall w \in W, \qquad (11.7)$$

$$\sum_{w:(v,w)\in F} y_{vw} = 1, \qquad \forall v \in V, \qquad (11.8)$$

$$y_{vw} \in \{0, 1\}, \qquad \forall (v, w) \in F. \qquad (11.9)$$

If we relax the binary constraints (11.9) to be nonnegativity constraints

$$y_{vw} \geq 0, \qquad \forall (v, w) \in F, \qquad (11.10)$$

then we get a linear program; a feasible solution is called a *fractional complete matching*. In Exercise 4.6 we showed that this linear program has the special property that each extreme point is integer. The exercise shows the following theorem.

Theorem 11.1 (Exercise 4.6). *For any bipartite graph $B = (V, W, F)$, each extreme point of the feasible region of (11.7), (11.8), and (11.10) has integer coordinates. Furthermore, given edge costs c_{vw}, $(v, w) \in F$, and a feasible fractional solution y_{vw}, $(v, w) \in F$, we can find, in polynomial time, a feasible integer solution $\hat{y}_{vw}$ such that*

$$\sum_{(v,w)\in F} c_{vw}\hat{y}_{vw} \leq \sum_{(v,w)\in F} c_{vw}y_{vw}.$$

We next show how this result can be applied to obtain the main result of this section, which is as follows.

Theorem 11.2. *If the linear program (11.1)–(11.3), (11.5), and (11.6) has a feasible (fractional) solution x of total cost C, then we can round it to an (integer) assignment of total cost at most C in which each machine is assigned total processing at most $2T$.*

Proof. We will prove this theorem by providing an algorithm that converts a feasible LP solution x to the required (integer) assignment. This fractional solution x assigns, in total, $\sum_{j=1}^{n} x_{ij}$ jobs to machine i; the integer assignment that we construct will be similar to this, and so we allocate $k_i = \lceil \sum_{j=1}^{n} x_{ij} \rceil$ "slots" for machine i to be assigned jobs. Furthermore, the algorithm will assign job j to machine i only if $x_{ij} > 0$.

We can model this restriction by constructing a bipartite graph $B = (J, S, E)$, where one side of the bipartite graph consists of *job nodes* $J = \{1, \ldots, n\}$, and the other side consists of *machine slots*

$$S = \{(i, s) : i = 1, \ldots, m, \ s = 1, \ldots, k_i\}.$$

(Note that $|S| \geq |J|$.) One natural idea is to simply include an edge $((i, s), j)$ in E whenever $x_{ij} > 0$; although this is a good start, we will need to refine this later.

We shall focus on assignments of the jobs that correspond to complete matchings in this graph B. Since an edge e that connects machine slot node (i, s) to job node j has the interpretation that job j is assigned to machine i, it is natural to set the cost of edge e equal to c_{ij}. Ideally, the graph B would have the following two properties:

1. B contains a fractional complete matching for J of cost C;
2. any (integer) complete matching for J in B corresponds to an assignment in which each machine is required to complete at most $2T$ time units of processing.

If we succeed in constructing such a bipartite graph B, then we can compute the desired assignment by finding the minimum-cost (integer) complete matching in B (for example, by the polynomial-time algorithm of Theorem 11.1). This matching must have cost at most C (by property (1) and Theorem 11.1), and must assign each machine total processing at most $2T$ (by property (2)).

Let us understand in detail why our graph B has the first property. Focus on any machine i. We can convert our LP solution x into a fractional complete matching y in B. Consider the slot nodes (i, s), $s = 1, \ldots, k_i$ as bins of capacity 1, and the values x_{ij}, $j = 1, \ldots, n$ as pieces of the n jobs to be packed in these bins. We can place the pieces in the bin corresponding to slot $(i, 1)$ until the next piece j would cause the bin to be packed with pieces of total size greater than 1. Suppose this piece j is of size x_{ij} and there is only capacity z remaining in the bin (where $z < x_{ij}$). Then we pack z of this job piece j (of size x_{ij}) into slot $(i, 1)$, and pack the remaining $x_{ij} - z$ in the next bin (or equivalently, slot $(i, 2)$). Whenever we pack a positive fraction of job j in slot (i, s), we set $y_{j,(i,s)}$ equal to that fraction; all other components of y are set to 0. It is easy to see that repeating this for each machine i yields a fractional complete matching in B of total cost $\sum_{i,j} c_{ij} x_{ij}$. See Figure 11.1 for an illustration.

However, as stated thus far, we do not have the second property. We will need to refine the construction of $B = (J, S, E)$. First, suppose that we include an edge $(j, (i, s)) \in E$ only if the corresponding value $y_{j,(i,s)} > 0$. Clearly, this does not affect the existence of a fractional complete matching y. Furthermore, let us refine our "bin-packing" procedure that constructs the solution y. Suppose that in packing the n

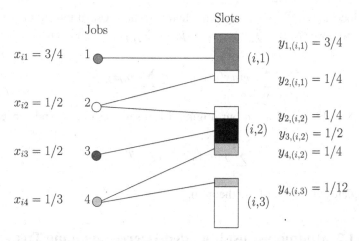

Figure 11.1. An example of how the fractional matching for B is created given x_{ij}.

pieces x_{ij}, $j = 1, \ldots, n$, into the k_i slots (or bins), we first sort the jobs so that their corresponding processing requirements p_{ij} are in non-increasing order. For ease of notation, suppose without loss of generality that

$$p_{i1} \geq p_{i2} \geq \cdots \geq p_{in}. \qquad (11.11)$$

We shall consider the graph B formed by including an edge $(j, (i, s))$ in E exactly when this bin-packing procedure places a positive fraction from x_{ij} into slot (i, s) (and hence makes the corresponding component of y positive).

Consider the slot (i, s), and focus on those jobs j for which some positive fraction is packed in the bin corresponding to this slot; let $max(i, s)$ denote the maximum processing requirement p_{ij} among these jobs. The total load assigned to machine i by any complete matching in B is at most

$$\sum_{s=1}^{k_i} max(i, s).$$

Since (11.6) holds, we know that $max(i, 1) \leq T$. We shall show that

$$\sum_{s=2}^{k_i} max(i, s) \leq T,$$

and hence the total load on machine i for any complete matching in B is at most $2T$. Observe that for each $s = 1, \ldots, k_i - 1$, we have that $\sum_j y_{j,(i,s)} = 1$, since we start the next bin only when we have completely filled the previous one. Thus, we can think of $\sum_j y_{j,(i,s)} p_{ij}$ as a weighted average of the relevant p_{ij} values, that is, those jobs for which a positive fraction is assigned to slot (i, s). By our ordering assumption (11.11), for each $s = 1, \ldots, k_i - 1$, we have that $max(i, s + 1) \leq \sum_j y_{j,(i,s)} p_{ij}$, and hence,

$$\sum_{s=1}^{k_i-1} max(i, s + 1) \leq \sum_{s=1}^{k_i-1} \sum_j y_{j,(i,s)} p_{ij} \leq \sum_{s=1}^{k_i} \sum_j y_{j,(i,s)} p_{ij}.$$

However, since $x_{ij} = \sum_s y_{j,(i,s)}$, by interchanging the order of the summations in the final expression, we see that $\sum_j \sum_s y_{j,(i,s)} p_{ij} = \sum_j p_{ij} x_{ij}$, and hence,

$$\sum_{s=1}^{k_i-1} max(i, s+1) \leq \sum_j p_{ij} x_{ij}.$$

Since x is a feasible solution for our original LP, it satisfies (11.3), and hence,

$$\sum_{s=1}^{k_i-1} max(i, s+1) \leq T,$$

which completes the proof of the theorem.   □

11.2 Minimum-Cost Bounded-Degree Spanning Trees

In this section, we consider the weighted case of a problem we considered in Sections 2.6 and 9.3. In those sections, we considered the problem of finding a spanning tree of a graph such that we minimized the maximum degree of the tree. Here, we consider the problem of finding a spanning tree of minimum cost such that the degree of node v is no more than some specified bound. We refer to this problem as the *minimum-cost bounded-degree spanning tree problem*. More formally, we are given as input an undirected graph $G = (V, E)$, costs $c_e \geq 0$ for all $e \in E$, a set $W \subseteq V$, and integer bounds $b_v \geq 1$ for all $v \in W$. Let OPT be the cost of the minimum spanning tree such that the degree of each node $v \in W$ is no more than b_v (if such a tree exists). In the first part of this section, we give an algorithm that finds a spanning tree of cost at most OPT such that each node $v \in W$ has degree at most $b_v + 2$. In the latter part of this section, we show that we can find a spanning tree of cost at most OPT such that each node $v \in W$ has degree at most $b_v + 1$. As we argued at the end of Section 2.6 for unweighted spanning trees, no better result is possible unless P = NP.

We begin by giving an integer programming formulation of the problem for a graph $G = (V, E)$. Given a vertex set $S \subseteq V$, let $E(S)$ be the subset of edges in E that have both endpoints in S, and let $\delta(S)$ be the subset of edges that have exactly one endpoint in S. We will denote $\delta(\{v\})$ by $\delta(v)$. We let $x_e \in \{0, 1\}$ indicate whether an edge e is in the spanning tree or not. Every spanning tree has exactly $|V| - 1$ edges, so we have

$$\sum_{e \in E} x_e = |V| - 1.$$

Furthermore, since for any set $S \subseteq V$ with $|S| \geq 2$, a spanning tree does not have a cycle in $E(S)$, we have

$$\sum_{e \in E(S)} x_e \leq |S| - 1.$$

Finally, we want the spanning tree to respect the degree bounds for all $v \in W$, so that we have

$$\sum_{e \in \delta(v)} x_e \leq b_v.$$

Relaxing the integrality constraints to $x_e \geq 0$ gives us the following linear programming relaxation of the problem:

$$\text{minimize} \sum_{e \in E} c_e x_e \tag{11.12}$$

$$\text{subject to} \sum_{e \in E} x_e = |V| - 1, \tag{11.13}$$

$$\sum_{e \in E(S)} x_e \leq |S| - 1, \qquad \forall S \subseteq V, |S| \geq 2, \tag{11.14}$$

$$\sum_{e \in \delta(v)} x_e \leq b_v, \qquad \forall v \in W, \tag{11.15}$$

$$x_e \geq 0, \qquad \forall e \in E. \tag{11.16}$$

We can use the ellipsoid method introduced in Section 4.3 to solve the linear program by giving a polynomial-time separation oracle. It is easy to check that the constraints (11.13), (11.15), and (11.16) are satisfied. To check that the constraints (11.14) are satisfied, we need to set up a sequence of maximum flow problems. We first explain the general max-flow construction, and then we modify it to check the constraints (11.14). We create a new graph G' where we add source and sink vertices s and t, edges (s, v) from the source to every vertex $v \in V$, and edges (v, t) from every vertex $v \in V$. The capacity of every edge e from G is $\frac{1}{2}x_e$, the capacity of every edge (s, v) is $\frac{1}{2}\sum_{e \in \delta(v)} x_e$, and the capacity of every edge (v, t) is 1. Then consider the capacity of any s-t cut $S \cup \{s\}$ for $S \subseteq V$. It contains edges (v, t) for all $v \in S$, all $e \in \delta(S) \cap E$, and (s, v) for all $v \notin S$. So its total capacity is

$$|S| + \frac{1}{2} \sum_{e \in \delta(S)} x_e + \frac{1}{2} \sum_{v \notin S} \sum_{e \in \delta(v)} x_e = |S| + \sum_{e \in \delta(S)} x_e + \sum_{e \in E(V-S)} x_e,$$

since adding up $\frac{1}{2}x_e$ for each $e \in \delta(v)$ where $v \notin S$ gives x_e for all edges e with both endpoints not in S plus $\frac{1}{2}x_e$ for all edges e with exactly one endpoint not in S. Using the fact that $\sum_{e \in E} x_e = |V| - 1$, this is equal to

$$|S| + |V| - 1 - \sum_{e \in E(S)} x_e = |V| + (|S| - 1) - \sum_{e \in E(S)} x_e.$$

Thus, the capacity of this cut is at least $|V|$ if and only if $\sum_{e \in E(S)} x_e \leq |S| - 1$. We want to make sure $|S| \geq 2$, so for each pair $x, y \in V$, we construct the max-flow instance as above, but alter the capacity of the edges (s, x) and (s, y) to be infinite. This ensures that any minimum s-t cut $S \cup \{s\}$ has $x, y \in S$. Then by the reasoning above, the value of the maximum flow for this instance will be at least $|V|$ if and only if constraints (11.14) are satisfied for all $S \supseteq \{x, y\}$. If the flow is at least $|V|$ for all pairs $x, y \in V$, then all constraints (11.14) are satisfied. If the flow value is less than $|V|$, then the corresponding minimum s-t cut $S \cup \{s\}$ will give a violated constraint.

We assume from here on that there is a feasible solution to this linear program. If there is no feasible solution, then obviously there is no tree in the graph G that has the given degree bounds.

$F \leftarrow \emptyset$
while $|V| > 1$ **do**
    Solve LP (11.12) on (V, E), get basic optimal solution x
    $E \leftarrow E(x)$
    Find $v \in V$ such that there is one edge (u, v) in $E(x)$ incident on v
    $F \leftarrow F \cup \{(u, v)\}$
    $V \leftarrow V - \{v\}$
    $E \leftarrow E - \{(u, v)\}$
return F

Algorithm 11.1. Deterministic rounding algorithm for finding a minimum-cost spanning tree.

As a warmup to the algorithm and its approach, we first show that if we have no degree bounds (that is, $W = \emptyset$), then we can find a spanning tree of cost no more than the value of the linear program (11.12); this gives us a minimum spanning tree. Given an LP solution x, define $E(x)$ to be the support of x; that is, $E(x) = \{e \in E : x_e > 0\}$. The algorithm for finding a minimum spanning tree depends on the following lemma. We defer the proof of the lemma for the moment.

Lemma 11.3. *For any basic feasible solution x to the linear program (11.12) with $W = \emptyset$, there is some $v \in V$ such that there is at most one edge of $E(x)$ incident on v.*

Our algorithm then works as follows. We maintain a set of edges F for our solution, which is initially empty. While there is more than one vertex in the current graph, we solve the linear program (11.12) for the current graph $G = (V, E)$, and obtain a basic optimal solution x. We remove from the edge set E all edges e for which $x_e = 0$. By Lemma 11.3, there exists some vertex $v \in V$ such that there is at most one edge of $E(x)$ incident on it; suppose the edge is (u, v). Then we add (u, v) to our solution set F, remove v and (u, v) from the graph, and repeat. Intuitively, each iteration finds a leaf v of the spanning tree, then recursively finds the rest of it. The algorithm is summarized in Algorithm 11.1.

Theorem 11.4. *Algorithm 11.1 yields a spanning tree of cost no more than the value of the linear program (11.12).*

Proof. We begin by showing that if the edge e^* is chosen to add to F in some iteration of the algorithm, then $x_{e^*} = 1$ in that iteration. To prove this, we first claim that $\sum_{e \in \delta(w)} x_e \geq 1$ for any vertex $w \in V$. Then for the edge $e^* = (u, v)$ chosen by the algorithm, we know that there is one edge in $E(x)$ incident on v, and therefore $x_{e^*} \geq 1$. To see that $\sum_{e \in \delta(v)} x_e \geq 1$, note that for $S = V - \{v\}$, the LP constraint (11.14) enforces that $\sum_{e \in E(S)} x_e \leq |S| - 1 = (|V| - 1) - 1 = |V| - 2$. But $\sum_{e \in E} x_e = |V| - 1$ by constraint (11.13) and also $\sum_{e \in \delta(v)} x_e = \sum_{e \in E} x_e - \sum_{e \in E(S)} x_e$. Therefore, $\sum_{e \in \delta(v)} x_e \geq (|V| - 1) - (|V| - 2) = 1$. Now consider the constraint (11.14) for $S = \{u, v\}$. This enforces $x_{e^*} \leq 1$, so it must be the case that $x_{e^*} = 1$.

We now prove by induction on the size of the graph that the algorithm produces a spanning tree of cost no more than the value of the linear program. In the base case, we have a graph with two vertices, and the algorithm returns a single edge e. By the above, we have $x_e = 1$, so that the value of the LP is at least $c_e x_e = c_e$, and the statement holds.

Now suppose that the statement holds for every graph with at most $k > 2$ vertices, and our graph has $k + 1$ vertices. We solve the LP, get a solution x, and find a vertex v such that there is only one edge $e^* = (u, v)$ in $E(x)$ incident on v. Let $V' = V - \{v\}$, and $E' = E(x) - \{e^*\}$. By the inductive hypothesis, we will find a spanning tree F' on (V', E') of cost at most the value of the LP on (V', E'); let x' be an optimal solution to this LP. Obviously $F' \cup \{e^*\}$ is a spanning tree of (V, E), so that the algorithm returns a spanning tree. To show that its cost is at most $\sum_{e \in E} c_e x_e$, we shall show that x_e for $e \in E'$ is a feasible solution to the LP on (V', E'). It then follows that the cost of the spanning tree returned is

$$\sum_{e \in F'} c_e + c_{e^*} \le \sum_{e \in E'} c_e x'_e + c_{e^*} x_{e^*} \le \sum_{e \in E'} c_e x_e + c_{e^*} x_{e^*} = \sum_{e \in E} c_e x_e,$$

as desired.

We now must show that x_e for $e \in E'$ is a feasible solution to the LP on (V', E'). Since the LP constraints (11.14) for (V', E') are a subset of the constraints for (V, E), x is feasible for them. Thus, it suffices to show that the first constraint holds, namely, $\sum_{e \in E'} x_e = |V'| - 1 = |V| - 2$. This follows since the only edges in $E - E'$ are e^*, which has $x_{e^*} = 1$, and edges such that $x_e = 0$. Thus, $\sum_{e \in E'} x_e = \sum_{e \in E} x_e - x_{e^*} = (|V| - 1) - 1 = |V'| - 1$, and x_e for $e \in E'$ is feasible for the LP on (V', E'). $\square$

Now we return to the minimum-cost bounded-degree spanning tree problem. Recall that we have a subset of vertices W such that we wish to find a tree with the degree of v at most b_v for all $v \in W$. We cannot hope for a result as strong as that of Lemma 11.3 for this problem, since we would be able to translate this into an algorithm to find an optimal tree. Instead, we will be able to show the following. This will lead to a result in which degree bounds are exceeded by at most two.

Lemma 11.5. *For any basic feasible solution x to the linear program (11.12), either there is some $v \in V$ such that there is at most one edge of $E(x)$ incident on v, or there is some $v \in W$ such that there are at most three edges of $E(x)$ incident on v.*

Note that Lemma 11.3 is a special case of this lemma; the second possibility cannot occur when $W = \emptyset$. We again defer the proof of this lemma, and instead show how it leads to the desired algorithm. As before, we maintain a solution set F, which is initially empty. We solve the linear program for the current graph (V, E) and current bound set W, and obtain a basic optimal solution x. We remove all edges e with $x_e = 0$ from the edge set. If, as before, there is some $v \in V$ such that there is at most one edge (u, v) in $E(x)$ incident on v, we add (u, v) to F, remove v from V, and remove (u, v) from E. If $u \in W$, we also decrease b_u by one. We then iterate. If instead there is some $v \in W$ such that there are at most three edges of $E(x)$ incident on v, we remove v from W and repeat. The algorithm is summarized in Algorithm 11.2.

We can now prove the following.

Theorem 11.6. *Algorithm 11.2 produces a spanning tree F such that the degree of v in F is at most $b_v + 2$ for $v \in W$, and such that the cost of F is at most the value of the linear program (11.12).*

Proof. In each step of the algorithm, we either add a spanning tree edge to F, or we remove a vertex from W. Thus, the algorithm will terminate in at most $(n - 1) + n = 2n - 1$ iterations.

$F \leftarrow \emptyset$
while $|V| > 1$ **do**
    Solve LP (11.12) on (V, E) and W, get basic optimal solution x
    $E \leftarrow E(x)$
    if $\exists\, v \in V$ such that there is one edge (u, v) in $E(x)$ incident on v **then**
        $F \leftarrow F \cup \{(u, v)\}$
        $V \leftarrow V - \{v\}$
        $E \leftarrow E - \{(u, v)\}$
        if $u \in W$ **then**
            $b_u \leftarrow b_u - 1$
    else
        $\exists\, v \in W$ such that there are at most three edges in $E(x)$ incident on v
        $W \leftarrow W - \{v\}$
return F

Algorithm 11.2. Deterministic rounding algorithm for finding a minimum-cost bounded-degree spanning tree.

Observe that the proof that the algorithm returns a spanning tree whose cost is at most the value of the linear program is almost identical to that of Theorem 11.4. In that proof we considered the graph (V', E') resulting from adding an edge (u, v) to our solution F, then removing v and (u, v) from the graph. We showed that the LP solution x for the graph (V, E) is feasible for the new graph (V', E') when restricted to the edges in E'. Here we also need to consider the set of degree bounds W, and show that x is feasible for the new graph (V', E') and the new degree bounds after b_u has been decreased by one. If x was feasible for the constraints (11.15) before, then $\sum_{e \in \delta(u)} x_e \le b_u$. Thus, after edge $e = (u, v)$ with $x_e = 1$ is removed from the graph, the solution x restricted to the remaining edges in E' will be feasible for the same constraint on the new graph (V', E') with the degree bound $b_u - 1$.

Now consider any vertex v initially in W. We show by induction on the algorithm that the degree of v in the solution F is at most $b_v + 2$. In each iteration, one of three things can happen. First, we can choose an edge incident on v and decrease b_v by 1, in which case the statement follows by induction. Second, we can choose an edge incident on v and remove v from the graph; in this case, we must have had $b_v \ge 1$ in order to have a feasible solution to the LP, so the statement holds. Third, we can remove v from W. In this case, we must have $b_v \ge 1$ in order for there to be any edges in $E(x)$ incident on v, yet there are at most three edges in $E(x)$ incident on v. Thus, in all future iterations we can add at most three edges incident on v, since all edges not in $E(x)$ are removed from the graph for all future iterations. Thus, v will have degree at most $b_v + 2$. $\qquad \square$

We can now turn to the proof of Lemma 11.5. In order to do this, we will need to introduce some definitions and notation. From here on, for the given solution x, we assume that all edges e such that $x_e = 0$ have been removed from the edge set; that is, $E = E(x)$.

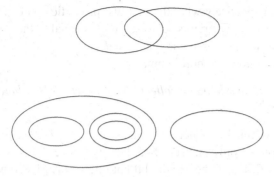

Figure 11.2. Top: two intersecting sets. Bottom: A laminar collection of sets.

Definition 11.7. *For $x \in \Re^{|E|}$ and a subset of edges F, we define $x(F) = \sum_{e \in F} x_e$.*

Definition 11.8. *For a solution x to LP (11.12), we say that a constraint (11.14) corresponding to a set $S \subseteq V$, $|S| \geq 2$, is* tight *if $x(E(S)) = |S| - 1$. A constraint (11.15) corresponding to a vertex $v \in W$ is* tight *if $x(\delta(v)) = b_v$.*

We may also say that the set $S \subseteq V$ is tight if $x(E(S)) = |S| - 1$ or that the vertex v is tight if $x(\delta(v)) = b_v$.

Definition 11.9. *We say two sets A and B are* intersecting *if $A \cap B$, $A - B$, and $B - A$ are all nonempty.*

Definition 11.10. *We say a collection of sets $\mathcal{S}$ is* laminar *if no pair of sets $A, B \in \mathcal{S}$ are intersecting.*

See Figure 11.2 for an example of intersecting sets and laminar set collections.

Definition 11.11. *For a subset of edges $F \subseteq E$, the* characteristic vector *of F is $\chi_F \in \{0, 1\}^{|E|}$, where $\chi_F(e) = 1$ if $e \in F$ and 0 otherwise.*

We are now able to state the following theorem, which we will need to prove Lemma 11.5.

Theorem 11.12. *For any basic feasible solution x to the linear program (11.12), there is a set $Z \subseteq W$ and a collection $\mathcal{L}$ of subsets of vertices with the following properties:*

1. *For all $S \in \mathcal{L}$, $|S| \geq 2$ and S is tight, and for all $v \in Z$, v is tight.*
2. *The vectors $\chi_{E(S)}$ for $S \in \mathcal{L}$ and $\chi_{\delta(v)}$ for $v \in Z$ are linearly independent.*
3. *$|\mathcal{L}| + |Z| = |E|$.*
4. *The collection $\mathcal{L}$ is laminar.*

We will defer the proof of this theorem for a moment, and will next show how Lemma 11.5 can be derived from the theorem. First, however, we observe that for any basic feasible solution x to the LP, there is a collection of sets $\mathcal{S}$ and set $Y \subseteq W$ such that the first three properties hold for $\mathcal{S}$ and Y; the key statement of the theorem is the last property, which states that for any basic feasible solution, there is a laminar collection of such sets. A basic solution is formed by taking $|E|$ linearly independent constraints from the linear program, setting them at equality, and solving the resulting linear system. This is precisely what the first two properties state. The third property states that the number of constraints set to equality is equal to the number of nonzero variables (recall that we have assumed that $E = E(x)$).

We first need the following short lemma.

Lemma 11.13. *Let $\mathcal{L}$ be a laminar collection of subsets of V, where each $S \in \mathcal{L}$ has $|S| \geq 2$. Then $|\mathcal{L}| \leq |V| - 1$.*

Proof. We can prove this by induction on the size of $|V|$. For the base case $|V| = 2$, obviously $\mathcal{L}$ can contain only one set of cardinality 2. For $|V| > 2$, pick a minimum cardinality set R in $\mathcal{L}$. Let V' be V with all but one vertex of R removed, and let $\mathcal{L}'$ be the sets in $\mathcal{L}$ restricted to the elements of V', with the set R removed. Note that $\mathcal{L}'$ fulfills the conditions of the lemma; it is still laminar, and any set must contain at least two elements. So $|\mathcal{L}'| \leq |V'| - 1$ by induction, and since $|\mathcal{L}'| = |\mathcal{L}| - 1$ and $|V'| \leq |V| - 1$, the lemma statement follows. $\square$

Now we recall the statement of Lemma 11.5, and give its proof.

Lemma 11.5. *For any basic feasible solution x to the linear program (11.12), either there is some $v \in V$ such that there is at most one edge of $E(x)$ incident on v, or there is some $v \in W$ such that there are at most three edges of $E(x)$ incident on v.*

Proof. We prove the statement by contradiction. If the statement is not true, then for every vertex $v \in V$, there are at least two edges of $E(x)$ incident on it, and for every $v \in W$, there are at least four edges of $E(x)$ incident on it. Then it must be the case that

$$|E(x)| \geq \frac{1}{2}(2(|V| - |W|) + 4|W|) = |V| + |W|.$$

However, by Theorem 11.12, we know that $|E(x)| = |\mathcal{L}| + |Z| \leq |\mathcal{L}| + |W|$ for laminar $\mathcal{L}$. Since each set $S \in \mathcal{L}$ has cardinality at least two, by Lemma 11.13, we get that $|E(x)| \leq |V| - 1 + |W|$, which is a contradiction. $\square$

Finally, we can turn to the proof of Theorem 11.12. The basic idea of the proof is simple, and has proven enormously useful in a number of different contexts. We start out with a collection of sets $\mathcal{S}$ that may not be laminar, and as long as we have two intersecting sets $S, T \in \mathcal{S}$, we show that we can "uncross" them and replace them with two nonintersecting sets. A first step in this proof is to show the following.

Lemma 11.14. *If S and T are tight sets such that S and T are intersecting, then $S \cup T$ and $S \cap T$ are also tight sets. Furthermore,*

$$\chi_{E(S)} + \chi_{E(T)} = \chi_{E(S \cup T)} + \chi_{E(S \cap T)}.$$

Proof. We begin by showing that $x(E(S))$ is supermodular; namely,

$$x(E(S)) + x(E(T)) \leq x(E(S \cap T)) + x(E(S \cup T)).$$

This follows by a simple counting argument: any edge in $E(S)$ or in $E(T)$ is in $E(S \cup T)$, while any edge in both $E(S)$ and $E(T)$ appears in both $E(S \cap T)$ and $E(S \cup T)$. The right-hand side may be greater than the left-hand side since edges with one endpoint in $S - T$ and the other in $T - S$ appear in $E(S \cup T)$ but not in $E(S)$ or $E(T)$.

Since S and T are intersecting, $S \cap T \neq \emptyset$. Thus, by the feasibility of x

$$(|S| - 1) + (|T| - 1) = (|S \cap T| - 1) + (|S \cup T| - 1) \geq x(E(S \cap T)) + x(E(S \cup T)).$$

By supermodularity,

$$x(E(S \cap T)) + x(E(S \cup T)) \geq x(E(S)) + x(E(T)).$$

Finally, since S and T are tight sets,

$$x(E(S)) + x(E(T)) = (|S| - 1) + (|T| - 1).$$

Thus, all of these inequalities must be met with equality, and $S \cap T$ and $S \cup T$ are tight sets. Furthermore, as $x(E(S \cap T)) + x(E(S \cup T)) = x(E(S)) + x(E(T))$, it must be the case that $\chi_{E(S)} + \chi_{E(T)} = \chi_{E(S \cup T)} + \chi_{E(S \cap T)}$, since we have assumed that the only edges in E have $x_e > 0$. $\qquad \square$

Let $\mathcal{T}$ be the collection of all tight sets for the LP solution x; that is, $\mathcal{T} = \{S \subseteq V : x(E(S)) = |S| - 1, |S| \geq 2\}$. Let $span(\mathcal{T})$ be the span of the set of vectors $\{\chi_{E(S)} : S \in \mathcal{T}\}$. We now show that we can find a laminar collection of sets with span at least that of $\mathcal{T}$.

Lemma 11.15. *There exists a laminar collection of sets $\mathcal{L}$ such that $span(\mathcal{L}) \supseteq span(\mathcal{T})$, where each $S \in \mathcal{L}$ is tight and has $|S| \geq 2$, and the vectors $\chi_{E(S)}$ for $S \in \mathcal{L}$ are linearly independent.*

Proof. Let $\mathcal{L}$ be a laminar collection of sets such that each $S \in \mathcal{L}$ is tight and has $|S| \geq 2$, and the vectors $\chi_{E(S)}$ for $S \in \mathcal{L}$ are linearly independent. We assume that $\mathcal{L}$ is the maximal such collection; that is, we cannot add any additional sets to $\mathcal{L}$ such that all of these properties continue to hold. We will give a proof by contradiction that $span(\mathcal{L}) \supseteq span(\mathcal{T})$; assume otherwise. Then there must be a tight set S with $|S| \geq 2$ such that $\chi_{E(S)} \in span(\mathcal{T})$ and $\chi_{E(S)} \notin span(\mathcal{L})$; we choose an S such that there is no other such set intersecting fewer sets in $\mathcal{L}$. Note that such an S must be intersecting with at least one set in $\mathcal{L}$; otherwise, $\mathcal{L}$ is not maximal.

Now pick a set $T \in \mathcal{L}$ such that S and T intersect. By Lemma 11.14, $\chi_{E(S)} + \chi_{E(T)} = \chi_{E(S \cap T)} + \chi_{E(S \cup T)}$ and both $S \cap T$ and $S \cup T$ are tight. We will argue that it cannot be the case that both $\chi_{E(S \cap T)} \in span(\mathcal{L})$ and $\chi_{E(S \cup T)} \in span(\mathcal{L})$. We know that $T \in \mathcal{L}$ so that $\chi_{E(T)} \in span(\mathcal{L})$, and we know that $\chi_{E(S)} = \chi_{E(S \cap T)} + \chi_{E(S \cup T)} - \chi_{E(T)}$. Thus, if both $\chi_{E(S \cup T)}$ and $\chi_{E(S \cap T)}$ are in $span(\mathcal{L})$, this implies $\chi_{E(S)} \in span(\mathcal{L})$, which contradicts our assumption that $\chi_{E(S)} \notin span(\mathcal{L})$. Hence, at least one of $\chi_{E(S \cap T)}$ and $\chi_{E(S \cup T)}$ is not in $span(\mathcal{L})$.

Without loss of generality, suppose that $\chi_{E(S \cap T)} \notin span(\mathcal{L})$; note that this implies that $\chi_{E(S \cap T)} \neq 0$, so that $|S \cap T| \geq 2$. We claim that $S \cap T$ must intersect fewer sets in $\mathcal{L}$ than S, and with this claim, we contradict the choice of S, since $S \cap T$ is tight, $|S \cap T| \geq 2$, and $\chi_{E(S \cap T)} \notin span(\mathcal{L})$. To prove the claim, we observe that any set in the laminar collection $\mathcal{L}$ intersecting $S \cap T$ must also intersect S; see Figure 11.3. However, S intersects T, while $S \cap T$ does not intersect T, so $S \cap T$ must intersect fewer sets in $\mathcal{L}$ than S. $\qquad \square$

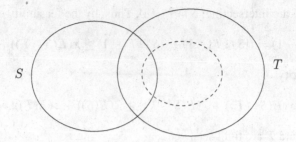

Figure 11.3. Proof of Lemma 11.15. The only sets from the laminar collection $\mathcal{L}$, with $T \in \mathcal{L}$, that can intersect $S \cap T$ must also intersect S.

We can now give the proof of Theorem 11.12, which we restate here.

Theorem 11.12. *For any basic feasible solution x to the linear program (11.12), there is a set $Z \subseteq W$ and a collection $\mathcal{L}$ of subsets of vertices with the following properties:*

1. *For all $S \in \mathcal{L}$, $|S| \geq 2$ and S is tight, and for all $v \in Z$, v is tight.*
2. *The vectors $\chi_{E(S)}$ for $S \in \mathcal{L}$ and $\chi_{\delta(v)}$ for $v \in Z$ are linearly independent.*
3. *$|\mathcal{L}| + |Z| = |E|$.*
4. *The collection $\mathcal{L}$ is laminar.*

Proof. As we said previously, we know that there exists a collection $\mathcal{S}$ and set $Y \subseteq W$ that have the first three properties of the theorem. Let $span(\mathcal{S}, Y)$ be the span of the set of vectors $\{\chi_{E(S)} : S \in \mathcal{S}\} \cup \{\chi_{\delta(v)} : v \in Y\}$. Since there are $|E|$ linearly independent vectors in this set and the vectors have $|E|$ coordinates, clearly $span(\mathcal{S}, Y) = \Re^{|E|}$. By Lemma 11.15, if $\mathcal{T}$ is the set of all tight sets, then there exists a laminar collection of tight sets $\mathcal{L}$ such that $span(\mathcal{L}) \supseteq span(\mathcal{T})$. Since $\mathcal{S} \subseteq \mathcal{T}$, then $\Re^{|E|} = span(\mathcal{S}, Y) \subseteq span(\mathcal{T}, Y) \subseteq span(\mathcal{L}, Y) \subseteq \Re^{|E|}$, so that $span(\mathcal{S}, Y) = span(\mathcal{L}, Y) = \Re^{|E|}$. From the proof of Lemma 11.15 the vectors $\chi_{E(S)}$ for all $S \in \mathcal{L}$ are linearly independent. We now let $Z = Y$, and as long as there exists some $v \in Z$ such that $\chi_{\delta(v)} \in span(\mathcal{L}, Z - v)$, we remove v from Z. Note that $span(\mathcal{L}, Z)$ never decreases, and so the span is always $\Re^{|E|}$. When this process terminates, the vectors $\chi_{E(S)}$ for $S \in \mathcal{L}$ and $\chi_{\delta(v)}$ for $v \in Z$ must be linearly independent, and furthermore since their span is $\Re^{|E|}$, we must have $|E| = |\mathcal{L}| + |Z|$.   □

To summarize, we have been able to show that we can find a spanning tree of cost at most OPT such that each node $v \in W$ has degree at most $b_v + 2$. To do this, we used the properties of a basic feasible solution; we showed that the basic optimal solution has structure in terms of a laminar collection of tight sets. This structure allows us to prove Lemma 11.5, which, informally speaking, states that either we can find a leaf of the tree or some node $v \in W$ that will have degree at most $b_v + 2$. The lemma leads naturally to an algorithm for finding the desired tree.

We now give an algorithm that finds a spanning tree of cost at most OPT such that each node $v \in W$ has degree at most $b_v + 1$. As with the previous algorithm, we find a basic optimal solution of a linear programming relaxation of the problem. The key to the algorithm is proving a stronger version of Lemma 11.5: we show that if $W \neq \emptyset$, we can find some $v \in W$ such that there are at most $b_v + 1$ edges of $E(x)$ incident on v. Thus, in our new algorithm, we will show that we will be able to remove degree bounds

---

while $W \neq \emptyset$ **do**

    Solve LP (11.12) on (V, E), W, get basic optimal solution x

    $E \leftarrow E(x)$

    Select $v \in W$ such that there are at most $b_v + 1$ edges in E incident on v

    $W \leftarrow W - \{v\}$

Compute minimum-cost spanning tree F on (V, E)

return F

Algorithm 11.3. Deterministic rounding algorithm for finding a minimum-cost bounded-degree spanning tree.

from the linear programming relaxation until none are left, in such a way that the cost of the solution to the corresponding relaxation does not increase. When all the degree bounds are removed, we will have a solution to the linear programming relaxation of the minimum spanning tree problem, and we previously saw in Theorem 11.4 that we can find a minimum spanning tree of cost at most the value of the linear programming relaxation.

As before, we define $E(x) = \{e \in E : x_e > 0\}$. Our algorithm will depend on the following lemma, whose proof we defer for a moment.

Lemma 11.16. *For any basic feasible solution x to the linear program (11.12) in which $W \neq \emptyset$, there is some $v \in W$ such that there are at most $b_v + 1$ edges incident on v in $E(x)$.*

Given the lemma, the algorithm is relatively straightforward. We solve the LP relaxation to obtain a basic optimal solution. All edges $e \in E$ such that $x_e = 0$ are removed from E. If $W \neq \emptyset$, the lemma states that there must exist some $v \in W$ such that there are at most $b_v + 1$ edges in $E(x)$. We remove v from W, since we know that when we obtain the minimum-cost spanning tree F, there can be at most $b_v + 1$ edges of F incident on v. If $W = \emptyset$, then by Theorem 11.4, we can compute a minimum spanning tree of cost at most the value of the linear programming relaxation. The algorithm is summarized in Algorithm 11.3. The following proof of the correctness of the algorithm is then not difficult.

Theorem 11.17. *Algorithm 11.3 produces a spanning tree F such that the degree of v in F is at most $b_v + 1$ for $v \in W$, and such that the cost of F is at most the value of the linear program (11.12).*

Proof. As in the proofs of Theorems 11.4 and 11.6, we show by induction that in each iteration, the LP solution x_e on (V, E) and W is feasible for the input (V, E') and W' for the next iteration. It is easy to see this since any time we remove an edge e from E, $x_e = 0$, which does not affect the feasibility of the solution. Also, we only remove vertices from W, imposing fewer constraints. Thus, the cost of the optimal LP solution on the input (V, E') and W' is no greater than that on the input (V, E) and W.

Since we remove a vertex v from W in each iteration, eventually $W = \emptyset$, and the algorithm computes a minimum spanning tree F on the final set of edges. By Theorem 11.4, this cost is at most the cost of the final linear programming solution.

Since the value of the linear program never increases as we modify E and W, the cost of the minimum spanning tree is at most the value of initial linear program (11.12).

Furthermore, we removed v from W only if there were at most $b_v + 1$ edges remaining in E incident on v. Thus, the computed spanning tree can have at most degree $b_v + 1$ for each vertex v in the initial set W.   □

We now turn to the proof of Lemma 11.16. As before, for the basic feasible solution x, we use the existence of a laminar collection $\mathcal{L}$ and a set of vertices Z as given in Theorem 11.12. We also need the following lemma.

Lemma 11.18. *For any $e \in E$ such that $x_e = 1$, $\chi_e \in span(\mathcal{L})$.*

Proof. By the proof of Theorem 11.12, the laminar collection $\mathcal{L}$ is such that $span(\mathcal{L}) \supseteq span(\mathcal{T})$, where $\mathcal{T}$ is the collection of all tight sets. Notice that if $x_e = 1$ for $e = (u, v)$, then the set $S = \{u, v\}$ is tight, since $x_e = x(E(S)) = |S| - 1 = 1$. Thus, $\chi_e = \chi_{E(S)} \in span(\mathcal{T}) \subseteq span(\mathcal{L})$.   □

We now restate Lemma 11.16 and give its proof.

Lemma 11.16. *For any basic feasible solution x to the linear program (11.12) in which $W \neq \emptyset$, there is some $v \in W$ such that there are at most $b_v + 1$ edges incident on v in $E(x)$.*

Proof. Assume the statement of the lemma is false, so that there are at least $b_v + 2$ edges in E incident on every $v \in Z$, with $W \neq \emptyset$. We derive the contradiction via a charging scheme, in which we assign each $v \in Z$ and each $S \in \mathcal{L}$ a certain nonnegative charge, possibly fractional. We will then show, by the falsity of the lemma statement, each $v \in Z$ and each $S \in \mathcal{L}$ receives a charge of at least one. This will imply that the total charge is at least $|Z| + |\mathcal{L}| = |E|$. However, we will also show that the total charge assigned must have been strictly less than $|E|$, giving the contradiction. Thus, there must exist some $v \in W \neq \emptyset$ such that there are at most $b_v + 1$ edges of E incident on v.

To carry out our charging scheme, for each $e \in E$ we assign a charge of $\frac{1}{2}(1 - x_e)$ to each endpoint of e that is in Z, and we assign a charge of x_e to the smallest $S \in \mathcal{L}$ that contains both endpoints of e, if such an S exists. Note then that have assigned a total charge of at most $(1 - x_e) + x_e = 1$ per edge $e \in E$.

Now we show that each $v \in Z$ and each $S \in \mathcal{L}$ receive a charge of at least one. Each $v \in Z$ receives a charge of $\frac{1}{2}(1 - x_e)$ from each edge of E incident on it. By hypothesis, there are at least $b_v + 2$ edges incident on v. Since $v \in Z$ implies v is tight, we know that $\sum_{e \in \delta(v)} x_e = b_v$. Thus, the total charge received by v is at least one, since

$$\sum_{e \in \delta(v)} \frac{1}{2}(1 - x_e) = \frac{1}{2}\left(|\delta(v)| - \sum_{e \in \delta(v)} x_e\right)$$

$$\geq \frac{1}{2}[(b_v + 2) - b_v]$$

$$= 1.$$

Now consider a set $S \in \mathcal{L}$. If S contains no other set $C \in \mathcal{L}$, then since S is a tight set, $\sum_{e \in E(S)} x_e = |S| - 1$, and the total charge assigned to S is $|S| - 1$. Since $|S| \geq 2$, the total charge assigned to S is at least one. Now suppose that S contains some $C \in \mathcal{L}$. We call a set $C \in \mathcal{L}$ a *child* of S if it is strictly contained in S, and no other set $C' \in \mathcal{L}$ that contains C is also strictly contained in S. Let $C_1, \ldots, C_k$ be the children of S. Recalling that the sets S and $C_1, \ldots, C_k$ are tight, we have that $x(E(S)) = |S| - 1$ and $x(E(C_i)) = |C_i| - 1$ and thus are integral. Furthermore, the $E(C_i)$ are disjoint and are contained in $E(S)$ by the laminarity of $\mathcal{L}$. Hence, the total charge assigned to S is

$$x(E(S)) - \sum_{i=1}^{k} x(E(C_i)) \geq 0.$$

However, it cannot be the case that $E(S) = \bigcup_{i=1}^{k} E(C_i)$ since then $\chi_{E(S)} = \sum_{i=1}^{k} \chi_{E(C_i)}$, which violates the second property of Theorem 11.12, which says that these vectors are linearly independent. Thus, it must be the case that the total charge assigned to S is

$$x(E(S)) - \sum_{i=1}^{k} x(E(C_i)) > 0,$$

and since

$$x(E(S)) - \sum_{i=1}^{k} x(E(C_i)) = (|S| - 1) - \sum_{i=1}^{k} (|C_i| - 1)$$

is integral, the difference must be at least one. Therefore, at least one unit of charge is assigned to S.

Finally, we show that the total charge is strictly less than $|E|$ via a three-case argument. First, if $V \notin \mathcal{L}$, then there must exist some edge e such that $e \notin E(S)$ for all $S \in \mathcal{L}$. The charge $x_e > 0$ is not made to any set, so that the total charge is strictly less than $|E|$. Second, if there exists some $e = (u, v) \in E$ with $x_e < 1$ such that one of its two endpoints is not in Z (say, $u \notin Z$), then the charge of $\frac{1}{2}(1 - x_e) > 0$ is not made to u, and again the total charge is strictly less than $|E|$. Finally, suppose that $V \in \mathcal{L}$ and for any $e \in E$ with $x_e < 1$, both endpoints of e are in Z. We will show that this case gives rise to a contradiction, so one of the first two cases must occur. We observe that $\sum_{v \in Z} \chi_{\delta(v)} = 2\chi_{E(Z)} + \chi_{\delta(Z)}$ and, by hypothesis, each edge $e \in \delta(Z) \cup E(V - Z)$ has $x_e = 1$. Now we show that we can express $2\chi_{E(Z)} + \chi_{\delta(Z)}$ by the sum of vectors $\chi_{E(S)}$ for $S \in \mathcal{L}$, which will contradict the linear independence of the vectors $\chi_{E(S)}$ for $S \in \mathcal{L}$ and $\chi_{\delta(v)}$ for $v \in Z$. By Lemma 11.18, for any $e \in \delta(Z) \cup E(V - Z)$, $\chi_e \in span(\mathcal{L})$ since $x_e = 1$. Thus, $\sum_{v \in Z} \chi_{\delta(v)} = 2\chi_{E(Z)} + \chi_{\delta(Z)} = 2\chi_{E(V)} - 2\sum_{e \in E(V-Z)} \chi_e - \sum_{e \in \delta(Z)} \chi_e$, and every term on the right-hand side is in $span(\mathcal{L})$; this proves that $\chi_{\delta(v)}$ for $v \in Z$ and $\chi_{E(S)}$ for $S \in \mathcal{L}$ are linearly dependent, which is a contradiction. □

In summary, we have been able to show that we can find a spanning tree of cost at most OPT with degree at most $b_v + 1$ for $v \in W$. We did this by proving a lemma showing that a basic feasible solution x to the linear programming relaxation of the problem must have some $v \in W$ such that at most $b_v + 1$ edges of $E(x)$ are incident on v. The proof of this lemma, given above, uses the structure of the basic feasible solution as a laminar collection of tight sets, as well as a charging scheme that uses fractional charges. In the next section we will use many of these same ideas in giving an approximation algorithm for another network design problem.

11.3 Survivable Network Design and Iterated Rounding

In this section, we turn to a generalization of the generalized Steiner tree problem that was introduced in Section 7.4. This problem is called the *survivable network design problem*. In this problem, we are given as input an undirected graph $G = (V, E)$, costs $c_e \geq 0$ for all $e \in E$, and connectivity requirements r_{ij} for all pairs of vertices $i, j \in V$, where $i \neq j$. The connectivity requirements are nonnegative integers. The goal is to find a minimum-cost set of edges $F \subseteq E$ such that for all pairs of vertices i, j with $i \neq j$, there are at least r_{ij} edge-disjoint paths connecting i and j in (V, F). The generalized Steiner tree problem is a special case of the survivable network design problem in which all $r_{ij} \in \{0, 1\}$.

The survivable network design problem is motivated by the telecommunications industry. We wish to design low-cost networks that can survive failures of the edges. In the case of $r_{ij} - 1$ edge failures, vertices i and j will still be connected in the resulting set of edges. We may wish to have certain pairs of vertices to be highly connected, with others with connectivity requirement 1 if it is not as crucial that they be connected in case of failures.

The problem can be modeled by the following integer program:

$$\text{minimize} \sum_{e \in E} c_e x_e$$

$$\text{subject to} \sum_{e \in \delta(S)} x_e \geq \max_{i \in S, j \notin S} r_{ij}, \qquad \forall S \subseteq V,$$

$$x_e \in \{0, 1\}, \qquad \forall e \in E.$$

Consider any pair of vertices i, j with $i \neq j$, and a set of edges F. By the max-flow/min-cut theorem, there are at least r_{ij} edge-disjoint paths connecting i and j in (V, F) if and only if every cut S separating i and j contains at least r_{ij} edges of F; that is, $|\delta(S) \cap F| \geq r_{ij}$. Hence, a set of edges F is feasible if and only if $|\delta(S) \cap F| \geq \max_{i \in S, j \notin S} r_{ij}$ for all $S \subseteq V$, which is exactly the constraint imposed by the integer program.

Note that this insight can be used to solve the following linear programming relaxation in polynomial time:

$$\text{minimize} \sum_{e \in E} c_e x_e$$

$$\text{subject to} \sum_{e \in \delta(S)} x_e \geq \max_{i \in S, j \notin S} r_{ij}, \qquad \forall S \subseteq V,$$

$$0 \leq x_e \leq 1, \qquad \forall e \in E.$$

We use the ellipsoid method introduced in Section 4.3 with the following separation oracle. Given a solution x, we first check that $0 \leq x_e \leq 1$ for all edges $e \in E$. We then create a max-flow instance for each pair of vertices $i, j, i \neq j$, with the capacity of each edge set to x_e. If the maximum flow that can be sent from i to j is at least r_{ij} for each $i, j \in V$, then by the argument above, we know that all the constraints are satisfied. If for some i, j, the maximum flow is less than r_{ij}, then there must be some cut S with $i \in S$, $j \notin S$, such that $\sum_{e \in \delta(S)} x_e < r_{ij}$, giving a violated constraint.

It will be useful to consider a more general form of the linear program above. We will consider the following linear program with functions f on the vertex set such that $f(S)$ is an integer for all $S \subseteq V$:

$$\text{minimize} \sum_{e \in E} c_e x_e \tag{11.17}$$

$$\text{subject to} \sum_{e \in \delta(S)} x_e \geq f(S), \qquad \forall S \subseteq V,$$

$$0 \leq x_e \leq 1, \qquad \forall e \in E.$$

Clearly the linear programming relaxation of the survivable network design problem corresponds to the case $f(S) = \max_{i \in S, j \notin S} r_{ij}$.

We will consider functions f that are *weakly supermodular*.

Definition 11.19. *A function $f : 2^V \to \mathbb{Z}$ is weakly supermodular if $f(\emptyset) = f(V) = 0$ and, for each two sets $A, B \subseteq V$, one of the following two statements holds:*

$$f(A) + f(B) \leq f(A \cap B) + f(A \cup B); \tag{11.18}$$

$$f(A) + f(B) \leq f(A - B) + f(B - A). \tag{11.19}$$

The function f that we use for the survivable network design problem falls into this class.

Lemma 11.20. *The function $f(S) = \max_{i \in S, j \notin S} r_{ij}$ is weakly supermodular.*

Proof. Trivially $f(\emptyset) = f(V) = 0$. We observe that $f(S) = f(V - S)$ for any $S \subseteq V$. Also, for any disjoint A, B, $f(A \cup B) \leq \max(f(A), f(B))$: choose $i \in A \cup B$ and $j \notin A \cup B$ attaining the maximum $\max_{i \in A \cup B, j \notin A \cup B} r_{ij}$ that defines $f(A \cup B)$. Then either $i \in A$ and $j \notin A$ or $i \in B$ and $j \notin B$, so that $\max(f(A), f(B)) \geq r_{ij} = f(A \cup B)$. We then observe that f obeys the following four inequalities:

$$f(A) \leq \max(f(A - B), f(A \cap B));$$
$$f(A) = f(V - A) \leq \max(f(B - A), f(V - (A \cup B)))$$
$$\qquad = \max(f(B - A), f(A \cup B));$$
$$f(B) \leq \max(f(B - A), f(A \cap B));$$
$$f(B) = f(V - B) \leq \max(f(A - B), f(V - (A \cup B)))$$
$$\qquad = \max(f(A - B), f(A \cup B)).$$

Then summing together the two inequalities involving the minimum of $f(A - B)$, $f(B - A)$, $f(A \cup B)$, and $f(A \cap B)$ gives the desired result; so, for instance, if $f(A - B)$ achieves the minimum of the four values, then we sum the first and last inequalities, which then implies $f(A) + f(B) \leq f(A \cup B) + f(A \cap B)$. $\qquad\square$

$F \leftarrow \emptyset$
$i \leftarrow 1$
while F is not a feasible solution **do**
    Solve LP (11.17) on edge set $E - F$ with function f_i, where
        $f_i(S) = f(S) - |\delta(S) \cap F|$, to obtain basic optimal solution x
    $F_i \leftarrow \{e \in E - F : x_e \geq 1/2\}$
    $F \leftarrow F \cup F_i$
    $i \leftarrow i + 1$
return F

Algorithm 11.4. Deterministic rounding algorithm for the survivable network design problem.

We now state a remarkable theorem that will allow us to obtain a 2-approximation algorithm for the survivable network design problem. We will first show how the theorem gives the approximation algorithm, then turn to the proof of the theorem.

Theorem 11.21. *For any basic feasible solution x to the linear program (11.17) such that f is a weakly supermodular function, there exists some edge $e \in E$ such that $x_e \geq 1/2$.*

Given the theorem, we have the following rather simple idea for an approximation algorithm for the survivable network design problem: we solve the linear programming relaxation, find all edges whose LP value is at least 1/2, and include them in our solution. We fix the value of these variables to 1, resolve the linear program, and repeat the process until we have a feasible solution to the problem. Intuitively, we are always rounding variables up by at most a factor of 2, which will lead to the performance guarantee of 2. There are a number of details to be taken care of, but this is the main idea.

We state the algorithm more formally in Algorithm 11.4. We let F be the set of edges in the solution; F is initially empty. In the ith iteration of the algorithm, we solve the linear program (11.17) on edge set $E - F$ with the function f_i, where $f_i(S) = f(S) - |\delta(S) \cap F|$. Given a basic optimal solution to this linear program, we set $F_i = \{e \in E - F : x_e \geq 1/2\}$, and add F_i to F. Because we iteratively round up the LP solution to create the final feasible solution, this technique is called *iterated rounding*.

To show that the algorithm works, we must show that each function f_i is again weakly supermodular, so that Theorem 11.21 applies; this will imply that $F_i \neq \emptyset$ in each iteration, and thus there are at most $|E|$ iterations before the algorithm terminates. We will also need to show that we can solve the linear program in each iteration. We start with the following lemma, which will be useful in showing that the f_i are weakly supermodular.

Lemma 11.22. *Pick any $z_e \geq 0$ for all $e \in E$, and let $z(E') = \sum_{e \in E'} z_e$ for any $E' \subseteq E$. Then for any subsets $A, B \subseteq V$,*

$$z(\delta(A)) + z(\delta(B)) \geq z(\delta(A \cup B)) + z(\delta(A \cap B))$$

and

$$z(\delta(A)) + z(\delta(B)) \geq z(\delta(A - B)) + z(\delta(B - A)).$$

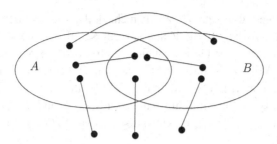

Figure 11.4. Proof of Lemma 11.22.

Proof. The proof is a simple counting argument; to prove each inequality, we show that an edge included in the sums on the right-hand side of the inequalities appears at least as many times on the left-hand side. See Figure 11.4 for an illustration. For instance, any edge whose two endpoints are in $A - B$ and $V - (A \cup B)$ appears in $\delta(A \cup B)$, $\delta(A - B)$, and $\delta(A)$, but not $\delta(A \cap B)$, $\delta(B - A)$, or $\delta(B)$. Thus, it is included once in the right-hand side and left-hand side of the first inequality, and once in the right-hand side and left-hand side of the second inequality. We simply need to check all possible cases for the four different places in which the two different endpoints of an edge can be. We note that an edge whose two endpoints are in $A - B$ and $B - A$ appears twice on the left-hand side of the first inequality, but not at all on the right-hand side; similarly, an edge whose two endpoints are in $A \cap B$ and $V - (A \cup B)$ appears twice on the left-hand side of the second inequality, but not on the right-hand side; thus, the inequalities can be strict.   □

Lemma 11.23. *For any $F \subseteq E$, the function $f_i(S) = f(S) - |\delta(S) \cap F|$ is weakly supermodular if f is weakly supermodular.*

Proof. Set $z_e = 1$ if $e \in F$ and $z_e = 0$ otherwise. Then it is equivalent to show that f_i is weakly supermodular when $f_i(S) = f(S) - z(\delta(S))$. It is clear that $f_i(\emptyset) = f_i(V) = 0$. Now pick any two subsets $A, B \subseteq V$. We note that for the function f, it is the case that either $f(A) + f(B) \leq f(A \cup B) + f(A \cap B)$ or $f(A) + f(B) \leq f(A - B) + f(B - A)$. Suppose the former holds. Then

$$\begin{aligned}
f_i(A) + f_i(B) &= f(A) + f(B) - z(\delta(A)) - z(\delta(B)) \\
&\leq f(A \cup B) + f(A \cap B) - z(\delta(A \cup B)) - z(\delta(A \cap B)) \\
&= f_i(A \cup B) + f_i(A \cap B),
\end{aligned}$$

where the inequality follows by hypothesis and by Lemma 11.22. The other case is identical.   □

Lemma 11.24. *For any $F \subseteq E$, we can solve the linear program (11.17) in polynomial time with edge set $E - F$ and function $g(S) = f(S) - |\delta(S) \cap F|$ when $f(S) = \max_{i \in S, j \notin S} r_{ij}$.*

Proof. We use the ellipsoid method with a separation oracle similar to the one given to solve the LP with the original function f. For a solution x, we first check that $0 \leq x_e \leq 1$ for all $e \in E - F$. Then for each pair of vertices i, j, with $i \neq j$, we create a maximum flow instance with the capacity of each edge $e \in E - F$ set to x_e and the capacity of each edge $e \in F$ set to 1. We then check that the flow between i and j is at least r_{ij}. If it is, then for any $i, j \in V$ and any cut S with $i \in S$ and $j \notin S$, it must be the case that the capacity is at least r_{ij}, which implies that $x(\delta(S)) + |\delta(S) \cap F| \geq r_{ij}$, which implies $x(\delta(S)) \geq r_{ij} - |\delta(S) \cap F|$. Since this holds for all pairs $i, j \in V$, then $x(\delta(S)) \geq g(S)$. Similarly, if for some pair $i, j \in V$, the maximum flow is less than r_{ij}, then the capacity of the minimum cut S with $i \in S$ and $j \notin S$ is less than r_{ij}. Then $x(\delta(S)) + |\delta(S) \cap F| < r_{ij}$, or $x(\delta(S)) < r_{ij} - |\delta(S) \cap F| \leq g(S)$, and this is a violated constraint. □

We can now prove that Theorem 11.21 implies that the algorithm is a 2-approximation algorithm.

Theorem 11.25. *Given Theorem 11.21, Algorithm 11.4 is a 2-approximation algorithm for the survivable network design problem.*

Proof. We prove a slightly stronger statement by induction on the number of iterations of the algorithm; in particular, we will show that the algorithm has a performance guarantee of 2 for any weakly supermodular function f. However, we do not know how to solve the linear program (11.17) in polynomial time for every weakly supermodular function. Hence, we claim a 2-approximation algorithm only for the survivable network design problem, since we do know how to solve the needed linear programs in polynomial time.

Let x be the solution to the original linear programming relaxation with function $f_1 = f$ for any weakly supermodular function f. For any subset $E' \subseteq E$ of edges, let $c(E') = \sum_{e \in E'} c_e$. The base case is straightforward: if after one iteration, $F = F_1$ is a feasible solution, then since $F_1 = \{e \in E : x_e \geq 1/2\}$, it is clear that $c(F) \leq 2 \sum_{e \in E} c_e x_e \leq 2 \, \mathrm{OPT}$.

Now suppose that the statement holds if the algorithm takes k iterations; we show that it holds if the algorithm takes $k + 1$ iterations. By induction, the cost of all the edges added from the second iteration onward is no more than twice the value of the LP solution for the weakly supermodular function f_2; that is, if x' is the solution found in the second iteration for the LP with function f_2, then $c(F - F_1) \leq 2 \sum_{e \in E - F_1} c_e x'_e$ since the algorithm finds a solution for function f_2 in k iterations. For $e \in F_1$, we know that $c(F_1) \leq 2 \sum_{e \in F_1} c_e x_e$, since $x_e \geq 1/2$ for all $e \in F_1$. To complete the proof, we will show that x is a feasible solution on the edges $E - F_1$ for the function f_2. Thus,

$$\sum_{e \in E - F_1} c_e x'_e \leq \sum_{e \in E - F_1} c_e x_e,$$

so that

$$c(F) = c(F - F_1) + c(F_1) \leq 2 \sum_{e \in E - F_1} c_e x'_e + 2 \sum_{e \in F_1} c_e x_e$$

$$\leq 2 \sum_{e \in E - F_1} c_e x_e + 2 \sum_{e \in F_1} c_e x_e$$

$$= 2 \sum_{e \in E} c_e x_e \leq 2 \, \mathrm{OPT}.$$

To see that x is feasible for the LP for the function f_2 on edges $E - F_1$, we note that for any $S \subseteq V$, $x(\delta(S)) \geq f_1(S)$ implies that

$$x(\delta(S) \cap (E - F_1)) = x(\delta(S)) - x(\delta(S) \cap F_1) \geq f_1(S) - x(\delta(S) \cap F_1)$$
$$\geq f_1(S) - |\delta(S) \cap F_1| = f_2(S),$$

where for the second inequality we use that $x_e \leq 1$. $\square$

We now turn to the proof of Theorem 11.21, and show that for any basic feasible solution x, $x_e \geq 1/2$ for some edge $e \in E$. We assume without loss of generality that $0 < x_e < 1$ for all $e \in E$; we can do this since if $x_e = 1$, then we are done, while if for some edge $e \in E$, $x_e = 0$, we can simply remove it from the graph. We will now need a definition.

Definition 11.26. *For the given solution x to LP (11.17), we say that a set $S \subseteq V$ is tight if $x(\delta(S)) = f(S)$.*

We are now able to state the following theorem, which we will need to prove Theorem 11.21.

Theorem 11.27. *For any basic feasible solution x to the linear program (11.17) with f a weakly supermodular function, there is a collection $\mathcal{L}$ of subsets of vertices with the following properties:*

1. *For all $S \in \mathcal{L}$, S is tight.*
2. *The vectors $\chi_{\delta(S)}$ for $S \in \mathcal{L}$ are linearly independent*
3. *$|\mathcal{L}| = |E|$.*
4. *The collection $\mathcal{L}$ is laminar.*

The proof of this theorem is almost identical to the proof of Theorem 11.12 in Section 11.2, and so we leave it as an exercise (Exercise 11.2).

We now turn to our proof of Theorem 11.21. We restate the theorem here for convenience. The proof is similar to the fractional charging argument used for the minimum-cost bounded-degree spanning tree problem in Lemma 11.16.

Theorem 11.21. *For any basic feasible solution x to the linear program (11.17) such that f is a weakly supermodular function, there exists some edge $e \in E$ such that $x_e \geq 1/2$.*

Proof. We give a proof by contradiction. Suppose that for all $e \in E$, $0 < x_e < \frac{1}{2}$. Given this hypothesis, we will give a charging scheme in which we distribute charge to the sets $S \in \mathcal{L}$ whose total is strictly less than $|E|$. However, we will also show that each $S \in \mathcal{L}$ receives a charge of at least one, for a total charge of at least $|\mathcal{L}| = |E|$. This will give our contradiction.

For each edge $e \in E$ we will distribute a charge of $1 - 2x_e > 0$ to the smallest set $S \in \mathcal{L}$ that contains both endpoints of e, if such a set exists, and for each endpoint v of e we distribute a charge of $x_e > 0$ to the smallest set $S \in \mathcal{L}$ containing v, if such a set exists. Both $1 - 2x_e$ and x_e are positive since we assume that $0 < x_e < 1/2$. Thus, the total charge distributed is at most $1 - 2x_e + 2x_e = 1$ per edge. However, notice that for any set $S \in \mathcal{L}$ not contained in any other set of $\mathcal{L}$, there must be edges $e \in \delta(S)$. These edges will not have both endpoints contained in some set $S \in \mathcal{L}$, and for these

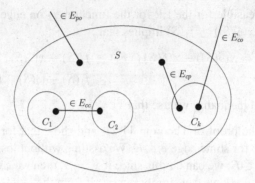

Figure 11.5. Illustration of the edge sets in the proof of Theorem 11.21.

edges we distribute charge strictly less than one since the charge $1 - 2x_e > 0$ for the edge is not distributed. Thus, the total charge distributed is strictly less than $|E|$.

Now we show that each $S \in \mathcal{L}$ receives a charge of at least one. We say a set $C \in \mathcal{L}$ is a *child* of S if it is strictly contained in S, and no other set $C' \in \mathcal{L}$ that contains C is also strictly contained in S. Let $C_1, \ldots, C_k$ be the children of S (if any exist). Since S and the C_i are in $\mathcal{L}$, they are all tight sets so that $x(\delta(S)) = f(S)$ and $x(\delta(C_i)) = f(C_i)$ for all i. Let $C = \bigcup_i C_i$. We now divide the edges in $E_S = \delta(S) \cup \bigcup_i \delta(C_i)$ into four sets (see Figure 11.5 for an illustration):

- E_{cc} is the set of edges $e \in E_S$ that have one endpoint in some C_i and the other in C_j for $j \neq i$ ("child-child edges"). By the charging scheme such edges contribute a charge of $1 - 2x_e$ to S since S is the smallest set to contain both endpoints.
- E_{cp} is the set of edges $e \in E_S$ that have one endpoint in C_i and the other in $S - C$ ("child-parent edges"). By the charging scheme such edges contribute a charge of x_e to S for the one endpoint in $S - C$, and a charge of $1 - 2x_e$ since S is the smallest set containing both endpoints of S. So the total charge given to S is $1 - x_e$ for each edge $e \in E_{cp}$.
- E_{po} is the set of edges $e \in E_S$ that have one endpoint in $S - C$ and the other outside S ("parent-out edges"). By the charging scheme such edges contribute a charge of x_e to S for the one endpoint in $S - C$.
- E_{co} is the set of edges of E_S in both $\delta(S)$ and $\delta(C_i)$ for some i ("child-out edges"). Such edges contribute no charge to S.

We claim that it cannot be the case that all edges of E_S are in E_{co}. If this were the case, then an edge is in $\delta(S)$ if and only if it is in $\delta(C_i)$ for some i, which implies $\chi_{\delta(S)} = \sum_{i=1}^{k} \chi_{\delta(C_i)}$. This contradicts Theorem 11.27, which states that the $\chi_{\delta(T)}$ are linearly independent for $T \in \mathcal{L}$.

Thus, at least one edge must be in E_{cc}, E_{cp}, or E_{po}; S receives a positive charge for each such edge, and the total charge received is $|E_{cc}| - 2x(E_{cc}) + |E_{cp}| - x(E_{cp}) + x(E_{po}) > 0$. By the definitions of the edge sets above, we note that

$$x(\delta(S)) - \sum_{i=1}^{k} x(\delta(C_i)) = x(E_{po}) - x(E_{cp}) - 2x(E_{cc}).$$

Then we have that the total charge received by S is

$$|E_{cc}| - 2x(E_{cc}) + |E_{cp}| - x(E_{cp}) + x(E_{po}) = |E_{cc}| + |E_{cp}|$$
$$+ \left(x(\delta(S)) - \sum_{i=1}^{k} x(\delta(C_i)) \right).$$

Since all sets are tight, this total charge is equal to

$$|E_{cc}| + |E_{cp}| + \left(f(S) - \sum_{i=1}^{k} f(C_i) \right).$$

Since this last expression is a sum of integers, and we know the total charge is positive, the total charge must be at least one.

Thus, each $S \in \mathcal{L}$ gets a charge of at least one, for a total charge of at least $|\mathcal{L}| = |E|$, but we distributed a total charge of strictly less than $|E|$, which gives the contradiction. $\square$

As we observed at the end of Section 7.4, the linear programming relaxation for the generalized Steiner tree problem has an integrality gap that is essentially 2. Since the generalized Steiner tree problem is a special case of the survivable network design problem, and the linear program used for the generalized Steiner tree problem is a special case of the linear program (11.17) we use for the survivable network design problem, the integrality gap of (11.17) is also essentially 2. Thus, we cannot obtain any better performance guarantee by comparing the value of the algorithm's solution to the value of the LP relaxation as we do in the deterministic rounding argument above.

As was mentioned at the beginning of the chapter, the motivation for studying the survivable network design problem comes from wanting to design low-cost networks that can survive failures in the edges of the network. Suppose we wish to design networks that can also survive failures in the vertices? In that case, we may wish for there to be r_{ij} vertex-disjoint paths between i and j for all $i, j \in V$. In Section 16.4, we show that this variant of the survivable network design problem is substantially harder to approximate than the edge-disjoint version we considered above.

Exercises

11.1 We consider a variant of the generalized assignment problem without costs. Suppose we are given a set of n jobs to be assigned to m machines. Each job j is to be scheduled on exactly one machine. If job j is scheduled on machine i, then it requires p_{ij} units of processing time. The goal is to find a schedule of minimum length, which is equivalent to finding an assignment of jobs to machines that minimizes the maximum total processing time required by a machine. This problem is sometimes called scheduling *unrelated* parallel machines so as to minimize the makespan. We show that deterministic rounding of a linear program can be used to develop a polynomial-time 2-relaxed decision procedure (recall the definition of a relaxed decision procedure from Exercise 2.4).

Consider the following set of linear inequalities for a parameter T:

$$\sum_{i=1}^{m} x_{ij} = 1, \qquad j = 1, \ldots, n,$$

$$\sum_{j=1}^{n} p_{ij} x_{ij} \leq T, \qquad i = 1, \ldots, m,$$

$$x_{ij} \geq 0, \qquad i = 1, \ldots, m, \ j = 1, \ldots, n$$

$$x_{ij} = 0, \qquad \text{if } p_{ij} > T.$$

If a feasible solution exists, let x be a basic feasible solution for this set of linear inequalities. Consider the bipartite graph G on machine nodes $M_1, \ldots, M_m$ and job nodes $N_1, \ldots, N_n$ with edges (M_i, N_j) for each variable $x_{ij} > 0$.

(a) Prove that the linear inequalities are a relaxation of the problem, in the sense that if the length of the optimal schedule is T, then there is a feasible solution to the linear inequalities.

(b) Prove that each connected component of G of k nodes has exactly k edges, and so is a tree plus one additional edge.

(c) If $x_{ij} = 1$, assign job j to machine i. Once all of these jobs are assigned, use the structure of the previous part to show that it is possible to assign at most one additional job to any machine. Argue that this results in a schedule of length at most $2T$.

(d) Use the previous parts to give a polynomial-time 2-relaxed decision procedure, and conclude that there is a polynomial-time 2-approximation algorithm for scheduling unrelated parallel machines to minimize the makespan.

11.2 In this exercise, we prove Theorem 11.27.

(a) First, prove the following. Given two tight sets A and B, one of the following two statements must hold:

- $A \cup B$ and $A \cap B$ are tight, and $\chi_{\delta(A)} + \chi_{\delta(B)} = \chi_{\delta(A \cap B)} + \chi_{\delta(A \cup B)}$; or
- $A - B$ and $B - A$ are tight, and $\chi_{\delta(A)} + \chi_{\delta(B)} = \chi_{\delta(A-B)} + \chi_{\delta(B-A)}$.

(b) Use the above to prove Theorem 11.27.

11.3 Consider the following LP relaxation for the traveling salesman problem:

$$\text{minimize} \sum_{e \in E} c_e x_e$$

$$\text{subject to} \sum_{e \in \delta(S)} x_e \geq 2, \qquad \forall S \subset V, S \neq \emptyset,$$

$$0 \leq x_e \leq 1, \qquad \forall e \in E.$$

Show that for any basic feasible solution x to the linear program, there must exist some $e \in E$ such that $x_e = 1$.

11.4 Recall the definition of a branching from Exercise 7.5: We are given a directed graph $G = (V, A)$, and a designated root vertex $r \in V$. A branching is a subset $F \subseteq A$ of arcs such that for every $v \in V$, there is exactly one directed path from r to v. Note that this implies that in F the indegree of any node (except the root) is 1.

In the *bounded-degree branching problem*, we are given degree bounds b_v, and the goal is to find a branching such that the outdegree of v is at most b_v for all $v \in V$. In the following, we will give a polynomial-time algorithm to compute a branching in which the outdegree of v is at most $b_v + 2$ for all $v \in V$, given that a branching exists with outdegree b_v for all $v \in V$.

Given the input graph $G = (V, A)$ and any subset $F \subseteq A$, let $\delta^+(S)$ be the set of all arcs in A with their tails in S and heads not in S, and let $\delta^-(S)$ be the set of all arcs in A with their heads in S and their tails not in S; furthermore, let $\delta_F^+(S) = \delta^+(S) \cap F$, and let $\delta_F^-(S) = \delta^-(S) \cap F$. Then consider the following linear programming relaxation, defined for a given set of arcs A, $F \subseteq A$ and $W \subseteq V$:

$$\text{minimize} \quad \sum_{a \in A} x_a$$

$$\text{subject to} \quad \sum_{a \in \delta^-(S)} x_a \geq 1 - |\delta_F^-(S)|, \qquad \forall S \subseteq V - r,$$

$$\sum_{a \in \delta^+(v)} x_a \leq b_v - |\delta_F^+(v)|, \qquad \forall v \in W,$$

$$0 \leq x_a \leq 1, \qquad \forall a \in A - F.$$

Consider the following algorithm for the problem. Initially, $F = \emptyset$ and $W = V$. While $A - F \neq \emptyset$, find a solution to the linear programming relaxation for A, F, and W. Remove from A any arc $a \in A - F$ such that $x_a = 0$. Add to F any arc $a \in A - F$ such that $x_a = 1$. Then for any $v \in W$ such that there are at most $b_v - |\delta_F^+(v)| + 2$ arcs coming out of v in $A - F$, remove v from W and add to F all outgoing arcs from v in $A - F$. When $A - F = \emptyset$, then output any branching rooted at r in F.

(a) Prove that the linear programming relaxation is a relaxation to the problem in the sense that if there is a feasible solution to the problem given the degree bounds, then there is a feasible solution to the linear programming relaxation.

(b) Prove that the following is true for any basic feasible solution x to the linear programming relaxation, for any A, $F \subseteq A$, and $W \subseteq V$: If $0 < x_a < 1$ for all $a \in A - F$, then there exists a set $Z \subseteq W$ and a collection $\mathcal{L}$ of subsets of V such that

1. $x(\delta^-(S)) = 1$ for all $S \in \mathcal{L}$ and $x(\delta^+(v)) = b_v - |\delta_F^+(v)|$ for all $v \in Z$;
2. the characteristic vectors $\chi_{\delta^-(S)}$ over all $S \in \mathcal{L}$ and $\chi_{\delta^+(v)}$ over all $v \in Z$ are linearly independent;
3. $|A - F| = |\mathcal{L}| + |Z|$;
4. $\mathcal{L}$ is laminar.

(c) Show that at the start of any iteration of the algorithm, every arc $a \in A - F$ has its tail in W.

(d) Prove that in each iteration, there must exist some $v \in W$ such that there are at most $b_v - |\delta_F^+(v)| + 2$ arcs coming out of v in $A - F$. (Hint: First show that if $|\mathcal{L}| < \sum_{a \in A - F} x_a + 2|W|$, then such a vertex in W must exist. Then design a charging argument that charges a total strictly less than $\sum_{a \in A - F} x_a + 2|W|$ such that each $S \in \mathcal{L}$ gets at least one unit of charge.)

(e) Prove that the algorithm runs in polynomial time and produces the desired output.

11.5 The *minimum k-edge-connected subgraph problem* takes as input an undirected graph $G = (V, E)$ and a positive integer k. The goal is to find the smallest set of edges $F \subseteq E$ such that there are at least k edge-disjoint paths between each pair of vertices.

Consider the following linear programming relaxation of the problem:

$$\text{minimize} \quad \sum_{e \in E} x_e$$

$$\text{subject to} \quad \sum_{e \in \delta(S)} x_e \geq k, \quad \forall S \subseteq V,$$

$$0 \leq x_e \leq 1, \quad e \in E.$$

(a) Prove that the linear program is indeed a relaxation of the problem.

(b) Prove that the linear program can be solved in polynomial time.

(c) Suppose we obtain a basic optimal solution to the LP relaxation and round up *every* fractional variable to 1. Prove that this gives a $(1 + \frac{4}{k})$-approximation algorithm for the problem.

11.6   In this problem, we revisit the generalized assignment problem from Section 11.1 and give an iterated rounding algorithm for it. We consider a slight generalization of the problem in which for each machine i there can be at most T_i units of processing assigned to i.

We now modify the linear programming relaxation of the problem given in Section 11.1. We let E denote a set of possible (i, j) pairs for which we can assign job j to machine i. Let $M = \{1, \dots, m\}$ be the set of machines and $J = \{1, \dots, n\}$ be the set of jobs. Initially, E consists of all (i, j) such that $i \in M$, $j \in J$, and $p_{ij} \leq T_i$. We also have a subset $M' \subseteq M$, where initially $M' = M$, and a subset $J' \subseteq J$, where initially $J' = J$. We also have a total amount of processing T'_i that can be assigned to machine $i \in M'$, where T'_i is initially T_i. Then the relaxation is as follows:

$$\text{minimize} \quad \sum_{(i,j) \in E} c_{ij} x_{ij}$$

$$\text{subject to} \quad \sum_{i \in M:(i,j) \in E} x_{ij} = 1, \quad \forall j \in J',$$

$$\sum_{j \in J:(i,j) \in E} p_{ij} x_{ij} \leq T'_i, \quad \forall i \in M',$$

$$x_{ij} \geq 0, \quad \forall (i, j) \in E.$$

Consider the following algorithm: While $J' \neq \emptyset$, we find a basic optimal solution to the LP relaxation. We remove from E any pair (i, j) such that $x_{ij} = 0$. If there is a variable $x_{ij} = 1$, then we assign job j to machine i; remove j from J' and reduce T'_i by p_{ij}. Let J_i be the jobs fractionally assigned to machine $i \in M'$, so that $J_i = \{j \in J : x_{ij} > 0\}$. If there is a machine i such that either $|J_i| = 1$, or $|J_i| = 2$ and $\sum_{j \in J_i} x_{ij} \geq 1$, then remove i from M'.

(a) Show that for any basic feasible solution x to the linear program, the following is true: there exist subsets $J'' \subseteq J'$ and $M'' \subseteq M'$ such that the LP constraint $\sum_{j \in J:(i,j) \in E} p_{ij} x_{ij} = T'_i$ for all $i \in M''$, the vectors corresponding to the LP constraints for J'' and M'' are linearly independent, and $|J''| + |M''|$ is equal to the number of variables $x_{ij} > 0$.

(b) Prove that for any basic feasible solution x to the LP, either there is some $(i, j) \in E$ such that $x_{ij} \in \{0, 1\}$, or there exists some $i \in M'$ with $|J_i| = 1$, or there exists some $i \in M'$ with $|J_i| = 2$ and $\sum_{j \in J_i} x_{ij} \geq 1$.

(c) Prove that the algorithm above returns a solution with total cost at most OPT, and such that machine i is assigned total processing time $2T_i$ for all $i \in M$.

Chapter Notes

We have seen in earlier sections some examples of the use of the structure of basic feasible solutions in approximation algorithms. As mentioned in the introduction, in Exercise 1.5, we saw that for a linear programming relaxation of the vertex cover problem, for any basic feasible solution x, each variable x_i is 0, 1, or 1/2. Also, in the algorithm for the bin-packing problem in Section 4.6, we used the fact that for any basic feasible solution to the linear programming relaxation, the number of nonzero variables is at most the number of distinct piece sizes.

The first more sophisticated use of the structure of a basic feasible solution in an approximation algorithm is due to Lenstra, Shmoys, and Tardos [215]. They give a 2-approximation algorithm for scheduling unrelated parallel machines. Their algorithm is given as Exercise 11.1. This work led to the result of Section 11.1 on the generalized assignment problem; the result we give there is due to Shmoys and Tardos [263]. This result does not use the properties of a basic feasible solution; it uses only feasibility. The alternative result in Exercise 11.6 for the generalized assignment problem that does use the properties of a basic feasible solution is due to Singh [268].

The idea of iterated rounding for obtaining approximation algorithms is due to Jain [175]; he introduced the algorithm for the survivable network design problem in Section 11.3. He also introduced the use of a charging scheme to prove Theorem 11.21. The proof we give is a simplification due to Nagarajan, Ravi, and Singh [230].

The first algorithm to achieve an additive factor of 2 for the minimum-cost bounded-degree spanning tree problem is due to Goemans [134]. Iterated rounding was then applied by Singh and Lau [269] to the problem; they obtain the approximation algorithm of Section 11.2 with the additive factor of 2. Singh and Lau also have the first algorithm bounding the degrees to within an additive factor of 1. We present a somewhat simplified version of this algorithm and analysis in Section 11.2 due to Lau and Singh [209] (see also Lau, Ravi, and Singh [208]) that draws upon work of Bansal, Khandekar, and Nagarajan [32] for a more general problem. Bansal et al. introduced the idea of a fractional charging scheme. The separation oracle we give for solving the linear program (11.12) is from Cunningham [85].

Exercise 11.2 is due to Jain [175]. The result of Exercise 11.3 was shown by Boyd and Pulleyblank [56] prior to all of the work on iterated rounding. Exercise 11.4 is due to Bansal et al. [32]. Exercise 11.5 is due to Gabow, Goemans, Tardos, and Williamson [120].

CHAPTER 12

Further Uses of Random Sampling and Randomized Rounding of Linear Programs

In this chapter, we revisit – for the final time – the uncapacitated facility location problem, and consider a randomized rounding algorithm for it. As we observed in Section 5.8, a natural randomized rounding algorithm is to open each facility i independently with probability equal to its associated variable in an optimal solution to the linear programming relaxation. As we will show, the difficulty with this algorithm is that it is possible that a client will not be near an open facility. However, we overcome this difficulty by using a combination of this randomized rounding algorithm and our previous randomized algorithm that uses clustering to ensure that each client is not too far away from an open facility. This will result in an approximation algorithm with a performance guarantee of $1 + \frac{2}{e} \approx 1.736$.

We also introduce a new problem, the single-source rent-or-buy problem, in which we must either rent or buy edges to connect a set of terminals to a root vertex. Here we make use once again of random sampling by using a sample-and-augment technique: we draw a random sample of the terminals, buy edges connecting them to the root, and then augment the solution to a feasible solution by renting whatever edges are needed to make the solution feasible.

We then turn to the Steiner tree problem introduced in Exercise 2.5; recall that the goal is to find a minimum-cost set of edges that connects a set of terminals. The Steiner tree problem is a special case of the prize-collecting Steiner tree problem, the generalized Steiner tree problem, and the survivable network design problem that we have considered in previous chapters; we introduced various LP rounding and primal-dual algorithms for these problems. For the Steiner tree problem, we introduce a new linear programming relaxation, and then combine both iterated and randomized rounding to obtain a good approximation algorithm.

Finally, we consider the maximum cut problem in dense graphs, and we obtain a polynomial-time approximation scheme for the problem by using a combination of most of our tools in randomization: random sampling, randomized rounding, and Chernoff bounds.

12.1 The Uncapacitated Facility Location Problem

In this section, we turn to another randomized rounding algorithm for the uncapacitated facility location problem. This algorithm will give us the best overall performance guarantee for this problem of all the discussions in this book. Recall that the input to the problem is a set of clients D and a set of facilities F, with facility costs f_i for all facilities $i \in F$, and assignment costs c_{ij} for all facilities $i \in F$ and clients $j \in D$. We assume that the clients and facilities are in a metric space and that the assignment cost c_{ij} is the distance between client j and facility i. The goal is to select a subset of facilities to open and an assignment of clients to open facilities so as to minimize the total cost of the open facilities plus the assignment costs.

Recall the following linear programming relaxation of the problem:

$$\text{minimize} \sum_{i \in F} f_i y_i + \sum_{i \in F, j \in D} c_{ij} x_{ij}$$

$$\text{subject to} \sum_{i \in F} x_{ij} = 1, \qquad \forall j \in D, \tag{12.1}$$

$$x_{ij} \le y_i, \qquad \forall i \in F, j \in D, \tag{12.2}$$

$$x_{ij} \ge 0, \qquad \forall i \in F, j \in D,$$

$$y_i \ge 0, \qquad \forall i \in F.$$

Recall also the dual of this LP relaxation:

$$\text{maximize} \quad \sum_{j \in D} v_j$$

$$\text{subject to} \quad \sum_{j \in D} w_{ij} \le f_i, \qquad \forall i \in F,$$

$$v_j - w_{ij} \le c_{ij}, \qquad \forall i \in F, j \in D,$$

$$w_{ij} \ge 0, \qquad \forall i \in F, j \in D.$$

In Sections 4.5 and 5.8, we said that given an optimal LP solution (x^*, y^*), a client j *neighbors* a facility i if $x_{ij}^* > 0$, and we set $N(j) = \{i \in F : x_{ij}^* > 0\}$. We set $N^2(j) = \{k \in D : k \text{ neighbors some } i \in N(j)\}$. We also showed the following lemma that relates the dual variable of a client to the cost of assigning the client to a neighboring facility.

Lemma 12.1 (Lemma 4.11). *If (x^*, y^*) is an optimal solution to the facility location LP and (v^*, w^*) is an optimal solution to its dual, then $x_{ij}^* > 0$ implies $c_{ij} \le v_j^*$.*

In Section 5.8, we considered a randomized rounding algorithm for the problem that clustered the clients and facilities as in the algorithm of Section 4.5, but then used randomized rounding to decide which facility in the cluster to open. In this section, we consider applying randomized rounding directly to decide which facilities to open. In particular, suppose we decide to open each facility i with probability y_i^*. Then the expected facility cost is $\sum_{i \in F} f_i y_i^*$, which is at most OPT, and if a neighbor of a given client j is open, then the service cost for j is at most v_j^* by the lemma above. If all clients have a neighbor open, then the total cost is $\sum_{i \in F} f_i y_i^* + \sum_{j \in D} v_j^* \leq 2 \cdot \text{OPT}$. However, it is possible that for a given client j, no neighbor of j is opened. Using $1 - x \leq e^{-x}$, the probability that no neighbor of j is opened is

$$\text{Pr[no neighbor of } j \text{ open]} = \prod_{i \in N(j)} \left(1 - y_i^*\right) \leq \prod_{i \in N(j)} e^{-y_i^*}.$$

By LP constraint (12.2), $x_{ij}^* \leq y_i^*$, and by LP constraint (12.1), $\sum_{i \in N(j)} x_{ij}^* = 1$, so that this probability is at most

$$\prod_{i \in N(j)} e^{-y_i^*} \leq \prod_{i \in N(j)} e^{-x_{ij}^*} = e^{-\sum_{i \in N(j)} x_{ij}^*} = e^{-1}.$$

It is possible that this upper bound on the probability can be achieved, and in this case we do not have a good way of bounding the cost of assigning the client to the nearest open facility. Thus, we need a more sophisticated approach.

The main idea of the algorithm in this section is to combine this randomized rounding with the clustering ideas of earlier chapters. This way, if a client j has no neighboring facility open via randomized rounding, then we know that there is some facility open that is not too far away.

Before we give the algorithm, we need a primal solution to the linear program that has a particular form. We say that a solution is *complete* if whenever $x_{ij}^* > 0$, then $x_{ij}^* = y_i^*$. It is possible to take any optimal solution to the linear program and create an equivalent complete solution with the same objective function value by making additional copies of each facility (where the facility costs and service costs of the copy are identical to the original). We leave this as an exercise (Exercise 12.1) and from here on assume that we have a complete solution.

We give the algorithm in Algorithm 12.1. As in the algorithm in Section 5.8, we choose cluster centers j_k via some criterion (here minimizing v_j^* among the remaining clients), then randomly choose a neighboring facility i_k to open according to the probabilities $x_{i_k j_k}^*$. Note that by completeness $x_{i_k j_k}^* = y_{i_k}^*$. After all clients end up in some cluster, for all facilities i not in some cluster, we open them independently with probability y_i^*.

Note that this algorithm is now not the same as opening each facility i with probability y_i^* independently: if a client j is chosen in some iteration, then exactly one of its neighboring facilities will be opened. Thus, the probability of a facility being opened is now dependent on the probability of other facilities being opened. The following lemma shows that this does not affect the bound on the probability that some neighbor of a given client is opened.

Lemma 12.2. *Given an arbitrary client $j \in D$, the probability that no neighbor of j is opened is at most $\frac{1}{e}$.*

Proof. We partition the facilities neighboring j into sets X_p as follows. Let X_k be the facilities in $N(j)$ in the cluster formed in the kth iteration, and let each facility i remaining at the end of the algorithm be put in its own set X_p. Let O_k be the event that some facility in X_k is opened. Note that by the structure of the algorithm, the events O_k are now independent.

Solve LP, get optimal, complete primal solution (x^*, y^*) and dual solution (v^*, w^*)
$C \leftarrow D$
$T \leftarrow F$
$k \leftarrow 0$
while $C \neq \emptyset$ **do**
   $k \leftarrow k + 1$
   Choose $j_k \in C$ that minimizes v_j^* over all $j \in C$
   Choose exactly one $i_k \in N(j_k)$ with probability $x_{i_k j_k}^* = y_{i_k}^*$
   Open i_k
   $C \leftarrow C - \{j_k\} - N^2(j_k)$
   $T \leftarrow T - N(j_k)$
foreach $i \in T$ **do** open i with probability y_i^*
Assign each client j to nearest open facility

Algorithm 12.1. Randomized rounding algorithm for the uncapacitated facility location problem.

Let Y_k^* be the probability that event O_k occurs. Then $Y_k^* = \Pr[O_k] = \sum_{i \in X_k} y_i^*$. Furthermore, by the completeness of the solution,

$$\sum_k Y_k^* = \sum_k \sum_{i \in X_k} y_i^* = \sum_k \sum_{i \in X_k} x_{ij}^*.$$

Then since the X_k partition $N(j)$ and by LP constraint (12.1),

$$\sum_k Y_k^* = \sum_k \sum_{i \in X_k} x_{ij}^* = \sum_{i \in F} x_{ij}^* = 1.$$

By following the reasoning as given earlier, we have that

$$\Pr[\text{no neighbor of } j \text{ open}] = \prod_k \left(1 - Y_k^*\right) \leq \prod_k e^{-Y_k^*} = e^{-\sum_k Y_k^*} = e^{-1}. \qquad \square$$

We can now prove the following theorem.

Theorem 12.3. *Algorithm 12.1 is a $(1 + \frac{3}{e})$-approximation algorithm for the uncapacitated facility location problem, where $1 + \frac{3}{e} \approx 2.104$.*

Proof. We follow the proof of Theorem 5.19. In iteration k, the expected cost of the facility opened is

$$\sum_{i \in N(j_k)} f_i x_{ij_k}^* \leq \sum_{i \in N(j_k)} f_i y_i^*,$$

using the LP constraint $x_{ij_k}^* \leq y_i^*$, so that the expected cost of facilities opened in this way is

$$\sum_k \sum_{i \in N(j_k)} f_i y_i^*.$$

We open each remaining facility $i \in F - \bigcup_k N(j_k)$ with probability y_i^*, so that the total expected cost of opening facilities is $\sum_{i \in F} f_i y_i^*$.

Given an arbitrary client $j \in D$, if some neighbor of j is not opened, then as argued in the proof of Theorem 4.13, we can assign j to some open facility in its cluster at cost at most $3v_j^*$. Note that for any given facility $i \in N(j)$, the probability that i is opened is y_i^*, so that although the probabilities that different $i \in N(j)$ are opened are dependent, the expected assignment cost for j given that some $i \in N(j)$ is opened is $\sum_{i \in N(j)} c_{ij} y_i^* = \sum_{i \in N(j)} c_{ij} x_{ij}^*$, with the equality following by the completeness of the solution. Thus, the expected assignment cost for j is

Pr[some neighbor of j is open] $\cdot$ E[assignment cost|some neighbor of j is open]

$+$ Pr[no neighbor of j is open] $\cdot$ E[assignment cost|no neighbor of j is open]

$$\leq 1 \cdot \sum_{i \in N(j)} c_{ij} x_{ij}^* + \frac{1}{e} \cdot (3v_j^*).$$

Therefore, the overall expected assignment cost is at most

$$\sum_{j \in D} \sum_{i \in F} c_{ij} x_{ij}^* + \frac{3}{e} \sum_{j \in D} v_j^*,$$

and the overall expected cost is

$$\sum_{i \in F} f_i y_i^* + \sum_{j \in D} \sum_{i \in F} c_{ij} x_{ij}^* + \frac{3}{e} \sum_{j \in D} v_j^* \leq \text{OPT} + \frac{3}{e} \cdot \text{OPT} = \left(1 + \frac{3}{e}\right) \text{OPT}. \quad \square$$

We can improve the algorithm to a $(1 + \frac{2}{e})$-approximation algorithm by making a small change to how client j_k is selected in the kth iteration, and by tightening the analysis. Following our notation in Section 5.8, we let C_j^* be the assignment cost incurred by j in the LP solution, so that $C_j^* = \sum_{i \in F} c_{ij} x_{ij}^*$. As in our algorithm in that section, in the kth iteration, we choose the client j that minimizes $v_j^* + C_j^*$ instead of choosing the client that minimizes v_j^*.

Let p_j denote the probability that no neighbor of client j is opened by the algorithm; we know $p_j \leq \frac{1}{e}$. The analysis in the theorem above is slightly loose in the sense that in analyzing the expected assignment cost, we bounded the probability that some neighbor of j is opened by 1. We can use the following lemma to make this part of the analysis slightly tighter. The proof of the lemma is quite technical, and so we omit it.

Lemma 12.4. *Let A_j be the expected assignment cost for j given that no neighbor of j is opened. Then the expected assignment cost of client $j \in D$ is at most $(1 - p_j)C_j^* + p_j A_j$.*

In Algorithm 12.1, we chose client j_k in the kth iteration to minimize v_j^*, which gave us a bound $A_j \leq 3v_j^*$. By choosing j_k to minimize $v_j^* + C_j^*$, we have that $A_j \leq 2v_j^* + C_j^*$ (as in the analysis in Theorem 5.19). Thus, we get that the expected assignment cost of the modified algorithm is

$$(1 - p_j)C_j^* + p_j(2v_j^* + C_j^*) = C_j^* + 2p_j v_j^* \leq C_j^* + \frac{2}{e} v_j^*.$$

Given that the expected facility cost is at most $\sum_{i \in F} f_i y_i^*$, we get that the overall expected cost is at most

$$\sum_{i \in F} f_i y_i^* + \sum_{j \in D} C_j^* + \frac{2}{e} \sum_{j \in D} v_j^* \leq \text{OPT} + \frac{2}{e} \text{OPT}.$$

This yields the following theorem.

Theorem 12.5. *Algorithm 12.1, modified to choose j_k to minimize $v_j^* + C_j^*$, is a $(1 + \frac{2}{e})$-approximation algorithm for the uncapacitated facility location problem, where $1 + \frac{2}{e} \approx 1.736$.*

12.2 The Single-Source Rent-or-Buy Problem

In this section, we consider the *single-source rent-or-buy problem*. The input for the problem is an undirected graph $G = (V, E)$ with edge costs $c_e \geq 0$ for all $e \in E$, a root vertex $r \in V$, a set of terminals $X \subseteq V$, and a parameter $M > 1$. We need to design a network connecting all terminals to the root; for each terminal we specify a path of edges from the terminal to the root. We say that a terminal *uses* an edge if the edge is on the terminal's path to the root. To build the paths, we can both buy and rent edges. We can buy edges at cost Mc_e, and once bought, any terminal can use the edge. We can also rent edges at cost c_e, but then we need to pay the rental cost for each terminal using the edge. The goal is to find a feasible network that minimizes the total cost. We can formalize this by letting $B \subseteq E$ be the set of edges that are bought, and letting R_t be the set of edges that are rented by terminal $t \in X$. Then for each $t \in X$, the set of edges $B \cup R_t$ must contain a path from t to the root r. Let $c(F) = \sum_{e \in F} c_e$ for any $F \subseteq E$. Then the total cost of the solution is $Mc(B) + \sum_{t \in X} c(R_t)$. We must find edges B to buy and R_t to rent that minimize this overall cost.

We will give a randomized approximation algorithm for the problem that cleverly trades off the cost of buying versus renting. The *sample-and-augment algorithm* draws a sample of terminals by marking each terminal t with probability $1/M$ independently. Let D be the random set of marked terminals. We then find a Steiner tree T on the set of terminals D plus the root, and buy the edges of T. To find a Steiner tree, we use the 2-approximation algorithm of Exercise 2.5 that computes a minimum spanning tree on the metric completion of the graph. We then augment the solution by renting paths from the unmarked terminals to the tree T. To do this, we find the shortest path from each unmarked t to the closest vertex in T, and rent these edges.

The analysis of the sample-and-augment algorithm begins by observing that the expected cost of buying the edges in the tree T is at most twice the cost of an optimal solution to the rent-or-buy problem.

Lemma 12.6.

$$E[Mc(T)] \leq 2\,\text{OPT}.$$

Proof. To prove the lemma, we demonstrate a Steiner tree T^* on the set of marked terminals such that the expected cost of buying the edges of T^* is at most OPT. Since we are using a 2-approximation algorithm to find T, the lemma statement then follows.

We consider an optimal solution to the problem: let B^* be the set of bought edges, and let R_t^* be the edges rented by terminal t. Consider the edges from B^* together with the union of edges of R_t^* over the marked terminals t. Note that this set of edges certainly contains some Steiner tree T^* on the set of marked terminals plus the root. We now want to analyze the cost of buying this set of edges. The essential idea of the analysis is that although we now have to pay M times the cost of the rented edges in each R_t^* for marked t, since we marked t with probability $1/M$, the expected cost of these edges will be the same as the renting cost of the optimal solution. To see this formally, if D is the random set of marked terminals, then

$$E[Mc(T^*)] \le Mc(B^*) + E[M \sum_{t \in D} c(R_t^*)]$$

$$= Mc(B^*) + M \sum_{t \in X} c(R_t^*)\Pr[t \in D]$$

$$= Mc(B^*) + \sum_{t \in X} c(R_t^*)$$

$$= \mathrm{OPT}. \qquad \qquad \qquad \square$$

To complete the analysis, we show that the expected renting cost is no more than the expected buying cost.

Lemma 12.7.

$$E\left[\sum_{t \in X} c(R_t)\right] \le E[Mc(T)].$$

Proof. To prove this, let us be a bit more precise about the algorithm; then we will alter the algorithm to give an equivalent algorithm, and prove the statement for the equivalent algorithm.

Let D be the (random) set of marked terminals. We run Prim's minimum spanning tree algorithm on the metric completion of the graph, starting with the root r (see Section 2.4 for a discussion of Prim's algorithm). Prim's algorithm maintains a set $S \subseteq D \cup \{r\}$ of vertices in the spanning tree, and chooses the cheapest edge e that has one endpoint in S and the other in $D - S$ to add next to the spanning tree; the endpoint of e in $D - S$ is then added to S.

We now alter the algorithm by not choosing D in advance. Rather, we choose the cheapest edge e with one endpoint in S and the other from the set of all terminals whose marking status has not been determined. Let t be the endpoint of e whose marking status is not determined. At this point, we decide, with probability $1/M$, whether to mark t. If t is marked, then we add t to D and to S, and add the edge e to the tree. If t is not marked, then we do not add t to D or S, and edge e is not added to the tree. Note that we get the same tree T on D via this process as in the case that the random set D was drawn before running the algorithm.

We let β_t for a terminal t be a random variable associated with the cost of connecting t to the tree via bought edges; we call it the buying cost. We let β_t of a marked terminal t be M times the cost of the edge that first connects it to the tree, and we let β_t be zero if t is not marked. In our modified algorithm above, β_t is the cost of the edge that connects t to S when t is marked. The total cost of the tree is then the sum of the buying costs of all the marked terminals in the tree, so that $\sum_{t \in D} \beta_t = Mc(T)$. In a similar way, we let ρ_t for a terminal t be a random variable giving the cost of renting edges to connect t to the tree.

Now consider a given terminal t at the time we decide whether to mark t or not. Let S be the set of vertices already selected by Prim's algorithm at this point in time, and let e be the edge chosen by Prim's algorithm with t as one endpoint and with the other endpoint in S. If we mark t, we buy edge e at cost Mc_e. If we do not mark t, then we could rent edge e at cost c_e, and since all the vertices in S are marked, this will connect t to the root; thus, $\rho_t \leq c_e$. Hence, the expected buying cost of t is $E[\beta_t] = \frac{1}{M} \cdot Mc_e = c_e$, whereas its expected cost of renting edges to connect t to the root is $E[\rho_t] \leq (1 - \frac{1}{M}) \cdot c_e \leq c_e$. Observe that this is true no matter what point in the algorithm t is considered. Thus,

$$E\left[\sum_{t \in X} c(R_t)\right] = E\left[\sum_{t \in X} \rho_t\right] \leq E\left[\sum_{t \in X} \beta_t\right] = E\left[\sum_{t \in D} \beta_t\right] = E[Mc(T)]. \qquad \square$$

The following theorem is then immediate.

Theorem 12.8. *The sample-and-augment algorithm described above is a randomized 4-approximation algorithm for the single-source rent-or-buy problem.*

Proof. For the solution $B = T$ and R_t computed by the randomized algorithm, we have that

$$E\left[Mc(T) + \sum_{t \in X} c(R_t)\right] \leq 2 \cdot E[Mc(T)] \leq 4\,\mathrm{OPT}. \qquad \square$$

In Exercise 12.2, we consider the multicommodity rent-or-buy problem, which is an extension of the single-source rent-or-buy problem to multiple source-sink pairs. We see that the sample-and-augment algorithm also leads to a good approximation algorithm for this problem.

12.3 The Steiner Tree Problem

The Steiner tree problem provides an excellent example of a problem for which our understanding of its combinatorial structure has worked hand in hand with the design and analysis of a linear programming-based approach to approximation algorithm design. Furthermore, we will combine two techniques already discussed for rounding LP solutions, by relying on an iterative use of randomized rounding. The *Steiner tree problem*, as discussed in Exercise 2.5, is as follows: Given an undirected graph $G = (V, E)$, and a subset of nodes $R \subseteq V$, along with a nonnegative edge cost $c_e \geq 0$ for each edge $e \in E$, find a minimum-cost subset of edges $F \subseteq E$, such that $G = (V, F)$ contains a path between each pair of nodes in R. As discussed in that exercise, by considering the metric completion of the graph, we may assume without loss of generality that the input graph G is complete, and that the costs satisfy the triangle inequality. In Section 7.4, we showed that the primal-dual method, based on a relatively

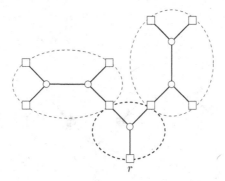

Figure 12.1. A Steiner tree. The terminals are squares, and the Steiner nodes are circles. The dashed ovals indicate the full components of the Steiner tree.

weak LP formulation, provides a 2-approximation algorithm for a more general problem in which the connectivity requirement must be satisfied for only specified pairs of nodes. The nodes in R for which there is a connectivity requirement are traditionally called *terminals*, whereas the remaining nodes are called *Steiner nodes*.

For the Steiner tree problem, a (minimal) feasible solution corresponds to a tree (a *Steiner tree*) in which all leaves are nodes in R; furthermore, there is a decomposition of each such Steiner tree into its *full components*, which will play a critical role in this discussion. A full component of a Steiner tree is a maximal subgraph in which *no* non-leaf node is a terminal. A Steiner tree and its decomposition into full components are shown in Figure 12.1. It is easy to see that if we start with the optimal Steiner tree, and this decomposition yields full components with node sets $V_1, V_2, \ldots, V_s$, then the full component on V_i must be an optimal Steiner tree for the input on the subgraph induced by V_i, $i = 1, \ldots, s$. Furthermore, it is also easy to see that if we contract the nodes in V_i in this optimal Steiner tree, then the tree resulting from this contraction must also be an optimal Steiner tree for the induced subproblem. Finally, an optimal Steiner tree for G that spans the set of nodes $V' \subseteq V$ must be a minimum spanning tree for the input induced by the subset V'. This suggests a very natural approach to designing an approximation algorithm (or even an optimization algorithm!): identify a full component to contract, contract that component, and iterate. Indeed, all known approximation algorithms for the Steiner tree problem with constant performance guarantee better than 2 are based on variants of this idea.

One natural approach to providing a stronger LP relaxation for the Steiner tree problem, as compared to the one discussed in Section 7.4, is to select one of the terminal nodes (arbitrarily) as a *root* node r, and to view each undirected edge connecting nodes u and v as two directed edges (u, v) and (v, u), both of cost equal to the cost of the original undirected edge. We then consider a directed network design problem in which we wish to select a subset F of these directed edges such that for each non-root node $v \in R$, there is a path from v to r using just edges in F. This gives rise to an integer programming formulation, known as the *bidirected cut formulation*, in which we require that for each nonempty subset $S \subseteq V - \{r\}$ with $S \cap R \neq \emptyset$, there exists an edge $(u, v) \in F$ that crosses this cut, that is, $u \in S$ and $v \notin S$. Let $\delta^+(S)$ be the set

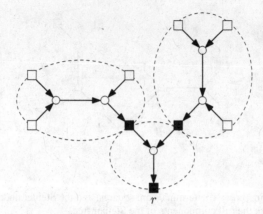

Figure 12.2. The Steiner tree of Figure 12.1, in which each full component is directed. The sink of each full component is indicated by a black square.

of arcs in which $(u, v) \in S$ when $u \in S$ and $v \notin S$. Let A be the set of arcs. Then the linear programming relaxation of this integer program is

$$\text{minimize} \sum_{e \in A} c_e y_e$$

$$\text{subject to} \sum_{e \in \delta^+(S)} y_e \geq 1, \qquad \forall S \subseteq V - \{r\}, S \cap R \neq \emptyset,$$

$$y_e \geq 0, \qquad \forall e \in A.$$

Although not the most direct proof, one consequence of Exercise 7.5 is that if we consider an input for which $V = R$ – that is, there are no Steiner nodes, and hence this is really a minimum spanning tree instance – then this LP relaxation of this bidirected cut formulation has integer extreme points, and hence the LP relaxation is the initial integer program.

We shall present algorithms for the Steiner tree problem that combine this idea with the notion of the full component decomposition. Again, we select one of the terminals as the root node r. Then, for any Steiner tree, we orient its edges toward the root, and decompose this tree into its full components. Each full component is now a directed graph (as shown in Figure 12.2). Furthermore, if we label each node in the graph with its distance (in terms of the number of edges in the (unique) path) to the root r, for each full component C, we shall call the node with minimum distance label the $sink(C)$ – of course, this sink must be a terminal node, and the induced directed Steiner tree on C is directed toward $sink(C)$, in much the same way that the entire Steiner tree is directed toward the root r. Such directed full components, with their specified sink nodes, will be the building blocks of our new integer programming formulation. Abusing notation slightly, let C now denote a directed full component with specified sink node; we let $R(C)$ denote the terminals of C (which includes $sink(C)$). Let $\mathcal{C}$ denote the set of all such directed full components.

We introduce a 0-1 decision variable x_C for each such directed full component $C \in \mathcal{C}$. Note that $c(C)$ denotes the total cost of the edges in the directed full component C. To specify a Steiner tree, we merely list its directed full components. Of course, we need to formulate a set of constraints that enforces that a given set of directed full components is, in fact, a feasible Steiner tree. We can do this again by cut constraints: for each subset $S \subseteq R - \{r\}$, we require that there is a directed full component C included such that $sink(C) \notin S$, but there exists some other terminal node $v \in R(C) - \{sink(C)\}$ such that $v \in S$. Extending the usual notation in which $\delta(S)$ denotes the set of edges that cross the cut S, we introduce the notation that $\Delta(S)$ is the set of directed full components that satisfy this cut-crossing condition.

Thus, we obtain the following linear programming relaxation of the Steiner tree problem:

$$\text{minimize} \quad \sum_{C \in \mathcal{C}} c(C) x_C \tag{12.3}$$

$$\text{subject to} \quad \sum_{C \in \mathcal{C} : C \in \Delta(S)} x_C \geq 1, \quad \forall S \subseteq R - \{r\}, \ S \neq \emptyset, \tag{12.4}$$

$$x_C \geq 0, \quad \forall C \in \mathcal{C}.$$

This LP reflects the beauty of mathematical notation: at a glance, it seems like a perfectly innocuous linear program. But encoded in this notation, we see that there are an exponential number of variables, *and* an exponential number of constraints. This means that we cannot make direct use of the ellipsoid method in order to solve this linear program in polynomial time. Fortunately, we can limit our attention to a weaker LP, without too great a loss in the quality of the bound that it provides: simply restrict attention to those full components with at most k terminals, where k is some fixed constant. If we do this for integer solutions, we obtain a formulation of the so-called *k-restricted Steiner tree problem*, and it has been shown that the optimal solution to this problem has the following strong property.

Theorem 12.9. *For each input to the Steiner tree problem, and for each fixed integer k, the optimal value of the k-restricted Steiner tree problem is within a factor of $1 + \frac{1}{\lfloor \log_2 k \rfloor}$ of the optimal value for the Steiner tree problem.*

We give a special case of this theorem as Exercise 12.6.

This suggests that we consider a relaxed version of the linear program (12.3), in which we replace $\mathcal{C}$ by the set of directed full components with at most k terminals. In fact, without loss of generality, we can be even more restrictive in setting up this linear program. Recall that in an optimal (integer) solution, we know that each full component must be an optimal Steiner tree on the given set of terminals. Similarly, in any optimal fractional solution, we can restrict attention to those variables x_C for which the directed full component C is an optimal Steiner tree on that set of terminals (with the specified sink node). Furthermore, since we have instances obeying the triangle inequality, we can assume without loss of generality that no Steiner node has degree two, since that node can be shortcut from the solution to yield a Steiner tree with one fewer node of no greater cost. Since the average degree of a node in a tree is less than 2 (in fact, exactly $2 - 2/n$ in an n-node graph), we see that in a full component with k terminals (each of degree one), there can be at most $k - 2$ Steiner nodes (each of degree at least 3). Once we specify the terminals and the Steiner nodes for a full component, then an optimal Steiner tree is a minimum spanning tree on this combined set of nodes, and so, with a specified sink, we know that there are at most kn^{2k-2} directed full components that need to be considered for the k-restricted component linear programming relaxation. Let $\mathcal{C}_k$ denote this restricted set of directed full components, and let $M = |\mathcal{C}_k|$.

By applying Theorem 12.9 to each full component in the support of the optimal fractional solution, it is straightforward to obtain the following corollary: if we consider the k-restricted LP to be a variant of the LP (12.3) in which each occurrence of the set $\mathcal{C}$ is replaced by the set $\mathcal{C}_k$, then the two optimal LP values are within a factor of $1 + \frac{1}{\lfloor \log_2 k \rfloor}$ of each other. Thus, if we can round the optimal solution of the k-restricted component LP to yield a Steiner tree, while losing a factor of α, then the resulting approximation algorithm is "nearly" an α-approximation algorithm, in that for any fixed $\epsilon > 0$, we can obtain an $(\alpha + \epsilon)$-approximation algorithm by setting k to a sufficiently large constant. Of course, we must still argue that the k-restricted component linear program is polynomial-time solvable, since there are still an exponential number of constraints. There are a number of approaches that suffice; once again, simple minimum-cut computations show that the inequalities corresponding to (12.4) either are all satisfied or identify a violated inequality. We leave the proof that the linear program is polynomial-time solvable to Exercise 12.5.

We can solve this LP relaxation, but how do we make use of the optimal fractional solution? We shall combine randomized rounding with an iterative rounding approach. We start with the minimum spanning tree on the graph induced by the set of terminals (which we call the *minimum terminal spanning tree*), and in each iteration, we randomly select a directed full component in proportion to its fractional value in the optimal fractional solution, contract that component by identifying its terminals, and then iterate. This process continues for a fixed number of iterations, at which point we settle for the final minimum terminal spanning tree to connect the remaining terminals. Since the set of terminals evolves over the execution of the algorithm, we shall let $mst(R')$ denote the cost of the minimum terminal spanning tree when $R' \subseteq R$ is the terminal set. In a given iteration, we start with a minimum terminal spanning tree T and perform a "contraction" defined by a directed full component C to yield a remaining set of terminals R'; the contraction reflects the commitment to include the edges in C in the solution, incurring a cost equal to $c(C)$, whereas it also "simplifies" the residual problem, providing a savings of

$$drop_T(C) = c(T) - mst(R').$$

The analysis of the algorithm is based on the following lemma that links the value of the fractional solution to these incremental improvements.

Lemma 12.10. *Let T be a terminal spanning tree, and let x be a feasible solution to the directed component cut-covering relaxation (12.3); then*

$$c(T) \le \sum_{C \in \mathcal{C}} drop_T(C) x_C. \tag{12.5}$$

Before proving this lemma, we first show how it provides the key to the analysis of our iterative approximation algorithm. Focus on one iteration of the algorithm; let T denote the minimum terminal spanning tree at the start of the iteration, let x denote the optimal fractional solution to the directed component relaxation, and let $\Sigma = \sum_C x_C$.

Let C denote the directed full component selected in this iteration (which occurred with probability x_C / Σ), and let T' denote the resulting minimum terminal spanning tree. Then, by taking into account the random selection of the component C, we see that

$$
\begin{aligned}
E[c(T')] &= c(T) - E[drop_T(C)] \\
&= c(T) - \sum_C (x_C / \Sigma) drop_T(C) \\
&\leq \left(1 - \frac{1}{\Sigma}\right) c(T) \\
&\leq \left(1 - \frac{1}{\Sigma}\right) \cdot 2\, \text{OPT},
\end{aligned}
$$

where OPT denotes the optimal value for the given Steiner tree input. In fact, we can strengthen this final inequality by the following lemma, which relates the cost of the minimum terminal spanning tree to the optimal value of the directed component linear programming relaxation.

Lemma 12.11. *For any input to the Steiner tree problem, the cost of the minimum terminal spanning tree T is at most twice the cost of the optimal fractional solution x for the directed component linear programming relaxation (12.3).*

Proof. We first transform x into a feasible fractional solution y to the bidirected cut relaxation for the input induced on the terminals R. The cost of y will be at most twice the cost of x, and by the integrality of the bidirected cut relaxation in this case (since then all nodes are terminals), we may conclude that the minimum terminal spanning tree costs no more than y. This completes the proof of the lemma.

To construct y, we initially set $y = 0$, then, in turn, consider each directed component C for which $x_C > 0$. Consider the "doubling" of each edge in the Steiner tree for this component C (ignoring edge directions), to yield an Eulerian graph. This Eulerian tour can then be shortcut to yield a cycle on the terminals of C, $R(C)$. We delete one edge of the cycle (chosen arbitrarily), and then orient the edges of this terminal spanning tree on $R(C)$ toward the root of the component, $sink(C)$. For each of the edges in this directed spanning tree, we increment its current value y_e by x_C. If we view each component C as providing capacity for x_C to flow from each terminal in $R(C)$ to the node $sink(C)$, then we see that we have provided exactly the same additional capacity from each terminal to $sink(C)$ in the shortcut solution that uses only terminal nodes. Since the feasibility of x ensures that for each node there is at least total capacity 1 from that node to the root, so must the modified construction for y. But this means that y is a feasible fractional solution for the bidirected cut relaxation, and this completes the proof of the lemma. □

Intuitively, if in each iteration we decrease the cost of a minimum terminal spanning tree by a factor of $(1 - 1/\Sigma)$, then if we apply the same technique for Σ iterations, we decrease the cost of the minimum terminal spanning tree by a factor that is at most $1/e$. Therefore, if we consider $\ell\Sigma$ iterations, we decrease the resulting cost by a factor of $(1/e)^\ell$. By Lemma 12.11, we know in fact that if we start with the minimum terminal spanning tree, the end result has an expected cost at most $2(1/e)^{\ell}$ times the optimal value of the directed component relaxation. However, in each iteration, this decrease is paid for by the connection cost $c(C)$ of the selected component C. Due to the random selection rule, the expected cost incurred is equal to $\sum_C (x_C / \Sigma) c(C)$, which is $1/\Sigma$ times the cost of the optimal fractional solution x for the current directed component relaxation. One technical convenience of bounding this cost by the optimal fractional value is that this value is non-increasing over the course of the algorithm (by again taking the capacity installation view of the directed component relaxation as in the proof of Lemma 12.11). Hence, after $\ell \Sigma$ iterations, we incur a total cost that is at most ℓ times the cost of the initial optimal solution to the directed component relaxation. In total, the result after $\ell \Sigma$ iterations has cost at most $(2e^{-\ell} + \ell)$ times this LP value; if we set ℓ so as to minimize this quantity, then $\ell = \ln 2$, and we obtain a performance guarantee (and an integrality gap) of $1 + \ln 2 \leq 1.694$.

This intuition oversimplifies one further technical issue – there is no reason that the variables of the relaxation need sum to Σ in each iteration. This can be avoided by the following simple workaround. We know that $\Sigma \leq M$, the number of variables in the k-restricted component LP in which we have only directed full components for the optimal Steiner tree on each set of at most k terminals. We add a dummy full component, corresponding to just the root node, and then can add the constraint that the variables must sum to M, and so we run the algorithm for $(\ln 2)M$ iterations, which is a polynomial bound. (It is significant to note that by stating the algorithm in this way, we have made it much less efficient, since an overwhelming fraction of the time, we will sample the dummy full component, which results in no contraction but incurs no additional cost.)

We turn next to gaining a greater structural understanding of $drop_T(C)$, which we will use to prove Lemma 12.10.

Let T be a minimum terminal spanning tree, and consider the contraction corresponding to some full component C, and hence we identify the nodes $R(C)$; what happens to the minimum terminal spanning tree? Since $|R(C)|$ nodes are replaced by 1 node, we need $|R(C)| - 1$ fewer edges to connect the resulting terminals. Suppose we first identify just two terminal nodes u and v. This is equivalent to having an edge connecting them of cost 0, and so the effect on the minimum terminal spanning tree is to delete from T the maximum-cost edge on the (unique) path between u and v in T. More generally, in identifying all of the vertices in $R(C)$, we can again consider the effect of adding an edge of cost 0 between each pair of vertices in $R(C)$. It is easy to see that a new minimum terminal spanning tree T' can be formed from a spanning tree on $R(C)$ (of cost 0) plus a subset of the edges in T: if this is not the case and there is a new edge e used in T' but not in T (other than the dummy edges of cost 0), then we could do an interchange and replace e by a cheapest edge in T that crosses the cut defined by deleting e from T'. Thus, we can define $Drop_T(C)$ as the set of $|R(C)| - 1$ edges in T that are deleted from the minimum terminal spanning tree by contracting the nodes in $R(C)$, and $drop_T(C)$ is the total cost of these edges. Notice also that we could find the set $Drop_T(C)$ by building an auxiliary complete graph with node set corresponding to $R(C)$, where the weight for each edge (u, v) is the maximum-cost edge in the path from u to v in T, and then finding a maximum-weight spanning tree in this auxiliary graph. One interpretation is that there is a correspondence between the edges of T in $Drop_T(C)$ and edges in the selected maximum-weight spanning tree in this auxiliary graph.

We now turn to the proof of Lemma 12.10.

Proof of Lemma 12.10. At the core of this proof is the integrality of the bidirected cut formulation for the minimum spanning tree problem. The basic steps of this proof are as follows: We construct an undirected multigraph $H = (R, F)$ with (new) edge costs, and devise a feasible fractional solution y to the bidirected cut formulation of cost equal to the right-hand side of (12.5); on the other hand, we show that any spanning tree of H has cost at least $c(T)$. The integrality of the formulation implies the lemma.

Consider in turn each directed full component C; each component C will cause us to include certain edges in H, and to adjust the fractional solution y, which is initially equal to 0. For the directed component C, consider the auxiliary (undirected) graph built on $R(C)$ in the construction above. Take the maximum-weight spanning tree on $R(C)$ (whose edges correspond to $Drop_T(C)$), and include each of these edges in H with cost equal to its weight in the auxiliary graph. Now direct this tree toward the node $sink(C)$, and for each edge e in this directed tree, increment y_e by x_C. It is clear that this process generates a fractional solution of total cost exactly equal to $\sum_C x_C drop_T(C)$.

We need to establish that y is a feasible fractional solution for the bidirected cut formulation for the multigraph H. The solution x is a feasible fractional solution to the directed component formulation, and we can view this as installing, for each component C, capacity x_C from each non-sink node in $R(C)$ to the node $sink(C)$; by the max-flow/min-cut theorem, the feasibility of x means that in total, these installations support a flow of 1 from each node in R to the root node r. However, the solution y does this as well; for each component C, we increment y so as to install an additional capacity of x_C (through a directed spanning tree) from each non-sink node in $R(C)$ to the node $sink(C)$. Hence, in total, we have installed sufficient capacity so that a flow of 1 can be sent from each terminal to the root. Hence, y is a feasible solution to the bidirected cut formulation.

Finally, we show that the cost of any spanning tree in H is at least $c(T)$. It suffices to show that if we consider G', which is the union of H and T, then T is a minimum spanning tree in G'. A sufficient condition for a spanning tree T to be minimum-cost is that the cost of each edge (u, v) not in T is at least the maximum cost in the path in T connecting u and v. But note that by our construction, each edge inserted in H has cost exactly equal to that maximum cost, and so T is a minimum spanning tree in G'. □

Putting the pieces together, we have now proved the following theorem.

Theorem 12.12. *The iterated randomized rounding algorithm yields a 1.694-approximation algorithm for the Steiner tree problem; furthermore, the integrality gap of the directed component relaxation is at most 1.694.*

In fact, a similar framework can be used to prove a significantly stronger performance guarantee of 1.5. The key observation is that when one selects a directed full component C and identifies its endpoints, not only does the minimum terminal spanning tree cost decrease, but the cost of the optimal Steiner tree decreases as well, albeit by a factor of

$(1 - 1/(2M))$ instead. Nonetheless, this allows for a somewhat different balancing of terms, and yields the stronger performance guarantee. Interestingly, this technique does not prove a stronger upper bound on the integrality gap of the directed component LP.

12.4 Everything at Once:
Finding a Large Cut in a Dense Graph

We now turn to a result that will require most of the tools we developed in Chapter 5: randomized rounding, Chernoff bounds, and random sampling. We will apply these to the maximum cut problem (MAX CUT) introduced in Section 5.1. Recall that in the maximum cut problem, the input is an undirected graph $G = (V, E)$ and nonnegative weights $w_{ij} \geq 0$ for each edge $(i, j) \in E$, and the goal is to partition the vertex set into two parts, U and $W = V - U$, so as to maximize the weight of the edges whose two endpoints are in different parts, one in U and one in W. In the case $w_{ij} = 1$ for all edges $(i, j) \in E$, we have an *unweighted* maximum cut problem.

In this section, we will show that we can obtain a polynomial-time approximation scheme for the unweighted maximum cut problem in dense graphs by using a sophisticated combination of the randomization techniques introduced in Chapter 5. Recall that a graph is dense if it has at least $\alpha \binom{n}{2}$ edges for some constant $\alpha > 0$. In Theorem 5.3 of Section 5.1, we gave a simple $\frac{1}{2}$-approximation algorithm for the maximum cut problem. The analysis shows that the algorithm finds a cut whose expected value is at least $\frac{1}{2} \sum_{(i,j) \in E} w_{ij}$. Thus, it must be the case that OPT $\geq \frac{1}{2} \sum_{(i,j) \in E} w_{ij}$. It follows that in an unweighted dense graph, we know that OPT $\geq \frac{\alpha}{2} \binom{n}{2}$.

Recall that in Section 5.12 we introduced a sampling technique for coloring dense 3-colorable graphs. We would like to use the same sampling technique for the maximum cut problem on unweighted dense graphs. That is, suppose we can draw a sample of the vertices of the graph and assume that we know whether each vertex of the sample is in U or W for an optimal cut. If the sample size is $O(\log n)$, we can enumerate all the possible placements of these vertices in U and W, including the one corresponding to an optimal cut. In the case of trying to color a 3-colorable graph, knowledge of the correct coloring of the sample was enough to infer the coloring of the rest of the graph. What can we do in this case? In the case of coloring, we showed that with high probability, each vertex in the graph had some neighbor in the sample S. Here we will show that by using the sample we can get an estimate for each vertex of how many neighbors are in U in an optimal solution that is accurate to within $\pm \epsilon n$. Once we have such estimates we can use randomized rounding of a linear program in order to determine which of the remaining vertices should be placed in U. Finally, we use Chernoff bounds to show that the solution obtained by randomized rounding is close to the optimal solution.

We draw our sample in a slightly different fashion than we did for the 3-coloring algorithm. Given a constant $c > 0$ and a constant ϵ, $0 < \epsilon < 1$, we draw a multiset S of exactly $(c \log n)/\epsilon^2$ vertices by choosing vertices at random with replacement. As in the case of 3-coloring a graph, we can now in polynomial time enumerate all possible ways of splitting the sample set S into two parts. Let us say that $x_i = 0$ if we assign vertex i to U and $x_i = 1$ if we assign vertex i to W. Let x^* be an optimal solution to the maximum cut problem. Let $u_i(x)$ be the number of neighbors of vertex i in U given an assignment x of vertices. Observe that $\sum_{i=1}^n u_i(x)x_i$ gives the value of cut for the assignment x: when $x_i = 1$ and $i \in W$, there are $u_i(x)$ edges from i to vertices in U, so that this sum counts exactly the set of edges in the cut. We can give a reasonably good estimate of $u_i(x)$ for all vertices i by calculating the number of neighbors of i that are in S and assigned to U, then scaling by $n/|S|$. In other words, if $\hat{u}_i(x)$ is our estimate of the neighbors of i in U, then

$$\hat{u}_i(x) = \frac{n}{|S|} \sum_{j \in S : (i,j) \in E} (1 - x_j).$$

Note that we can calculate this estimate given only the values of the x_j for $j \in S$.

To prove that these estimates are good, we will need the following inequality, known as *Hoeffding's inequality*.

Fact 12.13 (Hoeffding's inequality). *Let* $X_1, X_2, \ldots, X_\ell$ *be* ℓ *independent 0-1 random variables, not necessarily identically distributed. Then for* $X = \sum_{i=1}^\ell X_i$, $\mu = E[X]$, *and* $b > 0$,

$$\Pr[|X - \mu| \geq b] \leq e^{-2b^2/\ell}.$$

We can now prove bounds on the quality of the estimates.

Lemma 12.14. *With probability* $1 - 2n^{-2c}$,

$$u_i(x) - cn \leq \hat{u}_i(x) \leq u_i(x) + \epsilon n$$

for any given $i \in V$.

Proof. Let $N(i)$ be the neighbors of i in G; that is, $N(i) = \{j \in V : (i, j) \in E\}$. Let Y_j be a random variable for the jth vertex in S. If the jth vertex in S is some $k \in N(i)$, we let $Y_j = 1 - x_k$ and let $Y_j = 0$ otherwise. Note that the probability that $k \in N(i)$ is $|N(i)|/n$ since we chose the jth vertex of S randomly with replacement. Then the expected value of Y_j given that $j \in N(i)$ is $\frac{1}{|N(i)|} \sum_{k \in N(i)} (1 - x_k)$, so that the unconditional expected value of Y_j is

$$E[Y_j] = \frac{|N(i)|}{n} \cdot \frac{1}{|N(i)|} \sum_{k \in N(i)} (1 - x_k) = \frac{1}{n} u_i(x).$$

Thus, if $Y = \sum_{j=1}^{|S|} Y_j$, we have $\mu = E[Y] = \frac{|S|}{n} u_i(x)$. Note that $\hat{u}_i(x) = \frac{n}{|S|} Y$. If we now apply the Hoeffding inequality with $b = \epsilon|S|$, we have that

$$\Pr\left[\left| Y - \frac{|S|}{n} u_i(x) \right| \geq \epsilon|S| \right] \leq 2e^{-2(\epsilon|S|)^2/|S|} = 2e^{-2\epsilon^2|S|} = 2e^{-2c \ln n} = 2n^{-2c},$$

so that $\frac{|S|}{n} u_i(x) - \epsilon|S| \leq Y \leq \frac{|S|}{n} u_i(x) + \epsilon|S|$ with probability at least $1 - 2n^{-2c}$. Multiplying the inequalities by $n/|S|$, we get the desired result. $\square$

Since $|S|$ is sufficiently small, we can enumerate all the possible settings of the x_i for $i \in S$; one of these will correspond to an optimal solution x^*, and thus we will have good estimates $\hat{u}_i(x^*)$ for this particular setting. We will now turn to showing how to use these estimates to obtain a good cut. Note that in enumerating all possible settings of x_i for $i \in S$, we will not know which one corresponds to x^*. However, we will show that for the setting that corresponds to x^*, we will produce a cut of size at least $(1 - \epsilon')$ OPT, for a specified $\epsilon' > 0$. Thus, if we return the largest cut produced, we are guaranteed to produce a cut of size at least this large.

From now on, we assume that we have estimates $\hat{u}_i(x^*)$ for all i such that $u_i(x^*) - \epsilon n \leq \hat{u}_i(x^*) \leq u_i(x^*) + \epsilon n$. To produce a good cut given these estimates, we use randomized rounding. Consider the following linear program:

$$\text{maximize} \quad \sum_{i=1}^{n} \hat{u}_i(x^*) y_i$$

$$\text{subject to} \quad \sum_{j:(i,j)\in E} (1 - y_j) \geq \hat{u}_i(x^*) - \epsilon n, \quad i = 1, \ldots, n, \qquad (12.6)$$

$$\sum_{j:(i,j)\in E} (1 - y_j) \leq \hat{u}_i(x^*) + \epsilon n, \quad i = 1, \ldots, n,$$

$$0 \leq y_i \leq 1, \quad i = 1, \ldots, n.$$

Suppose that the variables y_i are integer. Then since $u_i(y) = \sum_{j:(i,j)\in E}(1 - y_j)$, the constraints enforce that $\hat{u}_i(x^*) - \epsilon n \leq u_i(y) \leq \hat{u}_i(x^*) + \epsilon n$. Note then that $y = x^*$ is a feasible solution for the linear program. Furthermore, if the objective function were $\sum_{i=1}^{n} u_i(x^*) y_i$ (rather than using the estimates $\hat{u}_i(x^*)$), then the value of the LP solution with $y = x^*$ would be OPT, since we earlier observed that $\sum_{i=1}^{n} u_i(x^*) x_i^*$ counts the number of edges in the cut of the assignment x^*.

We show below that by using the known estimates $\hat{u}_i(x^*)$ in the objective function instead of the unknown values $u_i(x^*)$, the value of this linear program is still nearly OPT. Our algorithm then will be to apply randomized rounding to the solution to the linear program. Using Chernoff bounds, we can then show that the solution obtained is only slightly smaller than that of the LP, and hence almost OPT.

Lemma 12.15. *The value of the linear programming relaxation (12.6) is at least* $(1 - \frac{4\epsilon}{\alpha})$ OPT.

Proof. As observed above, the solution $y = x^*$ is a feasible solution to the linear program. Since the objective function is $\sum_{i=1}^{n} \hat{u}_i(x^*) y_i$, the solution $y = x^*$ has value

$$\sum_{i=1}^{n} \hat{u}_i(x^*) x_i^* \geq \sum_{i=1}^{n} (u_i(x^*) - \epsilon n) x_i^*$$

$$\geq \text{OPT} - \epsilon n \sum_{i=1}^{n} x_i^*.$$

Since we assume there is at least one node in U in an optimal cut, we know that $\sum_{i=1}^{n} x_i^* \leq n - 1$. Then since we know that OPT $\geq \frac{\alpha}{2}\binom{n}{2}$, we have

$$\sum_{i=1}^{n} \hat{u}_i(x^*) x_i^* \geq \text{OPT} - \epsilon n(n - 1)$$

$$\geq \left(1 - \frac{4\epsilon}{\alpha}\right) \text{OPT}. \qquad \square$$

We now show that randomized rounding of the linear programming relaxation gives a good solution. Let y^* be an optimal solution to the linear program, and let $\bar{y}$ be the integer solution obtained from y^* by randomized rounding. We prove the following theorem.

Lemma 12.16. *For n sufficiently large, the randomized rounding of the linear program produces a solution of value at least $\left(1 - \frac{13\epsilon}{\alpha}\right)$ OPT with probability at least $1 - 2n^{-c+1}$.*

Proof. From the discussion, we know that the value of the integral solution $\bar{y}$ is $\sum_{i=1}^{n} u_i(\bar{y})\bar{y}_i$. We know from Lemma 12.15 that $\sum_{i=1}^{n} \hat{u}_i(x^*)y_i^*$ is close in value to OPT. We'll first show that $u_i(\bar{y})$ is close in value to $\hat{u}_i(x^*)$, and then that $\sum_{i=1}^{n} \hat{u}_i(x^*)\bar{y}_i$ is close in value to $\sum_{i=1}^{n} \hat{u}_i(x^*)y_i^*$, so that we prove that the solution $\bar{y}$ has value that is close to OPT.

First, we show that $u_i(\bar{y}) = \sum_{j:(i,j)\in E}(1 - \bar{y}_j)$ is close in value to $\hat{u}_i(x^*)$. To do this, observe that

$$
E[u_i(\bar{y})] = E\left[\sum_{j:(i,j)\in E} (1 - \bar{y}_j) \right]
$$
$$
= \sum_{j:(i,j)\in E} (1 - E[\bar{y}_j])
$$
$$
= \sum_{j:(i,j)\in E} (1 - y_j^*) = u_i(y^*).
$$

We now want to show that $u_i(\bar{y}) \geq (u_i(y^*) - \sqrt{(2c\ln n)u_i(y^*)})$ with high probability via a Chernoff bound. To do this, set $\delta_i = \sqrt{\frac{2c\ln n}{u_i(y^*)}} > 0$, let $Y_j = (1 - \bar{y}_j)$, and let $Y = \sum_{j:(i,j)\in E} Y_j = u_i(\bar{y})$, so that $\mu_i = E[Y] = u_i(y^*)$. By applying Corollary 5.28, we obtain that $u_i(\bar{y}) \geq (1 - \delta_i)u_i(y^*)$ with probability at least

$$
1 - e^{-\mu_i \delta_i^2/2} \geq 1 - e^{-u_i(y^*)\frac{c\ln n}{u_i(y^*)}} = 1 - n^{-c}.
$$

Thus, with probability at least $1 - n^{-c+1}$, $u_i(\bar{y})$ is close to $u_i(y^*)$ for all $i \in V$. Then we have that the value of the cut obtained by randomized rounding is

$$
\sum_{i=1}^{n} u_i(\bar{y})\bar{y}_i \geq \sum_{i=1}^{n}(1 - \delta_i)u_i(y^*)\bar{y}_i
$$
$$
\geq \sum_{i=1}^{n} \left(u_i(y^*) - \sqrt{(2c\ln n)u_i(y^*)} \right) \bar{y}_i
$$
$$
\geq \sum_{i=1}^{n} \left(\hat{u}_i(x^*) - \epsilon n - \sqrt{2cn\ln n} \right) \bar{y}_i,
$$

where the last inequality follows by the linear programming constraints of (12.6), since $u_i(y^*) = \sum_{j:(i,j)\in E}(1 - y_j^*) \geq \hat{u}_i(x^*) - \epsilon n$. Then since $\sum_{i=1}^{n} \bar{y}_i \leq n$, we have that

$$
\sum_{i=1}^{n} u_i(\bar{y})\bar{y}_i \geq \sum_{i=1}^{n} \hat{u}_i(x^*)\bar{y}_i - \epsilon n^2 - n\sqrt{2cn\ln n}. \tag{12.7}
$$

We would now like to bound the value of the term $\sum_{i=1}^{n} \hat{u}_i(x^*)\bar{y}_i$ and show that it is close to OPT. Note that its expected value is $\sum_{i=1}^{n} \hat{u}_i(x^*)y_i^*$, which is just the objective function value of the linear program, and hence close to OPT by Lemma 12.15. Let $Z = \max_i \hat{u}_i(x^*)$. We will show via a Chernoff bound that with high probability,

$$\sum_{i=1}^{n} \hat{u}_i(x^*)\bar{y}_i \geq \sum_{i=1}^{n} \hat{u}_i(x^*)y_i^* - \sqrt{2cZ \ln n \sum_{i=1}^{n} \hat{u}_i(x^*)y_i^*}.$$

Let $\delta = \sqrt{\frac{2cZ \ln n}{\sum_{i=1}^{n} \hat{u}_i(x^*)y_i^*}} > 0$, let $X_i = \hat{u}_i(x^*)\bar{y}_i/Z$, and let $X = \sum_{i=1}^{n} X_i$, so that $\mu = E[X] = \frac{1}{Z} \sum_{i=1}^{n} \hat{u}_i(x^*)y_i^*$. Note that since we have scaled by Z, either $X_i = 0$ or some value no greater than 1. Then by Corollary 5.28,

$$\Pr\left[\frac{1}{Z} \sum_{i=1}^{n} \hat{u}_i(x^*)\bar{y}_i \geq (1 - \delta)\frac{1}{Z} \sum_{i=1}^{n} \hat{u}_i(x^*)y_i^*\right] \geq 1 - e^{-\delta^2 \sum_{i=1}^{n} \hat{u}_i(x^*)y_i^*/2Z}$$

$$= 1 - n^{-c}.$$

Thus, with high probability we have that

$$\sum_{i=1}^{n} \hat{u}_i(x^*)\bar{y}_i \geq (1 - \delta) \sum_{i=1}^{n} \hat{u}_i(x^*)y_i^*$$

$$= \left(1 - \sqrt{\frac{2cZ \ln n}{\sum_{i=1}^{n} \hat{u}_i(x^*)y_i^*}}\right) \sum_{i=1}^{n} \hat{u}_i(x^*)y_i^*$$

$$= \sum_{i=1}^{n} \hat{u}_i(x^*)y_i^* - \sqrt{2cZ \ln n \sum_{i=1}^{n} \hat{u}_i(x^*)y_i^*}.$$

Using $Z \leq n$ and $\sum_{i=1}^{n} \hat{u}_i(x^*)y_i^* \leq n^2$, we have that

$$\sum_{i=1}^{n} \hat{u}_i(x^*)\bar{y}_i \geq \sum_{i=1}^{n} \hat{u}_i(x^*)y_i^* - n\sqrt{2cn \ln n}.$$

Plugging this into inequality (12.7), we obtain

$$\sum_{i=1}^{n} u_i(\bar{y})\bar{y}_i \geq \sum_{i=1}^{n} \hat{u}_i(x^*)y_i^* - 2n\sqrt{2cn \ln n} - \epsilon n^2.$$

Recall that $\sum_{i=1}^{n} \hat{u}_i(x^*)y_i^*$ is the objective function of the linear program, and its value is at least $(1 - \frac{4\epsilon}{\alpha})$ OPT by Lemma 12.15. Thus, the value of the randomized rounding solution, $\sum_{i=1}^{n} u_i(\bar{y})\bar{y}_i$, is

$$\sum_{i=1}^{n} u_i(\bar{y})\bar{y}_i \geq \left(1 - \frac{4\epsilon}{\alpha}\right) \text{OPT} - 2n\sqrt{2cn \ln n} - \epsilon n^2.$$

For n sufficiently large, $2n\sqrt{2cn \ln n} \leq \epsilon n(n - 1)/4$ and $\epsilon n^2 \leq 4\epsilon \binom{n}{2}$. Recall also that OPT $\geq \frac{\alpha}{2} \binom{n}{2}$. Thus, the value of the solution is at least

$$\left(1 - \frac{4\epsilon}{\alpha}\right) \text{OPT} - \frac{\epsilon}{\alpha} \text{OPT} - \frac{8\epsilon}{\alpha} \text{OPT},$$

or at least

$$\left(1 - \frac{13\epsilon}{\alpha}\right) \text{OPT}. \qquad \square$$

To recap, our algorithm draws a multiset S of exactly $(c \log n)/\epsilon^2$ vertices by choosing vertices randomly with replacement. We then enumerate all $2^{|S|}$ possible placements of the vertices in S on each side of the cut (in U and W) by setting x_j to either 0 or 1 for each $j \in S$. For each setting x, we get estimates $\hat{u}_i(x)$, which we use in the linear program (12.6), and apply randomized rounding to the solution of the linear program to obtain the cut. Since one of the settings of the x variables corresponds to an optimal cut x^*, during this iteration of the algorithm, the lemmas above will apply, and we will obtain a near-optimal cut. This gives the following theorem.

Theorem 12.17. *For n sufficiently large, the algorithm above obtains a cut of value at least $(1 - \frac{13\epsilon}{\alpha})\text{OPT}$ with probability at least $1 - 4n^{-c+1}$.*

Proof. From Lemma 12.14, we have that $u_i(x^*) - \epsilon n \leq \hat{u}_i(x^*) \leq u_i(x^*) + \epsilon n$ for all $i \in V$ with probability at least $1 - 2n^{-2c+1} \geq 1 - 2n^{-c+1}$ when we consider the solution x^* for our sample S. Given that the estimates hold, we have from Lemma 12.16 that, with probability at least $1 - 2n^{-c+1}$, the randomized rounding of the linear program produces a solution of value at least $(1 - \frac{13\epsilon}{\alpha})\text{OPT}$. Thus, the algorithm produces a solution of value at least $(1 - \frac{13\epsilon}{\alpha})\text{OPT}$ with probability at least $1 - 4n^{-c+1}$. $\qquad \square$

Exercises

12.1 Show how to transform any solution to the linear programming relaxation of the uncapacitated facility location problem into a complete solution as defined on page 311, so that whenever $x_{ij}^* > 0$, then $x_{ij}^* = y_i^*$.

12.2 In the *multicommodity rent-or-buy problem*, we are given an undirected graph $G = (V, E)$ with edge costs $c_e \geq 0$ for all $e \in E$, a set of k source-sink pairs s_i-t_i for $i = 1, \ldots, k$, and a parameter $M > 1$. For each source-sink pair, we need a path P_i in the solution connecting s_i to t_i. As in the single-source rent-or-buy problem, we can either buy edges e at cost Mc_e, which then any pair can use, or we can rent edges e at cost c_e, but every pair using edge e must pay the rental cost. If we let B be the set of bought edges, and R_i the set of rented edges for pair i, then there must be a path from s_i to t_i in the set of edges $B \cup R_i$ for each i, and the cost of this solution is $Mc(B) + \sum_{i=1}^{k} c(R_i)$.

Consider a sample-and-augment algorithm that samples every source-sink pair with probability $1/M$. Let D be the set of sampled pairs. We run the generalized Steiner tree algorithm of Section 7.4 on the demand pairs in D and buy the edges given by the algorithm; let these edges be B. Then for any s_i-t_i pair not in D we rent edges on the shortest path from s_i to t_i in which the edges in B are given cost 0.

(a) Show that the expected cost of the bought edges B is at most $2\,\text{OPT}$.

To analyze the cost of the rented edges, we use a notion of α-*strict cost shares* for the generalized Steiner tree problem. Suppose we have an instance of the generalized Steiner tree problem with s_i-t_i pairs for $i \in R$. We say we have an algorithm returning α-strict cost shares χ_i for all $i \in R$, if two conditions are met: first, the sum of the cost shares, $\sum_{i \in R} \chi_i$, is at most the optimum cost of the generalized Steiner tree on the pairs in R;

and second, for any $i \in R$, the algorithm running on the instances with source-sink pairs from $R - \{i\}$ returns a solution F such that the cost of the shortest path from s_i to t_i, treating edges in F as having cost 0, is at most $\alpha \chi_i$.

(b) Use the idea of cost shares to show that the expected cost of the rented edges is at most α OPT. (Hint: Define a random variable β_i to be $M\chi_i$ if $i \in D$ and 0 otherwise, and a random variable ρ_i to be the renting cost of the pair i if $i \notin D$ and 0 otherwise. Show that conditioned on the set $D - \{i\}$, the expected value of ρ_i is at most $\alpha\beta_i$.)

It is known that the primal-dual generalized Steiner tree algorithm of Section 7.4 can produce 3-strict cost shares.

(c) Show that the sample-and-augment algorithm given above is a randomized 5-approximation algorithm for the multicommodity rent-or-buy problem.

12.3 In the unweighted maximum directed cut problem, we are given as input a directed graph $G = (V, A)$, and the goal is to partition V into two sets U and $W = V - U$ so as to maximize the total weight of the arcs going from U to W (that is, arcs (i, j) with $i \in U$ and $j \in W$). Suppose that the graph (V, A) is dense; that is, for some constant $\alpha > 0$, the total number of arcs is at least αn^2. Give a polynomial-time approximation scheme for the unweighted maximum directed cut problem in dense graphs.

12.4 In this exercise, we revisit the *metric asymmetric traveling salesman problem* introduced in Exercise 1.3. Recall that we are given as input a complete directed graph $G = (V, A)$ with costs $c_{ij} \geq 0$ for all arcs $(i, j) \in A$, such that the arc costs obey the triangle inequality: for all $i, j, k \in V$, we have that $c_{ij} + c_{jk} \geq c_{ik}$. The goal is to find a tour of minimum cost, that is, a directed cycle that contains each vertex exactly once, such that the sum of the cost of the arcs in the cycle is minimized. As in Exercise 1.3, we will find a low-cost, strongly connected Eulerian graph and shortcut this to a tour. Recall that a directed graph is strongly connected if for any pair of vertices $i, j \in V$ there is a path from i to j and a path from j to i. A directed graph is Eulerian if it is strongly connected and the indegree of each vertex equals its outdegree.

We will show that we can obtain an $O(\log n)$-approximation algorithm for the problem via randomized rounding. We start by giving a linear programming relaxation of the problem. For each arc (i, j) in the input graph, we introduce a variable x_{ij}. For a subset of vertices, $S \subseteq V$, let $\delta^+(S)$ be all arcs that have their tail in S and their head not in S, and let $\delta^-(S)$ be all arcs that have their head in S and their tail not in S. For simplicity, we let $\delta^+(v) = \delta^+(\{v\})$ and $\delta^-(v) = \delta^-(\{v\})$. Then consider the following linear program:

$$
\begin{aligned}
\text{minimize} \quad & \sum_{(i,j)\in A} c_{ij} x_{ij} \\
\text{subject to} \quad & \sum_{(i,j)\in\delta^+(v)} x_{ij} = 1, \quad \forall v \in V, \\
& \sum_{(i,j)\in\delta^-(v)} x_{ij} = 1, \quad \forall v \in V, \\
& \sum_{(i,j)\in\delta^+(S)} x_{ij} \geq 1, \quad \forall S \subset V, S \neq \emptyset, \\
& x_{ij} \geq 0, \quad \forall (i, j) \in A.
\end{aligned}
$$

For notational simplicity, given a solution x to the LP and a set $F \subseteq A$, we will sometimes write $x(F)$ to denote $\sum_{(i,j)\in F} x_{ij}$.

Our algorithm is as follows. We obtain a solution x^* to the linear program. For an appropriate choice of constant C, we make $K = C \ln n$ copies of each arc (i, j), and then we apply randomized rounding to the resulting graph, including arc (i, j) with probability x_{ij}^*. Let z_{ij} be the number of copies of arc (i, j) in the resulting solution; note that z is a random variable. We note that z may not correspond to an Eulerian graph, so we must include additional arcs to make it Eulerian. Let $b_v = z(\delta^+(v)) - z(\delta^-(v))$ be the number of additional arcs coming in to vertex v needed to make the graph Eulerian (note that if b_v is negative we need to add $|b_v|$ arcs coming out of vertex v); we call b_v the demand of vertex v. We use a minimum-cost flow algorithm to find an integral vector $w \geq 0$ with $w(\delta^-(v)) - w(\delta^+(v)) = b_v$ for all $v \in V$ that minimizes $\sum_{(i,j) \in V} c_{ij} w_{ij}$.

(a) Show that the linear program above is a linear programming relaxation of the asymmetric traveling salesman problem.

(b) Show that by choosing C and ϵ properly, with high probability

$$(1 - \epsilon)x^*(\delta^+(S)) \leq z(\delta^+(S)) \leq (1 + \epsilon)x^*(\delta^+(S)),$$

for all $S \subset V$, $S \neq \emptyset$, and use this to show that with high probability

$$z(\delta^+(S)) \leq 2z(\delta^-(S))$$

for all $S \subset V$, $S \neq \emptyset$. (Hint: In an undirected graph with capacities on the edges, if λ is the capacity of the minimum cut, then there are at most $n^{2\alpha}$ cuts of capacity at most $\alpha\lambda$, where $n = |V|$. To apply this result, you will need to argue that in some sense the solution x^* is like a capacitated undirected graph.)

(c) It is known that in a directed graph with capacities u_{ij} for all $(i, j) \in A$ and demands b_v, there is a feasible flow satisfying all demands if $u(\delta^-(S)) \geq \sum_{v \in S} b_v$ for all $S \subset V$, $S \neq \emptyset$. Prove that $z(\delta^-(S)) \geq \sum_{v \in S} b_v$ for all $S \subset V$, $S \neq \emptyset$, and thus that for the minimum-cost flow w, $\sum_{(i,j) \in A} c_{ij} w_{ij} \leq \sum_{(i,j) \in A} c_{ij} z_{ij}$.

(d) Show that the algorithm is a randomized $O(\log n)$-approximation algorithm for the metric asymmetric traveling salesman problem.

12.5 Give a polynomial-time separation oracle for the directed component linear programming relaxation of the k-restricted Steiner tree problem (and hence a polynomial-time procedure to solve this linear program).

12.6 Consider the special case of Theorem 12.9 when the optimal Steiner tree is a complete binary tree, in which all terminals are leaves, and $k = 2^p$ for some integer p (in fact, $k = 4$ provides a good starting point); in this case, one can prove that the additional cost for small components is at most a factor of $1 + 1/p$. One approach is to produce many k-restricted Steiner trees from the unrestricted Steiner tree, and prove that the average cost among them has cost within the same factor $1 + 1/p$ of the original.

Chapter Notes

The approximation algorithms for the uncapacitated facility location problem in Section 12.1 are due to Chudak and Shmoys [77]. As of this writing, the best known approximation algorithm for this problem is a 1.5-approximation algorithm due to Byrka and Aardal [58].

The algorithm for the single-source rent-or-buy problem in Section 12.2 is due to Gupta, Kumar, and Roughgarden [149] (see also Gupta, Kumar, Pál, and Roughgarden [148]). Williamson and van Zuylen [289] have given a derandomization of this algorithm. An algorithm that marks vertices with a slightly different probability can be shown to give an improved performance guarantee; this result is due to Eisenbrand, Grandoni, Rothvoß, and Schäfer [98]. The sample-and-augment algorithm for the multicommodity rent-or-buy problem in Exercise 12.2 is due to Gupta et al. [148]. The fact that the primal-dual algorithm for the generalized Steiner tree problem gives 3-strict cost shares is due to Fleischer, Könemann, Leonardi, and Schäfer [115].

The result of Section 12.3 that gives a 1.694-approximation algorithm for the Steiner tree is due to Byrka, Grandoni, Rothvoß, and Sanità [59]. The first approximation algorithm for the Steiner tree, giving a performance guarantee of 2, is attributed to Moore and described in the 1968 paper of Gilbert and Pollak [130]. Zelikovsky [294] gave the first α-approximation algorithm for the Steiner tree problem with constant $\alpha < 2$. In many ways, it is completely analogous to the LP-based result discussed in this section. It focuses on the 3-restricted Steiner tree problem, and gives a greedy-based improvement approximation algorithm for that problem by starting with the minimum terminal spanning tree; it attempts to find the 3-node subgraph for which adding a Steiner node causes the greatest drop in net cost, and consequently introduces that full component (if there is a net drop at all). This yields an 11/6-approximation algorithm. Since that result, there have been many improvements, first by generalizing to a k-restricted Steiner tree, and using that as the basis for the approximation; Theorem 12.9 is due to Borchers and Du [53]. The best performance guarantee for a combinatorial algorithm is a 1.55-approximation algorithm due to Robins and Zelikovsky [254], which is a greedy algorithm. The monograph by Prömel and Steger [242] provides an excellent overview of the full range of work done on the Steiner tree as of its writing. Beyond the result presented here, Byrka et al. also prove a number of stronger results, most notably a ln 4-approximation algorithm (where ln 4 is less than 1.39). Our presentation was also strongly influenced by a more recent 1.55-approximation algorithm based on the same LP due to Chakrabarty, Könemann, and Pritchard [63], which matches the currently strongest integrality gap result known in this domain.

The result of Section 12.4 giving a polynomial-time approximation scheme for the maximum cut problem in unweighted dense graphs is due to Arora, Karger, and Karpinski [16]; Fernandez de la Vega [110] independently developed a different PTAS for the same case of the maximum cut problem. The Hoeffding inequality of Fact 12.13 is due to Hoeffding [166]. Arora et al. show that their techniques work for several other problems, such as the maximum directed cut problem in unweighted dense graphs, as given in Exercise 12.3. Since these results, several other approximation schemes have been developed for these problems and more general variants. Mathieu and Schudy [223] give a particularly simple algorithm for the maximum cut problem in unweighted dense graphs that draws a random sample, enumerates all possible cuts of the sample, and uses a greedy algorithm to augment it to a full solution.

Exercise 12.4 is due to Goemans, Harvey, Jain, and Singh [136]; an improvement of this result due to Asadpour, Goemans, Mądry, Oveis Gharan, and Saberi [25] gives a performance guarantee of $O(\log n / \log \log n)$. The bound on the number of cuts of capacity at most α times the minimum is due to Karger [183, 184]. The condition on the feasibility of a flow is known as Hoffman's circulation theorem and is due to Hoffman [167].

CHAPTER 13

Further Uses of Randomized Rounding of Semidefinite Programs

We introduced the use of semidefinite programming for approximation algorithms in Chapter 6. The algorithms of that chapter solve a vector programming relaxation, then choose a random hyperplane (or possibly many hyperplanes) to partition the vectors in some way. The central component of the analysis of these algorithms is Lemma 6.7, which says that the probability of two vectors being separated by a random hyperplane is proportional to the angle between them. In this chapter, we look at ways in which we can broaden both the analysis of algorithms using semidefinite programming, and the algorithms themselves.

To broaden our analytical techniques, we revisit two of the problems we discussed initially in Chapter 6. In particular, we consider the problem of approximating integer quadratic programs, which was introduced in Section 6.3, and the problem of coloring a 3-colorable graph, which was introduced in Section 6.5. In our algorithms in this chapter, we again solve vector programming relaxations of the problems, and choose a random hyperplane by drawing its components from the normal distribution. Here, however, our analysis of the algorithms will rely on several more properties of the normal distribution than we used in the previous chapter; in particular, it will be helpful for us to use bounds on the tail of the normal distribution.

We will also consider the application of semidefinite programming to the unique games problem. We have mentioned previously that several problems are hard to approximate assuming the unique games conjecture. In Section 13.3, we will define the unique games problem and give the unique games conjecture. The unique games problem is a type of constraint satisfaction problem, and the unique games conjecture states that it is NP-hard to satisfy a small fraction of the constraints even when it is known that the optimal solution satisfies almost all constraints. The unique games conjecture underlies various results on the hardness of approximation. We will give an approximation algorithm for the problem, though its performance guarantee does not refute the unique games conjecture. Interestingly, the algorithm for unique games does not use a random hyperplane, but instead relies on the geometric properties of vector programs.

13.1 Approximating Quadratic Programs

We begin the chapter by returning to the quadratic programming problem introduced in Section 6.3; recall the quadratic program (6.5):

$$\text{maximize} \sum_{1 \le i, j \le n} a_{ij} x_i x_j \tag{13.1}$$

$$\text{subject to } x_i \in \{-1, +1\}, \qquad i = 1, \ldots, n.$$

In Section 6.3, we restricted the objective function matrix $A = (a_{ij})$ to be positive semidefinite in order to guarantee that the optimal value is nonnegative. We were then able to obtain a $\frac{2}{\pi}$-approximation algorithm for that case. In this section, we instead restrict ourselves to any matrix A in which $a_{ii} = 0$ for all i, and obtain a much weaker approximation algorithm with performance guarantee $\Omega(1/\log n)$. In any solution to the quadratic program above, $\sum_{i=1}^{n} a_{ii} x_i^2 = \sum_{i=1}^{n} a_{ii}$, so these terms are simply a constant that is added to any solution to the problem.

We begin by showing that the optimal value for this case must be nonnegative, and thus it makes sense to talk about an approximation algorithm for this problem.

Lemma 13.1. *If $a_{ii} = 0$ for all i, then*

$$\text{OPT} \ge \frac{1}{n^2} \sum_{1 \le i < j \le n} |a_{ij} + a_{ji}|.$$

Proof. We will construct a solution $\bar{x}$ via randomization such that

$$E\left[\sum_{1 \le i, j \le n} a_{ij} \bar{x}_i \bar{x}_j \right] \ge \frac{1}{n^2} \sum_{1 \le i < j \le n} |a_{ij} + a_{ji}|.$$

This will prove the lemma.

Consider a complete undirected graph on n vertices, where each edge (i, j) for $i < j$ has weight $(a_{ij} + a_{ji})$. We construct a random matching M on the graph as follows: we pick an edge (i, j) of the graph at random, add it to the matching M, remove both of its endpoints i and j from the graph, and repeat until there is at most one vertex remaining. Since there are $n(n-1)/2$ edges in the graph, the probability that we choose any given edge for the matching in the first step is $2/n(n-1)$. Thus, the probability that any edge ends up in the matching is at least $1/n^2$; this is a very loose lower bound, but it is sufficient for our purposes.

We now construct the solution $\bar{x}$. Given the matching M, for each $(i, j) \in M$ with $i < j$, we set $\bar{x}_i = 1$ with probability $\frac{1}{2}$ and $\bar{x}_i = -1$ with probability $\frac{1}{2}$. We then set $\bar{x}_j = \bar{x}_i$ if $a_{ij} + a_{ji} \ge 0$ and $\bar{x}_j = -\bar{x}_i$ otherwise. Finally, for vertex i not in the matching (if n is odd), then we set $\bar{x}_i = 1$ with probability $\frac{1}{2}$ and $\bar{x}_i = -1$ with probability $\frac{1}{2}$. The crucial observation is that if $(i, j) \in M$, $E[(a_{ij} + a_{ji}) \bar{x}_i \bar{x}_j] = |a_{ij} + a_{ji}|$, while if $(i, j) \notin M$, then $E[(a_{ij} + a_{ji})\bar{x}_i\bar{x}_j] = 0$. Hence, we obtain that

$$E\left[\sum_{1 \leq i,j \leq n} a_{ij}\bar{x}_i\bar{x}_j\right] = E\left[\sum_{1 \leq i < j \leq n} (a_{ij} + a_{ji})\bar{x}_i\bar{x}_j\right]$$

$$= \sum_{1 \leq i < j \leq n : (i,j) \in M} \Pr[(i, j) \in M]E[(a_{ij} + a_{ji})\bar{x}_i\bar{x}_j|(i, j) \in M]$$

$$+ \sum_{1 \leq i < j \leq n : (i,j) \notin M} \Pr[(i, j) \notin M]E[(a_{ij} + a_{ji})\bar{x}_i\bar{x}_j|(i, j) \notin M]$$

$$\geq \frac{1}{n^2} \sum_{1 \leq i < j \leq n} |a_{ij} + a_{ji}|,$$

and the proof is complete. $\square$

As a first step toward an algorithm, we show that the quadratic programming problem with integer constraints, in which we must have $x_i \in \{-1, 1\}$, is actually equivalent, in terms of approximability, to a quadratic programming problem with linear constraints, in which we have $-1 \leq x_i \leq 1$. We will then provide an approximation algorithm for the case of linear constraints. In particular, consider the following program:

$$\text{maximize} \sum_{1 \leq i,j \leq n} a_{ij}y_iy_j \tag{13.2}$$

$$\text{subject to } -1 \leq y_i \leq 1, \qquad i = 1, \ldots, n.$$

We can show the following.

Lemma 13.2. *Assume that $a_{ii} = 0$ for all i. Then given any α-approximation algorithm for the program (13.2) with linear constraints, we can obtain a randomized α-approximation algorithm for the program (13.1) with integer constraints.*

Proof. We prove the lemma by showing that any solution $\bar{y}$ to the program (13.2) with linear constraints can be converted via randomized rounding to a solution $\bar{x}$ to the program (13.1) with integer constraints of the same expected value. To see this, set $\bar{x}_i = -1$ with probability $\frac{1}{2}(1 - \bar{y}_i)$ and $\bar{x}_i = 1$ with probability $\frac{1}{2}(1 + \bar{y}_i)$. Then for $i \neq j$

$$E[\bar{x}_i\bar{x}_j] = \Pr[\bar{x}_i = \bar{x}_j] - \Pr[\bar{x}_i \neq \bar{x}_j]$$

$$= \frac{1}{4}\left((1 - \bar{y}_i)(1 - \bar{y}_j) + (1 + \bar{y}_i)(1 + \bar{y}_j)\right)$$

$$- \frac{1}{4}\left((1 - \bar{y}_i)(1 + \bar{y}_j) + (1 + \bar{y}_i)(1 - \bar{y}_j)\right)$$

$$= \frac{1}{4}(2 + 2\bar{y}_i\bar{y}_j) - \frac{1}{4}(2 - 2\bar{y}_i\bar{y}_j)$$

$$= \bar{y}_i\bar{y}_j,$$

so that

$$E\left[\sum_{1 \leq i,j \leq n} a_{ij}\bar{x}_i\bar{x}_j\right] = \sum_{1 \leq i,j \leq n} a_{ij}\bar{y}_i\bar{y}_j,$$

given that $a_{ii} = 0$ for all i.

Let OPT_{lin} be the value of the optimal solution to the program (13.2) with linear constraints, and let OPT be the value of the optimal solution to the original program (13.1) with integer constraints. Note that $OPT_{lin} \geq OPT$, since every integer solution is feasible for the program with linear constraints. However, it is also true that $OPT \geq OPT_{lin}$, since given an optimal solution $\bar{y}$ to the program with linear constraints, the argument above implies there exists an integer solution of value at least as much. Hence, $OPT = OPT_{lin}$.

Thus, given any solution $\bar{y}$ to the program (13.2) with linear constraints of value at least $\alpha \, OPT_{lin}$, we can convert it in randomized polynomial time to an integer solution $\bar{x}$ to the program (13.1) of the same expected value, and thus of value at least $\alpha \, OPT_{lin} = \alpha \, OPT$. Therefore, given an α-approximation algorithm for the program (13.2), we can obtain a randomized α-approximation algorithm for the program (13.1). $\qquad\square$

We now give an $\Omega(1/\log n)$-approximation algorithm for the program (13.2), which, by Lemma 13.2, will imply an $\Omega(1/\log n)$-approximation algorithm for the original problem. We now let OPT stand for the optimal value of the program (13.2) with linear constraints (the proof of the lemma shows that the two values are identical). We use the same vector programming relaxation as we used in Section 6.3:

$$\text{maximize} \sum_{1 \leq i,j \leq n} a_{ij}(v_i \cdot v_j) \qquad\qquad (13.3)$$

$$\text{subject to } v_i \cdot v_i = 1, \qquad i = 1, \ldots, n,$$

$$v_i \in \Re^n, \qquad i = 1, \ldots, n.$$

Let Z_{VP} be the optimal value of the vector program. As we argued before, this program is a relaxation of the original program (13.1) with integer constraints, so that $Z_{VP} \geq OPT$. Our algorithm finds an optimal solution to the vector program (13.3) in polynomial time and obtains the vectors v_i. We find a random vector r, as usual, by drawing each component of r from $\mathcal{N}(0, 1)$, the normal distribution of mean 0 and variance 1. For a value of $T \geq 1$ to be chosen later, we let $z_i = (v_i \cdot r)/T$. Possibly z is infeasible if $z_i > 1$ or $z_i < -1$, so we create a solution y in which we clamp y_i to 1 (or -1) if that happens; in other words, we set

$$y_i = \begin{cases} z_i & \text{if } |z_i| \leq 1 \\ -1 & \text{if } z_i < -1 \\ 1 & \text{if } z_i > 1. \end{cases}$$

We return y as our solution. This algorithm is summarized in Algorithm 13.1.

We will be able to show that the expected value of the product $z_i z_j$ is the same as the inner product $v_i \cdot v_j$ scaled down by T^2. If it were the case that $|z_i| \leq 1$ for all i, then we could show that the expected value of the solution y would be Z_{VP}/T^2. However, possibly $|z_i| > 1$. By increasing T, we decrease the probability that this happens; we can show that the expected error incurred by the possibility that $|z_i| > 1$ is $O(n^2 e^{-T^2} OPT)$. By setting $T = \Theta(\sqrt{\ln n})$, we get a solution of expected value at least $Z_{VP}/\Theta(\ln n) \geq OPT /\Theta(\ln n)$ minus an error term of $O(OPT /n)$, which gives the desired performance guarantee for sufficiently large n.

```
Solve vector program (13.3), obtain vectors v_i
Draw random vector r
Set z_i = (v_i · r)/T
if |z_i| ≤ 1 then
    y_i ← z_i
else if z_i < −1 then
    y_i ← −1
else
    y_i ← 1
return y
```

Algorithm 13.1. Approximation algorithm for the quadratic programming problem.

We now prove the main lemmas we will need to obtain the result.

Lemma 13.3.

$$E[z_i z_j] = \frac{1}{T^2}(v_i \cdot v_j).$$

Proof. We want to calculate $E[z_i z_j] = \frac{1}{T^2} E[(v_i \cdot r)(v_j \cdot r)]$. The value of the vector program is not changed under a rotation of the vectors and r is spherically symmetric (by Fact 6.4), so we can rotate the vectors so that $v_i = (1, 0, \ldots)$ and $v_j = (a, b, 0, \ldots)$. Then for $r = (r_1, r_2, \ldots, r_n)$, where each r_i is drawn from $\mathcal{N}(0, 1)$, we have that $v_i \cdot r = r_1$ and $v_j \cdot r = ar_1 + br_2$. Therefore,

$$E[z_i z_j] = \frac{1}{T^2} E[r_1(ar_1 + br_2)] = \frac{1}{T^2}\left(aE[r_1^2] + bE[r_1 r_2]\right).$$

Because r_1 is drawn from $\mathcal{N}(0, 1)$, $E[r_1^2]$ is the variance of r_1 and is 1. Because r_1 and r_2 are drawn independently from $\mathcal{N}(0, 1)$, $E[r_1 r_2] = E[r_1]E[r_2] = 0$. Thus,

$$E[z_i z_j] = \frac{a}{T^2} = \frac{1}{T^2}(v_i \cdot v_j). \qquad \square$$

The expected value of the algorithm is

$$E\left[\sum_{1 \le i,j \le n} a_{ij} y_i y_j\right] = \sum_{1 \le i,j \le n} a_{ij} E[y_i y_j],$$

whereas the lemma above shows us that

$$\sum_{1 \le i,j \le n} a_{ij} E[z_i z_j] = \frac{1}{T^2}\sum_{1 \le i,j \le n} a_{ij}(v_i \cdot v_j) = \frac{1}{T^2} Z_{VP}.$$

In order to relate the expected value of the algorithm to the value of the semidefinite program, we consider the difference between $z_i z_j$ and $y_i y_j$ for each i, j. Let us denote this difference $\Delta_{ij} = z_i z_j - y_i y_j$. In the next lemma, we see that this difference is exponentially small in $-T^2$.

Lemma 13.4.

$$|E[\Delta_{ij}]| \le 8e^{-T^2}.$$

We defer the proof of this lemma for a moment. Given the lemma, we are able to obtain the proof of the performance guarantee of the algorithm.

Theorem 13.5. *For n sufficiently large, Algorithm 13.1 is a randomized $\Omega(1/\log n)$-approximation algorithm for approximating the quadratic program (13.2) if $a_{ii} = 0$ for all i.*

Proof. Via Lemma 13.3, we have that $E[z_i z_j] = \frac{1}{T^2}(v_i \cdot v_j)$. Then the expected value of the algorithm is

$$
\begin{aligned}
E\left[\sum_{1 \leq i,j \leq n} a_{ij} y_i y_j\right] &= \sum_{1 \leq i,j \leq n} a_{ij} E[y_i y_j] \\
&= \sum_{1 \leq i,j \leq n} a_{ij} E[z_i z_j] - \sum_{1 \leq i,j \leq n} a_{ij} E[\Delta_{ij}] \\
&= \frac{1}{T^2} \sum_{1 \leq i,j \leq n} a_{ij}(v_i \cdot v_j) - \sum_{1 \leq i,j \leq n} a_{ij} E[\Delta_{ij}] \\
&= \frac{1}{T^2} Z_{VP} - \sum_{1 \leq i,j \leq n} a_{ij} E[\Delta_{ij}] \\
&\geq \frac{1}{T^2} Z_{VP} - \left|\sum_{1 \leq i,j \leq n} a_{ij} E[\Delta_{ij}]\right| \\
&\geq \frac{1}{T^2} Z_{VP} - \sum_{1 \leq i<j \leq n} |a_{ij} + a_{ji}| \cdot |E[\Delta_{ij}]| \\
&\geq \frac{1}{T^2} Z_{VP} - 8e^{-T^2} \sum_{1 \leq i<j \leq n} |a_{ij} + a_{ji}|,
\end{aligned}
$$

where the last inequality follows from Lemma 13.4. Using Lemma 13.1, we know that $\sum_{1 \leq i<j \leq n} |a_{ij} + a_{ji}| \leq n^2 \cdot \text{OPT}$, so that the expected value of the algorithm is at least

$$
\frac{1}{T^2} Z_{VP} - 8n^2 e^{-T^2} \text{OPT} \geq \left(\frac{1}{T^2} - 8n^2 e^{-T^2}\right) \text{OPT}.
$$

Then if we set $T = \sqrt{3 \ln n}$, the expected value of the algorithm is at least

$$
\left(\frac{1}{3 \ln n} - \frac{8}{n}\right) \text{OPT}.
$$

For n larger than $e^8 \geq 128$, we have that $1/4 \ln n \geq 8/n$, so that the expected value of the algorithm is at least $(\frac{1}{3} - \frac{1}{4})\frac{\text{OPT}}{\ln n} = \frac{\text{OPT}}{12 \ln n}$. This proves that the algorithm is an $\Omega(1/\log n)$-approximation algorithm for n sufficiently large. $\square$

Finally, we turn to the proof of Lemma 13.4.

Proof of Lemma 13.4. Let X_i be the event that $y_i = z_i$ and X_j be the event that $y_j = z_j$. For notational simplicity, we will write expectations conditioned on X_i as E_i, expectations conditioned on $\bar{X}_i$ as $E_{\neg i}$, expectations conditioned on $X_i \wedge X_j$ as $E_{i,j}$, and so on. Then

$$|E[\Delta_{ij}]| \le |E_{i,j}[\Delta_{ij}] \Pr[X_i \wedge X_j]| + E_{\neg i,j}[|\Delta_{ij}|] \Pr[\bar{X}_i \wedge X_j]$$
$$+ E_{i,\neg j}[|\Delta_{ij}|] \Pr[X_i \wedge \bar{X}_j] + E_{\neg i,\neg j}[|\Delta_{ij}|] \Pr[\bar{X}_i \wedge \bar{X}_j]. \quad (13.4)$$

Observe that

$$E_{\neg i}[|\Delta_{ij}|] \Pr[\bar{X}_i] = E_{\neg i,j}[|\Delta_{ij}|] \Pr[\bar{X}_i \wedge X_j] + E_{\neg i,\neg j}[|\Delta_{ij}|] \Pr[\bar{X}_i \wedge \bar{X}_j]$$

and

$$E_{\neg j}[|\Delta_{ij}|] \Pr[\bar{X}_j] = E_{i,\neg j}[|\Delta_{ij}|] \Pr[X_i \wedge \bar{X}_j] + E_{\neg i,\neg j}[|\Delta_{ij}|] \Pr[\bar{X}_i \wedge \bar{X}_j].$$

Thus, since $E_{\neg i,\neg j}[|\Delta_{ij}|] \Pr[\bar{X}_i \wedge \bar{X}_j]$ is nonnegative, the right-hand side of (13.4) is at most

$$|E_{i,j}[\Delta_{ij}] \Pr[X_i \wedge X_j]| + E_{\neg i}[|\Delta_{ij}|] \Pr[\bar{X}_i] + E_{\neg j}[|\Delta_{ij}|] \Pr[\bar{X}_j].$$

We now bound these various terms. Given $X_i \wedge X_j$ (that is, $y_i = z_i$ and $y_j = z_j$), $\Delta_{ij} = 0$, so $E_{i,j}[\Delta_{ij}] = 0$. By symmetry, $E_{\neg i}[|\Delta_{ij}|] \Pr[\bar{X}_i] = E_{\neg j}[|\Delta_{ij}|] \Pr[\bar{X}_j]$, so it suffices to bound $E_{\neg i}[|\Delta_{ij}|] \Pr[\bar{X}_i]$. To do this, we recall that the density function $p(x)$ of the normal distribution $\mathcal{N}(0, 1)$ is

$$p(x) = \frac{1}{\sqrt{2\pi}} e^{-x^2/2},$$

and its cumulative distribution function is $\Phi(x) = \int_{-\infty}^{x} p(s)ds$. We will let $\overline{\Phi}(x) = 1 - \Phi(x) = \int_{x}^{\infty} p(s)ds$. We also recall from the proof of Lemma 13.3 that we can assume that $v_i = (1, 0, \ldots)$, $v_j = (a, b, 0, \ldots)$, where $|a| \le 1$ and $|b| \le 1$ since v_j is a unit vector. Further, $r = (r_1, r_2, \ldots, r_n)$, where each r_i is drawn independently from $\mathcal{N}(0, 1)$. Since the event $\bar{X}_i$ occurs when $|z_i| > 1$, or $|v_i \cdot r| > T$, we have

$$\Pr[\bar{X}_i] = 2\overline{\Phi}(T).$$

Also, using $|y_i y_j| \le 1$,

$$E_{\neg i}[|\Delta_{ij}|] \Pr[\bar{X}_i] \le E_{\neg i}[|y_i y_j| + |z_i z_j|] \Pr[\bar{X}_i] \le 2\overline{\Phi}(T) + E_{\neg i}[|z_i z_j|].$$

Since $z_i z_j = \frac{1}{T^2}(v_i \cdot r)(v_j \cdot r) = r_1(ar_1 + br_2)$, and $\bar{X}_i$ implies $|v_i \cdot r| > T$, we have that

$$E_{\neg i}[|z_i z_j|] = \frac{1}{T^2} \int_{-\infty}^{-T} \int_{-\infty}^{\infty} |r_1(ar_1 + br_2)| p(r_1)p(r_2)dr_2 dr_1$$

$$+ \frac{1}{T^2} \int_{T}^{\infty} \int_{-\infty}^{\infty} |r_1(ar_1 + br_2)| p(r_1)p(r_2)dr_2 dr_1$$

$$= \frac{2}{T^2} \int_{T}^{\infty} \int_{-\infty}^{\infty} |ar_1^2 + br_1 r_2| p(r_1)p(r_2)dr_2 dr_1$$

$$\le \frac{2}{T^2} \int_{T}^{\infty} |a| r_1^2 p(r_1)dr_1 + \frac{2}{T^2} \left(\int_{T}^{\infty} |br_1| p(r_1)dr_1 \right) \left(\int_{-\infty}^{\infty} |r_2| p(r_2)dr_2 \right).$$

We now bound each of these terms. Using integration by parts and $|a| \leq 1$, we obtain

$$
\int_T^\infty |a| r^2 p(r) dr \leq \frac{1}{\sqrt{2\pi}} \int_T^\infty r^2 e^{-r^2/2} dr
$$

$$
= \frac{1}{\sqrt{2\pi}} \left(-re^{-r^2/2} \Big]_T^\infty + \int_T^\infty e^{-r^2/2} dr \right)
$$

$$
= \frac{1}{\sqrt{2\pi}} T e^{-T^2/2} + \overline{\Phi}(T).
$$

Also, since $|b| \leq 1$,

$$
\int_T^\infty |br| p(r) dr \leq \frac{1}{\sqrt{2\pi}} \int_T^\infty r e^{-r^2/2} dr = -\frac{1}{\sqrt{2\pi}} e^{-r^2/2} \Big]_T^\infty = \frac{1}{\sqrt{2\pi}} e^{-T^2/2},
$$

and

$$
\int_{-\infty}^\infty |r| p(r) dr = 2 \int_0^\infty r p(r) dr = -\frac{2}{\sqrt{2\pi}} e^{-r^2/2} \Big]_0^\infty = \frac{2}{\sqrt{2\pi}}.
$$

Putting these pieces together, and using $T \geq 1$, we get

$$
E_{\neg i}[|\Delta_{ij}|] \Pr[\bar{X}_i] \leq 2\overline{\Phi}(T) + \frac{2}{T\sqrt{2\pi}} e^{-T^2/2} + \frac{2}{T^2} \overline{\Phi}(T) + \frac{2}{T^2\pi} e^{-T^2/2}
$$

$$
\leq 4\overline{\Phi}(T) + \frac{2}{T} e^{-T^2/2}.
$$

We can bound $\overline{\Phi}(T)$ for $T \geq 1$ with

$$
\overline{\Phi}(T) = \int_T^\infty p(x) dx \leq \int_T^\infty x p(x) dx = \frac{1}{\sqrt{2\pi}} \int_T^\infty x e^{-x^2/2}
$$

$$
= -\frac{1}{\sqrt{2\pi}} e^{-x^2/2} \Big]_T^\infty \leq \frac{1}{2} e^{-T^2/2}.
$$

Now we can put everything together. We have that

$$
|E[\Delta_{ij}]| \leq 2 E_{\neg i}[|\Delta_{ij}|] \Pr[\bar{X}_i] \leq 4e^{-T^2/2} + \frac{4}{T} e^{-T^2/2} \leq 8e^{-T^2/2},
$$

and we are done. $\square$

Before we move on, it is worth pausing for a moment to reflect on why the analysis above is necessary. Consider an alternative: suppose we solve the vector program and pick a random hyperplane r; if $z_i = (v_i \cdot r)/T$ is such that $|z_i| \leq 1$ for all i, return z_i as a solution; otherwise, return any nonnegative solution as given in Lemma 13.1. The probability that for a given i, $|z_i| > 1$ is the probability that $|v_i \cdot r| > T$, which is $2\overline{\Phi}(T) \leq e^{-T^2/2}$. If we set $T = O(\sqrt{\log n})$, then with high probability, for all i, $|z_i| \leq 1$. We already know that the expected value $E[z_i z_j] = (v_i \cdot v_j)/T^2$ by Lemma 13.3, so the expected value is within $\Omega(1/\log n)$ of Z_{VP}. Why isn't this easier? The problem with this analysis is that it does not consider the expected value of $E[z_i z_j]$ conditioned on $|z_i| \leq 1$ for all i, that is, the expected value of the solutions we actually return. Perhaps the value of solutions for which $|z_i| > 1$ is particularly high, and this is what makes the overall expectation large. It is this possibility that the above analysis of the error term Δ_{ij} considers.

13.2 Coloring 3-Colorable Graphs

In this section, we return to the problem discussed in Section 6.5 of coloring 3-colorable graphs with as few colors as possible. Our coloring algorithm in this section will work by repeatedly finding a large independent set in the graph. Recall from Section 10.2 that an independent set of vertices $S \subseteq V$ is one such that for all pairs i, j of vertices in S, there is no edge (i, j). Given an independent set in the graph, we can color all of its vertices the same color. We then remove the independent set from the graph, find another large independent set in the remaining graph, color all its vertices with a new color, and repeat. Clearly this process results in a feasible coloring of the graph. Now we bound the number of colors used. If in each iteration we find an independent set of size at least γ fraction of the remaining vertices, then after one iteration at most $(1 - \gamma)n$ vertices remain. After k iterations, $(1 - \gamma)^k n$ vertices remain. Since $(1 - \gamma)^k \leq e^{-\gamma k}$, using $1 - x \leq e^{-x}$, after $k = \frac{1}{\gamma} \ln n$ rounds, at most

$$(1 - \gamma)^k n \leq e^{-\gamma k} n = e^{-\ln n} n = 1$$

vertex remains, which we can color with its own color. Thus, if in each iteration we can find an independent set of size at least a γ fraction of the remaining number of vertices, then we can color the graph with $O(\frac{1}{\gamma} \ln n)$ colors overall. Let Δ be the maximum degree of the graph. We will modify the algorithm somewhat so that if Δ ever becomes smaller than a constant in the remaining graph, we simply use the greedy $\Delta + 1$ coloring algorithm of Exercise 6.4 to color the remaining graph; we state the constant below. This modification still yields an $O(\frac{1}{\gamma} \ln n)$ coloring algorithm.

To make matters slightly more complicated, the algorithm we give below for finding an independent set is a randomized algorithm that returns an independent set whose *expected* size is γn. We will argue below that we can simply run this algorithm $O(\frac{1}{\gamma} \ln n)$ times to get an independent set of size at least $\gamma n/2$ with high probability. If we let the random variable X denote the number of vertices not in the independent set, then if the expected size of the independent set is at least γn, it follows that $E[X] \leq n(1 - \gamma)$. Then by applying Markov's inequality (Lemma 5.25),

$$\Pr\left[X \geq n\left(1 - \frac{\gamma}{2}\right)\right] \leq \frac{E[X]}{n\left(1 - \frac{\gamma}{2}\right)} \leq \frac{n(1 - \gamma)}{n\left(1 - \frac{\gamma}{2}\right)} \leq 1 - \frac{\gamma}{2}.$$

Thus, the probability that the independent set has size smaller than $\gamma n/2$ is at most $1 - \frac{\gamma}{2}$, and the probability that the independent set has size at least $\gamma n/2$ is at least $\frac{\gamma}{2}$. Thus, if we run the algorithm at least $\frac{2c}{\gamma} \ln n$ times for some constant c, the probability that the algorithm does not return an independent set of size at least $\gamma n/2$ is at most

$$\left(1 - \frac{\gamma}{2}\right)^{\frac{2c}{\gamma} \ln n} \leq e^{-c \ln n} \leq \frac{1}{n^c}.$$

Solve vector program (13.5), get vectors v_i
Draw random vector r

$\epsilon \leftarrow \sqrt{\frac{2}{3}\ln\Delta}$
$S(\epsilon) \leftarrow \{i \in V : v_i \cdot r \geq \epsilon\}$
$S'(\epsilon) \leftarrow \{i \in S(\epsilon) : \forall(i,j) \in E, j \notin S(\epsilon)\}$
return $S'(\epsilon)$

Algorithm 13.2. Algorithm for finding a large independent set in a 3-colorable graph.

To find a large independent set, we will use a feasible solution to the following vector program:

$$\begin{aligned}
\text{minimize} \quad & 0 & & (13.5) \\
\text{subject to } v_i \cdot v_j &= -1/2, & \forall(i,j) &\in E, \\
v_i \cdot v_i &= 1, & \forall i &\in V, \\
v_i &\in \Re^n, & \forall i &\in V.
\end{aligned}$$

We use the objective function "minimize 0" since we are interested only in a feasible solution to the vector program. In Corollary 6.22, we showed that for any 3-colorable graph, there exists a feasible solution to this vector program. Given a feasible solution to the vector program, we choose a random vector $r = (r_1, r_2, \ldots, r_n)$ by drawing each r_i independently from the standard normal distribution $\mathcal{N}(0, 1)$. For a value of ϵ we specify momentarily, we find $S(\epsilon) = \{i \in V : v_i \cdot r \geq \epsilon\}$. The set $S(\epsilon)$ may not be independent, so we let $S'(\epsilon) \subseteq S(\epsilon)$ be all the $i \in S(\epsilon)$ that have no neighbors in $S(\epsilon)$. The set $S'(\epsilon)$ is independent, and we return it as our solution. We summarize this algorithm in Algorithm 13.2. We will show below that this algorithm produces an independent set of expected size at least $\Omega(n\Delta^{-1/3}(\ln\Delta)^{-1/2})$. In particular, we will choose $\epsilon = \sqrt{\frac{2}{3}\ln\Delta}$ for reasons explained later, and we would like $\epsilon \geq 1$, so we use the greedy coloring algorithm when $\Delta \leq e^{3/2} \leq 5$. Together with the previous discussion, this will yield an algorithm that colors any 3-colorable graph with $O(\Delta^{1/3}\sqrt{\ln\Delta}\log n)$ colors. In Exercise 13.1, this is shown to lead to a coloring algorithm that uses $\tilde{O}(n^{1/4})$ colors.

For our proofs we will need the following notation. As in the previous section, let the density function $p(x)$ of the normal distribution $\mathcal{N}(0, 1)$ be

$$p(x) = \frac{1}{\sqrt{2\pi}}e^{-x^2/2},$$

let its cumulative distribution function be $\Phi(x) = \int_{-\infty}^{x} p(s)ds$, and let $\overline{\Phi}(x) = 1 - \Phi(x) = \int_{x}^{\infty} p(s)ds$. We can now start with a simple lemma.

Lemma 13.6. *For any* $i \in V$, *the probability that* $i \in S(\epsilon)$ *is* $\overline{\Phi}(\epsilon)$, *so that* $E[|S(\epsilon)|] = n\overline{\Phi}(\epsilon)$.

Proof. The probability that any $i \in V$ is in $S(\epsilon)$ is equal to the probability that $v_i \cdot r \geq \epsilon$. By Fact 6.5, $v_i \cdot r$ is normally distributed. By the definition of $\overline{\Phi}$, the probability that $v_i \cdot r$ is at least ϵ is $\overline{\Phi}(\epsilon)$. $\qquad\square$

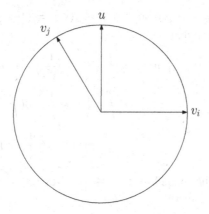

Figure 13.1. Figure for proof of Lemma 13.7.

Now we bound the probability that any vertex is not in $S'(\epsilon)$ given that it is in $S(\epsilon)$.

Lemma 13.7. *The probability that $i \notin S'(\epsilon)$ given that $i \in S(\epsilon)$ is at most $\Delta\overline{\Phi}(\sqrt{3}\epsilon)$.*

Proof. If $i \in S(\epsilon)$, then the only reason that i would not be in $S'(\epsilon)$ is because some neighbor j of i is also in $S(\epsilon)$. Thus,

$$\Pr[i \notin S'(\epsilon)|i \in S(\epsilon)] = \Pr[\exists(i, j) \in E : v_j \cdot r \geq \epsilon|v_i \cdot r \geq \epsilon].$$

Because i and j are neighbors, there is an edge $(i, j) \in E$. Thus, by the vector program (13.5), $v_i \cdot v_j = -1/2$. We can write that $v_j = -\frac{1}{2}v_i + \frac{\sqrt{3}}{2}u$ for a unit vector u orthogonal to v_i in the v_i-v_j plane (see Figure 13.1). Rewriting in terms of u, we have $u = \frac{2}{\sqrt{3}}(\frac{1}{2}v_i + v_j)$. Then if $v_i \cdot r \geq \epsilon$ and $v_j \cdot r \geq \epsilon$, this implies that $u \cdot r \geq \frac{2}{\sqrt{3}}(\epsilon + \frac{1}{2}\epsilon) = \sqrt{3}\epsilon$. Since u is orthogonal to v_i, by Fact 6.5, $u \cdot r$ is normally distributed and independent of $v_i \cdot r$. Thus, given that $v_i \cdot r \geq \epsilon$, the probability that $v_j \cdot r \geq \epsilon$ is at most the probability that the independent, normally distributed random variable $u \cdot r \geq \sqrt{3}\epsilon$, which happens with probability $\overline{\Phi}(\sqrt{3}\epsilon)$. Thus, $\Pr[v_j \cdot r \geq \epsilon|v_i \cdot r \geq \epsilon] \leq \overline{\Phi}(\sqrt{3}\epsilon)$. Since i has at most Δ neighbors, we have that

$$\Pr[\exists(i, j) \in E : v_j \cdot r \geq \epsilon|v_i \cdot r \geq \epsilon] \leq \sum_{j:(i,j)\in E} \Pr[v_j \cdot r \geq \epsilon|v_i \cdot r \geq \epsilon] \leq \Delta\overline{\Phi}(\sqrt{3}\epsilon),$$

and we are done. $\square$

Now if we can set ϵ so that $\overline{\Phi}(\sqrt{3}\epsilon)$ is at most $\frac{1}{2\Delta}$, then the probability that $i \notin S'(\epsilon)$ given that $i \in S(\epsilon)$ is at most $1/2$, which implies that the expected size of $S'(\epsilon)$ will be at least half the expected size of $S(\epsilon)$, or at least $\frac{n}{2}\overline{\Phi}(\epsilon)$. To determine an ϵ that gives this probability and a large independent set, we use the following bounds on $\overline{\Phi}$.

Lemma 13.8. *For $x > 0$,*

$$\frac{x}{1 + x^2}p(x) \leq \overline{\Phi}(x) \leq \frac{1}{x}p(x).$$

Proof. Note that $p'(s) = -sp(s)$, so that $\left(-\frac{1}{s}p(s)\right)' = \left(1 + \frac{1}{s^2}\right)p(s)$. To obtain the lower bound on $\overline{\Phi}$, observe that

$$\left(1 + \frac{1}{x^2}\right)\overline{\Phi}(x) = \int_x^\infty \left(1 + \frac{1}{x^2}\right)p(s)ds$$

$$\geq \int_x^\infty \left(1 + \frac{1}{s^2}\right)p(s)ds$$

$$= -\frac{1}{s}p(s)\Bigg]_x^\infty = \frac{1}{x}p(x).$$

Dividing both sides of the inequality by $1 + \frac{1}{x^2}$ gives the lower bound on $\overline{\Phi}(x)$. To obtain the upper bound, observe

$$\overline{\Phi}(x) = \int_x^\infty p(s)ds$$

$$\leq \int_x^\infty \left(1 + \frac{1}{s^2}\right)p(s)ds = \frac{1}{x}p(x)$$

as above.   □

We can now give the following theorem.

Theorem 13.9. *Algorithm 13.2 produces an independent set of expected size at least* $\Omega(n\Delta^{-1/3}(\ln \Delta)^{-1/2})$.

Proof. We set $\epsilon = \sqrt{\frac{2}{3}\ln \Delta}$. Recall from the discussion that we run the algorithm only on graphs such that $\epsilon \geq 1$.

By Lemma 13.8, we see that

$$\overline{\Phi}(\sqrt{3}\epsilon) \leq \frac{1}{\sqrt{3}\epsilon}\frac{1}{\sqrt{2\pi}}e^{-3\epsilon^2/2}$$

$$= \frac{1}{\sqrt{2\ln \Delta}}\frac{1}{\sqrt{2\pi}}e^{-\ln \Delta}$$

$$\leq \frac{1}{2\Delta}.$$

As argued above, by Lemma 13.7, this implies that the probability that $i \notin S'(\epsilon)$ given that $i \in S(\epsilon)$ is at most $1/2$. Thus, the expected size of $S'(\epsilon)$ is

$$E[|S'(\epsilon)|] = \sum_{i \in V} \Pr[i \in S'(\epsilon)|i \in S(\epsilon)]\Pr[i \in S(\epsilon)] \geq \frac{n}{2}\overline{\Phi}(\epsilon),$$

using Lemma 13.6. Using Lemma 13.8 and the fact that $\epsilon \geq 1$, we know that

$$\overline{\Phi}(\epsilon) \geq \frac{\epsilon}{1 + \epsilon^2}\frac{1}{\sqrt{2\pi}}e^{-\epsilon^2/2} \geq \frac{1}{2\epsilon}\frac{1}{\sqrt{2\pi}}e^{-(\ln \Delta)/3} = \Omega((\ln \Delta)^{-1/2}\Delta^{-1/3}).$$

Thus, the expected size of the independent set returned is $\Omega(n\Delta^{-1/3}(\ln \Delta)^{-1/2})$.   □

A somewhat improved algorithm is possible using the same semidefinite programming relaxation, and a slightly more improved algorithm is possible using a stronger semidefinite programming relaxation; see the notes at the end of the chapter for a discussion. However, the algorithms still use $O(n^c)$ colors to color a 3-colorable graph, for a constant c. Whether or not it is possible to obtain significantly better results (such as $O(\log^c n)$ colors) remains a large open question.

13.3 Unique Games

In this section, we introduce the unique games problem. The unique games problem is a type of *constraint satisfaction problem*. In a constraint satisfaction problem, we are given n variables $x_1, \ldots, x_n$ and a finite universe U of values for the variables. Furthermore, we are given m constraints that are represented as functions mapping some subset of the variables to either 0 or 1. Typically, these constraints are drawn from a particular class of k-ary functions $f : U^k \rightarrow \{0, 1\}$. The goal is to find a setting of the variables to values in U such that we maximize the number of constraints that are *satisfied*; we say that a constraint is satisfied if the corresponding function evaluates to 1 given the setting of the variables. We can also consider weighted versions of this problem in which a nonnegative weight $w_j \geq 0$ is given as input for the jth constraint, and the goal is to find a setting of the variables that maximizes the total weight of the satisfied constraints.

Several problems that we have seen thus far are kinds of constraint satisfaction problems. The maximum cut problem, studied in Sections 5.1, 6.2, and 12.4, is a weighted constraint satisfaction problem. Given the input graph $G = (V, E)$ with weights $w_{ij} \geq 0$ for all $(i, j) \in E$, the maximum cut problem corresponds to the weighted constraint satisfaction problem in which $U = \{0, 1\}$, there is a variable x_i for each vertex $i \in V$, and there is a constraint $f(x_i, x_j) = x_i \oplus x_j$ for each edge (i, j) with weight w_{ij}, where $\oplus$ is the exclusive-or function (which is 1 precisely when $x_i \neq x_j$). The maximum satisfiability problem, discussed in several sections in Chapter 5 starting in Section 5.1, is also a constraint satisfaction problem in which $U = \{\text{true}, \text{false}\}$; each constraint corresponds to a clause of the input and it is a Boolean function evaluating to 1 exactly when the clause is satisfied.

The *unique games problem* is a type of binary constraint satisfaction problem; that is, each constraint corresponds to a function on two variables. Furthermore, each function has the property that given the value of one of the two variables, there is exactly one value of the other variable for which the constraint is satisfied. For example, the constraint satisfaction problem given by the maximum cut problem above is a unique games problem on a universe of two elements because for any constraint on variables i and j (corresponding to an edge (i, j)), given the value of $x_i \in \{0, 1\}$, there is only one value of x_j for which the constraint is satisfied, and similarly given the value of x_j. In general, we will be interested in the unique games problem for universes U of various sizes.

In previous sections, we have mentioned that various theorems on the hardness of approximating particular problems depend on a conjecture involving the unique games problem. We are now in a position to state formally what this means. Informally, it means that it is NP-hard to distinguish between instances of the unique games problem in which almost all of the constraints can be satisfied and almost none of the constraints can be satisfied.

Conjecture 13.10 (Unique games conjecture). *Given any $\epsilon, \delta > 0$, there exists some $k > 0$ depending on ϵ and δ, such that for the unique games problem with a universe of size k, it is NP-hard to distinguish between instances in which at least a $1 - \epsilon$ fraction of the constraints can be satisfied and instances in which at most a δ fraction of the constraints can be satisfied.*

Because the unique games problem deals with binary constraints, it is typical to view it as a kind of undirected graph problem. In what follows, we will index the nodes of the graph by $u, v, w, \ldots$ and the values of the universe U by $i, j, \ldots$, with $U = [k] = \{1, \ldots, k\}$. We introduce a vertex u for each variable x_u and an undirected edge (u, v) for each constraint $f(x_u, x_v)$. For each edge (u, v), we introduce a permutation $\pi_{uv} : U \to U$, such that $\pi_{uv}(i) = j$ exactly when $f(i, j) = 1$. Such a permutation exists by the definition of the unique games problem, since each label for u maps to a unique label for v that satisfies the constraint and vice versa. The problem becomes one of finding *labels* for the vertices from the universe U such that as many of the edges are satisfied as possible; that is, if vertex u is labeled with $i \in U$ and vertex v is labeled with $j \in U$, edge (u, v) is satisfied if $\pi_{uv}(i) = j$, since this corresponds to the original constraint being satisfied.

Interestingly, it is easy to tell when all the edges (or constraints) are satisfiable or not. Given the graph of constraints, consider a connected component of the graph and choose an arbitrary vertex v of the component. Given a label i for v, the labels for all the neighbors of v are uniquely determined if we satisfy all of the edges from v to its neighbors; in particular, we must label a neighbor w of v with $\pi_{vw}(i)$. We say that we *propagate* the label i for v to the neighbors of v. Similarly, we can propagate the labels of the neighbors of v to the labels of the neighbors of the neighbors of v, and so on, until we have labels for all vertices in the connected component. We then check whether all the edges of the component are satisfied. We do this for all possible labels of v; if there is some labeling that satisfies all the edges of the component, one of the choices of a label for v will be correct, and will lead to the correct labeling of all vertices in the component. Thus, in polynomial time we can check whether all the edges of the graph are satisfiable. This shows that a crucial part of the unique games conjecture is checking whether almost all of the constraints are satisfiable, as opposed to checking whether all of the constraints are satisfiable.

At this point in time we do not know whether or not there exists an approximation algorithm for the unique games problem with a performance guarantee that would refute the unique games conjecture. In what follows, we give an algorithm that, given an instance of the unique games problem such that at least a $1 - \epsilon$ fraction of the constraints are satisfiable, outputs a solution satisfying at least a $1 - O(\sqrt{\epsilon \log n})$ fraction of the constraints. If $\epsilon = O(1/\log n)$, then the algorithm satisfies a constant fraction of the constraints.

We begin by giving an integer quadratic program that models the unique games problem. For each node $u \in V$ and each label $i \in [k]$, we create a variable $u_i \in \{0, 1\}$, where we set $u_i = 1$ if the node u is assigned the label i and 0 otherwise. Then since each node is assigned exactly one label, we have that $\sum_{i=1}^{k} u_i^2 = 1$ and that $u_i u_j = 0$ for $i \neq j$. Finally, since the edge (u, v) is satisfied exactly when u is assigned some label i and v is assigned the label $\pi_{uv}(i)$, we have that $\sum_{i=1}^{k} u_i v_{\pi_{uv}(i)} = 1$ exactly when edge (u, v) is satisfied, and is 0 otherwise. Hence, the following program models the unique games problem:

$$\text{maximize} \sum_{(u,v)\in E} \sum_{i=1}^{k} u_i v_{\pi_{uv}(i)} \tag{13.6}$$

$$\text{subject to} \sum_{i=1}^{k} u_i^2 = 1, \qquad \forall u \in V,$$

$$u_i u_j = 0, \qquad \forall u \in V, i \in [k], j \in [k], i \neq j,$$

$$u_i \in \{0, 1\}, \qquad \forall u \in V, i \in [k].$$

We can add some additional constraints that are redundant for this integer quadratic program, but will be useful when we consider a vector programming relaxation of the problem. We can assume that $(v_j - u_i)^2 \geq v_j^2 - u_i^2$, since the inequality holds for all possible assignments of 0 and 1 to v_j and u_i. Finally, for any $u, v, w \in V$ and $h, i, j \in [k]$, it is the case that $(w_h - u_i)^2 \leq (w_h - v_j)^2 + (v_j - u_i)^2$, again by checking all possible assignments of 0 and 1 to u_i, v_j, and w_h. We can view this inequality as a type of triangle inequality. These additional inequalities yield the following integer quadratic program, which also models the unique games problem:

$$\text{maximize} \sum_{(u,v)\in E} \sum_{i=1}^{k} u_i v_{\pi_{uv}(i)} \tag{13.7}$$

$$\text{subject to} \sum_{i=1}^{k} u_i^2 = 1, \qquad \forall u \in V,$$

$$u_i u_j = 0, \qquad \forall u \in V, i \in [k], j \in [k], i \neq j,$$

$$(v_j - u_i)^2 \geq v_j^2 - u_i^2, \qquad \forall u, v \in V, i, j \in [k],$$

$$(w_h - u_i)^2 \leq (w_h - v_j)^2 + (v_j - u_i)^2, \quad \forall u, v, w \in V, h, i, j \in [k],$$

$$u_i \in \{0, 1\}, \qquad \forall u \in V, i \in [k],$$

We relax the program (13.7) to a vector program by replacing all the scalar variables u_i with vectors u_i and multiplication with inner products. Since $u_i \cdot u_i = \|u_i\|^2$ and $(v_j - u_i) \cdot (v_j - u_i) = \|v_j - u_i\|^2$, we obtain

$$\text{maximize} \sum_{(u,v)\in E} \sum_{i=1}^{k} u_i \cdot v_{\pi_{uv}(i)} \tag{13.8}$$

$$\text{subject to} \sum_{i=1}^{k} \|u_i\|^2 = 1, \qquad \forall u \in V, \tag{13.9}$$

$$u_i \cdot u_j = 0, \qquad \forall u \in V, i \in [k], j \in [k], i \neq j, \tag{13.10}$$

$$\|v_j - u_i\|^2 \geq \|v_j\|^2 - \|u_i\|^2, \qquad \forall u, v \in V, i, j \in [k], \tag{13.11}$$

$$\|w_h - u_i\|^2 \leq \|w_h - v_j\|^2 + \|v_j - u_i\|^2, \quad \forall u, v, w \in V, h, i, j \in [k]. \tag{13.12}$$

$$u_i \in \Re^{kn}, \qquad \forall u \in V, i \in [k].$$

It is clear that this vector program is a relaxation of the integer quadratic program, and thus gives an upper bound on the number of constraints satisfiable in the unique games instance.

At a high level, our algorithm will work as follows. We solve the vector programming relaxation (13.8). We use this information to discard some number of constraints; for the remainder of the algorithm we will not care if we satisfy these constraints or not. The discarded edges will be of two types. First, we discard edges that contribute relatively little to the objective function. Second, we remove edges so as to break the graph into low-radius balls via the region-growing technique introduced in Section 8.3. For the center w of each ball, we randomly assign a label i to w with probability $\|w_i\|^2$; we can do this since $\sum_{i=1}^{k} \|w_i\|^2 = 1$ by constraint (13.9). Given that the center w is assigned the label i, then for every other vertex v in the ball, we assign v the label j that is closest to w_i in the sense that $\|w_i - v_j\|^2$ is minimized over all choices of label j. The fact that the ball is of low radius will imply that it is very likely, given an edge (u, v) with both endpoints in the ball, that the labels assigned to u and v satisfy the constraint (u, v).

Before we dive into the details of the algorithm, we need some notation. Suppose we are given a unique games instance that satisfies at least a $1 - \epsilon$ fraction of the constraints. Let $\delta = \sqrt{\epsilon \ln(n + 1)}$. Let u_i denote the optimal vectors from the vector program, and let $Z^* = \sum_{(u,v) \in E} \sum_{i=1}^{k} u_i \cdot v_{\pi_{uv}(i)}$ denote the value of the optimal solution to the vector program. If m is the number of constraints, then $Z^* \geq \text{OPT} \geq (1 - \epsilon)m$. For each edge (u, v) in the unique games instance, we define a length $\ell(u, v) = \frac{1}{2} \sum_{i=1}^{k} \|u_i - v_{\pi_{uv}(i)}\|^2$. The length of (u, v) captures how close the vectors for u are to the vectors for v that have labelings satisying edge (u, v); in particular the length $\ell(u, v)$ is zero when $u_i = v_{\pi_{uv}(i)}$ for all $i \in [k]$. Note that

$$\ell(u, v) = \frac{1}{2} \sum_{i=1}^{k} \|u_i - v_{\pi_{uv}(i)}\|^2$$

$$= \frac{1}{2} \sum_{i=1}^{k} \left(\|u_i\|^2 + \|v_{\pi_{uv}(i)}\|^2 - 2u_i \cdot v_{\pi_{uv}(i)} \right).$$

Using constraint (13.9) and that π_{uv} is a permutation, this implies

$$\ell(u, v) = \frac{1}{2} \left(2 - 2 \sum_{i=1}^{k} u_i \cdot v_{\pi_{uv}(i)} \right) = 1 - \sum_{i=1}^{k} u_i \cdot v_{\pi_{uv}(i)},$$

so that the length $\ell(u, v)$ is exactly one minus the contribution of (u, v) to the vector program objective function. Let L^* be the total length of all edges. Therefore,

$$L^* = \sum_{(u,v) \in E} \ell(u, v) = m - Z^* \leq m - (1 - \epsilon)m = \epsilon m.$$

We can now fill in some of the details of the algorithm. Again, the main intuition is that given a random assignment of a label to a node w, we will very likely be able to satisfy any edge whose endpoints are close to w in terms of the length ℓ. To that end, we want to break the graph up into components of low radius in terms of length ℓ. We first discard any edge (u, v) whose length $\ell(u, v) \geq \delta/4$; recall $\delta = \sqrt{\epsilon \ln(n + 1)}$. Note that since the total length of all edges is at most ϵm, we discard at most $4\epsilon m/\delta = 4\delta m/\ln(n+1)$ edges this way. We can then invoke the following lemma to remove at most another $O(\delta m)$ edges and break the graph into balls of low radius according to the edge lengths ℓ. As mentioned previously, we will do this via the region-growing technique. Let $d_\ell(u, v)$ be the distance between u and v in the graph given edge lengths ℓ. Let $B_\ell(u, r)$ be a ball of radius r around vertex u, so that $B_\ell(u, r) = \{v \in V : d_\ell(u, v) \leq r\}$.

Lemma 13.11. *There is a polynomial-time algorithm to remove at most $8\delta m$ edges from the graph so that the vertices of the graph are partitioned into t balls $B_1, \ldots, B_t$, where each ball B is centered at some vertex $w \in V$ and has radius at most $\delta/4$.*

Proof. Let the volume $V_\ell^*(w, r)$ of a ball of radius r around w be the usual notion as in Sections 8.3 and 8.4; that is, for $B = B_\ell(w, r)$ we set

$$V_\ell^*(w, r) = \frac{L^*}{n} + \sum_{e=(u,v):u,v \in B} \ell(u, v) + \sum_{e=(u,v):u \in B, v \notin B} (r - d_\ell(w, u)).$$

Note then that $V_\ell^*(w, r) \leq L^* + L^*/n$ for any $w \in V$ and any radius r. Then by Corollary 8.11, we can in polynomial time find a radius $r \leq \delta/4$ around any vertex $w \in V$ such that the number of edges with exactly one endpoint in $B_\ell(w, r)$ is at most

$$\frac{4}{\delta} \ln\left(\frac{V_\ell^*(w, \delta/4)}{V_\ell^*(w, 0)}\right) V_\ell^*(w, r) \leq \frac{4}{\delta} \ln\left(\frac{L^* + L^*/n}{L^*/n}\right) V_\ell^*(w, r) = \frac{4}{\delta} \ln(n+1) V_\ell^*(w, r).$$

Following the proof of Theorem 8.9 for the multicut problem, we select a vertex w in the graph. If there is another vertex v at distance more than $\delta/4$, we find a ball around w of radius $r \leq \delta/4$ and remove at most $\frac{4}{\delta} \ln(n+1)V_\ell^*(w, r)$ edges from the graph; we add this ball to our collection, and remove the vertices in the ball (and all adjacent edges) from the graph. We repeat until we select a vertex w in the remaining graph such that all vertices v in the remaining graph are no farther than $\delta/4$ away; the remaining graph then is the final ball in the collection, with w as its center. The total volume $V_\ell^*(w, r)$ over all balls $B_\ell(w, r)$ in the collection except the final ball is at most $2L^*$, so the total number of edges removed is at most

$$\frac{8}{\delta} \ln(n+1)L^* \leq \frac{8\epsilon m}{\delta} \ln(n+1) = 8\delta m,$$

using $L^* \leq \epsilon m$ and $\delta = \sqrt{\epsilon \ln(n+1)}$. $\qquad\square$

We now consider each ball B in the collection separately. We show in the following lemma that if we label the center w with label i with probability $\|w_i\|^2$, and label every other vertex $v \in B$ with the label j minimizing $\|w_i - v_j\|^2$, then the probability that any edge (u, v) with both $u, v \in B$ is satisfied is at least $1 - 3\delta$. Observe that the algorithm is easy to derandomize: We try all k labels for the center w. For each labeling of w, label the other $v \in B$ as above and see which label for w satisfies the most edges that have both endpoints in the ball. By the lemma, some choice of label for w will satisfy at least a $1 - 3\delta$ fraction of these edges.

The central idea of the lemma is as follows. Consider a path from w to v, and suppose we assign label i to w with probability $\|w_i\|^2$. Then consider two potential labels for v: the label for v that we get by propagating the label i from w to v along its path, and the label we get for v by assigning it the label j that minimizes $\|w_i - v_j\|^2$. We show that these labels disagree with probability at most 4 times the length of the path. Thus, for any edge (u, v) with both endpoints in the ball, since the ball has low radius and the length of (u, v) is short, it is likely that u and v are both assigned labels that satisfy (u, v).

Lemma 13.12. *For any ball B with center w and any edge (u, v) such that $u, v \in B$, the probability that the algorithm assigns labels such that (u, v) is satisfied is at least $1 - 3\delta$.*

Proof. Consider edge (u, v). Since u is in a ball of radius at most $\delta/4$ around w, we know there is a path of length at most $\delta/4$ from w to u. Let $w = u^0, u^1, \ldots, u^q = u$ be this path. Since we discarded every edge of length greater than $\delta/4$, we know that adding the edge (u, v) to this path makes a path from w of v of length at most $\delta/2$.

We want to be able to compute the label propagated to vertex u^t along this path if w is labeled with label i. Let π_t be the composition of the permutations $\pi_{wu^1}, \ldots, \pi_{u^{t-1}u^t}$ along the path from w to u^t, so that $\pi_t(i) = \pi_{u^{t-1}u^t}(\pi_{t-1}(i))$. Let $\pi_u = \pi_q$ (that is, the composition of all permutations along the path from w to u) and let π_v be the composition of π_u with π_{uv}, so that $\pi_v(i) = \pi_{uv}(\pi_u(i))$. Thus, if we label w with i, then $\pi_t(i)$ is the label propagated to u^t, $\pi_u(i)$ is the label propagated to u, and $\pi_v(i)$ is the label propagated to v.

For any vertex $z \in B$, let $A(z)$ be a random variable denoting the label assigned to vertex z by the algorithm. Let P be the event that the label $A(u)$ given to u by the algorithm is equal to the label obtained by taking the label $A(w)$ assigned to w by the algorithm and propagating it to u along the path; that is, P is the event that $A(u) = \pi_u(A(w))$. We will show that the probability that this event does not occur is at most 4 times the length of the path from w to u, and so is at most δ. Thus, the probability that these labels are the same is at least $1 - \delta$. Similarly, we can show that the probability that the label $A(v)$ assigned to v by the algorithm is equal to the label propagated to v, $\pi_v(A(v))$, is at least $1 - 4(\delta/2) = 1 - 2\delta$. Thus, with probability at least $1 - 3\delta$, $A(v) = \pi_v(A(w))$ and $A(u) = \pi_u(A(w))$ so that $A(v) = \pi_{uv}(A(u))$, and the edge (u, v) is satisfied.

Note that for any t,

$$\ell(u^t, u^{t+1}) = \frac{1}{2} \sum_{i=1}^{k} \|u_i^t - u_{\pi_{u^t u^{t+1}}(i)}^{t+1}\|^2 = \frac{1}{2} \sum_{i=1}^{k} \|u_{\pi_t(i)}^t - u_{\pi_{t+1}(i)}^{t+1}\|^2$$

by our definitions and since π_t is a permutation. Then by using the triangle inequality constraint (13.12), we see that

$$\frac{1}{2} \sum_{i=1}^{k} \|w_i - u_{\pi_u(i)}\|^2$$

$$\leq \frac{1}{2} \sum_{i=1}^{k} \left(\|w_i - u_{\pi_1(i)}^1\|^2 + \|u_{\pi_1(i)}^1 - u_{\pi_2(i)}^2\|^2 + \cdots + \|u_{\pi_{q-1}(i)}^{q-1} - u_{\pi_u(i)}^q\|^2 \right)$$

$$= \frac{1}{2} \sum_{i=1}^{k} \|w_i - u_{\pi_1(i)}^1\|^2 + \frac{1}{2} \sum_{i=1}^{k} \|u_{\pi_1(i)}^1 - u_{\pi_2(i)}^2\|^2 + \cdots + \frac{1}{2} \sum_{i=1}^{k} \|u_{\pi_{q-1}(i)}^{q-1} - u_{\pi_u(i)}^q\|^2$$

$$= \ell(w, u^1) + \ell(u^1, u^2) + \cdots + \ell(u^{q-1}, u^q)$$

$$\leq \delta/4, \tag{13.13}$$

since the path length is at most $\delta/4$. Let I be the set of labels i such that if we assign i to w then u is assigned a label different from its propagated value $\pi_u(i)$; that is, some $j \neq \pi_u(i)$ minimizes $\|w_i - u_j\|^2$. Then since we assign i to w with probability $\|w_i\|^2$, we have that

$$\Pr[A(u) \neq \pi_u(A(w))] = \sum_{i \in I} \|w_i\|^2.$$

We claim that for every $i \in I$, $\|w_i - u_{\pi_u(i)}\|^2 \geq \frac{1}{2}\|w_i\|^2$. Given the claim, we then have

$$\Pr[A(u) \neq \pi_u(A(w))] = \sum_{i \in I} \|w_i\|^2$$

$$\leq 2 \sum_{i \in I} \|w_i - u_{\pi_u(i)}\|^2$$

$$\leq 2 \sum_{i=1}^{k} \|w_i - u_{\pi_u(i)}\|^2$$

$$\leq 4 \cdot (\delta/4) = \delta,$$

where the last inequality follows from inequality (13.13). Since the length of the path from w to v is at most $\delta/2$, by a similar argument,

$$\Pr[A(v) \neq \pi_v(A(w))] \leq 4 \cdot (\delta/2) = 2\delta.$$

As we argued previously, this implies that edge (u, v) is satisfied with probability at least $1 - 3\delta$.

Now to prove the claim. We consider three cases. Assume that w is assigned the label i, and that j is the label for u that minimizes $\|w_i - u_j\|^2$. For simplicity of notation, let h be the propagated value $\pi_u(i)$; since $i \in I$, we know that $\pi_u(i) = h \neq j$. If $\|u_h\|^2 \leq \frac{1}{2}\|w_i\|^2$, then the inequality follows from the constraint (13.11), since

$$\|w_i - u_h\|^2 \geq \|w_i\|^2 - \|u_h\|^2 \geq \frac{1}{2}\|w_i\|^2.$$

Now suppose $\|u_j\|^2 \leq \frac{1}{2}\|w_i\|^2$. Then since j is the label that minimizes $\|w_i - u_j\|^2$, we have that

$$\|w_i - u_h\|^2 \geq \|w_i - u_j\|^2 \geq \|w_i\|^2 - \|u_j\|^2 \geq \frac{1}{2}\|w_i\|^2,$$

by constraint (13.11) and by hypothesis. Now suppose that neither condition holds, and both $\|u_h\|^2 \geq \frac{1}{2}\|w_i\|^2$ and $\|u_j\|^2 \geq \frac{1}{2}\|w_i\|^2$. By the triangle inequality constraint (13.12) and the fact that j is the label minimizing $\|w_i - u_j\|^2$, we have that

$$\|u_h - u_j\|^2 \leq \|w_i - u_h\|^2 + \|w_i - u_j\|^2 \leq 2\|w_i - u_h\|^2.$$

By constraint (13.10) and the fact $j \neq h$, it follows that $u_j \cdot u_h = 0$ so that

$$\|u_h - u_j\|^2 = \|u_h\|^2 + \|u_j\|^2 - 2u_h \cdot u_j = \|u_h\|^2 + \|u_j\|^2.$$

Thus,

$$\|w_i - u_h\|^2 \geq \frac{1}{2}\|u_h - u_j\|^2 = \frac{1}{2}\left(\|u_h\|^2 + \|u_j\|^2\right) \geq \frac{1}{2}\|w_i\|^2,$$

by hypothesis, and the claim holds. $\qquad\square$

We can now prove the following theorem.

Theorem 13.13. *Given an instance of the unique games problem satisfying a $1 - \epsilon$ fraction of the constraints, the algorithm above satisfies at least a $1 - 15\delta = 1 - O(\sqrt{\epsilon \log n})$ fraction of the constraints.*

Proof. When we remove all long edges, we remove at most $4\delta m / \ln(n + 1) \leq 4\delta m$ edges, and when we divide the graph up into balls, we remove at most $8\delta m$ edges. In each ball, we fail to satisfy at most a 3δ fraction of the edges with both endpoints in the balls, and so over all balls, we fail to satisfy at most $3\delta m$ edges. Thus, we fail to satisfy at most $(4 + 8 + 3)\delta m = 15\delta m$ edges, which gives the result. $\quad\square$

Somewhat better algorithms are known; these use the same vector programming relaxation of the unique games problem. One such algorithm shows the following.

Theorem 13.14. *Given a unique games instance in which at least a $1 - \epsilon$ fraction of the constraints are satisfiable, there is a polynomial-time algorithm that satisfies at least a $1 - O(\sqrt{\epsilon} \log k)$ fraction of the constraints.*

The following theorem shows that this result is essentially the best possible assuming that the unique games conjecture is true.

Theorem 13.15. *Assuming that the unique games conjecture is true, for any $\epsilon > 0$ there exists a k depending on ϵ such that for the unique games problem with universe size k, it is NP-hard to distinguish between instances in which a $1 - \epsilon$ fraction of constraints are satisfiable, and instances in which a $1 - \sqrt{2/\pi}\sqrt{\epsilon \log k} + o(1)$ fraction of constraints are satisfiable.*

Exercises

13.1 Show that the graph coloring algorithm of Section 13.2 can be used to color a 3-colorable graph with $\tilde{O}(n^{1/4})$ colors.

13.2 In this problem, we consider an unweighted version of the minimum multicut problem from Section 8.3. We are given a graph $G = (V, E)$ and k pairs of source-sink vertices, $s_i, t_i \in V$ for $i = 1, \ldots, k$. We wish to find a subset of edges $F \subseteq E$ that minimizes $|F|$ such that for each $i = 1, \ldots, k$, there is no s_i-t_i path in $(V, E - F)$.

Consider the following vector program:

$$\text{minimize} \quad \sum_{(i,j) \in E} (1 - v_i \cdot v_j)$$

$$\text{subject to} \quad v_{s_i} \cdot v_{t_i} = 0, \quad i = 1, \ldots, k,$$

$$v_j \cdot v_j = 1, \quad \forall j \in V,$$

$$v_j \in \Re^n, \quad \forall j \in V.$$

Consider the *demand graph* $H = (V, E')$, where $E' = \{(s_i, t_i) : i = 1, \ldots, k\}$. Let Δ be the maximum degree of a vertex in the demand graph. Suppose that the optimal value of the vector programming relaxation is $\epsilon|E|$. Consider the following algorithm, which is similar to the algorithm in Section 6.5 for coloring 3-colorable graphs. We draw

$t = \lceil \log_2(\Delta/\epsilon) \rceil$ random vectors $r_1, \ldots, r_t$. The t random vectors define 2^t different regions into which the vectors v_i can fall: one region for each distinct possibility of whether $r_j \cdot v_i \geq 0$ or $r_j \cdot v_i < 0$ for all $j = 1, \ldots, t$. Remove all edges (i, j) from the graph such that v_i and v_j are in different regions. If for any s_i-t_i pair, there still exists an s_i-t_i path, remove all edges incident on s_i. We now analyze this algorithm.

(a) Prove that the vector program is a relaxation of the unweighted minimum multicut problem.

(b) For any $(i, j) \in E$, prove that the probability that i and j are in different regions is at most $t \cdot \sqrt{1 - v_i \cdot v_j}$.

(c) Prove that for any $i = 1, \ldots, k$, the probability that we end up removing all the edges incident on i is at most $\Delta 2^{-t}$.

(d) Show that the expected number of edges removed is at most $O(\sqrt{\epsilon} \log(\Delta/\epsilon))|E|$.

For the final item, it may be useful to use *Jensen's inequality*, which states that for any convex function f (that is, $f''(x) \geq 0$) and any positive p_i,

$$f\left(\frac{\sum_i p_i x_i}{\sum_i p_i}\right) \leq \frac{1}{\sum_i p_i} \sum_i p_i f(x_i).$$

The arithmetic-geometric mean inequality given in Fact 5.8 is a special case of Jensen's inequality with $f(x) = -\log x$ and all the $p_i = 1$.

13.3 In this problem, we consider another algorithm for the unweighted minimum multicut problem from the previous exercise, using the same vector programming relaxation as above. As before, assume that the optimal value of the vector programming relaxation is $\epsilon|E|$, and that Δ is the maximum degree of a vertex in the demand graph. We set a threshold $\alpha = C\sqrt{\ln(\Delta/\epsilon)}$ for some constant C. Suppose we draw a random vector r. Consider the set $S(\alpha) = \{i \in V : v_i \cdot r \geq \alpha\}$, and $S'(\alpha) = S(\alpha) - \bigcup_{i=1}^k \{s_i, t_i : s_i, t_i \in S(\alpha)\}$; that is, $S'(\alpha)$ is all elements in $S(\alpha)$ except for the s_i, t_i pairs that both end up in $S(\alpha)$.

The following inequality will be useful for the analysis of the algorithm. Let v_i and v_j be unit vectors, and let r be a random vector. Let α be a quantity such that $\alpha > 1$ and $\overline{\Phi}(\alpha) < 1/3$. Then

$$\Pr[v_i \cdot r \geq \alpha \text{ and } v_j \cdot r < \alpha] = O\left(\sqrt{v_i \cdot v_j} \, \overline{\Phi}(\alpha) \sqrt{\log(1/\overline{\Phi}(\alpha))}\right).$$

(a) Give a randomized algorithm that works by repeatedly drawing random vectors r and considering the set $S'(\alpha)$ as defined above. Show that the expected size of the multicut returned by the algorithm is at most

$$\sum_{(i,j) \in E} \frac{\Pr[(i, j) \in \delta(S'(\alpha))]}{\Pr[i \in S'(\alpha) \text{ or } j \in S'(\alpha)]}.$$

(b) Prove that for any $(i, j) \in E$,

$$\frac{\Pr[(i, j) \in \delta(S'(\alpha))]}{\Pr[i \in S'(\alpha) \text{ or } j \in S'(\alpha)]} \leq O(\sqrt{v_i \cdot v_j})\alpha + \epsilon.$$

(c) Show that the randomized algorithm returns a multicut of size $O(\sqrt{\epsilon} \log(\Delta/\epsilon))|E|$ edges in expectation.

Chapter Notes

The approximation algorithm for quadratic programs given in Section 13.1 was rediscovered several times. To our knowledge, it first appeared in a paper of Nemirovski, Roos, and Terlaky [234], then later in papers of Megretski [224] and Charikar and Wirth [67]. Our presentation here follows that of Charikar and Wirth.

The approximation algorithm for coloring 3-colorable graphs of Section 13.2 is due to Karger, Motwani, and Sudan [182], but the analysis we present follows that of Arora, Chlamtac, and Charikar [15]. Exercise 13.1 is due to Karger et al. Through an improved algorithm and analysis, Arora et al. are able to color 3-colorable graphs with $O(n^{0.211})$ colors.

The unique games conjecture was first formulated in a paper of Khot [192]. Since then it has prompted a significant amount of research in algorithms and complexity theory, and has been used to show the conditional hardness of a quite significant number of results; we will say more about the conjecture in Chapter 16. The approximation algorithm for the unique games problem given here is due to Trevisan [282] with a slightly improved analysis due to Gupta and Talwar [150]. Charikar, Makarychev, and Makarychev [65] give the improved result mentioned in Theorem 13.14. The hardness result of Theorem 13.15 is due to Khot, Kindler, Mossel, and O'Donnell [193], together with a result of Mossel, O'Donnell, and Oleszkiewicz [227].

Exercises 13.2 and 13.3 are due to Steurer and Vishnoi [272]. The bound given in Exercise 13.3 is from Chlamtac, Makarychev, and Makarychev [72, Lemma A.2].

CHAPTER 14

Further Uses of the Primal-Dual Method

In this chapter, we give two somewhat more sophisticated applications of the standard primal-dual algorithm and analysis introduced in Chapter 7. We revisit the prize-collecting Steiner tree problem discussed in Sections 4.4 and 5.7, and give a primal-dual 2-approximation algorithm for it. We also revisit the feedback vertex set problem in undirected graphs introduced in Section 7.2, and give a primal-dual 2-approximation algorithm for this problem as well. In this case, we must give an alternative integer programming formulation for the problem since the previous formulation has an integrality gap that implies that the $O(\log n)$-approximation algorithm of Section 7.2 is the best possible (within constant factors) using the formulation of that section.

14.1 The Prize-Collecting Steiner Tree Problem

In this section, we revisit the prize-collecting Steiner tree problem introduced in Section 4.4 and further discussed in Section 5.7. We show that a primal-dual algorithm can be used to give a 2-approximation algorithm for the problem; this improves on the performance guarantee of the previously given algorithms, and the primal-dual algorithm does not require solving a linear programming relaxation. Recall that in this problem we are given an undirected graph $G = (V, E)$, edge costs $c_e \geq 0$ for all $e \in E$, a selected root vertex $r \in V$, and penalties $\pi_i \geq 0$ for all $i \in V$. The goal is to find a tree T that contains the root vertex r so as to minimize the cost of the edges in T plus the penalties of the vertices not in T; that is, $\sum_{e \in T} c_e + \sum_{i \in V - V(T)} \pi_i$, where $V(T)$ is the set of vertices in the tree.

We start by giving a different integer programming formulation of the problem. We have decision variables $x_e \in \{0, 1\}$ indicating if an edge $e \in E$ is part of the tree. We also have variables $z_X \in \{0, 1\}$ for all $X \subseteq V - r$, where $z_X = 1$ if X is the set of vertices not spanned by the tree and $z_X = 0$ otherwise. Then we need a constraint enforcing that for any subset $S \subseteq V$, either S is a subset of the set of vertices not spanned by the tree or some of S is being spanned by the tree. We do this with the constraint

$$\sum_{e \in \delta(S)} x_e + \sum_{X : X \supseteq S} z_X \geq 1,$$

since if $x_e = 1$ for some $e \in \delta(S)$, then at least some vertex in S is spanned by the tree. Let $\pi(X) = \sum_{i \in X} \pi_i$. Then we have the following integer programming formulation:

$$\text{minimize} \sum_{e \in E} c_e x_e + \sum_{X \subseteq V - r} \pi(X) z_X$$

$$\text{subject to} \quad \sum_{e \in \delta(S)} x_e + \sum_{X : X \supseteq S} z_X \geq 1, \qquad \forall S \subseteq V - r,$$

$$x_e \in \{0, 1\}, \quad \forall e \in E,$$

$$z_X \in \{0, 1\}, \quad \forall X \subseteq V - r.$$

As in the case of the shortest s-t path problem and the generalized Steiner tree problem in Sections 7.3 and 7.4, it can be shown via the max-flow/min-cut theorem that in any feasible solution there is a tree connecting the root r to every vertex i that is not in some set X for which $z_X = 1$.

If we replace the integrality conditions $x_e \in \{0, 1\}$ and $z_X \in \{0, 1\}$ with $x_e \geq 0$ and $z_X \geq 0$, and take the dual of this linear program, we obtain the following:

$$\text{maximize} \sum_{S \subseteq V - r} y_S$$

$$\text{subject to} \sum_{S : e \in \delta(S)} y_S \leq c_e, \qquad \forall e \in E,$$

$$\sum_{S : S \subseteq X} y_S \leq \pi(X), \qquad \forall X \subseteq V - r,$$

$$y_S \geq 0, \qquad \forall S \subseteq V - r.$$

Note that the dual LP has two types of constraints: one type associated with edges, and the other associated with sets of vertices. It will be convenient to introduce some notation regarding the constraint on sets.

Definition 14.1. *For a given set of vertices X such that $r \notin X$ and a dual feasible solution y, we say that $p(X, y, \pi) = \pi(X) - \sum_{S : S \subseteq X} y_S$ is the remaining potential of the set X.*

We now give our primal-dual algorithm in Algorithm 14.1. As in the case of the generalized Steiner tree algorithm, we maintain a feasible dual solution y (initially all zero) and an infeasible primal solution F (initially the empty set). We divide the connected components of F into two types: *active* and *inactive*. The connected component containing the root is always inactive. Any component C such that its potential $p(C, y, \pi)$ is zero is also inactive. Note that this corresponds to a tight dual constraint in which $\sum_{S : S \subseteq C} y_S = \pi(C)$, so we cannot increase the dual variable y_C without making the dual solution infeasible. We increase the dual variables associated with all active components uniformly until one of the two types of dual constraints becomes tight. If a constraint associated with an edge e becomes tight for some $e \in \delta(C)$ for some active

$y \leftarrow 0$
$F \leftarrow \emptyset$
$\ell \leftarrow 1$
while not all connected components of (V, F) are inactive **do**
    Let $\mathcal{C}$ be the set of all active connected components C of (V, F)
        $(p(C, y, \pi) > 0$ and $r \notin C)$
    Increase y_C for all C in $\mathcal{C}$ uniformly until either for some $e_\ell \in \delta(C')$, $C' \in \mathcal{C}$,
        $c_{e_\ell} = \sum_{S:e_\ell \in \delta(S)} y_S$ or for some $C \in \mathcal{C}$, $p(C, y, \pi) = 0$
    if for some $C \in \mathcal{C}$, $p(C, y, \pi) = 0$ **then**
        Make C inactive and remove C from $\mathcal{C}$
    else
        $F \leftarrow F \cup \{e_\ell\}$
        $\ell \leftarrow \ell + 1$
Let F' be the connected component of (V, F) containing r
for $k \leftarrow \ell - 1$ downto 1 **do**
    if $e_k \in F'$ **then**
        Let C be vertices connected to r by e_k
        if $p(C, y, \pi) = 0$ **then**
            Remove e_k from F' and remove all edges of F' with both endpoints
            in C
return F'

Algorithm 14.1. Primal-dual algorithm for the prize-collecting Steiner tree problem.

set C, we add e to F and continue. If a constraint associated with a set C becomes tight for some active set C (and its potential becomes zero), we make C inactive and continue. We end the main loop when all connected components of F are inactive.

As with the generalized Steiner tree algorithm, we have a final clean-up step in which we consider all the edges added to F in the reverse of the order in which they were added. We begin by letting F' be the connected component of F that contains the root vertex r. Then we iterate through the edges of F' in the reverse of the order in which they were added to F. Suppose we consider removing edge e. Removing e will disconnect some set of vertices C from the root. We check whether $p(C, y, \pi) = 0$. If it is, we remove from F' the edge e and all the edges of F' connecting vertices of C (so that F' remains a tree containing the root). Otherwise, we keep edge e.

We show that this algorithm gives us a performance guarantee of 2. As in the case of the generalized Steiner tree algorithm, this result follows from a lemma whose proof we will defer for a few moments.

Lemma 14.2. *Let F' be the tree returned by the algorithm, and let X be the vertices not spanned by F'. In any given iteration in which $\mathcal{C}$ is the set of active components,*

$$\sum_{C \in \mathcal{C}} |\delta(C) \cap F'| + |\{C \in \mathcal{C} : C \subseteq X\}| \leq 2|\mathcal{C}|.$$

From this lemma we can prove the performance guarantee.

Theorem 14.3. *Algorithm 14.1 is a 2-approximation algorithm for the prize-collecting Steiner tree problem.*

Proof. Let F' be the final tree containing the root, and let X be the vertices not spanned by F'. We first claim that X can be partitioned into sets $X_1, \ldots, X_k$ such that the potential $p(X_j, y, \pi) = 0$ for each set X_j. To see this, note that for any vertex in X either it was connected to the root before the edge deletion process or it was not. If it was not connected to the root, then it was in some inactive component I not containing the root, and I was inactive since the potential $p(I, y, \pi) = 0$. If the vertex was connected to the root before the edge deletion process, then it must have been disconnected in some step in which an edge was removed and a set of vertices I was disconnected from the root. But for this set, it must have been the case that the potential $p(I, y, \pi) = 0$. Hence, the claim follows.

Observe that the potential $p(I, y, \pi) = 0$ implies that $\pi(I) = \sum_{S \subseteq I} y_S$. We now rewrite the cost of the primal solution in terms of dual variables:

$$\sum_{e \in F'} c_e + \sum_{i \in X} \pi_i = \sum_{e \in F'} \sum_{S:e \in \delta(S)} y_S + \sum_{j=1}^{k} \pi(X_j)$$

$$= \sum_{S} |\delta(S) \cap F'| y_S + \sum_{j=1}^{k} \sum_{S \subseteq X_j} y_S.$$

We would like to show that this cost is less than twice the dual objective function; that is, we would like to show that

$$\sum_{S} |\delta(S) \cap F'| y_S + \sum_{j=1}^{k} \sum_{S \subseteq X_j} y_S \leq 2 \sum_{S \subseteq V - r} y_S. \tag{14.1}$$

As in the proof of Lemma 7.7, we do this by induction on the algorithm. Initially all dual variables are zero, and the inequality holds. Suppose that the inequality holds at the beginning of any given iteration. Let $\mathcal{C}$ be the active components in this iteration. Then in this iteration we increase each y_S for $S \in \mathcal{C}$ by the same amount (call it ϵ). This increases the left-hand side of (14.1) by

$$\epsilon \sum_{C \in \mathcal{C}} |F' \cap \delta(C)| + \epsilon \sum_{j=1}^{k} |\{C \in \mathcal{C} : C \subseteq X_j\}|$$

and the right-hand side by

$$2\epsilon |\mathcal{C}|.$$

However, by the inequality of Lemma 14.2, this means that the increase in the left-hand side is no greater than the increase in the right-hand side. Thus, if the inequality held before the increase of the dual variables in this iteration, it will also hold afterward. $\square$

We now conclude with the proof of the lemma.

Proof of Lemma 14.2. Given an iteration, let C be the set of active components, and let $\mathcal{I}$ be the set of connected components that are inactive. Note that the sets in $\mathcal{C}$ and $\mathcal{I}$ partition the set of vertices.

We begin by simplifying the inequality we must prove. Observe that if for some $C \in \mathcal{C}$, no vertex in C is spanned by the tree F', then $\delta(C) \cap F' = \emptyset$. Hence, if $C \subseteq X$, then $\delta(C) \cap F' = \emptyset$. Let $\mathcal{C}' = \{C \in \mathcal{C} : C \not\subseteq X\}$. Thus, the desired inequality is implied by showing

$$\sum_{C \in \mathcal{C}'} |\delta(C) \cap F'| \leq 2|\mathcal{C}'|.$$

As in the proof of Lemma 7.7 for the generalized Steiner tree, we consider the graph obtained by contracting each component in $\mathcal{C}'$ and $\mathcal{I}$ to a single node, ignoring components in $\mathcal{C} - \mathcal{C}'$; let V' be the resulting vertex set. Let T be the set of edges on V' from F' once the components in $\mathcal{C}'$ and $\mathcal{I}$ are collapsed; the edges in T form a tree as shown in Observation 7.9 and Lemma 7.7. We let $deg(v)$ for $v \in V'$ represent the degree of vertex v in this tree. We also color the vertices in V' with two different colors, red and blue: red vertices correspond to components from $\mathcal{C}'$ and blue vertices correspond to components from $\mathcal{I}$. Let R denote the set of red vertices in V' and B the set of blue vertices v that have $deg(v) > 0$. We can rewrite the desired inequality

$$\sum_{C \in \mathcal{C}'} |\delta(C) \cap F'| \leq 2|\mathcal{C}'|$$

in terms of this tree by showing $\sum_{v \in R} deg(v) \leq 2|R|$.

To prove this inequality, we claim that at most one blue vertex can have degree exactly one. If this is true, then we have that

$$\sum_{v \in R} deg(v) = \sum_{v \in R \cup B} deg(v) - \sum_{v \in B} deg(v).$$

Since the total degree of a forest is no more than twice the number of vertices in it minus one, and since all but one of the blue vertices in B have degree at least two by the claim, we have that this quantity is

$$\sum_{v \in R \cup B} deg(v) - \sum_{v \in B} deg(v) \leq 2(|R| + |B| - 1) - 2(|B| - 1) - 1 \leq 2|R|,$$

as desired.

Now to show the claim. At most one blue vertex corresponds to a component in the uncontracted graph containing the root. We show that all other blue vertices cannot have degree one. Suppose not, and there is a blue vertex v of degree one. Let $e \in F'$ be the edge incident on this vertex, and let $I \in \mathcal{I}$ be the corresponding component in the uncontracted graph, with $r \notin I$. First observe that because $e \in \delta(I)$, it is the case that e was added after the current iteration; otherwise, I would be part of a larger connected component containing e in the current iteration. Now when we considered e for removal, it joined some component C to the root. Since I remains connected to the root by e in the current iteration, it must be the case that $I \subseteq C$. Let $Q_1, \ldots, Q_k$ be the parts of C that were removed by later steps of the edge deletion process, from the point that e is considered down to the current iteration, so that I and the Q_j partition C (see

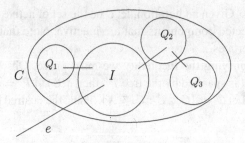

Figure 14.1. Part of the proof of Lemma 14.2.

Figure 14.1). Because the Q_j were removed, we know that $p(Q_j, y, \pi) = 0$. Because I is inactive and does not contain the root, it is also the case that $p(I, y, \pi) = 0$. By dual feasibility we know that

$$\pi(C) \geq \sum_{S \subseteq C} y_S \geq \sum_{S \subseteq I} y_S + \sum_{j=1}^{k} \sum_{S \subseteq Q_j} y_S.$$

Because the potentials of I and the Q_j are zero, the right-hand side is

$$\pi(I) + \sum_{j=1}^{k} \pi(Q_j) = \pi(C).$$

Thus, it must be the case that $\sum_{S \subseteq C} y_S = \pi(C)$, and that $p(C, y, \pi) = 0$. Hence, we should have removed edge e, which contradicts $e \in F'$, and we are done. $\qquad\square$

14.2 The Feedback Vertex Set Problem in Undirected Graphs

In this section, we return to the feedback vertex set problem in undirected graphs introduced in Section 7.2. Recall that in this problem we are given an undirected graph $G = (V, E)$ and nonnegative weights $w_v \geq 0$ for vertices $v \in V$, and the goal is to choose a minimum-cost subset of vertices $S \subseteq V$ such that every cycle C in the graph contains some vertex of S. Alternatively, we must find a minimum-weight set of vertices S such that the induced graph $G(V - S)$ is acyclic, where $G(V - S)$ is the graph induced by the vertex set $V - S$. We will sometimes use the shorthand $G - S$ for the graph induced on $V - S$.

In Section 7.2, we gave a primal-dual $O(\log n)$-approximation algorithm for the feedback vertex set problem. The algorithm used the following integer programming formulation for the problem, where $\mathcal{C}$ denotes the set of all cycles C in the graph:

$$
\begin{aligned}
\text{minimize} \quad & \sum_{v \in V} w_v x_v \\
\text{subject to} \quad & \sum_{v \in C} x_v \geq 1, \qquad \forall C \in \mathcal{C}, \\
& x_v \in \{0, 1\}, \quad \forall v \in V.
\end{aligned}
$$

In that section we claimed that the integrality gap of this formulation is known to be $\Omega(\log n)$, and so we cannot achieve a performance guarantee better than $O(\log n)$ using the integer programming formulation above.

However, we can devise a primal-dual 2-approximation algorithm by using an alternative integer programming formulation for the problem. To do this, we start by considering the number of edges that will need to be removed from the graph in order for the graph to be acyclic. Let $c(G)$ be the number of connected components in graph G. An acyclic subset of edges in a graph $G = (V, E)$ can have at most $|V| - c(G)$ edges. Therefore, we must remove at least $|E| - |V| + c(G)$ edges for the graph to become acyclic. Note that if we remove a vertex v and its incident edges, and $d(v)$ is the degree of vertex v, then it would seem that we remove $d(v)$ edges toward the overall goal of removing $|E| - |V| + c(G)$ edges. However, note that by removing v, we also reduce the number of vertices that need to be spanned by the remaining edges. In particular, in the remaining graph (with v removed), we now need to remove at least $(|E| - |d(v)|) - (|V| - 1) + c(G - v)$ edges for $G - v$ to become acyclic. Thus, removing v decreases the total number of edges we need to remove by

$$[|E| - |V| + c(G)] - [(|E| - d(v)) - (|V| - 1) + c(G - v)]$$
$$= d(v) - 1 + (c(G) - c(G - v)).$$

For simplicity of exposition, let us denote the quantity $c(G - v) - c(G) + 1$ by $b(v)$, so that removing v decreases the total number of edges we need to remove by $d(v) - b(v)$. We can formalize the reasoning above as follows.

Lemma 14.4. *For any feedback vertex set F of the graph $G = (V, E)$,*

$$\sum_{v \in F} (d(v) - b(v)) \geq |E| - |V| + c(G).$$

Proof. We know that if we remove F and its adjacent edges from the graph, the remaining set of edges is acyclic. Let $E(F)$ be the set of edges that have both endpoints in F. Then $\sum_{v \in F} d(v) - |E(F)|$ is an upper bound on the number of edges removed. Since $|V| - |F| - c(G - F)$ is an upper bound on the number of edges left over, we have that

$$|E| \leq \sum_{v \in F} d(v) - |E(F)| + |V| - |F| - c(G - F).$$

We now claim that we can show that

$$c(G) \leq \sum_{v \in F} (1 - b(v)) + |E(F)| + c(G - F). \tag{14.2}$$

Given the claim, if we add the two inequalities, we obtain

$$|E| + c(G) \leq \sum_{v \in F} (d(v) - b(v)) + |V|.$$

Subtracting $|V|$ from both sides gives the desired inequality.

We prove inequality (14.2) by induction on F; we will not need the fact that F is a feedback vertex set to prove the claim. It is easy to see that the claim holds if $F = \emptyset$

or $F = \{v\}$; in the latter case, this follows by the definition of $b(v)$ since

$$c(G) \leq (1 - b(v)) + c(G - v) = (1 - c(G - v) + c(G) - 1) + c(G - v) = c(G).$$

Suppose the claim holds for $F - v$; we now show it holds for F. Consider the neighbors of v in G. If we remove v from G, these are partitioned into at least $c(G - v) - c(G) = b(v) - 1$ additional connected components. Suppose we choose one distinct neighbor of v in each of these $b(v) - 1$ connected components. For each such neighbor, either the neighbor is already in F, and hence $E(F)$ includes the edge from v to this neighbor, or the neighbor is not in F, and removing v from $G - (F - v)$ will create a new connected component containing this neighbor. Thus, we have that $b(v) - 1$ is at most $|E(F)| - |E(F - v)|$ plus $c(G - F) - c(G - (F - v))$ or $0 \leq 1 - b(v) + |E(F)| - |E(F - v)| + c(G - F) - c(G - (F - v))$. By induction the inequality holds for $F - v$, so that

$$c(G) \leq \sum_{u \in F - v} (1 - b(u)) + |E(F - v)| + c(G - (F - v)).$$

Adding the previous inequality to this one gives inequality (14.2) for F. $\square$

Consider any subset $S \subseteq V$ of vertices. Let $G(S)$ be the subgraph of $G = (V, E)$ induced by S, let $d_S(v)$ for $v \in S$ be the degree of v in $G(S)$, and let $b_S(v)$ for $v \in S$ be the value of $b(v)$ in the graph $G(S)$. Let $f(S) = |E(S)| - |S| + c(G(S))$ be the minimum number of edges we need to remove to have a feedback vertex set in $G(S)$. Then by observing that $F \cap S$ is a feedback vertex set for $G(S)$, we have the following corollary to Lemma 14.4.

Corollary 14.5. *For any subset of vertices* $S \subseteq V$,

$$\sum_{v \in F \cap S} (d_S(v) - b_S(v)) \geq f(S).$$

We can now give the following integer program, which we claim models the feedback vertex set problem in undirected graphs:

$$\text{minimize} \sum_{v \in V} w_v x_v$$

$$\text{subject to} \sum_{v \in S} (d_S(v) - b_S(v)) x_v \geq f(S), \quad \forall S \subseteq V,$$

$$x_v \in \{0, 1\}, \quad \forall v \in V.$$

As before, the variable x_v denotes whether the vertex v is in the feedback vertex set or not. If a solution x corresponds to a feedback vertex set, then all the constraints are obeyed by Corollary 14.5. If a solution x does not correspond to a feedback vertex set, then there must exist a cycle C such that $x_v = 0$ for all $v \in C$. Now consider the constraint corresponding to C: the left-hand side will be zero, but we claim that $f(C) \geq 1$, and so the constraint will be violated. This will conclude the proof that the integer program indeed models the feedback vertex set problem. To see that $f(C) \geq 1$, note that since C is a cycle, $|E(C)| \geq |C|$, so that $f(C) = |E(C)| - |C| + c(G(C)) \geq c(G(C)) \geq 1$.

$y \leftarrow 0$
$F \leftarrow \emptyset$
$S \leftarrow V$
$\ell \leftarrow 0$
while F is not feasible (and $G(S)$ contains a cycle) **do**
    $\ell \leftarrow \ell + 1$
    Increase y_S until for some $v_\ell \in S$, $\sum_{C:v_\ell \in C}(d_C(v_\ell) - b_C(v_\ell))y_C = w_{v_\ell}$.
    $F \leftarrow F \cup \{v_\ell\}$
    $T \leftarrow \{v \in S : v$ not on some cycle in $G(S - v_\ell)\}$
    $S \leftarrow S - \{v_\ell\} - T$
$F' \leftarrow F$
for $k \leftarrow \ell$ downto 1 **do**
    if $F' - v_k$ is a feasible solution **then**
        Remove v_k from F'
return F'

Algorithm 14.2. Improved primal-dual algorithm for the feedback vertex set problem in undirected graphs.

The dual of the linear programming relaxation of the integer program is then

$$\text{maximize} \sum_{S \subseteq V} f(S)y_S$$

$$\text{subject to} \sum_{S:v \in S}(d_S(v) - b_S(v))y_S \leq w_v, \qquad \forall v \in S,$$

$$y_S \geq 0, \qquad \forall S \subseteq V.$$

Following the standard primal-dual algorithm as described in Chapter 7, we derive Algorithm 14.2. We start with a dual feasible solution of $y = 0$, and a primal infeasible solution of $F = \emptyset$. We maintain a set S of the vertices in the subgraph of G we are currently considering; initially, $S = V$. Then while F is not feasible (equivalently, $G(S)$ is not acyclic), we increase the dual variable y_S until some dual constraint becomes tight for some $v \in S$. We then add v to F, and remove v from S. We also remove from S all vertices that are no longer in a cycle in $G(S - v)$.

Once F is a feasible solution, we have a final clean-up step similar to that used for the generalized Steiner tree problem in Section 7.4. In particular, we iterate through the vertices of F in the reverse of the order in which they were added to F. We check to see whether the current vertex v can be removed from F without affecting its feasibility. If so, we remove it; otherwise, we leave v in F.

The clean-up step is designed to help prove the following lemma. We say that a feedback vertex set F is *minimal* for a graph G if for any $v \in F$, $F - v$ is not a feedback vertex set for G.

Lemma 14.6. *For the primal solution F' and dual solution y returned by Algorithm 14.2, for any $S \subseteq V$ such that $y_S > 0$, $F' \cap S$ is a minimal feedback vertex set for $G(S)$.*

Proof. The proof is by contradiction. Suppose there is some vertex $v_j \in F' \cap S$ such that $F' \cap S - v_j$ is a feedback vertex set for $G(S)$. By the construction of the cleanup step, we know that it must be the case that $\{v_1, \dots, v_{j-1}\} \cup F' - v_j$ must not be a feedback vertex set for G, since otherwise we would have removed v_j from F' in the cleanup step. Since $\{v_1, \dots, v_{j-1}\} \cup F' - v_j$ is not a feedback vertex set for G, while F' is a feedback vertex set for G, it must be the case that v_j is the unique vertex of $\{v_1, \dots, v_{j-1}\} \cup F'$ on some cycle C in G. Furthermore, $C \subseteq S$ since $v_j \in S$ and $\{v_1, \dots, v_{j-1}\} \cap C = \emptyset$, and thus by construction of the algorithm we cannot have removed any vertex of C from S in the iteration in which y_S is increased. Thus, since C is in $G(S)$ and $C \cap F' = \{v_j\}$, it cannot be the case that $F' \cap S - v_j$ is a feedback vertex set for $G(S)$.   □

As is typical for proofs of the analysis in primal-dual algorithms, the performance guarantee of the algorithm can be reduced to a combinatorial lemma. In this case, the lemma is as follows. We defer the proof for a moment.

Lemma 14.7. *For any graph G such that every vertex $v \in V$ is contained in some cycle, and for any minimal feedback feedback vertex set F for G,*

$$\sum_{v \in F} (d(v) - b(v)) \leq 2f(V) = 2(|E| - |V| + c(G)).$$

Given the lemma, we can now prove the performance guarantee of the algorithm.

Theorem 14.8. *Algorithm 14.2 is a 2-approximation algorithm for the feedback vertex set problem in undirected graphs.*

Proof. Let F' be the final feedback vertex set returned by the algorithm. Then by the standard primal-dual analysis,

$$\sum_{v \in F'} w_v = \sum_{v \in F'} \sum_{S: v \in S} (d_S(v) - b_S(v)) y_S$$
$$= \sum_{S \subseteq V} y_S \sum_{v \in F' \cap S} (d_S(v) - b_S(v)).$$

By Lemma 14.6, we know that if $y_S > 0$, then $F' \cap S$ is a minimal feedback vertex set for $G(S)$. By Lemma 14.7, we know that $\sum_{v \in F' \cap S} (d_S(v) - b_S(v)) \leq 2f(S)$ for the graph $G(S)$. Thus, we have that

$$\sum_{v \in F'} w_v \leq 2 \sum_{S \subseteq V} f(S) y_S \leq 2 \, \text{OPT},$$

by weak duality, since $\sum_{S \subseteq V} f(S) y_S$ is the dual objective function.   □

We now turn to the proof of Lemma 14.7.

Proof of Lemma 14.7. We know that $\sum_{v \in V} d(v) = 2|E|$, so subtracting this from both sides of the inequality leaves us to prove that

$$\sum_{v \in F} d(v) - \sum_{v \in V} d(v) - \sum_{v \in F} b(v) \leq 2(c(G) - |V|).$$

Doing some rearranging, we get

$$\sum_{v \notin F} d(v) \geq 2|V| - \sum_{v \in F} b(v) - 2c(G).$$

Note that $\sum_{v \notin F} d(v) = \sum_{v \notin F} d_{V-F}(v) + |\delta(F)|$ and that since $G(V - F)$ is a forest, $\sum_{v \notin F} d_{V-F}(v) = 2(|V| - |F| - c(G - F))$. Thus, the desired inequality is equivalent to proving that

$$2(|V| - |F| - c(G - F)) + |\delta(F)| \geq 2|V| - \sum_{v \in F} b(v) - 2c(G).$$

Rearranging terms again gives us

$$2|F| + 2c(G - F) \leq |\delta(F)| + \sum_{v \in F} b(v) + 2c(G). \qquad (14.3)$$

Since F is a minimal feedback vertex set of G, for each $v \in F$ there must be some cycle C_v in G such that v is the only vertex of F in the cycle, since otherwise we could remove v from F and still have a feedback vertex set. Therefore, each $v \in F$ must be adjacent to two edges from F to $V - F$ from the cycle C_v; we will call these edges *cycle edges*. Note then that we can charge the quantity $2|F|$ in the desired inequality to the cycle edges in $|\delta(F)|$. Observe also that the two cycle edges for any vertex $v \in F$ must both be adjacent to the same connected component of $G(V - F)$.

To complete the proof, we must show that for each component of $G(V - F)$, we can charge 2 against the right-hand side of the inequality (14.3) above. We show that we can appropriately charge the connected components of G, the noncycle edges of $\delta(F)$, or $b(v)$ for $v \in F$. Consider a given connected component S of $G(V - F)$. Note that by the hypothesis of the lemma, every vertex is in some cycle of the graph, so there must be at least two edges from F to S. Also note that if a cycle edge from some cycle C_v connects v to S, then the other cycle edge must connect v to S as well; it cannot connect some other connected component of $G(V - F)$ to v. We now give the charging scheme in a case analysis.

- If there are at least two noncycle edges from F to S, then we can charge 2 to $|\delta(F)|$ for these noncycle edges.
- If there are exactly two edges from F to S, and both are cycle edges corresponding to a cycle C_v, then either $v \cup S$ is a connected component of G and we can charge 2 to the corresponding connected component (that is, to the $2c(G)$ term), or removing v disconnects S from G, so that $b(v) = c(G - v) - c(G) + 1 \geq 2$, and we can charge 2 to $b(v)$.
- If there are three edges from F to S, two of which are cycle edges corresponding to a cycle C_v, then we can charge 1 to the noncycle edge in $|\delta(F)|$ and 1 to $b(v) \geq 1$.
- If there are four or more cycle edges from F to S, two of which correspond to a cycle C_v and two of which correspond to a cycle C_w, then we can charge 1 to $b(v) \geq 1$ and 1 to $b(w) \geq 1$.

See Figure 14.2 for an illustration of the cases.   □

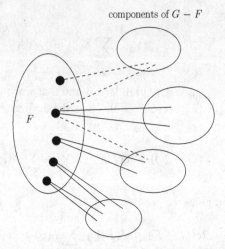

components of $G - F$

Figure 14.2. The final case analysis of Lemma 14.7. Solid lines represent cycle edges, and dashed edges noncycle edges. The four cases are illustrated in order by the four components of $G(V - F)$.

In Exercise 14.4, we give another integer programming formulation for the feedback vertex set problem and show that it can also lead to a primal-dual 2-approximation algorithm for the problem.

Exercises

14.1 Show that the performance guarantee of the primal-dual algorithm for the prize-collecting Steiner tree algorithm in Section 14.1 can be strengthened in the following way. Let T be the tree returned by the algorithm, and let y be the dual solution constructed by the algorithm. Show that

$$\sum_{e \in T} c_e + 2 \sum_{i \in V - V(T)} \pi_i \leq 2 \sum_{S \subseteq V - r} y_S.$$

This proves that the algorithm is *Lagrangean multiplier preserving* (see Section 7.7).

14.2 In the k-minimum spanning tree problem (k-MST), we are given an undirected graph $G = (V, E)$ with edge costs $c_e \geq 0$ for all $e \in E$, a root vertex $r \in V$, and a positive integer k. The goal is to find a minimum-cost tree spanning at least k vertices that include the root.

    (a) Give an integer programming formulation for the k-MST problem that has the same constraints as the integer program for the prize-collecting Steiner tree problem plus one additional constraint. Then apply Lagrangean relaxation to obtain an integer program in the same form as that for the prize-collecting Steiner tree problem modulo a constant term in the objective function.

    (b) Prove that an α-approximation algorithm that works in the case that the maximum distance from the root r is no more than OPT_k (the cost of an optimal tree spanning k vertices) can be used to produce an α-approximation algorithm for the general case.

(c) Using the prize-collecting Steiner tree algorithm as a subroutine and the analysis in Exercise 14.1, obtain a $(5 + \epsilon)$-approximation algorithm for the k-MST problem.

14.3 Show that the linear programming relaxation for the prize-collecting Steiner tree problem used in Section 14.1 is equivalent to the linear programming relaxation for the problem used in Sections 4.4 and 5.7.

14.4 There are other possible primal-dual 2-approximation algorithms for the feedback vertex set problem in undirected graphs other than the one given in the chapter. In this exercise, we derive another such algorithm.

    (a) Argue that for any feedback vertex set F,

$$\sum_{v \in F}(d(v) - 1) \geq |E| - |V| + 1.$$

    (b) Show that the following is an integer programming formulation of the feedback vertex set problem for $g(S) = |E(S)| - |S| + 1$:

$$\text{minimize} \quad \sum_{v \in V} w_v x_v$$

$$\text{subject to} \quad \sum_{v \in S}(d_S(v) - 1)x_v \geq g(S), \quad \forall S \subseteq V,$$

$$x_v \in \{0, 1\}, \quad v \in V.$$

    (c) A cycle is *semidisjoint* if at most one vertex of the cycle has degree greater than 2. Show that if every vertex of G has degree at least 2 and G contains no semidisjoint cycles, then for any minimal feedback vertex set F,

$$\sum_{v \in F}(d(v) - 1) \leq 2g(S).$$

    (d) Give a primal-dual algorithm for the problem based on the formulation above and prove that it is a 2-approximation algorithm. (Hint: The algorithm will need to increase a different dual variable if the graph contains a semidisjoint cycle.)

14.5 Consider the *prize collecting generalized Steiner tree problem*. In this problem, we are given an undirected graph $G = (V, E)$ with nonnegative costs $c_e \geq 0$ on $e \in E$. We are also given k source-sink pairs s_i-t_i, and a penalty $\pi_i \geq 0$ for each source-sink pair. We want to find a set of edges $F \subseteq E$ that minimizes the total cost of the edges in F plus the sum of the penalties of the s_i-t_i pairs that are not connected in (V, F).

    (a) Give an integer programming formulation of the problem with variables $y_i \in \{0, 1\}$ that indicate whether the pair s_i and t_i are connected in the solution. Using a linear programming relaxation of this formulation, give a randomized rounding $(1 - e^{-1/2})^{-1}$-approximation algorithm for the problem, where $(1 - e^{-1/2})^{-1} \approx 2.54$.

    (b) Let $\mathcal{X}$ be a collection of subsets of vertices. Let $\mathcal{S}_i$ be the collection of all sets S such that $|S \cap \{s_i, t_i\}| = 1$. We give another integer programming formulation of the problem. In our formulation, we will have 0-1 variables $z_{\mathcal{X}}$, where $z_{\mathcal{X}} = 1$ for $\mathcal{X}$ containing all sets S such that we have selected no edge in $\delta(S)$. Let $\pi(\mathcal{X})$ be the sum of all penalties π_i such that there exists some $S \in \mathcal{S}_i$ that is also in $\mathcal{X}$; that is,

$$\pi(\mathcal{X}) = \sum_{1 \leq i \leq k: \mathcal{X} \cap \mathcal{S}_i \neq \emptyset} \pi_i.$$

Then our formulation is

$$\text{minimize} \sum_{e \in E} c_e x_e + \sum_{\mathcal{X}} \pi(\mathcal{X}) z_{\mathcal{X}}$$

$$\text{subject to} \sum_{e \in \delta(S)} x_e + \sum_{\mathcal{X}: S \in \mathcal{X}} z_{\mathcal{X}} \geq 1, \qquad \forall S \subseteq V,$$

$$x_e \in \{0, 1\}, \qquad \forall e \in E,$$

$$z_{\mathcal{X}} \in \{0, 1\}, \qquad \forall \mathcal{X}.$$

Prove that this formulation models the prize-collecting generalized Steiner tree problem.

(c) Give a primal-dual 3-approximation algorithm for the prize-collecting generalized Steiner tree problem using the linear programming relaxation of the integer program above. For an easier variant of this problem, you do not need to explain how to detect in polynomial time when the dual constraint corresponding to the variables $z_{\mathcal{X}}$ becomes tight.

Chapter Notes

The prize-collecting Steiner tree algorithm of Section 14.1 is due to Goemans and Williamson [138].

    The first 2-approximation algorithms for the feedback vertex set problem in undirected graphs are due to Becker and Geiger [41] and Bafna, Berman, and Fujito [29], and were stated in terms of the local ratio technique. These algorithms were translated into primal-dual approximation algorithms by Chudak, Goemans, Hochbaum, and Williamson [74]; Exercise 14.4 is from this paper. The algorithm given in Section 14.2 is based on another primal-dual 2-approximation algorithm for the problem due to Fujito [117].

    The result of Exercise 14.1 is implicit in Goemans and Williamson [138], but made explicit independently by Blum, Ravi, and Vempala [51] and Goemans and Kleinberg [131]. The 5-approximation algorithm for the k-MST problem in Exercise 14.2 was first given by Garg [125]; the use of Lagrangean relaxation for the problem was made explicit by Chudak, Roughgarden, and Williamson [75]. The equivalence of the two prize-collecting Steiner tree formulations given in Exercise 14.3 is found in Williamson [287]. The prize-collecting generalized Steiner tree problem in Exercise 14.5 is defined by Hajiaghayi and Jain [154]; the two algorithms in the exercise are also from this paper.

CHAPTER 15

Further Uses of Cuts and Metrics

In Section 8.5, we introduced the idea of approximating one kind of metric with another one; namely, we looked at the idea of approximating a general metric with a tree metric. Here we will consider approximating a general metric with another metric more general than a tree metric, namely, an ℓ_1-embeddable metric. We show that we can approximate any metric (V, d) with an ℓ_1-embeddable metric with distortion $O(\log n)$, where $n = |V|$. The ℓ_1-embeddable metrics have a particularly close connection to cuts; we show that any such metric is a convex combination of the cut semimetrics we discussed at the beginning of Chapter 8. We show that the low-distortion embeddings into ℓ_1-embeddable metrics have applications to cut problems by giving an approximation algorithm for the sparsest cut problem.

In Section 15.2, we give an algorithm that finds a packing of trees called cut-trees into a graph; this packing allows us to solve a particular routing problem. In the subsequent section, we show that the cut-tree packing can be used in a way analogous to the probabilistic approximation of metrics by tree metrics in Section 8.5. In that section, we showed that given an algorithm to solve a problem on a tree metric, we could provide an approximate solution for the problem in a general metric with only an additional factor of $O(\log n)$ in the performance guarantee. Here we show that given an algorithm to solve a cut problem on trees, we can use a cut-tree packing to find a cut in general graphs with only an additional factor of $O(\log n)$ in the performance guarantee. We will see that the two results are intimately related. We use the algorithm to give an $O(\log n)$-approximation algorithm for the minimum bisection problem introduced in Section 8.4.

Finally, in Section 15.4, we return to a special case of the sparsest cut problem called the uniform sparsest cut problem, and we show how using a vector programming relaxation leads to an $O(\sqrt{\log n})$-approximation algorithm for the problem.

15.1 Low-Distortion Embeddings
and the Sparsest Cut Problem

In Section 8.5, we considered the idea of approximating a metric with a tree metric. Here we will consider approximating a general metric with another metric more general than a tree metric, namely, an ℓ_1-*embeddable metric*. Recall that if $x \in \Re^m$ and x^i is the ith component of the vector x then $\|x\|_1 = \sum_{i=1}^m |x^i|$.

Definition 15.1. *A metric* (V, d) *is an* ℓ_1-*embeddable metric (or embeds isometrically into* ℓ_1*) if there exists a function* $f : V \to \Re^m$ *for some* m *such that* $d_{uv} = \|f(u) - f(v)\|_1$ *for all* $u, v \in V$.

The function f is called the *embedding* of the metric into ℓ_1. It is not too hard to show that any tree metric is an ℓ_1-embeddable metric, and that the converse is not true; we leave this as an exercise to the reader (Exercise 15.1).

The ℓ_1-embeddable metrics are very closely related to cuts. We will show that any ℓ_1 metric (V, d) is a weighted sum of cuts of the vertex set V. To be clearer about what we mean, let $\chi_{\delta(S)}(u, v)$ be an indicator function for whether an edge (u, v) is in the cut S; that is, $\chi_{\delta(S)}(u, v) = 1$ if exactly one of u, v is in S and is 0 otherwise. Then we can show the following.

Lemma 15.2. *Let* (V, d) *be an* ℓ_1-*embeddable metric, and let* $f : V \to \Re^m$ *be the associated embedding. Then there exist* $\lambda_S \geq 0$ *for all* $S \subseteq V$ *such that for all* $u, v \in V$,

$$\|f(u) - f(v)\|_1 = \sum_{S \subseteq V} \lambda_S \chi_{\delta(S)}(u, v).$$

Furthermore, at most mn *of the* λ_S *are nonzero, and the* λ_S *can be computed in polynomial time.*

Proof. We start by considering the simple case that f embeds V into one dimension and $V = \{1, 2, \ldots, n\}$; that is, $f : \{1, \ldots, n\} \to \Re$. Let $x_i = f(i)$, and assume without loss of generality that $x_1 \leq x_2 \leq \cdots \leq x_n$. Then we consider cuts $\{1\}, \{1, 2\}, \ldots, \{1, 2, \ldots, n-1\}$, and let $\lambda_{\{1\}} = x_2 - x_1$, $\lambda_{\{1,2\}} = x_3 - x_2, \ldots, \lambda_{\{1,2,\ldots,n-1\}} = x_n - x_{n-1}$. Then observe that for any $i, j \in V$, where $i < j$,

$$|x_i - x_j| = x_j - x_i = \sum_{k=i}^{j-1} \lambda_{\{1,\ldots,k\}} = \sum_{S \subseteq V} \lambda_S \chi_{\delta(S)}(i, j).$$

For embeddings f into $m > 1$ dimensions, we generate the cuts and λ_S in each dimension using the process above as in the one-dimensional case; that is, we sort the vertices by the value of their component in that dimension, consider cuts S of the first i points ordered in that dimension, and set λ_S to be the distance in that dimension between the $(i + 1)$st and ith points. Then certainly at most mn of the λ_S are nonzero. If $x_u = f(u)$, x_u^i is the ith coordinate of x_u, and λ_S^i are the λ generated in the process for dimension i, we showed above that for any $u, v \in V$, $|x_u^i - x_v^i| = \sum_{S \subseteq V} \lambda_S^i \chi_S(u, v)$.

Then we get that

$$\| f(u) - f(v) \|_1 = \sum_{i=1}^{m} |x_u^i - x_v^i| = \sum_{i=1}^{m} \sum_{S \subseteq V} \lambda_S^i \chi_{\delta(S)}(u, v) = \sum_{S \subseteq V} \lambda_S \chi_{\delta(S)}(u, v),$$

as desired. Clearly the λ_S can be computed in polynomial time. $\square$

Not every metric is ℓ_1-embeddable, but we will show that every metric is in some sense not too far from an ℓ_1-embeddable metric. Consider the following definition.

Definition 15.3. *A metric (V, d) embeds into ℓ_1 with distortion α if there exists a function $f : V \to \Re^m$ for some m and r such that*

$$r \cdot d_{uv} \leq \| f(u) - f(v) \|_1 \leq r\alpha \cdot d_{uv}$$

for all $u, v \in V$.

The central result of this section is to show that there are relatively low-distortion embeddings into ℓ_1 for any metric.

Theorem 15.4. *Any metric (V, d) embeds into ℓ_1 with distortion $O(\log n)$, where $n = |V|$. Furthermore, the embedding $f : V \to \Re^{O(\log^2 n)}$ is computable with high probability in randomized polynomial time.*

This result is in some sense the best possible. In Exercise 15.2, the reader is asked to show that there exist distance metrics that cannot be embedded into ℓ_1 with distortion less than $\Omega(\log n)$.

To show an application of Theorem 15.4, we recall the *sparsest cut problem*, introduced in Exercise 8.6. In the sparsest cut problem, we are given an undirected graph $G = (V, E)$, costs $c_e \geq 0$ for all $e \in E$, and k pairs of vertices s_i, t_i with associated positive integer demands d_i. We want to find a set of vertices S that minimizes

$$\rho(S) \equiv \frac{\sum_{e \in \delta(S)} c_e}{\sum_{i:|S \cap \{s_i, t_i\}|=1} d_i}.$$

That is, the sparsest cut problem finds a cut that minimizes the ratio of the cost of the edges in the cut to the sum of the demands separated by the cut. In the exercise, the reader is asked to show that the following is an LP relaxation of the problem and is solvable in polynomial time, where $\mathcal{P}_i$ is the set of all s_i-t_i paths:

$$\text{minimize} \sum_{e \in E} c_e x_e$$

$$\text{subject to} \sum_{i=1}^{k} d_i y_i = 1,$$

$$\sum_{e \in P} x_e \geq y_i, \qquad \forall P \in \mathcal{P}_i, 1 \leq i \leq k,$$

$$y_i \geq 0, \qquad 1 \leq i \leq k,$$

$$x_e \geq 0, \qquad \forall e \in E.$$

Using this LP relaxation, we show below that we can obtain an $O(\log n)$-approximation algorithm for the sparsest cut problem via Theorem 15.4.

Theorem 15.5. *There is a randomized $O(\log n)$-approximation algorithm for the sparsest cut problem.*

Proof. To see this, suppose that we have an optimal solution (x, y) to the LP relaxation of the sparsest cut problem. Let $d_x(u, v)$ be the shortest path from u to v in the graph G using x_e as the length of edge e. By Theorem 15.4, we can obtain in randomized polynomial time an embedding $f : V \to \Re^{O(\log^2 n)}$ such that for some r, $\|f(u) - f(v)\|_1 \leq r \cdot O(\log n) \cdot d_x(u, v)$ and $\|f(u) - f(v)\|_1 \geq r \cdot d_x(u, v)$ for all $u, v \in V$. By Lemma 15.2, given the embedding f, we can find in polynomial time at most $O(n \log^2 n)$ nonzero λ_S such that $\|f(u) - f(v)\|_1 = \sum_{S \subseteq V} \lambda_S \chi_{\delta(S)}(u, v)$ for all $u, v \in V$. Let S^* be the minimum of $\rho(S)$ over all $S \subseteq V$ such that $\lambda_S > 0$; that is,

$$\rho(S^*) = \min_{S:\lambda_S>0} \rho(S) = \min_{S:\lambda_S>0} \frac{\sum_{e \in \delta(S)} c_e}{\sum_{i:|S \cap \{s_i, t_i\}|=1} d_i}.$$

We will show that $\rho(S^*) \leq O(\log n)\,\mathrm{OPT}$. Note that for any $S \subseteq V$, $\sum_{e \in \delta(S)} c_e = \sum_{e \in E} c_e \cdot \chi_{\delta(S)}(e)$ and $\sum_{i:|S \cap \{s_i, t_i\}|=1} d_i = \sum_i d_i \cdot \chi_{\delta(S)}(s_i, t_i)$. Using this and Fact 1.10, we have that

$$
\begin{aligned}
\rho(S^*) &= \min_{S:\lambda_S>0} \frac{\sum_{e \in \delta(S)} c_e}{\sum_{i:|S \cap \{s_i, t_i\}|=1} d_i} \\
&= \min_{S:\lambda_S>0} \frac{\sum_{e \in E} c_e \cdot \chi_{\delta(S)}(e)}{\sum_i d_i \cdot \chi_{\delta(S)}(s_i, t_i)} \\
&\leq \frac{\sum_{S \subseteq V} \lambda_S \sum_{e \in E} c_e \cdot \chi_{\delta(S)}(e)}{\sum_{S \subseteq V} \lambda_S \sum_{i=1}^k d_i \cdot \chi_{\delta(S)}(s_i, t_i)} \\
&= \frac{\sum_{e \in E} c_e \sum_{S \subseteq V} \lambda_S \chi_{\delta(S)}(e)}{\sum_{i=1}^k d_i \sum_{S \subseteq V} \lambda_S \chi_{\delta(S)}(s_i, t_i)} \\
&= \frac{\sum_{e=(u,v) \in E} c_e \|f(u) - f(v)\|_1}{\sum_{i=1}^k d_i \|f(s_i) - f(t_i)\|_1} \\
&\leq \frac{r \cdot O(\log n) \sum_{e=(u,v) \in E} c_e \cdot d_x(u, v)}{r \cdot \sum_{i=1}^k d_i \cdot d_x(s_i, t_i)},
\end{aligned}
$$

where the final inequality follows since the function f embeds $d_x(u, v)$ into ℓ_1 with distortion $O(\log n)$. Then noticing that $x_e \geq d_x(u, v)$ for all $e = (u, v) \in E$, and by the LP constraints $y_i \leq d_x(s_i, t_i)$ for all i and $\sum_{i=1}^k d_i y_i = 1$, we have that

$$
\begin{aligned}
\rho(S^*) &\leq O(\log n) \frac{\sum_{e=(u,v) \in E} c_e \cdot d_x(u, v)}{\sum_{i=1}^k d_i \cdot d_x(s_i, t_i)} \\
&\leq O(\log n) \frac{\sum_{e \in E} c_e x_e}{\sum_{i=1}^k d_i y_i} \\
&= O(\log n) \sum_{e \in E} c_e x_e \\
&\leq O(\log n) \cdot \mathrm{OPT}. \qquad \square
\end{aligned}
$$

If we look back at the proof of Theorem 15.5, we can observe that we aren't using all the properties required by a low-distortion embedding. In the proof of the performance guarantee, we need that for every edge $e = (u, v)$, $\|f(u) - f(v)\|_1 \leq r \cdot O(\log n)d_x(u, v)$, but we need only that $\|f(s_i) - f(t_i)\|_1 \geq r \cdot d_x(s_i, t_i)$ for every i, $1 \leq i \leq k$. With this weaker requirement, we can show that we can obtain a slightly stronger version of Theorem 15.4, and hence obtain a better approximation algorithm. In particular, we can obtain the following.

Theorem 15.6. *Given a metric (V, d) and k pairs of distinguished vertices, $s_i, t_i \in V$, $1 \leq i \leq k$, we can in randomized polynomial time compute an embedding $f : V \to \Re^{O(\log^2 k)}$ so that with high probability, $\|f(u) - f(v)\|_1 \leq r \cdot O(\log k) \cdot d_{uv}$ for all $u, v \in V$ and $\|f(s_i) - f(t_i)\|_1 \geq r \cdot d_{s_i t_i}$ for $1 \leq i \leq k$.*

Note that it is a generalization of Theorem 15.4 since we can take all $\binom{n}{2}$ pairs of vertices from V to be the s_i-t_i pairs, in which case the statement of Theorem 15.6 reduces to that of Theorem 15.4.

Using the theorem above we can get the following improved approximation algorithm simply by repeating the analysis of Theorem 15.5.

Corollary 15.7. *There is a randomized $O(\log k)$-approximation algorithm for the sparsest cut problem.*

We now turn to the proof of Theorem 15.6. We start by explaining how to map a metric (V, d) to points in Euclidean space. To do this, we will use a *Fréchet embedding*. Given (V, d) and a set of vertices $A \subseteq V$, define $d(u, A) = \min_{v \in A} d_{uv}$ for every $u \in V$.

Definition 15.8. *Given a metric space (V, d) and p subsets of vertices $A_1, \ldots, A_p$, a Fréchet embedding $f : V \to \Re^p$ is defined by*

$$f(u) = \big(d(u, A_1), d(u, A_2), \ldots, d(u, A_p)\big) \in \Re^p$$

for all $u \in V$.

A Fréchet embedding has the nice property that it is easy to compute given the sets A_i. It is also easy to show that the ℓ_1 distance between points is at most the dimension p times the original distance in the metric.

Lemma 15.9. *Given a metric (V, d) and the Fréchet embedding $f : V \to \Re^p$ defined above, for any $u, v \in V$, $\|f(u) - f(v)\|_1 \leq p \cdot d_{uv}$.*

Proof. For any $A \subseteq V$ and any $u, v \in V$, let w be the closest point in A to v so that $d(v, A) = d_{vw}$. Then $d(u, A) \leq d_{uw} \leq d_{uv} + d_{vw} = d_{uv} + d(v, A)$. Similarly, $d(v, A) \leq d_{uv} + d(u, A)$. Therefore, $|d(u, A) - d(v, A)| \leq d_{uv}$. Hence, we have that

$$\|f(u) - f(v)\|_1 = \sum_{j=1}^{p} |d(u, A_j) - d(v, A_j)| \leq p \cdot d_{uv}. \qquad \square$$

Now the central problem of the proof is picking good sets A_j so that the distance between any s_i-t_i pair in the embedding is some reasonable fraction of the distance from s_i to t_i. We will pick $O(\log^2 k)$ such sets using randomization, then show that with high probability the s_i-t_i distance in the embedding is at least $\Omega(\log k)d_{s_i t_i}$.

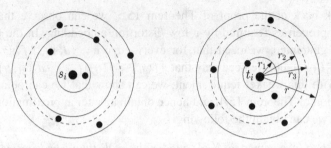

Figure 15.1. An example of the choices of radii r_t around s_i and t_i. The radius r_1 is the smallest such that $|B(s_i, r_1)| \geq 2$ and $|B(t_i, r_1)| \geq 2$. The radius r_2 is the smallest such that $|B(s_i, r_2)| \geq 4$ and $|B(t_i, r_2)| \geq 4$. The radius r is the smallest such that $|B(s_i, r)| \geq 8$ and $|B(t_i, r)| \geq 8$. Since $r \geq \frac{1}{4}d_{s_i t_i}$, but r_2 is less than this, $\hat{t} = 3$, and $r_{\hat{t}} = r_3 = \frac{1}{4}d_{s_i t_i}$.

This will give the result of Theorem 15.6 by setting $r = \Theta(\log k)$. The main lemma of the proof is as follows.

Lemma 15.10. *Given a metric space (V, d) with k distinguished pairs $s_i, t_i \in V$, we can pick $p = O(\log^2 k)$ sets $A_j \subseteq V$ using randomization such that a Fréchet embedding $f : V \to \Re^p$ gives $\|f(s_i) - f(t_i)\|_1 \geq \Omega(\log k) \cdot d_{s_i t_i}$ for $1 \leq i \leq k$ with high probability.*

Proof. To define the sets A_j, let $T = \bigcup_{i=1}^k \{s_i, t_i\}$. Assume that $|T|$ is a power of 2; if it is not, we can pick some additional s_i-t_i pairs and add them to T until it is. Let $\tau = \log_2(2k)$ so that $|T| = 2k = 2^\tau$. Let $L = q \ln k$ for some constant q to be chosen later. Then we define the sets $A_{t\ell}$ by picking $2^{\tau - t} = 2k/2^t$ vertices randomly from T with replacement, for $\ell = 1, \ldots, L$ and $t = 1, \ldots, \tau$. We will show that the Fréchet embedding f using these sets $A_{t\ell}$ has the desired properties. Note that we have chosen $L\tau = O(\log^2 k)$ sets, as desired.

Pick some i, $1 \leq i \leq k$. We will show that $\|f(s_i) - f(t_i)\|_1 \geq \Omega(Ld_{s_i t_i}) = \Omega((\log k)d_{s_i t_i})$ with high probability. Then this inequality will hold for all i, $1 \leq i \leq k$, with high probability.

We define a closed ball $B(u, r)$ of radius r around $u \in V$ to be the vertices in T within distance r of u, so that $B(u, r) = \{v \in T : d_{uv} \leq r\}$. The open ball $B^o(u, r)$ are all vertices in T that have distance strictly less than r from u, so that $B^o(u, r) = \{v \in T : d_{uv} < r\}$. We define a particular set of distances r_t with respect to the vertices s_i and t_i (for the arbitrary choice of i made above). We define $r_0 = 0$, and let r_t be the minimum distance r such that $|B(s_i, r)| \geq 2^t$ and $|B(t_i, r)| \geq 2^t$ for $t = 1, \ldots, \tau$. Define $\hat{t}$ to be the minimum index t so that $r_t \geq \frac{1}{4}d_{s_i t_i}$; we redefine $r_{\hat{t}} = \frac{1}{4}d_{s_i t_i}$. Then note that the balls of radius $r_{\hat{t}}$ around s_i and t_i don't intersect, so that $B(s_i, r_{\hat{t}}) \cap B(t_i, r_{\hat{t}}) = \emptyset$. See Figure 15.1 for an illustration. Since $|B(s_i, r_{\hat{t}-1})| \geq 2^{\hat{t}-1}$ and $|B(t_i, r_{\hat{t}-1})| \geq 2^{\hat{t}-1}$ and these balls also don't intersect, if $\hat{t} = \tau$, then $|B(s_i, r_{\hat{t}})| = |B(t_i, r_{\hat{t}})| = 2^{\tau-1}$ as there are 2^τ vertices total in T.

The idea of the proof is to show that for any $\ell = 1, \ldots, L$ and $t = 1, \ldots, \hat{t}$, the randomly chosen set $A_{t\ell}$ has a constant probability of having an intersection with the ball of radius r_{t-1} around one of terminals s_i, t_i and also having no intersection with the ball of radius r_t around the other terminal. Then with constant probability, the distance from one terminal to $A_{t\ell}$ is at most r_{t-1} and the distance from the other terminal to $A_{t\ell}$ is at least r_t, or $|d(s_i, A_{t\ell}) - d(t_i, A_{t\ell})| \geq r_t - r_{t-1}$. By applying a Chernoff bound (from Section 5.10), we will be able to show that with high probability for $t = 1, \ldots, \hat{\imath}$, $\sum_{\ell=1}^{L} |d(s_i, A_{t\ell}) - d(t_i, A_{t\ell})| \geq \Omega(L(r_t - r_{t-1}))$. This will allow us to conclude that with high probability,

$$\|f(s_i) - f(t_i)\|_1 \geq \sum_{t=1}^{\hat{\imath}} \sum_{\ell=1}^{L} |d(s_i, A_{t\ell}) - d(t_i, A_{t\ell})|$$

$$\geq \sum_{t=1}^{\hat{\imath}} \Omega(L(r_t - r_{t-1}))$$

$$= \Omega(Lr_{\hat{\imath}})$$

$$= \Omega(Ld_{s_i t_i}).$$

Note that it suffices to show the statement for t from 1 to $\hat{\imath}$, not from 1 to τ; since the sum of $r_t - r_{t-1}$ telescopes to $r_{\hat{\imath}}$ and $r_{\hat{\imath}} = \Omega(d_{s_i t_i})$, this is sufficient.

Assume that the ball around s_i defines the radius r_t so that $|B(s_i, r_t)| = 2^t$ but $|B^o(s_i, r_t)| < 2^t$; otherwise, we can switch the roles of s_i and t_i in the following discussion. Consider the event $E_{t\ell}$, which occurs when the randomly chosen set $A_{t\ell}$ has $A_{t\ell} \cap B^o(s_i, r_t) = \emptyset$ and $A_{t\ell} \cap B(t_i, r_{t-1}) \neq \emptyset$. If $E_{t\ell}$ occurs, then it must be the case that $d(s_i, A_{t\ell}) \geq r_t$ and $d(t_i, A_{t\ell}) \leq r_{t-1}$, which in turn implies that $|d(s_i, A_{t\ell}) - d(t_i, A_{t\ell})| \geq r_t - r_{t-1}$. We want to show that $\Pr[E_{t\ell}]$ is at least some constant. For notational simplicity, define $G = B(t_i, r_{t-1})$ (the "good set"), $B = B^o(s_i, r_t)$ (the "bad set"), and $A = A_{t\ell}$. Then we know that $|G| \geq 2^{t-1}$ by the definition of r_{t-1}, $|B| < 2^t$ by the assumption we made above on r_t, and $|A| = 2^{\tau-t} = |T|/2^t$; these statements are true even in the case $t = \hat{\imath}$. Recall $|T| = 2^\tau$. Then

$$\Pr[E_{t\ell}] = \Pr[A \cap B = \emptyset \wedge A \cap G \neq \emptyset]$$

$$= \Pr[A \cap G \neq \emptyset | A \cap B = \emptyset] \cdot \Pr[A \cap B = \emptyset]$$

$$\geq \Pr[A \cap G \neq \emptyset] \cdot \Pr[A \cap B = \emptyset].$$

Recall that the vertices in A are drawn randomly from T with replacement; if we want $A \cap B = \emptyset$, then each vertex drawn for A must be from $T - B$. The probability that one vertex drawn from T is not in B is $1 - \frac{|B|}{|T|}$. Thus,

$$\Pr[A \cap B = \emptyset] = \left(1 - \frac{|B|}{|T|}\right)^{|A|}.$$

Substituting bounds on the sizes of B and T, we obtain $\Pr[A \cap B = \emptyset] \geq (1 - 2^{t-\tau})^{2^{\tau-t}}$. Using $(1 - \frac{1}{x})^x \geq \frac{1}{4}$ for $x \geq 2$, we get that $\Pr[A \cap B = \emptyset] \geq \frac{1}{4}$ as long as $\tau - t \geq 1$; this is certainly true if $t \leq \hat{\imath} < \tau$, while if $t = \hat{\imath} = \tau$, we earlier observed that $|B| = |B^o(s_i, r_{\hat{\imath}})| \leq 2^{\tau-1}$, so the statement still holds. Similarly, using $1 - x \leq e^{-x}$, we obtain that

$$\Pr[A \cap G \neq \emptyset] = 1 - \left(1 - \frac{|G|}{|T|}\right)^{|A|} \geq 1 - e^{-|G||A|/|T|} \geq 1 - e^{-2^{t-1}/2^t} = 1 - e^{-1/2}.$$

Thus,

$$\Pr[E_{t\ell}] \geq \Pr[A \cap G \neq \emptyset] \cdot \Pr[A \cap B = \emptyset] \geq \frac{1}{4}(1 - e^{-1/2}) \geq 0.098$$

for $t \leq \hat{t}$.

Now we apply a Chernoff bound to show that the desired result occurs with high probability. Let $X_{t\ell}$ be a 0-1 random variable that is 1 if event $E_{t\ell}$ occurs, and let $X_t = \sum_{\ell=1}^{L} X_{t\ell}$ for $1 \leq t \leq \hat{t}$. Let $\mu = E[X_t] \geq 0.098L$. Observe that $\sum_{\ell=1}^{L} |d(s_i, A_{t\ell}) - d(t_i, A_{t\ell})| \geq X_t(r_t - r_{t-1})$. Applying the Chernoff bound of Lemma 5.26 and recalling that $L = q \ln k$ for some constant q, we get that the probability that $\Pr[X_t < \frac{1}{2}\mu] \leq e^{-L/8} = k^{-q/8}$. Then with probability at least $1 - k^{-q/8}$, $\sum_{\ell=1}^{L} |d(s_i, A_{t\ell}) - d(t_i, A_{t\ell})| \geq 0.049L(r_t - r_{t-1})$. Recalling that $\hat{t} \leq \tau = \log_2(2k)$, we have that with probability at least $1 - \frac{\log_2(2k)}{k^{q/8}}$,

$$\|f(s_i) - f(t_i)\|_1 \geq \sum_{t=1}^{\hat{t}} \sum_{\ell=1}^{L} |d(s_i, A_{t\ell}) - d(t_i, A_{t\ell})| \geq \sum_{t=1}^{\hat{t}} \Omega(L(r_t - r_{t-1})) \geq \Omega(Ld_{s_i t_i}),$$

as explained earlier. Since this probability holds for one arbitrary s_i-t_i pair, the probability that it holds for all s_i-t_i pairs is at least $1 - \frac{\log_2(2k)}{k^{q/8-1}}$. Choosing q sufficiently large gives the result with high probability. $\square$

Given the lemmas above, the proof of Theorem 15.6 is straightforward.

Proof of Theorem 15.6. We set $r = \Theta(L)$, where $L = q \ln k$ is the quantity used in the proof of Lemma 15.10. Then by that lemma $\|f(s_i) - f(t_i)\|_1 \geq r \cdot d_{s_i t_i}$ for all i with high probability. By Lemma 15.9, for all $u, v \in V$, $\|f(u) - f(v)\|_1 \leq O(\log^2 k)d_{uv} = r \cdot O(\log k)d_{uv}$, and the theorem is shown. $\square$

Note that we can consider embedding metrics (V, d) into metrics other than tree metrics or ℓ_1 metrics. For instance, consider the ℓ_p metric, where $\|x - y\|_p = \sqrt[p]{\sum_i (x^i - y^i)^p}$. Then we have the following definition.

Definition 15.11. *A metric* (V, d) *embeds into* ℓ_p *with distortion* α *if there exists a function* $f : V \to \Re^m$ *for some* m *and* r *such that*

$$r \cdot d_{uv} \leq \|f(u) - f(v)\|_p \leq r\alpha \cdot d_{uv}$$

for all $u, v \in V$.

The exercises consider embedding into ℓ_p metrics with low distortion.

Some recent work has shown that the sparsest cut problem may be quite difficult to approximate.

Theorem 15.12. *Assuming the unique games conjecture, there is no* α-*approximation algorithm for the sparsest cut problem for constant* α *unless* P = NP.

However, some recent work has used semidefinite programming to achieve improved results for the sparsest cut problem. We discuss a special case of the sparsest cut problem called the uniform sparsest cut problem in Section 15.4, and show that in this case one can achieve an $O(\sqrt{\log n})$-approximation algorithm for the problem.

15.2 Oblivious Routing and Cut-Tree Packings

In this section, we turn to routing problems. In routing problems, we are typically given an undirected graph $G = (V, E)$ with capacities $c_e \geq 0$ for all edges $e \in E$. We are also given a set of demands d_{uv} for all $u, v \in V$; each demand d_{uv} must be routed along some u-v path in the graph G; we will consider the case in which each demand d_{uv} can be split and sent along several different u-v paths. The total amount of demand (or total *flow*) using a given edge $e \in E$ is the sum over all u-v paths containing e of the amount of demand sent along that path. We would like to know if demands can be routed in such a way that the total flow on each edge is at most its capacity; more generally, we would like to know by how much we would have to exceed the given capacities in order to route the flows. The *congestion* ρ of a routing of demands is the minimum value such that the total flow on each edge e is at most ρc_e. We would like to find a routing that minimizes the overall congestion.

The problem as stated thus far is solvable in polynomial time; one can write a linear program that will find a routing with the minimum possible congestion. However, let us now consider a more difficult variant of the problem in which we do not know the demands d_{uv} in advance. We must still find a set of u-v paths for each $u, v \in V$, and for each path we specify the fraction of the demand that will be sent on that path; for example, our output for u, v may be three u-v paths P_1, P_2, P_3, and we specify that half the demand will be sent on P_1, a third on P_2, and the remaining sixth on P_3. We would like to find paths such that the congestion of routing on these paths is close to the minimum possible congestion no matter what demands d_{uv} we are given. This is the *oblivious routing problem*. We will give an $O(\log n)$-approximation algorithm for the problem, using some of the ideas from the probabilistic approximation of metrics by tree metrics as discussed in Section 8.7.

To begin, we will give some simple ideas about how to specify the paths, and then we will gradually refine them into ideas that will allow for the approximation algorithm. To start, it will be easier to express the capacity of edges in the graph by letting $c_{uv} = c_e$ for all $e = (u, v) \in E$, and $c_{uv} = 0$ for all $(u, v) \notin E$. An initial idea on how to give the u-v paths is via some spanning tree T in the graph G. Then for every $u, v \in V$, there is a unique u-v path in T. Furthermore, we can give a simple way of deciding if routing demands on the tree will come within some factor α of the optimal congestion for any set of demands d_{uv}. Consider any tree edge $(x, y) \in T$. Removing edge (x, y) from T splits it into two connected pieces, and induces a cut in the graph, consisting of all edges that have exactly one endpoint in each piece. If $S(x, y)$ is the set of vertices of one of the two connected pieces of T created by removing (x, y) from T, let $C(x, y)$ be the capacity of this cut; that is, $C(x, y) = \sum_{u \in S(x,y), v \notin S(x,y)} c_{uv}$. We observe that given any set of demands d, the amount of demand crossing this cut is $\sum_{u \in S(x,y), v \notin S(x,y)} d_{uv}$; let us denote this amount (for a given set of demands d) by $D(x, y)$. Thus, the flow per unit of capacity in the cut for *any* possible routing of this set of demands is at least $D(x, y)/C(x, y)$. Since this is the flow per unit capacity, some edge in this cut must have congestion at least $D(x, y)/C(x, y)$ in any possible routing.

Now we also observe that if we route paths in T along the paths uniquely defined by the tree, then the total amount of demand using edge (x, y) is exactly $D(x, y)$. Thus, if the capacity c_{xy} of edge $(x, y) \in T$ is at least $\frac{1}{\alpha}C(x, y)$, then the congestion

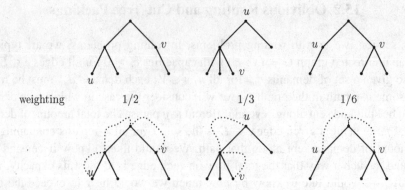

weighting   1/2   1/3   1/6

Figure 15.2. Two different ways of specifying a routing. On top is a weighted collection of trees. To route demand from u to v, we send 1/2 the demand along the u-v path in the first tree, 1/3 along the u-v path in the second tree, and 1/6 in the last tree. On the bottom is a weighted collection of trees in which each tree edge has an associated path (shown as a dotted line only for edges on the u-v path). To route demand from u to v, we send flow along the concatenation of the paths associated with each in the u-v path in the tree; we send 1/2 the demand along the concatenation of the paths in the first tree, 1/3 along the concatenation of paths in the second tree, and 1/6 along the concatenation of paths in the last tree.

on edge (x, y) in our routing is $D(x, y)/c_{xy} \leq \alpha D(x, y)/C(x, y)$. Since the minimum congestion needed by any routing is at least $D(x, y)/C(x, y)$, the congestion on edge (x, y) is then within a factor of α of the optimal congestion for routing the given set of demands d. Therefore, if for all $(x, y) \in T$, the capacity c_{xy} of edge (x, y) is at least $\frac{1}{\alpha}C(x, y)$, then routing the demands on the tree has congestion at most α times the optimal congestion. Notice that this condition does not depend on the demand set d, and so if it holds, it will be true for any set of demands.

To get the approximation factor α we desire, we modify our routing scheme in two ways. The first is to give a collection of trees T_i and a weighting λ_i of them, such that $\lambda_i \geq 0$ for all i and $\sum_i \lambda_i = 1$; see Figure 15.2. Now given any demand d_{uv} we send a λ_i fraction of it on the unique u-v path in tree T_i for each i. For edge $(x, y) \in T_i$, let $C_i(x, y)$ be the capacity of the cut induced by edge (x, y) in the tree T_i, and let $D_i(x, y)$ be the total demand crossing this cut for a given demand d; note that removing the same edge (x, y) from different trees T_i may induce different cuts. Then as argued above, for a given demand set d and for any i, the congestion of any routing of d is at least $D_i(x, y)/C_i(x, y)$, so any routing has congestion at least $\max_i D_i(x, y)/C_i(x, y)$. The total flow on edge (x, y) in our routing is $\sum_{i:(x,y)\in T_i} \lambda_i D_i(x, y)$. Thus, if

$$c_{xy} \geq \frac{1}{\alpha} \sum_{i:(x,y)\in T_i} \lambda_i C_i(x, y), \tag{15.1}$$

then the congestion along edge (x, y) in our routing is

$$\frac{\sum_{i:(x,y)\in T_i} \lambda_i D_i(x, y)}{c_{xy}} \leq \alpha \frac{\sum_{i:(x,y)\in T_i} \lambda_i D_i(x, y)}{\sum_{i:(x,y)\in T_i} \lambda_i C_i(x, y)} \leq \alpha \max_i \frac{D_i(x, y)}{C_i(x, y)}$$

by Fact 1.10. If inequality (15.1) holds for all edges (x, y), then our routing will have congestion at most α times the optimal congestion.

Although the condition given by inequality (15.1) is weaker than the condition on capacities for a single tree, in order to obtain the result we want we must modify our routing scheme in one additional way. For each tree T_i in our collection, and each edge $(x, y) \in T_i$, we specify a path in the graph G between the endpoints x and y. While this could be just the edge (x, y), it could also be some other path; for the tree T_i and edge $(x, y) \in T_i$, we denote the set of edges in this path by $P_i(x, y)$. We now have i index both the tree i and the associated paths $P_i(x, y)$ for all $(x, y) \in T_i$, so that a different index $i' \neq i$ may refer to the same tree (that is, $T_i = T_{i'}$) but with different paths. For a given demand d_{uv}, to route the λ_i fraction of the demand in tree T_i, we consider the unique path between u and v in the tree, and then we concatenate the paths $P_i(x, y)$ associated with each tree edge (x, y) along the path. This gives a path from u to v in the graph, and we route the demand along this path; see Figure 15.2. Now for any edge (u, v) in the graph, the total demand we route through it is the sum over all trees T_i of demand $\lambda_i D_i(x, y)$ for all edges $(x, y) \in T_i$ that have edge (u, v) in the associated path $P_i(x, y)$; that is,

$$\sum_i \lambda_i \sum_{(x,y) \in T_i : (u,v) \in P_i(x,y)} D_i(x, y).$$

Now suppose that for any edge $(u, v) \in E$, we have that its capacity is at least an α fraction of the weighted cuts associated with the paths using (u, v); that is,

$$c_{uv} \geq \frac{1}{\alpha} \sum_i \lambda_i \sum_{(x,y) \in T_i : (u,v) \in P_i(x,y)} C_i(x, y). \tag{15.2}$$

Then the congestion on (u, v) in our routing is

$$\frac{\sum_i \lambda_i \sum_{(x,y) \in T_i : (u,v) \in P_i(x,y)} D_i(x, y)}{c_{uv}} \leq \alpha \frac{\sum_i \lambda_i \sum_{(x,y) \in T_i : (u,v) \in P_i(x,y)} D_i(x, y)}{\sum_i \lambda_i \sum_{(x,y) \in T_i : (u,v) \in P_i(x,y)} C_i(x, y)}$$

$$\leq \alpha \max_i \frac{D_i(x, y)}{C_i(x, y)}.$$

As above, any routing will have congestion at least $\max_i D_i(x, y)/C_i(x, y)$. Thus, if inequality (15.2) holds for all $(u, v) \in E$, then our routing will have congestion within a factor α of the optimal congestion.

To find a collection of trees and associated paths, we will use a linear program. We have a decision variable α and decision variables λ_i. Each λ_i is the weight for a tree T_i together with paths $P_i(x, y)$ for the edges $(x, y) \in T_i$. We will minimize α subject to the constraint that inequality (15.2) holds for all $u, v \in V$; since $c_{uv} = 0$ for $(u, v) \notin E$, we will not choose any paths using (u, v). The LP is then

$$\text{minimize} \quad \alpha$$

$$\text{subject to} \quad \sum_i \lambda_i \sum_{(x,y) \in T_i : (u,v) \in P_i(x,y)} C_i(x, y) \leq \alpha c_{uv}, \qquad \forall u, v \in V,$$

$$\sum_i \lambda_i = 1,$$

$$\lambda_i \geq 0, \qquad \forall i.$$

We call the collection of trees found by this linear program a *cut-tree packing*. A cut-tree is a weighted tree T such that the weight of the edge (x, y) is exactly $C(x, y)$. One can view the LP above as trying to pack a convex combination of cut-trees into the graph G, stretching out each tree edge along a path, so as to minimize the overall factor by which each edge of G exceeds its capacity.

We can now show nonconstructively that the LP has a solution of value $O(\log n)$. The nonconstructive proof will then give us ideas for an algorithm to find the cut-tree packing. This will prove that we can find an $O(\log n)$-approximation algorithm for the oblivious routing problem.

Lemma 15.13. *The linear program has value $O(\log n)$.*

Proof. To prove this, we will take the dual of the linear program, then show that we can apply a result from the approximation of metrics by tree metrics in Section 8.7 to bound the value of the dual by $O(\log n)$. This will then bound the value of the primal by strong duality.

The dual of the linear program above is

$$\text{maximize} \quad z$$
$$\text{subject to} \quad \sum_{u,v \in V} c_{uv} \ell_{uv} = 1,$$
$$z \leq \sum_{(x,y) \in T_i} C_i(x, y) \sum_{(u,v) \in P_i(x,y)} \ell_{uv}, \quad \forall i,$$
$$\ell_{uv} \geq 0, \qquad\qquad \forall u, v \in V.$$

We will now begin modifying the dual solution to the point at which we can apply our knowledge of tree metrics to the problem. We will treat the dual variables ℓ_{uv} as the length of an edge between u and v. It will be useful to think of the shortest path distance between two $x, y \in V$ using edge lengths ℓ_{uv}; we will denote this distance as $d_\ell(x, y)$.

We first observe that the dual variable z is smaller than the sum over $(x, y) \in T_i$ of $C_i(x, y)$ times the length of the associated path from x to y. Therefore, we need to concentrate only on trees whose associated x-y paths are shortest paths using the edge lengths ℓ_{uv}. Thus, for all trees T_i we have that

$$z \leq \sum_{(x,y) \in T_i} C_i(x, y) d_\ell(x, y).$$

We can rewrite the dual as

$$\max_{\ell \geq 0: \sum_{u,v \in V} c_{uv} \ell_{uv} = 1} \min_i \sum_{(x,y) \in T_i} C_i(x, y) d_\ell(x, y).$$

We would now like to drop the restriction on the lengths ℓ that $\sum_{u,v \in V} c_{uv} \ell_{uv} = 1$. Observe that if we have lengths ℓ such that $\sum_{u,v \in V} c_{uv} \ell_{uv} = \beta > 0$, then if we multiply all the lengths ℓ_{uv} by $1/\beta$, we have that $\sum_{u,v \in V} c_{uv} \ell_{uv} = 1$. The shortest path lengths $d_\ell(x, y)$ also change by the same factor $1/\beta$, so that the dual objective function changes by a factor of $1/\beta$. Thus, we can rewrite the dual still further as

$$\max_{\ell \geq 0} \min_i \frac{\sum_{(x,y)\in T_i} C_i(x,y)d_\ell(x,y)}{\sum_{u,v\in V} c_{uv}\ell_{uv}}.$$

We recall from Theorem 8.25, combined with Theorem 8.19, that for any non-negative set of costs c_{uv} and any distance metric d_ℓ, we can find a tree met-ric (V, T) such that $d_\ell(u, v) \leq T_{uv}$ for all $u, v \in V$ and such that $\sum_{u,v\in V} c_{uv}T_{uv} \leq O(\log n)\sum_{u,v\in V} c_{uv}d_\ell(u, v)$. With two more observations, we will be done. First, we observe that $d_\ell(u, v) \leq \ell_{uv}$ for all $u, v \in V$ since the shortest path length between u and v is no more than the length of the u-v edge. Second, since $d_\ell(x, y) \leq T_{xy}$ for all $x, y \in V$, $\sum_{(x,y)\in T_i} C_i(x, y)d_\ell(x, y) \leq \sum_{(x,y)\in T_i} C_i(x, y)T_{xy}$. Further, observe that $\sum_{(x,y)\in T_i} C_i(x, y)T_{xy} = \sum_{u,v\in V} c_{uv}T_{uv}$, since any $u, v \in V$ contributes c_{uv} exactly to the cuts $C_i(x, y)$ corresponding to the edges (x, y) on the unique path in T_i from u to v. Putting all of this together, for any edge lengths $\ell \geq 0$, we have that

$$\sum_{(x,y)\in T_i} C_i(x, y)d_\ell(x, y) \leq \sum_{u,v\in V} c_{uv}T_{uv} \leq O(\log n) \sum_{u,v\in V} c_{uv}d_\ell(u, v)$$

$$\leq O(\log n) \sum_{u,v\in V} c_{uv}\ell_{uv}. \qquad (15.3)$$

Hence, for any edge lengths $\ell \geq 0$, there exists some tree T_i such that

$$\frac{\sum_{(x,y)\in T_i} C_i(x, y)d_\ell(x, y)}{\sum_{u,v\in V} c_{uv}\ell_{uv}} \leq O(\log n).$$

This proves that the optimal value of the dual is $O(\log n)$, and since by strong duality, the value of the primal is equal to the value of the dual, the original primal LP has value $O(\log n)$. $\qquad\square$

Finally, we can use our understanding from the lemma above to find an appro-priate collection of trees and corresponding paths such that we have an $O(\log n)$-approximation algorithm. One idea is to use the ellipsoid method of Section 4.3 to solve the dual linear program; the proof above shows that in a sense the tree metric algorithm can find a violated constraint if $z > \Omega(\log n)$. However, if the optimal z is much smaller than $O(\log n)$, we may not be able to find violated constraints. The idea for our approximation algorithm is to set up a different linear program so that we can indeed use the tree metric algorithm as a separation oracle for the ellipsoid method. We observe which tree metrics are used in defining the violated constraints, and then we find a cut-tree packing using only these trees; we show that this is sufficient to obtain the approximation algorithm.

Theorem 15.14. *There is an $O(\log n)$-approximation algorithm for the oblivious rout-ing problem.*

Proof. By the proof of the lemma above, we know that the value of the linear program is at most $Z = 4 \cdot 96 \ln(n + 1)$, since Theorem 8.25 and Theorem 8.19 show that given a metric d_ℓ defined by edge lengths ℓ, we can find a tree metric (V, T) such that $\sum_{u,v\in V} c_{uv}T_{uv} \leq 4 \cdot 96 \ln(n + 1) \sum_{u,v\in V} c_{uv}d_\ell(u, v)$. We now apply the ellipsoid method to a slightly different linear program. Consider the linear program as follows, where $\mathcal{I}$ is the set of indices of all possible trees and associated paths, and Z is treated as a constant. We are looking for a feasible solution to the problem, so we use the objective function of minimizing the constant 0. Then the linear program is

$$\text{minimize } 0$$
$$\text{subject to } \sum_{i \in \mathcal{I}} \lambda_i \sum_{(x,y) \in T_i : (u,v) \in P_i(x,y)} C_i(x, y) \leq Z c_{uv}, \qquad \forall u, v \in V,$$
$$\sum_{i \in \mathcal{I}} \lambda_i = 1,$$
$$\lambda_i \geq 0, \qquad \forall i \in \mathcal{I}.$$

The dual program is then

$$\text{maximize } \quad z - Z \sum_{u,v \in V} c_{uv} \ell_{uv}$$
$$\text{subject to } \quad z \leq \sum_{(x,y) \in T_i} C_i(x, y) \sum_{(u,v) \in P_i(x,y)} \ell_{uv}, \qquad \forall i \in \mathcal{I},$$
$$\ell_{uv} \geq 0, \qquad \qquad \forall u, v \in V.$$

Since we know that there is a feasible solution to the primal problem of value zero, the optimum solution to the dual problem must also be of value zero. We now show how to use the ellipsoid method on the dual program to obtain a polynomially sized set $\mathcal{T} \subseteq \mathcal{I}$ of tree/path indices such that the primal is feasible for $\mathcal{T}$. Once we have this, we can solve the primal in polynomial time, and obtain the desired cut-tree packing.

To do this, we use some knowledge of how the ellipsoid method works. When the separation oracle for the ellipsoid method declares that a given solution is feasible, the ellipsoid method makes an *objective function cut*; that is, it restricts its attention to all solutions having objective function value at least the value of the current solution (in the case of a maximization problem). In terms of the operations of the ellipsoid method, this is equivalent to the separation oracle returning a constraint stating that the objective function is at least the value of the current solution. As long as the ellipsoid method, in each step, imposes a constraint that retains an optimal solution, it will find an optimal solution in polynomial time (as long as the number of bits used to encode the constraints is also polynomial, as discussed in Section 4.3).

We now apply the ellipsoid method to the dual linear program. Our separation oracle works as follows. Given a solution (z, ℓ), we check to see if $z > Z \sum_{u,v \in V} c_{uv} \ell_{uv}$. If so, then we find a tree metric (V, T) such that $\sum_{u,v \in V} c_{uv} T_{uv} \leq Z \sum_{u,v \in V} c_{uv} d_\ell(u, v)$. By inequality (15.3) of Lemma 15.13, for this tree T where $P(x, y)$ is the shortest x-y path using lengths ℓ, we have that

$$\sum_{(x,y) \in T} C(x, y) \sum_{(u,v) \in P(x,y)} \ell_{uv} \leq Z \sum_{u,v \in V} c_{uv} d_\ell(u, v) \leq Z \sum_{u,v \in V} c_{uv} \ell_{uv} < z,$$

and we can return as a violated constraint the dual constraint associated with the index i of this tree T and the associated paths. If $z \leq Z \sum_{u,v \in V} c_{uv} \ell_{uv}$, then we declare the solution (z, ℓ) as feasible. Note in this case the objective function value is $z - Z \sum_{u,v \in V} c_{uv} \ell_{uv} \leq 0$. By the discussion above, the ellipsoid method will make an objective function cut, stating that the value of the objective function is at least $z - Z \sum_{u,v \in V} c_{uv} \ell_{uv}$. Since we know that the value of the optimal dual solution is zero, this does not remove any optimal solutions, and hence the ellipsoid method will find an optimal solution to the dual in polynomial time.

Now let $\mathcal{T} \subseteq \mathcal{I}$ be the set of all indices of trees and associated paths found by the separation oracle during the execution of the ellipsoid method above. We note that since the ellipsoid method ran in polynomial time, the size of $\mathcal{T}$ must be bounded by a polynomial in the input size. Also, we claim that if we set $\mathcal{I} = \mathcal{T}$ in the dual above, then it still has an optimal solution of value zero. To see this, we imagine running the ellipsoid method again on the dual with $\mathcal{I} = \mathcal{T}$. Since the only violated constraints returned are from $\mathcal{T}$, the execution of the ellipsoid method is identical to the previous execution of the ellipsoid method, and the same optimal solution of value zero is returned.

Since there is an optimal solution to the dual of value zero with $\mathcal{I} = \mathcal{T}$, there must also be a feasible solution to the primal for this set of trees. Now we can run a polynomial-time linear programming algorithm (such as the ellipsoid method) on a polynomially sized set of variables from $\mathcal{T}$, and this will yield a cut-tree packing of congestion at most $Z = O(\log n)$, as desired. $\qquad\square$

The connection between cut-tree packings and tree metrics can be shown to hold in the other direction as well. Suppose we are given as input a metric (V, d) and costs c_{uv} for all $u, v \in V$, and suppose we have a polynomial-time algorithm to find a cut-tree packing such that inequality (15.2) holds for some value α. In Exercise 15.7, we ask the reader to show that we can then derive a polynomial-time algorithm to find a tree metric (V, T) such that $d_{uv} \leq T_{uv}$ for all $u, v \in V$ and $\sum_{u,v \in V} c_{uv} T_{uv} \leq \alpha \sum_{u,v \in V} c_{uv} d_{uv}$. Thus, the two problems are reducible to each other.

15.3 Cut-Tree Packings and the Minimum Bisection Problem

In this section, we turn to additional applications of the cut-tree packings introduced in the previous section. When we discussed the probabilistic approximation of metrics by tree metrics in Section 8.5, we observed that it allowed us to translate the solution of problems on general metrics to problems on tree metrics with a loss of a factor of $O(\log n)$ in performance guarantee. In this section, we show that we can do the same for cut problems: we can reduce the solution of finding good cuts in general graphs to finding good cuts in trees with a loss of a factor of $O(\log n)$ in the performance guarantee.

To illustrate, we return to the problem of finding a minimum bisection, as introduced in Section 8.4. Recall that a set of vertices S is a *b-balanced cut* for $b \in (0, 1/2]$ if $\lfloor bn \rfloor \leq |S| \leq \lceil (1 - b)n \rceil$. Given an undirected graph $G = (V, E)$ with nonnegative edge costs $c_e \geq 0$ for all edges $e \in E$, and a $b \in (0, 1/2]$, the goal of the minimum b-balanced cut problem is to find the b-balanced cut S that minimizes the cost of the edges with exactly one endpoint in S. The minimum bisection problem is a special case in which $b = 1/2$.

In this section, we will show how to use cut-tree packings to find an $O(\log n)$-approximation algorithm for the minimum bisection problem. However, the algorithm and analysis we give here can be extended to many other cut problems as well. We give as exercises finding alternative $O(\log n)$-approximation algorithms for the minimum multicut problem (Exercise 15.5) and the sparsest cut problem (Exercise 15.6).

The algorithm itself is quite simple. Given the graph $G = (V, E)$ and edge costs c_e, we find a collection of trees and associated paths as discussed in the previous section, treating the edge costs c_e as capacities. Recall from the previous section that for a tree T_i and an edge $(x, y) \in T_i$, we consider the cut induced by removing (x, y) from T_i. Let $S(x, y)$ be the set of vertices in one of the two connected components of the tree remaining after (x, y) is removed. We denote the total cost of the edges in the cut by $C_i(x, y) = \sum_{e \in \delta(S_i(x,y))} c_e$. We let $P_i(x, y)$ be the path associated with the edge $(x, y) \in T_i$. For any $S \subseteq V$, let $c(\delta(S))$ denote the cost of the edges in G with exactly one endpoint in S, so that $c(\delta(S)) = \sum_{e \in \delta(S)} c_e$, and let $c_{T_i}(\delta(S))$ denote the cost of the tree edges of T_i with exactly one endpoint in S, so that $c_{T_i}(\delta(S)) = \sum_{(x,y) \in T_i \cap \delta(S)} C_i(x, y)$. Given the trees T_i from the collection, we find an optimal bisection $X_i \subseteq V$ in each tree T_i in which the cost of each edge $(x, y) \in T_i$ is $C_i(x, y)$; that is, we find the bisection X_i in T_i that minimizes $c_{T_i}(\delta(X_i))$. We show below that we can find an optimal bisection in a tree in polynomial time. Then over the trees T_i in the cut-tree packing, we return the bisection X_i that minimizes the cost in the graph G, that is, that minimizes $c(\delta(X_i))$.

In the following two lemmas, we relate the cost of any cut S in the graph G to its cost in T_i.

Lemma 15.15. *For any tree T_i and any $S \subseteq V$,*

$$c(\delta(S)) \leq c_{T_i}(\delta(S)).$$

Proof. By our definitions above, we can rewrite the right-hand side as

$$c_{T_i}(\delta(S)) = \sum_{(x,y) \in T_i \cap \delta(S)} C_i(x, y) = \sum_{(x,y) \in T_i \cap \delta(S)} \sum_{e : e \in \delta(S_i(x,y))} c_e.$$

Pick an arbitrary edge $e = (u, v)$ in G that is in $\delta(S)$. We will show that it must exist in the sum on the right-hand side. Since exactly one of u and v is in S, there must exist some edge in $\delta(S)$ on the path from u to v in T_i; call this edge (x, y). Then $(x, y) \in T_i \cap \delta(S)$ and $e = (u, v) \in \delta(S_i(x, y))$, so that c_e appears in the sum on the right-hand side. $\qquad\square$

Lemma 15.16. *Suppose we have an $O(\log n)$-congestion cut-tree packing of trees T_i as discussed in Section 15.2 for input graph G with edge costs c_e. Then for any cut $S \subseteq V$,*

$$\sum_i \lambda_i c_{T_i}(\delta(S)) \leq O(\log n) c(\delta(S)).$$

Proof. We recall the defining property of cut-tree packings, from inequality (15.2), where $P_i(x, y)$ is the path from x to y in G associated with the tree edge $(x, y) \in T_i$:

$$\sum_i \lambda_i \sum_{(x,y) \in T_i : (u,v) \in P_i(x,y)} C_i(x, y) \leq O(\log n) c_{uv}.$$

To prove the lemma, for each edge $(u, v) \in \delta(S)$, we remove the corresponding tree edges (x, y) for all $(x, y) \in T_i$ such that $(u, v) \in P_i(x, y)$. By the inequality above, the cost of the tree edges $(x, y) \in T_i$ removed (each multiplied by λ_i) is at most $O(\log n)c(\delta(S))$. If we can show that we have removed all tree edges $(x, y) \in \delta(S)$ for each tree T_i, then we have proven the lemma. Pick any tree edge $(x, y) \in \delta(S)$ for any tree T_i, and consider the corresponding path $P_i(x, y)$ between x and y. Because exactly one endpoint of (x, y) is in S, there must be some edge (u, v) on the path with exactly one endpoint in S, so that $(u, v) \in \delta(S)$. Thus, when we considered $(u, v) \in \delta(S)$, we must have removed the tree edge (x, y). □

Given the lemmas, the proof of the performance guarantee is straightforward, as we see below.

Theorem 15.17. *The algorithm above is an $O(\log n)$-approximation algorithm for the minimum bisection problem.*

Proof. Let $X^* \subseteq V$ be an optimal bisection of G. We know that in each tree T_i we have found an optimal bisection X_i, so that the cost of the bisection X^* costs at least as much; in other words, $c_{T_i}(\delta(X_i)) \leq c_{T_i}(\delta(X^*))$ for all trees T_i in the packing. Then by Lemma 15.15 we have that

$$\sum_i \lambda_i c(\delta(X_i)) \leq \sum_i \lambda_i c_{T_i}(\delta(X_i)).$$

By the observation above,

$$\sum_i \lambda_i c_{T_i}(\delta(X_i)) \leq \sum_i \lambda_i c_{T_i}(\delta(X^*)).$$

By Lemma 15.16 applied to the optimal bisection X^*, we have

$$\sum_i \lambda_i c_{T_i}(\delta(X^*)) \leq O(\log n)c(\delta(X^*)) = O(\log n)\,\text{OPT}.$$

Putting these together we have that

$$\sum_i \lambda_i c(\delta(X_i)) \leq O(\log n)\,\text{OPT}.$$

Thus, a convex combination of the costs of the bisections $c(\delta(X_i))$ is at most $O(\log n)\,\text{OPT}$, which implies that at least one of the bisections X_i must have cost at most $O(\log n)\,\text{OPT}$. Since the algorithm returns X_i minimizing $c(\delta(X_i))$, it is an $O(\log n)$-approximation algorithm. □

To finish off the proof, we must show how to find a minimum bisection in trees. We do this using dynamic programming.

Lemma 15.18. *There is a polynomial-time algorithm to find a minimum bisection in a tree.*

Proof. We assume that we are given as input a tree T on a set of vertices V with edge weights $c_e \geq 0$ for all $e \in T$. The algorithm we give below will work on rooted trees where internal nodes have either one or two children. If the tree has ℓ leaves, it will

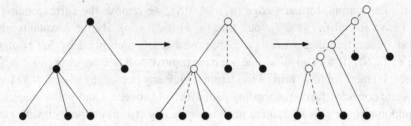

Figure 15.3. Modifying a tree into one in which all original vertices are leaves, and each internal node has at most two children. The new edges are dashed and have infinite cost. The new nodes have white interiors.

output the optimal cut S such that there are exactly $\lfloor \ell/2 \rfloor$ leaves in S; we will call this a *leaf bisection* of the tree. First we must show that we can transform our input into an input on which this leaf bisection algorithm will work. For any vertex $v \in V$ that is an internal node, we create a new node v', put it in the place of v, and then add an edge (v, v') of infinite cost. Now the leaves of the tree are all the vertices of V. We pick an arbitrary internal node as the root. For any internal node with more than two children, we create extra nodes and infinite cost edges so that each node has at most two children. See Figure 15.3 for the transformation such that all original vertices become leaves and each internal node has at most two children. Note that any solution in the modified tree that does not have infinite cost and gives a leaf bisection has a corresponding solution in the original tree of the same cost, and vice versa. For any node with $d \geq 3$ children, we end up creating $d - 2$ new nodes. Thus, we may create $O(n)$ new nodes, so any algorithm for finding a leaf bisection running in time polynomial in the number of nodes will also run in time polynomial in our original input size.

We now perform dynamic programming on the rooted tree, starting with the leaves and working our way up the tree, to find a minimum leaf bisection. For each internal node u with k leaves in its subtree, we create a table with entries for each integer $i \in [0, k]$. The table will give the minimum-cost set of edges we need to remove from u's subtree in order to have a cut with u on one side along with i leaves, and $k - i$ leaves on the other side of the cut. For a given internal node u with two children v_1 and v_2 having k_1 and k_2 leaves in their subtrees, respectively, we create entries for u's table for each $i \in [0, k_1 + k_2]$ by considering four different combinations; see Figure 15.4 for an illustration. First, we consider all $i_1 \in [0, k_1]$ and $i_2 \in [0, k_2]$ such that $i_1 + i_2 = i$; this captures the possible cuts in which u, v_1, and v_2 are all on the same side of the cut as the i leaves. Second, we consider all $i_1 \in [0, k_1]$ and $i_2 \in [0, k_2]$ such that $i_1 + (k_2 - i_2) = i$ while also removing the edge (u, v_2); this captures the possible cuts in which u and v_1 are on the same side of the cut as the i leaves, while v_2 is on the opposite side. Third, we consider all $i_1 \in [0, k_1]$ and $i_2 \in [0, k_2]$ such that $(k_1 - i_1) + i_2 = i$ while also removing the edge (u, v_1); this captures the possible cuts in which u and v_2 are on the same side of the cut as the i leaves, while v_1 is on the opposite side. Fourth, we consider all $i_1 \in [0, k_1]$ and $i_2 \in [0, k_2]$ such that $(k_1 - i_1) + (k_2 - i_2) = i$ while also removing both edges (u, v_1) and (u, v_2); this captures the possible cuts in which u is on the same side of the cut as the i leaves, but v_1 and v_2 are on the opposite side. Over all these possible combinations, we choose the combination of the least overall cost to store in the table entry for i. The case in which u has only a single child is similar.

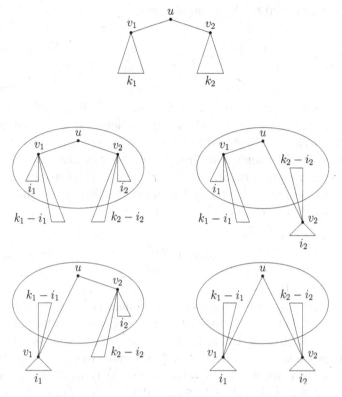

Figure 15.4. The four different cases of the dynamic program for an internal node u with two children v_1 and v_2 that have k_1 and k_2 leaves, respectively.

If there are ℓ leaves in the tree and n nodes, we consider $O(\ell)$ possible combinations per table entry, so that we take $O(\ell^2)$ time per internal node, and $O(n\ell^2) = O(n^3)$ time overall. To find the optimal leaf bisection, we consider the entry at the root node for $\lfloor \ell/2 \rfloor$. $\qquad \square$

15.4 The Uniform Sparsest Cut Problem

For our final algorithmic result of the book, we revisit the *sparsest cut problem*, introduced in Exercise 8.6 and discussed in Section 15.1. In the sparsest cut problem, we are given an undirected graph $G = (V, E)$, costs $c_e \geq 0$ for all $e \in E$, and k pairs of vertices s_i, t_i with associated positive integer demands d_i. We want to find a set of vertices S that minimizes

$$\rho(S) \equiv \frac{\sum_{e \in \delta(S)} c_e}{\sum_{i:|S \cap \{s_i, t_i\}|=1} d_i}.$$

That is, the sparsest cut problem finds a cut that minimizes the ratio of the cost of the edges in the cut to the demands separated by the cut. In this section, we will consider an interesting special case of the problem, the *uniform* sparsest cut problem. In this case, there is a single unit of demand between each distinct pair of vertices. Thus, the goal is to find a set of vertices S that minimizes

$$\rho(S) \equiv \frac{\sum_{e \in \delta(S)} c_e}{|S||V - S|}.$$

As with b-balanced cuts introduced in Section 8.4, finding a uniform sparsest cut is a popular choice in some divide-and-conquer applications. In unweighted problems (with $c_e = 1$ for all $e \in E$), the uniform sparsest cut problem finds the cut S that minimizes the ratio of the number of edges in the cut that do exist (that is, $|\delta(S)|$) to the number that could exist (that is, $|S||V - S|$). Additionally, finding the uniform sparsest cut is sometimes substituted for finding the edge expansion of unweighted graphs. The *edge expansion* $\alpha(S)$ of a cut $S \subseteq V$ for $|S| \leq n/2$ is

$$\alpha(S) \equiv \frac{|\delta(S)|}{|S|},$$

and the edge expansion of the graph is the minimum value of $\alpha(S)$ over all S with $|S| \leq n/2$. The cut that minimizes the edge expansion trades off the number of edges in the cut against the size $|S|$. Unlike the b-balanced cut problem, there is no arbitrary lower bound on the size of $|S|$ for the set S that minimizes the edge expansion; we can have $|S|$ small if the number of edges in the cut is small enough to justify it. When $|S| \leq n/2$, then $n/2 \leq |V - S| \leq n$, so that $\frac{1}{n}\alpha(S) \leq \rho(S) \leq \frac{2}{n}\alpha(S)$. Thus, the uniform sparsest cut problem in unweighted graphs approximates the edge expansion of the graph to within a factor of 2.

In Section 15.1, we considered a linear programming relaxation for the problem and used it to obtain an $O(\log k)$-approximation algorithm for the sparsest cut problem. Here we will consider a vector programming relaxation for the uniform sparsest cut problem, and show that it can be used to obtain an $O(\sqrt{\log n})$-approximation algorithm.

We start the discussion by giving an integer quadratic formulation of the problem. Consider the following formulation:

$$\text{minimize} \quad \frac{\frac{1}{4}\sum_{e=(i,j)\in E} c_e(x_i - x_j)^2}{\frac{1}{4}\sum_{i,j\in V: i\neq j}(x_i - x_j)^2}$$

$$\text{subject to } (x_i - x_j)^2 \leq (x_i - x_k)^2 + (x_k - x_j)^2, \qquad \forall i, j, k \in V, \qquad (15.4)$$

$$x_i \in \{-1, +1\}, \qquad\qquad\qquad \forall i \in V.$$

We claim that this models the uniform sparsest cut problem. Given a set $S \subseteq V$, then by setting $x_i = -1$ for all $i \in S$, and $x_i = 1$ otherwise, $\frac{1}{4}\sum_{(i,j)\in E} c_e(x_i - x_j)^2 = \sum_{e\in\delta(S)} c_e$ and $\frac{1}{4}\sum_{i,j\in V: i\neq j}(x_i - x_j)^2 = |S||V - S|$, so that the objective function is $\rho(S)$. It is easy to check that the constraints of the program are obeyed since the inequality (15.4) is trivially true if $x_i = x_j$, while if $x_i \neq x_j$, then either $x_i \neq x_k$ or $x_j \neq x_k$. Similarly, given a solution x to the integer quadratic program, let $S = \{i \in V : x_i = -1\}$, and the value of the objective function is $\rho(S)$.

We relax the formulation first as follows:

$$\text{minimize} \quad \frac{1}{n^2} \sum_{e=(i,j)\in E} c_e (y_i - y_j)^2$$

$$\text{subject to} \quad \sum_{i,j\in V: i\neq j} (y_i - y_j)^2 = n^2,$$

$$(y_i - y_j)^2 \leq (y_i - y_k)^2 + (y_k - y_j)^2, \qquad \forall i,j,k \in V.$$

Note that we do not require $y_i \in \{-1, 1\}$. Given an optimal solution x^* to the previous formulation, let $d = \sum_{i,j\in V: i\neq j} (x_i^* - x_j^*)^2$. Set $y_i = nx_i^*/\sqrt{d}$. Then

$$\sum_{i,j\in V: i\neq j} (y_i - y_j)^2 = \frac{n^2}{d} \sum_{i,j\in V: i\neq j} (x_i^* - x_j^*)^2 = n^2,$$

as required. Furthermore,

$$\frac{1}{n^2} \sum_{e=(i,j)\in E} c_e (y_i - y_j)^2 = \frac{1}{d} \sum_{e=(i,j)\in E} c_e (x_i^* - x_j^*)^2 = \frac{\frac{1}{4}\sum_{e=(i,j)\in E} c_e (x_i^* - x_j^*)^2}{\frac{1}{4}\sum_{i,j\in V: i\neq j} (x_i^* - x_j^*)^2},$$

and each constraint $(y_i - y_j)^2 \leq (y_i - y_k)^2 + (y_k - y_j)^2$ is satisfied since the corresponding constraint on x^* is satisfied. Thus, y is feasible for this program and has value equal to that of the optimal solution to the problem, so that this formulation is a relaxation.

We can now relax this formulation to a vector program. Note that $\|v_i - v_j\|^2 = (v_i - v_j) \cdot (v_i - v_j)$ for vectors $v_i \in \Re^n$, so that we have

$$\text{minimize} \quad \frac{1}{n^2} \sum_{e=(i,j)\in E} c_e \|v_i - v_j\|^2$$

$$\text{subject to} \quad \sum_{i,j\in V: i\neq j} \|v_i - v_j\|^2 = n^2,$$

$$\|v_i - v_j\|^2 \leq \|v_i - v_k\|^2 + \|v_k - v_j\|^2, \qquad \forall i,j,k \in V,$$

$$v_i \in \Re^n, \qquad \forall i \in V.$$

Given a solution y to the previous relaxation, we obtain a feasible solution to the vector program of the same objective function value by setting $v_i = (y_i, 0, \ldots, 0)$. Observe that unlike many previous vector programs we have studied, the vectors v_i are not constrained to be unit vectors.

Our algorithm for the problem is a variation on the random hyperplane technique that we have seen for rounding other vector programs. As usual, we pick a random vector $r = (r_1, \ldots, r_n)$ by drawing each coordinate from the normal distribution $\mathcal{N}(0, 1)$ with mean 0 and variance 1. The essence of the algorithm is that rather than simply partitioning the vectors according to whether $r \cdot v_i \geq 0$ or not, we instead consider a "fat" hyperplane, looking at vectors that have either significant positive projections on the random vector or significant negative projections on the random vector. We will show that aside from an easy exceptional case, with constant probability we obtain two sets of vectors L and R (with large positive and negative projections, respectively) that both have size $\Omega(n)$; see Figure 15.5 for an illustration. We then show that most of the

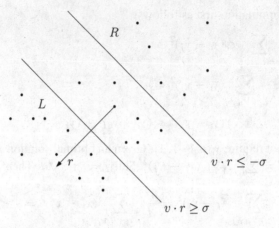

Figure 15.5. An illustration of the fat hyperplane rounding defining the two sets L and R.

pairs of points from these two sets are far apart; namely, for most $i \in L$ and $j \in R$, $\|v_i - v_j\|^2 = \Omega(1/\sqrt{\log n})$. This is the key to the result; once we have this, we see that

$$\sum_{i,j \in V: i \neq j} \|v_i - v_j\|^2 \geq \sum_{i \in L, j \in R} \|v_i - v_j\|^2 \geq \Omega(n^2/\sqrt{\log n}). \qquad (15.5)$$

We will show that we can easily find a cut S with $L \subseteq S \subseteq V - R$ such that

$$\rho(S) \leq \frac{\sum_{e=(i,j) \in E} c_e \|v_i - v_j\|^2}{\sum_{i \in L, j \in R} \|v_i - v_j\|^2}.$$

Thus, by inequality (15.5),

$$\rho(S) \leq O(\sqrt{\log n}) \frac{1}{n^2} \sum_{e=(i,j) \in E} c_e \|v_i - v_j\|^2 \leq O(\sqrt{\log n}) \, \text{OPT},$$

where the last inequality follows since $\frac{1}{n^2} \sum_{e=(i,j) \in E} c_e \|v_i - v_j\|^2$ is the objective function of the vector programming relaxation of the problem.

To begin stating the algorithm more formally, we first introduce some notation. For $i, j \in V$, let $d(i, j) = \|v_i - v_j\|^2$ and let $B(i, r) = \{j \in V : d(i, j) \leq r\}$. Note that d is a distance metric, since it obeys the triangle inequality due to the constraint in the vector program; because $d(i, j)$ is equal to the square of the ℓ_2 distance, it is sometimes called the ℓ_2^2 metric. For a set $S \subseteq V$, let $d(i, S) = \min_{j \in S} d(i, j)$. We let Δ stand for the desired distance between most of the pairs of vertices in L and R, so that our final goal is to show that we can find L and R where $|L|, |R| = \Omega(n)$ and for most $i \in L$ and $j \in R$, $d(i, j) \geq \Delta$ for $\Delta = \Omega(1/\sqrt{\log n})$.

The algorithm begins by checking to see whether a large fraction of the vertices are close together; in particular, the algorithm checks if there is a ball $B(i, \frac{1}{4})$ with at least $n/4$ vertices in it for some $i \in V$. If there is, this turns out to be an easy case that we handle separately, so we assume that there is no such ball. We choose a vertex o to maximize $|B(o, 4)|$; we will show that this guarantees that a large fraction of pairs of vertices are some constant distance apart and are not close to o. For a particular

---

if $\exists i \in V : |B(i, \frac{1}{4})| \geq \frac{n}{4}$ **then**
$\quad L' = B(i, \frac{1}{4})$
else
$\quad$ Pick $o \in V$ to maximize $|B(o, 4)|$
$\quad$ Pick random vector r
$\quad$ Let $L = \{i \in V : r \cdot (v_i - v_o) \geq \sigma\}$, $R = \{i \in V : r \cdot (v_i - v_o) \leq -\sigma\}$
$\quad$ Let $L' = L$, $R' = R$
$\quad$ **while** $\exists i \in L', j \in R' : d(i, j) \leq \Delta$ **do**
$\quad\quad L' \leftarrow L' - i;\ R \leftarrow R' - j$
$\quad$ Sort $i \in V$ by non-decreasing distance $d(i, L')$ to get $i_1, \ldots, i_n$
$\quad$ **return** $\{i_1, \ldots, i_k\}$ that minimizes $\min_{1 \leq k \leq n-1} \rho(\{i_1, \ldots, i_k\})$

Algorithm 15.1. Algorithm for rounding the vector programming relaxation of the uniform sparsest cut problem.

choice of constant σ, we consider two sets of vertices, $L = \{i \in V : r \cdot (v_i - v_o) \geq \sigma\}$ and $R = \{i \in V : r \cdot (v_i - v_o) \leq -\sigma\}$. We then pull out pairs of points from L and R if they are too close together; in particular, if for $i \in L$ and $j \in R$, $d(i, j) \leq \Delta$, then we remove i from L and j from R. As discussed above, our goal will be to show that the algorithm will work with $\Delta = C/\sqrt{\log n}$ for some constant C. We continue this process until no pair of points in L and R are within this distance of each other; let L' and R' be the resulting set of vertices after this removal process. We then sort the vertices $i \in V$ in order of their distance $d(i, L')$ from the set L', so that we have vertices $i_1, i_2, \ldots, i_n$. Finally, we consider the values of the sparsest cuts of all prefixes of this ordering; in particular, we consider $\rho(\{i_1\}), \rho(\{i_1, i_2\}), \ldots, \rho(\{i_1, \ldots, i_{n-1}\})$ and return the set $\{i_1, \ldots, i_k\}$ that gives the minimum of these values. The algorithm is summarized in Algorithm 15.1.

Before we state the main theorem, we first define a few terms that will allow us to state the theorems more easily. We will say that L and R are α-*large* if $|L| \geq \alpha n$ and $|R| \geq \alpha n$. In what follows, α will be some constant we state later. We say that L and R are Δ-*separated* if for all $i \in L$ and $j \in R$, $d(i, j) \geq \Delta$. We will need the following lemma.

Lemma 15.19. *If there is no $i \in V$ such that $|B(i, \frac{1}{4})| \geq \frac{n}{4}$, then with constant probability, L and R are α-large for a constant α.*

We defer the proof of this lemma until the end of the section; while it takes a bit of work, it is not hard and not part of the central difficulty of the result.

Now we state the central technical theorem of the analysis. As we sketched previously, this theorem implies that the algorithm returns a cut S with $\rho(S) \leq O(\sqrt{\log n})$ OPT with constant probability.

Theorem 15.20. *If L and R are α-large, then with constant probability, L' and R' are $\frac{\alpha}{2}$-large and are Δ-separated for $\Delta = C/\sqrt{\log n}$ for an appropriate choice of constant C.*

The proof of this theorem is easily the most lengthy and complex of the book, so we will work up to it slowly.

We start by showing that given that L' and R' are β-large and Δ-separated for some constant β, the algorithm has a performance guarantee of $O(1/\beta^2\Delta)$.

Theorem 15.21. *Given* $\Delta = O(1)$ *and a constant* $\beta \leq 1$, *suppose either that there exists an* $i \in V$ *such that* $|B(i, \frac{1}{4})| \geq \frac{n}{4}$ *or else that the sets* L' *and* R' *are* β-large *and* Δ-separated. *Then Algorithm 15.1 returns a solution to the uniform sparsest cut problem of value at most* $O(1/\beta^2\Delta)$ OPT.

Proof. We first claim that under the hypotheses of the theorem, the algorithm finds a set L' such that

$$\sum_{i,j\in V} |d(i, L') - d(j, L')| \geq \Omega(\beta^2 n^2 \Delta).$$

Given the claim, let $i_1, \ldots, i_n$ be the ordering of the vertices by non-decreasing distance $d(i, L')$. The algorithm returns a solution of value $\min_{1\leq k\leq n-1} \rho(\{i_1, \ldots, i_k\})$. Let $S_k = \{i_1, \ldots, i_k\}$, and let $\chi_{\delta(S)}(i, j) = 1$ if $|\{i, j\} \cap S| = 1$ and 0 otherwise. We can bound the cost of the solution found by the algorithm in a way similar to that in the proof of Theorem 15.5 for the sparsest cut problem:

$$\min_{1\leq k\leq n-1} \rho(S_k) = \min_{1\leq k\leq n-1} \frac{\sum_{e\in\delta(S_k)} c_e}{|S_k||V - S_k|} = \min_{1\leq k\leq n-1} \frac{\sum_{e\in E} c_e \chi_{\delta(S_k)}(e)}{\sum_{i,j\in V} \chi_{\delta(S_k)}(i, j)}.$$

By Fact 1.10, we have that

$$
\begin{aligned}
\min_{1\leq k\leq n-1} \frac{\sum_{e\in E} c_e \chi_{\delta(S_k)}(e)}{\sum_{i,j\in V} \chi_{\delta(S_k)}(i, j)} &\leq \frac{\sum_{k=1}^{n-1} |d(i_{k+1}, L') - d(i_k, L')| \sum_{e\in E} c_e \chi_{\delta(S_k)}(e)}{\sum_{k=1}^{n-1} |d(i_{k+1}, L') - d(i_k, L')| \sum_{i,j\in V} \chi_{\delta(S_k)}(i, j)} \\
&= \frac{\sum_{k=1}^{n-1} \sum_{e\in E} c_e \chi_{\delta(S_k)}(e)|d(i_{k+1}, L') - d(i_k, L')|}{\sum_{k=1}^{n-1} \sum_{i,j\in V} \chi_{\delta(S_k)}(i, j)|d(i_{k+1}, L') - d(i_k, L')|} \\
&= \frac{\sum_{e=(i,j)\in E} c_e |d(i, L') - d(j, L')|}{\sum_{i,j\in V} |d(i, L') - d(j, L')|} \\
&\leq \frac{\sum_{e=(i,j)\in E} c_e d(i, j)}{\Omega(\beta^2 n^2 \Delta)},
\end{aligned}
$$

where the inequality follows by the triangle inequality (in the numerator) and the claim (in the denominator). Then

$$\frac{\sum_{e=(i,j)\in E} c_e d(i, j)}{\Omega(\beta^2 n^2 \Delta)} = O(1/\beta^2\Delta)\frac{1}{n^2} \sum_{e=(i,j)\in E} c_e \|v_i - v_j\|^2 \leq O(1/\beta^2\Delta) \text{OPT},$$

since $\frac{1}{n^2} \sum_{e=(i,j)\in E} c_e \|v_i - v_j\|^2$ is the objective function of the vector programming relaxation of the problem.

We now need to prove the claim. If there is no $i \in V$ with $|B(i, \frac{1}{4})| \geq \frac{n}{4}$, then by hypothesis L' and R' are β-large and Δ-separated. Then we have that

$$\sum_{i,j\in V} |d(i, L') - d(j, L')| \geq \sum_{i\in L', j\in R'} |d(i, L') - d(j, L')| \geq |L'||R'|\Delta = \Omega(\beta^2 n^2 \Delta).$$

Now suppose there is an $i' \in V$ with $|B(i', \frac{1}{4})| \geq \frac{n}{4}$; the algorithm sets $L' = B(i', \frac{1}{4})$. By the constraint of the vector program we know that $\sum_{i,j \in V} d(i, j) = \sum_{i,j \in V} \|v_i - v_j\|^2 = n^2$. For any $i \in V$, there is some $j \in L'$ such that $d(i, L') = d(i, j)$, so $d(i, i') \leq d(i, j) + d(j, i') \leq d(i, L') + \frac{1}{4}$. Thus,

$$n^2 = \sum_{i,j \in V} d(i, j) \leq \sum_{i,j \in V} (d(i, i') + d(i', j))$$

$$= 2n \sum_{i \in V} d(i, i')$$

$$\leq 2n \sum_{i \in V} \left(d(i, L') + \frac{1}{4} \right)$$

$$= 2n \sum_{i \in V} d(i, L') + \frac{n^2}{2}.$$

Rearranging this inequality, we obtain

$$\sum_{i \in V} d(i, L') = \sum_{i \notin L'} d(i, L') \geq \frac{n}{4}.$$

Then

$$\sum_{i,j \in V} |d(i, L') - d(j, L')| \geq \sum_{j \in L', i \notin L'} d(i, L')$$

$$= |L'| \sum_{i \notin L'} d(i, L')$$

$$\geq \frac{n}{4} \sum_{i \notin L'} d(i, L') \geq \frac{n^2}{16} = \Omega(\beta^2 n^2 \Delta),$$

for $\Delta = O(1)$ and constant $\beta \leq 1$, which proves the claim.   □

The following corollary is now immediate from Lemma 15.19 and Theorems 15.20 and 15.21.

Corollary 15.22. *With constant probability, Algorithm 15.1 returns a set S such that* $\rho(S) \leq O(\sqrt{\log n}) \, \text{OPT}$.

We will now start working our way toward the proof of Theorem 15.20. As a warmup, we will show that we can weaken the result by obtaining Δ-separated sets L' and R' for $\Delta = C/\log n$ rather than $\Delta = C/\sqrt{\log n}$. This implies that the algorithm returns a solution of value at most $O(\log n) \, \text{OPT}$. Of course, we already have an $O(\log n)$-approximation algorithm for the uniform sparsest cut problem via the result of Section 15.1, but this will give us a start at the ideas behind the proof of the $O(\sqrt{\log n})$ performance guarantee. By Lemma 15.19, we assume that L and R are α-large. Then for any $i \in L$, $j \in R$, it must be that $(v_i - v_j) \cdot r = (v_i - v_o) \cdot r + (v_o - v_j) \cdot r \geq 2\sigma$ by the definition of L and R. However, we will show that it is very unlikely that $i \in L$ and $j \in R$ if $d(i, j) \leq \Delta = C/\log n$ since the probability that $(v_i - v_j) \cdot r \geq 2\sigma$ is $e^{-2\sigma^2 / \|v_i - v_j\|^2} \leq \frac{1}{n^c}$ for $C = \frac{2}{c}\sigma^2$. Thus, with probability at least $1 - \frac{1}{n^{c-2}}$ no pair of vertices $i \in L$ and $j \in R$ get deleted, so that both L' and R' are α-large and Δ-separated.

To prove this result, we will need a bound on the tail of the normal distribution. Recall that the density function $p(x)$ of the normal distribution $\mathcal{N}(0, 1)$ is

$$p(x) = \frac{1}{\sqrt{2\pi}}e^{-x^2/2},$$

and its cumulative distribution function is $\Phi(x) = \int_{-\infty}^{x} p(s)ds$. We let $\overline{\Phi}(x) = 1 - \Phi(x) = \int_{x}^{\infty} p(s)ds$ give the tail of the normal distribution. Then we have the following bounds.

Lemma 15.23. *Let $v \in \Re^n$ be a vector $v \neq 0$. Then for a random vector r and $\sigma \geq 0$,*

$$\Pr[v \cdot r \geq \sigma] \leq e^{-\frac{\sigma^2}{2\|v\|^2}}$$

and

$$\Pr[|v \cdot r| \leq \sigma] \leq \frac{2\sigma}{\|v\|}.$$

Proof. We recall from Fact 6.5 that $\frac{v}{\|v\|} \cdot r$ is distributed as $\mathcal{N}(0, 1)$. Thus,

$$\Pr[v \cdot r \geq \sigma] = \Pr\left[\frac{v}{\|v\|} \cdot r \geq \frac{\sigma}{\|v\|}\right] = \overline{\Phi}\left(\frac{\sigma}{\|v\|}\right).$$

Now if X is a random variable that is distributed as $\mathcal{N}(0, 1)$, then $\overline{\Phi}(t) = \Pr[X \geq t]$. Observe that for $\lambda \geq 0$ and $t \geq 0$, $\Pr[X \geq t] \leq \Pr[e^{\lambda X} \geq e^{\lambda t}]$, since $X \geq t$ implies $e^{\lambda X} \geq e^{\lambda t}$. Then by Markov's inequality (Lemma 5.25), $\Pr[e^{\lambda X} \geq e^{\lambda t}] \leq E[e^{\lambda X}]/e^{\lambda t}$. We calculate

$$E[e^{\lambda X}] = \int_{-\infty}^{\infty} e^{\lambda x} p(x)dx = \int_{-\infty}^{\infty} \frac{1}{\sqrt{2\pi}} e^{\lambda x - x^2/2} dx.$$

Making a change of variables $z = x - \lambda$, so that $z^2 = x^2 - 2\lambda x + \lambda^2$, we get

$$E[e^{\lambda X}] = \int_{-\infty}^{\infty} \frac{1}{\sqrt{2\pi}} e^{\lambda^2/2 - z^2/2} dz = e^{\lambda^2/2} \int_{-\infty}^{\infty} p(z)dz = e^{\lambda^2/2}.$$

Thus, $\overline{\Phi}(t) \leq E[e^{\lambda X}]/e^{\lambda t} = e^{\lambda^2/2 - \lambda t}$. Plugging in $\lambda = t$, we get $\overline{\Phi}(t) \leq e^{-t^2/2}$, so that $\overline{\Phi}\left(\frac{\sigma}{\|v\|}\right) \leq e^{-\frac{\sigma^2}{2\|v\|^2}}$, as desired.

For the second inequality,

$$\Pr[|v \cdot r| \leq \sigma] = \int_{-\sigma/\|v\|}^{\sigma/\|v\|} p(x)dx \leq \int_{-\sigma/\|v\|}^{\sigma/\|v\|} dx = \frac{2\sigma}{\|v\|}. \qquad \square$$

Now we can prove the weaker version of Theorem 15.20 with $\Delta = C/\log n$ substituted for $\Delta = C/\sqrt{\log n}$. By Lemma 15.19 and Theorem 15.21, this implies an algorithm with performance guarantee $O(\log n)$.

Theorem 15.24. *If L and R are α-large, then with high probability, Algorithm 15.1 finds α-large sets L' and R' that are Δ-separated for $\Delta = C/\log n$ and an appropriate choice of constant C.*

Proof. Pick any $i, j \in V$ such that $d(i, j) \le C/\log n$. By Lemma 15.23, we know that

$$\Pr[(v_i - v_j) \cdot r \ge 2\sigma] \le e^{-2\sigma^2/\|v_i - v_j\|^2} \le e^{-2\sigma^2 \log n/C} = n^{-2\sigma^2/C}.$$

Thus, if we set $C = \frac{2}{c}\sigma^2$, we have that this probability is at most n^{-c}. However, by construction we know that if $i \in L$ and $j \in R$ then

$$(v_i - v_j) \cdot r = [(v_i - v_o) + (v_o - v_j)] \cdot r \ge 2\sigma.$$

Thus, with high probability $(i, j) \notin L \times R$. Since there are at most n^2 pairs (i, j) such that $d(i, j) \le C/\log n$, with probability at least $1 - \frac{1}{n^{c-2}}$, no such pair is in $L \times R$, and thus no vertices are removed from L and R. Thus, if L and R are α-large, then with high probability, so are L' and R', and L' and R' are Δ-separated for $\Delta = C/\log n$. $\qquad\square$

The key to the proof of the $O(\sqrt{\log n})$ performance guarantee is similar to the proof of the $O(\log n)$ performance guarantee above. The proof of Theorem 15.20 will be a proof by contradiction. Suppose that L and R are α-large, and with constant probability, L' and R' are not $\frac{\alpha}{2}$-large. Then we will show that for a constant fraction of the probability space of random vectors r there exist pairs of vertices $i, j \in V$ such that $d(i, j) \le O(\sqrt{\log n})$ and such that $(v_i - v_j) \cdot r \ge \Omega(\sigma \log n)$. By Lemma 15.23, we know that the probability that $i, j \in V$ can have $(v_i - v_j) \cdot r \ge \Omega(\sigma \log n)$ is at most

$$e^{-\Omega(\sigma^2 \log^2 n)/\|v_i - v_j\|^2} \le e^{-\Omega(\sigma^2 \log n)} \le n^{-\Omega(\sigma^2)}.$$

Thus, over all pairs $i, j \in V$ such that $d(i, j) \le O(\sqrt{\log n})$, we know that the probability that any such pair i, j has $(v_i - v_j) \cdot r \ge \Omega(\sigma \log n)$ is $1/n^c$ for some constant c. Yet we will show that under these assumptions about L' and R', such pairs i and j must exist with constant probability, which is a contradiction.

To get some sense of how we will prove this, observe that if Theorem 15.20 is false, then with some constant probability, we remove at least $\Omega(n)$ pairs from $L \times R$; we can view this as a matching of vertices in L and R, where we know that for any $i \in L$ and $j \in R$ that get removed, $d(i, j) \le \Delta$ while $(v_i - v_j) \cdot r \ge 2\sigma$. For a given random vector r, let us call this set of matching edges $M(r)$. Thus, if the main theorem is false, for a constant fraction of the probability space of random vectors r, we have matchings $M(r)$ such that $|M(r)| = \Omega(n)$, and for any $(i, j) \in M(r)$, $(v_i - v_j) \cdot r \ge 2\sigma$. Let $\mathcal{M}$ be the set of these matching edges taken over the random vectors r for which L' and R' fail to be $\frac{\alpha}{2}$-large.

The crux of the proof of the $O(\sqrt{\log n})$ performance guarantee is to show that for a constant fraction of the probability space of random vectors r we can find paths of $k = \Theta(\log n)$ matching edges in $\mathcal{M}$ $(i_1, i_2), (i_2, i_3), \ldots, (i_{k-1}, i_k)$ such that $(v_{i_k} - v_{i_1}) \cdot r = \Omega(\sigma k) = \Omega(\sigma \log n)$. By the triangle inequality,

$$d(i_k, i_1) \le \sum_{j=1}^{k-1} d(i_{j+1}, i_j) \le (k-1)\Delta = O(\sqrt{\log n}),$$

and thus the pairs of vertices at the beginning and end of the paths give the desired contradiction. To see how we can get that $(v_{i_k} - v_{i_1}) \cdot r \ge \Omega(\sigma k)$ with constant probability, note that for each $j \in [1, k-1]$, $(v_{i_{j+1}} - v_{i_j}) \cdot r \ge 2\sigma$ for some fraction of the space of random vectors r. We would like to extend this to show that for a constant fraction of the probability space of random vectors r, it is the case that for all $j \in [1, k-1]$, $(v_{i_{j+1}} - v_{i_j}) \cdot r \geq \Omega(\sigma)$. Then we obtain what we desire: with constant probability we have that

$$(v_{i_k} - v_{i_1}) \cdot r = \left[\sum_{j=1}^{k-1} (v_{i_{j+1}} - v_{i_j}) \right] \cdot r \geq \Omega(\sigma k) = \Omega(\sigma \log n).$$

In fact, we will end up proving something weaker, but this gives some intuition of how the result is obtained.

In order to give ourselves the right start, we first prove one more intermediate result by showing that Theorem 15.20 holds for $\Delta = C/\log^{2/3} n$. To do this, we take the approach as described above, but with $\Delta = C/\log^{2/3} n$ and $k = \Theta(\log^{1/3} n)$. In particular, for a constant fraction of the probability space of random vectors r we find paths of $k = \Theta(\log^{1/3} n)$ matching edges in $\mathcal{M}$, $(i_1, i_2), (i_2, i_3), \ldots, (i_{k-1}, i_k)$ such that $(v_{i_k} - v_{i_1}) \cdot r \geq \Omega(\sigma k) = \Omega(\sigma \log^{1/3} n)$. Then by the triangle inequality, we know that $d(i_k, i_1) \leq (k-1)\Delta = O(\log^{-1/3} n)$. By Lemma 15.23 the probability that $(v_{i_k} - v_{i_1}) \cdot r \geq \Omega(\sigma \log^{1/3} n)$ is at most

$$e^{-\Omega(\sigma^2 \log^{2/3} n)/\|v_i - v_j\|^2} \leq e^{-\Omega(\sigma^2 \log n)} \leq n^{-\Omega(\sigma^2)}.$$

Thus, over all pairs $i, j \in V$ such that $d(i, j) \leq O(\log^{-1/3} n)$, we know that the probability that any such pair i, j has $(v_i - v_j) \cdot r \geq \Omega(\sigma \log^{1/3} n)$ is $1/n^c$ for some constant c. Yet if L' and R' are not $\frac{\alpha}{2}$-large with constant probability, then there exist such pairs with constant probability, which is a contradiction.

To start the proof, we give a more formal definition of the *matching graph* $\mathcal{M} = (V_M, A_M)$ in which we will find the desired paths. For a given Δ (either $\Delta = C/\sqrt{\log n}$ for the main result or $\Delta = C/\log^{2/3} n$ for the intermediate result), $\mathcal{M}$ will be a subgraph of $(V, \{(i, j) \in V \times V : d(i, j) \leq \Delta\})$. As above, we define $M(r)$ to be the set of edges (i, j) such that for the random vector r, we initially have $i \in L$, $j \in R$, and in some step of the algorithm i and j are removed from L and R, respectively. Since $i \in L$ and $j \in R$, $(v_i - v_j) \cdot r \geq 2\sigma$, and since they are removed, $d(i, j) \leq \Delta$. Note that the algorithm does not specify the order in which the pairs i, j are removed from L and R. We assume that this order is such that $(i, j) \in M(r)$ if and only if $(j, i) \in M(-r)$. We give each arc (i, j) in the graph a weight w_{ij} equal to the probability that the pair (i, j) is a matching edge in $M(r)$ for a randomly chosen vector r; that is, $w_{ij} = \Pr[(i, j) \in M(r)]$, where the probability is taken over the random vectors r. As we noted above, if $(i, j) \in M(r)$, then $(v_i - v_j) \cdot r \geq 2\sigma$, so that $\Pr[(v_i - v_j) \cdot r \geq 2\sigma] \geq w_{ij}$ (where the probability is over the choice of random vectors). Since $(i, j) \in M(r)$ if and only if $(j, i) \in M(-r)$, we have that $w_{ij} = w_{ji}$. We will show that if L' and R' fail to be $\frac{\alpha}{2}$-large given that L and R are α-large, then there is a subgraph $\mathcal{M}$ of $(V, \{(i, j) \in V \times V : d(i, j) \leq \Delta\})$ such that the weight of the outgoing arcs from any node is at least some constant δ. The next lemma shows that we can indeed construct the matching graph $\mathcal{M}$ to have this property.

Lemma 15.25. *If L and R are α-large, but with constant probability $q > 0$, L' and R' are not $\frac{\alpha}{2}$-large, then we can define the matching graph so that the total weight of arcs coming out of each vertex $i \in V_M$ is at least $\delta = q\alpha/8$.*

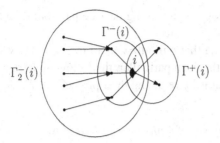

Figure 15.6. An illustration of the notation $\Gamma^-(i)$, $\Gamma_k^-(i)$, and $\Gamma^+(i)$.

Proof. Given the hypothesis of the lemma, with probability at least q, $|M(r)| \geq \frac{\alpha}{2}n$ over the distribution of random vectors r. Thus, given the definition of the weights in the graph, we know that the total weight of all arcs must be at least $q\alpha n/2$. To obtain the desired matching graph, we repeatedly remove all nodes whose outgoing arc weight is less than $q\alpha/8$. Note that since outgoing arc weight is equal to incoming arc weight, we remove arc weight at most $q\alpha/4$ per node removed. Thus, we remove at most weight $q\alpha n/4$ from the graph overall; since there was total weight at least $q\alpha n/2$, some of the graph must remain. We let V_M be the remaining nodes, and A_M the remaining arcs, with $\mathcal{M} = (V_M, A_M)$; each $i \in V_M$ has at least $\delta = q\alpha/8$ outgoing arc weight. $\square$

In the course of finding $\Theta(\log^{1/3} n)$-arc paths in the matching graph discussed above, we build up a set of paths, starting with an empty path for each node in V_M, and then extending each path by an additional arc, possibly eliminating some paths if we can't find an extension with the desired properties. At any point in the process of building up the paths, we characterize the paths by several properties. We say that the paths have *length* at most k if each path has at most k arcs in it. The *heads* of the paths are the vertices of V_M at which the paths end; we denote this set of vertices by H. The *tails* of the paths are the vertices at which the paths start. Since we will be extending the paths from the heads of the paths, we will pay special attention to them. We say that the paths have *projection* at least ρ with probability at least δ if for each $i \in H$, the probability is at least δ that there exists some path with tail j such that $(v_i - v_j) \cdot r \geq \rho$. For the most part, the set of paths will be defined implicitly as follows. Let $\Gamma_k^-(i)$ be the set of all vertices in V_M that can reach i in the matching graph via a path of k or fewer arcs; symmetrically, let $\Gamma_k^+(i)$ be the set of all vertices in V_M that can be reached from i in the matching graph via a path of k or fewer arcs. We will write $\Gamma^-(i) = \Gamma_1^-(i)$ and $\Gamma^+(i) = \Gamma_1^+(i)$, and for $S \subseteq V_M$, we let $\Gamma_k^+(S)$ be the set of all vertices in V_M that can be reached from the vertices in S in k or fewer arcs; see Figure 15.6 for an illustration. Thus, for a given head $i \in H$, we know there is a path of length at most k to i if there exists some $j \in \Gamma_k^-(i)$, and we extend paths by an extra arc by looking at the paths with heads in $\Gamma^+(i)$. Using the new notation, the paths of length at most k have projection at least ρ with probability at least δ if for each $i \in H$, $\Pr[\exists j \in \Gamma_k^-(i) : (v_i - v_j) \cdot r \geq \rho] \geq \delta$.

We will give below a procedure for extending the paths until we have a set of paths of length $O(\log^{1/3} n)$ having projection $\Omega(\sigma \log^{1/3} n)$ with constant probability. As we argued above, this is sufficient to give an $O(\log^{2/3} n)$ performance guarantee.

We will then explain how we can strengthen the path-building argument to obtain the $O(\sqrt{\log n})$ performance guarantee.

We now state a lemma that will allow us to trade off the various characteristics in the paths as we extend them. In particular, the following lemma will allow us to boost the probability of the paths by reducing their projection. We defer the proof to the end of the section.

Lemma 15.26. *For any set of paths of length at most k having projection at least ρ with probability at least $\beta \leq 1/2$, the same paths have projection at least $\rho - \gamma \sqrt{k\Delta}$ with probability at least $1 - e^{-\lambda^2/2}$ for any $\lambda \geq 0$ and any $\gamma \geq \sqrt{2\ln(1/\beta)} + \lambda$.*

We can now give the inductive proof that will allow us to construct the length $O(\log^{1/3} n)$ paths that result in the $O(\log^{2/3} n)$ performance guarantee.

Theorem 15.27. *Suppose L and R are α-large, but with constant probability $q > 0$, L' and R' are not $\frac{\alpha}{2}$-large. Then for each k, $0 \leq k \leq O(\log^{1/3} n)$, there exists a set of paths in the matching graph of length at most k with heads H_k, having projection $\sigma k/4$ with probability at least $1 - \delta/2$, such that $|H_k| \geq \left(\frac{\delta}{4}\right)^k |V_M|$.*

Proof. We will show that the statement of the theorem holds for $0 \leq k \leq K$, where

$$K = \left\lfloor \frac{7\sigma}{8\sqrt{2\Delta \ln(4/\delta)}} \right\rfloor = O(\log^{1/3} n).$$

For the base case we start with the set of paths being the collection of empty paths consisting of a single node, for each node in V_M, so that $H_0 = V_M$. Then trivially these paths have length 0, and projection 0 with probability 1.

Now for the inductive case: Suppose the statement holds true for $1 \leq k \leq K - 1$. We now carry out three steps to complete the inductive step: first, we extend the paths by an additional arc and increase the projection of the paths; second, we choose a subset of the heads of the extended paths in order to make sure the paths have reasonably good probability; and third, we apply Lemma 15.26 to boost the probability back to $1 - \delta/2$ while decreasing the projection only slightly.

For the first step, we extend the paths by an additional arc. By the induction hypothesis, for each $i \in H_k$, $\Pr[\exists j \in \Gamma_k^-(i) : (v_i - v_j) \cdot r \geq \sigma k/4] \geq 1 - \delta/2$. By Lemma 15.25, we know that the total weight of arcs leaving any i in the matching graph is at least δ, implying that $\Pr[\exists (i, \ell) \in A_M : (v_\ell - v_i) \cdot r \geq 2\sigma] \geq \delta$. Thus, for at least a $\delta/2$ fraction of the probability space of random vectors r, both statements are true, and for some $j \in \Gamma_k^-(i)$ and some $(i, \ell) \in A_M$, $(v_i - v_j) \cdot r \geq \sigma k/4$ and $(v_\ell - v_i) \cdot r \geq 2\sigma$. Thus, we can extend the path by the arc (i, ℓ), and this new path has projection

$$(v_\ell - v_j) \cdot r = [(v_\ell - v_i) + (v_i - v_j)] \cdot r = (v_\ell - v_i) \cdot r + (v_i - v_j) \cdot r$$
$$\geq \frac{1}{4}\sigma k + 2\sigma = \frac{1}{4}\sigma(k+1) + \frac{7}{4}\sigma.$$

This gives us a new set of length $k + 1$ paths, but now for the second step, we need to pick a subset of them so that the induction hypothesis holds. In particular, we pick a set $H_{k+1} \subseteq \Gamma^+(H_k)$ as the new heads of the paths. For each $\ell \in \Gamma^+(H)$, let $p(\ell)$ be the fraction of the probability space of random vectors r such that one of the paths constructed above has ℓ as its head. Observe that for each $i \in H_k$, we extended the path from i for a $\delta/2$ fraction of the random vectors r. Observe also that since for any random vector r, $M(r)$ is a matching, for a given r and different heads $i, i' \in H_k$, $i \neq i'$, it cannot be the case that the paths from i and i' are extended by edges to the same vertex ℓ. These two observations together imply that $\sum_{\ell \in \Gamma^+(H_k)} p(\ell) \geq \frac{\delta}{2}|H_k|$. Note that trivially $p(\ell) \leq 1$ for all $\ell \in \Gamma^+(H_k)$. Let the new set of heads H_{k+1} be those that have a significant probability of paths extended to them; in particular, we let $H_{k+1} = \{\ell \in \Gamma^+(H_k) : p(\ell) \geq \frac{\delta|H_k|}{4|\Gamma^+(H_k)|}\}$. Then we have

$$\frac{\delta}{2}|H_k| \leq \sum_{\ell \in \Gamma^+(H_k)} p(\ell) = \sum_{\ell \in \Gamma^+(H_k) - H_{k+1}} p(\ell) + \sum_{\ell \in H_{k+1}} p(\ell)$$

$$\leq |\Gamma^+(H_k) - H_{k+1}| \frac{\delta|H_k|}{4|\Gamma^+(H_k)|} + |H_{k+1}|$$

$$\leq \frac{\delta}{4}|H_k| + |H_{k+1}|,$$

so that $|H_{k+1}| \geq \frac{\delta}{4}|H_k|$. Thus, if we choose the paths constructed above that have their heads in H_{k+1}, we have that $|H_{k+1}| \geq \frac{\delta}{4}|H_k| \geq \left(\frac{\delta}{4}\right)^{k+1} |V_M|$. Also, as we argued above, for each $\ell \in H_{k+1}$, the projection of each path is $\frac{1}{4}\sigma(k+1) + \frac{7}{4}\sigma$ with probability at least $\frac{\delta|H_k|}{4|\Gamma^+(H_k)|} \geq \frac{\delta}{4}\frac{(\delta/4)^k |V_M|}{|\Gamma^+(H_k)|} \geq \left(\frac{\delta}{4}\right)^{k+1}$.

For the third and final step of the induction, we apply Lemma 15.26 to increase the probability of the paths by decreasing their projection by at most $\frac{7}{4}\sigma$. To achieve a probability of $1 - \delta/2$, we need to set $\beta = \left(\frac{\delta}{4}\right)^{k+1}$ and $\lambda = \sqrt{2\ln(2/\delta)}$, so that $1 - e^{-\lambda^2/2} = 1 - \delta/2$. Then we set

$$\gamma = \sqrt{2\ln(1/\beta)} + \lambda = \sqrt{2\ln(1/\beta)} + \sqrt{2\ln(2/\delta)}$$

$$= \sqrt{2(k+1)\ln(4/\delta)} + \sqrt{2\ln(2/\delta)}$$

$$\leq (\sqrt{k+1} + 1)\sqrt{2\ln(4/\delta)}$$

$$\leq 2\sqrt{k+1}\sqrt{2\ln(4/\delta)},$$

using $\delta \leq 1$ and $k \geq 1$. By the lemma, the projection of the length $k + 1$ paths decreases by at most $\frac{7}{4}\sigma$ exactly when $\gamma\sqrt{(k+1)\Delta} \leq \frac{7}{4}\sigma$. This inequality holds when

$$2(k+1)\sqrt{2\Delta \ln(4/\delta)} \leq \frac{7}{4}\sigma$$

or when

$$k+1 \leq \frac{.7\sigma}{8\sqrt{2\Delta \ln(4/\delta)}}.$$

This holds since $k + 1 \leq K$. $\qquad\square$

We can now summarize the discussion above in the following theorem.

Theorem 15.28. *If L and R are α-large, then with constant probability Algorithm 15.1 finds $\frac{\alpha}{2}$-large sets L' and R' that are Δ-separated for $\Delta = C/\log^{2/3} n$ and an appropriate choice of constant C.*

Proof. If L and R are α-large, but with constant probability $q > 0$, L' and R' are not $\frac{\alpha}{2}$-large for Δ, then by Lemma 15.25 we can define the matching graph, and by Theorem 15.27, we can find paths of length at most K having projection $\sigma K/4$ with probability at least $1 - \delta/2$. Let i, j be the head and tail of such a path (respectively); since the path has length at most K, we know that $d(i, j) \leq K\Delta$, so that $\|v_i - v_j\|^2 \leq K\Delta$. By Lemma 15.23, we know that

$$\Pr[(v_i - v_j) \cdot r \geq K\sigma/4] \leq e^{-K^2\sigma^2/32\|v_i-v_j\|^2} \leq e^{-K\sigma^2/32\Delta}.$$

By the definition of K in Theorem 15.27, $K/\Delta = \Theta(\Delta^{-3/2}) = \Theta(C^{-3/2} \log n)$, so that the probability is at most

$$e^{-\Theta(C^{-3/2} \log n)} = n^{-\Theta(C^{-3/2})}.$$

Thus, if we set C to an appropriate constant, we have that this probability is at most n^{-c}, and over all possible i, j pairs this probability is at most n^{-c+2}. For n sufficiently large, this contradicts the fact that such paths exist with probability at least $1 - \delta/2$. $\square$

Then from Lemma 15.19 and Theorems 15.21 and 15.28 we get the following corollary.

Corollary 15.29. *With constant probability, Algorithm 15.1 produces a set S such that $\rho(S) \leq O(\log^{2/3} n)\,\mathrm{OPT}$.*

We can now think about the limitations of Theorem 15.27 so that we can figure out how to extend these ideas to the proof of the $O(\sqrt{\log n})$ performance guarantee. We first observe that in our overall proof methodology, we are giving a proof by contradiction via the tail bound in Lemma 15.23. In order to get the contradiction, if our paths of length at most k from i to j have projection length at least $k\sigma$ we need that

$$\frac{(k\sigma)^2}{2\|v_i - v_j\|^2} \geq \frac{k\sigma^2}{2\Delta} = \Omega(\log n),$$

so that for the right choice of constants $e^{-(k\sigma)^2/2\|v_i-v_j\|^2} \leq 1/n^c$. Thus, we need that $k/\Delta = \Omega(\log n)$. Now let us consider how this limitation on k and Δ interacts with the proof of Theorem 15.27. In this proof, a key issue is that when we augment the length k paths to length $k + 1$, the probability of having a projection of $\Omega(\sigma(k + 1))$ drops significantly, from $1 - \delta/2$ to $\frac{\delta|H_k|}{4|\Gamma^+(H_k)|}$. We know that this probability is at least $\left(\frac{\delta}{4}\right)^{k+1}$, as shown in the proof. However, this means that in using Lemma 15.26 to increase the probability of the paths (while decreasing the projection) we must have $\gamma \geq \sqrt{2\ln(4/\delta)^k} = \Omega(\sqrt{k})$. In order to reduce the projection by at most σ, we need $\gamma\sqrt{k\Delta} \leq \sigma$, or $k = O(\sqrt{1/\Delta})$. Combined with the observation above that we need $k/\Delta = \Omega(\log n)$, this implies that $\Delta^{-3/2} = \Omega(\log n)$ or $\Delta = O(\log^{-2/3} n)$.

To improve the result, we will modify the way in which we augment paths so that when we increase the length of a path, the probability of having projection $\Omega(k\sigma)$ drops from $1 - \delta/2$ to something constant in δ. Then we apply Lemma 15.26, γ will be constant in δ, and in order to reduce the projection by at most σ, we will have $k = O(1/\Delta)$. Then since we need $k/\Delta = \Omega(\log n)$, this yields $\Delta^{-2} = \Omega(\log n)$ or $\Delta = O(\log^{-1/2} n)$, which will lead to the $O(\sqrt{\log n})$ performance guarantee.

In order to obtain this improvement, we will try to make sure that the set of vertices that can be reached from the heads of the paths is not too big in terms of the number of heads of paths $|H_k|$; in particular, we would like to make sure that $|\Gamma^+(H_k)| \le \frac{1}{8}|H_k|$. In this case, increasing the projection to $\Omega(\sigma(k+1))$ drops the probability from $1 - \delta/2$ to $\frac{\delta|H_k|}{4|\Gamma^+(H_k)|} \ge \delta^2/4$. To achieve this condition on $\Gamma_k^+(H_k)$, we will extend paths by some number of extra arcs until the desired condition is true. Note that if the condition is not true, then $|\Gamma^+(H_k)| > \frac{1}{8}|H_k|$, so that the number of vertices reached by extending the paths is increasing geometrically; thus, not many extra steps can be taken before all vertices are reachable and the condition is met. We will show that the extension does not decrease the projection and probability of the paths by too much, and the paths with heads in H_k will have length at most $4k$. We will use the following lemma to bound the decrease in projection and probability that we get by extending the paths.

Lemma 15.30. *Given any path of length at most k, having projection at least ρ with probability at least δ, then extending the path by any t arcs has projection at least $\rho - \lambda\sqrt{t\Delta}$ with probability at least $\delta - e^{-\lambda^2/2}$ for any $t \ge 0$ and $\lambda \ge 0$.*

Proof. Let $i \in H$ be the head of some set of paths of length at most k, let r be a random vector, and let $\ell \in \Gamma_t^+(i)$. If there exists $j \in \Gamma_k^-(i)$ such that $(v_i - v_j) \cdot r \ge \rho$ but $(v_\ell - v_j) \cdot r < \rho - \lambda\sqrt{t\Delta}$, then it must be the case that $(v_\ell - v_i) \cdot r < -\lambda\sqrt{t\Delta}$, or $(v_i - v_\ell) \cdot r > \lambda\sqrt{t\Delta}$. Note that since there is a path of length at most t from i to ℓ, $d(i, \ell) = \|v_i - v_\ell\|^2 \le t\Delta$. By Lemma 15.23, $\Pr[(v_i - v_\ell) \cdot r > \lambda\sqrt{t\Delta}] \le e^{-\frac{\lambda^2 t\Delta}{2t\Delta}} = e^{-\lambda^2/2}$. Thus, $\Pr[\exists j \in \Gamma_{k+t}^-(\ell) : (v_\ell - v_j) \cdot r > \rho - \lambda\sqrt{t\Delta}] \ge \delta - e^{-\lambda^2/2}$. $\square$

Now we can show the procedure for extending the paths.

Theorem 15.31. *Suppose L and R are α-large, but with constant probability $q > 0$, L' and R' are not $\frac{\alpha}{2}$-large. Assume $\delta \le 1/2$. Then for each k, $0 \le k \le O(\sqrt{\log n})$, there exists a set of paths in the matching graph of length at most $4k$, having projection $\sigma k/4$ with probability at least $1 - \delta/2$, such that $|H_k| \ge \left(\frac{\delta}{4}\right)^k |V_M|$ and $|H_k| \ge \delta|\Gamma^+(H_k)|$.*

Proof. We will show that the statement of the theorem holds for $0 \le k \le K$, where

$$K = \left\lfloor \frac{\sigma^2}{128\Delta \ln(2/\delta)} \right\rfloor = O(\sqrt{\log n}).$$

As in the proof of Theorem 15.27, in the base case we start with the paths being the collection of empty paths consisting of a single node, for each node in V_M, so that $H_0 = V_M$. Then trivially these paths have length 0, and projection 0 with probability 1. Furthermore, $|H_0| = |V_M| \ge \delta|\Gamma^+(H_0)| = \delta|V_M|$.

Now for the inductive case: Suppose the statement holds true for $1 \le k \le K - 1$. To carry out the inductive case, we take four steps: first, we extend the paths by an additional arc and increase their projection; second, we choose a subset of the heads of the extended paths in order to make sure the paths have reasonably good probability; third, we extend the paths still further by some additional arcs to make sure that $|H_{k+1}| \ge \delta|\Gamma^+(H_{k+1})|$ while losing a bit in the projection and probability; and fourth, we apply Lemma 15.26 to boost the probability back to $1 - \delta/2$ while decreasing the projection by a bit more.

The first two steps of the induction are identical to those in the proof of Theorem 15.27: we can use the current set of paths to construct paths that are one arc longer and have projection at least $\frac{1}{4}\sigma(k+1) + \frac{7}{4}\sigma$ with probability at least $\frac{\delta|H_k|}{4|\Gamma^+(H_k)|}$. By induction, $|H_k| \geq \delta|\Gamma^+(H_k)|$, so this probability is at least $\delta^2/4$. Let H'_{k+1} be the heads of these paths. By the proof of Theorem 15.27, we have that $|H'_{k+1}| \geq \frac{\delta}{4}|H_k| \geq \left(\frac{\delta}{4}\right)^{k+1}|V_M|$.

We now carry out the third step of the induction. Let t be the smallest nonnegative integer for which $|\Gamma_t^+(H'_{k+1})| \geq \delta|\Gamma_{t+1}^+(H'_{k+1})|$. We take each path in our current set of paths and consider the resulting set of paths obtained by adding any additional path of up to t arcs to its head; let the heads of the resulting set of paths be H_{k+1}. Then clearly $H_{k+1} = \Gamma_t^+(H'_{k+1})$, and by the choice of t we have the desired inductive statement that $|H_{k+1}| \geq \delta|\Gamma^+(H_{k+1})|$. Also, $H_{k+1} \supseteq H'_{k+1}$, so we still have $|H_{k+1}| \geq \left(\frac{\delta}{4}\right)^{k+1}|V_M|$.

We now bound the length of the paths. In carrying out the first step of the induction, we added one additional arc to the paths. In the third step, we added t additional arcs. Note that for any $t' < t$, it must have been the case that $\frac{1}{\delta}|\Gamma_{t'}^+(H'_{k+1})| < |\Gamma_{t'+1}^+(H'_{k+1})|$. Thus, in the third step we must have added at most $t \leq \log_{1/\delta} \frac{|H_{k+1}|}{|H'_{k+1}|}$ arcs. The total number of arcs added in the third step over all steps of the induction is then at most

$$\sum_{s=0}^{k} \log_{1/\delta} \frac{|H_{s+1}|}{|H'_{s+1}|}.$$

Since $|H'_{s+1}| \geq \frac{\delta}{4}|H_s|$, we have that the total length of the paths is at most

$$(k+1) + \sum_{s=0}^{k} \log_{1/\delta} \frac{|H_{s+1}|}{|H'_{s+1}|} = (k+1) + \log_{1/\delta} \left(\prod_{s=0}^{k} \frac{|H_{s+1}|}{|H'_{s+1}|} \right)$$

$$\leq (k+1) + \log_{1/\delta} \left(\left(\frac{4}{\delta}\right)^{k+1} \prod_{s=0}^{k} \frac{|H_{s+1}|}{|H_s|} \right)$$

$$\leq (k+1) + (k+1)\log_{1/\delta}\left(\frac{4}{\delta}\right) + \log_{1/\delta}\left(\frac{|V_M|}{|V_M|}\right)$$

$$\leq (k+1) + 3(k+1) \leq 4(k+1),$$

using $\delta \leq \frac{1}{2}$, $H_0 = V_M$, and $H_{k+1} \subseteq V_M$. Note that the proof above shows that the number t of extra arcs added in the third step of the induction is $t \leq 3(k+1)$.

We now apply Lemma 15.30 to determine the projection and probability of the paths with heads in H_{k+1}. As argued above, we know that the paths with heads in H'_{k+1} have projection at least $\frac{1}{4}(k+1)\sigma + \frac{7}{4}\sigma$ with probability at least $\delta^2/4$. By applying Lemma 15.30 with $\lambda = \sigma/\sqrt{t\Delta}$, we know that extending the paths by up to t additional arcs drops the projection by at most $\lambda\sqrt{t\Delta} = \sigma$ and the probability by at most $e^{-\lambda^2/2} = e^{-\sigma^2/2t\Delta}$. We would like the probability to decrease by at most $\delta^2/8$, so that it remains at least $\delta^2/8$. For this to be true, we need $e^{-\sigma^2/2t\Delta} \leq \frac{\delta^2}{8}$ or $-\frac{\sigma^2}{2t\Delta} \leq \ln\frac{\delta^2}{8}$ or $t \leq \frac{\sigma^2}{2\Delta\ln(8/\delta^2)}$. Recalling that $t \leq 3(k+1)$, the condition is true if

$$3(k+1) \leq \frac{\sigma^2}{2\Delta\ln(8/\delta^2)},$$

or

$$k + 1 \leq \frac{\sigma^2}{6\Delta \ln(8/\delta^2)}.$$

Since $\ln(8/\delta^2) \leq 3\ln(2/\delta)$ (because $\delta \leq 1$), the condition is met if

$$k + 1 \leq \frac{\sigma^2}{18\Delta \ln(2/\delta)},$$

which holds since $k + 1 \leq K$. Thus, the paths with heads in H_{k+1} have projection at least $\frac{1}{4}(k + 1)\sigma + \frac{3}{4}\sigma$ with probability at least $\delta^2/8$.

For the fourth and final step of the induction, we apply Lemma 15.26 to increase the overall probability of the paths while decreasing their projection somewhat. To achieve a probability of $1 - \delta/2$, we need to set $\beta = \delta^2/8$ and $\lambda = \sqrt{2\ln(2/\delta)}$ so that $1 - e^{-\lambda^2/2} = 1 - \delta/2$. Then we set

$$\gamma = \sqrt{2\ln(1/\beta)} + \lambda = \sqrt{2\ln(8/\delta^2)} + \sqrt{2\ln(2/\delta)} \leq \sqrt{2\ln(2/\delta)}(\sqrt{3} + 1)$$
$$\leq 3\sqrt{2\ln(2/\delta)}.$$

This reduces the projection of the paths by at most $\frac{3}{4}\sigma$ when $\gamma\sqrt{4(k+1)\Delta} \leq \frac{3}{4}\sigma$, or when

$$k + 1 \leq \frac{9\sigma^2}{64\gamma^2\Delta}.$$

This inequality holds if

$$k + 1 \leq \frac{\sigma^2}{128\Delta \ln(2/\delta)}.$$

This condition holds since $k + 1 \leq K$. Thus, the paths have projection at least $(k + 1)\sigma/4$ with probability at least $1 - \delta/2$. $\square$

The proof of the main theorem, Theorem 15.20, now follows from this theorem by a similar argument as used in the proof of Theorem 15.28.

Theorem 15.20. *If L and R are α-large, then with constant probability, L' and R' are $\frac{\alpha}{2}$-large and are Δ-separated for $\Delta = C/\sqrt{\log n}$ for an appropriate choice of constant C.*

Proof. If L and R are α-large, but with constant probability $q > 0$, L' and R' are not $\frac{\alpha}{2}$-large for Δ, then by Lemma 15.25 we can define the matching graph, and by Theorem 15.27 we can find paths of length at most $4K$ having projection $\sigma K/4$ with probability at least $1 - \delta/2$. Let i, j be the head and tail of such a path (respectively); since the path has length at most $4K$, we know that $d(i, j) \leq 4K\Delta$, so that $\|v_i - v_j\|^2 \leq 4K\Delta$. By Lemma 15.23, we know that

$$\Pr[(v_i - v_j) \cdot r \geq K\sigma/4] \leq e^{-K^2\sigma^2/32\|v_i - v_j\|^2} \leq e^{-K\sigma^2/128\Delta}.$$

By the definition of K in Theorem 15.31, $K/\Delta = \Theta(\Delta^{-2}) = \Theta(C^{-2}\log n)$, so that the probability is at most

$$e^{-\Theta(C^{-2}\log n)} = n^{-\Theta(C^{-2})}.$$

Thus, if we set C to an appropriate constant, we have that the probability is at most n^{-c}, and over all possible i, j pairs this probability is at most n^{-c+2}. For n sufficiently large this contradicts the fact that such paths exist with probability at least $1 - \delta/2$. □

We still have a few remaining lemmas to prove. To prove Lemma 15.26 we need a theorem whose proof is beyond the scope of this book; in order to state the theorem we need a few definitions. Given a set $A \subseteq \Re^n$, we let $\mu(A)$ denote the probability that a random vector $r \in A$. For $\gamma > 0$, we let $A_\gamma = \{r' \in \Re^n : \exists r \in A, \|r - r'\| \le \gamma\}$. Recall that $\Phi(x)$ is the cumulative distribution function of the standard normal probability distribution, and that $\overline{\Phi}(x) = 1 - \Phi(x)$. The statement of the theorem requires that A is a measurable set; we will not define what this means, but a set is measurable if it is the union of a countable number of halfspaces.

Theorem 15.32. *Given a measurable set $A \subseteq \Re^n$, let $\alpha \in [-\infty, +\infty]$ be such that $\mu(A) = \Phi(\alpha)$. Then $\mu(A_\gamma) \ge \Phi(\alpha + \gamma)$.*

We can now derive Lemma 15.26 from the theorem above; we restate the lemma here for convenience.

Lemma 15.26. *For any set of paths of length at most k having projection at least ρ with probability at least $\beta \le 1/2$, the same paths have projection at least $\rho - \gamma\sqrt{k\Delta}$ with probability at least $1 - e^{-\lambda^2/2}$ for any $\lambda \ge 0$ and any $\gamma \ge \sqrt{2\ln(1/\beta)} + \lambda$.*

Proof. Pick some i that is a head of a set of paths of length at most k. We let A be the set of random vectors r such that there exists $j \in \Gamma_k^-(i)$ with $(v_i - v_j) \cdot r \ge \rho$. We note that the set A is measurable since it is defined by a union of halfspaces (namely, $A = \bigcup_{j \in \Gamma_k^-(i)} \{r \in \Re^n : (v_i - v_j) \cdot r \ge \rho\}$. Pick any $r' \in A_\gamma$; there must be some $r \in A$ such that $\|r - r'\| \le \gamma$. Since the path has length at most k, we know that $\|v_i - v_j\|^2 \le k\Delta$. Then

$$(v_i - v_j) \cdot r' = (v_i - v_j) \cdot r + (v_i - v_j) \cdot (r' - r)$$
$$\ge \rho - \|r' - r\|\|v_i - v_j\| \ge \rho - \gamma\sqrt{k\Delta}.$$

Thus, given the random vectors in A_γ, we have the desired projection; we now determine the probability of drawing a random vector from A_γ.

By the hypothesis, $\mu(A) \ge \beta$, and $\beta \le 1/2$. Thus, if we choose α so that $\beta = \Phi(\alpha)$, we know $\alpha \le 0$ since the normal distribution is symmetric around 0. Also by symmetry, $\Phi(\alpha) = \overline{\Phi}(-\alpha)$. By applying Lemma 15.23, we know that $\beta = \overline{\Phi}(-\alpha) \le e^{-(-\alpha)^2/2}$, so that $-\alpha \le \sqrt{2\ln(1/\beta)}$. Since Φ is a non-decreasing function, if we choose α' so that $\mu(A) = \Phi(\alpha') \ge \beta = \Phi(\alpha)$, then $\alpha \le \alpha'$. By Theorem 15.32, we know $\mu(A_\gamma) \ge \Phi(\alpha' + \gamma) \ge \Phi(\alpha + \gamma)$, so all we need to do is give a lower bound on $\Phi(\alpha + \gamma)$. By the hypothesis $\gamma \ge \sqrt{2\ln(1/\beta)} + \lambda \ge -\alpha + \lambda$ so that $\alpha + \gamma \ge \lambda \ge 0$. Thus, by Lemma 15.23,

$$\mu(A_\gamma) \ge \Phi(\alpha + \gamma) = 1 - \overline{\Phi}(\alpha + \gamma) \ge 1 - e^{-(\alpha+\gamma)^2/2} \ge 1 - e^{-\lambda^2/2},$$

as desired. □

We finally give the proof of Lemma 15.19, which guarantees that with constant probability, the sets L and R are α-large. We restate the lemma here with values of the various constants filled in.

Lemma 15.33 (Lemma 15.19). *If there is no $i \in V$ such that $|B(i, \frac{1}{4})| \geq \frac{n}{4}$, then the sets $L = \{i \in V : (v_i - v_o) \cdot r \geq \sigma\}$ and $R = \{i \in V : (v_i - v_o) \cdot r \leq -\sigma\}$ are α-large with probability at least $a/32$, for $a = \frac{1}{\pi} \arccos(31/32)$, $\sigma = a^2/2^{14}$, and $\alpha = a/128$.*

Proof. We begin by showing that there are $\Omega(n^2)$ pairs of vertices i, j whose distance is at least $1/4$, and whose distance from o is at least $1/4$. First, we claim that by the algorithm's choice of $o \in V$, $|B(o, 4)| \geq \frac{3n}{4}$. Since o maximized $|B(o, 4)|$, if this is not the case, then for any $j \in V$, more than a fourth of the vertices have distance at least 4 to j, yielding

$$\sum_{i,j \in V} d(i, j) = \sum_{i \in V} \left(\sum_{j \in V} d(i, j) \right) > n \cdot \frac{n}{4} \cdot 4 = n^2.$$

This contradicts the vector programming constraint that $\sum_{i,j \in V} d(i, j) = \sum_{i,j \in V} \|v_i - v_j\|^2 = n^2$. Thus, it must be the case that $|B(o, 4)| \geq 3n/4$. Let $A = B(o, 4) - B(o, 1/4)$. By hypothesis, $|B(o, 1/4)| < n/4$, so that $|A| \geq n/2$. Then since for any $i \in V$, $|B(i, \frac{1}{4})| < \frac{n}{4}$, for any $i \in A$, there are at least $n/4$ other vertices $j \in A$ such that $d(i, j) > 1/4$ and $d(j, o) > 1/4$. This proves that the number of distinct pairs of vertices $i, j \in A$ such that $d(i, j) > 1/4$ is at least $n^2/16 \geq \frac{1}{8}\binom{n}{2}$.

We now wish to show that a constant fraction of A appears in each of L and R. We will say that vertices i and j are separated by the random vector r if either $(v_i - v_o) \cdot r \geq 0$ and $(v_j - v_o) \cdot r < 0$, or vice versa; we may also say that i and j are a separated pair. By the proof of Lemma 6.7, for a given pair $i, j \in A$ with $d(i, j) > 1/4$ the probability that i and j are separated is θ_{ij}/π, where θ_{ij} is the angle between the two vectors $v_i - v_o$ and $v_j - v_o$. By the law of cosines, we know that

$$\cos \theta_{ij} = \frac{\|v_i - v_o\|^2 + \|v_j - v_o\|^2 - \|v_i - v_j\|^2}{2\|v_i - v_o\|\|v_j - v_o\|}.$$

The angle is minimized when $\|v_i - v_o\|$ and $\|v_j - v_o\|$ are maximized and $\|v_i - v_j\|$ is minimized; we know that for $i, j \in A$, $i, j \in B(o, 4)$, so that $\|v_i - v_o\|^2 \leq 4$ and $\|v_j - v_o\|^2 \leq 4$, and by our choice of i, j, $\|v_i - v_j\|^2 > 1/4$. Thus, $\cos \theta_{ij} \leq (8 - 1/4)/8 = 1 - 1/32$, so that $\theta_{ij} \geq \arccos(1 - 1/32)$, and the probability that i and j are separated by the random vector when $i, j \in A$ and $d(i, j) > 1/4$ is at least some (small) constant $a = \frac{1}{\pi} \arccos(31/32)$. Thus, the expected number of distinct pairs of $i, j \in A$ separated by the random vector is at least $\frac{a}{8}\binom{n}{2}$.

We now bound the probability that the number of distinct pairs in A separated is less than half this, $\frac{a}{16}\binom{n}{2}$. If P is the total number of distinct pairs in A (so that $P \leq \binom{n}{2}$), this probability is equal to the probability that the number of distinct pairs not separated in A is at least $P - \frac{a}{16}\binom{n}{2}$. Let X be a random variable giving the number of nonseparated pairs in A; by the above, $E[X] \leq P - \frac{a}{8}\binom{n}{2}$. Using Markov's inequality (Lemma 5.25),

$$\Pr\left[X \geq P - \frac{a}{16}\binom{n}{2}\right] \leq \frac{E[X]}{P - \frac{a}{16}\binom{n}{2}}$$

$$\leq \frac{P - \frac{a}{8}\binom{n}{2}}{P - \frac{a}{16}\binom{n}{2}}$$

$$\leq \frac{\binom{n}{2}(1 - \frac{a}{8})}{\binom{n}{2}(1 - \frac{a}{16})}$$

$$\leq \frac{1 - a/8}{1 - a/16} \leq 1 - a/16.$$

If the number of separated pairs in A is indeed at least $\frac{a}{16}\binom{n}{2}$, then there must be at least $a(n-1)/32 \geq an/64$ vertices in A on each side of the random hyperplane; that is, there must be at least $an/64$ vertices $i \in A$ such that $(v_i - v_o) \cdot r \geq 0$ and at least $an/64$ vertices $i \in A$ such that $(v_i - v_o) \cdot r < 0$. Thus, with probability at least $a/16$, there are at least $an/64$ vertices of A on each side of the random hyperplane.

Applying Lemma 15.23 to the vectors $v_i - v_o$ for $i \in A$, we have that $\Pr[|(v_i - v_o) \cdot r| \leq \sigma] \leq 2\sigma/\|v_i - v_o\| \leq 4\sigma$ since $\|v_i - v_o\|^2 \geq 1/4$. Let Y be a random variable denoting the number of vertices $i \in A$ such that $|(v_i - v_o) \cdot r| \leq \sigma$, so that $E[Y] \leq 4\sigma n$. Applying Markov's inequality again, $\Pr[Y \geq an/128] \leq E[Y]/(an/128) \leq 4\sigma n/(an/128) = 512\sigma/a$. If we set $\sigma = a^2/(32 \cdot 512) = a^2/2^{14}$, this probability is at most $a/32$.

Therefore, the probability that there are fewer than $an/64$ vertices of A on some side of the random hyperplane or that there are at least $an/128$ vertices $i \in A$ such that $|(v_i - v_o) \cdot r| \leq \sigma$ is at most $1 - a/16 + a/32 = 1 - a/32$. Thus, with probability at least $a/32$ there are at least $an/64$ vertices of A on each side of the random hyperplane and there are at most $an/128$ vertices i such that $|(v_i - v_o) \cdot r| \leq \sigma$. Thus, with probability at least $a/32$, of the $an/64$ vertices $i \in A$ such that $(v_i - v_o) \cdot r \geq 0$, at least $an/128$ of them must have $(v_i - v_o) \cdot r \geq \sigma$, and of the $an/64$ vertices $j \in A$ such that $(v_j - v_o) \cdot r < 0$, at least $an/128$ of them must have $(v_j - v_o) \cdot r \leq -\sigma$. This implies that with probability at least $a/32$ there are at least $an/128$ vertices in each of L and R. $\qquad\square$

By building on some of the techniques introduced in this section, it is possible to do better for the general case of the sparsest cut problem than the $O(\log n)$-approximation algorithm given in Section 15.1.

Theorem 15.34. *There is an $O(\sqrt{\log n} \log \log n)$-approximation algorithm for the sparsest cut problem.*

Exercises

15.1 Show that every tree metric is an ℓ_1-embeddable metric, and that there is an ℓ_1-embeddable metric that is not equivalent to any tree metric (even on a larger set of nodes).

15.2 In this exercise, we will show that the distortion achieved by Theorem 15.4 is the best possible up to constant factors. For this, we need to look at distance metrics given by the shortest paths in an expander graph. An *expander graph* $G = (V, E)$ has the property that the number of edges in any cut is some constant factor times the smaller side of the cut; that is, there is some constant $\alpha > 0$ such that for any $S \subseteq V$ such that $|S| \leq |V|/2, |\delta(S)| \geq \alpha \cdot |S|$. There exist expanders such that every vertex in G has degree three.

(a) Given an expander $G = (V, E)$ with $c_e = 1$ for all $e \in E$, an s_i-t_i pair for each $j, k \in V$ with $j \neq k$, and $d_i = 1$ for all i, show that the sparsest cut has value at least $\Omega(1/n)$.

(b) Let G be an expander such that every vertex has degree three. Let (V, d) be the shortest path distance in G; that is, d_{uv} is the shortest path from u to v in G in which every edge has length 1. Show that for any vertex v, there are at most $n/4$ vertices u such that $d_{uv} \leq \log n - 3$.

(c) Given the graph and distance metric from the previous item, show that

$$\frac{\sum_{(u,v) \in E} d_{uv}}{\sum_{u,v \in V : u \neq v} d_{uv}} = O\left(\frac{1}{n \log n}\right).$$

(d) Using the items above, show that any expander with every vertex having degree three cannot be embedded into ℓ_1 with distortion less than $\Omega(\log n)$.

15.3 Show that by using semidefinite programming, for any metric space (V, d) one can compute an embedding $f : V \to \Re^{|V|}$ into ℓ_2 of minimum possible distortion.

15.4 Show that the Fréchet embedding given in the proof of Theorem 15.4 also gives an $O(\log n)$-distortion embedding into ℓ_p for any given $p \geq 1$.

15.5 Using cut-tree packings, give an alternative $O(\log n)$-approximation algorithm for the minimum multicut problem defined in Section 8.3. (Hint: Look at Exercise 7.2.)

15.6 Using cut-tree packings, give an alternative $O(\log n)$-approximation algorithm for the sparsest cut problem defined in Section 15.1.

15.7 Suppose we are given as input a metric (V, d) and costs c_{uv} for all $u, v \in V$, and suppose we have a polynomial-time algorithm to find cut-tree packing such that inequality (15.2) holds for some value α. Show that we can then derive a polynomial-time algorithm to find a tree metric (V, T) such that $d_{uv} \leq T_{uv}$ for all $u, v \in V$ and $\sum_{u,v \in V} c_{uv} T_{uv} \leq \alpha \sum_{u,v \in V} c_{uv} d_{uv}$.

15.8 Using the ideas of Theorem 15.14, prove that one can use the ellipsoid method to solve the linear programming relaxation of the bin-packing problem given in Section 4.6 to within an additive error of 1 in time that is polynomial in the number of different piece sizes m and $\log(n/s_m)$, where n is the total number of pieces and s_m is the size of the smallest piece.

15.9 Suppose we have a metric (V, d). Suppose we are also given a deterministic algorithm that for any costs $c_{uv} \geq 0$ for all $u, v \in V$ finds a tree metric (V', T) with $V' \supseteq V$ such that $d_{uv} \leq T_{uv}$ and $\sum_{u,v \in V} c_{uv} T_{uv} \leq O(\log n) \sum_{u,v \in V} c_{uv} d_{uv}$. Obtain a randomized algorithm that obtains a tree metric (V'', T') with $V'' \supseteq V$ such that $d_{uv} \leq T'_{uv}$ and $E[T'_{uv}] \leq O(\log n) d_{uv}$ for all $u, v \in V$.

Chapter Notes

The book of Deza and Laurent [87] contains a technical and in-depth treatment of the subject of cuts and metrics, though not from the point of view of approximation algorithms.

The study of the embedding of metrics into other metrics so as to minimize the distortion of the embedding has received a good deal of attention in the literature. In the area of approximation algorithms, this line of research was started with the results of Section 15.1. The main theorem of that section, Theorem 15.4, is essentially a result of Bourgain [55]. Bourgain's theorem did not give a polynomial-time algorithm; the result was made algorithmic by Linial, London, and Rabinovich [217]. Aumann and Rabani [26] and Linial et al. [217] independently derived the strengthened result in Theorem 15.6 and the $O(\log k)$-approximation algorithm for the sparsest cut problem. A deterministic version of the result is shown in Linial et al. Our proof follows the presentation in a survey of Shmoys [262].

Theorem 15.12 is due to Chawla, Krauthgamer, Kumar, Rabani, and Sivakumar [68].

The results of Sections 15.2 and 15.3 are due to Räcke [244]. Exercises 15.5 and 15.6 are from this paper as well. The duality between cut-tree packings and tree metrics has been shown in more general form by Andersen and Feige [8].

The improved result for the uniform sparsest cut problem of Section 15.4 is a breakthrough due to Arora, Rao, and Vazirani [22]; the discussion in this section follows an improved analysis due to Lee [212]. Arora, Rao, and Vazirani [21] also present a nontechnical overview of the result. The improvement for the general sparsest cut problem in Theorem 15.34 is due to Arora, Lee, and Naor [17] and is based on these earlier papers. Theorem 15.32 is due to Borell [54] and Sudakov and Tsirel'son [275].

Exercise 15.2 is from a combination of Leighton and Rao [214] and Linial et al. [217]. Exercise 15.4 is from Linial et al. [217]. Exercise 15.8 is from Karmarkar and Karp [187].

CHAPTER 16

Techniques in Proving the Hardness of Approximation

For this penultimate chapter, we turn from techniques for designing good approximation algorithms to techniques for proving that problems are hard to approximate within certain factors. Our coverage of this topic will be relatively brief: indeed, another book could be written on this subject alone.

We will look at several ways in which these results are proven. First, we start with reductions from NP-complete problems. We have already seen a few examples of such reductions in this book; for example, in Theorem 2.4, we showed that there is no α-approximation algorithm for the k-center problem for $\alpha < 2$ unless P = NP, and in Theorem 2.9 we argued that there is no $O(2^n)$-approximation algorithm for the general case of the traveling salesman problem unless P = NP. Second, we will look at reductions that preserve approximation; these are reductions from a problem Π to another problem Π' such that if there is an approximation algorithm with performance guarantee α for problem Π', then there is an approximation algorithm with performance guarantee $f(\alpha)$ for problem Π, where f is some function. These results yield hardness theorems via the contrapositive: if there is no $f(\alpha)$-approximation algorithm for problem Π unless P $-$ NP, then there is no α-approximation algorithm for problem Π' unless P = NP. Third, we will turn to a definition of NP in terms of probabilistically checkable proofs, or PCPs. These PCPs allow us to prove hardness of approximation results for a number of particular constraint satisfaction problems. We can then use approximation-preserving reductions from these constraint satisfaction problems to derive hardness results for a number of other problems. Fourth, we look at a particular problem called the label cover problem; reductions from label cover are used to prove certain kinds of hardness results. We will look at reductions to the set cover problem and two network design problems. Last, we can show reductions to problems from the unique games problem, which gives hardness results conditional on the truth of the unique games conjecture.

16.1 Reductions from NP-Complete Problems

An easy way to show hardness results is via a reduction from an NP-complete problem. A brief discussion of reductions and NP-completeness can be found in Appendix B. As discussed above, we have already seen several examples of this in the book. In particular, we have shown in Theorem 2.4 that there is no α-approximation algorithm for the k-center problem for $\alpha < 2$ unless P $=$ NP; we did this via a reduction from the dominating set problem, showing that we can find a dominating set of size at most k if and only if an instance of the k-center problem in which all distances are either 1 or 2 has optimal value 1. In Theorem 2.9, we showed that the general case of the traveling salesman problem has no $O(2^n)$-approximation algorithm unless P $=$ NP; we did this via a reduction from the Hamiltonian cycle problem. Theorem 3.8 shows that the bin-packing problem does not have an approximation algorithm with performance guarantee better than $3/2$ unless P $=$ NP via a reduction from the partition problem; we also showed that since the bin-packing problem does not have the rescaling property, we are able to give better performance guarantees if we have additional additive terms.

In most of these cases, we are able to reduce an NP-complete problem Π into a set of instances of a minimization problem of interest Π' in which the objective function has a small integer value. In these reductions, a "Yes" instance of Π maps to an instance of Π' of objective function value k, whereas a "No" instance maps into an instance of Π' with objective function value $k + 1$ or more. This proves that obtaining an approximation algorithm with performance guarantee better than $\frac{k+1}{k}$ is not possible unless P $=$ NP, since this would then allow us to distinguish between the "Yes" and "No" instances of NP-complete problem Π. For instance, with the bin-packing problem, the "Yes" instances of the partition problem are mapped in polynomial time to instances of the bin-packing problem that can be packed into two bins, while the "No" instances of the partition problem are mapped to instances requiring at least three bins. This implies that no performance guarantee better than $3/2$ is possible unless P $=$ NP. As is typical with all NP-completeness reductions, devising such reductions is something of an art.

We now give another such reduction. We consider the generalized assignment problem from Section 11.1, but without the costs of assigning jobs to machines. If we assign job j to machine i, it requires p_{ij} units of time to be processed on machine i. The goal of the problem is to find an assignment of jobs to machines that minimizes the maximum total processing time assigned to any machine. We considered this problem in Exercise 11.1, where we called it the problem of minimizing the makespan on unrelated parallel machines. Both the algorithms of Section 11.1 and Exercise 11.1 give a 2-approximation algorithm for this problem. By using a reduction directly from an NP-complete problem, we are able to show that it is NP-complete to decide whether there is a schedule of length at most 2 or one of length at least 3; this proves that there is no approximation algorithm with performance guarantee better than $3/2$ unless P $=$ NP.

We first prove a weaker result: we show that deciding whether there is a schedule of length at most 3 is NP-complete (where all processing times are integers). The reduction is from the *3-dimensional matching problem*, which is as follows: given disjoint sets $A = \{a_1, \ldots, a_n\}$, $B = \{b_1, \ldots, b_n\}$, and $C = \{c_1, \ldots, c_n\}$, along with a

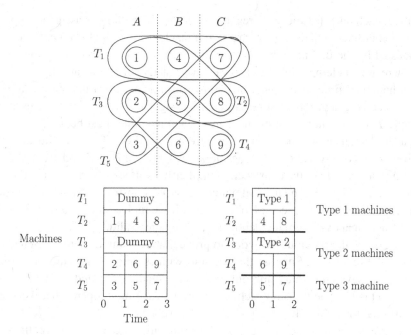

Figure 16.1. Illustration of the reduction from 3-dimensional matching to scheduling unrelated parallel machines. The 3-dimensional matching instance is given above with $F = \{T_1, \ldots, T_5\}$, where $A = \{1, 2, 3\}, B = \{4, 5, 6\}, C = \{7, 8, 9\}, T_1 = (1, 4, 7), T_2 = (1, 4, 8), T_3 = (2, 5, 8), T_4 = (2, 6, 9),$ and $T_5 = (3, 5, 7)$. The triples $T_2, T_4,$ and T_5 form a 3-dimensional matching. A corresponding schedule of length 3 (for the first reduction) is shown below on the left; a corresponding schedule of length 2 (for the second reduction) is shown below on the right. Note that in the second reduction $k_1 = 2, k_2 = 2,$ and $k_3 = 1$, so there is one type 1 dummy job, one type 2 dummy job, and no type 3 dummy job.

family $F = \{T_1, \ldots, T_m\}$, where each T_i, $i = 1, \ldots, m$, is a triple of elements, one from each of A, B, and C, does there exist a subset $F' \subseteq F$ such that each element of $A \cup B \cup C$ is contained in exactly one triple of F'? Such a subset is a called a *3-dimensional matching*.

The idea behind the reduction is quite simple. Given an instance of the 3-dimensional matching problem, we construct a scheduling input as follows. There is a job for each of the $3n$ elements in $A \cup B \cup C$, and there is a machine for each of the given m triples in F. The intuition is that we will embed a 3-dimensional matching as a "short" schedule. To do this, for each job j that corresponds to an element of the triple T_i, we set its processing time p_{ij} to 1, but otherwise we set the processing time to $+\infty$. Thus, given a 3-dimensional matching, we can schedule all $3n$ of these jobs on n of the machines. This leaves $m - n$ machines without any assigned jobs, and to make full use of this capacity, we complete the reduction by introducing $m - n$ additional jobs that require exactly 3 time units on each machine i, $i = 1, \ldots, m$. We shall call these additional jobs the *dummy* jobs, in contrast to the previous ones, which we shall call *element* jobs. Clearly, if there is a 3-dimensional matching, then there exists a schedule of length 3. See Figure 16.1 for an illustration.

However, suppose that there is a schedule of length 3 for a scheduling input obtained from this reduction. Fix one such schedule. Each of the $m - n$ dummy jobs must be scheduled; each takes 3 time units regardless of which machine is assigned to process it. Thus, in our fixed schedule, there are $m - n$ machines for which their entire capacity is exhausted by the dummy jobs, and exactly n machines for processing the element jobs. There are $3n$ element jobs, and so we have exactly sufficient capacity to schedule each of them for 1 time unit; hence, each must consume exactly 1 unit processing time. But then, each element job must be (uniquely) assigned to a machine i corresponding to a triple T_i that contains that element. And each machine must be assigned exactly three such element jobs, one from A, one from B, and one from C. But then these machines must correspond to a 3-dimensional matching of the ground set $A \cup B \cup C$.

Two minor notes: first, the construction implicitly assumes that $m \geq n$, but if $m < n$, then there cannot be a 3-dimensional matching, so we construct a trivial "no" instance of the scheduling problem; second, observe that if we replace the $+\infty$ with 3 (or 2) in the construction above, then the identical proof remains valid.

We can refine the previous reduction to prove that deciding if there is a schedule of length 2 is NP-complete. Suppose that we start with essentially the same construction as above, but have an element job only for each element of B and C. If we let each dummy job take 2 time units on each machine, we have the property that if there is a 3-dimensional matching, then there is a schedule of length 2. Of course, we no longer have the reverse implication – there might be a schedule of length 2, and yet there need not be a 3-dimensional matching in the original input. Consider such a schedule of length 2; there might be an element $a \in A$ such that there are two machines i and i' assigned to process element jobs for which $a \in T_i$ and $a \in T_{i'}$. Equivalently, if we let k denote the number of triples in F that contain this element a, then we are assigning a dummy job to $k - 2$ of their corresponding machines, instead of to $k - 1$, as desired. We can modify the construction of the dummy jobs to make sure that any schedule of length 2 has this additional property.

For each element $a \in A$, let k_a denote the number of triples in F that contain the element a. Instead of $m - n$ identical dummy jobs, let there be $k_a - 1$ dummy jobs of type a, for each of the n elements $a \in A$. (There are still $m - n$ dummy jobs in total.) Each dummy job of type a takes 2 time units on each machine i for which the triple T_i contains a, but takes $+\infty$ time units on each other machine. We also call a machine i of type a if $a \in T_i$. (Analogous to the case above where $m < n$, if some $k_a = 0$, then again construct a trivial "no" instance of the scheduling problem.)

Suppose that there is a 3-dimensional matching F'. For each $T_i \in F'$, schedule the jobs corresponding to their elements of B and C on machine i. For each of the n elements $a \in A$, this leaves $k_a - 1$ machines of type a that are still idle, and so we can schedule the $k_a - 1$ dummy jobs of type a on them. This is a schedule of length 2. See Figure 16.1 for an illustration of this reduction.

Conversely, suppose that there is a schedule of length 2. Each dummy job of type a must be scheduled on a machine of type a. Therefore, for each $a \in A$, there is exactly one machine of type a that is not processing a dummy job. Since there are $2n$ element jobs processed by the remaining n machines, each of these machines must be processing two element jobs in one time unit each. If the remaining machine of type a is processing b and c, then there is a triple (a, b, c) corresponding to it. Let F' be the set of n triples corresponding to machines that are not processing dummy jobs. Since each element job is scheduled exactly once, and there is one machine of each type scheduling element jobs, F' is a 3-dimensional matching.

We have proved the following theorem.

Theorem 16.1. *It is* NP-*complete to decide whether there exists a schedule of length at most 2, given an input of scheduling on unrelated parallel machines, where each job j is restricted to a subset of machines M_j, and takes time $p_j \in \{1, 2\}$ on any machine $i \in M_j$. Consequently, for any $\alpha < 3/2$, there is no α-approximation algorithm for the problem of minimizing the makespan on unrelated parallel machines, unless* P $=$ NP.

We conclude this section by showing one case in which a reduction from an NP-complete problem gives a very strong hardness result. We show this for the *edge-disjoint paths problem* in directed graphs introduced in Exercise 2.14. In this problem, we are given as input a directed graph $G = (V, A)$ and k source-sink pairs $s_i, t_i \in V$. The goal of the problem is to find edge-disjoint paths so that as many source-sink pairs as possible have a path from s_i to t_i. More formally, let $S \subseteq \{1, \ldots, k\}$. We want to find S and paths P_i for all $i \in S$ such that $|S|$ is as large as possible and for any $i, j \in S, i \neq j, P_i$ and P_j are edge-disjoint ($P_i \cap P_j = \emptyset$). In Exercise 2.14, we saw that a greedy algorithm gives an $\Omega(m^{-1/2})$-approximation algorithm for this problem. Here we show via a reduction from an NP-complete problem that we cannot do much better than this unless P $=$ NP; in particular, for any $\epsilon > 0$, we cannot obtain an $\Omega(m^{-\frac{1}{2}+\epsilon})$-approximation algorithm unless P $=$ NP.

The particular NP-complete problem we reduce from is simply the edge-disjoint paths problem in directed graphs in which $k = 2$; it has been shown that it is NP-complete to decide whether or not we can find edge-disjoint paths both from s_1 to t_1 and from s_2 to t_2 or only a single edge-disjoint path from s_1 to t_1, or from s_2 to t_2, but not both. Notice that this NP-complete problem immediately implies that we cannot get a ρ-approximation algorithm for the edge-disjoint paths problem in directed graphs for $\rho > 1/2$ unless P $=$ NP, but via a reduction we can prove a significantly stronger result than this.

Given an instance of the $k = 2$ problem on a graph $G = (V, A)$ and a constant $\epsilon > 0$, we create a new instance G' shown in Figure 16.2 where $k = |A|^{\lceil 1/\epsilon \rceil}$; to keep the two problems distinct, we call the source-sink pairs in G' a_i-b_i. The total number of arcs in G' is $O(k^2|A|) = O(k^{2+\epsilon})$. We make two observations about the relationship of G to G'. First, if there are two edge-disjoint paths in G from s_1 to t_1 and from s_2 to t_2, then it is clear that there are k edge-disjoint paths in G', one for each a_i-b_i pair. Second, if there are two edge-disjoint paths in G', from a_i to b_i and a_j to b_j for $i \neq j$, then we claim that there must be two edge-disjoint paths in G. This follows since the a_i-b_i and a_j-b_j paths must cross at some intersection in the graph G' that contains a copy of G; in order for the two paths to be edge-disjoint, there must be edge-disjoint s_1-t_1 and s_2-t_2 paths in G.

Thus, given an $\Omega(m^{-\frac{1}{2}+\epsilon})$-approximation algorithm for the edge-disjoint paths problem, we can decide whether the graph G has two edge-disjoint paths or only one by constructing G' in polynomial time as follows. If $|A|$ is smaller than some constant to be specified later, we simply do an exhaustive search to determine whether G has both paths or not; this takes constant time. If $|A|$ is larger than the constant, we create G'

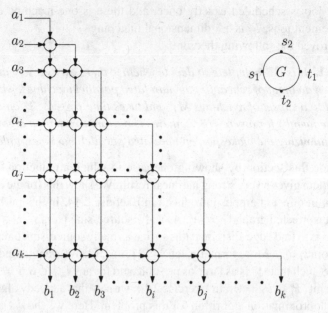

Figure 16.2. Illustration of the reduction from edge-disjoint paths problem for $k = 2$ to general k. Note that a copy of G is placed at the intersections of the various paths from the a_i to the b_i.

as given above and apply the approximation algorithm to it. If there is only one path in G, there is only one path in G'. If both paths exist in G, then we know that k paths exist in G', so that the approximation algorithm will find

$$\Omega\left((k^{2+\epsilon})^{-\frac{1}{2}+\epsilon}\right) \cdot k = \Omega\left(k^{\frac{3}{2}\epsilon+\epsilon^2}\right) = \Omega\left(|A|^{\frac{3}{2}+\epsilon}\right)$$

paths, and this is greater than 1 for $|A|$ larger than some constant. Thus, if the number of paths found in G' is greater than 1, then both paths exist in G; otherwise, only one does, and this decides an NP-complete problem in polynomial time. Thus, we have shown the following.

Theorem 16.2. *For any $\epsilon > 0$, there is no $\Omega(m^{-\frac{1}{2}+\epsilon})$-approximation algorithm for the edge-disjoint paths problem in directed graphs unless* P = NP.

16.2 Reductions that Preserve Approximation

In this section, we turn to the idea of an *approximation-preserving reduction*. We show how to reduce a problem Π to a problem Π' so that if there exists an α-approximation algorithm for Π', we can then get an $f(\alpha)$-approximation algorithm for Π, where f is some function. Then if we know that Π is hard to approximate to within some factor, the reduction implies that the problem Π' is also hard to approximate to within some factor.

We illustrate this type of reduction as follows. Consider the maximum satisfiability problem in which each clause has exactly three literals; we will call this variant of the problem MAX E3SAT. We will show a reduction to the maximum satisfiability problem in which each clause has at most two literals; this variant of the problem is called MAX 2SAT. In our reduction, we take each clause of the MAX E3SAT instance and create ten clauses for the MAX 2SAT instance; these ten clauses will involve the same variables x_i as used in the E3SAT instance, but for the jth E3SAT clause will introduce a new variable y_j to be used in the corresponding ten 2SAT clauses. In particular, suppose the jth E3SAT clause is $x_1 \vee x_2 \vee x_3$; we create the following ten clauses for the 2SAT instance:

$$x_1, x_2, x_3, \bar{x}_1 \vee \bar{x}_2, \bar{x}_2 \vee \bar{x}_3, \bar{x}_1 \vee \bar{x}_3, y_j, x_1 \vee \bar{y}_j, x_2 \vee \bar{y}_j, x_3 \vee \bar{y}_j.$$

We claim that if the E3SAT clause is satisfied by the assignment of values to x_1, x_2, and x_3, then we can set the variable y_j so that seven of the ten clauses are satisfied; if all of x_1, x_2, and x_3 are false, then we can set the variable y_j so that six of the ten clauses can be satisfied, but no more. To see this, consider the various cases: if all three of x_1, x_2, and x_3 are true, then setting y_j to true satisfies the first three and the last four clauses of the ten. If two of the three variables are true, then setting y_j true satisfies two of the first three, two of the next three, and three of the last four clauses. If one of the three variables is true, then setting y_j false satisfies one of the first three, all of the next three, and all of the last three clauses. If none of the three variables is true, then setting y_j to true satisfies none of the first three, all of the next three, and one of the last four clauses, whereas setting y_j to false satisfies none of the first three, all of the next three, and three of the last four clauses. We can give a similar reduction for any E3SAT clause.

Now we wish to relate the approximability of the MAX 2SAT instance to that of the MAX E3SAT instance. Suppose that the E3SAT instance has m clauses, and that an optimal solution satisfies k^* clauses, and thus $m - k^*$ clauses go unsatisfied. Note then that the optimal solution to the 2SAT instance will satisfy $7k^* + 6(m - k^*)$ clauses. Furthermore, suppose we have an α-approximation algorithm for the MAX 2SAT problem that satisfies seven clauses for $\tilde{k}$ of the ten clause groups, and six clauses for each of the $m - \tilde{k}$ remaining groups. Using the same setting of the variables x_i, we then satisfy $\tilde{k}$ clauses of the E3SAT instance. To relate the approximability of MAX 2SAT to MAX E3SAT, let I be the original instance of MAX E3SAT and let I' be the corresponding instance of MAX 2SAT. Let $\mathrm{OPT}(I) = k^*$ and $\mathrm{OPT}(I') = 7k^* + 6(m - k^*)$ be the optimal values of the two instances. We want to show that the α-approximation algorithm for MAX 2SAT gives us some $f(\alpha)$-approximation algorithm for MAX E3SAT. To do this, we see that

$$\mathrm{OPT}(I') - \alpha\,\mathrm{OPT}(I') \geq 7k^* + 6(m - k^*) - [7\tilde{k} + 6(m - \tilde{k})] = k^* - \tilde{k} = \mathrm{OPT}(I) - \tilde{k}.$$

We then have that

$$\tilde{k} \geq \mathrm{OPT}(I) - (1 - \alpha)\,\mathrm{OPT}(I').$$

To bound the value of the solution created for the E3SAT instance, we now need to relate $\mathrm{OPT}(I')$ to $\mathrm{OPT}(I)$. Recall from Section 5.1 that the simple randomized algorithm for the maximum satisfiability problem satisfies at least $\frac{7}{8}$ of the clauses of a MAX SAT instance in which each clause has exactly three literals, so that $k^* \geq \frac{7}{8}m$. Thus,

$$\text{OPT}(I') = 7k^* + 6(m - k^*) = k^* + 6m \leq k^* + \frac{48}{7}k^* = \frac{55}{7}\text{OPT}(I).$$

Plugging this inequality into the one above, we obtain that

$$\tilde{k} \geq \text{OPT}(I) - (1 - \alpha)\text{OPT}(I') \geq \text{OPT}(I) - (1 - \alpha)\frac{55}{7}\text{OPT}(I)$$

$$= \left(\frac{55}{7}\alpha - \frac{48}{7}\right)\text{OPT}(I).$$

Thus, given an α-approximation algorithm for the MAX 2SAT problem, we then have a $(\frac{55}{7}\alpha - \frac{48}{7})$-approximation algorithm for the MAX E3SAT problem. By using the contrapositive, if it is the case that we know that no ρ-approximation algorithm exists for MAX E3SAT for a given ρ unless P $=$ NP, then for any α such that $\frac{55}{7}\alpha - \frac{48}{7} \geq \rho$, we know that no α-approximation algorithm exists for MAX 2SAT unless P $=$ NP. In Theorem 5.2 we asserted that there can be no ρ-approximation algorithm for MAX E3SAT for constant $\rho > 7/8$ unless P $=$ NP. By determining the values of α for which $\frac{55}{7}\alpha - \frac{48}{7} > \frac{7}{8}$, we can draw the following conclusion.

Theorem 16.3. *There exists no α-approximation algorithm for the MAX 2SAT problem for constant $\alpha > \frac{433}{440} \approx 0.984$ unless* P $=$ NP.

We abstract the features of the reduction we used as follows; we will call this an *L-reduction*. An L-reduction from problem Π to problem Π' produces from an instance I of Π an instance I' of Π' in polynomial time such that for some constant a, $\text{OPT}(I') \leq a\,\text{OPT}(I)$. In addition, for a feasible solution to I' of value V', we can in polynomial time produce a solution to I of value V such that for some constant b, $|\text{OPT}(I) - V| \leq b|\text{OPT}(I') - V'|$. Because the parameters a and b are important in determining approximability, we will sometimes say that we have an *L-reduction with parameters a and b*; for instance, in our reduction of MAX E3SAT to MAX 2SAT above, we had an L-reduction with parameters $a = \frac{55}{7}$ and $b = 1$. For convenience, we make a formal definition of L-reduction below.

Definition 16.4. *Given two optimization problems Π and Π', we say we have an* L-reduction *(or an* L-reduction with parameters a and b*) from Π to Π' if for some $a, b > 0$*

1. *for each instance I of Π we can compute in polynomial time an instance I' of Π';*
2. $\text{OPT}(I') \leq a\,\text{OPT}(I)$;
3. *given a solution of value V' to I', we can compute in polynomial time a solution of value V to I such that*

$$|\text{OPT}(I) - V| \leq b|\text{OPT}(I') - V'|.$$

Notice then that if both Π and Π' are maximization problems, and if we have an α-approximation algorithm for problem Π', then we can obtain a solution for instance I of Π. We do this by producing in polynomial time the instance I' of Π', using the α-approximation algorithm to produce a solution of value $V' \geq \alpha\,\text{OPT}(I')$, then using the polynomial time algorithm to produce a solution to I of value V. Furthermore, we obtain that

$$V \geq \text{OPT}(I) - b(\text{OPT}(I') - V') \geq \text{OPT}(I) - b(1 - \alpha)\,\text{OPT}(I')$$
$$\geq \text{OPT}(I)(1 - ab(1 - \alpha)),$$

so that this algorithm is a $(1 - ab(1 - \alpha))$-approximation algorithm for Π. Similarly, if both Π and Π' are minimization problems, and we have an α-approximation algorithm for Π', we obtain from that an $(ab(\alpha - 1) + 1)$-approximation algorithm for Π. Again, so that it is easy to refer to these results later, we state these both as theorems.

Theorem 16.5. *If there is an L-reduction with parameters a and b from maximization problem Π to maximization problem Π', and there is an α-approximation algorithm for Π', then there is an $(1 - ab(1 - \alpha))$-approximation algorithm for Π.*

Theorem 16.6. *If there is an L-reduction with parameters a and b from minimization problem Π to minimization problem Π', and there is an α-approximation algorithm for Π', then there is an $(ab(\alpha - 1) + 1)$-approximation algorithm for Π.*

We observe that the quality of the L-reduction depends on the product ab; the smaller it is, the better the resulting approximation algorithm for Π. For instance, we can give a better L-reduction from MAX E3SAT to MAX 2SAT as follows. For the jth E3SAT clause $x_1 \vee x_2 \vee x_3$, we introduce the clauses $x_1 \vee x_3, \bar{x}_1 \vee \bar{x}_3, x_1 \vee \bar{y}_j, \bar{x}_1 \vee y_j$, $x_3 \vee \bar{y}_j, \bar{x}_3 \vee y_j$, and $x_2 \vee y_j$, with weights 1/2 on all clauses except the last, which has weight 1. Then it can be shown that for any assignment satisfying $x_1 \vee x_2 \vee x_3$, it is possible to set y_j so that clauses of total weight 3.5 are satisfied, while if all of x_1, x_2, and x_3 are false, then y_j can be set to satisfy clauses of weight 2.5, but no more. This gives an L-reduction with parameters $a = 1 + \frac{5}{2} \cdot \frac{8}{7} = \frac{27}{7}$ and $b = 1$, and thus an α-approximation algorithm for MAX 2SAT implies a $(1 - \frac{27}{7}(1 - \alpha))$-approximation algorithm for MAX E3SAT. As above, since there is no ρ-approximation algorithm for MAX E3SAT for constant $\rho > 7/8$ unless P = NP, we get the following theorem.

Theorem 16.7. *There is no α-approximation algorithm for MAX 2SAT for constant $\alpha > \frac{209}{216} \approx 0.968$ unless P = NP.*

We now give another L-reduction. Recall the maximum independent set problem from Section 10.2: given an undirected graph $G = (V, E)$, the goal is to find a subset $S \subseteq V$ of vertices of maximum cardinality such that for all $u, v \in S$, $(u, v) \notin E$. We show an L-reduction from MAX E3SAT to the maximum independent set problem. Given an E3SAT instance I with m clauses, we create a graph with $3m$ nodes, one for each literal in the E3SAT instance. For any clause, we add edges connecting the nodes corresponding to the three literals in the clause. Furthermore, for each node corresponding to a literal x_i, we add an edge connecting this node to each node corresponding to the literal $\bar{x}_i$. Call this instance I' for the maximum independent set problem; see Figure 16.3 for an illustration of the reduction.

Observe that given any solution to the independent set instance, we can obtain a solution to the E3SAT instance by setting to true any x_i whose corresponding literal node is in the independent set and to false any $\bar{x}_i$ whose corresponding literal node is in the independent set. This leads to a consistent assignment to the variables since there

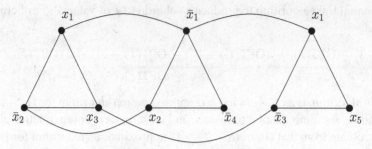

Figure 16.3. Illustration of the reduction from MAX E3SAT to the maximum independent set problem; the reduction is shown for the three clauses $x_1 \vee \bar{x}_2 \vee x_3$, $\bar{x}_1 \vee x_2 \vee \bar{x}_4$, and $x_1 \vee \bar{x}_3 \vee x_5$.

is an edge between each x_i node and each $\bar{x}_i$ node, so that only one of the two kinds of nodes can be in the independent set. If for some variable x_j neither kind of node is in the independent set, we set x_j arbitrarily. Notice that at most one literal node can be in the independent set for each clause; thus, we satisfy at least as many clauses as there are nodes in the independent set. Similarly, given any solution to the E3SAT instance, for each satisfied clause we can pick one of the literals that satisfies the clause (that is, a positive literal x_i set true or a negative literal $\bar{x}_i$ set false) and put the corresponding node in the independent set for an independent set of size at least the number of satisfied clauses. Thus, $\text{OPT}(I) = \text{OPT}(I')$, and for any solution V' to the independent set instance we can get a solution V to the E3SAT instance with $V \geq V'$. This implies that we have an L-reduction with parameters $a = b = 1$, so that any α-approximation algorithm for the maximum independent set problem yields an α-approximation algorithm for the MAX E3SAT problem. The following is then immediate.

Theorem 16.8. *There is no α-approximation algorithm for the maximum independent set problem for constant $\alpha > \frac{7}{8}$ unless P = NP.*

Let us give one last L-reduction before we move on to other types of approximation-preserving reductions. We give a reduction of the unweighted vertex cover problem in bounded degree graphs (where the vertex cover problem was introduced in Section 1.2) to the Steiner tree problem (given in Exercise 2.5 and Section 12.3). Given an instance I of the unweighted vertex cover problem in a connected graph $G = (V, E)$ in which each node has degree at most Δ, we create an instance I' of the Steiner tree problem as follows. We create a new graph G' in which the new vertex set V' has one vertex per vertex in V plus one vertex t_e per edge in E. The vertices from V will be nonterminals and the vertices t_e will be terminals. Let $T = \{e \in E : t_e\}$ be the set of terminals; then $V' = V \cup T$. For any $e = (u, v) \in E$, we set the cost $c_{t_e,u} = c_{t_e,v} = 1$, and for any pair of nonterminals $u, v \in V$, we set $c_{uv} = 1$. For any other pair of vertices $u, v \in V \cup T$, we set $c_{uv} = 2$. We give an illustration of the reduction in Figure 16.4.

Now we must show that this is an L-reduction. In the vertex cover instance, each vertex v can cover at most Δ edges, so that $\text{OPT}(I) \geq |E|/\Delta$. In the Steiner tree instance, we can build a tree by taking a path connecting just the terminals via edges of cost 2, so that $\text{OPT}(I') \leq 2(|T| - 1) \leq 2|E| \leq 2\Delta\,\text{OPT}(I)$, since $|E| = |T|$.

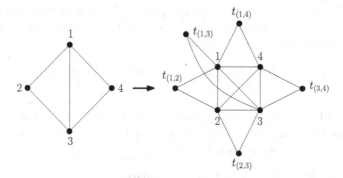

Figure 16.4. Illustration of the reduction from the unweighted vertex cover problem in bounded degree graphs to the Steiner tree problem. The vertex cover instance on the left is reduced to the Steiner tree instance on the right. Only edges with cost 1 in the Steiner tree instance are shown; all other edges have cost 2.

Observe that given a vertex cover $C \subseteq V$, we can build a Steiner tree of cost $|T| + |C| - 1$ as follows: build a tree of cost $|C| - 1$ on the nonterminals in C by using edges of cost 1, then connect each terminal t_e to the vertex $u \in C$ that covers e at a cost of $|T|$.

Similarly, given a Steiner tree of cost L, we show that we can convert it into a vertex cover with at most $L - (|T| - 1)$ vertices. We first take the Steiner tree and show that we can find another Steiner tree of cost at most L that uses no edges of cost 2. Removing any edge of cost 2 disconnects the tree into two components. If both components contain a nonterminal, then we can add the cost 1 edge between these two nonterminals and get a Steiner tree of lower cost. If one component does not contain a nonterminal, then it must have all cost 2 edges, and there is some terminal t_e for $e = (u, v)$ that is a leaf in the component. Replace the original cost 2 edge and remove the cost 2 edge incident on t_e. Since we assumed that G is connected, there is some other edge e' in G that is incident on either u or v; assume e' is incident on u. Then we can add the edges (t_e, u) and $(u, t_{e'})$ to the Steiner tree, both of which have cost 1. Since the terminal $t_{e'}$ must be in the Steiner tree, the terminal t_e is still connected and the tree has no greater cost. By repeating this process, we find a tree of cost no greater than L that uses only edges of cost 1. Then consider the set C of all nonterminals in the Steiner tree: since we use edges of cost 1 only, each terminal t_e for $e = (u, v)$ must have the edge (t_e, u) or (t_e, v) connecting it to either u or v in C, so that C must be a vertex cover. Furthermore, since the tree spans $|T| + |C|$ vertices with edges of cost 1, it has cost $|T| + |C| - 1 \leq L$, so that the vertex cover has size at most $L - (|T| - 1)$, as desired.

Thus, given a solution of cost Z' to the Steiner tree instance I', we can get a solution of size at most $Z \leq Z' - |T| + 1$ to the vertex cover problem, and given a solution of size Z to the vertex cover problem, we can get a solution of cost at most $Z + |T| - 1$ to the Steiner tree problem. Then in particular $\text{OPT}(I') = \text{OPT}(I) + |T| - 1$, which proves that $Z - \text{OPT}(I) = Z - \text{OPT}(I') + |T| - 1 \leq Z' - \text{OPT}(I')$. It follows that we have an L-reduction with parameters $a = 2\Delta$ and $b = 1$. Hence, we obtain the following.

Lemma 16.9. *Given an α-approximation algorithm for the minimum-cost Steiner tree problem, there is a $2\alpha\Delta$-approximation algorithm for the vertex cover problem in connected graphs of maximum degree Δ.*

The following theorem is known about the vertex cover problem in bounded degree graphs.

Theorem 16.10. *For any sufficiently large Δ, there exists $\epsilon > 0$ such that if a $(1 + \epsilon)$-approximation algorithm exists for the unweighted vertex cover problem in connected graphs of maximum degree Δ, then $P = NP$.*

Thus, we are able to infer the following corollary.

Corollary 16.11. *There exists $\epsilon' > 0$ such that if a $(1 + \epsilon')$-approximation algorithm exists for the minimum-cost Steiner tree problem, then $P = NP$.*

So far, all of the approximation-preserving reductions that we have seen are L-reductions; also, all were reductions from one problem to another. Next we will give an interesting example in which we have an approximation-preserving reduction from the maximum independent set problem to itself. We will use this reduction to show that there is no approximation algorithm possible with a constant performance guarantee for the maximum independent set problem unless $P = NP$.

Theorem 16.12. *If there exists an α-approximation algorithm for the maximum independent set problem, then there is also a $\sqrt{\alpha}$-approximation algorithm for the maximum independent set problem.*

Proof. Suppose we are given an α-approximation algorithm for the maximum independent set problem, and we have an input graph G. We would like to find a solution of value at least $\sqrt{\alpha}\, \text{OPT}(G)$, where $\text{OPT}(G)$ is the size of the maximum independent set in G. To do this, we create a new graph $G \times G$, with a vertex set $V' = V \times V$ and an edge set E' in which there is an edge between $(u_1, u_2) \in V'$ and $(v_1, v_2) \in V'$ if either $(u_1, v_1) \in E$ or $(u_2, v_2) \in E$.

Given an independent set S in G, we claim that $S \times S$ is an independent set in $G \times G$; this follows since for any $(u_1, u_2), (v_1, v_2) \in S \times S$, both $(u_1, v_1) \notin E$ and $(u_2, v_2) \notin E$ since S is independent. Furthermore, given any independent set $S' \subseteq V'$ in $G \times G$, we claim that both $S_1 = \{u \in V : \exists (u, w) \in S'\}$ and $S_2 = \{u \in V : \exists (w, u) \in S'\}$ are independent sets in G. To see this, if both $u, v \in S_1$, then there exist (u, w_1), $(v, w_2) \in S'$. Since S' is independent, there can be no edge $(u, v) \in E$; the argument for S_2 is identical. Thus, given an independent set S in G, we can find an independent set of size at least $|S|^2$ in $G \times G$. Also, given an independent set S' in $G \times G$, it is the case that $S' \subseteq S_1 \times S_2$, so that $|S'| \leq |S_1||S_2|$; if we take the larger of the two sets S_1 and S_2, then we have an independent set in G of size at least $\sqrt{|S'|}$. Thus, it must be the case that $\text{OPT}(G \times G) = \text{OPT}(G)^2$.

Given an α-approximation algorithm for the maximum independent set problem and an instance G, we construct the graph $G \times G$, use the approximation algorithm to find an independent set S' in $G \times G$ of size at least $\alpha\, \text{OPT}(G \times G)$, and then use this to find an independent set of size S in G of size at least $\sqrt{\alpha\, \text{OPT}(G \times G)} = \sqrt{\alpha}\, \text{OPT}(G)$. Thus, this is an $\sqrt{\alpha}$-approximation algorithm for the maximum independent set problem. $\quad\square$

By applying this reduction repeatedly, we can obtain the following result.

Corollary 16.13. *If there is a ρ-approximation algorithm for any constant $0 < \rho < 1$ for the maximum independent set problem, then there is a polynomial-time approximation scheme for the maximum independent set problem.*

Proof. Given $\epsilon > 0$, and the ρ-approximation algorithm, if $\rho > 1 - \epsilon$, then we are done. Otherwise if we apply the argument of the theorem above k times for $k \geq \log \log \frac{1}{\rho} - \log \log \frac{1}{1-\epsilon}$, then we have that $\rho^{1/2^k} \geq 1 - \epsilon$. If n is the size of the input graph, then the reduction creates a graph of size n^{2^k}, which is polynomial in the input size. Thus, we have a $(1 - \epsilon)$-approximation algorithm. $\square$

This argument yields the following.

Corollary 16.14. *There is no ρ-approximation algorithm for any constant ρ for the maximum independent set problem unless* P $=$ NP.

Proof. By Theorem 16.8, we know there is no α-approximation algorithm for the maximum independent set for $\alpha > 7/8$ unless P $=$ NP. Thus, by Corollary 16.13, there can be no ρ-approximation algorithm for any constant ρ unless P $=$ NP. $\square$

As a final example of a reduction from approximating one problem to approximating another, we give a reduction from the unweighted set cover problem (introduced in Section 1.2) to the metric uncapacitated facility location problem (introduced in Section 4.5). We show that if there is an α-approximation algorithm for the metric uncapacitated facility location problem with $\alpha < 1.463$, then there is a $(c \ln n)$-approximation algorithm for the unweighted set cover problem with $c < 1$. However, by Theorem 1.13, we know that no such algorithm for the unweighted set cover problem exists unless there is an $O(n^{O(\log \log n)})$ time algorithm for each NP-complete problem. This implies that there is no α-approximation algorithm for the metric uncapacitated facility location problem with $\alpha < 1.463$ unless there is an $O(n^{O(\log \log n)})$-time algorithm for each NP-complete problem.

The reduction is somewhat more involved than the previous reductions we have seen; in particular, we obtain an approximation algorithm for the unweighted set cover problem by making several calls to the α-approximation algorithm for the facility location problem. Given an instance of the set cover problem with ground set E and subsets $S_1, \ldots, S_m \subseteq E$, we create an instance of the uncapacitated facility location problem in which we set the clients $D = E$, and the set of facilities $F = \{1, 2, \ldots, m\}$. We let $c_{ij} = 1$ if the element corresponding to client j is in the set S_i, and let $c_{ij} = 3$ otherwise. Observe that these assignment costs are metric since for any facilities $h, i \in F$ and clients $j, l \in D$, $c_{ij} \leq c_{il} + c_{hl} + c_{hj}$.

In what follows, we let k be the size of the optimal set cover. Obviously, we do not know the size of the optimal set cover, so we run the following algorithm for each possible value of k from 1 to m, and return the smallest set cover found. We let the facility cost $f_i = \gamma |D| / k$ for all facilities $i \in F$ for a constant γ to be given later. Our algorithm will run the given α-approximation algorithm for the facility location problem multiple times; each time the algorithm finds all clients j assigned to facilities i with $c_{ij} = 1$; we then add the corresponding subsets S_i to our set cover and create

---

for $k \leftarrow 1$ to m **do**
  $I_k \leftarrow \emptyset$
  Let $D = E$, $F = [m]$ be the facility location instance
  while $D \neq \emptyset$ **do**
    $f_i \leftarrow \gamma |D|/k$ for all $i \in F$
    Run α-approximation algorithm on facility location instance
        with clients D, facilities F
    Let F' be facilities opened by approximation algorithm
    $I_k \leftarrow I_k \cup F'$
    Let D' be clients j such that $c_{ij} = 1$ for some $i \in F'$
    $F \leftarrow F - F', D \leftarrow D - D'$
return I_k that minimizes $|I_k|$

Algorithm 16.1. Algorithm for the unweighted set cover problem on elements E, sets $S_1, \ldots, S_m$, using α-approximation algorithm for the metric uncapacitated facility location problem as a subroutine.

a smaller facility location instance as above with the clients D corresponding to the uncovered elements and the facilities F to the unchosen sets. We continue until all elements are covered. The algorithm is summarized in Algorithm 16.1.

Theorem 16.15. *If there is an α-approximation algorithm for the metric uncapacitated facility location problem for $\alpha < 1.463$, then Algorithm 16.1 is a $(c \ln n)$-approximation algorithm for the unweighted set cover problem with $c < 1$ when n is sufficiently large.*

Proof. Assume that the optimal set cover has size k, and that we are currently in iteration k of the "for" loop. Let n_ℓ be the number of uncovered elements at the start of iteration ℓ of the "while" loop, and let $f^\ell = \gamma n_\ell/k$ be the facility cost in iteration ℓ for a constant γ; we will show later that we want $\gamma = 0.463$. Then there is a solution to the facility location problem of cost at most $f^\ell k + n_\ell$ in which we open the k facilities corresponding to the sets in the optimal set cover, and assign the n_ℓ clients corresponding to uncovered elements to these facilities with an assignment cost of 1 for each client. Given the α-approximation algorithm for the facility location problem, the solution returned by the algorithm has a cost of at most $\alpha(f^\ell k + n_\ell) = \alpha n_\ell(\gamma + 1)$, by the definition of f^ℓ.

Now consider the solution found by the algorithm in the ℓth iteration. Suppose it opens $\beta_\ell k$ facilities and of the n_ℓ clients in this iteration, $\rho_\ell n_\ell$ are assigned to facilities such that their assignment cost is 1. Since the other $(1 - \rho_\ell)n_\ell$ clients have assignment cost 3, the cost of this solution is

$$\beta_\ell k f^\ell + \rho_\ell n_\ell + 3(1 - \rho_\ell)n_\ell = n_\ell(\beta_\ell \gamma + 3 - 2\rho_\ell).$$

By the properties of the approximation algorithm, we know from above that this has cost at most $\alpha n_\ell(\gamma + 1)$, so we have that

$$\beta_\ell \gamma + 3 - 2\rho_\ell \leq \alpha(\gamma + 1), \tag{16.1}$$

or, rearranging,

$$\frac{\beta_\ell \gamma + 3 - 2\rho_\ell}{1 + \gamma} \leq \alpha < 1.463, \tag{16.2}$$

where the last inequality is by hypothesis.

Let c be a constant such that $0 < c < 1$ that we set later. We claim that if $\rho_\ell \leq 1 - e^{-\beta_\ell/c}$ for any ℓ, then $\alpha > 1.463$, a contradiction. Thus, it must the case that $\rho_\ell > 1 - e^{-\beta_\ell/c}$, and from this we shall now show that the algorithm returns a solution to the set cover problem using at most $(c' \ln n)k$ sets for some c', $c < c' < 1$, and for n sufficiently large. Since initially the number of elements to be covered is $n_1 = |E|$, and in the ℓth iteration we cover a ρ_ℓ fraction of them, we have that $n_{\ell+1} = (1 - \rho_\ell)n_\ell$. Since the algorithm ends when we cover all the elements, it must be the case that in the final, rth iteration, $\rho_r = 1$, $n_r \geq 1$, and $|E| \prod_{\ell=1}^{r-1}(1 - \rho_\ell) = n_r \geq 1$.

If the algorithm runs for r iterations of the "while" loop, the total number of sets chosen by the algorithm is $\sum_{\ell=1}^{r} \beta_\ell k$, so that the performance guarantee of the algorithm is $\sum_{\ell=1}^{r} \beta_\ell$. By our claim, $\rho_\ell > 1 - e^{-\beta_\ell/c}$ for all ℓ, so that $\beta_\ell < c \ln \frac{1}{1-\rho_\ell}$ for all ℓ. We also bound β_r in particular: by inequality (16.1), $\beta_r \gamma + 3 - 2\rho_r = \beta_r \gamma + 1 \leq \alpha(\gamma + 1)$. Given the choice of $\gamma = 0.463$, we obtain that $\beta_r \leq \alpha \left(1 + \frac{1}{\gamma}\right) \leq 4\alpha$. Thus, the performance guarantee of the algorithm is

$$\sum_{\ell=1}^{r} \beta_\ell = \sum_{\ell=1}^{r-1} \beta_\ell + \beta_r < c \sum_{\ell=1}^{r-1} \ln \frac{1}{1 - \rho_\ell} + 4\alpha = c \ln \prod_{\ell=1}^{r-1} \frac{1}{1 - \rho_\ell} + 4\alpha.$$

As we noted above, $|E| \prod_{\ell=1}^{r-1}(1 - \rho_\ell) \geq 1$, so that $\ln \prod_{\ell=1}^{r-1} \frac{1}{1-\rho_\ell} \leq \ln |E|$. Substituting this inequality into the one above, we have that the performance guarantee is

$$\sum_{\ell=1}^{r} \beta_\ell \leq c \ln \prod_{\ell=1}^{r-1} \frac{1}{1 - \rho_\ell} + 4\alpha \leq c \ln |E| + 4\alpha < c' \ln n$$

for some c' and n sufficiently large, where $c < c' < 1$. This follows since $n = |E|$ and α is constant.

Now to prove the claim that if $\rho_\ell \leq 1 - e^{-\beta_\ell/c}$ for some ℓ, then $\alpha > 1.463$. Suppose $\rho_\ell \leq 1 - e^{-\beta_\ell/c}$ for some ℓ. For fixed γ and c, set

$$f(\beta_\ell) = \frac{\beta_\ell \gamma + 1 + 2e^{-\beta_\ell/c}}{1 + \gamma} \leq \frac{\beta_\ell \gamma + 3 - 2\rho_\ell}{1 + \gamma}.$$

Thus, by inequality (16.2), $f(\beta_\ell) \leq \alpha$. This inequality remains true if we use a value of β_ℓ that minimizes the left-hand side of the inequality. The derivative $f'(\beta_\ell) = \frac{1}{1+\gamma}(\gamma - \frac{2}{c}e^{-\beta_\ell/c})$; it is zero for $\beta_\ell = c \ln \frac{2}{\gamma c}$. Because $f''(\beta_\ell) = \frac{2}{c^2(1+\gamma)}e^{-\beta_\ell/c} > 0$ for all values of β_ℓ, the function must achieve a minimum at $c \ln \frac{2}{\gamma c}$. For this value of β_ℓ the function has value

$$\frac{1}{1 + \gamma}\left(\gamma c \ln \frac{2}{\gamma c} + 1 + \gamma c\right).$$

Then if we choose $\gamma = 0.463$ and c close to 1, we get $\beta_\ell = 1.46305$, and $f(1.46305) \geq 1.46305$. Since this value of β_ℓ minimizes f, we know that $1.463 < f(\beta_\ell) \leq \alpha$, contradicting the fact that we had an α-approximation algorithm for $\alpha < 1.463$. Thus, it must be the case that $\rho_\ell > 1 - e^{-\beta_\ell/c}$ for all ℓ. □

We get the following corollary immediately from Theorem 1.13.

Corollary 16.16. *There is no α-approximation algorithm for the metric uncapacitated facility location problem with constant $\alpha < 1.463$ unless each problem in NP has an $O(n^{O(\log\log n)})$ time algorithm.*

The result above can be extended to a hardness result for the k-median problem. The extension is not difficult, and we leave it as an exercise for the reader.

Theorem 16.17. *There is no α-approximation algorithm for the k-median problem with constant $\alpha < 1 + \frac{2}{e} \approx 1.736$ unless each problem in NP has an $O(n^{O(\log\log n)})$ time algorithm.*

16.3 Reductions from Probabilistically Checkable Proofs

In this section, we turn to a definition of NP via a notion of probabilistically checkable proofs (PCPs). Probabilistically checkable proofs give us a direct way to show that certain constraint satisfaction problems cannot have particular performance guarantees unless P = NP. Then by using some of the approximation-preserving reductions of the previous section, we will see that PCPs imply hardness results for still other problems.

Before we define what we mean by a probabilistically checkable proof, it will be useful to recall a particular perspective on the problem class NP (see, for instance, Appendix B). Recall that the problem class NP concerns itself with decision problems; each instance of a decision problem is either a "Yes" instance or a "No" instance. For a given decision problem Π, Π is in NP if for any "Yes" instance of Π there is a short, easily verifiable "proof" that the instance is a "Yes" instance, while for any "No" instance, no short proof is convincing. For instance, for the problem of deciding whether a given 3SAT formula is satisfiable or not, a listing of the Boolean values to assign to each variable is a short proof that is easily verifiable: if the instance is a "Yes" instance, and is satisfiable, then it is easy to check that assigning the variables the values given in the proof in fact satisfies all the clauses, whereas if the instance is a "No" instance and is not satisfiable, then no possible assignment of values to variables leads to a satisfying assignment, and so no proof is convincing. More technically, we have a polynomial-time verification algorithm (or *verifier*) V that takes two inputs, the encoding x of the input instance and some proof y; the length of y must be bounded by a polynomial in the length of x (that is, the proof is short). If the instance is a "Yes" instance, then there exists some short proof y such that the verifier outputs "Yes"; we say that the verifier *accepts* the proof y. If the instance is a "No" instance, then for any short proof y, the verifier outputs "No"; we say that the verifier *rejects* all proofs y.

Surprisingly, it is possible to have a much weaker randomized concept of a verifier for any problem in NP. Instead of reading the entire proof y, the verifier will examine only some number of bits of the proof; it will decide which bits to look at by using some number of random bits. It performs some computation only on the bits of the proof, and based on this either accepts or rejects. Informally, for any "Yes" instance x of an NP problem Π, there exists a proof y such that the verifier almost certainly accepts (over all the possible choices of random bits), whereas for any "No" instance and for any proof y, the verifier rejects with reasonable probability. We formalize this notion as follows. For an instance whose encoding x is n bits long, the verifier will use $r(n)$ random bits to select $q(n)$ bits of the proof to examine. It selects a polynomial-time computable function $f : \{0, 1\}^{q(n)} \to \{0, 1\}$, and computes the function f on the $q(n)$ bits. It accepts if the function evaluates to 1, and rejects if the function evaluates to 0. If the input instance is a "Yes" instance, then there exists a polynomially sized proof y such that the verifier accepts with probability at least c, where the probability is taken over the $r(n)$ random bits used by the verifier; the parameter c is called the *completeness* of the verifier. If the input instance is a "No" instance, then for any polynomially sized proof y, the verifier will accept with probability at most $s < c$; the parameter s is called the *soundness* of the verifier. The class of decision problems that have such a verifier is denoted by $\mathrm{PCP}_{c,s}(r(n), q(n))$. We can capture the previous notion of a nonrandomized verifier by noting that if for a particular problem Π all proofs have length at most $p(n)$ for some polynomial p, then $\Pi \in \mathrm{PCP}_{1,0}(0, p(n))$; that is, the verifier uses no randomness, looks at all $p(n)$ bits of the proof, accepts a "Yes" instance with probability 1, and accepts a "No" instance with probability 0.

A truly astonishing fact is that it is possible to capture the class NP with a verifier that looks at just some small constant number of bits of the proof while using only a logarithmic amount of randomness.

Theorem 16.18 (PCP theorem). *There exists a positive constant k such that* $\mathrm{NP} \subseteq \mathrm{PCP}_{1,1/2}(O(\log n), k)$.

While we could now forge ahead and draw implications for the hardness of approximation from this theorem, it is worth spending a few moments to admire the view. Note that since the verifier uses $O(\log n)$ random bits, this is just enough randomness to index a polynomial number of locations in the proof since $2^{c \log n} = n^c$. Additionally, since there are 2^{2^k} different functions on k bits, the verifier selects one of a constant number of functions to evaluate in order to decide whether or not it accepts the proof. Thus, the verifier seems to have remarkably little power: it has just enough randomization to access any bit of the proof, is looking at only a constant number of bits, and is evaluating one of a constant number of functions, and yet this is enough to distinguish between "Yes" and "No" instances of a problem in NP with a reasonable probability!

We can now start to work out the implications of this theorem for the hardness of approximation. The central idea is that given the verifier, we can create from it an instance of a constraint satisfaction problem; in this instance we will try to determine the bits of the proof so as to maximize the verifier's probability of acceptance. Since there is a difference of a factor of 2 in the probability of acceptance (by the PCP theorem) between "Yes" and "No" instances of an NP-complete problem, approximating the maximum constraint satisfaction problem to some factor better than a half will imply that $\mathrm{P} = \mathrm{NP}$.

More formally, given an NP-complete problem Π, and a verifier for Π via the PCP theorem, we consider all $2^{c \log n} = n^c$ possible strings of random bits that the verifier could use. Let x_i be the ith bit of the proof, and let $\mathcal{F}$ be the collection of all possible functions on k bits. Given one of the random strings, for some $f \in \mathcal{F}$, the verifier computes a function $f(x_{i_1}, \ldots, x_{i_k})$. In our constraint satisfaction instance, we create a constraint $f(x_{i_1}, \ldots, x_{i_k})$. By the PCP theorem, for any "Yes" instance of Π, there exists some proof such that the verifier accepts with probability 1; this implies that there is some way of setting the variables $x_i \in \{0, 1\}$ so that all of the constraints $f(x_{i_1}, \ldots, x_{i_k})$ are satisfiable. Similarly, for any "No" instance of Π, for any proof, the verifier accepts with probability at most $1/2$; thus, for any setting of the variables $x_i \in \{0, 1\}$, at most half of the constraints can be satisfiable. Now suppose we have an α-approximation algorithm for this maximum constraint satisfaction problem with $\alpha > \frac{1}{2}$. If the constraint satisfaction instance corresponds to a "Yes" instance of Π, all the constraints are satisfiable, and so our approximation algorithm will satisfy strictly more than half the constraints. If the constraint satisfaction instance corresponds to a "No" instance of Π, at most half the constraints are satisfiable, and our approximation algorithm can satisfy at most half the constraints. Thus, by checking whether we have satisfied strictly more than half the constraints or at most half, we will be able to tell whether the instance of Π was a "Yes" instance or a "No" instance, yielding a polynomial-time algorithm for an NP-complete problem, implying P = NP. In general, if the PCP verifier has completeness c and soundness s, getting an α-approximation algorithm with $\alpha > s/c$ implies that P = NP.

Variants of the PCP theorem have been shown in which the verifier uses particular k-bit functions. Notice that this immediately implies hardness results for constraint satisfaction problems for these particular k-bit functions. For example, let $\text{odd}(x_1, x_2, x_3)$ be a 3-bit function such that $\text{odd}(x_1, x_2, x_3) = 1$ if the sum $x_1 + x_2 + x_3$ is odd and is 0 otherwise. Similarly, let $\text{even}(x_1, x_2, x_3)$ be a 3-bit function that is 1 if the sum of the bits is even and 0 otherwise. We can assume that the functions are always taken over distinct x_i. The following variation on the PCP theorem has been shown.

Theorem 16.19. *For any positive constants $\epsilon, \delta > 0$, it is the case that $NP \subseteq PCP_{1-\epsilon, 1/2+\delta}(O(\log n), 3)$, and the verifier is restricted to use only the functions* odd *and* even.

The resulting constraint satisfaction problem has constraints of the form $\text{odd}(x_i, x_j, x_k)$ and $\text{even}(x_i, x_j, x_k)$ in which the constraints are taken over distinct variables x_i; let us call this the *odd/even constraint satisfaction problem*. Given the discussion above, we have the following immediate corollary.

Corollary 16.20. *If for any constant $\alpha > 1/2$, there is an α-approximation algorithm for the odd/even constraint satisfaction problem, then* P = NP.

However, it is quite easy to see that there is a trivial $1/2$-approximation algorithm for the problem. If we set $x_i = 1$ for all i, then since the constraints are taken over distinct variables, it is the case that all odd constraints are satisfied. If we set $x_i = 0$ for all i, then all even constraints are satisfied. Since either the odd constraints or the even constraints make up at least half the constraints, one of the two settings satisfies at least half the constraints, yielding an easy $1/2$-approximation algorithm. Hence, the corollary above gives a sharp threshold in approximability; we can get a performance guarantee of $1/2$, but any better constant for a performance guarantee implies that P = NP.

The result of Theorem 16.19 has further implications for the MAX E3SAT problem. We will show an L-reduction from the odd/even constraint satisfaction problem to MAX E3SAT. For each odd(x_i, x_j, x_k) constraint, we create four clauses $x_i \vee x_j \vee x_k$, $\bar{x}_i \vee \bar{x}_j \vee x_k, \bar{x}_i \vee x_j \vee \bar{x}_k$, and $x_i \vee \bar{x}_j \vee \bar{x}_k$. We observe that if the variables are set so that odd(x_i, x_j, x_k) is satisfied, then all four of the clauses above are satisfied, whereas if the variables are set so that odd(x_i, x_j, x_k) is not satisfied, then exactly three of the four clauses are satisfied. For each even(x_i, x_j, x_k) constraint, we create four clauses $\bar{x}_i \vee x_j \vee x_k, x_i \vee \bar{x}_j \vee x_k, x_i \vee x_j \vee \bar{x}_k$, and $\bar{x}_i \vee \bar{x}_j \vee \bar{x}_k$. Again, if the variables are set so that even(x_i, x_j, x_k) is satisfied, then all four clauses are satisfied, whereas if even(x_i, x_j, x_k) is not satisfied, then exactly three of the four clauses are satisfied. Let I be the original odd/even constraint satisfaction instance, and I' our MAX E3SAT instance. Suppose an optimal solution to the odd/even constraint satisfaction problem satisfies k^* of m constraints, and our algorithm satisfies four clauses for $\tilde{k}$ of the groups of four clauses and three for each of the $m - \tilde{k}$ remaining groups of four clauses. Then the same settings of variables will satisfy $\tilde{k}$ constraints of the odd/even problem. Let $V' = 4\tilde{k} + 3(m - \tilde{k})$ be the number of E3SAT clauses satisfied by our algorithm, and $V = \tilde{k}$ be the number of odd/even constraints satisfied by the corresponding setting of the variables x_i. Then

$$\mathrm{OPT}(I) - V = k^* - \tilde{k} = [4k^* + 3(m - k^*)] - [4\tilde{k} + 3(m - \tilde{k})] = \mathrm{OPT}(I') - V'.$$

As we previously discussed, it is always possible to satisfy at least half of the m odd/even constraints, so that $k^* \geq \frac{1}{2}m$. Then

$$\mathrm{OPT}(I') = 4k^* + 3(m - k^*) = k^* + 3m \leq k^* + 6k^* = 7k^* = 7\,\mathrm{OPT}(I).$$

Thus, this is an L-reduction with parameters $a = 7$ and $b = 1$. Then from Theorem 16.5 we have that given an α-approximation algorithm for the MAX E3SAT problem, we have a $(7\alpha - 6)$-approximation algorithm for the odd/even constraint satisfaction problem. Given Corollary 16.20, we can deduce that if $7\alpha - 6 > \frac{1}{2}$, then an α-approximation algorithm for MAX E3SAT implies that P = NP. This yields the following theorem.

Theorem 16.21. *If for any constant $\alpha > 13/14 \approx 0.928$, there is an α-approximation algorithm for MAX E3SAT, then* P = NP.

However, we can derive a slightly stronger bound in the following way. Consider any NP-complete problem Π. By Theorem 16.19, for any "Yes" instance of Π, the corresponding instance of the odd/even constraint satisfaction problem has a solution that satisfies a $(1 - \epsilon)$ fraction of the constraints, while for any "No" instance of Π, the corresponding instance of the odd/even constraint satisfaction problem has no solution that satisfies more than a $\frac{1}{2} + \delta$ fraction of the constraints. Now consider the E3SAT instances created by the reduction above. If there is a solution that satisfies at least a $(1 - \epsilon)$ fraction of the m odd/even constraints, then the number of E3SAT clauses that are satisfiable in the reduction above is at least $4(1 - \epsilon)m + 3\epsilon m = (4 - \epsilon)m$. If no solution satisfies more than a $\frac{1}{2} + \delta$ fraction of the constraints, then at most $4\left(\frac{1}{2} + \delta\right)m + 3\left(\frac{1}{2} - \delta\right)m = \left(\frac{7}{2} + \delta\right)m$ E3SAT clauses are satisfiable. Thus, if in polynomial time we can distinguish between E3SAT instances in which at least $(4 - \epsilon)m$ of $4m$ clauses are satisfiable, and instances in which at most $\left(\frac{7}{2} + \delta\right)m$ of $4m$ clauses are satisfiable, we can distinguish between "Yes" and "No" instances of the

NP-complete problem Π in polynomial time, and P = NP. Note that we can distinguish between the two types of instances with an α-approximation algorithm for constant $\alpha > \frac{7}{8}$, since $\alpha \cdot 4(1 - \epsilon)m > \left(\frac{7}{2} + \delta\right)m$ for appropriate choices of ϵ, $\delta > 0$. This leads to Theorem 5.2.

Theorem 16.22 (Theorem 5.2). *If for any constant $\alpha > 7/8 = 0.875$, there is an α-approximation algorithm for MAX E3SAT, then* P = NP.

The reduction above is sometimes called a *gap-preserving reduction*. It preserves a "gap" in the fraction of constraints/clauses that can be satisfied that allows us to distinguish between "Yes" and "No" instances of NP-complete problems; the gap between satisfying at least a $(1 - \epsilon)$ fraction of odd/even constraints and at most a $\left(\frac{1}{2} + \delta\right)$ fraction of odd/even constraints is preserved in the E3SAT instances, in which we can satisfy at least a $\left(1 - \frac{\epsilon}{4}\right)$ fraction of the E3SAT clauses, or at most a $\left(\frac{7}{8} + \frac{\delta}{4}\right)$ fraction of the clauses. This gap allows us to infer that an α-approximation algorithm for MAX E3SAT with constant $\alpha > 7/8$ implies that P = NP.

There is also a direct proof of this result from the PCP theorem. We state it here because it will be useful to us later.

Theorem 16.23. *For any positive constant $\delta > 0$,* NP $\subseteq$ PCP$_{1,7/8+\delta}(O(\log n), 3)$, *and the verifier is restricted to use only functions that check the "or" of three bits or their negations.*

Thus, by our previous discussion, for any $\delta > 0$ no polynomial-time algorithm can distinguish between MAX E3SAT instances in which all clauses are satisfiable, and instances in which a $7/8 + \delta$ fraction of the clauses are satisfiable, unless P = NP.

We can also show a gap-preserving reduction from the odd/even constraint satisfaction problem to the MAX 2SAT problem, yielding an improved hardness bound for MAX 2SAT. For any even constraint even(x_i, x_j, x_k), we create the following twelve 2SAT clauses with four additional variables $y_{00}^\ell, y_{01}^\ell, y_{10}^\ell$, and y_{11}^ℓ for the ℓth constraint:

$$\bar{x}_i \vee \bar{y}_{00}^\ell, \bar{x}_j \vee \bar{y}_{00}^\ell, x_k \vee y_{00}^\ell,$$

$$x_i \vee \bar{y}_{01}^\ell, \bar{x}_j \vee \bar{y}_{01}^\ell, \bar{x}_k \vee y_{01}^\ell, \bar{x}_i \vee \bar{y}_{10}^\ell, x_j \vee \bar{y}_{10}^\ell, \bar{x}_k \vee y_{10}^\ell,$$

$$x_i \vee \bar{y}_{11}^\ell, x_j \vee \bar{y}_{11}^\ell, x_k \vee y_{11}^\ell.$$

We leave it as an exercise to the reader to verify that for any setting of x_i, x_j, and x_k such that the even constraint is satisfied, it is possible to set the y^ℓ variables such that eleven of the twelve clauses are satisfied, while if the even constraint is not satisfied, then there is a setting of the y^ℓ variables that satisfies ten of the twelve clauses, but no more. We further leave it to the reader to obtain a similar set of twelve 2SAT clauses for the odd constraint. With this reduction, if at least $(1 - \epsilon)m$ of m odd/even constraints are satisfiable, then at least $11(1 - \epsilon)m + 10\epsilon m = (11 - \epsilon)m$ of the $12m$ 2SAT clauses are satisfiable, while if only a $\left(\frac{1}{2} + \delta\right)m$ fraction of the odd/even constraints are satisfiable, then at most $11\left(\frac{1}{2} + \delta\right)m + 10\left(\frac{1}{2} - \delta\right)m = \left(\frac{21}{2} + \delta\right)m$ of the $12m$ clauses are satisfiable. Thus, if in polynomial time we can distinguish between 2SAT instances in which at least a $\frac{11}{12} - \frac{\epsilon}{12}$ fraction of the clauses are satisfiable and those in which at most a $\frac{21}{24} + \frac{\delta}{12}$ fraction of the clauses are satisfiable, then we can distinguish between

"Yes" and "No" instances of an NP-complete problem in polynomial time. We can distinguish between such instances with an α-approximation algorithm for the MAX 2SAT problem for constant $\alpha > 21/22$ since then $\alpha \cdot \left(\frac{11}{12} - \frac{\epsilon}{12}\right) > \frac{21}{24} + \frac{\delta}{12}$ for suitable choices of $\epsilon, \delta > 0$. Thus, we have the following theorem.

Theorem 16.24. *If for any constant $\alpha > 21/22$, there is an α-approximation algorithm for MAX 2SAT, then* P $=$ NP *(where $21/22 \approx 0.954$).*

16.4 Reductions from Label Cover

In this section, we define another problem, the label cover problem, that is frequently used in reductions for hardness of approximation results. The label cover problem has both a maximization and a minimization version. In the label cover problem, we have a bipartite graph (V_1, V_2, E). We have a set L_1 of possible labels for the vertices in V_1, and a set L_2 of possible labels for the vertices in V_2. For each edge $(u, v) \in E$, we have a nonempty relation $R_{uv} \subseteq L_1 \times L_2$ of acceptable labels for the edge. If u has a label $\ell_1 \in L_1$ and v has a label $\ell_2 \in L_2$, then the edge (u, v) is satisfied if $(\ell_1, \ell_2) \in R_{(u,v)}$. In the maximization version of the label cover problem, each vertex is assigned exactly one label, and the goal is to assign labels so as to satisfy as many edges as possible. In the minimization version of the problem, each vertex v is assigned a set of labels L_v so that for each edge $(u, v) \in E$, there is some label $\ell_1 \in L_u$ and some label $\ell_2 \in L_v$ so that $(\ell_1, \ell_2) \in R_{(u,v)}$. The goal of the minimization problem is to minimize the total number of labels used; that is, minimize $\sum_{u \in V_1} |L_u| + \sum_{v \in V_2} |L_v|$.

It is sometimes useful to ensure that the graph in the label cover instances is regular; that is, every $u \in V_1$ has the same degree d_1 and every $v \in V_2$ has the same degree d_2. We will call such instances (d_1, d_2)-*regular* label cover instances. If each vertex in both V_1 and V_2 has the same degree d, we will call the instance d-*regular*. Note that if the instance is d-regular, then $|V_1| = |V_2|$.

The maximization label cover problem is related to the unique games problem introduced in Section 13.3; in the case of unique games, we assume that the label sets are the same (so $L_1 = L_2$) and the relation R_{uv} on each edge (u, v) is in fact a permutation π_{uv} on the set of labels, so that for each potential label ℓ of u, there is a unique label $\pi_{uv}(\ell)$ that v can have that satisfies the edge, and vice versa.

We will show that it is hard to approximate both versions of the label cover problem given results we already know. Then we will use a reduction from the maximization version of the label cover problem to show that it is hard to approximate the set cover problem, and we will use a reduction from the minimization version of the label cover problem to show that it is hard to approximate two network design problems. In particular, we will show that it is hard to approximate a directed version of the generalized Steiner tree problem introduced in Section 7.4 and a vertex-connectivity version of the survivable network design problem introduced in Section 11.3.

In order to show that it is hard to approximate the maximization version of the label cover problem, we give a gap-preserving reduction from the MAX E3SAT problem. Given an instance of the MAX E3SAT problem, we create an instance of the label cover problem as follows. We create a vertex i in V_1 for each variable x_i in the E3SAT instance, and a vertex j in V_2 for each clause C_j. We create an edge (i, j) for $i \in V_1$ and $j \in V_2$ exactly when the variable x_i occurs in the clause C_j (whether positively or negatively). The labels L_1 for V_1 will be the set $L_1 = \{\text{true, false}\}$. The labels L_2 for V_2 will be all possible triples of Boolean values, so that $L_2 = L_1 \times L_1 \times L_1$; intuitively, we label $i \in V_1$ with the Boolean value b that is assigned to the variable x_i, and we label $j \in V_2$ with the three Boolean values (b_p, b_q, b_r) assigned to the three variables x_p, x_q, x_r in the clause. Note that for an edge (i, j), the variable x_i is one of the variables x_p, x_q, x_r in the clause C_j; that is, $i = p$ or $i = q$ or $i = r$. Then for an edge $(i, j) \in E$, the relation R_{ij} is the set of all $(b, (b_p, b_q, b_r)) \in L_1 \times L_2$ such that (b_p, b_q, b_r) satisfy the clause C_j and $b = b_i$. For example, if $x_1 \vee \bar{x}_2 \vee \bar{x}_3$ is the first E3SAT clause C_1, then we will have edges $(1, 1)$, $(2, 1)$, and $(3, 1)$ in the edge set, and the relation R_{11} is as follows (where each element in R_{11} is given in the form $(x_1, (x_1, x_2, x_3))$):

$$R_{11} = \big\{(\text{true}, (\text{true, true, true})), (\text{true}, (\text{true, true, false})), (\text{true}, (\text{true, false, true})),$$
$$(\text{true}, (\text{true, false, false})), (\text{false}, (\text{false, true, false})), (\text{false}, (\text{false, false, true})),$$
$$(\text{false}, (\text{false, false, false}))\big\}.$$

We note that given a label for clause C_j and an edge (i, j), there is at most one label for x_i that will satisfy the relation R_{ij}; for instance, in the example above, if C_1 is labeled (false, false, false), then only the label false for x_1 satisfies the relation. This is a useful property of these instances that we will exploit later in the section.

Now to show that this is a gap-preserving reduction. If there are m clauses in the E3SAT instance I, then there are $3m$ edges in the label cover instance I'. We claim that given a setting of the x_i that satisfies k clauses, we can construct a solution to the label cover instance that satisfies $3k + 2(m - k)$ edges. We obtain this solution by labeling every vertex $i \in V_1$ with the label corresponding to the setting of x_i. For each satisfied clause C_j, we label $j \in V_2$ with the corresponding setting of the three variables. For the three edges (i, j) incident on j, all three edges are satisfied. For each unsatisfied clause C_j, we label $j \in V_2$ with a label of variable settings that flips the setting of one of the variables so as to satisfy the clause. Then two of the three edges incident on j are satisfied and one is not (the one corresponding to the variable that was flipped). By the same logic, given any labeling of V_1, we can always modify the labels of V_2 so that each $j \in V_2$ has either 2 or 3 satisfied edges incident on it. Thus, given a solution to the label cover instance, we can assign each x_i in the E3SAT instance with the value of the label of $i \in V_1$. Each $j \in V_2$ that has three satisfied edges incident on it must correspond to a satisfied clause C_j in this assignment. Thus, if the label cover solution satisfies $3k + 2(m - k)$ edges, then k clauses of the E3SAT instance are satisfied.

We know from Theorem 16.23 that it is NP-hard to distinguish between E3SAT instances in which all m clauses are satisfiable, and those in which at most $\left(\frac{7}{8} + \delta\right) m$ clauses are satisfiable. By the reduction above, if all m clauses are satisfiable, then all $3m$ edges of the label cover instance are satisfiable, whereas if at most $\left(\frac{7}{8} + \delta\right) m$ clauses are satisfiable, then at most $3m \left(\frac{7}{8} + \delta\right) + 2m \left(\frac{1}{8} - \delta\right) = \left(\frac{23}{8} + \delta\right) m$ of the $3m$ edges of the label cover instance are satisfiable. Thus, distinguishing between the case in which all edges of the label cover instance are satisfiable and the case in which a $\left(\frac{23}{24} + \frac{\delta}{3}\right)$ fraction of the edges are satisfiable is NP-hard. Given an α-approximation algorithm for the maximization version of the label cover problem in which $\alpha > 23/24$, we can distinguish between these two types of instances. Thus, we obtain the following theorem.

Theorem 16.25. *If for any constant* $\alpha > \frac{23}{24}$ *there is an* α-*approximation algorithm for the maximization version of the label cover problem, then* $P = NP$.

We can show the same result for a different constant α for the $(5, 3)$-regular version of the label cover problem, though we do not give the details. In order to show this, we first claim that it is still hard to approximate the MAX E3SAT problem on instances in which each variable appears in exactly five clauses; in particular, in polynomial time we cannot distinguish between instances in which all clauses are satisfiable, and instances in which at most a ρ fraction of the clauses are satisfiable, for some constant $\rho < 1$. By following the same reduction as above, we obtain an instance of the maximization version of the label cover problem in which each $i \in V_1$ (corresponding to a variable x_i) has degree five, and each $j \in V_2$ (corresponding to a clause C_j) has degree exactly three. Thus, the instance is $(5,3)$-regular, and it is still hard to distinguish in polynomial time between instances in which all the edges are satisfiable, and instances in which at most an α fraction of the edges are satisfiable for some constant $\alpha < 1$. It is still also the case that given an edge $(u, v) \in E$, and a label ℓ_2 for $v \in V_2$, there is at most one label ℓ_1 for u such that $(\ell_1, \ell_2) \in R_{uv}$. Following the rest of the reduction above then gives the following.

Theorem 16.26. *If for a particular constant* $\alpha < 1$ *there is an* α *approximation algorithm for the maximization version of the label cover problem on* $(5,3)$-*regular instances, then* $P = NP$.

From the hardness of the label cover problem on $(5, 3)$-regular instances, we can derive the hardness of the maximization version of the label cover problem on d-regular instances for $d = 15$. Given a (d_1, d_2)-regular instance (V_1, V_2, E) with labels L_1 and L_2, we create a new instance (V_1', V_2', E') in which $V_1' = V_1 \times V_2$, $V_2' = V_2 \times V_1$, $L_1' = L_1$, and $L_2' = L_2$. For any $(u, v) \in V_1'$ and $(v', u') \in V_2'$, we create an edge $((u, v), (v', u')) \in E'$ exactly when $(u, v') \in E$ and $(u', v) \in E$; then $|E'| = |E|^2$. If we label $(u, v) \in V_1'$ with label ℓ_1 and $(v', u') \in V_2'$ with label ℓ_2, then (ℓ_1, ℓ_2) is in the relation $R'_{((u,v),(v',u'))}$ for the edge $((u, v), (v', u'))$ if and only if $(\ell_1, \ell_2) \in R_{uv'}$. By construction, for any fixed $(u', v) \in E$, there is a copy of the original instance: each edge (u, v') in the original instance corresponds to an edge $((u, v), (v', u'))$ in the new instance. If $(u, v) \in V_1'$ is labeled with ℓ_1 and $(v', u') \in V_2$ is labeled with ℓ_2, then the edge is satisfied in the new instance if and only if labeling $u \in V_1$ with ℓ_1 and $v' \in V_2$ with ℓ_2 satisfies the edge (u, v') in the original instance. Thus, if all edges are satisfiable in the original instance, then all edges will be satisfiable in the new instance, whereas if at most an α fraction of the edges are satisfiable in the original instance, then for each fixed $(u', v) \in E$, at most an α fraction of the corresponding set of edges $((u, v), (v', u'))$ are satisfiable. Since the edges of the new instance can be partitioned according to (u', v), it follows that if at most an α fraction of the edges of the original instance can be satisfied, then at most an α fraction of edges of the new instance can be satisfied. To see that the new instance is d-regular, fix any vertex $(u, v) \in V_1'$. Then since the original instance is (d_1, d_2)-regular, there are d_1 possible vertices $v' \in V_2$

such that (u, v') is an edge in the original instance, and d_2 possible vertices $u' \in V_1$ such that (u', v) is an edge in the original instance. Hence, there are $d = d_1 d_2$ edges $((u, v), (v', u'))$ incident on the vertex $(u, v) \in V_1'$. The argument that each vertex in V_2' has degree $d = d_1 d_2$ is similar. Finally, suppose in the original instance it was the case that given $(u, v) \in E$ and a label ℓ_2 for $v \in V_2$, there is at most one label ℓ_1 for u such that $(\ell_1, \ell_2) \in R_{uv}$. Then in the new instance, given an edge $((u, v), (v', u')) \in E'$ and a label ℓ_2 for $(v', u') \in V_2'$, again there can be at most one ℓ_1 for $(u, v) \in V_1'$ such that (ℓ_1, ℓ_2) is in the relation for the edge. We thus have the following result.

Theorem 16.27. *If for a particular constant $\alpha < 1$ there is an α-approximation algorithm for the maximization version of the label cover problem on 15-regular instances, then* P = NP.

We can prove a theorem with a much stronger hardness bound by using a technique similar to the one we used for the independent set problem, and reducing the maximization version of the label cover problem to itself. Given an instance I of the maximization version of the label cover problem with vertex sets V_1 and V_2, label sets L_1 and L_2, edges E, and relations R_{uv} for all $(u, v) \in E$, we create a new instance I' of the problem with vertex sets $V_1' = V_1^k = V_1 \times V_1 \times \cdots \times V_1$ and $V_2' = V_2^k$, with label sets $L_1' = L_1^k$ and $L_2' = L_2^k$, and with edge set $E' = E^k$ for any positive integer k. Consider an edge $(u, v) \in E'$; let $u \in V_1'$ be a vertex such that $u = (u_1, \ldots, u_k)$, where each $u_i \in V_1$, and let $v \in V_2'$ be a vertex such that $v = (v_1, \ldots, v_k)$, where each $v_i \in V_2$, so that $(u_i, v_i) \in E$ for all i. Then the relation R_{uv}' for edge $(u, v) \in E'$ is given so that if u is labeled with $(\ell_1', \ell_2', \ldots, \ell_k') \in L_1'$ and v is labeled with $(\ell_1'', \ell_2'', \ldots, \ell_k'') \in L_2'$, then the pair of labels is in R_{uv}' if and only if $(\ell_i', \ell_i'') \in R_{u_i,v_i}$ for all $i = 1, \ldots, k$. Suppose it is the case in the original instance that given a label ℓ_2 for $v \in V_2$ and an edge (u, v) then there is at most one label $\ell_1 \in L_1$ for u such that $(\ell_1, \ell_2) \in R_{uv}$ (as we argued is true for the hard instances of Theorem 16.27); then this property also holds for this new instance. Similarly, if the original instance is d-regular, then the new instance is d^k-regular. If the size of the original instance I is n, then the size of the new instance I' is $O(n^{O(k)})$. If $m = |E| = \text{OPT}(I)$ and all edges of the original instance can be satisfied, then by labeling each of the new vertices with the corresponding k-tuple of labels, we can satisfy all $m^k = |E'|$ edges of the new instance, so that $\text{OPT}(I') = m^k$. However, if $\text{OPT}(I)$ is somewhat less than m, then the following theorem shows that the optimum of the new instance is much smaller.

Theorem 16.28. *There is a constant $c > 0$, such that for any label cover instance I with m edges and $L = |L_1| + |L_2|$ total labels, if $\text{OPT}(I) = |E|(1 - \delta)$, then $\text{OPT}(I') \le |E'|(1 - \delta)^{\frac{ck}{\log L}}$.*

The proof of this theorem is highly nontrivial, and we will not give it here.

From the reduction above, we can derive the stronger hardness result. We first observe that in our reduction from MAX E3SAT to the label cover problem, we use $L = 2 + 8 = 10$ labels. Now we apply Theorem 16.28 for some fixed k. As we stated above, there is no polynomial-time algorithm that can distinguish between d-regular label cover instances that satisfy all edges and those that satisfy some constant fraction $\alpha < 1$ of edges unless P = NP. Then by the theorem, with $\delta > 0$ for some constant δ, we know that if $\text{OPT}(I) = |E|$, then $\text{OPT}(I') = |E'|$, while if $\text{OPT}(I) = |E|(1 - \delta)$, then $\text{OPT}(I') \leq |E'|(1 - \delta)^{\frac{ck}{\log 10}}$. Thus, for any fixed k, if we have a polynomial-time algorithm that can distinguish between whether all $|E'|$ edges are satisfied in I' and only $|E'|(1 - \delta)^{\frac{ck}{\log 10}}$ edges are satisfied, then we can distinguish whether $\text{OPT}(I) = |E|$ and $\text{OPT}(I) = |E|(1 - \delta)$, and then P = NP. This implies that a performance guarantee better than $(1 - \delta)^{\frac{ck}{\log 10}}$ for the maximization version of the label cover problem is not possible for a particular constant $\delta > 0$ unless P = NP. We state this conclusion as follows.

Theorem 16.29. *There is a constant $c > 0$, such that for any positive integer k, we cannot distinguish between d-regular instances I of the maximization label cover problem in which $\text{OPT}(I) = |E|$ and $\text{OPT}(I) = |E|(1 - \delta)^{\frac{ck}{\log 10}}$ for some constant $\delta > 0$ unless each problem in NP has an algorithm running in time $O(n^{O(k)})$.*

We can easily derive the following corollary.

Corollary 16.30. *There is no α-approximation algorithm for any constant $\alpha \leq 1$ for the maximization version of the label cover problem unless P = NP.*

Proof. Given any α-approximation algorithm for constant α, if we set k so that $(1 - \delta)^{\frac{ck}{\log 10}} < \alpha$, then k is constant, and so $O(n^{O(k)})$ is a polynomial. Hence, in polynomial time we will be able to distinguish between label cover instances in which all edges are satisfied and those in which at most a $(1 - \delta)^{\frac{ck}{\log 10}}$ fraction of edges are satisfied. $\qquad\square$

Using Theorem 16.29, we can get a very strong hardness bound if we are willing to weaken the hypothesis that P $\neq$ NP. If we set $k = C(\log|E|)^{\frac{1-\epsilon}{\epsilon}}$ for some $\epsilon > 0$, then for an appropriate choice of C we have $\frac{ck^\epsilon}{\log 10} \log_2(1 - \delta) \leq -(\log|E|)^{1-\epsilon}$, which implies that $\frac{ck}{\log 10} \log_2(1 - \delta) \leq -(k \log|E|)^{1-\epsilon}$ or $(1 - \delta)^{ck/\log 10} \leq 2^{-\log^{1-\epsilon}|E|^k} = 2^{-\log^{1-\epsilon}|E'|}$. However, to create the instance I' requires $O(|E|^{O(k)}) = O(|E|^{O(\log^{O((1-\epsilon)/\epsilon)}|E|)})$ time. Thus, if we have a polynomial-time algorithm that can distinguish between the case in which all $|E'|$ edges of I' are satisfiable, and those in which at least $2^{-\log^{1-\epsilon}|E'|}|E'|$ edges are satisfiable, this implies only that NP has algorithms that run in time $O(n^{O(\log^c n)})$ for some constant c. The running time $O(n^{O(\log^c n)})$ for constant c is sometimes called *quasipolynomial time*. This gives us the following theorem.

Theorem 16.31. *For any $\epsilon > 0$, there is no $2^{-\log^{1-\epsilon} m}$-approximation algorithm for the maximization version of the label cover problem with d-regular instances unless NP has quasipolynomial-time algorithms.*

We can use the hardness of the maximization version of the label cover problem to derive a slightly weakened version of the hardness of the unweighted set cover problem claimed in Theorems 1.13 and 1.14. We will show the following.

Theorem 16.32. *There is no $(\frac{1}{32} \log N)$-approximation algorithm for the unweighted set cover problem (where N is the size of the ground set of elements) unless each problem in NP has an algorithm running in time $O(n^{O(\log \log n)})$.*

We will need the following version of the hardness of the maximization version of the label cover problem, which we can derive from our prior results. We will also need a property that we observed earlier, namely, that for these hard instances, given a label $\ell_2 \in L_2$ for $v \in V_2$, and an edge (u, v), then there is at most one label $\ell_1 \in L_1$ for $u \in V_1$ such that $(\ell_1, \ell_2) \in R_{uv}$.

Lemma 16.33. *There exist d-regular instances of the maximization version of the label cover problem such that we cannot distinguish in polynomial time between instances in which all edges are satisfiable and those in which at most a $1/\log^2(|L_1||E|)$ fraction of the edges are satisfiable unless each problem in NP has an algorithm running in time $O(n^{O(\log \log n)})$.*

Proof. We apply Theorem 16.29 with $k = \frac{2 \log 10}{c} \log_{1/(1-\delta)} (\log |L_1||E|) = O(\log \log n)$, where n is the input size of the label cover instance. The reduction takes time $O(n^{O(k)}) = O(n^{O(\log \log n)})$, and we cannot distinguish between instances in which all the edges are satisfiable, and those in which at most a $(1 - \delta)^{\frac{ck}{\log 10}} = (1 - \delta)^{2 \log_{1/(1-\delta)}(\log |L_1||E|)} = 1/\log^2(|L_1||E|)$ fraction of edges are satisfiable. $\square$

The basic idea of the reduction is that given a label cover instance as in Lemma 16.33, we will create a set cover instance in which there is a set $S_{u,i}$ for each $u \in V_1$ and $i \in L_1$, and a set $S_{v,j}$ for each $v \in V_2$ and $j \in L_2$. The ground set of elements will be a set $E \times U$ for some set U; let $N = |E||U|$ be the number of ground elements. We will construct these sets so that given some edge (u, v) in the label cover instance, and labels $(i, j) \in R_{uv}$, then either the set cover must have chosen the sets $S_{u,i}$ and $S_{v,j}$, or it must have chosen $\Omega(\log N)$ times more sets to cover the elements in the ground set from $\{(u, v)\} \times U$.

To obtain sets with this property, we will need the notion of a partition system. A *partition system* on a universe U of size s with t pairs of sets for a parameter h consists of a set $U = \{1, \ldots, s\} = [s]$, and t pairs of sets $(A_1, \bar{A}_1)$ (where $\bar{A}_1 = U - A_1$), $(A_2, \bar{A}_2), \ldots, (A_t, \bar{A}_t)$. Furthermore, if from each of h of the pairs of sets we choose one set from the pair, the union of these h sets is a strict subset of U. More formally, if we choose h distinct indices $i_1, i_2, \ldots, i_h$ and for each index i_j let either $B_{i_j} = A_{i_j}$ or $B_{i_j} = \bar{A}_{i_j}$, then $\bigcup_{j=1}^{h} B_{i_j} \subset U$. We will later show how such a partition system can be constructed with size $s = |U| = 2^{2h+2} t^2$; we will later set $t = |L_1|$ and $h = \log |L_1||E|$, and will show that $h = \Omega(\log N)$. Intuitively, we will want to create the sets so that if for an edge (u, v) of the label cover instance, we have $(i, j) \in R_{uv}$, then one set $S_{u,i}$ contains $\{(u, v)\} \times A_k$ for some index k and $S_{v,j}$ contains $\{(u, v)\} \times \bar{A}_k$. Thus, their union contains $\{(u, v)\} \times U$, while otherwise it will take at least $h = \Omega(\log N)$ sets to contain $\{(u, v)\} \times U$.

We now give the construction following this intuition. Given the partition system with universe U with $t = |L_1|$ pairs of sets $(A_1, \bar{A}_1), \ldots, (A_t, \bar{A}_t)$ with parameter $h = \log |L_1||E|$, we create a set cover instance as follows. As stated previously, the ground set of elements will be the set $E \times U$, and we create a set $S_{u,i}$ for each $u \in V_1$ and $i \in L_1$, and a set $S_{v,j}$ for each $v \in V_2$ and $j \in L_2$. Recall that for the hard instances of the label cover problem, for any edge $(u, v) \in E$ and any label $j \in L_2$, there is at most one label $i \in L_1$ such that $(i, j) \in R_{uv}$. Then for all $u \in V_1$ and $i \in L_1$ we set

$$S_{u,i} = \{((u, v), a) : v \in V_2, (u, v) \in E, a \in A_i\}$$

and

$$S_{v,j} = \left\{((u, v), a) : u \in V_1, (u, v) \in E, (i, j) \in R_{uv}, a \in \bar{A}_i\right\}.$$

In the definition of $S_{v,j}$ note that given j and edge (u, v), there is at most one $(i, j) \in R_{uv}$, and hence the set $\bar{A}_i$ is well defined.

We argue that this gives us the hardness result that we want. First, given a solution to the label cover instance that satisfies all edges, we claim that there is a solution to the set cover instance that uses only $|V_1| + |V_2|$ sets; in particular if $u \in V_1$ is labeled with i, then we choose set $S_{u,i}$, and if $v \in V_2$ is labeled with j, then we choose set $S_{v,j}$. Since $(i, j) \in R_{uv}$, it is the case that

$$\{(u, v)\} \times U = \{(u, v)\} \times (A_i \cup \bar{A}_i) \subseteq S_{u,i} \cup S_{v,j}.$$

Since all edges are satisfied, it is the case that $\{(u, v)\} \times U$ is contained in the union of all selected sets for all $(u, v) \in E$, and thus the entire ground set is covered.

Next, we need to argue that given a relatively small solution to the set cover instance, we can satisfy a relatively large fraction of the edges of the label cover instance.

Lemma 16.34. *Given a solution to the set cover instance using at most $\frac{h}{8}(|V_1| + |V_2|)$ sets, we can find in polynomial time a solution to the label cover instance satisfying at least $\frac{2}{h^2}|E|$ edges.*

Proof. For $u \in V_1$, let n_u be the number of sets $S_{u,i}$ in the set cover, and for $v \in V_2$, let n_v be the number of sets $S_{v,j}$ in the set cover. Let $E_1 = \{(u, v) \in E : n_u \geq h/2\}$ and let $E_2 = \{(u, v) \in E : n_v \geq h/2\}$. Since there are at most $\frac{h}{8}(|V_1| + |V_2|)$ sets in the set cover solution, there can be at most $1/4$ of the vertices in $V_1 \cup V_2$ that have n_u or n_v at least $h/2$. Since the label cover instance is d-regular, $|E_1 \cup E_2| \leq \frac{1}{2}|E|$. Let $E_0 = E - E_1 - E_2$. Then for any edge $(u, v) \in E_0$, $n_u + n_v < h$, so that the number of sets $S_{u,i}$ and $S_{v,j}$ in the set cover is less than h. By the property of partition system, then, in order for the elements in $\{(u, v)\} \times U$ to be covered, it must be the case that for (u, v) there are labels $i \in L_1$ and $j \in L_2$ such that sets $S_{u,i}$ and $S_{v,j}$ are in the set cover and $S_{v,j} \supseteq \{(u, v)\} \times \bar{A}_i$, implying that $(i, j) \in R_{uv}$. Suppose that for each $u \in V_1$ we pick a label i for u by randomly choosing a set $S_{u,i}$ from all such sets in the set cover, and similarly for all $v \in V_2$. For each edge $(u, v) \in E_0$, since there is at least one labeling out of the $(h/2)^2$ possible choices of labels for u and v that will satisfy the edge, the probability that the edge is satisfied is at least $1/(h/2)^2 = 4/h^2$. Thus, the expected number of satisfied edges is at least

$$\sum_{(u,v) \in E_0} \frac{4}{h^2} = \frac{4}{h^2}|E_0| \geq \frac{2}{h^2}|E|.$$

We can derandomize the algorithm using the method of conditional expectations. $\square$

We can now prove the desired theorem on the hardness of the set cover problem.

Theorem 16.32. *There is no* $(\frac{1}{32} \log N)$-*approximation algorithm for the unweighted set cover problem (where N is the size of the ground set of elements) unless each problem in NP has an algorithm running in time $O(n^{O(\log \log n)})$.*

Proof. Given the label cover instance (V_1, V_2, E) with label sets $|L_1|$ and $|L_2|$, we set $h = \log |E||L_1|$ and $t = |L_1|$. Then the size of the partition system has $s = |U| = 2^{2h+2}t^2 = 4(|E||L_1|)^2|L_1|^2 = 4|E|^2|L_1|^4$. By construction of the set cover instance, the size of the ground set is $N = |E||U| = 4|E|^3|L_1|^4 \leq (|E||L_1|)^4$ if $|E| \geq 4$; then $h \geq \frac{1}{4} \log N$. Given an instance of the label cover problem in which all edges are satisfiable, we know that there is a solution to the set cover instance in which we need $|V_1| + |V_2|$ sets. If for such instances we can obtain a set cover of size at most $\frac{h}{8}(|V_1| + |V_2|)$, then by Lemma 16.34 we can obtain a solution to the maximization version of the label cover problem satisfying at least a $2/h^2 > 1/\log^2(|L_1||E|)$ fraction of the edges; this will allow us to distinguish between instances of the label cover problem in which all of the edges are satisfiable and instances in which at most a $1/\log^2(|L_1||E|)$ fraction of edges are satisfiable. If we have an approximation algorithm for the unweighted set cover problem with performance guarantee at most $h/8$, we can distinguish such instances in polynomial time. Note that $h/8 = \frac{1}{8} \log |E||L_1| \geq \frac{1}{32} \log N$. Thus, by Lemma 16.33, there cannot be an approximation algorithm for the unweighted set cover problem with performance guarantee $\frac{1}{32} \log N$ unless each problem in NP has an algorithm running in time $O(n^{O(\log \log n)})$. □

To finish the hardness result for the set cover problem, we need to give the construction of the partition system. There is a deterministic algorithm for constructing systems of size $2^{2h+2}t^2$; however, we give a simpler randomized algorithm that needs a somewhat smaller size.

Lemma 16.35. *Given h and t, there is a randomized algorithm for constructing a partition system of size $s = 2^h h \ln(4t) \leq 2^{2h+2}t^2$ with high probability.*

Proof. We pick each set A_i uniformly at random from the set 2^U of all possible subsets of U. Suppose we select one particular set of h indices $i_1 < i_2 < \cdots < i_h$ and sets B_{i_j} such that for each j either $B_{i_j} = A_{i_j}$ or $B_{i_j} = \bar{A}_{i_j}$. There are $\binom{t}{h} 2^h$ ways to select these indices and choose the sets B_{i_j}. For a given choice, consider the probability that $\bigcup_{j=1}^{h} B_{i_j} = U$. By the random construction of the sets A_i, the probability that any given $u \in U$ is in this union is independent of the probability that any other $u' \in U$ is in the union. The probability that $u \notin \bigcup_{j=1}^{h} B_{i_j}$ is the probability that for each index j, for the pair $(A_{i_j}, \bar{A}_{i_j})$ the element u is not in the set we choose. For each pair, the probability that u is not in the chosen set is $1/2$, and so the probability is $1/2^h$. Thus,

$$\Pr\left[\bigcup_{j=1}^{h} B_{i_j} = U\right] = \left(1 - \frac{1}{2^h}\right)^s.$$

Thus, the probability that the sets A_i do not form a partition system is at most

$$\binom{t}{h} 2^h \left(1 - \frac{1}{2^h}\right)^s \leq (2t)^h e^{-s/2^h} = (2t)^h \cdot e^{-h \ln(4t)} \leq \frac{1}{2^h}.$$

Given a choice of $h = \log|L_1||E|$, the sets A_i form the desired partition system with probability at least $1 - \frac{1}{|E||L_1|}$. □

We now turn to proving bounds on the approximability of the minimization version of the label cover problem. To do this, we will show that a $2^{\log^{1-\epsilon} m}$-approximation algorithm for d-regular instances of the minimization version of the label cover problem implies a $2^{-\log^{1-\epsilon} m}$-approximation algorithm for d-regular instances of the maximization version of the problem, which implies that NP has quasipolynomial-time algorithms. We first need the following lemma.

Lemma 16.36. *Given a d-regular instance of the label cover problem and a solution that uses at most $K(|V_1| + |V_2|)$ labels and satisfies all the edges, there is a polynomial-time algorithm to choose a single label per vertex so that at least $1/32K^2$ edges are satisfied.*

Proof. This lemma is similar to Lemma 16.34, which we used in the reduction to the set cover problem. We give a randomized algorithm for the problem, and assert that by using the method of conditional expectations we can get a deterministic version that does at least as well. Let L_v be the set of labels assigned to node $v \in V_1 \cup V_2$, and let $n_v = |L_v|$ be the number of labels in the set assigned a node $v \in V_1 \cup V_2$. For each $v \in V_1 \cup V_2$ we select a single label at random from L_v and assign it to v. For each edge (u, v) there exists some label $i \in L_u$ and $j \in L_v$ such that (u, v) is satisfied, so that the probability that the random choice of labels satisfies (u, v) is at least $\frac{1}{n_u n_v}$.

Let $E_1 = \{(u, v) \in E : n_u \geq 4K\}$ and let $E_2 = \{(u, v) \in E : n_v \geq 4K\}$. Since the total number of labels used is at most $K(|V_1| + |V_2|)$, at most $1/4$ of the nodes in $V_1 \cup V_2$ have at least $4K$ labels. Since the instance is d-regular, $|E_1 \cup E_2| \leq \frac{1}{2}|E|$. Let $E_0 = E - E_1 - E_2$, so that $|E_0| \geq \frac{1}{2}|E|$. Then the expected number of satisfied edges by choosing a label uniformly at random is

$$\sum_{(u,v) \in E} \frac{1}{n_u n_v} \geq \sum_{(u,v) \in E_0} \frac{1}{n_u n_v} \geq \sum_{(u,v) \in E_0} \frac{1}{(4K)(4K)} \geq \frac{|E|}{32K^2}.$$ □

Now we can prove the hardness of the minimization version of the label cover problem.

Theorem 16.37. *For any $\epsilon > 0$, there is no $2^{\log^{1-\epsilon} m}$-approximation algorithm for d-regular instances of the minimization version of the label cover problem unless NP has quasipolynomial-time algorithms.*

Proof. We prove this by a gap-preserving reduction from the hardness of the maximization version of the label cover problem for d-regular instances given in Theorem 16.31. Suppose we have an α-approximation algorithm for d-regular instances of the minimization version of the label cover problem. Given a d-regular instance (V_1, V_2, E) of the maximization problem in which all edges are satisfiable, we know that only $|V_1| + |V_2|$ labels are needed to satisfy all edges, so that the algorithm will return a solution using at most $\alpha(|V_1| + |V_2|)$ labels. Then by Lemma 16.36, we can get a solution to the maximization problem that satisfies at least a $1/32\alpha^2$ fraction of the edges. If $1/32\alpha^2 > 2^{-\log^{1-\epsilon} m}$, then we would be able to distinguish between instances of the maximization problem in which all edges are satisfied and those in which at most a $2^{-\log^{1-\epsilon} m}$ fraction of the edges can be satisfied. Hence, it must be the case that $\alpha \geq \frac{1}{\sqrt{32}} \cdot 2^{\frac{1}{2}\log^{1-\epsilon} m} = 2^{\frac{1}{2}(\log^{1-\epsilon} m - 5)}$, unless NP has quasipolynomial-time algorithms. For sufficiently large m, $\frac{1}{2}(\log^{1-\epsilon} m - 5) \geq \log^{1-2\epsilon} m$, so that there cannot be a $2^{\log^{1-\epsilon'} m}$-approximation algorithm for the minimization version of the label cover problem unless NP has quasipolynomial-time algorithms, for $\epsilon' = 2\epsilon$. Since the hardness result for the maximization problem holds for any $\epsilon > 0$, the result also holds for the minimization problem for any $\epsilon' > 0$. $\qquad\square$

The minimization version of the label cover problem is useful for proving the hardness of network design problems. In particular, we reduce the minimization version of the label cover problem to the directed generalized Steiner tree problem, and then show how this leads to the hardness of a vertex-connectivity version of the survivable network design problem. The *directed generalized Steiner tree problem* is a version of the generalized Steiner tree problem (introduced in Section 7.4) in directed graphs. We are given as input a directed graph $G = (V, A)$, nonnegative costs $c_a \geq 0$ for all arcs $a \in A$, and k pairs of vertices $s_i, t_i \in V$. The goal is to find a minimum-cost subset of arcs $F \subseteq A$ such that there is an s_i-t_i path in the set of selected arcs; that is, there is a directed path from s_i to t_i in (V, F) for all i.

Lemma 16.38. *Given an α-approximation algorithm for the directed generalized Steiner tree problem, we can obtain an α-approximation algorithm for the minimization version of the label cover problem.*

Proof. Given an instance of the minimization version of the label cover problem, we reduce it to an instance of the directed generalized Steiner tree problem. Given any feasible solution to the label cover instance, we can create a feasible solution to the generalized Steiner tree instance whose cost is equal to the number of labels used. Furthermore, given any feasible solution to the generalized Steiner tree instance, we can obtain a feasible solution to the label cover instance using labels equal to the cost of the generalized Steiner tree instance. Thus, the optimal values of the two instances are exactly the same. Also, we can use an α-approximation algorithm for the directed generalized Steiner tree problem to give an α-approximation algorithm for the label cover problem by first reducing the label cover instance to a generalized Steiner tree instance, running the α-approximation algorithm on it, and then translating the feasible solution obtained back to a feasible solution for the label cover instance. If OPT_{LC} is the value of an optimal solution to the label cover instance, and OPT_{GST} is the value of an optimal solution to the generalized Steiner tree instance, then this algorithm produces a solution to the label cover instance of value at most $\alpha \, \text{OPT}_{GST} = \alpha \, \text{OPT}_{LC}$.

Let (V_1, V_2, E) be the input graph for the label cover instance, let L_1 and L_2 be the labels, and let R_{uv} be the relation for each $(u, v) \in E$. We create an instance of the directed generalized Steiner tree problem as follows. We create a vertex set $V = V_1 \cup V_2 \cup (V_1 \times L_1) \cup (V_2 \times L_2)$. We will denote the vertices in $V_1 \times L_1$ and $V_2 \times L_2$ by pairs such as (u, ℓ_1) and (v, ℓ_2). We also create a set of arcs $A = A_1 \cup A_2 \cup A_3$, where $A_1 = \{(u, (u, \ell_1)) : u \in V_1, \ell_1 \in L_1\}$, $A_2 = \{((u, \ell_1), (v, \ell_2)) : u \in V_1, \ell_1 \in L_1, v \in V_2, \ell_2 \in L_2, (\ell_1, \ell_2) \in R_{uv}\}$, and $A_3 = \{((v, \ell_2), v) : v \in V_2, \ell_2 \in L_2\}$. We set the cost of arcs in A_1 and A_3 to be 1, and the cost of arcs in A_2 to be 0. For each edge $(u, v) \in E$, we create an s_i-t_i pair with $s_i = u$ and $t_i = v$.

Given a feasible labeling for the label cover instance, with label sets L_u for each $u \in V_1$, and L_v for each $v \in V_2$, we create a feasible solution to the generalized Steiner tree instance as follows. For $u \in V_1$ and each label $\ell_1 \in L_u$, we add arc $(u, (u, \ell_1))$ to the solution, and for each $v \in V_2$ and each label $\ell_2 \in L_v$, we add arc $((v, \ell_2), v)$. We know that for each edge (u, v) in the label cover instance, there is some $\ell_1 \in L_u$ and $\ell_2 \in L_v$ such that $(\ell_1, \ell_2) \in R_{uv}$; we then add the arc $((u, \ell_1), (v, \ell_2))$ to the solution. This arc allows there to be a directed path from u to v by taking the arcs $(u, (u, \ell_1))$, $((u, \ell_1), (v, \ell_2))$, and $((v, \ell_2), v)$. Thus, for each s_i-t_i pair, there is a directed path in the solution. Clearly the cost of the generalized Steiner tree solution is equal to the number of labels in the label cover solution.

Given a feasible solution F to the generalized Steiner tree instance, we convert it to a feasible solution to the label cover instance in a similar way. For each arc $(u, (u, \ell_1)) \in F$, we label $u \in V_1$ with label $\ell_1 \in L_1$, and for each arc $((v, \ell_2), v) \in F$, we label $v \in V_2$ with label $\ell_2 \in L_2$. Note that the total number of labels used is exactly equal to the cost of the set of arcs F. We now need to argue that this labeling is a feasible solution for the minimization version of the label cover problem. Because F is a feasible solution to the generalized Steiner tree instance, for the s_i-t_i pair in which $s_i = u$ and $t_i = v$, there must be some path in the directed graph (V, A) from u to v, and this must use an arc $(u, (u, \ell_1))$ from A_1, an arc $((u, \ell_1), (v, \ell_2))$ from A_2, and an arc $((v, \ell_2), v)$ from A_3, where by the definition of A_2 it must be the case that $(\ell_1, \ell_2) \in R_{uv}$. Since the arcs $(u, (u, \ell_1))$ and $((v, \ell_2), v)$ are in F, we must have labeled u with ℓ_1 and v with ℓ_2. □

We can now derive the following corollary; it follows from the theorem above combined with the fact that the number of vertices n in the Steiner tree instance is related by a polynomial to the number of edges m in the label cover instance.

Corollary 16.39. *There is no $O(2^{\log^{1-\epsilon} n})$-approximation algorithm for the directed generalized Steiner tree problem for any $\epsilon > 0$ unless NP has quasipolynomial-time algorithms.*

We conclude this section by considering a vertex-connectivity version of the survivable network design problem introduced in Section 11.3. As in the survivable network design problem, we are given as input an undirected graph $G = (V, E)$, costs $c_e \geq 0$ for all $e \in E$, and connectivity requirements r_{ij} for all pairs of vertices $i, j \in V$, where $i \neq j$. The goal is to find a minimum-cost set of edges $F \subseteq E$ such that for all pairs of vertices i, j with $i \neq j$, there are at least r_{ij} vertex-disjoint paths connecting i and j in (V, F); by this we mean that the only vertices that the paths have in common are the endpoints i, j. In Section 11.3, we gave a 2-approximation algorithm for the case in which we needed r_{ij} edge-disjoint paths between i and j. However, the vertex-connectivity version is substantially harder. We will prove the following theorem.

Theorem 16.40. *Given an α-approximation algorithm for the vertex-connectivity version of the survivable network design problem in which there is some k such that each $r_{ij} \in \{0, k\}$, there is an α-approximation algorithm for the directed generalized Steiner tree problem.*

From the theorem, we get the following corollary immediately.

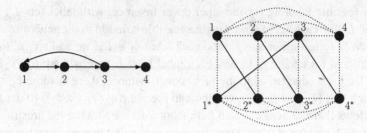

Figure 16.5. Illustration of the reduction from the directed generalized Steiner tree problem to the vertex-connectivity version of the survivable network design problem. The directed graph is on the left, and the corresponding undirected graph is on the right. The nonarc edges are dotted, and the arc edges are solid. We suppose that we need to find a path from vertex 1 to vertex 4 in the generalized Steiner tree instance; this translates to finding five vertex-disjoint paths between vertex 1 and vertex 4* in the survivable network design instance.

Corollary 16.41. *There is no $O(2^{\log^{1-\epsilon} n})$-approximation algorithm for the vertex-connectivity version of the survivable network design problem in which each $r_{ij} \in \{0, k\}$ for any $\epsilon > 0$ unless* NP *has quasipolynomial-time algorithms.*

To prove the theorem, we give a reduction from the directed generalized Steiner tree problem to the vertex-connectivity version of the survivable network design problem. Given the directed graph $G = (V, A)$ with costs $c_a \geq 0$ for all arcs $a \in A$, we create an undirected graph $G' = (V', E')$ as follows. For the vertex set V', we let V^* be a copy of the vertex set V, and set $V' = V^* \cup V$. We let $u^* \in V^*$ denote the copy of $u \in V$. For each $u, v \in V, u \neq v$, we create an edge (u, v) of cost 0, and for each $u^*, v^* \in V^*$, $u^* \neq v^*$, we create an edge (u^*, v^*). We also create edges (u, u^*) of cost 0 for each $u \in V$. Finally, for each arc $a = (u, v) \in A$ of cost c_a, we create an edge (u, v^*) of cost c_a. We call this latter set of edges *arc edges*, and the prior set of edges *nonarc edges*; let $N' \subseteq E'$ be all the nonarc edges. For any set of arcs $F \subseteq A$, we denote the corresponding set of arc edges by F'; that is, for each arc $(u, v) \in F$, we have the edge $(u, v^*) \in F'$. Let c_e denote the cost of each edge $e \in E'$, and let $k = |V| + 1$. For each s_i-t_i pair in the generalized Steiner tree instance, we set $r_{s_i, t_i^*} = k$, and for all other pairs of vertices $u, v \in V', u \neq v$, we set $r_{uv} = 0$. See Figure 16.5 for an illustration of the reduction.

The following lemma is the key to proving Theorem 16.40.

Lemma 16.42. *Let $F \subseteq A$ be a set of arcs from $G = (V, A)$, and let $s, t \in V$ be two vertices from G. Then there is a directed path from s to t in (V, F) if and only if there are $k = |V| + 1$ vertex-disjoint paths in $(V', N' \cup F')$ between $s \in V'$ and $t^* \in V'$.*

Proof. See Figure 16.6 for an illustration of the proof. First, assume there is a simple path from s to t in (V, F); let the path P be $s, u_1, \ldots, u_r, t$. From P, we construct the k vertex-disjoint paths in $(V', N' \cup F')$. For the first arc in P, (s, u_1), we construct the path $(s, u_1^*), (u_1^*, t^*)$. For the last arc in P, (u_r, t), we construct the path $(s, u_r), (u_r, t^*)$. For all other arcs (u_i, u_{i+1}) in P (for $1 \leq i \leq r - 1$), we construct the path (s, u_i), $(u_i, u_{i+1}^*), (u_{i+1}^*, t^*)$. For all vertices $v \notin \{s, t, u_1, \ldots, u_r\}$, we construct the path (s, v), $(v, v^*), (v^*, t^*)$. Finally, we construct the two paths $(s, s^*), (s^*, t^*)$ and $(s, t), (t, t^*)$. Observe that all of these paths are vertex-disjoint. We have one path for each of the

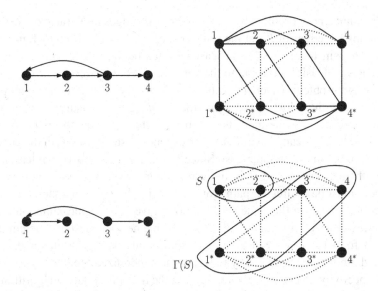

Figure 16.6. Illustration of the proof of Lemma 16.42. The instances on the top show a case in which a path from 1 to 4 exists, and there are five vertex-disjoint paths between 1 and 4* in the corresponding survivable network design instance; the edges in the vertex-disjoint paths are solid, while the other edges are dotted. The instances on the bottom show a case in which a path from 1 to 4 does not exist; the set $S = \{1, 2\}$ and $\Gamma(S) = \{1^*, 2^*, 3, 4\}$ are shown in the survivable network design instance. Since $|\Gamma(S)| = 4$, and all paths between 1 and 4* must use a vertex in $\Gamma(S)$, it is not possible to have five vertex-disjoint paths between 1 and 4*.

$r + 1$ arcs in P, one path for each of the $|V| - (r + 2)$ vertices not in the path, plus two more paths for a total of $(r + 1) + (|V| - (r + 2)) + 2 = |V| + 1 = k$.

Now assume there is no path from s to t in (V, F). Then there must be a set $S \subseteq V$ with $s \in S$, and $t \notin S$, such that there is no arc of F leaving S. Consider the same set of vertices $S \subseteq V'$, and consider the edges of $N' \cup F'$ with one endpoint in S and the other in $V' - S$. Let $\Gamma(S) \subseteq V'$ be the set of endpoints of these edges that are not in S. We claim that $|\Gamma(S)| < k$, and that $t^* \notin \Gamma(S)$. Given the claim, we can show that there cannot be k vertex-disjoint paths from s to t^* in $(V', N' \cup F')$ as follows. Observe that since $s \in S$ and $t^* \notin S \cup \Gamma(S)$, any vertex-disjoint path from s to t^* must pass through one of the vertices of $\Gamma(S)$. But since $|\Gamma(S)| < k$, there cannot be k such paths.

To prove the claim, we enumerate the vertices in $\Gamma(S)$. Note that every vertex $v \in V - S$ must be in $\Gamma(S)$ since $(s, v) \in N'$. Also, for each $u \in S$, $(u, u^*) \in N'$, so that $u^* \in \Gamma(S)$; thus there are at least $|V - S| + |S| = |V| = k - 1$ vertices in $\Gamma(S)$. Observe that this accounts for all edges in N' with exactly one endpoint in S. For any $v \in V - S$, it cannot be the case that $v^* \in \Gamma(S)$, since this would imply that there is some arc edge $(u, v^*) \in F'$ with $u \in S$, $v \notin S$, which would imply that the arc $(u, v) \in F$ is leaving S, a contradiction. Since for any $v \in V - S$, $v^* \notin \Gamma(S)$, this implies that $|\Gamma(S)| = |V| = k - 1$, and that $t^* \notin \Gamma(S)$ since $t \notin S$. $\qquad \square$

It is now straightforward to prove Theorem 16.40.

Proof of Theorem 16.40. Given any feasible solution F to the instance of the directed generalized Steiner tree problem, we construct a feasible solution of the same cost to the vertex-connectivity problem by taking the nonarc edges in N' (at zero cost) and the corresponding arc edges in F' (at the same cost as those in F). Then by Lemma 16.42, for each s_i-t_i pair, there must be at least k vertex-disjoint paths between s_i and t_i^*, and so we have a feasible solution to the vertex-connectivity version of the survivable network design problem. Given a feasible solution to the vertex-connectivity problem, we can assume without loss of generality that it includes all nonarc edges in N', since these have zero cost. So assume the solution to the vertex-connectivity problem is $N' \cup F'$; from this we can construct the corresponding set of arcs F in the generalized Steiner tree problem of the same cost. Since for each i there must be at least k vertex-disjoint paths between s_i and t_i^* in the vertex-connectivity problem, then by Lemma 16.42, there must be a directed path from s_i to t_i in (V, F). Thus, the optimal values of the two instances are the same. Furthermore, given an α-approximation algorithm for the vertex-connectivity version of the survivable network design problem in which $r_{ij} \in \{0, k\}$ for all i, j, we can give an α-approximation algorithm for the directed generalized Steiner tree problem by reducing the generalized Steiner tree instance to a vertex-connectivity instance as above, running the α-approximation algorithm on it to obtain a solution $N' \cup F'$, and then returning the corresponding set of arcs F at cost at most α times the cost of an optimal solution. $\qquad\square$

16.5 Reductions from Unique Games

In this section, we return to the unique games problem introduced in Section 13.3. Recall that in the unique games problem, we are given as input an undirected graph $G = (V, E)$, and a set of labels L. Also, for each $(u, v) \in E$, we are given a permutation π_{uv}. The goal of the problem is to assign a label from L to each vertex in V so as to *satisfy* as many edges as possible; we say that edge (u, v) is satisfied if when u is labeled with label i and v is labeled with label j, then $\pi_{uv}(i) = j$.

We also recall the unique games conjecture, which states that it is NP-hard to distinguish between instances of the unique games problem in which almost all of the edges can be satisfied and almost none of the edges can be satisfied.

Conjecture 16.43 (Unique games conjecture (UGC)). *Given any $\epsilon, \delta > 0$, there exists some $k > 0$ depending on ϵ and δ, such that for the unique games problem with $|L| = k$, it is NP-hard to distinguish between instances in which at least a $1 - \epsilon$ fraction of the edges can be satisfied, and instances in which at most a δ fraction of the edges can be satisfied.*

In this section, we show how reductions from the UGC can be used to prove hardness results (conditional on the truth of the conjecture, of course). For this purpose, it will be useful to give a special case of the unique games problem called MAX 2LIN(k). The unique games conjecture for MAX 2LIN(k) can be shown to be equivalent to the original unique games conjecture, though we will not show the equivalence here. In MAX 2LIN(k), we assume that $L = \{0, 1, \ldots, k - 1\}$, and that the permutation π_{uv} is given by a constant $c_{uv} \in \{0, \ldots, k - 1\}$ such that if u is labeled with $x_u \in L$ and v is labeled with $x_v \in L$ then $\pi_{uv}(x_u) = x_v$ if and only if $x_u - x_v = c_{uv} (\text{mod } k)$. The problem is called MAX 2LIN(k) since the permutation is linear in the labels, since the linear equation relates two variables, and since it is over a universe of size k. We will call the associated conjecture the *linear* unique games conjecture, which is as follows.

Conjecture 16.44 (Linear unique games conjecture (LUGC)). *Given any $\epsilon, \delta > 0$, there exists some $k > 0$ depending on ϵ and δ, such that for the MAX 2LIN(k) version of the unique games problem with $L = \{0, \dots, k - 1\}$, it is* NP-*hard to distinguish between instances in which at least a $1 - \epsilon$ fraction of the edges can be satisfied, and instances in which at most a δ fraction of the edges can be satisfied.*

We begin by showing a strong connection between MAX 2LIN(k) and the multicut problem introduced in Section 8.3; this gives the hardness result for the multicut problem we claimed in Theorem 8.10. Additionally, it will give us an approximation algorithm for MAX 2LIN(k) that is better than the approximation algorithm given for the more general unique games problem in Section 13.3. Recall that in the multicut problem we are given an undirected graph $G = (V, E)$ with nonnegative costs $c_e \geq 0$ for all edges $e \in E$. We are also given a set of distinguished source-sink pairs of vertices s_1-$t_1, \dots, s_k$-t_k. The goal is to find a minimum-cost set of edges F whose removal disconnects all s_i-t_i pairs; that is, for every i, $1 \leq i \leq k$, there is no path connecting s_i and t_i in $(V, E - F)$.

To show the connection between the two problems, we give a reduction from MAX 2LIN(k) to the multicut problem. Given an instance of MAX 2LIN(k) with input graph $G = (V, E)$, label set $L = \{0, \dots, k - 1\}$, and constants $c_{uv} \in L$ for all $(u, v) \in E$, we create an instance of the multicut problem as follows. We let $V' = V \times L$, and we create an edge between $(u, i) \in V'$ and $(v, j) \in V'$ if and only if $(u, v) \in E$ and $i - j = c_{uv}(\text{mod } k)$. Let E' be this set of edges, and let $G' = (V', E')$. Note that $|E'| = k|E|$ and $|V'| = k|V|$. We let the cost of each edge in E' be 1 (that is, we consider an unweighted instance of the problem). Finally, we create a source-sink pair consisting of the pair of vertices (u, i) and (u, j) for each $u \in V$ and each pair $i \neq j$ with $i, j \in L$.

We can now show the following two lemmas connecting the value of the MAX 2LIN(k) instance to the new multicut instance.

Lemma 16.45. *For any ϵ such that $0 \leq \epsilon \leq 1$, given any feasible solution to the MAX 2LIN(k) instance that satisfies at least $(1 - \epsilon)|E|$ edges, there is a feasible solution to the multicut instance of cost at most $\epsilon|E'|$.*

Proof. Suppose we have a labeling of G that satisfies at least $(1 - \epsilon)|E|$ edges of G; let $x_u \in \{0, \dots, k - 1\}$ be the label given to $u \in V$. We now obtain a multicut of G' by partitioning its vertex set V' into k parts, $V'_0, \dots, V'_{k-1}$, and removing all edges whose endpoints are in different parts. We let the cth part $V'_c = \{(u, x_u + c(\text{mod } k)\}$ for all $u \in V$. We first observe that this is indeed a multicut of G' since (u, i) and (u, j) end up in different parts of the partition for $i \neq j$ and $i, j \in \{0, \dots, k - 1\}$. Now we determine the cost of the multicut. Consider any edge $((u, i), (v, j)) \in E'$ such that (u, i) and (v, j) end up in different parts of the partition; we show that (u, v) must not be satisfied by the labeling. By construction of E', we know that $i - j = c_{uv}(\text{mod } k)$. We also know that (u, i) and (v, j) are in different parts of the partition; suppose $(u, i) \in V'_c$

and $(v, j) \in V'_{c'}$ for $c \neq c'$. Then $i = x_u + c \pmod{k}$ and $j = x_v + c' \pmod{k}$, so that

$$c_{uv} = i - j \pmod{k} = (x_u + c) - (x_v + c') \pmod{k} = (x_u - x_v) + (c - c') \pmod{k}$$
$$\neq x_u - x_v \pmod{k},$$

since $c \neq c'$. Thus, the edge $(u, v) \in E$ is not satisfied in the solution to the MAX 2LIN(k) problem. Since each edge (u, v) in the MAX 2LIN(k) instance corresponds to k edges in the multicut instance, the total number of edges removed in the multicut can be at most k times the number of unsatisfied edges in the MAX 2LIN(k) solution. Thus, if at most $\epsilon|E|$ edges are not satisfied in the MAX 2LIN(k) solution, at most $\epsilon k|E| = \epsilon|E'|$ edges are in the multicut. $\square$

Lemma 16.46. *For any ϵ such that $0 \leq \epsilon \leq 1$, given any feasible solution to the multicut instance of cost at most $\epsilon|E'|$, there is a solution to the MAX 2LIN(k) instance that satisfies at least $(1 - 2\epsilon)|E|$ edges.*

Proof. Suppose that if we remove the edges in the multicut solution from G', the graph is partitioned into ℓ components. We randomly index the corresponding partition of the vertex set V' from 1 to ℓ, so that we have $V'_1, \ldots, V'_\ell$. We use this partition to determine a labeling for the MAX 2LIN(k) instance: in particular, for each $u \in V$, there is some part V'_c of least index c such that some vertex $(u, i) \in V'_c$ for some label $i \in L$ and no vertex $(u, j) \in V'_{c'}$ for $c' < c$. Because the partition is given by a multicut, we know that there can be no other $(u, j) \in V'_c$ for $j \neq i$. We then label u with i. We say that the part V'_c *defines* u.

In order to analyze the number of edges satisfied by this labeling, consider an edge $(u, v) \in E$. Consider the k corresponding edges in E', and let ϵ_{uv} be the fraction of these k edges that are in the multicut. Then for a $1 - \epsilon_{uv}$ fraction of these edges, both endpoints (u, i) and (v, j) are inside the same part of the partition. Suppose some such part V'_c contains both endpoints (u, i) and (v, j) of an edge $((u, i), (v, j))$ and the part defines both u and v. Then the labeling of u and v will satisfy $(u, v) \in E$ since u is labeled with i, v is labeled with j, and the edge $((u, i), (v, j))$ implies that $i - j = c_{uv} \pmod{k}$, so that the labels satisfy the edge (u, v). We call such a part of the partition a *good part*; there are $(1 - \epsilon_{uv})k$ good parts of the partition. We now analyze the probability that a good part of the partition defines both u and v. This probability gives us a lower bound on the probability that the edge (u, v) is satisfied. To do this, we analyze the probability that some other part (a *bad part*) defines a label for u or v. Since $\epsilon_{uv}k$ edges corresponding to (u, v) are in the multicut, there are at most $2\epsilon_{uv}k$ parts of the partition for which one of the following three things is true: it contains a vertex (u, i) but no vertex (v, j); it contains a vertex (v, j) but no vertex (u, i); or it contains both (u, i) and (v, j), but there is no edge $((u, i), (v, j))$. If any such part is ordered first, a good part will not define the labels for u and v. Suppose there are $b \leq 2\epsilon_{uv}k$ bad parts. Thus, the probability that edge $(u, v) \in E$ is not satisfied by the labeling is at most the probability that of the $b + (1 - \epsilon_{uv})k$ total good and bad parts of the partition, one of the bad parts is ordered first. This is at most

$$\frac{b}{b + (1 - \epsilon_{uv})k} \leq \frac{2\epsilon_{uv}k}{2\epsilon_{uv}k + (1 - \epsilon_{uv})k} = \frac{2\epsilon_{uv}}{1 + \epsilon_{uv}} \leq 2\epsilon_{uv}.$$

Therefore, the overall expected number of edges that are not satisfied by the random labeling is at most $2 \sum_{(u,v)\in E} \epsilon_{uv}$. By the definition of ϵ_{uv}, there are $k \sum_{(u,v)\in E} \epsilon_{uv}$ edges of $|E'|$ in the multicut. Thus, if the multicut has cost $k \sum_{(u,v)\in E} \epsilon_{uv} \leq \epsilon |E'| = \epsilon k |E|$, then $\sum_{(u,v)\in E} \epsilon_{uv} \leq \epsilon |E|$. Then the expected number of edges not satisfied is at most $2\epsilon |E|$, so that the expected number of satisfied edges is at least $(1 - 2\epsilon)|E|$. $\square$

Although the lemma above gives a randomized algorithm for obtaining a solution to the MAX 2LIN(k) instance from the solution to the multicut instance, it is not hard to convert this to a deterministic algorithm. We leave this as an exercise to the reader.

Corollary 16.47. *There is a deterministic polynomial-time algorithm such that given any feasible solution to the multicut instance of cost at most $\epsilon |E'|$, the algorithm finds a solution to the MAX 2LIN(k) instance that satisfies at least $(1 - 2\epsilon)|E|$ edges.*

From these two lemmas, we can derive the following corollaries.

Corollary 16.48. *Given the unique games conjecture, for any constant $\alpha \geq 1$, there is no α-approximation algorithm for the multicut problem unless* P = NP.

Proof. We use the equivalence of the unique games conjecture and the linear unique games conjecture. Suppose for some constant $\alpha \geq 1$, an α-approximation algorithm for the multicut problem exists. Then choose any ϵ, δ such that $\epsilon < \frac{1-\delta}{2\alpha}$. Given an instance of the MAX 2LIN(k) problem, we create a multicut instance as described above, apply the α-approximation for the multicut problem, and then use Corollary 16.47 to transform the multicut solution back into a solution to the MAX 2LIN(k) instance in polynomial time. Given an instance of the MAX 2LIN(k) problem in which at least $(1 - \epsilon)|E|$ constraints can be satisfied, we know by Lemma 16.45 that the corresponding multicut instance has an optimal solution of cost at most $\epsilon |E'|$. Given the approximation algorithm, we find a multicut of cost at most $\epsilon \alpha |E'|$. Then by Corollary 16.47, the MAX 2LIN(k) solution we obtain from this multicut satisfies at least $(1 - 2\epsilon \alpha)|E|$ constraints. Given a MAX 2LIN(k) instance in which at most $\delta |E|$ constraints can be satisfied, our algorithm will in the end satisfy at most $\delta |E|$ constraints. If $\epsilon < \frac{1-\delta}{2\alpha}$, then $(1 - 2\epsilon \alpha)|E| > \delta |E|$, and our algorithm can in polynomial time distinguish between MAX 2LIN(k) instances in which at least $(1 - \epsilon)|E|$ constraints are satisfied, and instances in which at most $\delta |E|$ are satisfied. Given the unique games conjecture, this implies that P = NP. $\square$

Corollary 16.49. *There is a polynomial-time algorithm for MAX 2LIN(k), such that given any instance that satisfies at least a $1 - \epsilon$ fraction of the edges, the algorithm can satisfy at least a $1 - O(\epsilon \log n)$ fraction of the edges.*

Proof. Given the MAX 2LIN(k) instance, we create a multicut instance as described above, apply the approximation algorithm from Section 8.3, and then use Corollary 16.47 to transform the multicut solution back into a solution to the MAX 2LIN(k) instance. The number of source-sink pairs in the multicut instance is $nk(k - 1)/2$, so that the performance guarantee of the multicut algorithm is $O(\log nk) = O(\log n)$, treating k as a constant. By hypothesis, the MAX 2LIN(k) instance satisfies at least a $1 - \epsilon$ fraction of the edges, so that the optimal solution to the multicut problem must cost at most $\epsilon |E'|$. The approximation algorithm then must find a solution that costs at most

$O(\epsilon \log n)|E'|$, and by the algorithm of Corollary 16.47, we must obtain a solution to the MAX 2LIN(k) instance that satisfies at least $(1 - O(\epsilon \log n))|E|$ edges.   □

To conclude this section, we give a high-level sketch of the proof of Theorem 6.11, the theorem giving a hardness bound for the maximum cut problem conditional on the unique games conjecture. We restate the theorem here.

Theorem 6.11. *Given the unique games conjecture, there is no α-approximation algorithm for the maximum cut problem with constant*

$$\alpha > \min_{-1 \leq x \leq 1} \frac{\frac{1}{\pi} \arccos(x)}{\frac{1}{2}(1 - x)} \geq 0.878$$

unless P $=$ NP.

The proof of this theorem gives many ideas that are used in other proofs showing the hardness of approximation for other problems conditional on the unique games conjecture. However, the entire proof is too complex to give here; instead we sketch the ideas so that the reader will have familiarity with them when they are encountered elsewhere.

To start the proof, we need another equivalent formulation of the unique games conjecture. The unique games conjecture is equivalent to the case in which all instances are bipartite graphs in which the degree of the vertices in one part are the same.

Conjecture 16.50 (Bipartite unique games conjecture). *Given any $\epsilon, \delta > 0$, there exists some $k > 0$ depending on ϵ and δ, such that for the unique games problem with $|L| = k$ on bipartite graphs in which all vertices in one part have the same degree, it is NP-hard to distinguish between instances in which at least a $1 - \epsilon$ fraction of the edges can be satisfied, and instances in which at most a δ fraction of the edges can be satisfied.*

We will sketch the proof of the following theorem.

Theorem 16.51. *Assuming the bipartite unique games conjecture, for any positive constant $\gamma > 0$ and any $\rho \in (-1, 0)$, NP $\subseteq$ PCP($\log n$, 2), where the verifier has completeness at least $\frac{1}{2}(1 - \rho) - \gamma$, has soundness at most $\frac{1}{\pi} \arccos(\rho) + \gamma$, and accepts if the two bits are not equal.*

Given the theorem, the hardness of the maximum cut problem follows easily.

Proof of Theorem 6.11. Following the discussion of Section 16.3, for any instance of an NP-complete problem Π and a verifier for Π via Theorem 16.51, we create a graph with a vertex for each possible bit of the proof. For each of the possible $2^{c \log n} = n^c$ strings of random bits that the verifier could use, we create an edge corresponding to the two bits of the proof that the verifier checks. We know that for any "Yes" instance of the problem Π, it is possible to set the bits of the proof to 0 and 1 such that at least a $\frac{1}{2}(1 - \rho) - \gamma$ fraction of the verifier's tests pass. This corresponds to partitioning the graph into two parts: one part consists of vertices corresponding to bits that are set to 0, and the other corresponds to bits that are set to 1. Since at least $\frac{1}{2}(1 - \rho) - \gamma$ of the verifier's tests pass, this implies that at least a $\frac{1}{2}(1 - \rho) - \gamma$ fraction of all edges are in the cut (since the values of the two endpoints are different). Similarly, for any "No" instance of the problem, at most a $\frac{1}{\pi} \arccos(\rho) + \gamma$ fraction of the edges can be in the cut. Thus, if we have an α-approximation with constant α such that

$$\alpha > \frac{\frac{1}{\pi} \arccos(\rho) + \gamma}{\frac{1}{2}(1 - \rho) - \gamma},$$

then we can distinguish between "Yes" and "No" instances of Π in polynomial time and thus P = NP. Since this holds for any $\gamma > 0$ and any $\rho \in (-1, 0)$, we have that there is no α-approximation algorithm for constant α with

$$\alpha > \min_{\rho \in (-1,0)} \frac{\frac{1}{\pi} \arccos(\rho)}{\frac{1}{2}(1 - \rho)}$$

unless P = NP. To complete the proof, it suffices to observe that

$$\min_{\rho \in (-1,0)} \frac{\frac{1}{\pi} \arccos(\rho)}{\frac{1}{2}(1 - \rho)} = \min_{\rho \in [-1,1]} \frac{\frac{1}{\pi} \arccos(\rho)}{\frac{1}{2}(1 - \rho)};$$

that is, the minimum of the ratio over the range $[-1, 1]$ is in fact achieved on the range $(-1, 0)$. $\square$

We now explain how the PCP proofs for the "Yes" instances of the bipartite unique games conjecture (those in which at least a $1 - \epsilon$ fraction of the edges are satisfiable) are encoded. Let $G = (V_1, V_2, E)$ be the instance of the unique games problem with label set L, such that every vertex in V_1 has the same degree. For each vertex $v \in V_1 \cup V_2$ of the bipartite graph (V_1, V_2, E), we want to encode its label. To do this, we create a function $f_v : \{0, 1\}^k \rightarrow \{0, 1\}$. To encode the fact that vertex v is labeled with label i, we set the function f_v so that it is 1 exactly when the ith bit of its input is 1, and is 0 if the ith bit is 0. Such a function is sometimes called a *dictator*; its value is dictated completely by one of the input bits (in this case, $f_v(x_1, \ldots, x_k) = x_i$). A block of the PCP proof will be devoted to encoding f_v; we will do this by listing the value of f_v on all 2^k input strings from $\{0, 1\}^k$. Note that this is a particularly inefficient encoding; to encode one of k possible labels takes only $\lceil \log_2 k \rceil$ bits, whereas 2^k bits is larger by a doubly exponential factor. For this reason, this encoding is sometimes known as the *long code*. However, since k is a constant, the length 2^k is also constant, and the length of the proof is $(|V_1| + |V_2|)2^k$, which is polynomial in the size of the unique games instance.

We now need to define a few concepts in order to explain the test that the verifier will use to check the proof. We say that the *influence* of the ith bit on a function $f : \{0, 1\}^k \rightarrow \{0, 1\}$ is the probability (taken over all inputs to f) that the function's value changes if the ith input bit is flipped. We call this quantity Inf_i, so that

$$\text{Inf}_i(f) = \Pr_{x \in \{0,1\}^k} [f(x) \neq f(x_1, \ldots, x_{i-1}, 1 - x_i, x_{i+1}, \ldots, x_k)].$$

Notice that for a dictator function f that depends on the ith bit, $\text{Inf}_i(f) = 1$, while $\text{Inf}_j(f) = 0$ for all other $j \neq i$. We will say that a function f is *far from being a dictator* if the influence of every bit is low. Given an input $x \in \{0, 1\}^k$, we consider the possible introduction of noise that flips the bits of x independently. We write $y \sim_\rho x$ if we obtain y by randomly flipping the bits of x so that for each i, $y_i = x_i$ with probability $\frac{1}{2}(1 + \rho)$ and $y_i = 1 - x_i$ with probability $\frac{1}{2}(1 - \rho)$ for $\rho \in [-1, 1]$. Finally, we define the concept of the *noise sensitivity* of a function $f : \{0, 1\}^k \to \{0, 1\}$. The noise sensitivity is the probability taken over all inputs x that $f(x)$ is different from $f(y)$ for $y \sim_\rho x$; a function with high noise sensitivity is one whose output is likely to change in the presence of noise. We denote noise sensitivity by NS so that

$$\text{NS}_\rho(f) = \Pr_{x \in \{0,1\}^k, y \sim_\rho x} [f(x) \neq f(y)].$$

There is a more general definition of noise sensitivity for non-Boolean functions that reduces to this one in the case of Boolean functions.

We now observe that for a dictator Boolean function f, it is easy to state the noise sensitivity; if the dictator depends on bit i, then it is just the probability that the ith bit is flipped, so that for a dictator f, $\text{NS}_\rho(f) = \frac{1}{2}(1 - \rho)$. Furthermore, if a function is far from being a dictator, the following can be shown.

Theorem 16.52. *For every $\rho \in (-1, 0)$ and $\gamma > 0$ there exists a β (depending on ρ and γ) such that if $f : \{0, 1\}^k \to [0, 1]$ has $\text{Inf}_i(f) \leq \beta$ for all i, then*

$$\text{NS}_\rho(f) \leq \frac{1}{\pi} \arccos(\rho) + \gamma.$$

The discussions of noise sensitivity above are suggestive of the proof of Theorem 16.51. Suppose we choose a vertex $v \in V_1 \cup V_2$ at random, choose an input $x \in \{0, 1\}^k$ at random, pick $y \sim_\rho x$, and check if the proof bits corresponding to $f_v(x)$ and $f_v(y)$ are equal. By the discussion above, if f_v is a dictator, then $f_v(x) \neq f_v(y)$ with probability $\frac{1}{2}(1 - \rho)$, while if f_v is far from being a dictator, this probability is at most $\frac{1}{\pi} \arccos(\rho) + \gamma$. Thus, we should be able to test whether the proof encodes a labeling in the proper way by performing this test; the test will pass with the completeness probability if the proof does indeed encode a labeling and will pass with at most the soundness probability if each encoded function is far from being a dictator.

However, we need to test more than simply whether the encoding is that of dictator functions; we want to check whether almost all of the edges are satisfied by the encoded labeling, or whether almost none of the edges are satisfied. We will use the following notation in devising the appropriate test. For $x \in \{0, 1\}^k$, and a permutation π on the label set $\pi : [k] \to [k]$, we let $x \circ \pi$ denote the set of bits $x_{\pi(1)}, x_{\pi(2)}, \ldots, x_{\pi(k)}$. Note that for an edge $(v, w) \in E$, if v and w have labels i and j such that $\pi_{vw}(i) = j$, and if f_v and f_w are the dictator functions encoding the labels i and j, respectively, then for any $x \in \{0, 1\}^k$, $f_v(x) = f_w(x \circ \pi_{vw})$. Furthermore, if there are two edges (v, w) and (v, u), and we have labels i for v, j for w, and h for u, such that $\pi_{vw}(i) = j$ and $\pi_{vu}(i) = h$, and if f_v, f_w, and f_u are dictator functions encoding the appropriate labels for v, w, and u, then for any $x \in \{0, 1\}^k$, $f_v(x) = f_w(x \circ \pi_{vw}) = f_u(x \circ \pi_{vu})$.

We can now give the verifier's test: for a bipartite unique games instance (V_1, V_2, E) in which all vertices in V_1 have the same degree, it picks a vertex $v \in V_1$ uniformly at random, then picks two neighbors of v uniformly and independently, $w, u \in V_2$. It picks $x \in \{0, 1\}^k$ uniformly at random, and draws $y \sim_\rho x$. Finally, it looks at the two bits $f_w(x \circ \pi_{vw})$ and $f_u(y \circ \pi_{vu})$ and accepts only if the two bits are different.

We can now prove the completeness of the verifier's test.

Lemma 16.53. *For any $\rho \in [-1, 1]$, if at least a $1 - \epsilon$ fraction of the edges of the unique games instance are satisfiable, then there is a proof such that the verifier accepts with probability at least $(1 - 2\epsilon) \cdot \frac{1}{2}(1 - \rho)$.*

Proof. We observe that since each vertex in V_1 has the same degree, if we choose v randomly, and choose a neighbor w of v randomly, then (v, w) is a randomly chosen edge, and similarly (v, u). The probability that (v, w) is not satisfied is at most ϵ, and similarly for (v, u). Hence, the probability that both edges are satisfied is at least $1 - 2\epsilon$.

We assume that the proof is an encoding of the appropriate dictator function f_v for each $v \in V_1 \cup V_2$. By the reasoning above, if the edges (v, w) and (v, u) are satisfied, then $f_w(x \circ \pi_{vw}) = f_u(x \circ \pi_{vu})$. Now if we draw $y \sim_\rho x$, the probability that the bit of x that dictates the value of f_u is flipped in y is $\frac{1}{2}(1 - \rho)$. Thus, given that both (v, w) and (v, u) are satisfied, the probability that $f_w(x \circ \pi_{vw}) \neq f_u(y \circ \pi_{vu})$ is $\frac{1}{2}(1 - \rho)$. Therefore, the overall probability that the verifier accepts is at least $(1 - 2\epsilon) \cdot \frac{1}{2}(1 - \rho)$. $\square$

We note that given the value of ρ and a $\gamma > 0$, we can choose the values of ϵ and δ in the unique games instance. Thus, we get the following corollary.

Corollary 16.54. *For any $\rho \in [-1, 1]$ and any $\gamma > 0$, if at least a $1 - \epsilon$ fraction of edges of the unique games instance are satisfiable, then there is a proof such that the verifier accepts with probability at least $\frac{1}{2}(1 - \rho) - \gamma$.*

The proof of soundness is the technically difficult part of the proof, and we state only the very high-level idea here. Suppose there exists a proof such that the verifier accepts with probability greater than $\frac{1}{\pi} \arccos(\rho) + \gamma$. For a given $v \in V_1$ with degree d, define $g_v(z) = \frac{1}{d} \sum_{w \in V_2 : (v, w) \in E} f_w(z \circ \pi_{vw})$. Let p_v be the probability that the verifier accepts given that it chooses vertex v. Then it can be shown that $p_v = \mathrm{NS}_\rho(g_v)$. If the verifier accepts with probability at least $\frac{1}{\pi} \arccos(\rho) + \gamma$, then it is possible to show that for a $\gamma/2$ fraction of vertices $v \in V_1$, it is the case that $\mathrm{NS}_\rho(g_v) \geq \frac{1}{\pi} \arccos(\rho) + \gamma/2$. By Theorem 16.52, any such function g_v must have a bit i such that its influence is large. These large-influence coordinates are then used to construct a solution to the unique games instance that satisfies more than a δ fraction of its edges. The soundness theorem proved is as follows.

Theorem 16.55. *For any $\rho \in (-1, 0)$ and any $\gamma > 0$, if at most a δ fraction of edges of the unique games instance are satisfiable, then there is no proof such that the verifier accepts with probability more than $\frac{1}{\pi} \arccos(\rho) + \gamma$.*

The unique games conjecture has been used to prove the hardness of many other problems in a way similar to that above: the test of a labeling encoded as a dictatorship function via the long code reduces to the problem of interest.

Chapter Notes

As mentioned in the beginning of the chapter, complete coverage of the topic of the hardness of approximation would be a book in itself. At this time that book has not yet been written. However, there is some coverage of the topic in the book on complexity theory by Arora and Barak [14], as well as the books on approximation algorithms by Ausiello, Crescenzi, Gambosi, Kann, Marchetti-Spaccamela, and Protasi [27] and Vazirani [283]. An older survey of Arora and Lund [18] is still well worth reading; there is also an excellent, more recent survey by Trevisan [281]. Also useful are lecture notes from a workshop organized by Harsha and Charikar [156].

Our coverage of hardness results is roughly chronological; that is, some of the first proofs of the hardness of approximation were by reduction from NP-complete problems. It was then observed that there were relationships between the approximability of various problems, such that the hardness of one problem would imply the hardness of another. In the early 1990s, the PCP theorem was proven. This result and subsequent work showed the hardness of various constraint satisfaction problems, and by using the approximation-preserving reductions previously known, other hardness results were derived. During this time, the label cover problem was derived as a way of showing the hardness of still other problems. As mentioned previously, the unique games problem and the unique games conjecture were introduced by Khot [192] in the early 2000s. Since that time, there has been a substantial amount of work done on deriving hardness results from the unique games conjecture.

In Section 16.1, the results showing the hardness of scheduling unrelated parallel machines via a reduction from the 3-dimensional matching problem are due to Lenstra, Shmoys, and Tardos [215]. The result showing the hardness of the edge-disjoint paths problem is due to Guruswami, Khanna, Rajaraman, Shepherd, and Yannakakis [153].

In Section 16.2, the concept of an L-reduction was formalized by Papadimitriou and Yannakakis [240] in the paper that introduced the problem class MAX SNP. This paper defined a particular class of problems and showed that unless P = NP, either all problems in the class have polynomial-time approximation schemes or no problem in the class has a PTAS; the PCP theorem then proved that none of the problems in the class have approximation schemes. The L-reduction from MAX E3SAT to MAX 2SAT is actually the original reduction showing the NP-completeness of MAX 2SAT due to Garey, Johnson, and Stockmeyer [124]. The L-reduction from MAX E3SAT to the maximum independent set problem is due to Papadimitriou and Yannakakis [240]. The L-reduction from vertex cover in bounded degree graphs to the Steiner tree problem is due to Bern and Plassmann [44]. The reduction of the maximum independent set problem to itself, showing that either there is a polynomial-time approximation scheme for the problem or no constant factor is possible, is due to Garey and Johnson [123]. The reduction of the set cover problem to the uncapacitated facility location problem is due to Guha and Khuller [146]; the observation that the same reduction can be extended to the k-median problem is due to Jain, Mahdian, Markakis, Saberi, and Vazirani [176].

The PCP theorem of Section 16.3 is due to Arora, Lund, Motwani, Sudan, and Szegedy [19], building on previous work of Feige, Goldwasser, Lovász, Safra, and Szegedy [108] and Arora and Safra [23]. The definition of NP in terms of probabilistically checkable proofs is due to Arora and Safra [23], though with different parameters from those given in the PCP theorem. Since the proof of the PCP theorem, there has been a significant stream of work improving the various parameters of the theorem. Theorem 16.19 is a significant example of this, showing that the verifier needs to read only three bits of the proof and use the functions odd and even. This theorem is due to Håstad [159], as is Theorem 16.23 on a variant of the PCP theorem that has completeness 1 and proves the hardness of MAX E3SAT to within a factor of 7/8. Dinur [89] has substantially simplified the very complicated original proof; Radhakrishnan and Sudan [245] give a presentation of Dinur's result. The gap-preserving reduction from odd/even constraint satisfaction to MAX 2SAT at the end of the section is from Bellare, Goldreich, and Sudan [42].

The label cover problem was introduced in a paper of Arora, Babai, Stern, and Sweedyk [13] as a way of capturing certain aspects of two-prover interactive proofs. The definition of the label cover problem given there is somewhat different from the one we give here. The hardness of approximating MAX E3SAT in which each variable appears in exactly five clauses is due to Feige [107]. The reduction we use from (d_1, d_2)-regular instances to d-regular instances follows an analogous reduction in Lund and Yannakakis [220] for the underlying two-prover interactive proof systems. Theorem 16.28 follows from a theorem known as the parallel repetition theorem, which again is used in the underlying context of two-prover interactive proof systems; the parallel repetition theorem is due to Raz [250]. The proof of the hardness of the set cover problem is due to Lund and Yannakakis [220]; our presentation follows lecture notes of Khot [191]. The reduction from the minimization version of the label cover problem to the directed generalized Steiner tree problem is due to Dodis and Khanna [92]. The reduction from the directed generalized Steiner tree problem to the vertex-connectivity version of the survivable network design problem is due to Lando and Nutov [207]; this result for the vertex-connectivity version of the survivable network design problem had been earlier shown by Kortsarz, Krauthgamer, and Lee [204] in a more complicated proof.

As mentioned previously, the unique games problem and the unique games conjecture were introduced by Khot [192], originally for bipartite graphs; hence, the bipartite unique games conjecture is in fact the original conjecture. The equivalence of the unique games conjecture and the linear unique games conjecture was shown by Khot, Kindler, Mossel, and O'Donnell [193]. The reduction from MAX 2LIN to multicut we show is due to Steurer and Vishnoi [272]. Previously a more complicated proof showed that multicut is not approximable to within any constant given the unique games conjecture; this prior work is by Chawla, Krauthgamer, Kumar, Rabani, and Sivakumar [68]. The result on the hardness of the maximum cut problem is due to Khot et al. [193] together with a result of Mossel, O'Donnell, and Oleszkiewicz [227]. The overview of the result we give here follows closely lecture notes by Khot from a workshop on the hardness of approximation mentioned earlier [156]. The unique games conjecture continues to prove to be a source of strong hardness results. Raghavendra [248] and Raghavendra and Steurer [249] have given essentially the best possible approximation algorithm for any constraint satisfaction problem given the unique games conjecture; Raghavendra [248] shows that the hardness bound for a given constraint satisfaction matches the integrality gap of a natural SDP, while Raghavendra and Steurer give an algorithm for rounding the SDP with performance guarantee matching the integrality gap. Resolving the status of the conjecture is a very interesting open question in the area of approximation algorithms.

CHAPTER 17

Open Problems

The design of approximation algorithms has reached a period of relative maturity as a discipline. We hope that the wealth of results presented herein makes a strong case that this is so. However, we also believe that there is much work remaining, with many more fundamental contributions yet to be discovered.

We will outline a few questions to highlight some of the research that we speculate might have the potential to surprise us with new directions for this area. Since "top 10" lists are the norm not just for year-end film critics and late-night show hosts, we will structure these thoughts in that format.

For many optimization problems, the ultimate result is a performance guarantee with a matching lower bound (based on a complexity-theoretic assumption, at least until the time that questions such as P vs. NP are resolved). For a significant fraction of this book, we have been concerned with designing α-approximation algorithms for some constant α – polynomial-time algorithms that find solutions of objective function value within a factor of α of optimal. Implicitly, we were seeking the best value α that is achievable for the given problem at hand.

One of the significant developments of the past decade is the introduction of the unique games conjecture, as discussed in Section 16.5. This conjecture provides a stronger complexity-theoretic hypothesis on which to base lower bounds for performance guarantees, and recent work has shown that tight bounds on performance guarantees follow for a wide swath of optimization problems. Consequently, before turning our attention to questions of algorithm design, our Open Problem 0 is the resolution of Conjecture 16.43, the unique games conjecture of Khot [192]. Of course, it is possible that the conjecture is false, but that there are still no polynomial-time or even quasipolynomial-time algorithms to distinguish nearly satisfiable instances of the unique games problem from instances in which very few constraints are satisfiable, and this would imply similar complexity bounds for all hardness results relying on the unique games conjecture.

Problem 1: the metric traveling salesman problem. The metric traveling salesman problem, as introduced in Section 2.4, has repeatedly been the source of inspiration for a wide gamut of algorithmic advances. Christofides [73] presented his 3/2-approximation

453

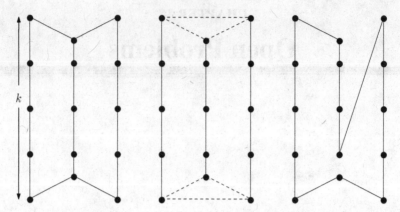

Figure 17.1. Illustration of the worst example known for the integrality gap for the metric TSP. The figure on the left gives a graph, and the costs c_{ij} are the shortest path distances in the graph. The figure in the center gives the LP solution, in which the dotted edges have value $1/2$, and the solid edges have value 1. The figure on the right gives the optimal tour.

algorithm for this problem nearly 35 years ago, and yet no improved performance guarantee has been obtained in the intervening years. This is even more remarkable in light of the state of knowledge concerning the natural linear programming relaxation given in Exercise 11.3. For this LP, we know that its integrality gap is at most 3/2 (shown by Wolsey [291], and later by Shmoys and Williamson [266]), but no example worse than 4/3 is known (see Figure 17.1). Our first open problem is to give an improved algorithm for the TSP, and in particular to show that one can obtain a 4/3-approximation algorithm based on this linear program. We note that Oveis Gharan, Saberi, and Singh have announced a result (not yet published at this writing) that gives a glimmer of hope for this problem; the result slightly improves upon the bound of 3/2 for the special case in which the metric is given by shortest path distances in an unweighted undirected graph.

Problem 2: the asymmetric traveling salesman problem. There are still many problems for which we might be able to obtain constant approximation algorithms (even assuming that P is not equal to NP), and yet no such algorithm is known. Perhaps most notable among this class of problems is the metric asymmetric variant of the traveling salesman problem. Exercises 1.3 and 12.4 give $O(\log n)$-approximation algorithms for this problem, and recent elegant work of Asadpour, Goemans, Mądry, Oveis Gharan, and Saberi [25] improves this to a performance guarantee of $O(\log n/\log \log n)$. As our second open problem, we ask for a constant approximation algorithm for the metric asymmetric TSP. Again, the natural approach is via the LP relaxation given in Exercise 12.4. Even progress on the following special case would be of interest: this is the so-called *no-wait flowshop scheduling problem*. In this problem, the input consists of n jobs, and their processing requirements on each of m machines; let p_{ij} denote the processing requirement of job j, $j = 1, \ldots, n$, on machine i, $i = 1, \ldots, m$. Each job must be processed first on machine 1, then on machine 2, and so forth, through machine m. Furthermore, this processing must take place over a continuous period of time, or in other words, the processing on machine $i + 1$ must start at the moment that it finishes on machine i (that is, without waiting). The aim is to sequence the jobs so as to minimize the time by which they have all completed. This problem is NP-hard, and yet no constant approximation algorithm is known for it.

Problem 3: the bin-packing problem. The ultimate approximation algorithm result for a problem (in which all feasible solutions have integer objective function values) is to show that, despite the NP-completeness of deciding if there exists a feasible solution of value k, it is nonetheless possible to find a feasible solution in polynomial time of objective function value at most one off from the optimal. For example, we saw such results in Section 2.7 for the edge coloring problem, and in Section 9.3 for the minimum-degree spanning tree problem. There are not many natural optimization problems for which such a result might still be achievable, but the bin-packing problem is the foremost candidate, at least in terms of its previous importance in the development of approximation algorithms. In Section 4.6, we have seen a polynomial-time algorithm for the bin-packing problem that uses $O(\log^2 n)$ extra bins (beyond the optimal), but although Karmarkar and Karp [187] obtained this result nearly 30 years ago, there has been no progress on this problem in the interim, and this is our third open problem. Showing that one can compute a packing with only a constant number of extra bins would be remarkable progress; again there is an LP relaxation (the one used in the Karmarkar–Karp result) for which we have no evidence that it cannot be the basis for such a result.

Problem 4: a primal-dual algorithm for the survivable network design problem. Although we are often tempted to measure progress solely in terms of the performance guarantees that can be achieved, there are other axes of progress. For example, a significant fraction of the results in this text are based on a linear programming or semidefinite programming relaxation; however, not all of those results are created equal. Some are rounding results, whereas others are based on a primal-dual approach. Although both have the advantage of providing an instance-by-instance *a fortiori* guarantee, the first approach is saddled by the fact that the relaxation must be solved first. While solving these relaxations can be done in polynomial time, it is important to note that solving these relaxations can be computationally quite demanding, such as when we have an exponential number of constraints in the LP and rely on the ellipsoid method for its polynomial-time solvability (or on the simplex method in practice). For our fourth open problem, we focus on the survivable network design problem; in Section 11.3, we presented the iterative rounding 2-approximation algorithm of Jain [175]. For the case in which the connectivity requirements are 0-1, the primal-dual 2-approximation algorithm of Section 7.4 is known, but for the general case, the best known performance guarantee for a primal-dual algorithm is $O(\log R)$, where R is the maximum connectivity requirement (that is, $R = \max_{i,j} r_{ij}$); this result is due to Goemans, Goldberg, Plotkin, Shmoys, Tardos, and Williamson [135]. Our fourth open problem is to design a primal-dual 2-approximation algorithm for this optimization problem.

Problem 5: a relaxation-based algorithm for the capacitated facility location problem. Whether via a primal-dual algorithm or a rounding-based approach, results that rely on a particular relaxation have a distinct advantage over the alternative – such an algorithm provides an instance-by-instance *a fortiori* guarantee. In fact, due to recent work by Raghavendra [248], we know that the ultimate performance guarantee can be obtained surprisingly often via a semidefinite programming relaxation. Among the problems for which such a relaxation-based result is still unknown, foremost is the capacitated variant of the uncapacitated facility location problem introduced in Section 4.5 and discussed extensively throughout this volume. The only difference between the capacitated and uncapacitated variants is that each potential facility has a given limit (or capacity) on the number of client nodes that it can serve. There are elegant local search algorithms for the capacitated problems, starting with the work of Korupolu, Plaxton, and Rajaraman [205], but no such relaxation-based result is known, and this is our fifth open problem.

Problem 6: the generalized Steiner tree problem. There is a rich literature of fundamental optimization problems for which a well-known constant approximation algorithm has remained the benchmark despite substantial effort to improve upon it in the intervening years (such as the metric TSP). For the last 15 years, the majority of these questions have been settled via advances in complexity theory; indeed, proving the unique games conjecture would settle far more of these, and we focus only on those problems not known to be related to this conjecture (and its variants). For our sixth open problem, we turn to a special case of the survivable network design problem just discussed, the generalized Steiner tree problem introduced in Section 7.4. For even this special case, the best known performance guarantee is the factor of 2 first obtained by Agrawal, Klein, and Ravi [4], and more than 20 years have passed without improvement on this basic problem. Of course, we hope that ideas that generate progress in this case will lead to comparable improvement for the survivable network design problem in general.

Problem 7: scheduling unrelated parallel machines. A final example of an improved constant that we would like to highlight is for the problem of finding a schedule of minimum length on unrelated machines, which was introduced in Exercise 11.1 and Section 16.1. The best performance guarantee known for this problem is the factor of 2 first obtained by Lenstra, Shmoys, and Tardos [215]; furthermore, they also proved the NP-hardness of a performance guarantee better than 3/2 (as we showed in Section 16.1). There has been no progress on either the upper or lower bound in the intervening 25 years, and so our seventh open problem is, for some $\alpha < 2$, to provide an α-approximation algorithm. One particular ray of hope for this problem lies in a very recent result of Svensson [276] for the special case in which each job has a given processing time, but is restricted to be processed on a specified subset of machines – in other words, for each job, its finite machine-dependent processing times are all identical. This special case is often referred to as requiring that $p_{ij} \in \{p_j, \infty\}$. The NP-hardness result given in Section 16.1 still applies to this special case, and yet Svensson proves a performance guarantee of 1.9412.

Problem 8: scheduling related parallel machines with precedence constraints. Complexity-theoretic techniques have also been extremely successful over the past decade in squashing our hopes for constant approximation algorithms for problems where none were known. However, there are still a few central open problems of this type, and for our eighth open problem we would like to highlight one of these. One of the earliest approximation algorithm results is that of Graham [142], who gave a 2-approximation algorithm for scheduling precedence-constrained jobs on identical parallel machines (given in Exercise 2.3). We have already mentioned a generalization of this machine environment, when the parallel machines are unrelated. However, there is a natural model in between unrelated and identical machines, in which the machines run at different speeds, but do so uniformly for all jobs; in other words, the time that it takes for a given machine to process a particular job is always equal to the inherent processing requirement of the job divided by that machine's speed. This is the model of related parallel machines given in Exercise 2.4. Surprisingly, no constant approximation algorithm is known for this problem when the jobs have precedence constraints; the best result known for this problem is an $O(\log m)$-approximation algorithm due to Chudak and Shmoys [76] (see also Chekuri and Bender [69]).

Problem 9: coloring 3-colorable graphs. Coloring problems have played an integral role in the history of the development of approximation algorithms. While much has been accomplished, several basic problems remain. Foremost among them is the problem discussed in Sections 6.5 and 13.2, finding a good vertex coloring for a graph known to be 3-colorable. Here the state of the art provides algorithms with guarantees of the form $O(n^\epsilon)$, starting with the algorithm of Wigderson [286] given in Section 6.5 that uses $O(\sqrt{n})$ colors. However, there are no complexity-theoretic barriers known to obtaining a polynomial-time algorithm that uses $O(\log n)$ colors for a 3-colorable graph, and to do so is our ninth open problem.

Problem 10: a primal-dual algorithm for the maximum cut problem. Finally, we have already noted that semidefinite programming has been shown to be the basis for the ultimate performance guarantee for a wide swath of problems. However, while semidefinite programming is in P, the state of the art for solving SDPs in practice is quite far from what is known for LP, even in light of recent work to quickly obtain near-optimal solutions for the SDP itself. Hence, the appeal of primal-dual algorithms in this context is particularly profound. Our last open problem is to return to the starting point of semidefinite programming in approximation algorithms, the maximum cut problem, and to derive a direct primal-dual algorithm that matches the performance guarantee of the algorithm presented in Section 6.2.

One final footnote should be added to this list. One surprise, at least to us, is that none of the problems on this list was of this form: for the following problem for which there is an approximation algorithm with constant performance guarantee, show that there exists a polynomial-time approximation scheme. It is not that no such problems exist, but none appeared to us to be of the same level of centrality to the field as the problems listed above. Nonetheless, we view this as a testament to which the interplay between algorithm design and complexity theory has served to yield a thorough understanding of this level of performance guarantee. We believe that similar understanding for other thresholds will follow, and we hope that this list might provide some guideposts along the way.

APPENDIX A

Linear Programming

In this appendix we give a quick overview of linear programming. In linear programming, we find a nonnegative, rational vector x that minimizes a given linear objective function in x subject to linear constraints on x. More formally, given an n-vector $c \in \mathbb{Q}^n$, an m-vector $b \in \mathbb{Q}^m$, and an $m \times n$ matrix $A = (a_{ij}) \in \mathbb{Q}^{m \times n}$, an *optimal solution* to the linear programming problem

$$\text{minimize} \sum_{j=1}^{n} c_j x_j$$

$$(P) \qquad \text{subject to} \sum_{j=1}^{n} a_{ij} x_j \geq b_i, \qquad i = 1, \ldots, m, \qquad \text{(A.1)}$$

$$x_j \geq 0, \qquad j = 1, \ldots, n, \qquad \text{(A.2)}$$

is an n-vector x that minimizes the linear *objective function* $\sum_{j=1}^{n} c_j x_j$ subject to the *constraints* (A.1) and (A.2). The vector x is called the *variable*. Any x that satisfies the constraints is said to be *feasible* or is a *feasible solution*, and if such an x exists, the linear program is said to be *feasible*. We say that we *solve* the linear program if we find an optimal solution x. If there does not exist any feasible x, the linear program is called *infeasible*. The term *linear program* is frequently abbreviated to *LP*. There are very efficient, practical algorithms to solve linear programs; LPs with tens of thousands of variables and constraints are solved routinely.

One could imagine variations and extensions of the linear program above: for example, maximizing the objective function rather than minimizing it, having equations in addition to inequalities, and allowing variables x_j to take on negative values. However, the linear program (P) above is sufficiently general that it can capture all these variations, and so is said to be in *canonical form*. To see this, observe that maximizing $\sum_{j=1}^{n} c_j x_j$ is equivalent to minimizing $-\sum_{j=1}^{n} c_j x_j$, and that an equation $\sum_{j=1}^{n} a_{ij} x_j = b_i$ can be expressed as a pair of inequalities $\sum_{j=1}^{n} a_{ij} x_j \geq b_i$ and $-\sum_{j=1}^{n} a_{ij} x_j \geq -b_i$. Finally, a variable x_j that is allowed to be negative can be expressed in terms of two nonnegative variables x_j^+ and x_j^- by substituting $x_j^+ - x_j^-$ for x_j in the objective function and the constraints.

Another variation of linear programming, called *integer linear programming* or *integer programming*, allows constraints that require variable x_j to be an integer. For instance, we can require that $x_j \in \mathbb{N}$, or that x_j be in a bounded range of integers, such as $x_j \in \{0, 1\}$. Unlike linear programming, there is currently no efficient, practical algorithm to solve general integer programs; in fact, many quite small integer programs are very difficult to solve. Integer programming is known to be NP-complete, so no efficient algorithm is likely to exist. Nevertheless, integer programming remains a useful tool because it is a compact way to model problems in combinatorial optimization, and because there are several important special cases that do have efficient algorithms.

Linear programming has a very interesting and useful concept of *duality*. To explain it, we begin with a small example. Consider the following linear program in canonical form:

$$\text{minimize } 6x_1 + 4x_2 + 2x_3$$

$$\text{subject to } 4x_1 + 2x_2 + x_3 \geq 5,$$

$$x_1 + x_2 \geq 3,$$

$$x_2 + x_3 \geq 4,$$

$$x_i \geq 0, \qquad \text{for } i = 1, 2, 3.$$

Observe that because all variables x_j are nonnegative, it must be the case that the objective function $6x_1 + 4x_2 + 2x_3 \geq 4x_1 + 2x_2 + x_3$. Furthermore, $4x_1 + 2x_2 + x_3 \geq 5$ by the first constraint. Thus, we know that the value of the objective function of an optimal solution to this linear program (called the *optimal value* of the linear program) is at least 5. We can get an improved lower bound by considering combinations of the constraints. It is also the case that $6x_1 + 4x_2 + 2x_3 \geq (4x_1 + 2x_2 + x_3) + 2 \cdot (x_1 + x_2) \geq 5 + 2 \cdot 3 = 11$, which is the first constraint summed together with twice the second constraint. Even better, $6x_1 + 4x_2 + 2x_3 \geq (4x_1 + 2x_2 + x_3) + (x_1 + x_2) + (x_2 + x_3) \geq 5 + 3 + 4 = 12$, by summing all three constraints together. Thus, the optimal value of the LP is at least 12.

In fact, we can set up a linear program to determine the best lower bound obtainable by various combinations of the constraints. Suppose we take y_1 times the first constraint, y_2 times the second, and y_3 times the third, where the y_i are nonnegative. Then the lower bound achieved is $5y_1 + 3y_2 + 4y_3$. We need to ensure that

$$6x_1 + 4x_2 + 2x_3 \geq y_1(4x_1 + 2x_2 + x_3) + y_2(x_1 + x_2) + y_3(x_2 + x_3),$$

which we can do by ensuring that no more than six copies of x_1, four copies of x_2, and two copies of x_3 appear in the sum; that is, $4y_1 + y_2 \leq 6$, $2y_1 + y_2 + y_3 \leq 4$, and $y_1 + y_3 \leq 2$. We want to maximize the lower bound achieved subject to these constraints, which gives the linear program

$$\text{maximize } 5y_1 + 3y_2 + 4y_3$$
$$\text{subject to} \qquad 4y_1 + y_2 \le 6,$$
$$2y_1 + y_2 + y_3 \le 4,$$
$$y_1 + y_3 \le 2,$$
$$y_i \ge 0, \qquad i = 1, 2, 3.$$

This maximization linear program is called the *dual* of the previous minimization linear program, which is referred to as the *primal*. It is not hard to see that any feasible solution to the dual gives an objective function value that is a lower bound on the optimal value of the primal.

We can create a dual for any linear program; the dual of the canonical form LP (P) above is

$$\text{maximize } \sum_{i=1}^{m} b_i y_i$$

(D) $\qquad$ subject to $\displaystyle\sum_{i=1}^{m} a_{ij} y_i \le c_j, \qquad \text{for } j = 1, \ldots, n,$ $\qquad$ (A.3)

$$y_i \ge 0, \qquad \text{for } i = 1, \ldots, m. \qquad \text{(A.4)}$$

As in our small example, we introduce a variable y_i for each linear constraint in the primal, and try to maximize the lower bound achieved by summing y_i times the ith constraint, subject to the constraint that the variable x_j not appear more than c_j times in the sum.

We now formalize our argument above that the value of the dual of the canonical form LP is a lower bound on the value of the primal. This fact is called *weak duality*.

Theorem A.1 (Weak duality). *If x is a feasible solution to the LP (P), and y a feasible solution to the LP (D), then $\sum_{j=1}^{n} c_j x_j \ge \sum_{i=1}^{m} b_i y_i$.*

Proof.

$$\sum_{j=1}^{n} c_j x_j \ge \sum_{j=1}^{n} \left(\sum_{i=1}^{m} a_{ij} y_i \right) x_j \qquad \text{(A.5)}$$

$$= \sum_{i=1}^{m} \left(\sum_{j=1}^{n} a_{ij} x_j \right) y_i$$

$$\ge \sum_{i=1}^{m} b_i y_i, \qquad \text{(A.6)}$$

where the first inequality follows by the feasibility of y (via dual inequalities (A.3)) and $x_j \ge 0$, the next equality by an interchange of summations, and the last inequality by the feasibility of x (via primal inequalities (A.1)) and $y_i \ge 0$. $\qquad \square$

A very surprising, interesting, and useful fact is that when both primal and dual LPs are feasible, their optimal values are exactly the same! This is sometimes called *strong duality*.

Theorem A.2 (Strong duality). *If the LPs (P) and (D) are feasible, then for any optimal solution x^* to (P) and any optimal solution y^* to (D), $\sum_{j=1}^{n} c_j x_j^* = \sum_{i=1}^{m} b_i y_i^*$.*

As an example of this, for the small, three-variable LP and its dual we saw earlier, the optimal value is 14, achieved by setting $x_1^* = 0$, $x_2^* = 3$, and $x_3^* = 1$ in the primal, and $y_1^* = 0$, $y_2^* = 2$, and $y_3^* = 2$ in the dual. A proof of Theorem A.2 is beyond the scope of this appendix, but one can be found in the textbooks on linear programming referenced in the notes at the end of Chapter 1.

An easy but useful corollary of strong duality is a set of implications called the *complementary slackness conditions*. Let $\bar{x}$ and $\bar{y}$ be feasible solutions to (P) and (D), respectively. We say that $\bar{x}$ and $\bar{y}$ obey the complementary slackness conditions if $\sum_{i=1}^{m} a_{ij} \bar{y}_i = c_j$ for each j such that $\bar{x}_j > 0$ and if $\sum_{j=1}^{n} a_{ij} \bar{x}_j = b_i$ for each i such that $\bar{y}_i > 0$. In other words, whenever $\bar{x}_j > 0$ the dual constraint that corresponds to the variable x_j is met with equality, and whenever $\bar{y}_i > 0$ the primal constraint that corresponds to the variable y_i is met with equality.

Corollary A.3 (Complementary slackness). *Let $\bar{x}$ and $\bar{y}$ be feasible solutions to the LPs (P) and (D), respectively. Then $\bar{x}$ and $\bar{y}$ obey the complementary slackness conditions if and only if they are optimal solutions to their respective LPs.*

Proof. If $\bar{x}$ and $\bar{y}$ are optimal solutions, then by strong duality the two inequalities (A.5) and (A.6) must hold with equality, which implies that the complementary slackness conditions are obeyed. Similarly, if the complementary slackness conditions are obeyed, then (A.5) and (A.6) must hold with equality, and it must be the case that $\sum_{j=1}^{n} c_j \bar{x}_j = \sum_{i=1}^{m} b_i \bar{y}_i$. By weak duality, $\sum_{j=1}^{n} c_j x_j \geq \sum_{i=1}^{m} b_i y_i$ for any feasible x and y, so therefore $\bar{x}$ and $\bar{y}$ must both be optimal. $\qquad\square$

So far we have focused on the case in which the LPs (P) and (D) are feasible, but of course it is possible that one or both of them are infeasible. The following theorem tells us that if the primal is infeasible and the dual is feasible, the dual must be *unbounded*: that is, given a feasible y with objective function value z, then for any $z' > z$ there exists a feasible y' of value z'. Similarly, if the dual is infeasible and the primal is feasible, then the primal is unbounded: given feasible x with objective function value z, then for any $z' < z$ there exists a feasible x' with value z'. If an LP is not unbounded, we say it is *bounded*.

Theorem A.4. *For primal and dual LPs (P) and (D), one of the following four statements must hold: (1) both (P) and (D) are feasible; (2) (P) is infeasible and (D) is unbounded; (3) (P) is unbounded and (D) is infeasible; or (4) both (P) and (D) are infeasible.*

Sometimes in the design of approximation algorithms it is helpful to take advantage of the fact that if an LP is feasible, there exist feasible solutions of a particular form, called *basic feasible solutions*. Furthermore, if an optimal solution exists, then there exists a *basic optimal solution*; that is, an optimal solution that is also a basic feasible solution. Most linear programming algorithms will return a basic optimal solution. Consider the canonical primal LP: There are $n + m$ constraints and n variables. A basic solution is obtained by selecting n of the constraints, treating them as equalities, and solving the resulting $n \times n$ linear system (assuming the system is consistent and the n constraints are linearly independent). The solution might not be feasible since we ignored some of the constraints. The oldest and most frequently used linear programming algorithm, called the *simplex method*, works by moving from basic solution to basic solution, at each step swapping a constraint outside of the linear system for another in the linear system in a particular manner, eventually reaching a basic feasible solution, then finally a basic optimal solution.

NP-Completeness

In this appendix, we briefly review the concepts of NP-completeness and reductions. We will use the knapsack problem of Section 3.1 as a running example. Recall that in the knapsack problem, we are given a set of n items $I = \{1, \ldots, n\}$, where each item i has a value v_i and a size s_i. All sizes and values are positive integers. The knapsack has capacity B, where B is also a positive integer. The goal is to find a subset of items $S \subseteq I$ that maximizes the value $\sum_{i \in S} v_i$ of items in the knapsack subject to the constraint that the total size of these items is no more than the capacity; that is, $\sum_{i \in S} s_i \leq B$.

Recall the definition of a polynomial-time algorithm.

Definition B.1. *An algorithm for a problem is said to run in polynomial time, or said to be a polynomial-time algorithm, with respect to a particular model of computer (such as a RAM) if the number of instructions executed by the algorithm can be bounded by a polynomial in the size of the input.*

More formally, let x denote an *instance* of a given problem; for example, an instance of the knapsack problem is the number n of items, the numbers s_i and v_i giving the sizes and values of the items, and the number B giving the size of the knapsack. To present the instance as an input to an algorithm A for the problem, we must encode it in bits in some fashion; let $|x|$ be the number of bits in the encoding of x. Then $|x|$ is called the *size* of the instance or the *instance size*. Furthermore, we say that A is a polynomial-time algorithm if there exists a polynomial $p(n)$ such that the running time of A is $O(p(|x|))$.

We will need the concept of a decision problem. A decision problem is one whose output is either "Yes" or "No." It is not difficult to think of decision problems related to optimization problems. For instance, consider a decision variant of the knapsack problem in which, in addition to inputs B, and v_i and s_i for every item i, there is also an input C, and the problem is to output "Yes" if the optimum solution to the knapsack instance has value at least C, and "No" otherwise. The instances of a decision problem can be divided into "Yes" instances and "No" instances, that is, instances in which the correct output for the instance is "Yes" (or "No"). The class P contains all *decision problems* that have polynomial-time algorithms.

Roughly speaking, the class NP is the set of all decision problems such that for any "Yes" instance of the problem, there is a short, easily verifiable "proof" that the answer is "Yes." Additionally, for each "No" instance of the problem, no such "proof" is convincing. What kind of "short proof" do we have in mind? Take the example of the decision variant of the knapsack problem given above. For any "Yes" instance, in which there is a feasible subset of items of value at least C, a short proof of this fact is a list of the items in the subset. Given the knapsack instance and the list, an algorithm can quickly verify that the items in the list have total size at most B, and total value at least C. Note that for any "No" instance, no possible list of items will be convincing.

We now attempt to formalize this rough idea as follows. A short proof is one whose encoding is bounded by some polynomial in the size of the instance. An easily verifiable proof is one that can be verified in time bounded by a polynomial in the size of the instance and the proof. This gives the following definition.

Definition B.2. *A decision problem is said to be in the problem class NP if there exists a verification algorithm $A(\cdot, \cdot)$ and two polynomials, p_1 and p_2, such that*

1. *for every "Yes" instance x of the problem, there exists a proof y with $|y| \leq p_1(|x|)$ such that $A(x, y)$ outputs "Yes";*
2. *for every "No" instance x of the problem, for all proofs y with $|y| \leq p_1(|x|)$, $A(x, y)$ outputs "No";*
3. *the running time of $A(x, y)$ is $O(p_2(|x| + |y|))$.*

NP stands for *nondeterministic polynomial time*.

Observe that nothing precludes a decision problem in NP from having a polynomial-time algorithm. However, the central problem of complexity theory is whether *every* problem in NP has a polynomial-time algorithm. This is usually expressed as the question of whether the class P of decision problems with polynomial-time algorithms is the same as the class NP or, more succinctly, whether P = NP.

As an approach to this problem, it has been shown that there are problems in NP that are representative of the entire class, in the sense that if they have polynomial-time algorithms, then P = NP, and if they do not, then P $\neq$ NP. These are the NP-*complete* problems. To define NP-completeness, we will need the notion of a *polynomial-time reduction*.

Definition B.3. *Given two decision problems A and B, there is a polynomial-time reduction from A to B (or A reduces to B in polynomial time) if there is a polynomial-time algorithm that takes as input an instance of A and produces as output an instance of B and has the property that a "Yes" instance of B is output if and only if a "Yes" instance of A is input.*

We will use the symbol $\preceq$ to denote a polynomial-time reduction so that we write $A \preceq B$ if A reduces to B in polynomial time. Sometimes the symbol $\leq_m^P$ is used in the literature to denote a polynomial-time reduction. We can now give a formal definition of NP-completeness.

Definition B.4 (NP-complete). *A problem B is NP-complete if B is in NP, and for every problem A in NP, there is a polynomial-time reduction from A to B.*

The following theorem is now easy to show.

Theorem B.5. *Let B be an* NP-*complete problem. If B has a polynomial-time algorithm, then* P $=$ NP.

Proof. It is easy to see that P $\subseteq$ NP. To show that NP $\subseteq$ P, pick any problem $A \in$ NP. For any instance of the problem A, we can run our polynomial-time reduction from A to B and use the polynomial-time algorithm for B. We return "Yes" if this algorithm returns "Yes," and "No" otherwise. By the properties of the polynomial-time reduction, this algorithm correctly decides whether the instance is a "Yes" instance of A, and does so in polynomial time. $\square$

A useful property of NP-complete problems is that once we have an NP-complete problem B it is often easy to prove that other problems are also NP-complete. As we will see, all we have to do is show that a problem A is in NP, and that $B \preceq A$. This follows as an easy corollary of the transitivity of polynomial-time reductions.

Theorem B.6. *Polynomial-time reductions are transitive: that is, if* $A \preceq B$ *and* $B \preceq C$, *then* $A \preceq C$.

Corollary B.7. *If* A *is in* NP, B *is* NP-*complete, and* $B \preceq A$, *then* A *is also* NP-*complete.*

Proof. All we need to show is that for each problem C in NP, there is a polynomial-time reduction from C to A. Because B is NP-complete, we know that $C \preceq B$. By hypothesis, $B \preceq A$. By Theorem B.6, $C \preceq A$. $\square$

Many thousands of problems have been shown to be NP-complete. We list two of them here. In the *partition problem*, we are given as input positive integers $a_1, \ldots, a_n$ such that $\sum_{i=1}^{n} a_i$ is even. We must decide whether there exists a partition of $\{1, \ldots, n\}$ into sets S and T such that $\sum_{i \in S} a_i = \sum_{i \in T} a_i$. In the *3-partition problem*, we are given as input positive integers $a_1, \ldots, a_{3n}, b$, such that $b/4 < a_i < b/2$ for all i, and such that $\sum_{i=1}^{3n} a_i = nb$. We must decide whether there exists a partition of $\{1, \ldots, 3n\}$ into n sets T_j such that $\sum_{i \in T_j} a_i = b$ for all $j = 1, \ldots, n$. By the condition on the a_i, each T_j must contain exactly three elements. The decision version of the knapsack problem given at the beginning of the section is also NP-complete. However, as shown in Section 3.1, we know that this problem has a pseudopolynomial-time algorithm. This brings up an interesting distinction among the NP-complete problems. Some NP-complete problems, such as the knapsack and partition problems, are NP-complete only when it is assumed that their numeric data are encoded in binary. As we have seen, the knapsack problem has a polynomial-time algorithm if the input is encoded in unary (recall that in a unary encoding the number 7 would be encoded as 1111111). The partition problem also has a polynomial-time algorithm if the input is encoded in unary. Other problems, however, such as the 3-partition problem above, are NP-complete even when their numeric data are encoded in unary. We call such problems *strongly* NP-*complete* or, sometimes, *unary* NP-*complete*. In contrast, problems such as the knapsack and partition problems are called *weakly* NP-*complete* or *binary* NP-*complete*.

Definition B.8. *A problem B is* strongly NP-complete *if it is* NP-*complete even when its numeric data are encoded in unary. A problem C is* weakly NP-*complete if it has* *a pseudopolynomial-time algorithm (that is, it has a polynomial-time algorithm if its numeric data are encoded in unary).*

We conclude this section by defining the term NP-*hard*, which can be applied to either optimization or decision problems. Roughly speaking, it means "as hard as the hardest problem in NP." To be more precise, we need to define an *oracle*. Given a decision or optimization problem A, we say that an algorithm has A as an oracle (or has *oracle access* to A) if we suppose that the algorithm can solve an instance of A with a single instruction.

Definition B.9 (NP-hard). *A problem A is* NP-hard *if there is a polynomial-time algorithm for an* NP-*complete problem B when the algorithm has oracle access to A.*

For example, the knapsack problem is NP-hard because given oracle access to it, we can solve the decision version of the knapsack problem in polynomial time: we simply check whether the value of the optimal solution is at least the value C for the decision problem, and output "Yes" if so, and otherwise "No."

The term "NP-hard" is most frequently applied to optimization problems whose corresponding decision problems are NP-complete; it is easy to see that such optimization problems are indeed NP-hard, as we saw for the knapsack problem above. It is also easy to see that if A is NP-hard and there is a polynomial-time algorithm for A, then $P = NP$.

Bibliography

[1] A. A. Ageev and M. I. Sviridenko. An 0.828-approximation algorithm for the uncapacitated facility location problem. *Discrete Applied Mathematics*, 93:149–156, 1999.

[2] A. A. Ageev and M. I. Sviridenko. Approximation algorithms for maximum coverage and max cut with given sizes of parts. In G. Cornuéjols, R. E. Burkard, and G. J. Woeginger, editors, *Lecture Notes in Computer Science*, vol. 1610, *Integer Programming and Combinatorial Optimization*, pages 17–30. Springer-Verlag, Berlin, Germany, 1999.

[3] A. A. Ageev and M. I. Sviridenko. Pipage rounding: a new method of constructing algorithms with proven performance guarantee. *Journal of Combinatorial Optimization*, 8:307–328, 2004.

[4] A. Agrawal, P. Klein, and R. Ravi. When trees collide: an approximation algorithm for the generalized Steiner problem on networks. *SIAM Journal on Computing*, 24:440–456, 1995.

[5] F. Alizadeh. Interior point methods in semidefinite programming with applications to combinatorial optimization. *SIAM Journal on Optimization*, 5:13–51, 1995.

[6] N. Alon, Y. Azar, G. J. Woeginger, and T. Yadid. Approximation schemes for scheduling. In *Proceedings of the 8th Annual ACM-SIAM Symposium on Discrete Algorithms*, pages 493–500, 1997.

[7] N. Alon, R. M. Karp, D. Peleg, and D. West. A graph-theoretic game and its application to the k-server problem. *SIAM Journal on Computing*, 24:78–100, 1995.

[8] R. Andersen and U. Feige. Interchanging distance and capacity in probabilistic mappings. *CoRR*, abs/0907.3631, 2009. Available at http://arxiv.org/abs/0907.3631. Accessed June 4, 2010.

[9] D. L. Applegate, R. E. Bixby, V. Chvátal, and W. J. Cook. *The Traveling Salesman Problem: A Computational Study*. Princeton University Press, Princeton, NJ, USA, 2006.

[10] S. Arnborg and A. Proskurowski. Linear time algorithms for NP-hard problems restricted to partial k-trees. *Discrete Applied Mathematics*, 23:11–24, 1989.

[11] S. Arora. Polynomial time approximation schemes for Euclidean traveling salesman and other geometric problems. *Journal of the ACM*, 45:753–782, 1998.

[12] S. Arora. Approximation schemes for NP-hard geometric optimization problems: a survey. *Mathematical Programming*, 97:43–69, 2003.

[13] S. Arora, L. Babai, J. Stern, and Z. Sweedyk. The hardness of approximate optima in lattices, codes, and systems of linear equations. *Journal of Computer and System Sciences*, 54:317–331, 1997.

[14] S. Arora and B. Barak. *Computational Complexity: A Modern Approach*. Cambridge University Press, New York, NY, USA, 2009.

[15] S. Arora, E. Chlamtac, and M. Charikar. New approximation guarantee for chromatic number. In *Proceedings of the 38th Annual ACM Symposium on the Theory of Computing*, pages 215–224, 2006.

[16] S. Arora, D. Karger, and M. Karpinski. Polynomial time approximation schemes for dense instances of NP-hard problems. *Journal of Computer and System Sciences*, 58:193–210, 1999.

[17] S. Arora, J. R. Lee, and A. Naor. Euclidean distortion and the sparsest cut. *Journal of the American Mathematical Society*, 21:1–21, 2008.

[18] S. Arora and C. Lund. Hardness of approximations. In D. S. Hochbaum, editor, *Approximation Algorithms for NP-Hard Problems*, chapter 10. PWS Publishing Company, Boston, MA, USA, 1997.

[19] S. Arora, C. Lund, R. Motwani, M. Sudan, and M. Szegedy. Proof verification and the hardness of approximation problems. *Journal of the ACM*, 45:501–555, 1998.

[20] S. Arora, P. Raghavan, and S. Rao. Approximation schemes for Euclidean k-medians and related problems. In *Proceedings of the 30th Annual ACM Symposium on the Theory of Computing*, pages 106–113, 1998.

[21] S. Arora, S. Rao, and U. Vazirani. Geometry, flows, and graph-partitioning algorithms. *Communications of the ACM*, 51:96–105, 2008.

[22] S. Arora, S. Rao, and U. Vazirani. Expander flows, geometric embeddings and graph partitioning. *Journal of the ACM*, 56, 2009. Article 5.

[23] S. Arora and S. Safra. Probabilistic checking of proofs: a new characterization of NP. *Journal of the ACM*, 45:70–122, 1998.

[24] V. Arya, N. Garg, R. Khandekar, A. Meyerson, K. Munagala, and V. Pandit. Local search heuristics for k-median and facility location problems. *SIAM Journal on Computing*, 33:544–562, 2004.

[25] A. Asadpour, M. X. Goemans, A. Mądry, S. Oveis Gharan, and A. Saberi. An $O(\log n / \log \log n)$-approximation algorithm for the asymmetric traveling salesman problem. In *Proceedings of the 21st Annual ACM-SIAM Symposium on Discrete Algorithms*, pages 379–389, 2010.

[26] Y. Aumann and Y. Rabani. An $O(\log k)$ approximate min-cut max-flow theorem and approximation algorithm. *SIAM Journal on Computing*, 27:291–301, 1998.

[27] G. Ausiello, P. Crescenzi, G. Gambosi, V. Kann, A. Marchetti-Spaccamela, and M. Protasi. *Complexity and Approximation: Combinatorial Optimization Problems and Their Approximability Properties*. Springer-Verlag, Berlin, Germany, 1999.

[28] B. Awerbuch and Y. Azar. Buy-at-bulk network design. In *Proceedings of the 38th Annual IEEE Symposium on Foundations of Computer Science*, pages 542–547, 1997.

[29] V. Bafna, P. Berman, and T. Fujito. A 2-approximation algorithm for the undirected feedback vertex set problem. *SIAM Journal on Discrete Mathematics*, 12:289–297, 1999.

[30] B. S. Baker. Approximation algorithms for NP-complete problems on planar graphs. *Journal of the ACM*, 41:153–180, 1994.

[31] E. Balas. The prize collecting traveling salesman problem. *Networks*, 19:621–636, 1989.

[32] N. Bansal, R. Khandekar, and V. Nagarajan. Additive guarantees for degree-bounded directed network design. *SIAM Journal on Computing*, 39:1413–1431, 2009.

[33] R. Bar-Yehuda. One for the price of two: a unified approach for approximating covering problems. *Algorithmica*, 27:131–144, 2000.

[34] R. Bar-Yehuda, K. Bendel, A. Freund, and D. Rawitz. *Local ratio*: a unified framework for approximation algorithms. *In Memorium*: Shimon Even 1935–2004. *ACM Computing Surveys*, 36:422–463, 2004.

[35] R. Bar-Yehuda and S. Even. A linear time approximation algorithm for the weighted vertex cover problem. *Journal of Algorithms*, 2:198–203, 1981.

[36] R. Bar-Yehuda and S. Even. A local-ratio theorem for approximating the weighted vertex cover problem. *Annals of Discrete Mathematics*, 25:27–46, 1985.

[37] R. Bar-Yehuda, D. Geiger, J. Naor, and R. M. Roth. Approximation algorithms for the feedback vertex set problem with applications to constraint satisfaction and Bayesian inference. *SIAM Journal on Computing*, 27:942–959, 1998.

[38] R. Bar-Yehuda and D. Rawitz. On the equivalence between the primal-dual schema and the local ratio technique. *SIAM Journal on Discrete Mathematics*, 19:762–797, 2005.

[39] Y. Bartal. Probabilistic approximation of metric spaces and its algorithmic applications. In *Proceedings of the 37th Annual IEEE Symposium on Foundations of Computer Science*, pages 184–193, 1996.

[40] Y. Bartal. On approximating arbitrary metrics by tree metrics. In *Proceedings of the 30th Annual ACM Symposium on the Theory of Computing*, pages 161–168, 1998.

[41] A. Becker and D. Geiger. Optimization of Pearl's method of conditioning and greedy-like approximation algorithms for the vertex feedback set problem. *Artificial Intelligence*, 83:167–188, 1996.

[42] M. Bellare, O. Goldreich, and M. Sudan. Free bits, PCPs, and nonapproximability – towards tight results. *SIAM Journal on Computing*, 27:804–915, 1998.

[43] M. Bellare, S. Goldwasser, C. Lund, and A. Russell. Efficient probabilistically checkable proofs and applications to approximation. In *Proceedings of the 25th Annual ACM Symposium on the Theory of Computing*, pages 294–304, 1993.

[44] M. Bern and P. Plassmann. The Steiner problem with edge lengths 1 and 2. *Information Processing Letters*, 32:171–176, 1989.

[45] D. P. Bertsekas and J. N. Tsitsiklis. *Introduction to Probability*. Athena Scientific, Nashua, NH, USA, second edition, 2008.

[46] D. Bertsimas and C.-P. Teo. From valid inequalities to heuristics: a unified view of primal-dual approximation algorithms in covering problems. *Operations Research*, 46:503–514, 1998.

[47] D. Bertsimas and J. N. Tsitsiklis. *Introduction to Linear Optimization*. Athena Scientific, Belmont, MA, USA, 1997.

[48] D. Bienstock, M. X. Goemans, D. Simchi-Levi, and D. Williamson. A note on the prize collecting traveling salesman problem. *Mathematical Programming*, 59:413–420, 1993.

[49] G. Birkhoff. Tres observaciones sobre el algebra lineal [in Spanish]. *Revista Facultad de Ciencias Exactas, Puras y Aplicadas Universidad Nacional de Tucumán, Serie A (Matemáticas y Física Teórica)*, 5:147–151, 1946.

[50] R. G. Bland, D. Goldfarb, and M. J. Todd. The ellipsoid method: a survey. *Operations Research*, 29:1039–1091, 1981.

[51] A. Blum, R. Ravi, and S. Vempala. A constant-factor approximation algorithm for the k-MST problem. *Journal of Computer and System Sciences*, 58:101–108, 1999.

[52] H. L. Bodlaender. Planar graphs with bounded treewidth. Technical Report RUU-CS-88-14, Utrecht University, Department of Computer Science, Netherlands, 1988.

[53] A. Borchers and D.-Z. Du. The k-Steiner ratio in graphs. *SIAM Journal on Computing*, 26:857–869, 1997.

[54] C. Borell. The Brunn-Minkowski inequality in Gauss space. *Inventiones Mathematicae*, 30:207–216, 1975.

[55] J. Bourgain. On Lipschitz embedding of finite metric spaces in Hilbert space. *Israel Journal of Mathematics*, 52:46–52, 1985.

[56] S. C. Boyd and W. R. Pulleyblank. Optimizing over the subtour polytope of the travelling salesman problem. *Mathematical Programming*, 49:163–187, 1991.

[57] Y. Boykov, O. Veksler, and R. Zabih. Fast approximate energy minimization via graph cuts. *IEEE Transactions on Pattern Analysis and Machine Intelligence*, 23:1222–1239, 2001.

[58] J. Byrka and K. Aardal. An optimal bifactor approximation algorithm for the metric uncapacitated facility location problem. *SIAM Journal on Computing*, 39:2212–2231, 2010.

[59] J. Byrka, F. Grandoni, T. Rothvoß, and L. Sanità. An improved LP-based approximation for Steiner tree. In *Proceedings of the 42nd Annual ACM Symposium on the Theory of Computing*, pages 583–592, 2010.

[60] G. Călinescu, H. Karloff, and Y. Rabani. An improved approximation algorithm for MULTIWAY CUT. *Journal of Computer and System Sciences*, 60:564–574, 2000.

[61] T. Carnes and D. Shmoys. Primal-dual schema for capacitated covering problems. In A. Lodi, A. Panconesi, and G. Rinaldi, editors, *Lecture Notes in Computer Science*, vol. 5035, *Integer Programming and Combinatorial Optimization*, pages 288–302. Springer, New York, NY, USA, 2008.

[62] R. D. Carr, L. K. Fleischer, V. J. Leung, and C. A. Phillips. Strengthening integrality gaps for capacitated network design and covering problems. In *Proceedings of the 11th Annual ACM-SIAM Symposium on Discrete Algorithms*, pages 106–115, 2000.

[63] D. Chakrabarty, J. Könemann, and D. Pritchard. Integrality gap of the hypergraphic relaxation of Steiner trees: A short proof of a 1.55 upper bound. *Operations Research Letters*, 38:567–570, 2010.

[64] M. Charikar and S. Guha. Improved combinatorial algorithms for facility location problems. *SIAM Journal on Computing*, 34:803–824, 2005.

[65] M. Charikar, K. Makarychev, and Y. Makarychev. Near-optimal algorithms for unique games. In *Proceedings of the 38th Annual ACM Symposium on the Theory of Computing*, pages 205–214, 2006.

[66] M. Charikar and B. Raghavachari. The finite capacity dial-a-ride problem. In *Proceedings of the 39th Annual IEEE Symposium on Foundations of Computer Science*, pages 458–467, 1998.

[67] M. Charikar and A. Wirth. Maximizing quadratic programs: extending Grothendieck's inequality. In *Proceedings of the 45th Annual IEEE Symposium on Foundations of Computer Science*, pages 54–60, 2004.

[68] S. Chawla, R. Krauthgamer, R. Kumar, Y. Rabani, and D. Sivakumar. On the hardness of approximating multicut and sparsest-cut. *Computational Complexity*, 15:94–114, 2006.

[69] C. Chekuri and M. Bender. An efficient approximation algorithm for minimizing makespan on uniformly related machines. *Journal of Algorithms*, 41:212–224, 2001.

[70] C. Chekuri, S. Guha, and J. Naor. The Steiner k-cut problem. *SIAM Journal on Discrete Mathematics*, 20:261–271, 2006.

[71] H. Chernoff. A measure of asymptotic efficiency for tests of a hypothesis based on the sum of observations. *Annals of Mathematical Statistics*, 23:493–507, 1952.

[72] E. Chlamtac, K. Makarychev, and Y. Makarychev. How to play unique games using embeddings. In *Proceedings of the 47th Annual IEEE Symposium on Foundations of Computer Science*, pages 687–696, 2006.

[73] N. Christofides. Worst-case analysis of a new heuristic for the travelling salesman problem. Report 388, Graduate School of Industrial Administration, Carnegie Mellon University, Pittsburgh, PA, USA, 1976.

[74] F. A. Chudak, M. X. Goemans, D. S. Hochbaum, and D. P. Williamson. A primal-dual interpretation of two 2-approximation algorithms for the feedback vertex set problem in undirected graphs. *Operations Research Letters*, 22:111–118, 1998.

[75] F. A. Chudak, T. Roughgarden, and D. P. Williamson. Approximate k-MSTs and k-Steiner trees via the primal-dual method and Lagrangean relaxation. *Mathematical Programming*, 100:411–421, 2004.

[76] F. A. Chudak and D. B. Shmoys. Approximation algorithms for precedence-constrainted scheduling problems on parallel machines that run at different speeds. *Journal of Algorithms*, 30:323–343, 1999.

[77] F. A. Chudak and D. B. Shmoys. Improved approximation algorithms for the uncapacitated facility location problem. *SIAM Journal on Computing*, 33:1–25, 2003.

[78] V. Chvátal. A greedy heuristic for the set-covering problem. *Mathematics of Operations Research*, 4:233–235, 1979.

[79] V. Chvátal. *Linear Programming*. W. H. Freeman, New York, NY, USA, 1983.

[80] W. Cook and P. Seymour. Tour merging via branch-decomposition. *INFORMS Journal on Computing*, 15:233–248, 2003.

[81] W. J. Cook, W. H. Cunningham, W. R. Pulleyblank, and A. Schrijver. *Combinatorial Optimization*. Wiley & Sons, New York, NY, USA, 1998.

[82] T. H. Cormen, C. E. Leiserson, R. L. Rivest, and C. Stein. *Introduction to Algorithms*. MIT Press, Cambridge, MA, USA, third edition, 2009.

[83] G. Cornuejols, M. L. Fisher, and G. L. Nemhauser. Location of bank accounts to optimize float: an analytic study of exact and approximate algorithms. *Management Science*, 23:789–810, 1977.

[84] G. Cornuéjols, J. Fonlupt, and D. Naddef. The traveling salesman problem on a graph and some related integer polyhedra. *Mathematical Programming*, 33:1–27, 1985.

[85] W. H. Cunningham. Minimum cuts, modular functions, and matroid polyhedra. *Networks*, 15:205–215, 1985.

[86] E. Dahlhaus, D. S. Johnson, C. H. Papadimitriou, P. D. Seymour, and M. Yannakakis. The complexity of multiterminal cuts. *SIAM Journal on Computing*, 23:864–894, 1994.

[87] M. M. Deza and M. Laurent. *Geometry of Cuts and Metrics*. Springer, Berlin, Germany, 1997.

[88] E. W. Dijkstra. A note on two problems in connexion with graphs. *Numerische Mathematik*, 1:269–271, 1959.

[89] I. Dinur. The PCP theorem by gap amplification. *Journal of the ACM*, 54, 2007. Article 12.

[90] I. Dinur, E. Mossel, and O. Regev. Conditonal hardness for approximate coloring. *SIAM Journal on Computing*, 39:843–873, 2009.

[91] I. Dinur and S. Safra. The importance of being biased. In *Proceedings of the 34th Annual ACM Symposium on the Theory of Computing*, pages 33–42, 2002.

[92] Y. Dodis and S. Khanna. Designing networks with bounded pairwise distance. In *Proceedings of the 31st Annual ACM Symposium on the Theory of Computing*, pages 750–759, 1999.

[93] R. Durrett. *The Essentials of Probability*. Duxbury Press, Belmont, CA, USA, 1994.

[94] R. Durrett. *Elementary Probability for Applications*. Cambridge University Press, New York, NY, USA, 2009.

[95] J. Edmonds. Optimum branchings. *Journal of Research of the National Bureau of Standards B*, 71B:233–240, 1967.

[96] J. Edmonds. Matroids and the greedy algorithm. *Mathematical Programming*, 1:127–136, 1971.

[97] K. Edwards. The complexity of colouring problems on dense graphs. *Theoretical Computer Science*, 43:337–343, 1986.

[98] F. Eisenbrand, F. Grandoni, T. Rothvoß, and G. Schäfer. Connected facility location via random facility sampling and core detouring. *Journal of Computer and Systems Sciences*, 76:709–726, 2010.

[99] P. Erdős. Gráfok páros körüljárású részgráfjairól [On bipartite subgraphs of graphs, in Hungarian]. *Matematikai Lapok*, 18:283–288, 1967.

[100] P. Erdős and L. Pósa. On the maximal number of disjoint circuits of a graph. *Publicationes Mathematicae Debrecen*, 9:3–12, 1962.

[101] P. Erdős and J. L. Selfridge. On a combinatorial game. *Journal of Combinatorial Theory B*, 14:293–301, 1973.

[102] G. Even, J. Naor, S. Rao, and B. Schieber. Fast approximate graph partitioning algorithms. *SIAM Journal on Computing*, 28:2187–2214, 1999.

[103] G. Even, J. Naor, S. Rao, and B. Schieber. Divide-and-conquer approximation algorithms via spreading metrics. *Journal of the ACM*, 47:585–616, 2000.

[104] S. Even, A. Itai, and A. Shamir. On the complexity of timetable and multicommodity flow problems. *SIAM Journal on Computing*, 5:691–703, 1976.

[105] J. Fakcharoenphol, S. Rao, and K. Talwar. Algorithms column: Approximating metrics by tree metrics. *SIGACT News*, 35:60–70, 2004.

[106] J. Fakcharoenphol, S. Rao, and K. Talwar. A tight bound on approximating arbitrary metrics by tree metrics. *Journal of Computer and System Sciences*, 69:485–497, 2004.

[107] U. Feige. A threshold of ln n for approximating set cover. *Journal of the ACM*, 45:634–652, 1998.

[108] U. Feige, S. Goldwasser, L. Lovász, S. Safra, and M. Szegedy. Interactive proofs and the hardness of approximating cliques. *Journal of the ACM*, 43:268–292, 1996.

[109] U. Feige and G. Schechtman. On the optimality of the random hyperplane rounding technique for MAX CUT. *Random Structures and Algorithms*, 20:403–440, 2002.

[110] W. Fernandez de la Vega. MAX-CUT has a randomized approximation scheme in dense graphs. *Random Structures and Algorithms*, 8:187–198, 1996.

[111] W. Fernandez de la Vega and G. L. Lueker. Bin packing can be solved within $1 + \epsilon$ in linear time. *Combinatorica*, 1:349–355, 1981.

[112] M. C. Ferris, O. L. Mangasarian, and S. J. Wright. *Linear Programming with MATLAB*. Society for Industrial and Applied Mathematics and the Mathematical Programming Society, Philadelphia, PA, USA, 2007.

[113] G. Finn and E. Horowitz. A linear time approximation algorithm for multiprocessor scheduling. *BIT*, 19:312–320, 1979.

[114] M. L. Fisher, G. L. Nemhauser, and L. A. Wolsey. An analysis of approximations for maximizing submodular set functions – II. *Mathematical Programming Study*, 8:73–87, 1978.

[115] L. Fleischer, J. Könemann, S. Leonardi, and G. Schäfer. Simple cost sharing schemes for multicommodity rent-or-buy and stochastic Steiner tree. In *Proceedings of the 38th Annual ACM Symposium on the Theory of Computing*, pages 663–670, 2006.

[116] D. Fotakis. A primal-dual algorithm for online non-uniform facility location. *Journal of Discrete Algorithms*, 5:141–148, 2007.

[117] T. Fujito. Approximating node-deletion problems for matroidal properties. *Journal of Algorithms*, 31:211–227, 1999.

[118] M. Fürer and B. Raghavachari. Approximating the minimum degree spanning tree to within one from the optimal degree. In *Proceedings of the 3rd Annual ACM-SIAM Symposium on Discrete Algorithms*, pages 317–324, 1992.

[119] M. Fürer and B. Raghavachari. Approximating the minimum-degree Steiner tree to within one of optimal. *Journal of Algorithms*, 17:409–423, 1994.

[120] H. N. Gabow, M. X. Goemans, É. Tardos, and D. P. Williamson. Approximating the smallest k-edge connected spanning subgraph by LP-rounding. *Networks*, 53:345–357, 2009.

[121] D. Gale. Optimal assignments in an ordered set: An application of matroid theory. *Journal of Combinatorial Theory*, 4:176–180, 1968.

[122] M. R. Garey and D. S. Johnson. "Strong" NP-completeness results: motivation, examples, and implications. *Journal of the ACM*, 25:499–508, 1978.

[123] M. R. Garey and D. S. Johnson. *Computers and Intractability: A Guide to the Theory of NP-Completeness*. W. H. Freeman and Company, New York, NY, USA, 1979.

[124] M. R. Garey, D. S. Johnson, and L. Stockmeyer. Some simplified NP-complete graph problems. *Theoretical Computer Science*, 1:237–267, 1976.

[125] N. Garg. A 3-approximation for the minimum tree spanning k vertices. In *Proceedings of the 37th Annual IEEE Symposium on Foundations of Computer Science*, pages 302–309, 1996.

[126] N. Garg, V. V. Vazirani, and M. Yannakakis. Approximate max-flow min-(multi)cut theorems and their applications. *SIAM Journal on Computing*, 25:235–251, 1996.

[127] N. Garg, V. V. Vazirani, and M. Yannakakis. Primal-dual approximation algorithms for integral flow and multicut in trees. *Algorithmica*, 18:3–20, 1997.

[128] G. Gens and E. Levner. Complexity of approximation algorithms for combinatorial problems: a survey. *SIGACT News*, 12:52–65, 1980.

[129] G. V. Gens and E. V. Levner. On approximation algorithms for universal scheduling problems [in Russian]. *Izvestiya Akademii Nauk SSSR, Tehnicheskaya Kibernetika*, 6:38–43, 1978.

[130] E. N. Gilbert and H. O. Pollak. Steiner minimal trees. *SIAM Journal on Applied Mathematics*, 16:1–29, 1968.

[131] M. Goemans and J. Kleinberg. An improved approximation ratio for the minimum latency problem. *Mathematical Programming*, 82:111–124, 1998.

[132] M. X. Goemans. A supermodular relaxation for scheduling with release dates. In W. H. Cunningham, S. T. McCormick, and M. Queyranne, editors, *Lecture Notes in Computer Science*, vol. 1084, *Integer Programming and Combinatorial Optimization*, pages 288–300. Springer-Verlag, Berlin, Germany, 1996.

[133] M. X. Goemans. Improved approximation algorithms for scheduling with release dates. In *Proceedings of the 8th Annual ACM-SIAM Symposium on Discrete Algorithms*, pages 591–598, 1997.

[134] M. X. Goemans. Minimum bounded-degree spanning trees. In *Proceedings of the 47th Annual IEEE Symposium on Foundations of Computer Science*, pages 273–282, 2006.

[135] M. X. Goemans, A. V. Goldberg, S. Plotkin, D. B. Shmoys, É. Tardos, and D. P. Williamson. Improved approximation algorithms for network design problems. In *Proceedings of the 5th Annual ACM-SIAM Symposium on Discrete Algorithms*, pages 223–232, 1994.

[136] M. X. Goemans, N. J. A. Harvey, K. Jain, and M. Singh. A randomized rounding algorithm for the asymmetric traveling salesman problem. *CoRR*, abs/0909.0941, 2009. Available at http://arxiv.org/abs/0909.0941. Accessed June 10, 2010.

[137] M. X. Goemans and D. P. Williamson. New 3/4-approximation algorithms for the maximum satisfiability problem. *SIAM Journal on Discrete Mathematics*, 7:656–666, 1994.

[138] M. X. Goemans and D. P. Williamson. A general approximation technique for constrained forest problems. *SIAM Journal on Computing*, 24:296–317, 1995.

[139] M. X. Goemans and D. P. Williamson. Improved approximation algorithms for maximum cut and satisfiability problems using semidefinite programming. *Journal of the ACM*, 42:1115–1145, 1995.

[140] M. X. Goemans and D. P. Williamson. The primal-dual method for approximation algorithms and its application to network design problems. In D. S. Hochbaum, editor, *Approximation Algorithms for NP-Hard Problems*, chapter 4. PWS Publishing Company, Boston, MA, USA, 1997.

[141] T. F. Gonzalez. Clustering to minimize the maximum intercluster distance. *Theoretical Computer Science*, 38:293–306, 1985.

[142] R. L. Graham. Bounds for certain multiprocessor anomalies. *Bell System Technical Journal*, 45:1563–1581, 1966.

[143] R. L. Graham. Bounds on multiprocessing timing anomalies. *SIAM Journal on Applied Mathematics*, 17:416–429, 1969.

[144] M. Grötschel, L. Lovász, and A. Schrijver. The ellipsoid method and its consequences in combinatorial optimization. *Combinatorica*, 1:169–197, 1981.

[145] M. Grötschel, L. Lovász, and A. Schrijver. *Geometric Algorithms and Combinatorial Optimization*. Springer-Verlag, Berlin, Germany, 1988.

[146] S. Guha and S. Khuller. Greedy strikes back: improved facility location algorithms. *Journal of Algorithms*, 31:228–248, 1999.

[147] A. Gupta. Steiner points in tree metrics don't (really) help. In *Proceedings of the 12th Annual ACM-SIAM Symposium on Discrete Algorithms*, pages 220–227, 2001.

[148] A. Gupta, A. Kumar, M. Pál, and T. Roughgarden. Approximation via cost-sharing: simpler and better approximation algorithms for network design. *Journal of the ACM*, 54, 2007. Article 11.

[149] A. Gupta, A. Kumar, and T. Roughgarden. Simpler and better approximation algorithms for network design. In *Proceedings of the 35th Annual ACM Symposium on the Theory of Computing*, pages 365–372, 2003.

[150] A. Gupta and K. Talwar. Approximating unique games. In *Proceedings of the 17th Annual ACM-SIAM Symposium on Discrete Algorithms*, pages 99–106, 2006.

[151] A. Gupta and K. Tangwongsan. Simpler analyses of local search algorithms for facility location. *CoRR*, abs/0809.2554, 2008. Available at http://arxiv.org/abs/0809.2554. Accessed November 19, 2010.

[152] V. Guruswami and S. Khanna. On the hardness of 4-coloring a 3-colorable graph. *SIAM Journal on Discrete Mathematics*, 18:30–40, 2004.

[153] V. Guruswami, S. Khanna, R. Rajaraman, B. Shepherd, and M. Yannakakis. Near-optimal hardness results and approximation algorithms for edge-disjoint paths and related problems. *Journal of Computer and System Sciences*, 67:473–496, 2003.

[154] M. Hajiaghayi and K. Jain. The prize-collecting generalized Steiner tree problem via a new approach of primal-dual schema. In *Proceedings of the 17th Annual ACM-SIAM Symposium on Discrete Algorithms*, pages 631–640, 2006.

[155] L. A. Hall, A. S. Schulz, D. B. Shmoys, and J. Wein. Scheduling to minimize average completion time: off-line and on-line approximation algorithms. *Mathematics of Operations Research*, 22:513–544, 1997.

[156] P. Harsha, M. Charikar, M. Andrews, S. Arora, S. Khot, D. Moshkovitz, L. Zhang, A. Aazami, D. Desai, I. Gorodezky, G. Jagannathan, A. S. Kulikov, D. J. Mir, A. Newman, A. Nikolov, D. Pritchard, and G. Spencer. Limits of approximation algorithms: PCPs and unique games (DIMACS tutorial lecture notes). *CoRR*, abs/1002.3864, 2010. Available at http://arxiv.org/abs/1002.3864. Accessed June 2, 2010.

[157] R. Hassin. Approximation schemes for the restricted shortest path problem. *Mathematics of Operations Research*, 17:36–42, 1992.

[158] J. Håstad. Clique is hard to approximate within $n^{1-\epsilon}$. *Acta Mathematica*, 182:105–142, 1999.

[159] J. Håstad. Some optimal inapproximability results. *Journal of the ACM*, 48:798–859, 2001.

[160] D. S. Hochbaum. Approximation algorithms for the set covering and vertex cover problems. *SIAM Journal on Computing*, 11:555–556, 1982.

[161] D. S. Hochbaum. Heuristics for the fixed cost median problem. *Mathematical Programming*, 22:148–162, 1982.

[162] D. S. Hochbaum, editor. *Approximation Algorithms for NP-Hard Problems*. PWS Publishing Company, Boston, MA, USA, 1997.

[163] D. S. Hochbaum and D. B. Shmoys. A best possible heuristic for the k-center problem. *Mathematics of Operations Research*, 10:180–184, 1985.

[164] D. S. Hochbaum and D. B. Shmoys. A unified approach to approximation algorithms for bottleneck problems. *Journal of the ACM*, 33:533–550, 1986.

[165] D. S. Hochbaum and D. B. Shmoys. Using dual approximation algorithms for scheduling problems: theoretical and practical results. *Journal of the ACM*, 34:144–162, 1987.

[166] W. Hoeffding. Probability inequalities for sums of bounded random variables. *Journal of the American Statistical Association*, 58:13–30, 1963.

[167] A. J. Hoffman. Some recent applications of the theory of linear inequalities to extremal combinatorial analysis. In R. Bellman and M. Hall, Jr., editors. *Proceedings of Symposia in Applied Mathematics*, vol. X, *Combinatorial Analysis*, pages 113–127. American Mathematical Society, Providence, RI, USA, 1960.

[168] A. J. Hoffman. On simple combinatorial optimization problems. *Discrete Mathematics*, 106/107:285–289, 1992.

[169] K. Hogstedt, D. Kimelman, V. T. Rajan, T. Roth, and M. Wegman. Graph cutting algorithms for distributed applications partitioning. *ACM SIGMETRICS Performance Evaluation Review*, 28:27–29, 2001.

[170] I. Holyer. The NP-completeness of edge coloring. *SIAM Journal on Computing*, 10:718–720, 1981.

[171] R. A. Horn and C. R. Johnson. *Matrix Analysis*. Cambridge University Press, New York, NY, USA, 1985.

[172] W.-L. Hsu and G. L. Nemhauser. Easy and hard bottleneck location problems. *Discrete Applied Mathematics*, 1:209–215, 1979.

[173] O. H. Ibarra and C. E. Kim. Fast approximation algorithms for the knapsack and sum of subset problems. *Journal of the ACM*, 22:463–468, 1975.

[174] J. R. Jackson. Scheduling a production line to minimize maximum tardiness. Research Report 43, Management Science Research Project, University of California at Los Angeles, USA, 1955.

[175] K. Jain. A factor 2 approximation algorithm for the generalized Steiner network problem. *Combinatorica*, 21:39–60, 2001.

[176] K. Jain, M. Mahdian, E. Markakis, A. Saberi, and V. V. Vazirani. Greedy facility location algorithms analyzed using dual fitting with factor-revealing LP. *Journal of the ACM*, 50:795–824, 2003.

[177] K. Jain and V. V. Vazirani. Approximation algorithms for metric facility location and k-median problems using the primal-dual schema and Lagrangian relaxation. *Journal of the ACM*, 48:274–296, 2001.

[178] D. S. Johnson. *Near-Optimal Bin Packing Algorithms*. PhD thesis, Massachusetts Institute of Technology, Cambridge, MA, USA, June 1973.

[179] D. S. Johnson. Approximation algorithms for combinatorial problems. *Journal of Computer and System Sciences*, 9:256–278, 1974.

[180] M. Jünger and W. Pulleyblank. New primal and dual matching heuristics. *Algorithmica*, 13:357–380, 1995.

[181] N. Kahale. On reducing the cut ratio to the multicut problem. Techical Report 93-78, DIMACS, Rutgers, Piscataway, NJ, USA, 1993.

[182] D. Karger, R. Motwani, and M. Sudan. Approximate graph coloring by semidefinite programming. *Journal of the ACM*, 45:246–265, 1998.

[183] D. R. Karger. Global min-cuts in RNC, and other ramifications of a simple min-cut algorithm. In *Proceedings of the 4th Annual ACM-SIAM Symposium on Discrete Algorithms*, pages 21–30, 1993.

[184] D. R. Karger. Minimum cuts in near-linear time. *Journal of the ACM*, 47:46–76, 2000.

[185] D. R. Karger, P. Klein, C. Stein, M. Thorup, and N. E. Young. Rounding algorithms for a geometric embedding of minimum multiway cut. *Mathematics of Operations Research*, 29:436–461, 2004.

[186] O. Kariv and S. L. Hakimi. An algorithmic approach to network location problems. II: the p-medians. *SIAM Journal on Applied Mathematics*, 37:539–560, 1979.

[187] N. Karmarkar and R. M. Karp. An efficient approximation scheme for the one-dimensional bin-packing problem. In *Proceedings of the 23rd Annual IEEE Symposium on Foundations of Computer Science*, pages 312–320, 1982.

[188] J. O. Kephart, G. B. Sorkin, W. C. Arnold, D. M. Chess, G. J. Tesauro, and S. R. White. Biologically inspired defenses against computer viruses. In *Proceedings of the International Joint Conference on Artificial Intelligence*, pages 985–996, 1995.

[189] L. G. Khachiyan. A polynomial algorithm in linear programming [in Russian]. *Doklady Akademii Nauk SSSR*, 244:1093–1096, 1979.

[190] S. Khanna, N. Linial, and S. Safra. On the hardness of approximating the chromatic number. *Combinatorica*, 20:393–415, 2000.

[191] S. Khot. Lecture notes from Fall 2004, Georgia Tech CS 8002: PCPs and the hardness of approximation, lecture 3: hardness of set cover. Available at http://www.cs.nyu.edu/~khot/pcp-lecnotes/lec3.ps. Accessed June 2, 2010.

[192] S. Khot. On the power of unique 2-prover 1-round games. In *Proceedings of the 34th Annual ACM Symposium on the Theory of Computing*, pages 767–775, 2002.

[193] S. Khot, G. Kindler, E. Mossel, and R. O'Donnell. Optimal inapproximability results for MAX-CUT and other 2-variable CSPs? *SIAM Journal on Computing*, 37:319–357, 2007.

[194] S. Khot and O. Regev. Vertex cover might be hard to approximate to with 2-ϵ. *Journal of Computer and System Sciences*, 74:335–349, 2008.

[195] H. Kise, T. Ibaraki, and H. Mine. Performance analysis of six approximation algorithms for the one-machine maximum lateness scheduling problem with ready times. *Journal of the Operations Research Society of Japan*, 22:205–224, 1979.

[196] P. Klein and R. Ravi. A nearly best-possible approximation algorithm for node-weighted Steiner trees. *Journal of Algorithms*, 19:104–115, 1995.

[197] J. Kleinberg and É. Tardos. Approximation algorithms for classification problems with pairwise relationships: metric labeling and Markov random fields. *Journal of the ACM*, 49:616–639, 2002.

[198] J. Kleinberg and É. Tardos. *Algorithm Design*. Pearson Education, Boston, MA, USA, 2006.

[199] J. M. Kleinberg. *Approximation Algorithms for Disjoint Paths Problems*. PhD thesis, Massachusetts Institute of Technology, Cambridge, MA, USA, May 1996.

[200] D. E. Knuth. *The Art of Computer Programming*, vol. 2, *Seminumerical Algorithms*. Addison-Wesley, Reading, MA, USA, third edition, 1998.

[201] D. Kőnig. Grafok és alkalmazásuk a determinánsok és a halmazok elméletére [in Hungarian]. *Mathematikai és Természettudományi Értesítő*, 34:104–119, 1916.

[202] G. Konjevod, R. Ravi, and F. Sibel Salman. On approximating planar metrics by tree metrics. *Information Processing Letters*, 80:213–219, 2001.

[203] B. Korte and J. Vygen. *Combinatorial Optimization*. Springer, Berlin, Germany, fourth edition, 2007.

[204] G. Kortsarz, R. Krauthgamer, and J. R. Lee. Hardness of approximation for vertex-connectivity network design problems. *SIAM Journal on Computing*, 33:704–720, 2004.

[205] M. R. Korupolu, C. G. Plaxton, and R. Rajaraman. Analysis of a local search heuristic for facility location problems. *Journal of Algorithms*, 37:146–188, 2000.

[206] A. A. Kuehn and M. J. Hamburger. A heuristic program for locating warehouses. *Management Science*, 9:643–666, 1963.

[207] Y. Lando and Z. Nutov. Inapproximability of survivable networks. *Theoretical Computer Science*, 410:2122–2125, 2009.

[208] L. C. Lau, R. Ravi, and M. Singh. *Iterative Methods in Combinatorial Optimization*. Cambridge University Press, New York, NY, USA, 2011.

[209] L. C. Lau and M. Singh. Iterative rounding and relaxation. To appear in *RIMS Kôkyûroku Bessatsu*, 2008. Available at http://www.cse.cuhk.edu/~chi/papers/relaxation.pdf. Accessed November 19, 2010.

[210] E. Lawler, J. Lenstra, A. Rinnooy Kan, and D. Shmoys. *The Traveling Salesman Problem: A Guided Tour of Combinatorial Optimization*. John Wiley & Sons, Chichester, UK, 1985.

[211] E. L. Lawler. Fast approximation algorithms for knapsack problems. *Mathematics of Operations Research*, 4:339–356, 1979.

[212] J. R. Lee. Distance scales, embeddings, and metrics of negative type. Unpublished manuscript, 2005. Available at http://www.cs.washington.edu/homes/jrl/papers/soda05-full.pdf. Accessed November 19, 2010.

[213] T. Leighton and S. Rao. An approximate max-flow min-cut theorem for uniform multicommodity flow problems with applications to approximation algorithms. In *Proceedings of the 29th Annual IEEE Symposium on Foundations of Computer Science*, pages 422–431, 1988.

[214] T. Leighton and S. Rao. Multicommodity max-flow min-cut theorems and their use in designing approximation algorithms. *Journal of the ACM*, 46:787–832, 1999.

[215] J. K. Lenstra, D. B. Shmoys, and É. Tardos. Approximation algorithms for scheduling unrelated parallel machines. *Mathematical Programming*, 46:259–271, 1990.

[216] K. J. Lieberherr and E. Specker. Complexity of partial satisfaction. *Journal of the ACM*, 28:411–421, 1981.

[217] N. Linial, E. London, and Y. Rabinovich. The geometry of graphs and some of its algorithmic applications. *Combinatorica*, 15:215–245, 1995.

[218] L. Lovász. On the ratio of optimal integral and fractional covers. *Discrete Mathematics*, 13:383–390, 1975.

[219] L. Lovász. On the Shannon capacity of a graph. *IEEE Transactions on Information Theory*, IT-25:1–7, 1979.

[220] C. Lund and M. Yannakakis. On the hardness of approximating minimization problems. *Journal of the ACM*, 41:960–981, 1994.

[221] N. Maeda, H. Nagamochi, and T. Ibaraki. Approximate algorithms for multiway objective point split problems of graphs [in Japanese]. *Surikaisekikenkyusho Kôkyûroku*, 833:98–109, 1993.

[222] S. Mahajan and H. Ramesh. Derandomizing approximation algorithms based on semidefinite programming. *SIAM Journal on Computing*, 28:1641–1663, 1999.

[223] C. Mathieu and W. Schudy. Yet another algorithm for dense max cut: go greedy. In *Proceedings of the 19th Annual ACM-SIAM Symposium on Discrete Algorithms*, pages 176–182, 2008.

[224] A. Megretski. Relaxations of quadratic programs in operator theory and system analysis. In A. A. Borichev and N. K. Nikolski, editors, *Systems, Approximation, Singular Integral Operators, and Related Topics: International Workshop on Operator Theory and Applications, IWOTA 2000*, pages 365–392. Birkhäuser, Basel, Switzerland, 2001.

[225] J. S. B. Mitchell. Guillotine subdivisions approximate polygonal subdivisions: a simple polynomial-time approximation scheme for geometric TSP, k-MST, and related problems. *SIAM Journal on Computing*, 28:1298–1309, 1999.

[226] M. Mitzenmacher and E. Upfal. *Probability and Computing: Randomized Algorithms and Probabilistic Analysis*. Cambridge University Press, New York, NY, USA, 2005.

[227] E. Mossel, R. O'Donnell, and K. Oleszkiewicz. Noise stability of functions with low influences: Invariance and optimality. *Annals of Mathematics*, 171:295–341, 2010.

[228] R. Motwani and P. Raghavan. *Randomized Algorithms*. Cambridge University Press, New York, NY, USA, 1995.

[229] C. Nagarajan and D. P. Williamson. Offline and online facility leasing. In A. Lodi, A. Panconesi, and G. Rinaldi, editors, *Lecture Notes in Computer Science*, vol. 5035, *Integer Programming and Combinatorial Optimization*, pages 303–315. Springer, Berlin, Germany, 2008.

[230] V. Nagarajan, R. Ravi, and M. Singh. Simpler analysis of LP extreme points for traveling salesman and survivable network design problems. *Operations Research Letters*, 38:156–160, 2010.

[231] G. L. Nemhauser and L. E. Trotter, Jr. Vertex packings: Structural properties and algorithms. *Mathematical Programming*, 8:232–248, 1975.

[232] G. L. Nemhauser and L. A. Wolsey. *Integer and Combinatorial Optimization*. Wiley, New York, NY, USA, 1988.

[233] G. L. Nemhauser, L. A. Wolsey, and M. L. Fisher. An analysis of approximations for maximizing submodular set functions – I. *Mathematical Programming*, 14:265–294, 1978.

[234] A. Nemirovski, C. Roos, and T. Terlaky. On maximization of quadratic form over intersection of ellipsoids with common center. *Mathematical Programming*, 86:463–473, 1999.

[235] Y. Nesterov. Semidefinite relaxation and nonconvex quadratic optimization. *Optimization Methods and Software*, 9:141–160, 1998.

[236] Y. Nesterov and A. Nemirovskii. *Interior-Point Polynomial Algorithms in Convex Programming*. Society for Industrial and Applied Mathematics, Philadelphia, PA, USA, 1994.

[237] C. H. Norton. *Problems in Discrete Optimization*. PhD thesis, Massachusetts Institute of Technology, Cambridge, MA, USA, September 1993.

[238] C. H. Papadimitriou and K. Steiglitz. *Combinatorial Optimization: Algorithms and Complexity*. Prentice-Hall, Englewood Cliffs, NJ, USA, 1982. Reprinted by Dover Publications, Mineola, NY, USA, 1998.

[239] C. H. Papadimitriou and S. Vempala. On the approximability of the traveling salesman problem. *Combinatorica*, 26:101–120, 2006.

[240] C. H. Papadimitriou and M. Yannakakis. Optimization, approximation, and complexity classes. *Journal of Computer and System Sciences*, 43:425–440, 1991.

[241] C. Phillips, C. Stein, and J. Wein. Minimizing average completion time in the presence of release dates. *Mathematical Programming*, 82:199–223, 1998.

[242] H. J. Prömel and A. Steger. *The Steiner Tree Problem: A Tour through Graphs, Algorithms, and Complexity*. Vieweg, Braunschweig, Germany, 2002.

[243] M. Queyranne. Structure of a simple scheduling polyhedron. *Mathematical Programming*, 58:263–285, 1993.

[244] H. Räcke. Optimal hierarchical decompositions for congestion minimization in networks. In *Proceedings of the 40th Annual ACM Symposium on the Theory of Computing*, pages 255–264, 2008.

[245] J. Radhakrishnan and M. Sudan. On Dinur's proof of the PCP theorem. *Bulletin of the American Mathematical Society*, 44:19–61, 2007.

[246] R. Rado. Note on independence functions. *Proceedings of the London Mathematical Society*, s3-7:300–320, 1957.

[247] P. Raghavan and C. D. Thompson, Randomized rounding: a technique for provably good algorithms and algorithmic proofs, *Combinatorica*, 7: 365–374, 1987.

[248] P. Raghavendra. Optimal algorithms and inapproximability results for every CSP? In *Proceedings of the 40th Annual ACM Symposium on the Theory of Computing*, pages 245–254, 2008.

[249] P. Raghavendra and D. Steurer. How to round any CSP. In *Proceedings of the 50th Annual IEEE Symposium on Foundations of Computer Science*, pages 586–594, 2009.

[250] R. Raz. A parallel repetition theorem. *SIAM Journal on Computing*, 27:763–803, 1998.

[251] A. Rényi. *Probability Theory*. North-Holland, Amsterdam, Netherlands, 1970.

[252] N. Robertson and P. D. Seymour. Graph minors. II. Algorithmic aspects of tree-width. *Journal of Algorithms*, 7:309–322, 1986.

[253] N. Robertson and P. D. Seymour. Graph minors. X. Obstructions to tree-decomposition. *Journal of Combinatorial Theory B*, 52:153–190, 1991.

[254] G. Robins and A. Zelikovsky. Tighter bounds for graph Steiner tree approximation. *SIAM Journal on Discrete Mathematics*, 19:122–134, 2005.

[255] D. J. Rosenkrantz, R. E. Stearns, and P. M. Lewis II. An analysis of several heuristics for the traveling salesman problem. *SIAM Journal on Computing*, 6:563–581, 1977.

[256] S. Ross. *A First Course in Probability*. Prentice Hall, Englewood Cliffs, NJ, USA, eighth edition, 2009.

[257] S. Sahni and T. Gonzalez. P-complete approximation problems. *Journal of the ACM*, 23:555–565, 1976.

[258] S. K. Sahni. Algorithms for scheduling independent tasks. *Journal of the ACM*, 23:116–127, 1976.

[259] H. Saran and V. V. Vazirani. Finding k cuts within twice the optimal. *SIAM Journal on Computing*, 24:101–108, 1995.

[260] F. Schalekamp and D. B. Shmoys. Universal and *a priori* TSP. *Operations Research Letters*, 36:1–3, 2008.

[261] A. S. Schulz and M. Skutella. Scheduling unrelated machines by randomized rounding. *SIAM Journal on Discrete Mathematics*, 15:450–469, 2002.

[262] D. B. Shmoys. Cut problems and their application to divide-and-conquer. In D. S. Hochbaum, editor, *Approximation Algorithms for NP-Hard Problems*, chapter 5. PWS Publishing Company, Boston, MA, USA, 1997.

[263] D. B. Shmoys and É. Tardos. An approximation algorithm for the generalized assignment problem. *Mathematical Programming*, 62:461–474, 1993.

[264] D. B. Shmoys, É. Tardos, and K. Aardal. Approximation algorithms for facility location problems. In *Proceedings of the 29th Annual ACM Symposium on the Theory of Computing*, pages 265–274, 1997.

[265] D. B. Shmoys, J. Wein, and D. P. Williamson. Scheduling parallel machines on-line. *SIAM Journal on Computing*, 24:1313–1331, 1995.

[266] D. B. Shmoys and D. P. Williamson. Analyzing the Held-Karp TSP bound: a monotonicity property with application. *Information Processing Letters*, 35:281–285, 1990.

[267] N. Z. Shor. Cut-off method with space extension in convex programming problems [in Russian]. *Kibernetika*, 13:94–95, 1977.

[268] M. Singh. *Iterative Methods in Combinatorial Optimization*. PhD thesis, Carnegie Mellon University, Pittsburgh, PA, USA, May 2008.

[269] M. Singh and L. Lau. Approximating minimum bounded degree spanning trees to within one of optimal. In *Proceedings of the 39th Annual ACM Symposium on the Theory of Computing*, pages 661–670, 2007.

[270] W. E. Smith. Various optimizers for single-stage production. *Naval Research Logistics Quarterly*, 3:59–66, 1956.

[271] J. Spencer. *Ten Lectures on the Probabilistic Method*. Society for Industrial and Applied Mathematics, Philadelphia, PA, USA, 1987.

[272] D. Steurer and N. K. Vishnoi. Connections between unique games and multicut. Report TR09-125, Electronic Colloquium on Computational Complexity, Potsdam, Germany, 2009. Available at http://eccc.hpi-web.de/report/2009/125/. Accessed November 19, 2010.

[273] G. Strang. *Linear Algebra and Its Applications*. Brooks/Cole, Stanford, CT, USA, fourth edition, 2005.

[274] G. Strang. *Introduction to Linear Algebra.* Wellesley-Cambridge Press, Wellesley, MA, USA, fourth edition, 2009.

[275] V. N. Sudakov and B. S. Tsirel'son. Extremal properties of semi-spaces for spherically symmetric measures [in Russian]. In V. N. Sudakov, editor, *Zapiski Nauchnykh Seminarov LOMI*, vol. 41, *Problems of the Theory of Probability Distributions. Part II*, pages 14–24. Nauka, Leningrad, Russia, 1974.

[276] O. Svensson. Santa Claus schedules jobs on unrelated machines. *CoRR*, abs/1011.1168, 2010. Available at http://arxiv.org/abs/1011.1168. Accessed November 4, 2010.

[277] C. Swamy. Correlation clustering: maximizing agreements via semidefinite programming. In *Proceedings of the 15th Annual ACM-SIAM Symposium on Discrete Algorithms*, pages 519–520, 2004.

[278] A. Tamir. An $O(pn^2)$ algorithm for the p-median and related problems in tree graphs. *Operations Research Letters*, 19:59–64, 1996.

[279] L. Trevisan. Positive linear programming, parallel approximation, and PCP's. In J. Diaz and M. Serna, editors, *Lecture Notes in Computer Science*, vol. 1136, *Algorithms – ESA '96*, pages 62–75. Springer-Verlag, Berlin, Germany, 1996.

[280] L. Trevisan. Parallel approximation algorithms by positive linear programming. *Algorithmica*, 21:72–88, 1998.

[281] L. Trevisan. Inapproximabilité des problèmes d'optimisation combinatoire [Inapproximability of combinatorial optimization problems, in French]. In V. T. Paschos, editor, *Optimisation combinatoire*, vol. 2, *Concepts avancés*, chapter 3 (Séries Informatique et systèmes d'information). Lavoisier, Paris, France, 2005. English version available at http://www.cs.berkeley.edu/~luca/pubs/inapprox.pdf. Accessed June 2, 2010.

[282] L. Trevisan. Approximation algorithms for unique games. *Theory of Computing*, 4:111–128, 2008. Online journal available at http://theoryofcomputing.org.

[283] V. V. Vazirani. *Approximation Algorithms.* Springer, Berlin, Germany, second edition, 2004.

[284] V. G. Vizing. On an estimate of the chromatic class of a p-graph [in Russian]. *Diskretnyǐ Analiz*, 3:25–30, 1964.

[285] H. Whitney. On the abstract properties of linear dependence. *American Journal of Mathematics*, 57:509–533, 1935.

[286] A. Wigderson. Improving the performance guarantee of approximate graph coloring. *Journal of the ACM*, 30:729–735, 1983.

[287] D. P. Williamson. *On the Design of Approximation Algorithms for a Class of Graph Problems.* PhD thesis, MIT, Cambridge, MA, USA, September 1993. Also appears as Tech Report MIT/LCS/TR-584.

[288] D. P. Williamson. The primal-dual method for approximation algorithms. *Mathematical Programming*, 91:447–478, 2002.

[289] D. P. Williamson and A. van Zuylen. A simpler and better derandomization of an approximation algorithm for single source rent-or-buy. *Operations Research Letters*, 35:707–712, 2007.

[290] H. Wolkowicz, R. Saigal, and L. Vandenberghe, editors. *Handbook of Semidefinite Programming: Theory, Algorithms, and Applications.* Kluwer Academic Publishers, Boston, MA, USA, 2000.

[291] L. A. Wolsey. Heuristic analysis, linear programming and branch and bound. *Mathematical Programming Study*, 13:121–134, 1980.

[292] L. A. Wolsey. Mixed integer programming formulations for production planning and scheduling problems. Invited talk at the 12th International Symposium on Mathematical Programming, MIT, Cambridge, MA, USA, 1985.

[293] M. Yannakakis. On the approximation of maximum satisfiability. *Journal of Algorithms*, 17:475–502, 1994.

[294] A. Z. Zelikovsky. An 11/6-approximation algorithm for the network Steiner problem. *Algorithmica*, 9:463–470, 1993.

[295] L. Zhao, H. Nagamochi, and T. Ibaraki. Greedy splitting algorithms for approximating multiway partition problems. *Mathematical Programming*, 102:167–183, 2005.

[296] D. Zuckerman. Linear degree extractors and the inapproximability of max clique and chromatic number. *Theory of Computing*, 3:103–128, 2007. Online journal available at http://theoryofcomputing.org.

Author Index

Subject Index

Printed in the United States
By Bookmasters